INTERNATIONAL MIGRATION

# International Migration
## *Prospects and Policies in a Global Market*

---

*Edited by*
DOUGLAS S. MASSEY
J. EDWARD TAYLOR

UNIVERSITY PRESS

OXFORD
UNIVERSITY PRESS

Great Clarendon Street, Oxford OX2 6DP

Oxford University Press is a department of the University of Oxford.
It furthers the University's objective of excellence in research, scholarship,
and education by publishing worldwide in

Oxford New York

Auckland Bangkok Buenos Aires Cape Town Chennai
Dar es Salaam Delhi Hong Kong Istanbul Karachi Kolkata
Kuala Lumpur Madrid Melbourne Mexico City Mumbai Nairobi
São Paulo Shanghai Taipei Tokyo Toronto

Oxford is a registered trade mark of Oxford University Press
in the UK and in certain other countries

Published in the United States
by Oxford University Press Inc., New York



First published 2004



British Library Cataloguing in Publication Data
Data available

Library of Congress Cataloging in Publication Data
Data available

ISBN 0-19-926900-9

1 3 5 7 9 10 8 6 4 2

Typeset by Newgen Imaging Systems (P) Ltd., Chennai, India
Printed in Great Britain
on acid-free paper by
Biddles Ltd., King's Lynn, Norfolk

# Contents

# List of Tables

# *List of Figures*

# 1

# Introduction

DOUGLAS S. MASSEY AND J. EDWARD TAYLOR

In 2000, the total world population of immigrants—people living outside their country of birth or citizenship—reached approximately 160 million. If these people were united in a single country, they would create a "nation of immigrants" with the sixth largest population on earth, larger than Japan, Pakistan, or the Russian Federation. The world population of immigrants increased at a rate of 2.8 million per year between 1985 and 1990 and more than 4 million per year between 1990 and 1997, compared with 0.8 million per year between 1965 and 1975. The breakup of the Soviet Union and Yugoslavia added 20 million new international migrants to the world in 1991, as borders moved across people instead of people across borders.

Most of the world's immigrants live in developing, not developed, countries. However, the recent growth in immigration has mostly been to developed countries. Together with the fact that immigrants often are concentrated in a few regions and economic sectors, this makes immigration one of the most visible and volatile issues throughout the "North" (the industrialized or developed countries of immigration, as opposed to the developing nations of emigration in the "South"). Not only has immigration been rising; its composition is also changing. From North African venders in the streets of Florence to Mexican and Hmong meat packers in Iowa to Brazilian and Indonesian factory workers in Japan, immigrants are increasingly diverse in their origins, destinations, and characteristics.

The remittance income that migrants send home, according to conservative estimates by the International Monetary Fund (1999), surpassed $95 billion in 1998, outstripping total official development assistance and making migrants the chief export of many countries in terms of the foreign exchange they generate. Migrant remittances are equivalent to more than one half the value of total merchandise exports in the Dominican Republic, Egypt, El Salvador, Jordan, Yemen, and Greece.

Recognizing how vital migrant remittances are to their economies, some labor-abundant developing nations have designed and implemented policies to train and place workers abroad and to harness more of the income they earn for development. Meanwhile, migrant host countries in Europe, North America, and Asia are taking an increasingly restrictionist stance towards immigrants and refugees, instituting policies that attempt—usually without much success—to reduce the flow of migrants into their territories. In most cases, countries do not have a clear idea of how many immigrants they host or send abroad, let alone how to control immigration effectively or influence its impacts.

Such is the conflicting landscape of international migration trends and policies as we enter the twenty-first century. The International Union for the Scientific Study of Population (IUSSP) brought together a panel of world migration experts to assess the existing and emerging trends and issues surrounding international migration. Their work, presented at a symposium convened in Barcelona on May 7 through 10, 1997, is showcased in this volume. The conference was organized by the IUSSP Committee on South–North Migration and sponsored by the IUSSP together with the Ortega and Gasset Cultural Institute of Spain and the Government of Catalonia. The subjects of the conference papers span a spectrum of key issues confronting migrant-sending and host countries, including international migration trends, patterns, and determinants; immigration and refugee policies; the social and economic integration of immigrants; and the impacts of migration and remittances in migrant-sending regions. The papers offer insights critical to understanding the determinants and impacts of international migration and designing domestic and international migration policies.

This volume and the conference that created it are the second and final component of the Committee on South–North Migration's work. It complements the critical analysis of international migration theory published in the book *Worlds in Motion: Understanding International Migration at the End of the Millennium* (Oxford University Press, 1998; Massey et al. 1999) and in a series of journal articles (Massey et al. 1993, 1994; Taylor et al. 1996*a,b*). Three themes emerge from the chapters in this volume and the discussion they generated at the conference.

## PATTERNS AND CHARACTERISTICS OF INTERNATIONAL MOVEMENT

World immigration is increasing and its character is changing. The world's population of immigrants has increased at a rate exceeding world population growth and the potential for future growth in international migration is nothing less than staggering. First, there is a widening income gap between rich and poor countries. According to the World Bank, the ratio of per capita incomes in high- and low-income countries was 11:1 in 1870 and 52:1 in 1985. Second, the transportation and communication revolutions have put migration to distant lands within the reach as well as the imaginations of more and more people. Third, newly emerging economies, in particular China, are beginning to enter the world labor market in a much bigger way than before. Finally, despite recent increases in world migration, only a small share of the world's people (just 2.3 per cent in the mid-1990s) live outside of their country of birth or citizenship. That is, nearly 98 per cent of the world's population does not migrate internationally, a huge reservoir of potential emigrants. The percentage of people not migrating is even higher for Asia, which is home to 60 per cent of the world's population but only 10 per cent of all international migrants.

As international migration expands, its diversity in terms of origins and destinations, as well as social, demographic, and economic characteristics, increases. Developed countries currently take in a disproportionate and growing share of the world's international migrants. Within developed countries, immigrants are changing the demographic makeup of communities that previously were not major immigrant destinations. Increasing diversity shows up in the number of countries of origin represented in immigration flows to developed countries. In virtually every developed country, the number of countries of origin accounting for three quarters of all immigrants rose between 1965–9 and 1990–4. For example, 18 countries accounted for 75 per cent of the total inflow to the United States in 1965–9. In 1990–4, no fewer than 27 countries accounted for the same share (Zlotnik 1998). In the case of Eastern and Central Europe, an entirely new region has appeared on the international migration stage. Meanwhile, Asian migration flows have become enormously more complex. Chapters in this volume document the diversification of international migration in terms of gender, skills and occupations, and recruitment.

## THE COMPLEXITY OF EFFECTS AT ORIGIN AND DESTINATION

The effects of migration are becoming increasingly multifaceted, both at places of migrant origin and at migrant destinations. In the South, the economic impacts of out-migration appear to be framed by two extremes. In some sending areas, migration has set in motion a development dynamic, as income remitted by migrants loosens various kinds of production and investment constraints that typically confront households in poor developing economies. In others, relatively lucrative migration activities have drained local economies of their labor and capital, crowding out local production of tradable goods and leading some communities and regions to specialize in migration.

At migrant destinations, as researchers attempt the complex calculus of immigration's costs and benefits (see Smith and Edmonston 1998; and U.S. Commission on Immigration Reform 1997), governments implement policies to reduce the negative fiscal impacts, almost certainly with adverse consequences for the economic integration of immigrants and especially their children. Immigrants' increasing geographic and socio-demographic diversity means that their influences are being felt in new areas and by new groups in host societies.

## POLICY MISMATCHES AND UNINTENDED CONSEQUENCES

Three kinds of policy mismatches are evident from the chapters in this volume. First, there is a widening rift between migrant-export policies in sending countries and immigration policies in migrant destination countries, with possibilities for heightened

North–South tensions over migration (see the chapters by de Wenden, Hugo, Stahl, and Battistella). Second, there are contradictions between immigration policies and realities in developed countries, with the consequence that immigration policies rarely achieve their stated goals and frequently produce outcomes the opposite of what policy makers intended (see Chapter 19 by Bean and Spener). Third, there is a striking juxtaposition and, in some eyes, contradiction in the policies that increase the free movement of goods and capital across nations but leave migration—the movement of people—off the negotiating table (see Chapters 7 and 15 by Martin and de Wenden).

## THE ORGANIZATION OF THIS BOOK

This volume is organized into three parts. Part I, which follows this Introduction, is entitled "Prospects." It examines emerging trends and factors influencing international migration throughout the world. Part II, entitled "Policies in Sending Nations," considers the effects of immigration at places of origin and undertakes a critical evaluation of policies that have been implemented or proposed to manage them. Part III, which focuses on "Policies in Receiving Nations," examines the consequences of immigration in places of destination and assesses the efficacy of policies that receiving nations have used in an effort to control the number, characteristics, and effects of immigrants.

### *Prospects*

Our assessment of the prospects for international migration begins with an analysis of the extent to which international migration influences, and is influenced by, population growth. Hania Zlotnik provides a straightforward demographic assessment of the interplay between population growth, immigration, and emigration. She finds that, in most countries, the net effect of international migration on population growth is small. The relatively few countries where net immigration makes a sizeable contribution to population growth are concentrated in the North, but there are almost as many developing countries in which immigration substantially affects population growth. Zlotnik finds no simple relationship between natural population increase and net migration. That is, rapid population growth in and of itself does not fuel emigration.

Thus, the causes of international migration are not demographic, but political, social, and economic. Post-1989 political transformations in Central and Eastern Europe instantly added some 20 million people to the world's population of immigrants. Some observers forecast massive emigration from this region to western Europe as a result. International migration from Central and Eastern Europe did, indeed, increase dramatically after 1990. But the mass exodus to the West failed to materialize. Marek Okólski explores this paradox, investigating why sharp increases in international migration between the countries of Central and Eastern Europe did not spill over into extra-regional migration. He argues that the region has acquired the attributes of a self-contained migration system (Kritz et al. 1992). Whether this system will persist in coming years or become simply an eastward extension of an expanding European migration system depends on the success of economic reforms in creating and sustaining poles of attraction linked to regions of expulsion that are distinct from the West European system.

In Chapter 4, Aderanti Adepoju points out that African history is deeply rooted in migration, and that international migration from African countries persists today. Most of this migration, however, is within the continent rather than between Africa and the rest of the world. Adepoju examines trends in immigration within and from Africa, concentrating on the nexus of demographic, political, ethnic, economic, and ecological variables shaping African population movements. He argues that African migration is likely to increase in the future, as economic and political crises swell refugee flows and stimulate labor migration. Migration networks will direct this migration to new destinations inside and outside the African region. Extra-regional migration is likely to be increasingly undocumented, given restrictive immigration and refugee policies in developed countries.

Contemporary international migration in Asia is unprecedented in terms of its scale, diversity, and impacts, with every country in the region and a broadening population base being influenced by migration. In its sheer magnitude, the migration potential in Asia is overwhelming, yet our understanding of it is quite limited. Graeme Hugo offers a detailed analysis of emerging trends and issues in Asian–Pacific international migration. Asian migration includes very large outflows to other regions along with complex and growing intra-regional population movements. No longer limited to narrowly defined social groups, Hugo argues that international migration is increasingly becoming part of the "calculus of choice" by Asians assessing their future options. He foresees international migration becoming more institutionalized, facilitated by governments and by private agencies promoting migration for profit. An already huge reservoir of Asians seeking to emigrate will increase at a faster rate than the total Asian population in coming years. This is especially true for educated youth, due to mismatches between the supply of skilled workers and economies' ability to absorb them. Challenging the "brain drain" paradigm, Hugo argues that the loss of highly trained individuals to international migration is having beneficial impacts upon most sending countries.

Argentina has historically been one of the world's great countries of immigration. Alicia Maguid reviews the history of Argentine immigration to reveal a marked transformation in the origins of immigrants from Europe to bordering countries of South America. She then examines the role of border-country immigrants in the metropolitan Buenos Aires labor market, which lies at the center of a Southern Cone migration subsystem and constitutes a magnet for workers from Chile, Bolivia, Uruguay, and Paraguay. Maguid contends that the Buenos Aires labor market has become segmented along immigration lines. Immigrants from neighboring countries are selectively inserted into manual jobs, particularly in construction and domestic service. These jobs are rejected by the native population because of their low wages, instability, limited benefits, and hazardous working conditions.

Her findings mirror those from U.S. research by Piore (1979), Dickens and Lang (1985), Taylor (1992), and others. As the employment rate falls, the immigrant workers appear to be concentrated increasingly in two economic sectors: construction and services, particularly domestic services. It seems that the space the labor market allows for immigrant workers narrows when the labor market contracts. In general, the concentration of immigrants is highest in those sectors which have always been more flexible and unfavorable in terms of salary levels and working conditions.

As the foregoing examples illustrate, contemporary international migration unfolds in a context of the globalization of markets. Governments in developed countries as well as less developed countries increasingly regard trade liberalization as an alternative to migration. In his analysis of Mexico–U.S. migration, the largest sustained international flow of migrants anywhere in the world, Philip Martin challenges the argument that trade liberalization necessarily offers alternatives to migration, at least in the short run. He argues that economic integration policies like the North American Free Trade Agreement only provide a basis for reducing international migration between member countries in the long run. In the short run, they are likely to increase migration pressures, resulting in a "migration hump." Although developed in the context of NAFTA, his core arguments are relevant for understanding the likely effect of economic integration on migration in other world regions.

Central to any consideration of international migration is the issue of economic integration. Min Zhou's study of employment patterns among immigrants in the United States questions the human capital view that workers' skills determine their mobility and earnings in the labor market. She finds evidence that human capital alone does not account for the economic success of immigrants. Although immigrants are made to believe that their labor market experience should be commensurate with their skills, they often encounter barriers based on group membership, not individual characteristics. Immigrant workers gain access to U.S. labor markets by either accepting low wages or taking jobs for which they are overqualified. Although functional as strategies for labor market entry, both actions violate the mainstream cultural value of equity. This chapter also reveals differences in employment experience by immigrant group and gender, the analysis of which requires new theoretical frameworks.

## *Policies in sending nations*

The effects of international migration on regions of origin have been a source of controversy among researchers and policymakers. In part, the controversy stems from the contextual specificity and inherently unequal distributions of these effects, raising questions like "why does international migration appear to promote development in some migrant-sending areas but not in others?" and "which social groups benefit from immigration, which lose, and why?" Thus, the consequences of international migration are contentious because they are multifaceted and complex and the policy responses are rarely simple.

For many years, researchers and policymakers thought about the effects of migration apart from its determinants. Recently, a new genre of migration theory and research, coined the new economics of labor migration (Stark 1991), has emerged to challenge traditional migration models and suggest new policy options. It views migration decisions as being made not by individual economic actors, but rather, within larger units of related people—families, households, even communities. It also recognizes that the motives for migration are more diverse than simply to maximize income; they also may include minimizing risks and loosening constraints associated with various types of market failures common in developing countries, especially in rural areas from which many migrants originate. This new perspective opens up an array of potential influences of migration and remittances on migrant-sending and migrant-receiving areas, including indirect influences unrecognized by traditional approaches.

Drawing on insights from the new economics of labor migration, Taylor presents evidence to show that migrant remittances contribute substantially to income in migrant-sending areas, both directly and indirectly. He argues that many of the negative findings of past migration-and-development research are due to researchers' failure to take account of the indirect effects of migration and remittances in their analysis. Directly, remittances benefit the households that receive them. Indirectly, they loosen constraints on production activities by providing migrant households with capital and insurance against income loss. Households with migrants spend remittances on goods and services supplied by others. Through these expenditures, remittances create income linkages that transmit the impacts of remittances from the remittance-receiving households to others in the migrant-sending economy. For policymakers, understanding these direct and indirect influences of migration is crucial in designing programs and policies to harness remittances for development.

Graeme Hugo and Charles Stahl review the actions that governments of migrant sending nations have employed to shape the extent, character, and direction of labor exports. They consider policies designed to influence remittance flows, the reabsorption of returnees, and investments in human resource development among potential migrants (in anticipation of the skill and occupational needs of labor-importing countries). Hugo and Stahl conclude that there are significant differences in governments' abilities to influence different types of migration, for example, labor exports through officially sanctioned programs versus illegal migration. Their analysis indicates that, although governments have implemented a diversity of strategies to influence emigration, these policies have been developed largely in a research vacuum.

Considerable research has documented the powerful role of networks in driving international migration. Although considerable research has been carried out on migration networks, little is known about the commercialization of international migration—the involvement of profit-motivated intermediaries in organizing migrant flows. Private firms often take the place of social networks when the latter are insufficiently developed or where migration, including clandestine migration, is complicated by long distances and difficult border crossings. However, they do so at a price, and the fees charged by labor recruiters reduce the economic returns from migration for individual migrants and their families.

Manolo Abella offers an economic analysis of labor recruitment, focusing on what determines the recruiters' share of the economic returns from international migration.

His analysis highlights a policy conundrum. Intermediaries are notorious for exploiting migrants, which creates a rationale for developing public recruitment institutions. However, public employment offices are usually less effective in finding job offers abroad than their private counterparts. As a result, most prospective migrants seek the services of private intermediaries even when public alternatives exist, despite the risk of fraud and high fees.

Because of the circularity of international migration, the economic and social reintegration of return migrants has become an important policy concern. Emigrant reintegration is particularly important when economic crises abroad provoke the sudden return of large numbers of migrant workers. Graziano Battistella addresses the question of what policies can be implemented to facilitate the reintegration of return migrants. He focuses on the Philippines, but his analysis is germane for other migrant-sending countries. Battistella concludes that, even though return migration is a permanent feature of international labor migration, no country has succeeded in dealing with it adequately. He argues that the best policies are not those specifically designed for migrants, but rather, policies designed for the whole population on which returning migrants can capitalize. Successful migrant reintegration programs require cooperation between migrant sending and receiving countries.

Beyond producing economic effects, international migration shapes and is influenced by identities. Richard Bedford's assessment of mobility, identity, and development in Oceania challenges conventional approaches that view fragmented microstates as isolated entities scattered across a vast ocean. An enduring feature of migration in Oceania, he argues, is the high level of circulation of population between the islands and countries of the Pacific rim. Bedford views this circulation as part of an ongoing process of expanding worlds of action and interaction of islanders, which has been going on for centuries in this "sea of islands," but which has accelerated very rapidly over the past twenty years. He identifies new trends in Oceania migration research at the end of the millennium, including new perspectives on the meaning of mobility for peoples whose societies and cultures are multi-local in character rather distinctive and separate places of migrant origin and destination. This perspective reflects a new emphasis on transnational communities in migration research, here as in other parts of the world.

## *Policies in receiving nations*

Nation states are crucial players in international migration, designing policies that attempt to influence the scale, direction, composition, and effects of population movements. A great deal of research has considered the influence of immigration policies on the characteristics and qualities of immigrants. A large body of literature, for example, concludes that immigrant occupational skills have declined over time in the United States (LaLonde and Topel 1992; Borjas 1994). Guillermina Jasso critiques these studies for failing to distinguish immigrants by their immigration status when assessing the skills of entering cohorts of immigrants. She points out that more recent immigrants are less likely to have permanent resident status, and the legal compositions of different cohorts may be correlated with skills.

Drawing from a new survey of immigrants in the United States, Jasso tests the "declining immigrant quality" (Borjas 1994) hypothesis while controlling for immigration status. She finds no evidence of declining skills among female immigrants, suggesting that cohort decline in skills is only a male phenomenon. Cohort change dynamics differ not only by gender but also by visa class and origin country, producing a mix of increases and decreases in occupational earnings. Jasso attributes a significant portion of the observed decline in immigrant skills to changes in U.S. immigration law and policies other than family reunification.

Most migrant-receiving countries have moved towards increasingly restrictive immigration policies, and those in Europe are no exception. Indeed, the control of immigration has become a major preoccupation of the European Union. Catherine Withol de Wenden examines European immigration policies at two levels: accords encompassing all or a subset of European states; and the tapestry of policies in specific countries. She demonstrates that policies on both levels are becoming increasingly restrictionist. She also identifies a tension between country concerns, shaped largely by public opinion, for sovereignty over borders, and the extension of Common European policies into the immigration arena. Despite a convergence in European policies with respect to entry, disparities in policies related to stay persist, including residence, social rights, and access to nationality. De Wenden identifies a divergence in European country policies related to asylum and the treatment of unauthorized or irregular migrants. The future trend, however, will be towards a strengthening of the Europe-wide decision process with respect to immigration policies.

Growing restrictionism in immigration policies extend into the asylum/refugee policy arena. Danièle Joly and Astri Suhrke offer a detailed assessment of changing European concepts and practices of asylum. They argue that a new asylum regime emerged in Europe during the late 1980s and early 1990s, distinguished by an attempt to limit asylum under the 1951 United Nations convention. The new regime extends beyond Europe's borders, including interventions in countries of origin in an effort to preempt mass outflows of asylum seekers (the so-called "comprehensive refugee policies"), and it increasingly offers only temporary protection to refugees.

Immigration presents both promise and challenges to European welfare states. On one hand, immigration is blamed for the financial crises endemic in sustaining generous welfare arrangements. On the other, immigrants promise short-term relief to the demographic crisis predicted for almost all European countries, in which many pensioners will have to be supported by a relatively small working-age population. This is clearly exemplified in Germany's pension schemes, which have been sustained for some time by migrant workers' contributions. Martin Baldwin-Edwards assesses the implications of immigration for Europe's welfare states and concludes that the social protection of migrants across the E.U. is fragmented and sometimes tenuous, with variation between countries, at different phases of the immigrant cycle, between different legal statuses and among different nationalities. As European welfare regimes undergo radical restructuring, there is the possibility of incorporating noncitizens in a rational ordered manner. However, Baldwin-Edwards finds it doubtful that European countries will be able to escape their histories of racial exclusion and construct inclusive market-based welfare systems.

The United States is by far the world's largest immigrant destination, and traditionally it has been one of the most open in terms of immigrants' access to the welfare state. Since 1996, it has, however, become a laboratory for testing the effectiveness of restrictionist immigration through welfare policies. The 1996 Personal Responsibility and Work Opportunity Reconciliation Act, for example, systematically discriminates against noncitizens in the provision of U.S. public benefits. As Fix and Zimmermann point out, this legislation signals a marked departure from an inclusive social welfare policy that made legal immigrants eligible for public benefits on largely the same terms as citizens, to one that systematically discriminates against noncitizens. The authors argue that new welfare policies in the United States have introduced deep structural changes related to civic membership, social policy, and federalism that will be hard to undo, even if the anti-immigrant attitudes and policies of the 1990s ultimately recede.

In the United States, restrictionism is also explicit in immigration policies such as the 1996 Illegal Immigration Reform and Individual Responsibility Act, which set higher income thresholds for immigrant sponsors and authorized new "expedited removal" procedures at U.S. ports of entry (Musalo et al. 2000). This legislation, however, was preceded by the 1986 Immigration Reform and Control Act, which launched a massive militarization of the 1,900-mile Mexico–U.S. border in an effort to prevent the entry of undocumented migrants. Frank Bean and David Spener assess how effective this militarization has been. Their analysis reveals an often-contradictory quilt of immigration policies that produce unintended consequences and raise challenging questions about the effectiveness of states as control agents in an era that increasingly emphasizes the importance of relatively unrestricted global markets, especially financial and commercial ones. Spener and Bean suggest that at least certain kinds of immigrant flows are either uncontrollable or so strongly sustained by existing social and economic forces that effective control would be prohibitively expensive in financial or political terms.

## CONCLUSIONS

As we enter the new millennium, it is likely that the international migration trends identified in this volume will continue, creating new challenges for sending and host countries and highlighting the importance of more concerted efforts to understand and address these challenges. Some of the key trends that emerge from this work include

(1) Larger and more diverse international migrant flows, driven by widening income inequalities across nations, improvements in transportation and communications, expanding formal and informal recruitment networks, sending-country policies that encourage and train people for work abroad, and structural changes in the economies and societies of migrant-sending and host countries—changes that are themselves shaped by migration;

(2) Continuing economic integration among nations, including the formation of new trade blocks, with labor migration largely absent from the negotiating table. By promoting trade and investment, market liberalization may reduce economic pressures for international migration in the long run by bringing capital to would-be migrants in their home countries as an alternative to having people migrate to capital in developed countries. Nevertheless, in the short run, market liberlization is likely to create labor–market dislocations that intensify migration pressures;

(3) Reluctance by developed countries to receive immigrants and refugees and integrate them into their economies and societies. This may trigger new political conflicts between North and South in the immigration arena, while intensifying social conflicts involving immigrants, their children, and other groups within developed countries.

How policymakers respond to these challenges will be instrumental in determining whether the twenty-first century will be a time of intensifying North–South conflict or of cooperation with regard to migration. Cooperative efforts are critical to ease potential North–South migration tensions, to facilitate the economic and social integration of immigrants in host countries, and to enhance the potential for turning migration into development in migrant-sending areas. Ultimately, economic development in regions of population expulsion is a prerequisite for easing migration pressures.

## References

Borjas, George J. (1994). "The Economics of Immigration," *Journal of Economic Literature*, 32: 1667–717.

Dickens, William T., and Lang, Kevin. (1985). "A Test of Dual Labor Market Theory," *American Economic Review*, 75: 792–805.

International Monetary Fund (1999). *Balance of Payments Statistical Yearbook*. Washington, DC: International Monetary Fund.

Kritz, Mary, Lim, Lean L., and Zlotnik, Hania (eds.) (1992). *International Migration Systems: A Global Approach*. Oxford: Oxford University Press.

LaLonde, Robert, and Topel, R. (1991). "Labor Market Adjustments to Increased Immigration," in John Abowd and Richard Freeman (eds.), *Immigration, Trade, and the Labor Market*. Chicago: University of Chicago Press, pp. 167–200.

Massey, Douglas S., Arango, Joaquín, Hugo, Graeme, Kouaouci, Ali, Pellegrino, Adela, and Taylor, J. Edward (1993). "Theories of International Migration: An Integration and Appraisal," *Population and Development Review*, 19: 431–66.

—————————— (1994). "International Migration: The North American Case," *Population and Development Review*, 20: 699–751.

———————————— (1999). *Worlds In Motion: Understanding International Migration at the End of the Millennium*. Oxford: Oxford University Press.

Musalo, Karen, Gibson, Lauren, Night, Stephen, and Taylor, J. Edward (2000). "The Expedited Removal Study Releases Its Third Report," *Interpreter Releases*, 77: 1189–96.

Piore, Michael J. (1979). *Birds of Passage: Migrant Labor in Industrial Societies.* New York: Cambridge University Press.

Smith, James P., and Edmonston, Barry (eds.) (1998). *The New Americans: Economic, Demographic, and Fiscal Effects of Immigration.* Washington, DC: National Academy Press.

Stark, Oded (1991). *The Migration of Labor.* Cambridge: Basil Blackwell.

Taylor, J. Edward (1992). "Earnings and Mobility of Legal and Illegal Immigrant Workers in Agriculture," *American Journal of Agricultural Economics,* 74: 889–96.

—— Massey, Douglas S., Arango, Joaquín, Hugo, Graeme, Kouaouci, Ali, and Pellegrino, Adela (1996*a*). "International Migration and National Development," *Population Index,* 62: 181–212.

—— —— —— —— —— —— (1996*b*). "International Migration and Community Development," *Population Index,* 62: 397–418.

United States Commission on Immigration Reform (1997). *Migration Between Mexico and the United States: Binational Study.* Mexico City: Editorial y Litografia Regina de los Angeles, S.A.

Wheeler, Charles (1999). "Affidavit of Support: A Year in Review," *Immigration Bulletin,* 4: 97–105.

Zlotnik, Hania (l998). "International Migration 1965–96: An Overview," *Population and Development Review,* 24: 429–68.

# PART I

# PROSPECTS

# 2

# Population Growth and International Migration

HANIA ZLOTNIK

Whereas international migration in its net form is a component of population growth and therefore a direct determinant of the latter, the nature and strength of population growth's potential effects on international migration are debatable. In this chapter, I examine the influence of net international migration on population growth and then consider available evidence on the influence of population growth on international migration.

## INTERNATIONAL MIGRATION AS A COMPONENT OF POPULATION GROWTH

The growth of a population between any two points in time, $t_0$ and $t_1$, equals the number of births ($B$) minus the number of deaths ($D$) plus the number of immigrants ($I$) minus the number of emigrants ($E$), all relative to the period $t_0$ to $t_1$. Thus, if $P_1$ is the population at time $t_1$ and $P_0$ is the population at time $t_0$, then:

$$P_1 - P_0 = B - D + I - E. \tag{2.1}$$

The number of births minus the number of deaths is defined as the natural increase of the population (denoted by $NI$), whereas the number of immigrants minus the number of emigrants constitutes the net number of international migrants gained or lost by the population and denoted by $NM$:

$$P_1 - P_0 = NI + NM. \tag{2.2}$$

Dividing both sides of eqn (2.2) by the population at the mid-point of the period $t_0$ to $t_1$ and by the length of that period to obtain annual rates, eqn (2.2) becomes

$$r = n + m \tag{2.3}$$

where $r$ is the annual rate of growth of the population, $n$ is the rate of natural increase, and $m$ is the net migration rate.

During most of this century rates of natural increase in developed countries have differed markedly from those of developing countries. Having undergone the demographic transition earlier, developed countries were exhibiting by 1960 lower rates of natural increase than their developing counterparts. Then, as fertility began to fall in one group of developing countries after another, the diversification of those rates increased. By the early 1990s, developed countries, including countries with economies in transition, were characterized by very low rates of natural increase (averaging 0.22 per cent for all developed countries combined) and in a number of developed countries the number of deaths was surpassing the number of births, resulting in negative rates of natural increase.

Among developing countries the rates of natural increase estimated for the period 1990–5 varied considerably, ranging, at the regional level, from a high of 2.7 per cent per year in Africa to 1 per cent per year in Eastern Asia. Moderate to low levels of natural increase predominated in South America, the Caribbean and southeastern Asia, whereas in South Asia and Central America natural increase was still on the moderate to high range.

Although trends in natural increase are fairly well documented in most regions of the world, much less is known about net migration levels. Because a majority of countries in the world lack data on international migration flows, one must resort to indirect estimates to obtain a comprehensive view of the likely impact of net migration on population growth. For instance, if a country lacks data on international migration flows but conducts population censuses at regular intervals, and if it has adequate registration systems of births and deaths, then estimates of net migration over the intercensal period can be obtained on the basis of eqn (2.2).

For such indirect estimates to be free from bias, however, the listing of births, deaths, and persons in the census must be free from coverage errors. Changes in the completeness of coverage from one census to the next, if not corrected, will produce biased estimates of net migration. Errors in estimation will also arise if the completeness of vital registration differs from that achieved by censuses. To obtain accurate estimates of net migration using eqn (2.2), therefore, it is necessary to ensure that data on population counts and on births and deaths are adjusted so as to reflect full coverage. If the goal is to estimate migration rates rather than numbers of migrants, less stringent conditions must be fulfilled, namely that the completeness of coverage of the data on births, deaths and population be the same.

In preparing estimates and projections of the population of each of the countries of the world, the Population Division of the United Nations assesses, to the extent possible, the various data sources available for each country. For developed countries, official estimates of changes in population size and of fertility and mortality rates are generally used to derive the estimates required. For developing countries, where data are often less complete and reliable, a variety of indirect techniques is used to estimate the components of population growth, particularly fertility and mortality rates. Whenever possible, estimates of international migration are based on actual information, whether the latter is the number of refugees as reported by UNHCR or actual information on inflows and outflows of migrants.

In its 1996 revision of *World Population Prospects*, the United Nations (1998) was able to derive estimates of net migration for 1990–5 using official statistics for about a third of the world's countries. In a sixth of the nations estimates were obtained by applying eqn (2.2) or a variation of it; and in another sixth they were derived indirectly from information on the foreign or refugee stock. Finally, for about a third of the countries of the world, net international migration was considered to be negligible.

In this section, I draw upon these population estimates and projections (United Nations 1998) to examine the contribution that net international migration has made to population growth. Attention will focus on the period 1960–95, which falls within the "estimation" period, as distinguished from the "projection" period. It must be borne in mind, however, that a number of countries lack data for the 1990s and, consequently, the 1990–5 "estimates" are likely to be extrapolations of past trends rather than actual estimates.

Because population estimates and projections are presented by 5-year periods, it is possible to derive net migration estimates for every quinquennium over the period 1950–95. In fact, the published data include estimates of population size for every year that is a multiple of 5 and the number of births and deaths occurring over each succeeding quinquennium. The estimates of net migration that those numbers imply are not published, partly because they were thought unlikely to be reliable indicators of migration over each quinquennium.

Because data on population size are commonly available only once every decade (or less in some cases), it is advisable to consider decennial estimates of net migration (or even those corresponding to longer periods) to reduce the effects of errors over short periods, thus adding stability to the results. Because our interest is in the effect of migration on population growth since the onset of the demographic transition in developing countries, the period considered will be 1960–95. This period also encompasses major policy changes that have contributed to the increase of international migration from developing to developed countries.

The UN estimates permit me to calculate two indicators of international migration: the net number of international migrants over the period 1960–95, derived using eqn (2.2), and the annual net migration rate, derived according to eqn (2.3). Given that the annual rate of natural increase can also be calculated, it is possible to ascertain the extent to which net migration contributes either to an increase or reduction in population growth, compared with natural increase alone. To measure the relative contribution of net migration to population growth, the former is expressed as a proportion of the latter. Given that natural increases from 1960 to 1995 were generally positive, when this ratio is positive it implies that net migration contributed to population growth over the period; when it is negative it means that emigration counterbalanced natural increase to reduce population growth.

The 1996 estimates give the annual rate of net migration and net migration as a proportion of natural increase for each of 164 countries during 1960–95 (United Nations 1998). The number of countries covered is smaller than the number currently in existence because the data do not allow separate consideration of successor states to the former Ethiopia, the former Yugoslavia, or the former USSR. During most of the period of interest, however, Ethiopia, Yugoslavia, and the USSR were single countries, justifying their retention as single cases for this analysis.

Table 2.1 presents five-number summaries of the distribution of different migration measures across the 164 countries. For each migration index it shows the lower

**Table 2.1.** *Five-number summary of distributions of countries according to different indicators of net international migration over the period 1960–95*

| Indicator of net migration | Lower bound | Lower quartile | Median | Upper quartile | Upper bound |
|---|---|---|---|---|---|
| Net number of migrants (000) | −6,733.0 | −453.0 | −44.0 | 126.0 | 19,837 |
| Net migration rate (%) | −1.9 | −0.2 | −0.1 | 0.1 | 3.4 |
| Net migration/Natural increase (%) | −71.2 | −11.1 | −2.6 | 4.2 | 646.0 |

*Source*: United Nations (1998).

and upper bounds of the distribution, its upper and lower quartiles, and the median. In terms of net international migration, the median value for the world indicated a net loss of 44,000 persons between 1960 and 1995. In other words, more than half of all countries in the world must have experienced a net loss during the period. Only sixty countries experienced positive net migration over the period, including seventeen of the twenty-eight western market economies. Most developing countries experienced net emigration. In terms of annual average rates of international migration, the median value was negative and the quartile points imply that for half of the countries of the world, annual net migration rates differed little from zero, ranging from −0.2 to 0.1 per cent. At the upper and lower tails of the distribution, however, net migration was responsible for an average annual gain of 3.4 per cent in the United Arab Emirates and an average annual loss of 1.9 per cent in Samoa.

The five-number summary for net migration as a percentage of natural increase indicates a distribution highly skewed to the right. It is only among countries that experience net gains from migration that the net balance accounts for a high proportion of total population growth. At the lower end of the distribution, net emigration contributed to a reduction of population ranging from 11 to 71 per cent of natural increase in a quarter of the countries of the world. However, most of these countries were very small: a majority (twenty-eight out of forty-two) had mid-period populations below four million; and seventeen had less than a million inhabitants.

The quartile values shown in Table 2.1 also indicate that in half the countries of the world, net migration constituted a very small part of population growth, either positive or negative (ranging from −11 to 4 per cent). In general, therefore, these estimates confirm the conclusion of Keyfitz (1971) that the level of emigration that a growing population would have to sustain over the long run in order to become stationary was not likely to be achieved in practice.

Realistic levels of emigration can be expected to have virtually no effect on the long-term demographic evolution of developing country populations.

Given the skewed nature of the distributions of these indicators of net migration, it is instructive to consider those cases that are statistical outliers (those whose distance to the median was twice the interquartile range). Table 2.2 presents outliers with respect to net number of international migrants during the period. At the upper end of the distribution, the countries experiencing the largest absolute gains through

Table 2.2. *Countries or areas identified as statistical outliers by total net migration 1960–95*

| Country or area | Net migrants (thousands) | Net migration rate (percentage) | Rate of natural increase (percentage) | Net migration as percentage of natural increase |
|---|---|---|---|---|
| United States | 19,837 | 0.25 | 0.77 | 32.5 |
| Germany | 7,725 | 0.29 | 0.04 | 646.0 |
| Canada | 3,999 | 0.48 | 0.91 | 53.4 |
| Saudi Arabia | 3,668 | 0.94 | 2.69 | 34.9 |
| France | 3,459 | 0.19 | 0.49 | 38.6 |
| India | 3,148 | 0.01 | 2.01 | 0.7 |
| Former USSR | 3,097 | 0.03 | 0.85 | 4.1 |
| Australia | 2,911 | 0.61 | 0.93 | 65.0 |
| Iran | 2,390 | 0.15 | 2.82 | 5.4 |
| Ivory Coast | 1,435 | 0.47 | 2.76 | 17.0 |
| United Arab Emirates | 1,379 | 3.42 | 1.84 | 186.0 |
| Zaire | 1,270 | 0.12 | 2.71 | 4.4 |
| Israel | 1,160 | 0.87 | 1.68 | 51.5 |
| Portugal | −1,275 | −0.39 | 0.69 | −56.3 |
| Egypt | −1,514 | −0.10 | 2.27 | −4.2 |
| Sri Lanka | −1,601 | −0.33 | 1.98 | −16.6 |
| Rwanda | −1,750 | −1.26 | 3.02 | −41.7 |
| Morocco | −1,780 | −0.27 | 2.50 | −10.7 |
| Former Yugoslavia | −1,793 | −0.25 | 0.84 | −30.1 |
| Colombia | −1,860 | −0.21 | 2.40 | −8.6 |
| Vietnam | −2,175 | −0.11 | 2.17 | −5.3 |
| China | −2,190 | −0.01 | 1.72 | −0.4 |
| Pakistan | −3,271 | −0.10 | 2.75 | −3.7 |
| Philippines | −3,684 | −0.22 | 2.63 | −8.4 |
| Bangladesh | −3,863 | −0.13 | 2.38 | −5.5 |
| Afghanistan | −4,161 | −0.78 | 2.45 | −31.9 |
| Mexico | −6,733 | −0.30 | 2.72 | −11.0 |

*Source*: United Nations (1998).

immigration are the United States and Germany (reunified), with gains of nearly 20 million and 8 million persons, respectively. Australia, Canada, and Israel, all countries favoring migration for settlement, are likewise among the outliers. France, a former labor-importing country, along with current importers Saudi Arabia and the United Arab Emirates, also appear on the list, as does Ivory Coast, which hosts a large expatriate labor force. Iran is listed because of the large number of refugees it contains, and the prominence of India and Zaire is also related to their status as receivers of forced migrants.

At the lower end of the distribution, Mexico and Afghanistan appear as the two main sources of emigrants, the former being the major source of migrants to the United States and the latter a major source for refugees during the 1980s. Other outliers include former and current labor exporting countries, such as Morocco, Portugal, and ex-Yugoslavia (sources of labor for European countries) as well as Bangladesh, Egypt, Pakistan, the Philippines, and Sri Lanka (sources for western and south-eastern Asia) and Colombia (the main source for Venezuela). In the case of the former Yugoslavia, forced migration also played a part in increasing its emigration. Rwanda and Vietnam appear as outliers because they are major sources of refugees, although in the case of Rwanda the situation is fluid and, at the time of this writing, massive return movements were already beginning. Lastly, China appears as an important source of emigrants. However, a large proportion of these migrants went to Hong Kong and would technically cease to be defined as international migrants as of mid-1997 when the former colony became a Special Administrative Region within the People's Republic of China.

Among those countries estimated to have received the largest number of immigrants, net migration made a major contribution to population growth in Germany and the United Arab Emirates. Germany's net migration rate was equivalent to 6.5 times the rate of natural increase recorded during 1960–95 and in the United Arab Emirates the net migration rate was nearly double the rate of natural increase. However, the high ratio for Germany owed much to the low level of natural increase experienced during 1960–95 (0.04 per cent per annum) and does not necessarily imply a high net migration rate. In contrast, for the United Arab Emirates, the high net migration rate of 3.4 per cent was still larger than the significant 1.8 per cent rate of natural increase, implying that the population of the country grew 5.3 per cent per annum during 1960–95. Net migration also contributed strongly to growth in Australia, Canada, and Israel (where it was over 50 per cent of natural increase) and moderately to the growth of France, Saudi Arabia, and the United States (where it was slightly over a third of natural increase).

Among the countries losing large numbers of migrants, net emigration reduced population growth by the equivalent of 56 per cent of natural increase in Portugal, 42 per cent in Rwanda and by about a third of natural increase in the former Yugoslavia and Afghanistan. For all other countries or areas characterized by large numbers of emigrants, net emigration generally reduced population growth equivalent only to a small proportion of natural increase.

Table 2.3 presents the countries or areas that qualify as outliers according to net migration rate. There are fifteen outliers at each end of the distribution. Among them, the majority are countries with very small populations: ten out of the fifteen at the upper end had a mid-period population under 1 million and so did nine of fifteen at the lower end of the distribution. Only four countries out of these thirty had populations of at least 4 million: Australia, Hong Kong, and Saudi Arabia among countries experiencing high net immigration and Afghanistan among those experiencing high net emigration. Table 2.3 suggests that net migration made sizeable contributions to population growth only among countries that experienced positive net migration

Table 2.3. *Countries or areas identified as statistical outliers by rate of net migration 1960–95*

| Country or area | Net migration rate (percentage) | Rate of natural increase (percentage) | Net migration as percentage of natural increase | Average population size (thousands) | Net number of migrants (thousands) |
|---|---|---|---|---|---|
| United Arab Emirates | 3.42 | 1.84 | 186 | 1,150 | 1,379 |
| Qatar | 3.15 | 1.70 | 186 | 296 | 327 |
| Djibouti | 2.31 | 2.01 | 115 | 342 | 277 |
| Western Sahara | 2.23 | 2.17 | 103 | 140 | 109 |
| Macau | 1.08 | 1.36 | 80 | 301 | 114 |
| Saudi Arabia | 0.94 | 2.69 | 35 | 11,165 | 3,668 |
| Gambia | 0.92 | 2.04 | 45 | 732 | 235 |
| Israel | 0.87 | 1.68 | 52 | 3,820 | 1,160 |
| Gabon | 0.84 | 1.31 | 64 | 781 | 231 |
| Brunei | 0.73 | 2.49 | 29 | 188 | 48 |
| Bahrain | 0.70 | 2.51 | 28 | 357 | 87 |
| Bahamas | 0.67 | 1.82 | 37 | 194 | 46 |
| Australia | 0.61 | 0.93 | 65 | 14,071 | 2,991 |
| Luxembourg | 0.61 | 0.13 | 456 | 361 | 77 |
| Hong Kong | 0.60 | 1.30 | 46 | 4,599 | 961 |
| Gaza Strip | −0.68 | 3.24 | −21 | 547 | −129 |
| Fiji | −0.71 | 2.60 | −27 | 589 | −147 |
| Martinique | −0.73 | 1.58 | −46 | 331 | −85 |
| Belize | −0.74 | 2.99 | −25 | 153 | −40 |
| Barbados | −0.76 | 1.11 | −69 | 246 | −66 |
| Afghanistan | −0.78 | 2.45 | −32 | 15,218 | −4,161 |
| Trinidad and Tobago | −0.80 | 1.99 | −40 | 1,065 | −298 |
| Cape Verde | −0.82 | 2.69 | −31 | 291 | −84 |
| Lebanon | −1.01 | 2.36 | −43 | 2,433 | −857 |
| Jamaica | −1.08 | 2.25 | −48 | 2,049 | −774 |
| Liberia | −1.17 | 3.13 | −37 | 1,581 | −646 |
| Rwanda | −1.26 | 3.02 | −42 | 3,963 | −1,750 |
| Guyana | −1.29 | 2.36 | −55 | 699 | −316 |
| Suriname | −1.45 | 2.54 | −57 | 358 | −182 |
| Samoa | −1.90 | 2.98 | −64 | 139 | −92 |

*Source*: United Nations (1998).

during 1960–95. In countries that qualified as outliers that had experienced net emigration, the relative impact of net migration on population growth was smaller.

Table 2.4 considers outliers according to net migration as a percentage of natural increase. There are twenty-four outliers at the upper end of the distribution and fourteen at the lower end. Aside from confirming that the distribution is markedly

Table 2.4. *Countries or areas identified as statistical outliers with respect to net migration as a percentage of natural increase 1960–95*

| Country or area | Net migration as percentage of natural increase | Net migration rate (percentage) | Rate of natural increase (percentage) | Average population size (thousands) | Net number of migrants (thousands) |
|---|---|---|---|---|---|
| Germany | 645 | 0.29 | 0.04 | 77,133 | 7,725 |
| Luxembourg | 456 | 0.61 | 0.13 | 361 | 77 |
| United Arab Emirates | 186 | 3.42 | 1.84 | 1,150 | 1,379 |
| Qatar | 186 | 3.15 | 1.70 | 296 | 327 |
| Austria | 146 | 0.22 | 0.15 | 7,547 | 592 |
| Djibouti | 115 | 2.31 | 2.01 | 342 | 277 |
| Western Sahara | 103 | 2.23 | 2.17 | 140 | 109 |
| Sweden | 84 | 0.21 | 0.25 | 8,134 | 598 |
| Macau | 80 | 1.08 | 1.36 | 301 | 114 |
| Switzerland | 78 | 0.36 | 0.46 | 6,264 | 788 |
| Australia | 65 | 0.61 | 0.93 | 14,071 | 2,991 |
| Gabon | 64 | 0.84 | 1.31 | 781 | 231 |
| Belgium | 55 | 0.10 | 0.19 | 9,640 | 347 |
| Canada | 53 | 0.48 | 0.91 | 23,655 | 3,999 |
| Israel | 52 | 0.87 | 1.68 | 3,820 | 1,160 |
| Hong Kong | 46 | 0.60 | 1.30 | 4,599 | 961 |
| Gambia | 45 | 0.92 | 2.04 | 732 | 235 |
| France | 39 | 0.19 | 0.49 | 51,894 | 3,459 |
| Bahamas | 37 | 0.67 | 1.82 | 194 | 46 |
| Saudi Arabia | 35 | 0.94 | 2.69 | 11,165 | 3,668 |
| Singapore | 34 | 0.50 | 1.46 | 2,481 | 430 |
| United States | 32 | 0.25 | 0.77 | 226,637 | 19,837 |
| Denmark | 31 | 0.09 | 0.29 | 4,902 | 151 |
| Brunei | 29 | 0.73 | 2.49 | 188 | 48 |
| Liberia | −37 | −1.17 | 3.13 | 1,581 | −646 |
| Trinidad and Tobago | −40 | −0.80 | 1.99 | 1,065 | −298 |
| Rwanda | −42 | −1.26 | 3.02 | 3,963 | −1,750 |
| Lebanon | −43 | −1.01 | 2.36 | 2,433 | −857 |
| Malta | −45 | −0.37 | 0.83 | 339 | −44 |
| Martinique | −46 | −0.73 | 1.58 | 331 | −85 |
| Bulgaria | −48 | −0.20 | 0.43 | 8,188 | −582 |
| Jamaica | −48 | −1.08 | 2.25 | 2,049 | −774 |
| Guyana | −55 | −1.29 | 2.36 | 699 | −1,275 |
| Portugal | −56 | −0.39 | 0.69 | 9,321 | −1,275 |
| Suriname | −57 | −1.45 | 2.54 | 358 | −182 |
| Samoa | −64 | −1.90 | 2.98 | 139 | −92 |
| Barbados | −69 | −0.76 | 1.11 | 246 | −66 |
| Hungary | −71 | −0.09 | 0.12 | 10,045 | −303 |

*Source*: United Nations (1998).

skewed to the right, the higher number of outliers at the upper end reveals that net migration makes a larger contribution to increasing the populations of countries that are net receivers of migrants than it does to reducing the populations of countries that are net senders. Among some net receivers, migration is responsible for increasing population growth by at least as much as natural increase and, in a few cases, by factors of two to six. The case of Germany has already been highlighted, net migration also contributed significantly to the growth of Austria, Belgium, Denmark, France, Luxembourg, Sweden, and Switzerland. Even though net migration is modest in these countries, natural increase is even lower, yielding a relative large ratio of net migration to natural increase.

In traditional countries of immigration such as Australia, Canada, and the United States, natural increase is somewhat higher so that net migration tends to make a lower but still important contribution to population growth. In countries or areas such as Gabon, Hong Kong, Israel, Macau, and Singapore, where natural increase is moderate, the contribution of net migration also tends to be moderate in relative terms. Of greater interest are countries such as Brunei, Djibouti, the Gambia, Qatar, Saudi Arabia, the United Arab Emirates, and the Western Sahara. In these countries natural increase is quite high, but net migration, nonetheless, accounts for a high proportion of total growth. In contrast to the prior table, a large number of the outliers listed in Table 2.4 have large populations, including Australia, Canada, France, Germany, and the United States, meaning that net international migration was making sizeable contributions to population growth in major countries in the developed world.

From the perspective of emigration, the contribution of net migration to a reduction in population growth has generally been moderate. Even in the most extreme case, Hungary, net migration reduced population growth by the equivalent of 71 per cent of natural increase. However, natural increase in Hungary has historically been very low. Net emigration was more likely to play a significant role in lowering growth in countries with small populations, especially in island nations. Among the fourteen countries or areas identified as outliers in Table 2.4, six had mid-period populations below one million and only three had more than 5 million inhabitants (Bulgaria, Hungary, and Portugal). Furthermore, six of the countries listed as outliers in Table 2.4 were occupied islands.

## EFFECT OF POPULATION GROWTH ON INTERNATIONAL MIGRATION

Given that most Western market economy countries experienced positive net migration over the period 1960–95 while most developing countries experienced net emigration, a common view of the dynamics of international migration is that international migrants move mainly from developing to developed countries. Such a view has been reinforced by neoclassical economics, which posits that countries with large endowments of labor relative to capital will tend to have low equilibrium wages, whereas those with limited endowments of labor relative to capital will tend to have high market wages, yielding a wage differential that entices workers to move from low-wage to high-wage countries.

It is, thus, common to argue that large economic and demographic imbalances between developed and developing countries predict rising rates of immigration to developed countries because developing countries will be incapable of absorbing the projected increase in the labor force (Emmerij 1993; Golini, Righi, and Bonifazi 1993). However, evidence to validate this claim has generally not been provided. Given that the economic and demographic imbalances have existed for at least 40 years, it is worth considering whether the data analyzed so far can shed light on the existence of a relationship between population growth and international migration.

Figure 2.1 presents scatter diagrams of the rate of natural increase plotted against the net migration rate, each estimated for the 1960–95 period on the basis of the official population estimates for 1966 and projections of the United Nations (United Nations 1998). When all countries are considered, there is no clear relationship between the two variables. When a line relating net migration to natural increase was fitted to the observations, it yielded a negative coefficient for natural increase but neither that coefficient nor the constant was statistically significant.

Given that the inclusion of all countries might confound the effect of natural increase on countries of net immigration with that on countries of net emigration, Fig. 2.2 explores whether a stronger relationship might be found by considering only the countries of net emigration. A line fitted only to the points whose net migration was not positive produced again a negative slope (implying that the higher the natural increase the more negative the net migration became), which was statistically significant at the 4 per cent level. That is, among the countries of net emigration,

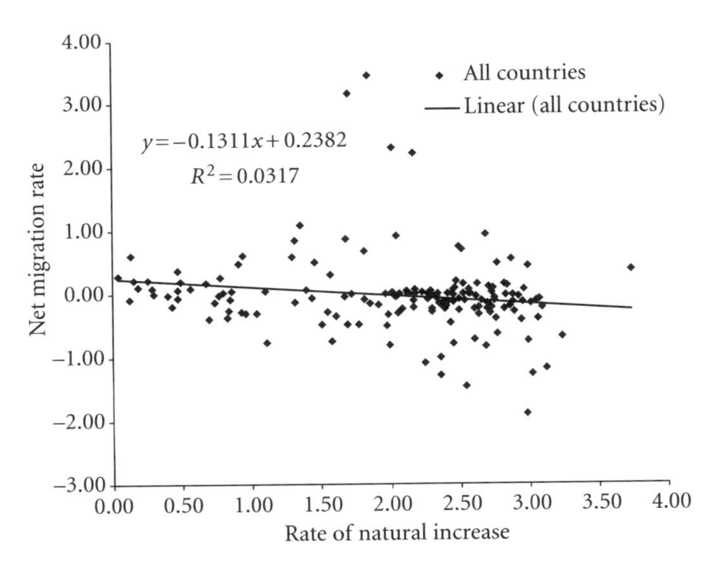


**Figure 2.1.** *Scatterplot of the net migration rate against the rate of natural increase 1960–95*

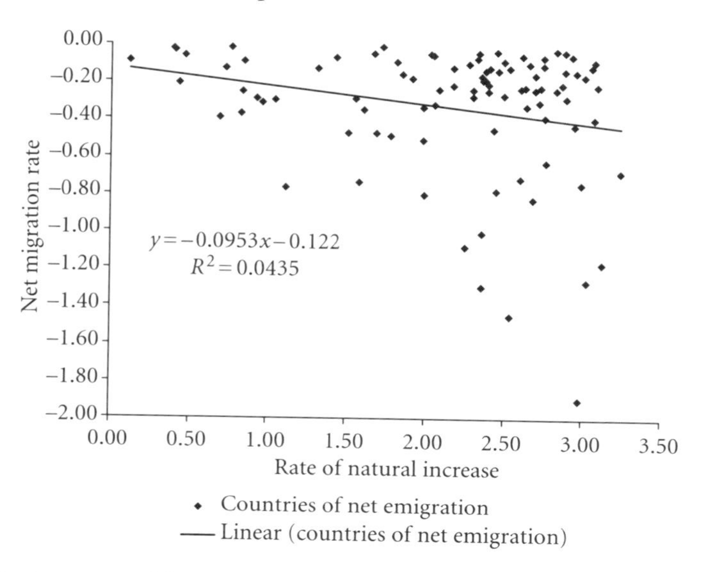


**Figure 2.2.** *Scatterplot of the net migration rate against the rate of natural increase 1960–95: countries with net emigration*

these data suggest that there is the expected relation between net migration and natural increase. However, the fact that countries of net emigration had to be preselected weakens the value of the relationship found.

Lastly, in order to control to some extent for the confounding effects of level of development, a set of countries that excluded the Western market economies was considered. The third plot in Fig. 2.3, labeled "developing countries and countries with economies in transition," is the result. It shows more clearly than the first diagram that there is a great variation in the rates of net migration associated with a given rate of natural increase. The inclusion of both countries experiencing net immigration and those experiencing net emigration leads again to poor results in fitting a line to the data: the coefficient of natural increase is negative but not significant.

In sum, the relation between net migration and natural increase according to the only global set of estimates available does not seem to be strong enough to merit further exploration. Although among net emigration countries higher rates of natural increase are associated with somewhat higher net emigration rates, the relationship can go in either direction when both countries of net immigration and countries of net emigration are considered simultaneously.

Let us consider the claims made about the relation between population growth and migration between developing and developed countries from another perspective. The fact that, at the global level, developed countries and particularly the Western market economies record a positive net migration balance with the rest of the world does not mean that all migrants from developing countries necessarily go to developed countries (or to Western market economy countries). When one focuses on

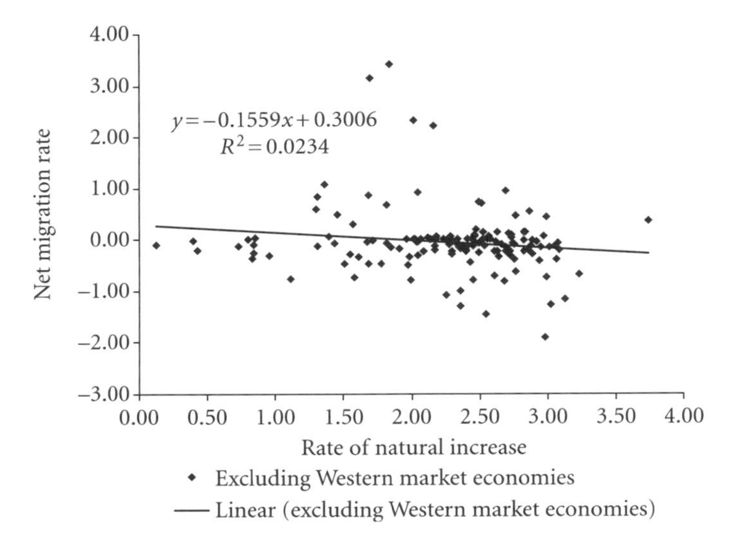


**Figure 2.3.** *Scatterplot of the net migration rate against the rate of natural increase 1960–95: developing countries and economies in transition*

**Table 2.5.** *Percentage of the migrant inflow directed to selected developed countries originating in developing countries 1960–94*

| Receiving country | 1960–4 | 1965–9 | 1970–4 | 1975–9 | 1980–4 | 1985–9 | 1990–4 | Total 1960–94 |
|---|---|---|---|---|---|---|---|---|
| Australia | 7.0 | 11.5 | 22.4 | 43.9 | 41.5 | 53.1 | 60.4 | 31.7 |
| Canada | 12.3 | 20.9 | 42.5 | 55.6 | 62.1 | 70.8 | 77.3 | 49.6 |
| Belgium | 21.7 | 20.5 | 22.6 | 29.1 | 28.4 | 26.5 | 24.2 | 24.7 |
| Germany (West) | — | 14.2 | 26.4 | 32.8 | 29.0 | 20.6 | 16.0 | 22.3 |
| Netherlands | 16.1 | 24.2 | 21.2 | 33.5 | 37.4 | 39.5 | 42.7 | 31.7 |
| Sweden | 4.7 | 5.9 | 11.1 | 23.2 | 33.1 | 45.2 | 42.7 | 24.4 |
| United Kingdom | — | 46.3 | 44.7 | 54.5 | 51.8 | 44.0 | 28.5 | 46.5 |
| United States | 41.7 | 55.7 | 70.5 | 80.9 | 85.2 | 87.9 | 86.1 | 78.2 |

*Note*: Data for Australia, Canada, and the United States are classified by place of birth; those for Belgium and the Netherlands are by country of citizenship; and those for Germany, Sweden, and the United Kingdom are by place of previous or intended residence. Data for Belgium do not cover the years 1961 and 1962 and stop in 1990; those for Canada cover the period 1961–92; those for Germany stop at 1992; and those for Netherlands, Sweden, and the United Kingdom stop at 1993. The data for the United States exclude migrants whose status was regularized under the Immigration Reform and Control Act of 1986.

*Sources*: Zlotnik (1991, 1998).

migrant flows registered by Western market economy countries, it transpires that the proportion of those flows originating in developing countries is not always high.

Table 2.5, for instance, shows the percentage of migrants to eight developed countries accounted for by developing countries. The data are presented in 5-year periods from 1960 to 1994, and the overall total for 1960–94 is also shown. Focusing on that total, it is clear that there is a wide variation in the importance of migration from developing to developed market economies. The percentage of migrants originating in developing countries varied from 22 per cent in West Germany to 78 per cent in the United States. In addition, whereas Australia, Canada, the Netherlands, Sweden and the United States experienced a generally increasing trend in the percentage of migrants originating in the developing world, Belgium, West Germany, and the United Kingdom did not.

Table 2.6 presents information on migrant inflows to the same Western market economy countries in terms of numbers rather than percentages. The data show that not only has the percentage of migrants originating in developing countries declined in some receiving countries but, in addition, there has been a reduction in the absolute number of migrants that originate in developing countries, especially between 1985–9 and 1990–4. That trend is observed most clearly in Australia, Belgium, Western Germany, Sweden, and the United Kingdom.

Although these reductions are generally small and, at the overall level, are more than counterbalanced by the large increase registered by the United States, they are, nevertheless, symptomatic of changes in the policies and control practices of receiving countries, which have been adopting measures to prevent the admission of migrants from developing countries. That is, those who claim that international migration between developing and developed countries will necessarily occur as economic and demographic disparities increase usually fail to take account of the barriers that prevent international migration from becoming a reality in most of the world.

Table 2.7 presents data on net migration by region of origin (developing versus developed countries) for all those receiving countries that gather information on both migrant inflows and outflows. These data corroborate that fact that the net number of migrants from developing countries declined between 1985–9 and 1990–4 in several European countries and in Australia.

To examine the linkage between rates of natural increase and levels of emigration to Western market economy countries more fully, data on gross and net migration to the eight receiving countries listed in Tables 2.6 and 2.7 were used to calculate the number of migrants originating in the various developing regions. The resulting estimates are presented in Table 2.8 in two forms: the upper panel includes the gross number of migrants for all countries (the equivalent of data on inflows presented in Table 2.6), whereas the lower panel includes the net number of migrants for countries having information on outflows (those listed in Table 2.7) plus the gross inflow to Canada and the United States. Table 2.8 also shows the rates of natural increase of each region considered and for selected periods. These rates are derived from the 1996 Revision of the World Population Prospects (United Nations, 1998).

Although these data are far from ideal, they nevertheless provide a rough indication of whether a strong relationship exists. In fact, the data presented probably overstate the relative importance of migration from developing countries to developed countries since many of the developed countries excluded from the group

**Table 2.6.** *Gross inflow of international migrants to selected developed countries by region of origin 1960–94 (thousands)*

| Receiving country and area of origin | 1960–4 | 1965–9 | 1970–4 | 1975–9 | 1980–4 | 1985–9 | 1990–4 | Total 1960–94 |
|---|---|---|---|---|---|---|---|---|
| *Australia* | | | | | | | | |
| Total inflow | 558 | 781 | 612 | 345 | 470 | 616 | 463 | 3,844 |
| Developing countries | 39 | 90 | 137 | 151 | 195 | 327 | 280 | 1,219 |
| Developed countries | 520 | 691 | 475 | 193 | 275 | 289 | 183 | 2,626 |
| *Canada* | | | | | | | | |
| Total inflow | 352 | 910 | 794 | 651 | 570 | 690 | 698 | 4,655 |
| Developing countries | 43 | 190 | 337 | 361 | 354 | 488 | 540 | 2,315 |
| Developed countries | 309 | 720 | 457 | 289 | 216 | 201 | 158 | 2,350 |
| *Belgium* | | | | | | | | |
| Total inflow | 207 | 328 | 323 | 291 | 239 | 248 | 63 | 1,700 |
| Developing countries | 45 | 67 | 73 | 85 | 68 | 66 | 15 | 419 |
| Developed countries | 175 | 261 | 250 | 207 | 171 | 183 | 47 | 1,294 |
| *Germany (West)* | | | | | | | | |
| Total inflow | — | 3,531 | 4,356 | 2,673 | 2,511 | 4,066 | 4,324 | 21,434 |
| Developing countries | — | 502 | 1,151 | 866 | 729 | 838 | 691 | 4,777 |
| Developed countries | — | 3,029 | 3,215 | 1,771 | 1,782 | 3,227 | 3,633 | 16,657 |
| *Netherlands* | | | | | | | | |
| Total inflow | 289 | 355 | 446 | 488 | 397 | 453 | 474 | 2,901 |
| Developing countries | 47 | 86 | 94 | 163 | 149 | 179 | 202 | 902 |
| Developed countries | 242 | 269 | 351 | 324 | 249 | 274 | 272 | 1,981 |
| *Sweden* | | | | | | | | |
| Total inflow | 146 | 227 | 217 | 207 | 161 | 232 | 217 | 1,407 |
| Developing countries | 7 | 13 | 24 | 48 | 53 | 105 | 93 | 343 |
| Developed countries | 139 | 214 | 193 | 159 | 108 | 127 | 124 | 1,064 |
| *United Kingdom* | | | | | | | | |
| Total inflow | — | 1,078 | 1,027 | 933 | 932 | 1,161 | 959 | 6,088 |
| Developing countries | — | 499 | 459 | 508 | 483 | 510 | 369 | 2,829 |
| Developed countries | — | 578 | 567 | 424 | 449 | 650 | 589 | 3,258 |
| *United States* | | | | | | | | |
| Total inflow | 1,419 | 1,759 | 1,923 | 2,413 | 2,825 | 3,507 | 6,046 | 19,928 |
| Developing countries | 592 | 1,000 | 1,356 | 1,951 | 2,406 | 3,083 | 5,206 | 15,593 |
| Developed countries | 827 | 795 | 568 | 462 | 419 | 424 | 840 | 4,335 |

*Note*: Data for Australia, Canada, and the United States are classified by place of birth; those for Belgium and the Netherlands are by country of citizenship; and those for Germany, Sweden, and the United Kingdom are by place of previous or intended residence. Data for Belgium do not cover the years 1961 and 1962 and stop in 1990; the data for Canada cover the period 1961–92; those for Germany stop at 1992; and those for Netherlands, Sweden, and the United Kingdom stop at 1993. The data for the United States exclude migrants legalized under the Immigration Reform and Control Act of 1986.

*Source*: Zlotnik (1991).

**Table 2.7.** *Net number of immigrants to selected developed countries by area of origin 1960–94 (thousands)*

| Receiving Country and area of origin | 1960–64 | 1965–9 | 1970–4 | 1975–9 | 1980–4 | 1985–9 | 1990–4 | Total 1960–94 |
|---|---|---|---|---|---|---|---|---|
| *Australia* | | | | | | | | |
| Total net Flow | 516 | 671 | 473 | 272 | 397 | 508 | 320 | 3,157 |
| Developing countries | 36 | 85 | 131 | 146 | 189 | 318 | 260 | 1,165 |
| Developed countries | 479 | 586 | 342 | 126 | 208 | 190 | 60 | 1,991 |
| *Belgium* | | | | | | | | |
| Total net flow | 101 | 120 | 85 | 26 | −54 | −9 | 20 | 291 |
| Developing countries | 36 | 39 | 44 | 45 | 22 | 22 | 9 | 218 |
| Developed countries | 54 | 81 | 41 | −19 | −76 | −30 | 10 | 62 |
| *Germany (West)* | | | | | | | | |
| Total Net Flow | — | 987 | 1,521 | 32 | 15 | 1,868 | 2,430 | 6,863 |
| Developing countries | — | 349 | 676 | 170 | −52 | 342 | 380 | 1,764 |
| Developed countries | — | 738 | 855 | −138 | 67 | 1,526 | 2,050 | 5,099 |
| *Netherlands* | | | | | | | | |
| Total net flow | 33 | 53 | 140 | 189 | 87 | 175 | 241 | 919 |
| Developing countries | 27 | 53 | 68 | 127 | 94 | 130 | 171 | 670 |
| Developed countries | 6 | 0 | 72 | 62 | −6 | 45 | 70 | 249 |
| *Sweden* | | | | | | | | |
| Total net flow | 70 | 128 | 38 | 87 | 24 | 122 | 111 | 581 |
| Developing countries | 1 | 4 | 8 | 34 | 36 | 90 | 76 | 250 |
| Developed countries | 69 | 123 | 30 | 53 | −12 | 32 | 35 | 331 |
| *United Kingdom* | | | | | | | | |
| Total net Flow | — | −388 | −252 | −106 | −138 | 121 | 50 | −713 |
| Developing countries | — | 144 | 75 | 110 | 58 | 189 | 107 | 683 |
| Developed countries | — | −532 | −327 | −216 | −6 | −69 | −57 | −1,397 |

*Note*: Data for Australia are classified by place of birth; those for Belgium and the Netherlands are by country of citizenship; and those for Germany, Sweden, and the United Kingdom are by place of previous or intended residence. The data for Belgium do not cover the years 1961 and 1962 and stop in 1990; those for Germany stop at 1992; and those for Netherlands, Sweden, and the United Kingdom stop at 1993.

*Sources*: Zlotnik (1991, 1998).

of receivers have tended to receive greater numbers of migrants from other developed countries rather than from the developing world (Zlotnik 1994). In any event, Table 2.8 shows that during the 1960s, when there was not a great differentiation among developing regions in rates of natural increase, developing countries were the source of relatively few migrants to developed countries. Indeed, most migrants to developed countries originated in other developed countries where the rate of natural increase was already quite low (0.96 per cent per year).

During the 1970s, the number of migrants originating in developing countries increased markedly but mostly because of policies adopted by the receiving countries

**Table 2.8.** *Rate of natural increase and levels of gross and net emigration, 1960–94*

| Region of origin | Rate of natural increase | | | Annual gross migration (000) | | | |
|---|---|---|---|---|---|---|---|
| | 1960–70 | 1990–5 | 1960–95 | 1960–9 | 1970–9 | 1980–9 | 1990–4 |
| World | 2.00 | 1.48 | 1.74 | 1,220 | 1,843 | 2,088 | 3,451 |
| *Developing Countries* | 2.44 | 1.81 | 2.11 | 326 | 853 | 1,181 | 1,688 |
| Sub-Saharan Africa | 2.58 | 2.84 | 2.59 | 27 | 58 | 66 | 115 |
| W. Asia and N. Africa | 2.69 | 2.27 | 2.44 | 70 | 232 | 167 | 214 |
| Southern Asia | 2.34 | 1.97 | 2.17 | 27 | 74 | 125 | 172 |
| E. and S.E. Asia | 2.25 | 1.23 | 1.75 | 43 | 161 | 318 | 415 |
| Latin America | 2.76 | 1.82 | 2.27 | 141 | 299 | 475 | 741 |
| Europe in Transition | 1.08 | 0.25 | 0.81 | 110 | 171 | 219 | 732 |
| Developed Countries | — | — | — | 894 | 990 | 907 | 1,762 |
| | | | | **Maximum net migration (000)** | | | |
| World | — | — | — | 692 | 906 | 1,251 | 2,436 |
| *Developing Countries* | — | — | — | 254 | 641 | 954 | 1,498 |
| Sub-Saharan Africa | — | — | — | 8 | 21 | 37 | 84 |
| W. Asia and N. Africa | — | — | — | 46 | 116 | 46 | 147 |
| Southern Asia | — | — | — | 21 | 61 | 105 | 153 |
| E. and S.E. Asia | — | — | — | 40 | 150 | 300 | 387 |
| Latin America | — | — | — | 134 | 285 | 461 | 724 |
| Europe in Transition | — | — | — | 82 | 62 | 101 | 442 |
| Developed Countries | — | — | — | 439 | 265 | 297 | 938 |

*Source*: Zlotnik (1991) and United Nations (1998).

(particularly Australia, Canada, and the United States) which made possible the selective admission of persons from the developing world. The flows that ensued were determined by economic, political, and cultural considerations, and tended not to correlate well with demographic variables relative to the region of origin. Thus, among the developing regions, North Africa and West Asia as well as Latin America generated similar numbers of emigrants settling in developed countries, and their rates of natural increase were high. Yet, East and Southeast Asia, with a lower rate of natural increase than even sub-Saharan Africa or South Asia generated more emigrants than these regions put together.

By the early 1990s, the rates of natural increase of developing regions had become more differentiated owing to the sharp fertility declines experienced by most regions during the 1970s and 1980s. Thus, the range of variation of the rates of natural increase among developing regions rose from scarcely 0.5 percentage points in the 1960s to 1.6 percentage points in the 1990s. The marked difference between rates of natural increase in developing versus developed regions persisted and the relation between natural increase and emigration levels became clearer: by the 1990s those regions experiencing the highest rates of natural increase (sub-Saharan Africa and Western Asia and Northern Africa) were generating considerably lower numbers of emigrants to developed countries than regions with lower rates of natural increase, including Eastern and southeastern Asia, Latin America and, especially, the developed countries. A similar conclusion is reached if instead of considering the rates of natural increase for 1990–5 the average annual rates for the period 1960–95 are used. Therefore, these data do not lend support to the claim that population growth per se leads to international migration.

There is no other evidence linking overall emigration levels from developing to developed countries to population growth rates in developing countries. However, some studies have explored the determinants of emigration to the United States. Yang (1995), for instance, focuses on the determinants of legal permanent immigration from 137 countries to the United States over the period 1982–6 and shows that the migrant stock already in the United States is the most important predictor of the level of emigration from the country of origin. In addition, the economic, military, and cultural involvement of the United States in the sending country has a positive and significant effect on the volume of emigration from that country to the United States, whereas an indicator of modernization of the country of origin which includes population size has a significant but negative effect on emigration to the United States. However, these findings are difficult to interpret because composite indices are used as independent variables. In a model that includes an index of population pressure constructed on the basis of the 1981–5 population growth rate of the country of origin, total fertility over the same period and the percentage of the population under age 15 in 1980, the resulting index has a positive and significant effect on the level of emigration to the United States.

Kritz (1995) explores the effect of population growth (measured by the rate of natural increase), population size, population density, and total fertility on the annual number of emigrants to the United States by using data on the number of permanent legal immigrants admitted by the United States over the period 1989–93, but excluding persons who adjusted their status as a result of the regularization program established by the Immigration Reform and Control Act of 1986. She finds that countries with the lowest total fertility and low rates of natural increase are more likely to be the origin of migrants to the United States than countries with the highest rates of natural increase or total fertility.

Using regression analysis Kritz corroborates Yang's findings regarding the strong effect that the migrant stock originating in specific countries and already present in the United States has in determining emigration levels from the corresponding countries of origin. Population size is also found to have a positive effect on emigration levels whereas total fertility and the rate of natural increase have negative effects. However, only population size maintains its significance when other factors are controlled for, including distance from the United States, total fertility, size of the migrant stock already in the United States, the human development index and the growth of GDP per capita. That is, these findings provide no support for the claim that population growth in countries of origin fuels migration to the United States. However, they also imply that countries with larger populations are more likely to send migrants to the United States, especially if they are located near that country and if their welfare status, as measured by the human development index, is poor.

In another chapter, Kritz (1996) explores the effect of population size and population growth on emigration rates to the United States using essentially the same data. Emigration rates are calculated as the total number of immigrants originating in a given country and admitted by the United States during 1989–93 divided by the country's population in 1985. She finds that countries with high rates of natural increase are less likely to experience high rates of emigration to the United States. Similarly, countries with large populations and countries located at greater distances from the United States are also less likely to experience high emigration rates to that country. Kritz, therefore, concludes that emigration rates to the United States are lower from countries that have rapid population growth and that geographic proximity is, in fact, a more important correlate of migration to the United States than population growth. Only among the oil-producing countries of Western Asia, characterized by both rapid population growth and high GNP, does population growth contribute to increase emigration rates (Kritz 1997).

Although both Kritz and Yang consider only the legal component of migration to the United States, their findings are likely to be robust to the addition of illegal flows which are concentrated more heavily on a small number of countries of origin, most of which are in the immediate vicinity of the United States. Despite their possible shortcomings, the studies cited confirm that the relationship between population growth and emigration levels is not as strong as is often assumed.

## CONCLUSION

This chapter has considered available evidence on the relationship between international migration and population growth for the 164 countries or areas into which the world was divided in 1990. The data show that, for ninety-three of the 164 countries or areas considered, the impact of international migration on population growth during the 1960–95 period was small, with net international migration increasing or reducing the growth due to natural increase by at most 12 per cent. For a further thirty-eight countries (those identified as statistical outliers), the contribution of net international migration to population growth was sizeable, with migration raising or decreasing natural increase by at least 29 per cent but, in most cases, by less than 100 per cent.

Only in a few cases did the contribution of net migration to population growth surpass that of natural increase. The fact that countries where net migration made a sizeable contribution to population growth inclued a large number of the Western market economies, including most traditional countries of immigration, validates the view that the developed countries of "the North" are experiencing the major demographic effects of net immigration. However, it is important to underscore that there are almost as many developing countries or areas where, despite relatively high rates of natural increase, the impact that net migration has had in increasing population growth has been substantial.

Given the large economic and demographic disparities existing between developed and developing countries, it has been argued that migration from developing to developed countries will necessarily rise as developing countries become increasingly incapable of absorbing the large increases expected in the labour force. Since such disparities have been very much in evidence during 1960–95, the data available were used to explore whether past experience validates such expectations. The analysis presented in this chapter shows that that there is no simple or unidirectional relation between natural increase and net migration since, expecially at relatively high levels of natural increase, there are a number of countries experiencing high net immigration and others experiencing high net emigration. Thus, although there is a tendency for net emigration to dominate as natural increase rises, the relation is weak. That is, rapid population growth, per se, does not necessarily fuel emigration.

In conclusion, migration has always been an important process leading to the redistribution of population. At the beginning of the twentieth century, it was a major component of the population growth of the relatively sparsely populated countries of overseas European expansion. By the end of the century, international migration has become a key component of the population growth of most of the highly developed market economy countries of Europe and has remained an important determinant of population growth in Northern America and Australia. From the optic of a world divided into a developing "South" and a developed "North," international migration is often seen as the main process leading to the redistribution of population. When very low levels of natural increase are achieved and sustained, international migration can indeed play a role in affecting population growth, but it too would need to be sustained. Unless net migration increases exponentially, it cannot counterbalance over the long run the effects of either a positive or a negative rate of natural increase (Keyfitz 1971; Espenshade, Bouvier, and Arthur 1982) and, at least during the twentieth century, no major region has experienced anything akin to an exponential growth in net migration over a prolonged period.

## References

Emmerij, Louis (1993). "The International Situation, Economic Development and Employment," in *The Changing Course of International Migration.* Paris: Organization for Economic Cooperation and Development.

Espenshade, Thomas, Bouvier, Leon F., and Arthur, Brian (1982). "Immigration and the Stable Population Model," *Demography*, 19: 125–33.

Golini, Antonio, Righi, Alessandra, and Bonifazi, Corrado (1993). "Population Vitality and Decline: The North–South Contrast," in *The Changing Course of International Migration.* Paris: Organization for Economic Cooperation and Development.

Keyfitz, Nathan (1971). "Migration as a Means of Population Control," *Population Studies*, 25: 63–72.

Kritz, Mary M. (1995). "Population Growth and International Migration: Is There a Link?" Occasional Paper No. 1, Migration Policy in Global Perspective Series, The International Center for Migration, Ethnicity and Citizenship, New York.

Kritz, Mary M. (1996). "U.S. Investment, Population Growth and GNP as Determinants of Emigration to the USA," Paper presented at the Annual Meeting of the American Sociological Association, New York City, New York, August 1996.

—— (1997). "Investment, Population Growth and GNP as Determinants of U.S. Immigration," Population and Development Program, Cornell University. Mimeo.

United Nations (1995). *World Population Prospects: the 1994 Revision.* New York: United Nations.

—— (1998). *World Population Prospects: The 1996 Revision.* New York: United Nations.

Yang, Philip Q. (1995). *Post-65 Immigration to the United States: Structural Determinants.* Westport, Conn.: Praeger.

Zlotnik, Hania (1991). "South-to-North Migration since 1960: The View from the North," *Population Bulletin of the United Nations*, 31/32: 17–37.

—— (1994). "International Migration: Causes and Effects," in Laurie Ann Mazur (ed.), *Beyond the Numbers: A Reader on Population, Consumption, and the Environment.* Washington, DC: Island Press, pp. 359–77.

—— (1998). "International migration 1965–96: An Overview," *Population and Development Review*, 24: 429–68.

# 3

# The Effects of Political and Economic Transition on International Migration in Central and Eastern Europe

MAREK OKÓLSKI

International migration in Central and Eastern Europe is a striking example of how quickly population processes respond to political and economic transformations. Before 1990, not only emigration, but all international travel was severely limited throughout the region. Aside from short bursts of politically driven emigration from Hungary (following the 1956 uprising), Czechoslovakia (after the 1968 Warsaw Pact invasion), and Poland (after the 1980 liberalization), movement was restricted and mostly limited to settled migration for purposes of family reunification, the "repatriation" of selected ethnic minorities, or controlled movements of workers within the framework of the Soviet-sponsored economic union, the Council of Mutual Economic Assistance (COMECON). Since the onset of the transition to a market economy and democratic rule, this picture has radically changed.

First, the rate of international migration, both documented and undocumented, has substantially increased. Second, despite widely shared expectations to the contrary, this movement, for the most part, did not spill over the region's boundaries into the West, but was contained within Central and Eastern Europe (CEE, which includes the former Council of Mutual Economic Assistance, including the new post-Soviet entities but excluding the ex-German Democratic Republic). Third, the number and complexity of links between sending and receiving countries grew dramatically, a shift attributable to the emergence of new states and their growing connection to nations both inside the region (e.g. Albania and Ukraine) and outside of it (e.g. Afghanistan, China, India, Sri Lanka, and Vietnam). Fourth, population mobility shifted from a predominance of long-term, settled migration to recurrent short-term movements. Fifth, population flows diversified dramatically with respect to socioeconomic origins, bringing about large-scale movements that were unknown in the past. Finally, the pace of change was exceptional, occurring so rapidly that after less than a decade, the momentum may already have passed (Okólski 1998*a*).

These new migratory patterns may follow naturally from the establishment of democratic order, the rule of law, functioning markets, and viable institutions in civil society, and not reflect the emergence of any extraordinary "push" or "pull" factors. Several questions, nonetheless, arise: How stable and durable will the new trends prove to be? What is the absolute and relative importance of each of the above factors in current flows? Does Central and Eastern Europe constitute a coherent if not uniform migratory system and if so, what are its distinctive features? These are the major issues dealt with in this chapter.

In this chapter, the focus will be on international migration after 1990. A perspective of a decade is really not sufficient to predict whether current trends will continue, not only because the time of observation is short, but also because certain migratory phenomena have only just emerged and are not well-captured by available statistics. Rampant data deficiencies are another factor hampering the analysis. Data problems are exacerbated by the fact that the political and economic situation in the region remains greatly differentiated, complex, and far from stable. Under these circumstances, quantitative data are necessarily limited.

Using the data available, in this chapter I discuss the significance of particular population movements and migration trends, their regional specificity, their heterogeneity within regions, their likely stability, and the principal factors responsible for them. I argue that since 1989, population movements in the region reflect the interplay of three different kinds of imbalances within and between countries: demographic, economic, and political. This perspective may be summarized in terms of three general propositions derived from a review of prior research (see Chesnais 1992; Okólski 1992; Ardittis 1994; Fassmann and Munz 1994*a,b*; Salt, Singleton, and Hogarth 1995; Frejka, 1996*a,b*):

1. International migration rates are generally high within CEE as a result of distinctive demographic realities: the existence of emigrant communities in destination countries throughout the world, a relatively high rate of natural increase within the region, and a relatively large proportion of the population living in rural areas.
2. The principal economic motivation for international migration is the desire of CEE inhabitants to improve their standard of living. The peripheral status of CEE economies creates a sense of economic relative deprivation relative to the rest of Europe, creating a latent potential for emigration.
3. East–West relations have played a decisive political role in shaping population movements at the macro level.

Various combinations of these propositions may be invoked to explain CEE migration over the last half a century. They are also consistent with the fundamental assumptions of migration theory. Although some observers have emphasized the natural *immobility* of human populations (Kubat and Hoffmann-Nowotny 1982), historically certain peoples have been significantly more mobile than others, and what follows unambiguously from a review of migration theories (United Nations 1997) is that what overcomes the natural inclination toward immobility is typically the aspiration to enhance material well-being. Politics, however, strongly conditions the intensity and direction of any migratory flow. Although economic factors represent a necessary condition for voluntary mass migration, therefore, political factors are usually the sufficient condition that allow it to materialize.

## NEW MIGRATION TRENDS

Migration statistics and analyses for CEE countries are replete with confusing and misleading concepts, definitions, and sources. The reasons for this are manifold. In general, the concepts (and, consequently, the definitions and data) are inherited from a pre-1990 past and were designed to measure heavily controlled, poorly differentiated, and atrophic flows of people rather than diverse and quickly changing movements that are associated with the present market economy. As a result, they do not capture very well the migration patterns that have become prominent during the transition period (Organization for Economic Cooperation and Development 1992).

Seven types of migration flows are relevant to the post-1990 era and are broadly depicted in Table 3.1. In the following paragraphs I attempt to describe the relative

**Table 3.1.** *Major types of population movements in Central and Eastern European countries during the pre-transition and transition periods*

| Type of migration | In-migrants | | Out-migrants | |
|---|---|---|---|---|
| | Documented | Undocumented | Documented | Undocumented |
| *Migration for settlement* | | | | |
| Ethnically motivated repatriation | + | | v ++ | v |
| Family reunification | + | | v + | v |
| Other reasons | | + | v + | v |
| *Labor migration*[a] | v ++ | + | v ++ | + |
| *Other non-settlement migration*[b] | v ++ | | v ++ | |
| *Incomplete migration*[c] | | + | | + |
| *Asylum and refugee migration* | + | | + | |
| *Transit migration* | | | | |
| Migrants in temporary protected status[d] | + | | + | |
| Readmitted foreigners | + | | + | |
| Migrants being trafficked | | + | | + |
| Illicit migrants[e] | | + | | + |
| *Non-migration mobility* | | | | |
| Tourists | v ++ | | v ++ | |
| Passengers in transit | v ++ | | v ++ | |
| Daily migrants | + | + | + | + |

*Note*: v significant in pre-transition period; + significant in transition period; ++ significant in both periods, higher in latter.

[a] Migration for work but not settlement, excluding incomplete migrants.
[b] Migration for study, professional training, business, etc.
[c] Short-term circular migration to earn money.
[d] Persons qualifying for temporary protected status.
[e] Unrelated to trafficking.

importance, geographical specificity, social origins, continuity with the past, and political relevance of each type of flow. Recent work on CEE migration has mentioned three categories of migration as most characteristic (if not most important) in the mobility of the 1990s: transit movements directed toward the West, movements of persons in need of protection, and movements between successor states of the ex-USSR (see Frejka 1996*b*; Salt 1996; Garson, Redor, and Lemaitre 1997; United Nations 1997). Whereas the third category pertains only to the three Baltic states and twelve countries of the Commonwealth of Independent States, the first two apply to all CEE countries.

Among the above three categories, movement between Russia and ex-Soviet states has been the largest. For decades during the Soviet era, the various republics of the USSR were subject to colonization by ethnic Russians; but with the decline and breakup of the Soviet Union these former colonists and their descendants have sought to return. The outflow began as early as the mid-1970s, although net in-migration into Russia averaged only 162,000 during the period 1976–90. The breakthrough year was 1993, when net immigration to Russia suddenly increased to 356,000. During the peak year of 1994 some 1.1 million persons moved from former Soviet republics into Russia, while 227,000 others moved from Russia to Soviet successor states, yielding a positive immigration of 916,000 persons.

Although the number fell to 433,000 3 years later, net immigration in 1994 alone was nearly six times greater than the annual average for 1986–90. Between January 1, 1990 and December 31, 1997, almost 5.7 ex-Soviet citizens moved to or from Russia (4.6 million immigrants and 1.1 million emigrants), the vast majority being ethnic Russians. Population exchanges with Russia accounted for half of all movement within the former USSR during the 1990s. Altogether more than 11 million documented migrations for settlement took place between Soviet successor states through 1996.

In contrast to fairly regular flows between former Soviet republics, migration by persons in need of protection cannot be estimated, even approximately. Relevant movements include internally displaced persons from various parts of the ex-USSR (mainly non-European successor states), assisted war victims, persons from Bosnia–Herzegovina, persons from former Soviet republics qualifying for temporary protected status, refugees or asylum seekers (some from within CEE but above all from Africa and Asia), and, according to some accounts, forcibly displaced members of non-titular nationalities (ethnicities) in the former Soviet Union.

Given their irregular status, data on these migrants are generally not accurate. Often, counts of persons in need of protection overlap with other categories of international movers, such as tourists, leading to double counting. Nevertheless, estimates based on official statistics produced by governments in some CEE countries are helpful in drawing a broad picture of movements made by persons in need of protection. In Hungary, for example, about 60,000 refugees from Romania and 75,000 temporarily protected persons from ex-Yugoslavia were registered between 1988 and 1995, along with at least 20,000 refugees from other countries (Jungbert 1996).

Since 1990, practically all CEE nations have experienced a large inflow of persons in need of protection from outside the region (Salt 1996). Some of these people have come from nations far away from the host country. In 1996, for example, Belarus was estimated to contain more than 5,000 asylum seekers from countries such as Afghanistan, Bolivia, China, Ethiopia, Iran, Pakistan, Somalia, and Vietnam, in addition to some 30,000 refugees from former Soviet republics (Marach 1996).

By far the largest sub-category of persons in need of protection, however, consists of persons fleeing armed conflicts in ex-Yugoslavia and the ex-USSR, although these estimates are inconsistent and often contradictory (Ryvkina 1996). Displaced persons from the former Yugoslavia seem to have gone mostly to western countries. As of 1996, only 442,000 refugees from Bosnia–Herzegovina remained in the ex-Yugoslavia compared with 601,000 in nations outside the region. On the list of the twenty-five most important host countries compiled by UNHCR in Sarajevo, six were in the CEE region (Albania, Bulgaria, the Czech Republic, Hungary, Poland, and the Slovak Republic—see United Nations 1996).

Most persons fleeing violence in the former Soviet Union went to other CEE nations. According to UN estimates, by the end of 1992 conflicts in the ex-USSR had generated 700,000 refugees and 2.3 million internally displaced persons, which by 1996 had dropped to 500,000 and 1.3 million, respectively (United Nations 1997). Figures from the Russian Central Statistical Office, however, indicate a rising tide of refugees, with the estimated number going from 160,000 on January 1, 1993 to 970,000 on January 1, 1996 (Ryvkina 1996). The concept of a refugee in Russia includes four sub-categories of foreign citizens arriving in Russia: refugees/asylum seekers from outside of the ex-USSR, forcibly displaced Russians (compelled to abandon their residence in a former Soviet republic), forcibly displaced non-Russians, and members of non-Russian ethnic groups spontaneously returning to the places of historical origin (from other former Soviet republics). While the first sub-category is statistically negligible, and the second consists of only 79,000 persons, it is the last two subcategories that count (United Nations 1996).

Finally, the last but certainly not least among the three principal flows, transit migrants, can only be assessed on the basis of guesswork, as their status is almost entirely irregular, semi-legal, and sometimes even criminal. Nevertheless, the volume of transit migration appears to be high and similar to that of persons in need of protection. It has become customary in analyses of CEE migration to reserve the term of "transit migrants" for two distinct groups of people: those from CEE countries that do not border a western country (or at least a preferred destination country) and those from developing nations. Both sets of people are driven by a desire to move to the west and are united in their relative inability to do so.

Country-of-origin bears substantially on the legality or regularity of a migrant's stay in a transit country, as well as the number of stages in the migratory process, the sophistication and cost of the trip, and the likelihood of getting stuck in a transit country should entry to the West prove impossible. While the number of transit migrants from outside CEE nations is on the rise, the number from within the region appears to be shrinking (United Nations, 1998). Thus the overall increase can be attributed to increased entry by persons originating in far-away countries, who as a rule are in an illegal or irregular status.

Very rough estimates for 1993 suggest that at least 100,000 migrants transited through Poland and another 100,000–140,000 went through the Czech Republic, the two most popular countries for final stage migration (International Organization for Migration 1994). In the same year, tens of thousands of persons were believed to be transiting through Bulgaria, Hungary, Romania and the Slovak Republic (Frejka 1996*b*). It, thus, appears that the "Balkan route," which bypasses the ex-USSR, has lost the importance it once had around 1990 (International Organization for Migration 1994).

Most transit routes and movements now go through the ex-USSR, which represents a northern "Baltic route" to the West. In the middle of 1996, for example, the stock of transit migrants in Belarus alone exceeded 300,000 persons (Sipaviciene 1996) and at any point in time many more transit migrants are probably in Ukraine and Russia. Most of these migrants originate in south Asia—mainly in countries of the Indian subcontinent. One example of the "tremendous build-up of South Asian transit migrants in Russia" is the estimated 200,000 illegal foreigners residing in the Moscow region at any one time. Among those apprehended for illegal entry to Lithuania in 1996, the largest number (27 per cent) were from Sri Lanka (International Organization for Migration 1997).

Transit migration is typically multistage and time consuming, with long periods spent idle in transit countries. A series of IOM-sponsored studies reveals the great determination and ingenuity of transit migrants and their traffickers. According to IOM estimates, the average transit migrant visits 5–6 countries before finally (if ever) arriving in the West (International Organization for Migration 1995, 1997). Transit migrants use a combination of transportation modes in moving and are assisted by a network of highly specialized and efficient traffickers.

For a variety of reasons, transit migrants are difficult to expel, even when apprehended. These reasons for this difficulty include the lack of readmission agreements between states, the absence of a record of actual border crossing, the presentation of false evidence on citizenship, the request of asylum or refugee status immediately after apprehension, and inadequate resources. As a result, transit migration generates a non-negligible inflow of *de facto* permanent immigrants, owing to the relatively high incidence of failed migration.

Other migrant flows observed in post-1989 CEE have generally been accorded less importance for two principal reasons. First, moves begun in one of the above categories may end up being unsuccessful, in the sense that the migrants fail to reach their intended destination and are unable to find secure and acceptable shelter in the transit country. These people, who I call "incomplete migrants," represent a kind of "time bomb" that may be transformed into other kinds of migrants in the future. Second, other migratory flows are much smaller and less stable, and some have even been decreasing.

The omission of permanent emigration to the West from Table 3.1 might appear puzzling, for it was practically the only kind of migration that counted before 1989, and initially during the transition its volume appeared to increase. However, after a short-lived surge in 1989, major western receiving countries began to record *declining* numbers of migrants from CEE nations (Organization for Economic Cooperation and Development 1996). Germany offers an excellent illustration of the trend. The inflow of ethnic Germans peaked in 1989–90, asylum seekers in 1991–3, and regular migrants in 1991–2. In each case, the flows leveled off shortly after the peak (Garson, Redor, and Lemaitre 1997).

In certain CEE nations, outflows, irrespective of how large they were before 1990, soon stabilized and either became negligible (as in the Baltic States), were substantially reduced (as in Poland), or actually turned positive (as in the Czech Republic). Much of the decline was attributable to the exhaustion of stocks of ethnic Germans in the East. For example, the departure of ethnic Germans from Poland declined from 250,000 in 1989 to 134,000 in 1990 and gradually fell thereafter to an annual level of just 2,000 (Salt 1996).

An important part of the upsurge stemmed from the liberalization of emigration policies among nations (such as Bulgaria) that had not permitted any emigration before 1989. As a result, these countries built up a large "backlog" of people who were determined to leave, a substantial portion of whom quickly exited once they could. In Bulgaria, annual emigration averaged 152,000 in the period 1989–90, but by 1991–5 the volume had dropped to 56,000 (Bobeva 1996). In Romania the decline was from 71,000 in 1990–1 to 23,000 in 1992–5 (Gheorghiu 1996). The earliest emigrants were often "privileged minorities" (Germans and Jews) who followed the footsteps of coethnics from other CEE countries that had already liberalized exit controls (such as Poland).

Later emigration expanded beyond these minorities, but after an initial increase these migrations also began to diminish. The annual number of Bulgarian asylum seekers registered in the European Union, for example, fell from 21,000 in 1990–2 to 15,000 in 1993–4, while comparable figures for Romanians were 78,000 and 53,000 (with just 21,000 in 1994—see Eurostat 1996).

Successor states of the ex-USSR also recorded a dramatic increase in emigration to the West in 1990–1, but the outflow quickly leveled off. In Russia, annual emigration averaged 96,000 in 1990–1 but was only marginally higher at 105,000 during 1992–6 (United Nations 1996; Zayonchkovskaya 1996). It seems very unlikely that these movements will boom in the near future. To the extent that migration to the West continues, it increasingly involves the temporary migration of persons in irregular status rather than the permanent settlement of documented immigrants (Garson, Redor, and Lemaitre 1997).

Even labor migration to the West appears to be rather small, particularly if one restricts consideration to trips of at least 3 months in length. Even in Poland, which sends abroad more migrant workers than any other CEE country, the numbers recorded in the 1990s do not significantly differ from those recorded in the late 1980s (100,000–150,000 per year—see Okólski 1996). Increases reported by certain western countries pertain mainly to seasonal and frontier workers, and above all to temporary workers who disguise themselves as tourists. Even taking into account these very short term migrants, the total number of persons going to the West each year does not appear to exceed 250,000, which is relatively little.

Finally, mention should be made of two other categories that became novelties in many CEE nations after 1989: permanent settlers and labor migrants. With the transition to a market economy, countries throughout the region were surprised by sudden inflows of migrants intending to stay for a long time or even establish permanent residence, in great contrast to situation before 1990, when settlement was very rare and limited to complicated individual cases. Even in Hungary, the leader as far as immigration is concerned, official statistics indicate that permanent arrivals never exceeded 37,000 annually through 1990, and in three other countries where the inflow was significant (the Czech Republic, Hungary, and Poland) only 5,000–7,000 entered each year (Juhasz 1996; Maresova 1996; Okólski 1996).

After 1990, in contrast, many of these nations became popular destinations for large numbers of long-term immigrants, both regular and irregular. In 1995, for example, the foreign population of the Czech Republic housed roughly 159,0000 foreigners in regular status and 150,000–200,000 in irregular status (Maresova 1996). In some CEE nations the proportion of foreigners (mostly irregular) reached levels observed in the West. It is estimated, for example, that in 1995 foreign nationals accounted for 9–11 per cent of Prague's population and 4–6 per cent of Budapest's, with large concentrations of immigrants from Asia, especially China and Vietnam (United Nations 1996). Certain parts of the Czech Republic, Hungary, and Poland have already witnessed the establishment of "immigrant strongholds" capable of serving as foundations for future arrivals (see Lukowski 1997; Nyiri 1997; Drbohlav 1997*a*,*b*).

After an initial increase between 1990 and 1993, however, the number of documented workers stabilized at relatively low levels. The number of foreign citizens with valid work permits in mid-1996 stood at around 19,200 in Hungary, 13,500 in Poland, and 2,800 in the Slovak Republic, with Bulgaria and Romania reporting figures of just 100–200 persons (Hudek 1996; Juhasz 1996; Lubyova 1996; Okólski 1996). Moreover, with one significant exception, there has been little change in labor migration since 1994.

The Czech Republic is the only country to report a rise in documented labor migration, with as many as 67,000 foreigners holding work permits (including numerous Slovaks) and 39,000 registered entrepreneurs (Maresova 1996). Czechoslovakia was already known, of course, as a labor-importer in the pre-transition period, although from the late 1980s to 1992 the number of registered foreign workers had declined from around 100,000 to 15,000 (United Nations 1997). All CEE countries are estimated to contain tens of thousands of foreigners in irregular employment (Salt 1996).

## DISTINCTIVENESS AND HOMOGENEITY

The variety of migratory flows, kinds of migrants, and country-specific patterns make it difficult to depict current migration trends in general terms. The OECD Secretariat, however, notes a growth of flows between neighboring countries that share a common historical, economic, and cultural tradition (Organization for Economic Cooperation and Development 1996), and certain distinctive regional characteristics may be identified. Although these are not always obvious at first sight, three regional characteristics of CEE migration stand out.

First, the CEE region has increasingly become a migratory entity unto itself, as noted by those who have labeled it a "new migration space" (Morokvasic and de Tinguy 1993) and a "new regional migration pole" (Garson, Redor, and Lemaitre 1997). The number and size of international movements between CEE nations is considerable, even if one discounts those between USSR successor states. Moreover, intra-regional migration generally prevails over that between CEE nations and third countries. The region, thus, appears to have acquired the attributes of a stable migration system, in the sense described by Kritz, Lim, and Zlotnik (1992). That is, it encompasses a defined geographic area, is mostly self-contained, and internal political and economic diversity produces a variety of push and pull forces for migrants.

The compactness and geographic integrity of the region, along with its relative cultural homogeneity, make movements within CEE more attractive and less risky than movements beyond its boundaries. Moreover, within individual countries, the principal categories of migrants and the size of flows are relatively orderly and stable. The coincidence of massive population movements within the region combined with moderate outflows beyond it contradicts alarmist predictions of a massive westward exodus that were widely broadcast in 1990 and 1991. These forecasts went wrong in one important respect: although the scale of population movements was indeed large, most of the migration was contained within the region itself rather than being directed to the West.

Second, a large proportion of migrants arriving in CEE countries are in irregular status, at least at some point in their migratory career. Indeed, the region appears to be rather tolerant with respect to visiting and resident foreigners from within the CEE. In general, governments are reluctant to enact legislation and undertake administrative measures to cope with this new migratory reality, and the transitional and fluid nature of the legal environment in most CEE countries is conducive to irregular residence.

Transit migrants are just one of several categories of irregular migration. Irregularity is also widespread among short-term labor migrants, particularly those employed in the shadow economy, as irregular labor migration seems to overwhelm its regular counterpart throughout the region (Salt 1996). Long-term settlers display a similar tendency toward irregularity. Surveys in the Czech Republic and Poland reveal the existence of rather large communities of settled foreign families in which nearly all household members have failed to regularize, and most have few prospects of doing so (Drbohlav 1997*a,b*; Lukowski 1997). Even in Poland, which imports about as many workers as it exports, most departing Poles are in regular status while arriving foreigners are irregular (Okólski 1994). In Germany, especially, most of the irregular Polish workers of the 1980s were regularized during the 1990s.

Third, post-1989 movements between CEE nations not only defy registration; often they also do not even conform to conventional definitions of migration itself. A new type of international movement has emerged to become ubiquitous throughout the region and is poorly captured by the definitions and typologies now in use

(Morokvasic 1996). I have termed this form of movement *incomplete migration* (Okólski 1998*b*).

The essence of incomplete migration is its quasi-migratory character. Although incomplete migrants may not strictly fit the usual definition of a migrant, to a large degree they realize the economic functions of a migrant and often spend a considerable portion of their time outside countries of origin. Incomplete migrants are characterized by three basic traits: (1) a "loose" social status and flexible occupational position in the country of origin; (2) irregularity of status and work in the country of destination; and (3) the maintenance of close and steady contacts with people at home (through frequent visits, regular phone calls, periodic remitting of money, and long periods of residence at home, often for reasons of "professional necessity"). The survival of incomplete migrants depends largely on activities related to migration itself, such as interregional trading or cross-border petty commerce. Quite frequently, the migrants do not have access to regular employment, steady income, or social benefits in the home country.

Many incomplete migrants enter as tourists ("false tourists" or "overstaying tourists"). Jazwinska and Okólski (1996) report how a single job (say in domestic service) may be filled by multiple friends or family members who rotate in and out on short-term tourist visas. Incomplete migration also includes many circular migrants (shuttle or pendular movers—see United Nations 1997) and a relatively small, but by no means negligible, number of short-term labor migrants, along with dependents, foreign students, and various kinds of people admitted for humanitarian reasons (Aktar and Ogelman 1994; de Tinguy and Withol de Wenden 1994; Sik 1997; Wallace, Bedzir, and Chmouliar 1997; Morokvasic 1996; Iglicka 1998). Some short-term, incomplete migrants may become long-term settlers working in the shadow economy.

The distinct features of CEE migration notwithstanding, the region would probably have to be characterized differently if the successor states of the Soviet Union were excluded, especially Russia and Ukraine. Most migrants to the rest of CEE come from these two countries. Other countries in the region generally report near-zero outflows to CIS and Baltic states (with minor exceptions such as Bulgaria). Thus, a more exclusive geographic definition of CEE would probably yield smaller intraregional flows. Thus, a distinctive feature, if not a peculiarity, of CEE migration is that it, to a large degree, consists of movements generated internally within the former USSR.

In spite of some inter-country differences and a few exceptions, CEE nations were relatively homogeneous with respect to pre-transition migration patterns. Repressive emigration policies necessarily made their basic trends quite similar. Ironically, what most CEE nations had in common before 1989 was the *nonexistence* of most forms and categories of movement. This homogeneity, however, could not have been maintained into the 1990s, even if all countries had introduced identical migratory roles (which they did not). After 1992, the mosaic of migratory trends in CEE became very complex. Owing to space limitations, I simply sketch out that diversity as of the mid-1990s.

First, though overall population mobility is generally high across the region, it is low in three countries (the Czech Republic, Hungary, and the Slovak Republic) and moderate in three others (Estonia, Latvia, and Lithuania). Second, the long-term balance of migration with the West is significantly positive in just one country (the Czech Republic) and negligible in two or three others (Hungary, the Slovak Republic, and perhaps Lithuania). Other CEE nations have large negative balances, with the nations in the CIS taking the lead.

Third, with respect to intra-regional flows of long-term immigrants, six countries experience net emigration (Bulgaria, Estonia, Latvia, Lithuania, Romania, and Ukraine) and six experience net immigration (in descending order, Russia, the Czech Republic, Hungary, Poland, the Slovak Republic, and probably also Belarus). Fourth, only Poland and Albania, and to a lesser degree Romania, send significant numbers of migrant workers to the West. The Czech Republic and Russia are the only countries with a positive (albeit tiny) migrant–worker balance. In Russia, an estimated 100,000 documented foreigners are currently employed, mostly in joint ventures with western capital, and another 200,000 are working in irregular status (Knabe 1996). These figures far exceed the number of Russians estimated to be working abroad. For other countries, flows of labor to and from the West seem to be more or less even (Hungary) or very small (all remaining countries).

Fifth, Russia and the Czech Republic, along with Hungary, Poland, and probably the Slovak Republic, are the only net importers of labor from other CEE countries. Ukraine, Belarus, Bulgaria, and Romania are net exporters of labor (in descending order of importance) and Albania and the Baltic are very weakly involved in intra-regional labor exchanges. Sixth, Albania, Bulgaria, Romania and a few CIS countries continue to send asylum seekers either to other countries in the region, as well as to the West, whereas Russia and Hungary receive the largest numbers of people in need of protection.

Finally, in some countries (notably Hungary, the Slovak Republic, and the Baltic states), the intensity of international flows is diminishing. In Albania and CIS countries, and particularly Russia, however, population movements continue to be intense and rather unstable. In the Czech Republic, the inflow might still be growing slightly but the outflow is already near zero. Outflows from Bulgaria, Poland, and Romania have reached a plateau, whereas in Poland the inflow shows signs of both increase and instability. In Bulgaria and Romania the inflow is negligible, and therefore relatively stable.

In sum, even when migrants are classified into the broadest categories, movement within CEE is heterogeneous and diversified and can hardly be considered a single "migratory space" with common characteristics. There is no distinct dividing line to separate one group of countries from another and almost every one of the above seven criteria leads to a substantially different division of CEE nations. Obviously, however, there is a strong internal bond that creates intra-regional movements at rather high level.

At the same time, from the viewpoint of migratory links with other parts of the world, at least three distinct subregional patterns can be distinguished. The first comprises countries with very weak outflows but rather strong inflows, with the quintessential example being the Czech Republic. The second includes countries with high outflows and high inflows, with Poland being the typical representative. The third is made up of countries with strong outflows and weak inflows, such as Ukraine. This differentiation should be taken into account in all analyses of migratory trends in the transition period, in particular, those aiming to assess the impact of CEE migration on the situation elsewhere in Europe.

## INTERPRETATIONS

In order to understand the future of CEE migration, one needs to consider the stability of current trends and judge, those that are likely to continue and those that are not. For those that are not likely to continue, one needs to specify the new directions that future trends might take. Both tasks require insight into, if not a causal analysis of, the determinants of migration among CEE nations. However, as the foregoing sections have revealed, the trends are unusually complex and diverse, and this complexity, when combined with the inadequacy of data and the scarcity of causal analyses, renders this task formidable if not impossible. Despite these difficulties, I attempt to draw a few relevant conclusions and interpret them with respect to the postulates outlined at the beginning of this chapter.

My first postulate was that populations within CEE are characterized by a relatively high propensity to migrate rooted in a distinctive regional demography. In those countries where population flows were brought to a standstill between 1950 and 1988, high mobility was restored quickly after 1989. Although there are no real exceptions to the trend of rising international migration in the post-Soviet period, there are significant differences across countries with respect to the forms and directions of movement. Many countries recorded a striking decline in long-term outflows, including emigration for settlement, that was more than offset by a sizeable elevation of short-term and incomplete migration. At the same time, quite unexpectedly, all countries in the region witnessed a substantial influx of foreigners from outside the CEE region, in great contrast the pre-transition era.

The high population mobility now prevailing in CEE may be understood in terms of the two remaining postulates, one suggesting that the root causes of the high mobility are economic and the other insisting that they are political. In fact, push and pull factors within the region become active when both economic and political imbalances occur. To illustrate, I first consider a set of migratory flows with a relatively high degree of homogeneity in the region—specifically, movements between successor states of the USSR, which are the largest and most similar in terms of their root causes.

The underlying reason for this migration was the dissolution of the Soviet Union itself, although there *are* certain differences in the immediate reasons for migration among the four major sub-categories. Refugees and internally displaced people were generated mostly by "political rivalries and inter-ethnic strife" in the newly independent states (Shamshur 1996). Those who undertook more or less voluntary moves in the past, such as ethnic Russians who colonized non-Russian republics during the Soviet era, are now migrating back to their historic/sentimental homelands out of a fear of nationalism, socio-cultural or economic discrimination, and even persecution.

Likewise, the reason for the repatriation of certain ethnic groups deported from their historical territories under Stalinism (such as the Crimean Tartars) is that they never accepted their fate in the first place, and have simply been waiting for the moment when they could return. Finally, some regular and irregular migrants move in search of a higher quality of life, better jobs, and greater earning opportunities. Clearly, these first three categories (of which the third is least numerous) are almost exclusively motivated by political factors. Only in the last category, which is relatively small, are migrants significantly influenced by economic factors (Shamshur 1996).

Another relatively homogenous set of flows involve transit migration. Practically all transit migrants have a common objective: to limit their stay in CEE and get to the West as soon as possible. For these migrants, it is the new geopolitical situation of the CEE region that is attractive. Relatively liberal rules of admission in most CEE nations and the fluidity of their legal regimes, combined with increasingly restrictive rules for admission in western Europe, virtually exhausts the list of factors explaining transit migration (Salt 1996). Hence, once again, political circumstances matter more and the role of economic considerations is negligible.

A similar interpretation might be made of persons in need of protection (other than those migrating within the ex-USSR). Although they are relatively few in number, their movements are inherently political, as many such persons only pretend to be in need of protection. In order to improve their chances of reaching a western country and avoiding deportation, many people register as refugees within CEE nations but are really in transit to the West. Other cases comprise bona fide refugees, fleeing countries in turmoil from which access to the West is rather difficult and which are located relatively near CEE. Their choice of a CEE destination is frequently accidental and rather of the "second best" type.

There is only one quantitatively large category of migration whose rise in recent years may be interpreted simultaneously in both political and economic terms: incomplete migration. Although both factors are relevant in explaining the remaining three types of flows (migrant workers, emigrants to the West, and immigrants into CEE), their quantitative significance has been low and declining in recent years. Nonetheless, in all four cases it is reasonable to assume that political developments within CEE and in western receiving nations have been of crucial importance in establishing potential opportunities for, and also constraints on, international mobility.

The major political factor affecting movements since 1989 has been a dramatic liberalization of migration policies throughout CEE (although not entirely coherent in all countries). This liberalization involved the abolition of exit visas, the removal of restrictions on the issuance of passports, the modification of nationality laws, the abandonment of entry visas, the softening of non-visa barriers for Europeans as well as many non-Europeans, the introduction of a legal basis for the contract employment of foreigners, the ratification of the Geneva Convention on Refugees, and the establishment of a framework for labor migration to the West (Garson, Redor, and Lemaitre 1997).

These reforms were paralleled by important changes in the migration policies of Western countries. Along with the lifting of visa requirements for citizens of certain CEE nations (such as Poland), readmission agreements with those countries have been concluded, and more rigorous admission rules have been enforced (Frejka 1996*b*). For example, asylum applicants and ethnic Germans from certain CEE nations have become subject to much tighter scrutiny than before 1990. At the same time, however, modified guest worker schemes have been developed in some Western countries (such as Germany) that allow labor inflow from CEE nations under rules that strictly control access to western employment and seek to impose a "rotation principle" (Salt 1996; United Nations 1997), allegedly to provide legal pathways for migrants who would inevitably find other, more clandestine ways into Western labor markets (Kuptsch and Oishi 1995).

The effect of these political factors on migration from CEE nations has undoubtedly been great, if only by offering potential migrants some freedom of choice. But these factors, though greatly facilitating the cross-border movement of people, have made it much more difficult for persons from CEE to emigrate permanently to the West, or, more precisely, to be admitted for permanent settlement (or at least a long-term stay).

Economic factors operate at both the micro and macro levels. The importance of macroeconomic factors has been underscored by Garson, Redor, and Lemaitre (1997). First, the market transition has yielded an excess in the supply of labor (in contrast to the situation before 1989), and hence, relatively high levels of unemployment in regimes that offer few social protections to the unemployed, thus compelling many unemployed persons (particularly the young, the unskilled, and recent school leavers) to seek employment in the West.

Second, macroeconomic theory generally holds that the intensity of international exchange with respect to goods is inversely associated with the intensity of exchange with respect to people. As CEE trade was redirected away from its previous emphasis on COMECON nations and toward exchanges with the West, the outflow of labor to western countries decreased while labor migration between CEE nations increased. Likewise, the inflow of western capital in the form of direct foreign investment, produced a decrease in the outflow of labor from CEE nations by creating better paid jobs, although there was a strong differentiation between countries that absorbed relatively large quantities of capital (where migratory pressures diminished) and those that did not (where they persisted).

The liberalization of centrally planned economies also revealed comparative advantages among different CEE countries, as well as other differences with respect to labor market development, the structure of international trade, and the quantity and nature of capital inflows. These differences produced widening income differentials between CEE nations, with varying effects on international migration (United Nations 1997).

The above reasoning leads to a somewhat disappointing conclusion—that the fundamental macroeconomic forces operating with the CEE region might exert opposite, mutually contradictory influences on international migration depending on where and how they play out. Whereas some macroeconomic developments might stimulate migration from certain CEE nations to other CEE or western nations, other macroeconomic trends might inhibit such movement and even lead to an inflow of foreigners from outside the region.

Apart from this rather confusing assessment, there is also the question of how plausible macroeconomic arguments are given the relatively immature nature of markets in most CEE nations and the high degree of state protectionism and interventionism that still remain. Barta and Url (1997) divide the process of market transition into four phases—adjustment, restructuring, recovery, and growth. Whereas a few CEE nations have entered the phase of recovery, most are only at the stage of restructuring and none have yet reached growth.

Microeconomic theory argues that market transformations alter the decision-making environment for individuals and enhances the role of collective household strategies in adapting to structural change, notably through migration (Jazwinska and Okólski 1996). An important consequence of the market reforms implemented since 1989 has been a growing freedom of choice and a rise in independent decision-making by individuals and households in both labor and consumer markets. These reforms mean that more people must take greater risks, and acquire more competence and responsibility in decision-making, which brings about a differentiation in wage levels and career prospects, usually to the advantage of the younger and better educated (Okólski 1998*c*).

In the context of a rapidly changing and unstable economic and political environment, these circumstances have led to a polarization of people into two opposing strategies, one dynamic, risk-taking and future-oriented, and thus open to mobility, and the other conservative, risk-minimizing and survival-oriented that is less conducive to change of any sort. The latter strategy was initially adopted in response to the shocks of transition by a majority of households and individuals in CEE nations, yielding a decline in population mobility (Okólski 1997). Migrants were recruited primarily from those adopting the former strategy, people who were relatively young, predominantly urban, and if unemployed often voluntarily so by their own choice.

There might be a number of motivations behind migration undertaken in response to structural change, but most seem to have a common denominator: the accumulation of capital in order to achieve a stable adaptation to the conditions of a market economy (Schmidt-Hauer 1993). Under conditions of declining real incomes typical during the early stages of market transition, some households decide to invest in migration, sending family members abroad to earn money in hopes of diversifying sources of household income sources through remittances (or other benefits) to decrease the risks inherent in the transition (see Taylor, this volume; and Stark 1991). For many would-be entrepreneurs, including peasants seeking to transform themselves into modern farmers, migration also constitutes an effort to acquire the initial capital necessary to finance productive investments. For others, migration may simply be defensive strategy against social degradation (Jazwinska and Okólski 1996; Morokvasic 1996).

Considering both macro and micro processes, massive incomplete migration (predominantly within the CEE region but also to the West) might be interpreted as follows.

The *sine qua non* for migration to occur was political liberalization after 1989, which expanded individual freedom of choice. Once begun, incomplete migration fed on the shifting, transitory character of political and economic reality, the creation of deep structural economic imbalances in one country or a group of countries, the inadequacy of legal codes and inefficient law enforcement, and floating social and economic structures. The list of more specific factors is too long to be quoted here, but two deserve mention if only because they are often overlooked by researchers.

One is the emergence of a powerful incentive to seek additional income abroad—to maintain pre-transition standards of living during a period of dramatic decline in real income and a scarcity of jobs in the home country. The second factor is the emergence of large masses of unemployed, "loosely employed" or "rootless" people with no practical obstacles to travel. In the case of migrants from ex-Soviet republics, particularly, a striking characteristic is that they have a lot of time to spare and the price of their time is very cheap. Under such circumstances, it scarcely matters what profit (if any) is made out of migration, as such people are often seen carrying from one country to another very small quantities of cash or merchandise.

At present, this form of incomplete migration seems most relevant to people from Belarus and Ukraine (but also some other countries) who formally remain employed in their home countries but who are not producing, not being paid, or only earning a fraction of what they are entitled to, owing to the economic slump and the decline in factory production. For such people, migration is often a matter of survival.

More sophisticated forms of incomplete migration—such as the monopolization of certain seasonal jobs in specific markets or the rotation of migrants from the same household or community to irregular employment in the same job—mainly migrants from Poland who travel to the West, taking advantage of the experience acquired by other Poles during their pioneering migrations in the 1980s (Jazwinska and Okólski 1996). Recent migration surveys conducted in Poland reveal many farm households where working age members are engaged in incomplete migration outside the country and the work is being done by irregular migrants from the former Soviet Union.

In sum, motivations for incomplete migration appear to be largely economic, with the distinct exception of movements undertaken by Polish migrants, who are successors to the pendular migrants first identified by Morokvasic (1992). While the adaptive strategies and related migratory behaviors might seem perfectly normal, the economic environment which gave rise to incomplete migration is not. Rather, it is characterized by various structural imbalances, market imperfections, legal loopholes that create a fertile ground for this kind of international population mobility.

The determinants of regular, documented migration to the West are vastly different, depending on the direction of movement and position of the worker in the host country. Since these movements result from sovereign individual decisions, the political foundations on which they rest constitute a necessary initial condition. A large majority of laborers originating in the CEE region are Polish, nearly half of whom are seasonal workers in Germany. However, no systematic explanation based on transition-related factors can be offered for the migratory motives of these people.

Although the ultimate determinants are definitely pull factors, the root causes seem to be diversified and almost randomly distributed, for several reasons.

First, the number of those who can actually manage to work in the West at any moment is a tiny minority of those ready to do so. Furthermore, workers who were in irregular employment in the Federal Republic of Germany in the 1980s constitute a large part of this group and previously established links with German employers appear to be the biggest single factor discriminating those who acquired legal permission to work in Germany and those who did not. In other words, new regulations adopted in the West, especially in Germany, simply helped to regularize the status quo. Despite official agreements reached by respective governments, workers from regions of Poland particularly stricken by unemployment do not seem to enjoy preferential access to the German labor market (Okólski 1994, 1995, 1996).

A large proportion of documented migrant workers within CEE nations are top-level professionals posted by their companies. For them, the macroeconomic situation that brought their firms to CEE is practically the only factor that matters. The remaining and relatively much larger category of foreign workers (though small compared with the total labor force) is made up of low-skilled workers from CEE countries that are lagging behind in undertaking economic reforms, as well as those individuals from remote countries (such as China and Vietnam) who set up small businesses in the region. Regardless of the small size of these flows, their existence is of utmost importance because it reflects what the normal operation of a properly functioning market, which suggests that labor markets in transition economies are beginning to emit clear signals.

Ethnic factors have also been instrumental in bringing numerous immigrants into the region. Owing to post-1945 boundary changes or other political factors, many people found themselves as minorities in their own homelands, and were thus highly motivated to emigrate. Until 1990 they were effectively prevented from moving to their "titular motherlands" and afterward they were often treated more as repatriated nationals rather than immigrants. The case of Romanians of Hungarian origin, who migrated in large numbers to Hungary in 1989 and 1990, also suggest the existence of decisive push factors, such as deplorable and deteriorating living conditions and a highly unstable political situation. In this case, ethnic considerations were of crucial importance in just one thing: selecting the country of destination.

There are two remaining components of immigration to CEE that are statistically non-negligible: re-emigration (particularly of young persons) and the immigration of foreign citizens from "alien" ethnic backgrounds. In these cases, push factors appear to be relatively unimportant, at least with respect to choice of destination country. Instead, the improved economic performance and growing political stability of the receiving country cannot be overestimated. Nonetheless, at the moment these flows remain small in quantitative terms.

The only category of movement reflecting the same set of determinants across all countries in the region is emigration to the West. This outflow is highly constrained by the absorptive capacity (operationalized through entry controls) of the destination countries (although restrictions may also be imposed by origin nations). When the supply of potential emigrants grossly exceeds the demand for them, the problem becomes politicized. Before 1989, for example, many western countries opened "side doors" for the immigration from CEE, but usually only for specifically defined groups and for specific political purposes. Since the transition, the political motives for admitting immigrants from CEE have been gradually disappearing, and most western nations have steady sought to close the doors on people arriving from CEE nations.

The case of Polish citizens searching for a way into western countries in the early 1990s serves as a good illustration. Owing to the strategic importance of Poland in undermining of the Soviet system, Poles were readily accepted as the immigrants by many western countries during the 1980s. After 1990, however, the various side doors were closed, even the one that had been most widely open in the pre-transition period, that opened for ethnic Germans. The only "loophole" that remains for Poles is the U.S. visa lottery. The pressure of Polish applicants was so great that between 1992 and 1994, Poles obtained a majority of the visas given away to lucky winners. In 1995 the lottery met with so many applications from Polish citizens (six times greater than the next largest country), that in 1996 it was removed from the list of eligible countries (Okólski 1995). Thus, restrictive immigration policies in western countries appear to have done little to dampen motivations for emigration to the West.

In many CEE countries, emigration is no longer the only possible response to a structural imbalance. Other feasible choices have emerged both at home and abroad, which brings the discussion to one final question: what factors have helped transform the westward outflow from long-term to short-term migration? As already observed, a powerful force that decreased the number of persons immigrating from CEE to western nations was a tightening of admission rules by the latter. Despite the relatively high migratory potential of many CEE countries, however, people have generally become much less desperate to emigrate to the West. One of the reasons for this is the adoption of liberal exit rules which enable migrants to go and return at any time, and to do so as many times as they wish, which in reality open the way for multiple short-term migration. As a result, after 1989 circulation of the same persons contributed much more to the increase in the volume of migration than the increase in the number of persons migrating (Jazwinska and Okólski 1996).

The popularity of short-term migration (not only under the guise of tourism), which in the 1990s "absorbed" a substantial part of the potential long-term migration, reflects one more factor: a change in the migration-related cost-benefit ratio. While the costs of migration rose with the removal of rail and air subsidies, the dismantling of institutional protections for migrants, and increased risks of deportation, there was no meaningful increase in benefits, as increased earnings were offset by a decline in their purchasing power. As a result, movements involving short distances and a relatively short stay abroad became much more profitable.

One final determinant of movement of within CEE has been the emergence of new economic and political diversity among countries of the region. This diversity has substantially reinforced historical peculiarities of migration within particular countries and has led to intra-regional differentiation of migration trends, which vary according to the degree of political liberty enjoyed by the population, the extent of political corruption, the scope of social security, the level of economic performance, wage levels, the size of shadow economy, etc.

The analysis of this section suggests that most of the important CEE migrations of the 1990s had their source in political developments, either within the region or elsewhere in the world, although some flows reflected an interplay of political and economic factors. Incomplete migration, in particular, has risen as populations have adapted to liberation from the ban on free movement in combination with internal economic imbalances, such as the rise of shadow economy and a radical drop in the demand for low-skilled labor. Nonetheless, particular flows to or from particular CEE countries stemmed from significantly different sets of determinants, reflecting the great diversity of migration flows throughout the region. This diversity makes it very difficult to evaluate recent migration trends in terms of their stability and future course of development.

## STABILITY OF TRENDS IN TRANSITION

In discussing the stability of current CEE migration trends, I considered four distinct types of migration: the ethnicity-related movements between the ex-Soviet republics, transit migrations, incomplete migration, and all other important flows described earlier. As for the first type, movements within the ex-USSR presently show strong signs of subsiding. The main reason is obvious: these movements are presently at a point in their cycle where the pool of potential migrants can only shrink. The transformation of a rising trend (observed through 1994) into a declining trend (clearly visible in recent years) appears to be relatively stable, although it does not preclude a further shifting of flows to countries outside the former Soviet Union. In particular, the many recent migrants who still live in makeshift arrangements under a deteriorated standard of living might decide to undertake migration once again, this time to countries to the west of former Soviet boundaries.

Trends in transit migration are surprisingly stable, despite the fact that national origins are somewhat volatile and subject to abrupt changes. A number of CEE nations have, rather unwillingly, assumed the role of *cordonne sanitaire* for the new "fortress of Europe," the European Union. With the exception of Turkey, CEE nations offer the only land access to Europe from the Third World and they have, thus, increasingly become targets for migration from Asia and Africa. Since the migratory potential of developing countries is expected to grow (Salt 1996; United Nations 1997), transit migration through CEE will probably also rise. The only uncertainty is which countries will be most affected. The admission of certain countries into the European Union (or any transitory phase towards this), may shift the critical migration staging area (presently Poland and the Czech Republic) a little eastward (Ukraine and Belarus).

Incomplete migration, meanwhile, might soon be contracting, as the suspended economic reforms in countries containing most incomplete migrants cannot continue indefinitely (Ukraine, Belarus, Romania, and a few other countries). Ukraine, for instance, aspires to the status of a reliable and independent European partner, whereas Belarus aims to have a closer partnership with Russia. For these countries, economic reforms would seem to be a matter of survival. Bolder introduction of industrial restructuring and macroeconomic stabilization packages might quickly remove many of the incentives for interrupted movement. Should this happen, incomplete migration would be reduced to its pre-1989 form of occasional movements of petty traders devoid of strong economic and social consequences (see Morokvasic 1992; Jazwinska and Okólski 1996).

The last category of migratory flows includes "all others," most of which flourished immediately after the onset of the transition (such as emigration to the West). In general, these movements all stabilized within a relatively short time, mostly by 1992. The principal determinants of these flows were political and, to a lesser degree, economic and their character was discrete and revolutionary. Because of this, after a short period of adaptation these flows started to "normalize" in political and economic terms and to display a relatively smooth course and continuity. Relative stability seems to be characteristic of all movements in CEE except for transit migration, movements within the former USSR, and, especially, movements by persons in need of protection, mainly the victims of armed and other grave conflicts. The relevant trend is particularly hard to predict, but who can predict wars?

The foregoing review suggests that the era of vast and sudden changes in population movement might already be past, and that CEE migration within the next few years will witness no major swings. Possibly the most likely and far-reaching change would involve the emergence of large-scale emigration from the ex-USSR owing to the failure of economic reforms, political destabilization, and social disorder. In this case, the outflow would almost certainly be directed towards the West.

Another potential change, though not particularly likely, might be the acceleration of economic reforms in Russia, Ukraine, and Belarus, which could produce a dramatic decline in the intensity of incomplete migration and a substantial influx of migrant workers to these countries. A contrasting hypothesis is that limited trade between the ex-USSR and the rest of the region will produce an acceleration of outflows from European portions of the former USSR to other destinations in Central and Eastern Europe. Low levels of trade and economic cooperation in general will stimulate migration, mainly in the form of movements of temporary workers. These flows will probably be fostered by market signals from potential countries of destination such as the Czech Republic and Hungary, which are soon projected to suffer from meaningful labor shortages. Garson, Redor, and Lemaitre (1997) suggest that in the absence of closer regional cooperation, the receiving countries of CEE will have little choice but to accept this reinforced inflow from the former Soviet Union.

New migratory trends will also likely follow from the accession of a limited number of CEE nations into the European Union. Anticipatory movements of people from the countries excluded from the accession to other, more fortunate countries might occur on a large scale. The first to consider such migration will probably be members of groups having ethnic homelands in newly admitted nations. They will be followed by persons who already have extensive experience traveling to these nations, such as former migrant workers or people involved in incomplete migration. Ukraine, especially, seems to be a major reservoir for such potential anticipatory migrants.

In the light of the growing demographic pressure on labor markets projected for several CEE nations over the next 10 years (e.g. Poland and the Czech Republic) western countries might begin to admit more migrant workers from the region in order to avoid later massive uncontrolled immigration. A closer integration of these nations within the European Union, inspired *inter alia* by an idea of alleviating labor market imbalances across regions, would lead to a similar outcome, although it would require a fundamental change in the region's educational systems and a greater convergence between education and training systems, which seems unlikely (see Biffl 1997). At the same time, however, increasing trade between CEE and the West, and foreign direct investment in the region, which is very probable in view of closer links with the European Union, will to some extent discourage uncontrolled emigration (Garson, Redor, and Lemaitre 1997).

Finally, CEE might embark on the path of intensified regional economic integration. This is even less probable in the near future than a decisive economic push in the largest post-Soviet states. If it were to occur, however, after a certain time-lag, characterized by temporarily elevated people movements (a migration hump—see Martin 1993; Martin and Taylor 1996) regional integration would greatly diminish pressures for large migratory flows within the region and between CEE and the West (Garson, Redor, and Lemaitre 1997). Most probable would be a limited integration, for example, among countries aspiring to European Union membership whose migration volume in general is already very low.

One thing is certain, both in the near and more remote future: movements of population within and from CEE countries will continue because they will be taking place in freer societies (Salt 1996). Moreover, due to unusual opportunities for migrants generated by the dynamics of transition in various countries, intra-regional flows will tend to prevail over outflows from the region, and undocumented movements will predominate over documented ones.

## References

Aktar, C., and Ogelman, N. (1994). "Recent developments in East-West migration: Turkey and the Petty Traders," *International Migration*, 32: 343–54.

Ardittis, S. (1994). *The Politics of East-West Migration*. London/New York: Macmillan/St.Martin's Press.

Barta, V., and Url, T. (1997). "Economies in transition: long-term growth potential, capital accumulation and labour-capital substitutability in five Central European countries," in G. Biffl (ed.), *Migration, Free Trade and Regional Integration in Central and Eastern Europe*. Vienna: Verlag Oesterreich, pp. 67–100.

Biffl, G. (1997). "Migration, labour market and regional integration: the role of the education system," in G. Biffl (ed.), *Migration, Free Trade and Regional Integration in Central and Eastern Europe*. Vienna: Verlag Oesterreich, pp. 269–90.

Bobeva, D. (1996). "SOPEMI report for Bulgaria," Paper presented to the Meeting of the SOPEMI Correspondents. 2–4 December, Paris.

Chesnais, J. C. (1992). "Migration from eastern to western Europe, past (1946–1989) and future (1990–2000)," *in People on the Move: New Migration Flows in Europe.* Strasbourg: Council of Europe Press, pp. 11–40.

Drbohlav, D. (1997*a*). "Imigranti v Ceske Republice (s durazem na Ukrajinske pracovniky a 'zapadni' firmy operujici v Praze) [Immigrants in the Czech Republic (with an emphasis on Ukrainian workers and 'western' firms operating in Prague)]," Report to the Research Support Scheme, Prague.

—— (1997*b*). "Ukrainian workers operating in the Czech Republic," Paper presented to the ISS/FES International Conference on Central and Eastern Europe—New Migration Space. 11–13 December, Pultusk (Poland).

—— (1998). "Information on the Migration Situation in the Territory of the Czech Republic," Ministry of the Interior, Czech Republic.

Eurostat (1996). "Asylum-Seekers in Europe 1985–1995," Eurostat/Statistics in Focus: Population and Social Conditions, No. 1.

Fassmann, H., and Munz, R. (eds.) (1994*a*). *European Migration in the Late Twentieth Century: Historical Patterns, Actual Trends, and Social Implications.* Aldershot: Edward Elgar.

—— —— (1994*b*). "European east–west migration, 1945–1992." *International Migration Review*, 28: 520–38.

Frejka, T. (ed.) (1996*a*). *International Migration in Central and Eastern Europe and the Commonwealth of Independent States.* New York and Geneva: United Nations.

—— (1996*b*). "Overview," in Frejka T. (ed.), *International Migration in Central and Eastern Europe and the Commonwealth of Independent States.* New York and Geneva: United Nations, pp. 1–16.

Garson, J. P., Redor, D., and Lemaitre, G. (1997). "Regional integration and the outlook for temporary and permanent migration in Central and Eastern Europe," in G. Biffl (ed.), *Migration, Free Trade and Regional Integration in Central and Eastern Europe.* Vienna: Verlag Oesterreich, pp. 299–333.

Gheorghiu, D. (1996). "SOPEMI report for Romania," Paper presented to the Meeting of the SOPEMI Correspondents. 2–4 December, Paris.

Hudek, L. (1996). "Contribution of Mr. Ludovit Hudek, Minister of Interior of the Slovak Republic." Paper presented to the 6th Conference of European Ministers Responsible for Migration Affairs. 16–18 June, Warsaw.

Iglicka, K. (1998). "The economics of petty trade on the eastern Polish border," in K. Iglicka and K. Sword (eds.), *Challenges of East–West Migration for Poland.* London/New York: Macmillan/St.Martin's Press.

International Organization for Migration (1994). *A series of five volumes: Transit Migration in Bulgaria; Transit Migration the Czech Republic; Transit Migration in Poland; Transit Migration in Russia and Transit Migration in Ukraine.* Budapest: Migration Information Programme/International Organization for Migration.

International Organization for Migration (1995). *Transit Migration in Hungary.* Budapest: Migration Information Programme/International Organization for Migration.

International Organization for Migration (1997). *The Baltic Route: the Trafficking of Migrants through Lithuania.* Budapest: Migration Information Programme/International Organization for Migration.

Jazwinska, E., and Okólski, M. (eds.) (1996). *Causes and Consequences of Migration in Central and Eastern Europe.* Podlasie and Slask Opolski: Basic Trends in 1975–1994. Warsaw: Instytut Studiow Spolecznych/Friedrich Ebert Stiftung.

Juhasz, J. (1996). "SOPEMI report for Hungary," Paper presented to the Meeting of the SOPEMI Correspondents. 2–4 December, Paris.

Jungbert, B. (1996). "Hungary," Paper presented to the NACC Seminar on Economic Aspects of the Impact of Migrations and Refugees on State Security. 16–17 September, Warsaw.

Knabe, B. (1996). "Re-emigration as a contribution to transformation processes in East European countries (the case of the Russian Federation)," Paper presented to the NACC Seminar on Economic Aspects of the Impact of Migrations and Refugees on State Security. 16–17 September, Warsaw.

Kritz, M., Lim, L. L., and Zlotnik, H. (eds.) (1992). *International Migration Systems: A Global Approach.* London: Clarendon Press.

Kubat, Daniel, and Hoffman-Nowanty, H. J. (1982). "International and Internal Migration: Toward a New Paradigm," in T. Bottomore, S. Nowak, and M. Sokowlska (eds.), *The State of the Art.* London: Sage Publications, pp. 201–32.

Kuptsch, C., and Oishi, N. (1995). "Training abroad: German and Japanese schemes for workers from transition economies or developing countries," *ILO International Migration Papers,* No. 3, Geneva.

Lubyova, M. (1996). "SOPEMI report for the Slovak Republic," Paper presented to the Meeting of the SOPEMI Correspondents. 2–4 December, Paris.

Lukowski, W. (1997). "Czy Polska stanie sie krajem imigracyjnym?" [Will Poland become an immigration country?]. ISS Working Papers, No. 12, Warsaw.

Lukowski, Wojciech (1997). "Polska Stanie sie Krajem Imigragyyjnym?," Working Paper, Center of Migration Studies, Institute of Social Studies, University of Warsaw.

Marach, D. I. (1996). "On the migration situation in the Republic of Belarus," Paper presented to the NACC Seminar on Economic Aspects of the Impact of Migrations and Refugees on State Security. 16–17 September, Warsaw.

Maresova, J. (1996). "SOPEMI report for the Czech Republic," Paper presented to the Meeting of the SOPEMI Correspondents. 2–4 December, Paris.

Martin, P. L. (1993). *Trade and Migration: NAFTA and Agriculture.* Washington, DC: Institute for International Economics.

—— and Taylor, J. E. (1996). "The anatomy of a migration hump," in J. E. Taylor (ed.), *Development Strategy, Employment and Migration: Insights from Models.* Paris: OECD, pp. 43–62.

Morokvasic, M. (1992). "Une migration pendulaire: les Polonais en Allemagne," *Hommes et Migrations,* 1155: 31–7.

—— (1996). "Entre l'Est et l'Ouest, des migrations pendulaires," in M. Morokvasic and H. Rudolph (eds.), *Migrants. Les nouvelles mobilites en Europe.* Paris/Montreal: L'Harmattan pp. 119–57.

—— and Tinguy, A. de (1993). "Entre l'est et l'ouest. Un nouvel espace migratoire," in G. Mink and C. Szurek (eds.), *Cet etrange post-communisme: Rupture et transitions.* Paris: La Decouverte, pp. 305–20.

Nyiri, P. (1997). "Organisation and integration in a new overseas Chinese community," Paper presented to the ISS/FES International Conference on Central and Eastern Europe—New Migration Space. 11–13 December, Pultusk (Poland).

—— (1999). *New Chinese Migrants in Europe: The Case of the Chinese Community in Hungary.* London: Ashgate.

Organization for Economic Cooperation and Development (1992). *Trends in International Migration.* Organization for Economic Cooperation and Development, Paris.

—— (1996). "Recent trends in migration movements and policies (note by the Secretariat)," Paper presented to the Working Party on Migration, Organization for Economic Cooperation and Development. 13–14 June, Paris.

Okólski, M. (1992). "Migratory movements from countries of central and eastern Europe," in *People on the Move: New Migration Flows in Europe.* Strasbourg: Council of Europe Press, pp. 83–116.

—— (1994). "Trends in international migration. Poland—SOPEMI 1994 report," OECD, Paris.

—— (1995). "Trends in international migration. Poland—SOPEMI 1995 report," OECD, Paris.

—— (1996). "SOPEMI report for Poland," Paper presented to the Meeting of the SOPEMI Correspondents. 2–4 December, Paris.

—— (1997). "How to improve the economic analysis of labour migration in Central and Eastern Europe?" in G. Biffl (ed.), *Migration, Free Trade and Regional Integration in Central and Eastern Europe.* Vienna: Verlag Oesterreich, pp. 351–8.

—— (1998*a*). "Regional dimension of international migration in Central and Eastern Europe," *Genus*, 54: 1–26.

—— (1998*b*). "Incomplete migration. A new form of mobility in Central and Eastern Europe: the case of Polish and Ukrainian migrants," Paper presented to the EAPS Conference on International Migration: Challenges for European Populations. 25–27 June, Bari.

—— (1998*c*). "Recent migration in Poland:trends and causes. A preliminary assessment," in K. Iglicka and K. Sword (eds.), *Challenges of East-West Migration for Poland.* London: Macmillan.

Ryvkina, R. (1996). "Refugees as factor of social tension in Russia," Paper presented to the NACC Seminar on Economic Aspects of the Impact of Migrations and Refugees on State Security. 16–17 September, Warsaw.

Salt, J. (1996). "Current trends in international migration in Europe," Paper presented to the 6th Conference of European Ministers Responsible for Migration Affairs. 16–18 June, Warsaw.

—— Singleton, A., and Hogarth, J. (1995). *Europe's International Migrants: Data Sources, Patterns and Trends.* London: HMSO.

Schmidt-Hauer, Ch. (1993). *Russland in Aufruhr. Innenansichten aus einem rechtlosen Reich.* Munchen/Zurich: Piper.

Shamshur, O. (1996). "The former Soviet Union," in T. Frejka (ed.), *International Migration in Central and Eastern Europe and the Commonwealth of Independent States.* New York and Geneva: United Nations, pp. 137–41.

Sipaviciene, A. (1996). "SOPEMI report for the Baltic States," Paper presented to the Meeting of the SOPEMI Correspondents. 2–4 December, Paris.

Stark, O. (1991). *The Migration of Labor.* Cambridge: Basil Blackwell.

Tinguy, A. de, and Withol de Wenden, C. (eds.) (1994). "Est: ces immigres qui viendraient du froid," *Panoramiques* (special issue), 14.

United Nations (1996). International Migration Bulletin, No. 9 (November), 1996. United Nations Economic Commission for Europe, Geneva.

—— (1997). *World Population Monitoring, 1997. Issues of International Migration and Development: Selected Aspects.* New York: United Nations.

—— *Transit Migration in Central Europe.* Geneva: United Nations Economic Commission for Europe.

Wallace, C., Bedzir, V., and Chmouliar, O. (1997). "Spending, saving or investing social capital: the case of shuttle traders in post-communist Central Europe," Institute for Advanced Studies, Vienna, East European Series, No. 43.

Zayonchkovskaya, Z. (1996). "The Russian Federation," in T. Frejka (ed.), *International Migration in Central and Eastern Europe and the Commonwealth of Independent States.* New York and Geneva: United Nations, pp. 119–29.

# 4

## Trends in International Migration in and from Africa

ADERANTI ADEPOJU

Spatial mobility is a fundamental social and historical aspect of African life. Indeed, Africa is rooted in migration; evidence suggests that the human race began there and migrated outward. Today, it persists as a region of considerable migration, both voluntary and involuntary. What sets it apart from other regions, however, is that most African international migration is intra-continental, consisting of regional movements by refugees, nomads, undocumented migrants, and seasonal labor migrants.

Deteriorating economic, social, political, and ecological conditions across the continent have produced changes in the direction, pattern, composition, and dynamics of African migration. Successive political and economic crises have triggered flows to new destinations without any prior historical, political, or economic links to countries of emigration. As the various crises have intensified, moreover, migratory outflows have increased in both size and effect. The adoption of policies of structural adjustment seems to have accelerated the pace of out-migration in the context of economic stagnation.

Emigrants to northern countries include skilled workers, students, semi-skilled and unskilled workers, and, in recent years, autonomous female migrants. In response to the imposition of restrictive immigration policies in the north, migration destinations have diversified and the outflow has feminized. The spread of intertwined political and economic crises to traditional labor-importing nations in west Africa, such as Ivory Coast, have increased the lure of nations to the south, such as Botswana and the Republic of South Africa. Increasingly, skilled professionals see these countries as viable alternatives compared with Europe, the United States, and the Persian Gulf. At the same time, undocumented migrants make their way northward in clandestine fashion through intermediate countries, often stopping at new destinations in Europe, the United States, and the Middle East, as well as in Central and Southern Africa. In this chapter, I outline the complex web of interrelated factors associated with migratory movements within and from sub-Saharan Africa.

### THE DETERMINANTS OF EMIGRATION

Rapid population growth has combined with unstable politics, escalating ethnic conflict, persistent economic decline, poverty, and environmental deterioration to shape trends and patterns of international migration in Africa. Broader international trends also affect the region—globalization, regional integration, network formation, political transformation, and the entry of multinational corporations in search of cheap labor. Although the specter of African refugees has captured the attention of the world (reflecting the large number of people involved, the traumatic conditions they face, and the massive foreign assistance they require), other forms of international migration have also increased—namely the circulation of low-wage labor, the permanent exit of skilled workers, and the clandestine migration of undocumented workers at all skill levels. Moreover, unlike refugee flows, which are largely confined to sub-Saharan Africa, these newer forms of migration are more often directed to countries in the north.

## *Demography and labor force growth*

Spiraling population growth and unemployment lie at the root of much international migration in Africa, as elsewhere in the developing world. The current rate of natural increase of 2.5 per cent per year means that Africa's population doubles every 27 years. During the 1990s, the region's population grew more rapidly than economic production in thirty-five countries of fifty-two nations. Only seventeen countries experienced a rate of GDP growth that exceeded that of population (United Nations 1996*b*: 22). Fertility remains high, and in only a few countries is the demographic transition under way; and even in these places population momentum ensures that large numbers of people will enter the labor force for years to come. Rapid population growth places a tremendous strain on the region's development as the disparity between labor force growth and job creation creates migratory pressures by generating high rates of under- and unemployment.

The most visible effects of Africa's ongoing economic crisis are in urban labor markets. With employment stagnating and rural–urban migration proceeding at annual rates of 6–8 per cent, newcomers are forced into the informal sector where, by the early 1990s, two-fifths of the urban labor force was "employed." Deepening unemployment in towns and cities reflects the incapacity of the urban sector to act as a "sponge" for the rapidly growing workforce, compelling people to consider alternative destinations away from what Findley (1997) has labeled "oversized metropolitan areas with undersized job opportunities."

Unemployment rates of 33 per cent or more among secondary and university graduates—the cream of the region's youth—illustrate the extent of the potential crisis. African populations are strikingly young, with some 43 per cent under the age of 15. Very few countries, even those in the developed world, can create jobs fast enough to meet the needs of such a burgeoning youth population. Unemployment among those aged 15–24 is generally twice that of the labor force as a whole and young people comprise between 60 and 75 per cent of the region's unemployed, even though they represent just a third of the labor force (International Labour Office 1994: 24).

Migration is a crucial link in the chain of events linking high fertility to labor force growth and unemployment. Although a high rate of population growth does not *necessarily* translate into migration, in the context of a deteriorating economy it provides a trigger for migration to be set in motion. This is precisely what is occurring in Africa, where millions of additional people join the labor force each year, adding to the large pool of unemployed and underemployed workers. Over the past decade, the region has experienced steady economic deterioration exacerbated by the imposition of stern adjustment measures, yielding a situation of daunting proportions.

## *Economic decline, structural adjustment, and debt*

Africa is caught in a vicious cycle whereby poor education, poor health, and malnutrition forestall economic growth to perpetuate poverty. According to the United Nations (1996*a*), "the damage wrought by decades of economic crisis is visible in today's deteriorating health and education structures." Africa is a region of contradictions: rich in resources, it is nevertheless the world's poorest major region. Of the world's forty-eight countries ranked "low" in terms of human development indicators, 77 per cent are in sub-Saharan Africa (United Nations 1996*b*). Across the continent, illiteracy remains high and health conditions continue to deteriorate. Owing to the failure of development planning to improve living conditions, the 1980s came to be known as the lost decade and the 1990s fared even worse, with absolute declines in many leading indicators (United Nations Development Program 1993).

Most African countries have been implementing structural adjustment programs for more than a decade. To adhere to the dictates from the International Monetary Fund and World Bank, governments have been forced to reduce the size of the public sector, in many countries the leading source of jobs, and the private sector has generally followed suit to drive up rates of unemployment for both family heads and young people (Adepoju 1993). In several African countries, the costs of structural adjustment have reduced access to education, health, food, and social services by removing subsidies, thus reducing the overall welfare of families, particularly the poor (Adepoju 1996). Cost-recovery strategies call for families to pay the full cost of health and education at a time when family heads are increasingly jobless. Parents unable to pay school fees grudgingly withdraw their children, faced with a burden that is heaviest for the poor, Africa's majority. The United Nations Development Program (1992) reports that the average African today is less well educated, less well fed, less well employed, and less well paid than in the immediate aftermath of independence. The destruction of the African middle class and the dismal economic forecasts for the foreseeable future combine to stimulate emigration.

External debt is another major constraint to development in Africa. At $313 billion in 1994, it was equivalent to 234 per cent of Africa's total export income and 83 per cent of its GDP, representing the highest debt burden for any world region (United Nations 1996*a*). As of 1994, average per capita spending for debt service was $43, compared with only $35 on education and health. With nearly two-thirds of its export earnings devoted to debt service, the region's capacity to mobilize resources for socioeconomic development and employment is severely constrained.

African economies have also been disrupted by civil war, political violence, and economic mismanagement, usually in the context of an overtaxed ecosystem, yielding local conditions that fall below the critical threshold for tolerance, forcing many to leave in search of a safer haven. Recent experiences in Togo, Congo, Cameroon, Sierra Leone, Ethiopia, Ghana, Uganda, Rwanda, and Nigeria amply demonstrate this phenomenon. Whether from village to town, town to city, country to country, or continent to continent, migration always responds to the pull of opportunity and the push of poverty (United Nations Development Program 1993). For many Africans, the push of abject poverty is more compelling than the pull of better living conditions abroad.

The story is not always negative, however. In Ivory Coast, Mali, Ghana, and Uganda, the removal of marketing boards that formerly paid farmers below market value for their products has enhanced rural incomes and reduced rural out-migration. In some cases, it has even stimulated return migration to rural areas. During the early 1990s, migrants from Burkina Faso returned home from Ivory Coast while others left urban for rural areas as living conditions in cities worsened. These trends will no doubt continue as countries continue to implement policies of structural economic adjustment.

### *Ethnopolitical conflict*

A large number of African nations contain multiple ethnic groups, especially those located south of the Sahara. Multiethnic states evince a high potential for emigration because inter-ethnic rivalries for scarce state resources and privileges bring about the cultural and political repression of minorities (United Nations High Commissioner for Refugees 1993). Conflicts between African ethnic groups often lead to mass exodus, internal displacement, and exile (Nnoli 1996). In 1989, for example, thousands of black African agriculturalists were forced to flee Mauritania for Senegal when the government undertook a program of "Arabization" whereby black-owned lands were seized for redistribution to Moors.

Poverty and economic decline exacerbate disputes between social groups. Under conditions where state resources are scarce, as in Africa, conflicts over access may become explosive, as the case of Rwanda demonstrates. There, ethnicity was rooted in an unequal distribution of power and land between the minority Tutsis and the majority Hutus; and behind this historical dispute lay intense demographic pressure on increasingly unproductive land (the country's population density ranks among the highest in the world).

Political instability resulting from political, religious, and ethnic conflicts is unusually strong as a determinant of migration in Africa. All over the continent, the explosion of ethnic violence has uprooted millions of people. During 1969–90, seventeen of the world's forty-three refugee-causing civil wars occurred in Africa, including high intensity civil wars such as those in Angola, Liberia, and Mozambique (Schmeidl 1996) as well as lower intensity conflicts in Sudan, Somalia, and Burundi. Ethnic rebellions, in which minorities fight for their rights against governments unwilling to treat citizens equally, were recorded in seventeen countries of the region, most of which produced major refugee flows. In states that lack a coherent central government, in particular, places such as Liberia and Somalia, people are often forced to flee struggles between clan- and ethnic-based warlords.

The Horn of Africa—Ethiopia, Djibouti, Sudan, and Somalia—has long been noted for generating millions of refugees. For decades, these countries produced large numbers of refugees fleeing conflict and drought. Later the focus shifted to West Africa, where prolonged internal conflicts in Liberia and Sierra Leone produced millions of refugees to the Ivory Coast and Guinea, as well as thousands of internally displaced persons. More recently, the spotlight has shifted to the Great Lakes region, where Burundi and Rwanda have become major sources for refugee migration. Although Rwanda is an impoverished and strategically irrelevant country, in 1994 it was the scene of major genocide that led to the outflow of two million refugees, who joined the one million Rwandan Tutsis already exiled from the country by earlier conflicts. Equally dramatic was the sudden return of nearly 700,000 Rwandan refugees from eastern Congo in late 1996 followed shortly by the forced repatriation of some 500,000 more from Tanzania.

External involvement in regional conflicts often increases the severity of violence, as occurred in Angola and Mozambique during the Cold War. Dictatorial regimes that systematically abused human rights were often tolerated by western democracies because they were anti-communist. But these regimes often fomented the emigration of skilled professionals by targeting students, intellectuals, and union leaders for harassment and intimidation. According to the International Organization for Migration (1996), sub-Saharan Africa lost 30 per cent of its highly skilled professionals between 1960 and 1987, mostly to Europe. Between 1986 and 1990 alone some 50,000–60,000 middle and high level managers emigrated from Africa in response to deteriorating economic and political conditions (International Organization for Migration 1996: 7).

Turbulent African politics have interacted with deteriorating economies to worsen the situation. Repressive totalitarian regimes frequently divert scarce resources away from economic development toward the military. When coupled with inconsistent policies and widespread corruption, the resulting loss of state capacity scares away investors to stifle development (United Nations 1996*a*). The collapse of the state itself promotes out-migration by people looking to escape repression and disorder (Adekanye 1996).

Although the African political landscape may appear to have undergone remarkable transformations in recent years, the shift to multi-party democracy has often been more apparent than real, yielding little more than cosmetic changes. In some countries, the transition to multi-party democracy has diverted attention away from needed economic policy reforms (World Bank 1994). The notable exception is the Republic of South Africa, a country previously ruled by a racist apartheid regime that was a destabilizing force in the region.

In several countries, such as Angola and Mozambique, and to a lesser extent Liberia, basic elements of infrastructure (schools, hospitals, homes, businesses) were devastated by war as family members were scattered far and wide, causing an entire generation of Africans to grow up without basic necessities. If this were not bad enough, human capital has often been threatened by total destruction in countries torn by civil war, often years after the hostilities have ceased. It is currently estimated that 5–10 million land mines are scattered about the countryside in nations such as Angola, Mozambique, and even parts of Zimbabwe. In addition to posing major threats to civilians, land mines also hinder the return of refugees to traditional farming occupations and prevents the rehabilitation of the agrarian economy.

## *Ecological deterioration*

Obviously, solutions to the region's refugee problems lie as much in the political as the economic sphere, but a notable contributing factor in Africa has always been the environment. African agriculture, in particular, is vulnerable to a lack of rain, depleted soil resources, and civil conflicts, yielding frequent crop failures that generate massive internal displacements to augment the already large pool of labor migrants. The physical geography of Africa is heterogeneous, embracing fragile arid and semi-arid ecosystems that coexist with more stable rainforests and coastal lowlands. National resource endowments are determined primarily by the local ecology. Although certain stable ecologies support the cultivation of lucrative cash crops, most arid regions are stretched to the limit by subsistence farming and the rearing of livestock.

The seasonality and the precariousness of the weather has strongly influenced the African ecology (Union for African Population Studies 1992). In recent decades, desertification has considerably expanded Africa's arid zones, affecting some 300 million people and now covering almost half of the continent (United Nations 1996*a*). As of the late 1980s, there were already some 10 million environmental refugees in Africa, with another 135 million people living on soils deemed vulnerable to desertification; 80 per cent of all pasture and range lands are threatened by soil erosion. In the last quarter of the twentieth century land productivity was estimated to have declined by 25 per cent (United Nations 1996*b*).

Poverty and landlessness are the culmination of a host of interrelated factors—small farm sizes, marginal ecological conditions, depleted soil, low farm productivity, intense population pressure, a lack of access to credit, and institutional constraints. Sub-Saharan Africa was the only developing region to register a decline in per capita food production during the period 1990–5 (United Nations 1996*b*). Landlessness and rural poverty generate emigration because small, unproductive landholdings yield low incomes that farmers must supplement with earnings from non-farm activities. Given the limited opportunities for earning in most villages, this need turns directly into out-migration.

In other words, a stagnant rural economy underlies much of Africa's high rate of out-migration. Unable to satisfy their needs and aspirations within the local opportunity structure, migrants quite literally move in search of something better (Findley et al. 1995). Migration often persists even in the face of worsening urban employment conditions because work opportunities, however inadequate they may be in urban areas, are more abundant than in rural areas. Cities also provide educational opportunities for the migrants' children, who constitute the bulk of potential emigrants.

The rudimentary nature of the technology available to most Africans makes it very difficult to fight environmental degradation, especially in the context of rapid population growth, increasing demand for land, and a fickle and often hostile climate. In addition, certain "mega-projects" dreamed up by development planners, such as hydroelectric dams, have contributed to the displacement of rural families and the destruction of natural habitat (Adepoju 1997*a*,*b*). In what has increasingly become a no-win battle, the deteriorating environment is worsened by recurrent floods and drought, periodically occasioning a massive loss of resources and the displacement of whole families and communities (Findley et al. 1995).

During 1983–5, for example, the outflow from the Kayes region of Mali more than doubled in response to a scarcity of rain. According to Findley and Sow (1988), drought-related circulation accounted for 63 per cent of all migration in the region, up from 25 per cent just prior to the onset of the drought. Circulatory migration also stems from periodic downturns in the urban economy and the increasing difficulty of finding stable, remunerative urban work. But in the main, circular migration of long duration from the Sahel, especially from Mali to France and other parts of Africa, has been a strategy for overcoming drought-related deprivation.

Migration as a response to cyclical downswings and seasonal shortages has long been part of the way of life of the Soninke people of Mali, and the cyclical nature of their movement is strongly maintained by the agricultural system they practice. For this ethnic group, migration is the most common response to drought given the absence of irrigation, inadequate hydraulic resources, and a dependence on subsistence agriculture.

## EMIGRATION AS A SURVIVAL STRATEGY

Thus, migration is commonly used by Africans to ensure the survival of their families or to pursue economic mobility to supplement dwindling household resources. Households generally select and invest in a family member who is viewed to have the greatest potential for generating migrant earnings and sending remittances. Propelled by the economic crisis, migration has become central as a coping mechanism to secure family survival. Analyses of African responses to structural adjustment amply demonstrate that, in the final analysis, it is the family rather than its individual members that determines which coping mechanisms are employed and the economic role played by each family member (Adepoju 1997*a*). Decisions about who should migrate, where, and for how long are still sanctioned, if not completely controlled, by the family so as to promote inter-generational flows of resources within the family. Because migration is used as a means of crisis management, however, it is not necessarily sustainable in the long run.

Africa's extended-family structure facilitates the subdivision of the family into two or more units that continue to function as an economic whole even when spatially separated. Indeed, a new phenomenon of "dual households" has emerged among families trying to maximize economic returns by combining earnings from places of origin and destination. Dual-residence strategies enable families to function as an extended structure in the face of migration-induced separation. Indeed, Findley and Sow (1988) have shown that migrants from the Sahel are especially likely to maintain several residences simultaneously. The expectation is that migrants will maintain close contact with family members left behind through visitations and especially remittances.

Another family survival strategy involves selective migration for education. A family adopting this strategy sponsors one or more members as migrants to gain education in the city. They invest in the person's education expecting to reap rewards when he or she obtains a job in the formal sector of the urban economy (Oucho 1990). The city-based family member typically feels compelled to remit regularly a substantial proportion of his or her earned income to support family members left behind at home.

For many families, remittances are a lifeline and the dominant source of income to pay for rent, home construction, medical expenses, school fees, business investment, and a variety of other activities. Surveys confirm that African migrants regularly remit home through both formal and informal channels. In some resource-poor African countries, the importance of remittances—especially those in hard foreign currencies—is given considerable attention by governments, which work actively to encourage labor migration (Adepoju 1990). In Senegal, for example, household budget surveys reveal that dependence on migrant remittances is considerable: between 30 and 70 per cent, and in a few cases as much as 80 per cent, of family needs are covered by remittances (International Labor Organization 1994). Similar findings have been reported for Mali (Findley and Sow 1988), Lesotho (Milazi 1995) and to a lesser extent Burkina Faso (Cordell, Gregory, and Piche 1996).

## CHANGING PATTERNS OF MIGRATION

Whether the migrants stay within their country, migrate outside their country but within Africa, or go to another continent depends on both regional opportunities and foreign constraints. The unstable economic situation in African cities and the continued weakness of the agricultural sector have drawn more people into circular migration. As the economic instability has deepened, however, fewer migrants have been able to find stable and remunerative work in traditional regional destinations. Consequently, circulation and repeat migration have expanded to a wider variety of alternative destinations, often to places without any historical, political, or economic links to the countries of emigration.

For example, just as the economic crisis began to reduce employment within Africa, the Gulf States became particularly attractive as destinations for highly skilled professionals. But even countries such as Saudi Arabia and Kuwait have been showing signs of economic stagnation in recent years, rendering growing counties such as South Africa and Botswana relatively more attractive to migrants. Skilled professionals, in particular, pressured by uncertain economic conditions at home, have found their booming economies to be convenient alternatives to Europe, the United States, and the Gulf (Adepoju 1991, 1995). Indeed, less than 1.5 per cent of sub-Saharan Africans living outside their country live in countries of the European Union (Schmid 1996, quoting Collinson 1993). The proportion becomes even more insignificant if we include in the denominator the millions of refugees who have relocated to nations bordering zones of crisis and conflict.

The migration of skilled Africans has antecedents in the 1960s, when developing countries engaged in an unprecedented expansion of education (Fadayomi 1996) and was latter spurred by a combination of economic, social, and political factors. In the 1970s, highly qualified, experienced workers in trades and professions migrated from Zimbabwe, Zambia, Senegal, Ghana, and Uganda, to South Africa and even destinations outside of Africa. Since the 1980s, emigration to Europe, North America and the oil-rich countries of the Middle East has intensified. A recent World Bank study noted, for instance, that some 23,000 qualified academics emigrate from Africa each year in search of better working conditions, and 10,000 Nigerian academics are now employed in United States alone (World Bank 1995).

One of the most striking effects of economic stagnation has been the shrinking of budgets allocated to higher education, causing depressed academic salaries, the erosion of research grants, and increasing student unrest. Paradoxically, about 100,000 foreign experts now work in Africa, far more than worked there at independence and about the same as the number of Africans working in Western Europe and North America. These foreign experts occupy positions that are not available to qualified Africans, and account for 35 per cent of the region's annual official development aid. Most aid agencies are unwilling to pay for local staff, insisting that staff come from the donor countries and obliging African governments to employ expatriates as part of the overall aid package (International Organization for Migration 1996).

Although the tempo of migration to South Africa has increased recently since the demise of the apartheid regime and its spectacular political transformation, that country has its own domestic problems, with unemployment being one of the thorniest. No more than 7 per cent of young South Africans who complete their education can find work, and an estimated 40 per cent of the country's workforce, 6 million mostly black persons, was unemployed in 1995, up from 30 per cent in 1980. South Africa's share of world gold output fell from 50 per cent in 1980 to just 23 per cent in 1995, as this natural resource has become increasingly costly to extract. At the same time, mechanization has reduced labor inputs by miners from traditional sources in Lesotho, Botswana, Swaziland, Malawi, and Mozambique (*The Economist*, November 2, 1996, p. 79). South Africa would have to grow at 7 per cent per year (rather than the current figure of 4 per cent) just to create enough jobs to accommodate the annual number of school-leavers.

## *Feminization of migration*

The traditional pattern of migration in Africa—male-dominated, long-term, long-distance, and autonomous—is increasingly feminizing. Anecdotal evidence reveals a striking increase in migration by women, who had traditionally remained at home while men moved around in search of paid work. A significant share of these women are autonomous migrants who move independently to fulfill their own economic needs; they are not simply joining a husband or other family member. Nonetheless, migration in Africa still remains very much a "family matter," with non-migrant members of the family intimately involved in and affected by migration decision-making (Adepoju 1997*a*).

The increase in autonomous female migration is not confined by national borders: professional women from Nigeria, Ghana, and to some extent, Tanzania now engage in international migration, often leaving their spouses behind at home to care for children. Female nurses and doctors have been recruited from Nigeria to work in Saudi Arabia, while some have taken advantage of the handsome pay packages in the United States to work for a spell of time there in order to accumulate savings to survive harsh economic conditions at home. Others migrate with their children to pursue studies in the United States and the United Kingdom, given that the educational system in Nigeria has virtually collapsed (Adepoju 1991, 1997*a*; Adekanye 1996).

The relatively new phenomenon of female migration constitutes an important change in gender roles for Africa, creating new challenges for public policy. In Ivory Coast, for instance, female migration from Burkina Faso has intensified in spite of the ongoing economic crisis in the receiving society. This is possible because women generally cluster in the informal commercial sector, which is less affected by economic crisis than the wage sector where most male migrants work. The emergence of migrant females as breadwinners puts pressure on traditional gender roles within the African family.

Thus, like men, women increasingly participate in migration as a family survival strategy. At the same time, traditional male labor migration has also promoted new roles for the women they leave behind. As jobs became tighter during the 1980s and 1990s and remittances thinned out, many families relied on women and their farming activities for day-to-day support (Findley 1997). Women become the *de facto* resource managers and decision-makers, particularly within the agricultural sector. The gendered division of family labor has also been upset by the loss of male employment through urban job retrenchment and structural adjustment, forcing women to seek additional income generating activities to support the family.

## *Diversification of destinations*

Africans constitute about half of the world's estimated 80 million international migrants (Schmid 1996). Close to 35 million Africans already live outside their country of birth and this number is expected to rise (Russell 1993). Findley (1997) estimates that 5.3 million of these international migrants were living in other parts of sub-Saharan Africa, with the greatest numbers coming from the landlocked Sahelian nations of Burkina Faso (about 1 million) and Mali (about 400,000), which together accounted for one-fourth of all African emigrants.

In recent years, African migration has become more varied and spontaneous. Many who migrate no longer adhere to classic geographic patterns, but explore a much wider set of destinations than those where traditional seasonal work can be found. This diversification is evident in rising levels of both temporary and long-term circulation. Findley (1997) notes the greater diversification of destinations among Sahelian international migrants, which more and more include small and medium-sized cities and rural areas. This shift away from major metropolitan areas reflects the serious problems they confront as a result of recession, structural adjustment, and the disadvantageous terms of trade for African products.

A trend toward greater emigration off the continent is also evident, with growing movements among African countries as well as to Europe and America. The emigration of Malians to France, for example, is increasingly chosen by experienced migrants who have contracts and potential support there. As a result, traditional seasonal and circulatory patterns of movement are being replaced by more diverse patterns involving complicated itineraries. With economic success not necessarily guaranteed even by circulation between two places, more migrants must move among multiple destinations to "patch together" a decent living (Findley 1997).

There is some evidence to support a pattern of replacement migration, whereby migrants of rural origin move to the towns to occupy positions vacated by nationals who emigrate abroad, as seems to be occurring in Mali, Burkina Faso, Ivory Coast, Gabon, and Senegal (where urban workers go to France) as well as in Egypt (whose migrants to the Gulf). In some instances, immigrants from neighboring countries occupy positions vacated by nationals emigrating abroad, yielding a stepwise migration pattern, first from rural areas to cities and then from cities to foreign destinations. As a result, international migration has become increasingly flexible with respect to the timing of moves and destinations, as migrants come to regard cross-border movements as fundamentally the same as internal migration (Findley et al. 1995).

## *Commercialization of migration*

For a long time, Sahelians, particularly those from Mali, emigrated mainly to France in order to engage in menial wage labor. This pattern is rapidly changing. A large proportion of Sahelian migrants in the Ivory Coast, France, and Italy can be classified as commercial migrants, especially those from Senegal. Sudarkasa (1974/5) observed such a phenomenon among Nigerian emigrants to Ghana in the early 1960s. What sets the Sahelians apart is their departure for unconventional destinations to which they had no prior linguistic, cultural, or colonial ties. Initially the emigration focused on Zambia, and when its economy collapsed, it shifted to South Africa following the demise of the apartheid regime. More recently Sahelians have been moving to Italy, Portugal, Germany, Belgium, and Spain, although there they encounter an increasingly hostile reception, with growing xenophobia, apprehension of foreigners, and anti-immigrant political mobilizations. As a result, a growing number are crossing the Atlantic to seek greener pastures as petty traders in the United States.

A notable example is the migration the Sufi brotherhood of Senegal to New York. These people—known as the Mourides—formerly worked the peanut basin in Senegal when peanuts were that country's primary cash-crop. As the soil deteriorated, however, farmers began to emigrate, initially to France but, in the 1980s, increasingly to the United States, where they established themselves in petty commerce. As the first Francophone Africans to arrive "en masse" in New York, they started out as street vendors, but after sustained harassment by city officials, the settled as merchants in a specific neighborhood (Ebin 1996). Once this base was established the momentum was set in motion and "follow-up" immigration blossomed.

The opening up of South Africa in 1994 was followed by an influx of migrants from various parts of the sub-Saharan region, including Nigeria, Senegal, Sierra Leone, Zaire, Kenya, and Uganda. Some of these nationals had earlier entered the Republic's then nominally independent homelands—Ciskei, Bophuthatswana, Transkei, and so on—clandestinely during the period of apartheid. The numbers were small and the immigrants remained underground. They were mostly skilled professionals—teachers, university professors, doctors, lawyers, nurses, and engineers—a situation that set them apart from the traditional migrants from the neighboring states, whose nationals were mostly unskilled mine workers and farm laborers. Traders and students from the Congo followed in 1991–4 as Zaire's economy, polity, and society virtually collapsed. The post-apartheid wave of immigrants from Senegal, Nigeria, and Sierra Leone consisted mostly of street vendors and traders seeking to capitalize on the relatively affluent market of the new post-apartheid republic (Bouillon 1996).

## *The emergence of illegal migration*

African migrants have increasingly adopted more sophisticated, daring, and evasive methods to enter northern countries, even as they tighten border controls. Movements are more clandestine and spontaneous, involving riskier passages and trafficking via more diverse transit points, for example, through Senegal to Spain en route Las Palmas. Some migrants enter host countries as tourists or students and later work without officially changing their status. Others travel via an intermediate country such as Gambia, Cape Verde, or Guinea Conakry to obtain false documentation for a fee en route to Spain, Portugal, Italy, or Libya (invariably via another country), giving rise to a multipolar and multidimensional migratory system. While some continue with traditional two-step moves from village to coastal city and to European capital, many others pursue varied itineraries through Sahelian or coastal African cities to reach their ultimate destination, Europe (Findley et al. 1995).

The closing of France to legal immigration from its African colonies and the Maghreb opened the door to illegal immigration and caused migrants to explore other destinations, legally or otherwise. Illegal immigration into Europe is boosted by poverty in source countries and more recently, political persecution and wars have increased the pressure to emigrate. This is especially true of Algeria, some of whose citizens hold dual nationality with France. Most undocumented migrants enter Europe through intervening countries such as Morocco, Algeria, and especially Tunisia. Undocumented migrants from African to Europe are likely to be curbed by the stringent immigration policies and new "safeguards" put in place (Milazi 1996).

Given the rising barriers to legal and illegal entry, migrant trafficking, hitherto a rare phenomenon, has increased and a growing number of young people are involved in daredevil ventures to gain entry into Europe. Individual stowaways engage in life-threatening ventures hidden onboard ships destined for southern Europe, and recently to as far as East Asia. Unscrupulous agents exploit desperate youths with promises of passage to Italy, Spain, and France via, for instance, Dakar and Las Palmas. Most of these people get stranded in Dakar, and others who manage to find their way into Europe get apprehended and deported on arrival or soon thereafter (Adepoju 1996).

According to Milazi (1996) since the early 1980s France has witnessed the influx of 4 million visibly "different" new immigrants, including many illegals. A large share of the new migrants are Muslim and Arab-speaking people from former colonies in North Africa and the Maghreb. In France, they were subjected to considerable anti-foreign sentiment. Muslims are believed to represent a danger from outside, are visible both culturally and religiously, and they have erected mosques in the heart of Paris, a nominally Catholic community.

In South Africa, about 91,000 illegal immigrants were apprehended and sent home by the new government after the end of apartheid in 1994, representing a 50 per cent jump in the number of expulsions over the prior three years. Three quarters were Mozambicans; others came from Nigeria, Sierra Leone, Ethiopia, and Zambia. These so-called "illegals" were accused of being involved in criminal activities; of infiltrating cities, townships, and squatter camps and taking away native housing; of adding to the decay of inner cities; of taking the jobs of locals; of working for lower wages and tolerating substandard working conditions; of exploiting South African girls by marrying them to obtain residence permits, and so on. To counter undocumented immigration, the government overhauled the system of border control and introduced new forge-proof passports and identity cards. In addition, "marriages of convenience" were more closely policed and employers who hired illegal immigrants were penalized (*The Economist*, March 4, 1995, p. 48).

## POLICY PERSPECTIVES

One cannot fully understand migration and its dynamics or prescribe appropriate policy actions without a thorough analysis of the economic, political, and demographic situations of both sending and receiving societies, as well as the prevailing policy regimes, especially at points of destination. Within the context of the labor market, the characteristics of migrants—their skill composition, demographic profile, and so on—are of considerable concern. As Schmid (1996) succinctly summed it up, "a mix of economic factors, ecological or social—demographic factors and conflict-related political factors attract or expel groups of people to and from states." I now address policy issues emanating from these sets of interlocking factors.

I begin with a few questions raised to focus my consideration of policy options for the region (Adepoju and Hammar 1996): What are the alternatives to migration in general and to international migration in particular? Is there, in fact, a "crisis" of migration in Africa? Perhaps the correct question should not be "why is migration accelerating in the face of poverty and deteriorating living conditions?" Rather, it should be "why is there not even *greater* emigration in the face of such dire conditions? And, finally, what are the types of migrants and their patterns of migration? What prospects are there at the end of the tunnel for Africa's economic malaise, political turmoil, excruciating external debt burden, and the vacillating effects of the structural adjustment?

Perhaps the real problem, and therefore the focus of policy should be economic development, not migration. Evidence suggests that migration proceeds with or without development, but that some types of migration respond to coherent changes in development policy. The political landscape, the sociopolitical effects of structural adjustment, and endemic ethnic conflicts have dampened any optimism that the region will emerge in the twenty-first century less distressed than it was in the 1980s, a period widely regarded as "the lost decade."

International migration will become more important and more visible in Africa in the future for several reasons. First, the prospects for internal migration in the region are increasingly limited and, in fact, shrinking as a result of generalized poverty, unemployment, inadequate land and socioeconomic insecurity. Consequently, some of the migration that would otherwise take place internally is likely to become replacement migration in urban areas and sequentially emerge as external emigration. Second, the prospects for South–South migration are not very encouraging. Several southern countries that have hosted immigrants from Africa in the past, especially those of the Persian Gulf, are undergoing simmering political upheaval and their economies need fundamental restructuring. The era of large-scale labor importation in the Gulf appears to be over.

In Europe, meanwhile, traditional receiving countries have tightened the requirements for entry and increased border controls. Immigration laws have been overhauled and apparent loopholes blocked. At the same time, the screening of those already living in these countries, especially France, has intensified to detect and deport those of irregular status. In spite of all this, it is certain that the pressure for labor migration in search of jobs abroad will intensify, as employment is simply not going to be available in Africa for the millions of people who will enter the labor market annually.

In Africa, more than in any other region, economic recovery and improved living conditions depend crucially on the successful resolution of ongoing economic malaise. Without improvement in this arena, effective and sustainable development is a mirage (Cornia and Helleiner 1994). But the goal is not in sight. The debt burden has dramatically reduced the capacity of African governments to mobilize resources for development. At the same time, foreign direct investment to Africa declined from 10 per cent in 1987–91 to 5 per cent in 1992–4 and to a mere 3.6 per cent in 1995 (United Nations 1996*a*). Thus, the alleviation of poverty and debt relief are crucial for future economic development in the region. In this context, the international community has a responsibility to help promote sustainable development and strategies that could alleviate poverty in the region and hence, forestall pressures for emigration.

Since meaningful development cannot take place in conditions of conflict, African governments must strengthen the democratization process and improve the quality of governance to ensure a greater and more effective participation of the people in politics and development. Governments should also redirect their huge military and security expenditures to much-needed socioeconomic investment. As experience shows for several African countries (Togo, Zaire, Liberia, Burundi, Rwanda, Sierra Leone, Somalia, Sudan), the absence of peace and stability discourages investment and leads to capital flight. African governments must realize that development is as much a political and economic undertaking. The Organization of African Unity's Mechanism for Conflict Prevention, Management and Resolution is a welcome initiative that has contributed to the peace process in Angola, Ethiopia, Eritrea, Mozambique, and Comores. So are the efforts of non-governmental organizations to promote better governance, facilitate conflict resolution, and undertake post-conflict reconstruction (United Nations 1996*b*). Such efforts should be sustained.

A familiar recommendation is to develop alternatives to migration in the source countries by helping them stimulate domestic employment to prevent large-scale migration. Clearly, persistent economic difficulties in Africa will spur additional migrants and the huge economic differentials between the North and South will lure many people northward despite strict entry requirements and tightened border controls. Experience shows that wherever such spectacular differentials exist, migratory flows, in regular but increasingly in irregular legal situations, are directed from impoverished countries to more affluent societies.

The sharp contrast between Mozambique and South Africa is illustrative: per capita income in the former nation is thirty-seven times that in the latter (*The Economist*, September 2, 1996, p. 35). As a result, even when South Africa erected electric barbed fences along its border with Mozambique, desperate migrants ventured and continued to risk entry. In the meantime, South Africa is undertaking a regularization drive for current undocumented migrants even as it seeks passage of tougher legislation to curb illegal immigration. But these are short-sighted strategies: in the long run, the security of South Africa lies not in these measures but in helping to stimulate the economic growth of its neighbors.

In the short term, economic growth and the development of human capabilities have the potential to enhance both the capacity and the desire of Africans to migrate. Movement will therefore continue, but advances will ultimately reduce the pressure to migrate, diminishing the "excess demand" for migration and, with it, migratory potential. National policies in population and development catering to the needs of the individual are therefore critical to reducing migratory potential. Long-term initiatives designed to provide jobs, land, rural development, access to credit, and a means of livelihood for the poor are crucial policy tools (Sadik 1993). Such programs, to be effective, must be built on the individual and, in the African context, the family.

The disadvantageous terms of trade for Africa's primary products, the unstable economic situation in the cities, coupled with the deteriorating agricultural sector will provoke different patterns of migration, traditionally directed to the cities, but increasingly destined for other countries. At the same time, the global economic downturn and the political and economic constraints on international migration in traditional recipient countries have taxed the ingenuity of emigrants, forcing them to increasingly diversify migration destinations.

The future is bleak for the region's emigrants, in view of the current restrictive policies being implemented in countries of the North and the inability of countries in the region to absorb more migrants. Four of the region's major migrant-receiving countries—Gabon, Libya, RSA, and Zambia—have begun expelling illegal immigrants. The European Community now gives preference to migrants from Eastern Europe over those from Africa, especially Sahelians. France, where domestic unemployment remains high, and influenced by xenophobic public opinion, has shipped planeloads of Sahelians back to their countries of origin.

These events in Europe should encourage Africa to act decisively in fostering regional integration. Sub-regional and regional economic organizations might facilitate intra-regional labor mobility and promote self-reliant development. The free movement of persons has already been institutionalized by the Preferential Trade Area (PTA) and the Common Market for Eastern and Southern Africa (COMESA), and most notably by the Economic Community for West African States (ECOWAS). Thus, integration is likely to accelerate, paving the way for closer economic cooperation and labor migration in the region. The problems posed by, and the policy responses to, migration, circulation, permanent residence, and settlement are quite different. Of particular concern in the region is the residence rights of aliens, especially in countries bound together in regional unions like ECOWAS.

In 1993, the Abuja treaty for the establishment of the African Economic Community came into force. Sub-regional groupings—such as the recently relaunched secretariat for East African Cooperation (EAC), COMESA, the Arab Maghreb Union (AMU) of North Africa, and the integration of RSA into the Southern African Development Community (SADC) in 1994—offer promise for helping to facilitate intra-regional labor mobility (Akande 1996).

Above all, since the growth of the labor force continues to outstrip employment growth and prompt emigration, the formulation and implementation of comprehensive population policies targeted at moderating population growth through fertility decline is an inevitable long-term strategy. Such a policy should be programmed within a national macroeconomic framework and explicitly address the population growth–labor force growth–employment–migration continuum.

## References

Adekanye, J. B. (1996). "Conflicts, Loss of State Capacities and Migration in Contemporary Africa," Report of Indepth Research on Emigration Dynamics in Sub-Saharan Africa (mimeo).

—— (1998). "Conflicts, loss of state capacities and migration dynamics in Sub-Saharan Africa," in Appleyard, R. (Ed.) *Emigration Dynamics in Developing Countries.* Vol. 1: Sub-Saharan Africa. Aldershot: Ashgate. pp. 165–206.

Adelman, H. (1966). "State Crime and Migration," Paper presented at the ISPAC International Conference on Migration and Crime: Global and Regional Problems and Responses. Courmayeur, 5–8 October.

Adepoju, A. (1990). "State of the Art: Review of Migration in Africa." In *Union for African Population Studies, Conference on Role of Migration in African Development: Issues and Policies for the 1990s*. Dakar, Senegal: Union for African Population Studies, pp. 3–41.

—— (1991). "South-North Migration: The African Experience," *International Migration*, 29(2): 205–21.

—— (1993). " 'Introduction," in A. Adepoju (ed.), *The Impact of Structural Adjustment on the Population of Africa: The Implications for Education, Health and Employment*. London: James Currey, pp. 1–6.

—— (1995). "Emigration Dynamics in Sub-Saharan Africa," *International Migration* 33(3/4), 315–90.

—— (1996). "Population, Poverty, Structural Adjustment Programmes and Quality of Life in Sub-Saharan Africa," PHRDA Research Paper No. 1. Dakar: PHRDA.

—— (1997*a*). "Introduction," in A. Adepoju (ed.), *Family, Population and Development in Africa*. London: Zed Books, pp. 1–24.

—— (1997*b*). "Emigration Dynamics in Sub-Saharan Africa: The Economic, Demographic, Political, and Ecological Conditions and Policy Implications," Background Document for The Twelfth Seminar on Migration: Managing International Migration in Developing Countries: International Organization for Migration, Geneva, 28 and 29 April.

—— and Hammar, T. (1996). "Introduction," in A. Adepoju and T. Hammar (eds.), *International Migration to and from Africa: Dimensions, Challenges and Prospects*. Dakar, Senegal: PHRDA and CEIFO, pp. 7–11.

Akande, J. (1996). "The Changing Obligations Arising from Bilateral and Sub-Regional International Legal Treaties and Instruments Relating to Migration and their Integration in National Law and Administrative Practice," Report of indepth research on Emigration Dynamics in Sub-Saharan Africa (mimeo).

—— (1998). "International legal treaties and instruments relating to migration in Sub-Saharan Africa," in Appleyard, R. (Ed.) *Emigration Dynamics in Developing Countries. Vol. 1: Sub-Saharan Africa*. Aldershot: Ashgate, pp 338–362.

Bouillon, A. (1996). "La Nouvelle Migration Africaine en Afrique du Sud. Immigrants d'Afrique Occidentale et Centrale a Joannesburg," Paper presented at Colloque Systemes et Dynamiques des Migrations Internationales Ouest-Africaines, IFAN/OSRORM, Dakar (3–6 December).

Collinson, S. (1993). *Europe and International Migration*. London: Pinter Publishers.

Cordell, D. D., Gregory, J. W., and Piche, V. (1996). *Hoe and Wage: A Social History of a Circular migration system in West Africa*. Boulder: Westview Press.

Cornia, G. A., and Helleiner, G. K. (1994). *From Adjustment to Development in Africa: Conflict, Controversy, Convergence, Consensus?* Houndmills, UK: Macmillan Press.

Ebin, V. (1996). "Negociations et Appropriations: Les Revendications des Migrants Senegalais a New York," Paper delivered at IFAN/ORSTOM Colloque Systems et Dynamiques des Migrations Internationales Ouest-Africaines, Dakar.

Fadayomi, T. O. (1996). "Brain Drain and Brain Gain in Africa: Causes, Dimensions and Consequences," in A. Adepoju and T. Hammar (eds.), *International Migration to and from Africa: Dimensions, Challenges and Prospects*. Dakar, Senegal: PHRDA and CEIFO, pp. 143–159.

Findley, F., Traore, S., Ouedraogo, D., and Diarra, S. (1995). "Emigration from the Sahel," *International Migration*, 33(3/4):

Findley, S. (1997). "Migration and Family Interactions in Africa," in A. Adepoju (ed.), *Family, Population and Development in Africa*. London: Zed Books, pp. 109–138.

Findley, Sally, and Salif Sow. (1998). "From Season to Season: Agriculture, Poverty, and Migration in the Senegal River Valley, Mali," In Reginal Appleyard (ed.) *Emigration Dynamics in Developing Countries, Volume 1: Sub-Saharan Africa*. Aldershot, UK: Ashgate, pp. 69–144.

International Labor Organization (1994). *World Labor Report: 1994.* Geneva: International Labor Organization.

International Organization for Migration (1996). *Emigration Dynamics in Sub-Saharan Africa: A IOM/UNFPA Workshop.* Geneva: International Organisation for Migration.

Milazi, D. (1995). "Emigration Dynamics in Southern Africa," *International Migration*, 33(3/4): 521–56.

—— (1996). "Immobility: Low Intercontinental Emigration from Sub-Saharan Africa—A Sociological Investigation," in A. Adepoju and T. Hammar (eds.), *International Migration to and from Africa: Dimensions, Challenges and Prospects.* Dakar, Senegal: PHRDA and CEIFO, pp. 89–111.

Nnoli, O. (1996). "Ethnicity, Ethnic Conflict and Emigration Dynamics in Sub-Saharan Africa," Report of indepth research on Emigration Dynamics in Sub-Saharan Africa (mimeo).

—— (1998). "Ethnicity, ethnic conflict and emigration dynamics in Sub-Saharan Africa," in Appleyard, R. (ed.) Emigration Dynamics in Developing Countries. Vol. 1: Sub-Saharan Africa. Aldershot: Ashgate, pp. 207–263.

Oucho, J. O. (1990). "Migrant Linkages in Africa: Retrospects and Prospects," Paper presented at the Union of African Population Studies Conference on the Role of Migration in African Development: Issues and policies for the 1990s, Dakar.

—— (1995). "Emigration Dynamics of Eastern African Countries," *International Migration*, 33(3/4), 391–434.

Russell, S. S. (1993). "International Migration," in K. A. Foote, K. H. Hill, and L. Martin (eds.), *Demographic Change in Sub-Saharan Africa.* Washington, DC: National Academy Press, pp. 297–349.

Sadik, N. (1993). *The State of World Population 1993*, New York: United Nations Fund for Population Activities.

Schmeidl, S. (1996). "Hard Times in Countries of Origin," in *Migration and Crime.* Milan: ISPAC, pp. 127–36.

Schmid, A. (1996). "Introduction," in *Migration and Crime.* Milan: ISPAC, pp. 1–23.

Sudarkasa, N. (1974/5). "Commercial Migration in West Africa with Special Reference to the Yoruba in Ghana," *African Urban Notes*, Series B. No. 1.

Union for African Population Studies (1992). *Conference on Population and Environment in Africa: Solicited Papers* (Botswana, 14–19 September). Dakar: Union for African Population Studies.

United Nations (1996*a*). *The United Nations System-wide Special Initiative on Africa.* New York: United Nations.

—— (1996*b*). *African Recovery 10(2).* New York: United Nations.

United Nations Development Program (1992). *Human Development Report: 1992.* New York: Oxford University Press.

—— (1994). *Human Development Report: 1994.* New York: Oxford University Press.

United Nations High Commissioner for Refugees. (1993). "Refugees: Focus." *Ethnic Conflicts 93.* Geneva: United Nations.

World Bank (1994). *The World Bank Annual Report 1994.* Washington, DC: World Bank.

—— (1995). "Rethinking Teaching Capacity in African Universities: Problems and Prospects," Study commissioned by The Working Group on Higher Education under the donors to African Education in 1993 Findings, African Region, No 33. Washington, DC: World Bank.

# 5

# International Migration in the Asia–Pacific Region: Emerging Trends and Issues

GRAEME HUGO

As home to 58 per cent of the world's population, the Asia–Pacific region looms large in any discussion of global population processes. Although Asia historically experienced considerable international movement, contemporary migratory flows are unprecedented in their scale, complexity, and impact. Every country in the region is now influenced by international migration, and labor migration has become part of the calculus of choice for people throughout the region. Although permanent migration by persons seeking refuge, family reunion, asylum, or work has grown markedly, the circulation of business people, students, and tourists has increased even more.

Although the Asia–Pacific migration system may be hugely complex, it is characterized by three distinctive features: (1) the existence of large outflows to other migratory regimes—notably to North America, the Middle East, and Western Europe; (2) the emergence of smaller but still significant inflows into the region of highly skilled professionals from developed nations (Hugo 1994); and (3) growing intra-regional movements of workers between countries of labor surplus and labor shortage, in addition to continued movements by refugees and other migrants.

The complexity of Asian migration is heightened by the region's remarkable cultural, ethnic, religious, and social variation, as well as by large interregional differences in rates of economic growth. Per capita GDP ranges from a low of around $200 in Vietnam to a high of $35,000 in Japan. There are also huge variations in demographic conditions (Hugo 1998). Replacement-level fertility was achieved decades ago in countries such as Japan, Taiwan, Singapore, and South Korea and the number of young people entering the labor force in these nations has now leveled off and begun to decline. In contrast, fertility has just begun to fall in other nations, such as Vietnam, Cambodia, and Burma, yielding annual rates of labor force growth of 2 per cent or more. Very often, labor surplus nations are located "cheek by jowl" alongside labor shortage nations.

Although international migration may have been significant during the colonial era (Hugo 1980), from World War II through the mid-1970s it was minor in both scale and impact. Since then, however, international population movements within Asia have greatly increased in size and complexity, reflecting the economic, political, demographic, and social transformations that have swept the region. Despite this recent growth, research on international migration is limited, for several reasons.

First, the recency of many of the flows means that there are few demographers, economists, sociologists, or geographers within the region who possess the training and experience necessary for international migration research. Second, data on international migration are of very poor quality in most countries. Consequently, it is not possible to establish the scale and composition of migration with any accuracy, let alone to address its causes and consequences (see the *Asia-Pacific Migration Journal*, Vol. 4, No. 4, 1995, for a critical assessment of data sources). Third, much transnational movement is clandestine; indeed, undocumented migrants probably exceed those who are documented by a considerable margin (Hugo 1996*a*).

Although several journals have emerged in recent years to provide outlets for research on international migration in Asia, much information remains buried in government reports and unpublished student dissertations. The literature also suffers from the usual shortcomings that bedevil investigators in other regions: the studies are predominantly descriptive, they do not address theoretical issues, and they provide little basis for generalization (Massey et al. 1994). Moreover, as Goss and Lindquist (1995) have pointed out, "researchers have been more occupied with evaluating the consequences of international labour migration on national economics, communities and households than with identifying the processes that lead individuals to pursue employment overseas." As a result, governments throughout Asia are formulating policies and interventions in a vacuum of theoretical and substantive knowledge.

## MAJOR TYPES OF INTERNATIONAL MIGRATION

An important trend within Asia has been a diversification of the types of international migration. In this section I briefly describe the major features of the Asia–Pacific migration system and discuss its recent evolution, drawing on the more detailed analyses of Pongsapich (1995), Bedford and Lidgard (1996), Martin (1996), Rallu (1996), Stahl and PECC-HRD Task Force (1996), and Martin, Mason, and Tsay (1995). That international migration has become ubiquitous in Asia is evident from Table 5.1, which presents UN estimates of the stock of immigrants residing in different Asian countries as of 1995. India housed the largest absolute number of immigrants (8.7 million), followed by Pakistan (7.3 million), and Iran (3.6 million). In relative terms, however, the most immigrant-dependent country is the oil-exporting principality of Brunei, where foreigners comprise 30 per cent of the population, followed by Singapore (15.5 per cent), Iran (6.2 per cent), and Pakistan (6.1 per cent).

### *Refugees*

Some of the largest forced movements in history have recently occurred in Asia. Although the end of the Cold War brought the promise of smaller refugee flows, Asia continues to produce more refugees than any other region, accounting for around two-thirds of the global total over the last 15 years. The 1990s witnessed a considerable

**Table 5.1.** *Stocks of international migrants and refugees in Asian countries, 1995*

| Region and country | International migrants | | Refugees |
|---|---|---|---|
| | Number | Percentage | |
| *Eastern Asia* | | | |
| China | 345,518 | 0.0 | 287,096 |
| North Korea | 36,816 | 0.2 | 0 |
| Japan | 867,667 | 0.7 | 9,061 |
| Mongolia | 9,998 | 0.5 | 0 |
| South Korea | 900,229 | 2.1 | 0 |
| *South Central Asia* | | | |
| Afghanistan | 29,993 | 0.2 | 29,993 |
| Bangladesh | 800,093 | 0.7 | 116,338 |
| Bhutan | 8,239 | 0.5 | 0 |
| India | 8,659,775 | 1.0 | 286,730 |
| Iran | 3,587,697 | 6.2 | 2,236,350 |
| Maldives | 2,702 | 1.3 | 0 |
| Nepal | 400,737 | 2.1 | 123,237 |
| Pakistan | 7,272,000 | 6.1 | 1,055,435 |
| Sri Lanka | 21,081 | 0.1 | 13 |
| *South Eastern Asia* | | | |
| Brunei | 76,832 | 30.2 | 0 |
| Cambodia | 22,064 | 0.3 | 10 |
| Indonesia | 95,837 | 0.1 | 97 |
| Laos | 14,486 | 0.4 | 0 |
| Malaysia | 745,401 | 4.2 | 5,308 |
| Myanmar | 100,000 | 0.2 | 0 |
| Philippines | 37,860 | 0.1 | 669 |
| Singapore | 417,808 | 15.5 | 12 |
| Thailand | 313,750 | 0.6 | 100,817 |
| Vietnam | 21,000 | 0.0 | 5,000 |

reduction in the number of refugees in Asia, however, and by 1995 its 5.12 million refugees constituted just 35 per cent of the total. The right-hand column of Table 5.1 shows the distribution of refugees among Asian nations in 1995. The massive displacement of people from Afghanistan to the neighboring states of Pakistan and Iran is immediately evident, with 2.2 million refugees in the former and 1.0 million in the latter. Relatively large refugee populations are also observed in China, Bangladesh, India, Nepal, and Thailand.

The large exodus of Indochinese refugees is not fully captured by the data in Table 5.1, as most Indochinese are resettled to third countries outside the region. Indeed, a distinctive feature of the refugee migration from Southeast Asia is the extent of third country resettlement, overwhelmingly to western nations such as the United States, Australia, or Canada, where they appear to be part of South–North migration. With political change and the opening up of Indochina, refugee flows declined in the 1990s. As late as 1992 there still were large numbers of Indochinese in China (287,000 Vietnamese and 4,200 Laotians), Hong Kong (60,000 Vietnamese), Indonesia (18,700 Vietnamese), Malaysia (12,500 Vietnamese), the Philippines (18,000 Vietnamese), and Thailand (370,000 Cambodians, 59,000 Laotians, and 15,700 Vietnamese). But by the beginning of 1996 there were only 37,000 Vietnamese left in refugee scattered camps across Asia. Some 80,000 people were voluntarily repatriated after 1989 in addition to forced repatriations carried out in Malaysia, the Philippines, and Hong Kong.

In addition to the refugee flows out of Afghanistan and Indochina, smaller but locally significant flows have emerged in recent years. Perhaps the most substantial has been the outflow of Rohinga Muslims from Myanmar to Bangladesh. In 1992 alone, some 300,000 such refugees entered Bangladesh seeking to escape religious persecution by the Buddhist majority (Rogge 1993: 4). Another important refugee movement has consisted of political refugees from Myanmar, where crackdowns by the military government led to significant outflows of students and intellectuals to Thailand, mostly to Bangkok. As of 1991, the UN High Commissioner for Refugees registered 70,000 Myanmarese refugees in Thailand.

### *South–North migration*

For more than two centuries the United States, Canada, Australia, and New Zealand have accepted immigrants and they are among the relatively few countries that continue to support active immigration programs. Until the late 1960s, however, policies discriminated in favor of Europeans and against Asians. Since the elimination of discriminatory quotas and the introduction of selection criteria based on skills and family reunification, the entry of Asians into traditional countries of immigration has increased substantially, a fact that is readily apparent from Table 5.2, which documents the increase in Asian immigration to four nations.

In North America the inflow from Asia increased sharply starting in the 1970s. Whereas during the 1960s a third of all immigrants to the United States, and two-thirds of those to Canada, were from Europe, over the next decade the share of Europeans fell dramatically in both settings—to 18 per cent in the United States and 36 per cent in Canada during the 1980s. By the 1990s, the share of Europeans had fallen to just 15 per cent in the United States and 19 per cent in Canada.

In contrast, from the 1960s to the 1990s the share of immigrants from Asia grew dramatically, going from 13 to 31 per cent in the United States and from 14 to 57 per cent in Canada. In Australia and New Zealand, the inflow of Asians accelerated more during the 1980s than the 1970s. Whereas just 11 per cent of immigrants to Australia and a tiny fraction of those to New Zealand came from Asia during the 1960s, by the 1990s the share of Asian immigrants had risen to 29 per cent in Asia and 52 per cent in New Zealand.

Europe has also become an important destination for Asian emigrants, as is evident from the data in Table 5.3, which shows the composition of immigration to Europe by

Table 5.2. *Immigration to North America, Australia, and New Zealand by region of origin and period*

| Nationality | 1960s(%) | 1970s(%) | 1980s(%) | 1990s(%) |
|---|---|---|---|---|
| *United States* | | | | |
| Europe | 33.8 | 17.8 | 10.4 | 14.9 |
| Asia | 12.9 | 35.3 | 37.3 | 30.8 |
| Americas | 51.7 | 44.1 | 49.3 | 47.3 |
| Other | 1.6 | 2.8 | 3.0 | 7.0 |
| *N* | 3,321 | 4,493 | 7,338 | 7,605 |
| *Canada* | | | | |
| Europe | 69.0 | 35.7 | 25.7 | 19.0 |
| Asia | 13.5 | 32.9 | 46.9 | 57.1 |
| Americas | 14.3 | 23.8 | 20.5 | 15.6 |
| Other | 3.2 | 7.6 | 6.9 | 8.3 |
| *N* | 788 | 996 | 1,092 | 1,039 |
| *Australia* | | | | |
| Europe | 80.1 | 57.9 | 36.0 | 20.7 |
| Asia | 3.2 | 11.3 | 27.3 | 29.4 |
| Americas | 2.4 | 4.4 | 3.6 | 2.8 |
| Pacific Islands | 1.5 | 7.0 | 13.9 | 15.4 |
| Other | 12.8 | 19.4 | 19.2 | 31.7 |
| *N* | 1,113 | 957 | 1,084 | 901 |
| *New Zealand* | | | | |
| Europe | | 58.6 | 38.1 | 21.9 |
| Asia | | 0.0 | 25.6 | 51.6 |
| Americas | | 5.1 | 5.8 | 3.3 |
| Pacific Islands | | 36.3 | 27.4 | 12.0 |
| Other | | 0.0 | 3.1 | 11.2 |
| *N* | | 187 | 111 | 306 |

*Sources*: U.S. Immigration and Naturalization Service (2002); Statistics Canada (2002); Australian Department of Immigration and Multicultural Affairs (2001); New Zealand Immigration Service (2002).

Table 5.3. *Average annual number of immigrants to selected European countries by region of origin, 1960–89*

| Region | 1960–4 | 1965–9 | 1970–4 | 1975–9 | 1980–4 | 1985–9 |
|---|---|---|---|---|---|---|
| Developed Countries | 89.9% | 79.5% | 72.1% | 63.4% | 65.2% | 72.4% |
| Sub-Saharan Africa | 1.8 | 3.4 | 3.9 | 4.6 | 4.4 | 4.2 |
| North Africa-Middle East | 6.2 | 8.9 | 17.1 | 18.4 | 14.7 | 9.3 |
| Asia | 1.5 | 6.2 | 5.3 | 10.3 | 12.7 | 12.5 |
| Latin America-Caribbean | 0.6 | 1.9 | 1.6 | 3.3 | 2.8 | 2.1 |
| Total (000) | 729.2 | 1,100.5 | 1,297.4 | 912.0 | 842.9 | 1,229.4 |

*Source*: Zlotnik (1993).

region of origin. Whereas fewer than 2 per cent of immigrants to Europe during the 1960s were Asian, by the late 1980s their share had risen to nearly 13 per cent. These figures only include documented immigrants, moreover. Were unauthorized immigrants to be factored in, the percentage of Asians would clearly be larger.

### *Overseas contract workers*

The greatest growth in Asian international migration has involved the nonpermanent movement of people for contract labor. Temporary labor migration has its historical roots in "contract coolie" systems initiated by colonial powers during the nineteenth century (Hugo 1980). The first major post-independence contract labor migration occurred in the late 1960s and early 1970s in the former South Vietnam, where multinational contractors sought to advance large infrastructure projects with the help of workers imported from South Korea, the Philippines, and Thailand.

The most important impetus to international labor migration came in 1973, however, with the Arab Oil Boycott, which increased petroleum prices sufficiently to allow the nations of the Gulf Cooperation Council (GCC) to undertake massive infrastructure development. The resulting construction boom often involved the same international contractors who had worked in South Vietnam, and their earlier experience with labor recruiters facilitated the participation of Asian workers in very large numbers.

South Asia already had a long history of migration to the Gulf, but after 1973 the volume expanded rapidly and came to include Eastern and Southeastern Asians as well. Although India and Pakistan accounted for 97 per cent of Asian workers in the Middle East during 1975, by the late 1990s the share had fallen below a third. At the same time, the relative number from Southeast Asia grew from 2 per cent to more than half. Whereas workers in the early years were mainly involved in infrastructure development, more recently they have moved into service occupations. At the same time, women have become increasingly important, with many migrating for employment as domestic servants. Over the last decade, destinations have also become more diverse, with other Asian nations overtaking the Middle East as points of destination. Much of this intra-Asian movement is undocumented and is, thus, excluded from official statistics. In general, undocumented migration consists of unskilled and semi-skilled men, as well as women in domestic service.

In the contemporary situation it is possible to classify Asian nations according to whether they gain or lose migrant workers to other Asian destinations. Table 5.4 shows large Asian nations where the transition to low fertility did not commence until the 1970s or later and simultaneously exporters and importers of labor. In contrast, Japan, Korea, and several Newly Industrialized Countries (NICs), which experienced early, sustained, and rapid fertility decline, experienced labor shortages that produced major inflows of both documented and undocumented migrants.

Although countries such as Korea and Taiwan were mainly regions of emigration during the first three decades of the postwar period, they later went through a migratory transition to become significant nations of immigration. This transition

**Table 5.4.** *Classification of Asian nations by pattern of immigration/emigration in late 1990s*

| Mainly emigration | Mainly immigration | Both immigration and emigration |
|---|---|---|
| Philippines | South Korea | Malaysia |
| China | Japan | Thailand |
| India | Taiwan | |
| Bangladesh | Hong Kong | |
| Sri Lanka | Singapore | |
| Pakistan | Brunei | |
| Laos | | |
| Indonesia | | |
| Burma | | |
| Cambodia | | |
| Vietnam | | |
| Nepal | | |

was much more rapid than occurred historically in Europe and represents a distinctive feature of Asian international migration (Martin 1993, 1994; Fields 1994; Skeldon 1994; Vasuprasat 1994). Two countries in the region—Malaysia and Thailand—are midway through the migratory transition and record substantial numbers of both emigrants and immigrants, notably from nearby labor surplus nations such as Indonesia, Bangladesh, and Myanmar.

Careful study of Asian international migration is difficult because of a lack of good data from receiving countries, many of which are not anxious to publicize the extent of their dependence on foreign labor. Even in migrant-sending countries, the data are frequently limited in detail and accuracy (Athukorala and Wickramasekara 1996). Data on stocks of migrants enumerated in national census generally only represent the "tip of the iceberg" because of the constant coming and going of migrants. The influence of emigration on sending regions is often much greater than that suggested by cross-sectional stocks of immigrants. Undocumented migration is also larger than indicated by official sources. Hence, it is difficult to build up an accurate picture of the scale of Asian international migration.

The stranding of hundreds of thousands of Asian workers in Kuwait by the Iraqi invasion of 1990 drew attention to the large number of Asian immigrants in the Middle East. As of mid-1989, 86 per cent of Kuwait's 863,000-person workforce was foreign, and of its 744,000 foreign workers about 400,000 (54 per cent) were Asian (Asian Regional Program on International Labour Migration 1990). This figure includes some 130,000 Indian workers whose annual remittances totaled $205 million (US), as well as 105,000 Bangladeshis (remittances of $250 million), 100,000 Pakistanis ($350 million), 100,000 Sri Lankans ($60 million), 63,000 Filipinos ($40 million), 16,000 Vietnamese and 12,000 Thais (see *Far Eastern Economic Review*, August 30, 1990: 8).

**Table 5.5.** *Official deployment of overseas contract workers from Asian sending countries, 1963–98*

| Country | Annual deployment in 1990s | | Total deployment 1970s to 1990s | |
|---|---|---|---|---|
| | Year | Number | Period | Number |
| Bangladesh | 1994 | 186,203 | 1976–94 | 1,594,289 |
| Burma | 1995 | 415,000 | 1989–92 | 35,248 |
| China | 1994 | 219,000 | 1982–94 | 740,347 |
| India | 1994 | 366,425 | 1976–94 | 3,549,782 |
| Indonesia | 1997 | 235,275 | 1969–98 | 2,113,237 |
| South Korea | 1982 | 34,632 | 1963–92 | 1,884,606 |
| Philippines | 1994 | 719,600 | 1975–94 | 4,677,000 |
| Pakistan | 1994 | 114,019 | 1971–94 | 2,324,673 |
| Sri Lanka | 1994 | 130,027 | 1979–94 | 679,304 |
| Thailand | 1995 | 445,000 | 1973–95 | 1,529,644 |
| Vietnam | 1995 | 195,000 | 1997 | 178,000 |
| Total | | 3,061,901 | | 19,306,130 |

*Sources*: ILO ARTEP; AKAN Indonesia; *Asian Migrant*, 6, 1, 1993; Asian Migrant, 5, 2, 1998; Stahl and PECC-HRD Task Force (1996); *Asian and Pacific Migration Journal*, 4, 4, 1995; *Saigon Times Daily*, September 17, 1997; *Straits Times*, November 11, 1997.

Table 5.5 summarizes official statistics on the number of emigrants from major sending countries. Even when focusing on documented migrants, the total deployed is around 2.3 million per year and the cumulative total is 15 million. Pre-eminent among sending nations is the Philippines, which Brillantes (1997) estimates to have sent more than 6 million of its nationals out for work during the 1990s. This estimate suggests that official data seriously underestimate the numbers involved (see the figure of 4.7 million reported in Table 5.5).

To consider the extent of underestimation, I collaborated with labor specialists in and outside of Indonesia to estimate roughly the number of Indonesians working overseas. Although official statistics put the total at 235,000 in 1997, my consultations set it at 2.4 million, with 1.9 million in Malaysia, another 425,000 in Saudi Arabia, and immigrant populations of 32,000 or less scattered across Hong Kong, Singapore, Taiwan, South Korea, and Japan. The data for Vietnam are similarly incomplete, with only 178,000 Vietnamese reported to be working overseas in the late 1990s. In contrast, Hiebert (1990: 20) estimates that "over 180,000 Vietnamese work in Eastern Europe [alone], mostly in light industry and building construction, under bilateral 'labour co-operation' agreements signed in 1980. Part of their salaries goes to repay Vietnam's debts to these countries, while the workers use the rest to feed themselves and buy local products to send home." The recent increase in contract labor migration from China is of particular interest, given the size of its potential labor supply (Saywell 1997). According to official statistics, annual labor emigration from China

**Table 5.6.** *Main East and Southeast Asian labor exporting countries: percentage of overseas workers deployed to Middle East and Asian destinations, 1980–94*

| Country of origin and region of destination | 1980 | 1986 | 1990 | 1994 |
|---|---|---|---|---|
| *Philippines* | | | | |
| Middle East | 84 | 73 | 65 | 54 |
| Asia | 11 | 22 | 27 | 36 |
| *Indonesia* | | | | |
| Middle East | 74 | 83 | 72 | 60 |
| Asia | 8 | 4 | 39 | 36 |
| *Thailand* | | | | |
| Middle East | 97 | 87 | 43 | 10 |
| Asia | 3 | 12 | 47 | 89 |
| *South Korea* | | | | |
| Middle East | 97 | 85 | n.a. | n.a. |
| Asia | 3 | 9 | n.a. | n.a. |
| *China* | | | | |
| Middle East | 97 | 81 | 50 | 10 |
| Asia | 3 | 16 | 22 | 65 |

*Source*: Stahl and PECC-HRD Task Force (1996).

increased from 35,000 persons per year in the early 1980s to 219,000 in 1994, when a total of 740,000 were registered as working overseas.

Although the Middle East remains an important destination for contract workers for Asia, Table 5.6 suggests that over time it has declined in significance. Whereas a majority of labor migrants from the Philippines and Indonesia still go to the Middle East, the percentage has fallen, from a peak of 84 per cent in the Philippines in 1980 down to 54 per cent in 1994, and from a peak of 74 per cent in Indonesia in 1980 down to 60 per cent by 1994 (although not shown, similar trends prevail in India and Pakistan). In contrast the percentage of Asian workers going to destinations elsewhere in Asia rose from 11 to 36 per cent in the Philippines and from 8 to 36 per cent in Indonesia. These trends would be even more pronounced if undocumented migrants were included. The vast majority of Thai and Chinese migrants go to destinations in Asia rather than the Middle East.

According to data provided by Birks, Sinclair and Associates (1992) and Stahl (1996), the total stock of Asian workers in nations of the GCC stood at 4.34 million in 1992, with 1.43 million from India, 828,000 from Pakistan, 508,000 from Bangladesh, 453,000 from Sri Lanka, 500,000 from the Philippines, and 450,000 from Indonesia. South Korea and Thailand sent far fewer workers to the Gulf, with 97,000 and 81,000, respectively. Thus, South Asians still dominate among Asian workers in the Gulf region, although Filipinos and Indonesians are increasing rapidly.

In Newly Industrialized Countries such as South Korea and Singapore, the demand for workers now outstrips the supply and contract labor emigration has declined precipitously. In Singapore, for example, annual economic growth is in the order of 7 per cent per year whereas the number of people aged 15–29 is projected to decline by 25 per cent between 1985 and 2000 (Salem 1988). The shortfall in entry-level workers is filled by some 520,000 foreigners, mostly from other Asian countries, notably Malaysia (Wong 1997). Singapore is only one of several countries in the region that is now attracting substantial numbers of workers from elsewhere in the region. Indeed, the data in Table 5.7 reveals that the stock of migrant workers in Asia (6.2 million) is now greater than the stock in the Middle East (4.3 million).

Labor markets throughout Asia increasingly overlap and interpenetrate, yielding migration not just of the unskilled, but of skilled and professional workers as well. Singapore's Economic Development Board currently offers a recruitment service to companies seeking skilled workers from overseas and in 1995 led recruitment missions

**Table 5.7.** *Growth of foreign labor in selected Asian countries, 1969–98*

| Country and year | Estimated stock of migrant workers | Country and year | Estimated stock of migrant workers |
|---|---|---|---|
| *Japan* | | *South Korea* | |
| 1969 | 696,000 | 1980 | 0 |
| 1984 | 841,000 | 1990 | 41,487 |
| 1993 | 1,320,000 | 1992 | 66,100 |
| 1994 | 1,354,011 | 1994 | 78,000 |
| 1995 | 1,360,000 | 1998 | 291,816 |
| *Taiwan* | | *Singapore* | |
| 1980 | 0 | 1970 | 14,000 |
| 1991 | 53,700 | 1973 | 100,000 |
| 1994 | 246,500 | 1989 | 128,000 |
| 1995 | 296,745 | 1993 | 180,000 |
| 1998 | 270,000 | 1998 | 530,000 |
| *Malaysia* | | *Thailand* | |
| 1984 | 500,000 | 1993 | 200,000 |
| 1992 | 1,102,000 | 1994 | 600,000 |
| 1996 | 2,300,000 | 1996 | 1,000,000 |
| 1998 | 2,000,000 | 1997 | 1,300,000 |
| *Brunei* | | *Hong Kong* | |
| 1971 | 11,000 | 1990 | 227,600 |
| 1986 | 26,000 | 1994 | 368,500 |
| 1988 | 31,400 | *Total* | |
| 1994 | 62,326 | Most recent year | 6,182,642 |

*Source*: Abella (1995); Stahl and PECC-HRD Task Force (1996); Martin et al. (1995); *Agence France Presse*, July 2, 1996; Azizah (1997); Wong (1997); *Asian Migration News*, November 2, 1998; *Migration News*, October 30, 1998; *Central News Agency*, January 14, 1999.

**Table 5.8.** *Employment sector of foreign workers in Taiwan and Malaysia and from Indonesia*

| Industrial sector | Taiwan 1994 | Indonesia 1989–94 | Malaysia 1991 |
|---|---|---|---|
| Agriculture/Plantation(%) | 0.8 | 22.5 | 45.8 |
| Manufacturing | 68.6 | 0.0 | 3.4 |
| Construction | 21.6 | 0.1 | 26.6 |
| Social/Personal Services | 8.9 | 60.7 | 19.1 |
| Transport | 0.0 | 13.9 | 0.0 |
| Other | 0.1 | 3.8 | 5.1 |
| Total (*N*) | 199,553 | 642,268 | 1,200,920 |

*Source*: Hugo (1995*a*); Stahl and PECC-HRD Task Force (1996).

to the United States, Britain, India, and Australia on behalf of fifty Singapore-based companies. These visits yielded 2,127 scientists, researchers, and entrepreneurs, plus another 5,363 other skilled workers, mainly from India and China (Hiebert 1996: 67).

Despite the growth of skilled migration, most overseas contract workers continue to be employed in poorly paid, low status jobs that require little skill and are eschewed by local citizens. This pattern is evident in Table 5.8, which shows foreign contract workers by industry of employment in Taiwan and Malaysia, as well as among labor migrants leaving Indonesia. In each case, the bulk of migrants continue to work in unskilled occupations, typically in agriculture, construction, manufacturing, or the service sector, especially domestic work.

## North–South migration

The colonial period witnessed a substantial movement by European functionaries and company employees to Asia, often with families. Similarly, the rapid growth and restructuring of Asian economies has been accompanied by an influx of skilled workers and business people from developed nations in Europe, North America, Japan, and Australasia. These nations also attract professionals and skilled workers from Asian nations whose educational systems produce more graduates than the local economies can absorb, with the prime exemplars being India, the Philippines, Pakistan, Sri Lanka, and Bangladesh.

The long-term immigration of professionals, business people, and technical workers from developed countries reflects two broader socioeconomic trends. The first is the massive growth of investment by multinational corporations in Asia's developing markets, which brings a large number of intra-company transferees into the region. In 1994, for example, some 690,000 Japanese were officially registered as living overseas, mostly in Asia and the Pacific (Okunishi 1995: 141). Second, the mismatch between what many national educational systems produce and what rapidly growing economies demand in the way of skills creates a strong supply-side effect. Indonesia, for example, has been forced to import engineers, accountants, financial experts, and managers from abroad, even though it suffers from high levels of under- and unemployment (Hugo 1996*b*).

The end result has been a remarkable influx of highly trained people from developed nations into the region. As of 1994, Hong Kong housed 23,700 British, 29,900 Americans, 24,700 Canadians, 18,700 Australians, and 17,600 Japanese, in addition to another 11,500 from the Philippines, 23,800 from Thailand, 19,500 from India, 19,700 from Indonesia and 13,800 from Malaysia (these numbers were substantially reduced after the Asian Economic Crisis of 1997). In addition to documented workers, many skilled workers enter Asian nations with tourist visas and subsequently take a job (*Manila Chronicle*, December 16, 1994).

An important element in the North–South flow is the reverse of the South–North flow mentioned earlier. A phrase frequently heard in emerging Asian markets is "reverse brain drain," which refers to nationals who return home after many years living and working abroad. This movement began gathering momentum in the late 1980s in response to labor shortages in various NICs. The movement accelerated in the early 1990s when dynamic economic growth across Asia coincided with recessions in Europe and North America. Several Asian nations—notably South Korea and Taiwan—adopted specific policies of recruiting back former emigrants who possessed technical, professional, and business skills.

Some business migrants from Hong Kong established citizenship in Canada or Australia as a form of insurance, only to return home quickly. In the United States, Arnold (1989: 890–1) reports that a significant number of Asian "immigrants" have not really moved to the United States despite receiving "green cards," which they use more as travel documents. Migrants from Hong Kong, Korea, and Taiwan are quite likely to keep one foot in each country and never really establish U.S. residency, even though technically it is a legal requirement. Visits to the United States are only made often enough to keep the Immigration and Naturalization Service from revoking their permanent residence visas.

In recent years, Canada, the United States, and Australia have witnessed a rise in a phenomenon known as "astronauting," whereby Hong Kong immigrants acquire residence visas and establish their families in the host country but move back and forth themselves, maintaining homes and businesses at both locations. For example, of thirty principal immigrants from Hong Kong sampled in the 1991 prototype for Australia's Longitudinal Survey of Immigrants, only one person could be re-interviewed a year later. The most frequent reason for this loss to follow-up was "gone to former home country temporarily." An investigation of arrivals and departures for the other twenty-eight missing respondents revealed that all returned to Hong Kong.

"Astronauting" is not restricted to immigrants from Hong Kong. Indeed, some 14 per cent of all primary immigrants interviewed in the prototype survey were reported to have returned home temporarily and another 1 per cent were said to have gone back permanently (8 per cent could not be contacted). According to Hugo and Gartner (1993), the percentage of immigrants who had returned home after one year stood at 48 per cent among those from Hong Kong, 37 per cent among those from

Malaysia, 36 per cent among those from Taiwan, and 26 per cent among those from South Africa, compared with an average of just 5 per cent across other countries.

## *Student migration*

The substantial increase in Asian temporary labor migration has been more than matched by the expansion of moves associated with tourism, business, and education. In Australia, for example, the number of visitors almost trebled over the last decade, going from 930,400 in 1982–3 to 3,966,200 in 1995–6, with 45 per cent of the latter coming from Asia. The increase in student visas has been particularly dramatic, with the number of full-paying Asian students rising from 6,624 in 1987 to 68,125 in 1995 (Shu and Hawthorne 1996).

In the United States similar trends prevail: the number of foreign university students increased from 82,709 in 1965 to 453,787 in 1995; and the equivalent figures for Canada were 11,284 and 35,451 (see Kritz and Caces 1989; UNESCO 1997). Since 1980 more than half of all U.S. doctorates in engineering went to foreigners, with Asians being predominant among overseas graduates (Tran 1990). There has also been an increasing flow of Asian students to Japan, and in 1990 some 60,000 researchers from less developed countries were estimated to be undertaking training there (Cross 1990: 66). In 1994, Malaysia paid 49.9 billion in Malaysian currency for the education of nationals overseas, mostly in developed nations (*Do Rosario Far Eastern Economic Review*, April 27, 1995: 44).

There is undoubtedly a strong connection between student migration and the eventual settlement of Asians abroad. Students may overstay their visas, adjust status to that of legal resident, simply return home to file a petition for re-entry as an immigrant. Unfortunately, few data exist to establish the extent to which these processes presently occur. In Australia the overstay rate among students declined from 12 per cent in May 1989 to under 1 per cent in December 1993; at the latter date 13,687 student overstayers made up a fifth of all the total (DIEA 1994). Much of recent immigration into Australia from Malaysia and Singapore can be traced to linkages established while in a student status (Dawkins et al. 1991; Lewis 1994). As Low, Toh, and Soon (1991) note, "studying abroad... exposes the young to external influences and may initiate ideas of migration to the extent that they can be practised. The brain drain problem is a real one in Singapore, and it is one which they can ill afford."

It is increasingly apparent also that the availability of high quality educational opportunities for children is one important factor motivating Asian migrants to settle in Australia. Sullivan and Gunasekeran (1993), for example, found that immigrants from Singapore and Malaysia were motivated primarily by the superior educational and career opportunities they saw for their children in Australia. This has led many countries to become concerned about a student-led brain drain. In China, for example, some 220,000 students are estimated to have gone abroad since 1979 but only 75,000 have returned (Plafker 1995). Although this loss was obviously exacerbated by the Tienanmen Square Uprising (Goldstein 1994), the trend remains general rather than historically specific. Although the Chinese State Education

Commission has strict rules about returning, only 40,000 of the 220,000 Chinese students who went abroad were state funded (Plafker 1995).

New forms of student migration are also beginning to occur in Asia. These include the movement of "trainees" to work in Japanese companies, ostensibly to gain experience and upgrade their skills but more transparently to overcome labor shortages in the host country. The official count of foreign "trainees" admitted to Japan quadrupled between 1982 and 1992, and Furuya (1995: 8) suggests that the 43,627 registered trainees accepted in 1992 (88.1 per cent from Asia) actually understate the true number. The practice of transforming labor migrants into "trainees" through reclassification is also common in South Korea, which began to experience its own labor shortages in the 1990s. At present, the Korean Ministry of Labor has a quota of 20,000 of foreign "technical trainees" permitted in low-end manufacturing.

## EMERGING ISSUES IN ASIAN MIGRATION

### *Remittances*

There are many issues of significance associated with labor migration but the generation of foreign exchange through remittances is of particular importance. Remittances were once considered to be of limited value and of small scale, but more careful and detailed measurement of remittance flows has led to a significant revision of conventional wisdom (Russell and Teitelbaum 1992). In several Asian countries (e.g. Pakistan, India, Sri Lanka, Bangladesh, Philippines), remittances are among the most important sources of foreign exchange, and in many cases they are the top source. In such places, exporting workers has replaced exporting commodities as the principal means of generating foreign earnings.

Table 5.9 illustrates the absolute and relative importance of remittances in three labor exporting nations. From 1980 through 1995 total remittances grew from $33 million (U.S.) to $356 million, a tenfold increase in just 15 years. Despite this increase, however, remittances remain a small factor in the huge Indonesian economy, constituting only around 1 per cent of both imports and exports. Although official statistics underestimate migrant earnings, which are often carried in person or sent with returning friends or relatives, adjusting for this underestimation does not change the overall picture. In specific regions of Indonesia from which migrants are selectively drawn, however, remittances do have significant effects (Hugo 1996*a*).

In the Philippines, remittances play a more important role in the national economy. Between 1980 and 1995 the flow of remittances through official channels increased from $421 million to $4.9 billion (*Xinhua News Agency*, April 2, 1996), and by the latter date constituted 37 per cent of total exports and 21 per cent of total imports. The 65,000 female domestics employed in Singapore that year sent back $106 million all by themselves, an average of $1,630 per person (Meng, *Straits Times*, March 17, 1996). The central importance of international migration in the Filipino economy is indicated by the fact that remittances almost covered the $6 billion trade gap in 1995 and were three times larger than direct foreign investment (Tiglao 1996),

Table 5.9. *Main Southeast Asian labor exporting countries: workers' remittances relative to exports and imports in US$ Million, 1980–95*

| Country and year | Total remittances | Total merchandise | | Remittances as percentage | |
|---|---|---|---|---|---|
| | | Exports | Imports | Exports | Imports |
| *Indonesia* | | | | | |
| 1980 | $33 | $21,908 | $10,834 | 0.1% | 0.3% |
| 1992 | 264 | 33,825 | 27,280 | 0.8 | 1.0 |
| 1995 | 356 | 40,054 | 31,985 | 0.9 | 1.1 |
| *Philippines* | | | | | |
| 1980 | 421 | 5,744 | 8,295 | 7.3 | 5.0 |
| 1992 | 2,222 | 9,790 | 15,465 | 22.7 | 14.4 |
| 1995 | 4,930 | 13,304 | 22,546 | 37.1 | 21.9 |
| *Thailand* | | | | | |
| 1979 | 191 | 5,240 | 7,158 | 3.6 | 2.7 |
| 1992 | 1,500 | 32,473 | 40,466 | 4.6 | 3.7 |
| 1995 | 1,900 | 45,262 | 54,459 | 4.2 | 3.5 |

*Source*: Hugo (1996*a*: p. 8, 1996*c*: p. 3); World Bank (1996).

and these figures only include money sent through official channels. The importance of unofficial channels was brought home in 1990 when the Philippine National Bank extended its services to Italy, the Netherlands, Germany, and Spain and per capita labor income from Europe immediately doubled (Russell 1992).

By far the largest source for remittances to the Philippines is the United States. Migrants there were responsible for $1.7 billion or 57 per cent of the total received in 1994. Other important sources are Western Europe, the Persian Gulf, and several of the East Asian "tigers," such as Hong Kong, Taiwan, Singapore, and Japan. The Middle East is presently declining as a source of earnings for the Philippines, dropping from $173 million in 1993 to $130 million in 1994. In contrast, remittances from Asian destinations climbed from $75 million to $381 million and constituted 13 per cent of the 1994 total.

## *The feminization of migration*

A distinctive feature of Asian migration is the extensive involvement of women. Among immigrants to developed countries, women outnumber their males in official statistics (Hugo 1997). But legal immigration is only one of several kinds of migration of varying distance, legality, motivation, and permanency. Women have increasingly been recruited as overseas contract workers, for example, and they now predominate in the outflow of labor from several countries. According to official statistics from the Indonesian Manpower Ministry, women have outnumbered men among contract workers every year since 1984. Indeed, by 1998–9 there were only eighteen men for every 100 women among workers processed by the ministry (Hugo 1995*b*).

The main sources for female migration are the Philippines, Indonesia, Sri Lanka, Thailand, and Bangladesh. In the 1950s, they mainly went to the Middle East, but more recently they have included Hong Kong, Singapore, and Malaysia among their destinations. By the early 1990s, some 1.7 million Asian women were estimated to be working as maids outside their home country (*Straits Times*, May 13, 1995).

Despite this feminization, gender has been neglected as a topic in Asian migration research. The role and status of women is undergoing rapid and profound change throughout Asia, as indicated by rising education, increasing labor force participation, and the growing use of contraceptives. Little is known about the impact of these changes on population mobility, or whether or not international migration empowers or subordinates women. Too much of the region's research remains gender-blind or, even worse, relegates women to the category of "associational" migrants, even though independent migration is clearly gathering pace.

The fact that Asian women do often move for marriage, domestic duties, and jobs in entertainment or the sex industry means they are uniquely vulnerable to exploitation. Indonesian women, for example, have been documented to experience serious difficulties as contract workers (Robinson 1991) and the incidence of problems is particularly high when they work in countries such as Saudi Arabia. Cases of physical mistreatment, excessive workloads, and sexual assault are given prominent media coverage. Newspapers report women returning to Indonesia only to find that their husbands have remarried and used their remittances to start a new life, and of women being raped by Middle Eastern employers and then rejected by their families upon their return.

In Saudi Arabia, particularly, women are especially vulnerable as protective labor legislation does not apply to domestic workers. If a female servant is judged to be unsatisfactory and asked to leave before the end of her contract, she is expected to refund all travel costs paid by her employer. A woman is also required to produce three eye-witnesses to lodge a complaint against a Saudi employer. As one Indonesian commentator put it, "the Middle Eastern employer is in a stronger position than the Indonesian worker in any dispute" (Anon 1984: 14).

The sex trade has become a significant element in the international migration of Asian women, who increasingly are recruited to work as entertainers and prostitutes throughout the region as well as in developed countries such as Japan and Australia. Thailand and the Philippines are important source countries for sex workers. According to Brockett (1996), there is a well-established migratory circuit to Japan, Taiwan, and Australia with social networks linking key players in the sex industry across several nations.

A survey by the *Far Eastern Economic Review* (December 14, 1995) revealed the growing scale of trafficking of women. This trade is largely in the hands of organized crime. The main routes for the smuggling of women begin in Burma, China, and Laos and proceed to Thailand. From there the women are smuggled to Japan, Taiwan, Malaysia, and Australia. Japan alone is estimated to house 150,000 foreign sex workers, mostly Thais and Filipinos (Sherry, Lee, and Vatikiotis 1995: 24).

Women have not only become more important in clandestine flows, but in all forms of international movement, reflecting the changing role and status of women in the region. Women, for example, are increasingly represented among students and manual laborers. In Flores, East Indonesia young men have been traveling for decades to Sabah in East Malaysia to work on plantations and construction projects. In the past, the few women who traveled did so in the company of men. Since 1990, however, young women from Flores have begun to migrate to Malaysia autonomously to work as domestic servants, mess cooks, and housemaids (Hugo 1996*a*).

Governments have increasingly become involved in managing the international migration of women. The Philippines has long had special training institutes designed to prepare nurses for the U.S. labor market. The Indonesian government initiated a similar training program and provides a compulsory course to prepare women to work as domestic servants in the Middle East. Governments have increasingly scrutinized the mail order bride services that have sprung up to market Filipino (and, to a lesser extent, Thai) women to men in Australia, Japan, the United States, and Europe.

On the surface, increased migration by Asian women would appear to offer them social and economic improvement. Frequently moves are between contexts where, other things equal, one might expect some empowerment to occur (rural to urban, familial labor to enterprise production, traditional to modern). Leaving home often involves moving away from the immediate control of a traditional, patriarchal family to a situation where women are paid for their work and retain control over their earnings. For the first time they may live away from home and are exposed to a range of new, nontraditional ideas and to a wider range of people.

Although such transitions can and do result in empowerment, this outcome is by no means automatic. Indeed, migration can operate to preserve and even strengthen the status quo with respect to gender relations (Hugo 1997) and many female migrants from Asia continue to move into very vulnerable situations, creating a pressing need for policies and programs to protect their rights (Lim and Oishi 1996).

## *Undocumented migration*

An important trend in recent years has been the increase in undocumented Asian migration. Table 5.10 presents recent estimates to indicate the scale of this movement. Undocumented migration is especially strong in Japan and the four NIC "tigers," where strict immigration regulations have combined with substantial labor shortages in unskilled areas to encourage illegal movement from labor surplus areas. One of the most substantial movements, from Indonesia to Malaysia, involves more than 1 million workers, who constitute 10 per cent of the Malaysian workforce and substantially more than 1 per cent of the Indonesian workforce (Azizah 1997). In recent years, China has also become a significant source for illegal migrants, with people smuggling estimated to run at around 200,000 to the US, 150,000 to Russia, 100,000 to Thailand, and smaller flows to other nations (UNECE 1994).

Thailand also has become a major focus for illegal migration from Burma, Laos, Cambodia, and Bangladesh. In 1994 it was estimated that Thailand had half a

**Table 5.10.** *Estimates of the numbers of illegal migrants in selected countries in the mid–late 1990s*

| Country | Estimate | Source |
|---|---|---|
| Australia | 80,000 | *The Australian*, May 17, 1994 |
| Japan | 300,000 | *Japan Times*, June 15, 1998 |
| South Korea | 98,688 | *Asian Migration News*, Nov. 1998 |
| Philippines | 600,000 | *Manila Chronicle*, Aug. 1994 |
| Taiwan | 180,000 | *China Post*, May 2, 1994 |
| Malaysia | 1,000,000 | *The Star*, Feb. 1998 |
| Singapore | 250,000 | Prasai (1993) |
| Thailand | 1,000,000 | *Straits Times*, May 2, 1998 |

million illegal migrants, including 300,000 from Burma, 100,000 from China, 50,000 from South Asia and 10,000 from Indo-China (*Straits Times*, March 17, 1994) but more recent estimates put it at around one million (*Asia Pulse*, May 21, 1997). In Japan it is possible to calculate the number of visa overstayers to estimate the number of undocumented migrants. As Stahl and the PECC-HRD Task Force (1996) have shown, there were virtually no illegal foreign workers in 1985, but by 1994 there were some 288,000 overstayers. Moreover, "if to this figure we add those who are working on currently valid nonwork visas, then it is conceivable that the numbers working illegally would exceed 500,000, an estimate consistent with several Japanese sources" (p. 8).

## *The immigration industry*

A distinctive and pervasive feature of international migration in Asia is the involvement of a varied group of recruiters, lawyers, agents of various kinds, immigration officials, and an array of different gatekeepers. Much of the migration emanating in Asia is at least facilitated, and is often initiated, by these intermediaries. This is certainly the case for international labor migration, especially for the segment that is clandestine. While employer recruitment has also been significant in North America (Massey et al. 1994), it seems to be even more important in Asia, although this fact is frequently overlooked or given only passing mention by researchers.

The neglect of the immigration industry is partly an artefact of methodologies that focus on the migrants, their families, and their communities of origin and destination, but which fail to gather data on recruiters or other informal and formal institutional actors who initiate and facilitate migration. These gatekeepers are often very difficult (and at times even dangerous) to study, not only because of commercial considerations but especially because many operate outside the law. The high level of profitability associated with people smuggling and the "new slave trade" in workers who are effectively indentured to their owners has led syndicates formerly involved in the drug trade to move into the immigration arena.

The role of such groups goes back to the slave trade, which once prospered in Asia, as well as to the "contract coolie" trade of the late nineteenth and early twentieth centuries. A variety of institutions were instrumental in promoting the immigration of Chinese to Southeast Asia at this time. A complex array of shipping companies, agents, brokers, innkeepers, and carriers were implicated in a massive out-migration of Chinese that extended over more than a century (Hicks 1993, chapter 2; Shozo 1995). Such arrangements have persisted up to the present, with Chinese emigration now organized by traffickers known as shetou or snakeheads (Thuno 1996; Pieke 1997; Chin 1999).

The few studies which have examined the role of the immigration industry in Asia have shown how important the activities of recruiters can be in persuading potential migrants to move (Hugo and Singhanetra-Renard 1987; Spaan 1994; Goss and Lindquist 1995). Private agencies are involved in most contract-labor migration as well as in much permanent migration out of Asia. The number of immigration agents and lawyers is growing rapidly in both origin and destination nations. However, the visible legal component is only part, and perhaps only a small part, of the global people smuggling industry.

In Indonesia, for example, agents variously known as calo, taikong, tauke, or mandor are highly organized and are crucial in facilitating migration to Malaysia. They operate both within and outside existing legal constraints. Habir (1984) describes the range of roles these middlemen play: recruiting the workers, arranging their moves, and obtaining jobs and lodging for them at points of destination. These agents generally have extensive networks on both sides of the border and often take money from prospective migrants but do not deliver the services promised.

A detailed study in Indonesia illustrates the complex role played by the taikong in promoting the movement of East Javans to Malaysia, with the illegal migrant being passed from one intermediary to another across a chain of contacts that link origin and destination areas (Spaan 1994). Each element in the chain receives a small payment in classic "involutionary" fashion (Hugo 1975). It is a safe and trusted network because it starts in the home village with a calo who has to bear the results of a failure in the system or of exploitation. Such illegal networks are often much more trusted and reliable than official systems, in which there is not the same degree of personalized local accountability. Moreover, official channels often involve costly delays in obtaining documentation and a great deal of waiting before the migration can actually take place.

Drawing on Giddens' (1990) theory of structuration, Goss and Lindquist (1995) argue that "international migration is best examined not as a result of individual motivations and structural determinations, although these must play a part in any explanation, but as the articulation of agents with particular interests and playing specific roles within an institutional environment, drawing knowledgeably upon sets of rules in order to increase access to resources" (p. 345).

### *Government involvement*

Governments are important in promoting emigration from Asia. According to Pieke (1997), "chain migration—coupled with the push of poverty in the Chinese countryside and the pull of prosperity in Europe—is but part of the story of post-war Chinese migration; political factors have often been equally if not more important in promoting or inhibiting the migrant flow" (p. 3). It was government actions, for example, that effectively closed China in the 1950s, 1960s, and early 1970s, thereby preventing prospective emigrants in areas like Guandong and Zhejiang from joining friends and relatives in Europe. It was decolonization in Southeast Asia that led to the massive outflow of overseas Chinese to Europe. Finally, visa restrictions in Europe strongly influenced the size and composition of Chinese communities there: by forcing students to return home, they deprived Europe of a brain drain that has enriched the United States and Australia.

Although policy analyses generally focus on the efforts of destination countries to control the size, composition, and duration of immigration, throughout Asia the export of labor has become an important part of development planning, simultaneously permitting nations to reduce pressure upon national and regional labor markets, while enhancing their foreign exchange earnings and providing workers with skills and training. Indeed, as was pointed out earlier, labor export has become an important foreign exchange earning activity, outweighing most commodity exports.

To maximize the scale and benefits of labor export, national governments have put in place a number of policies and programs. Most labor surplus nations in Asia have established labor export agencies within the government bureaucracy, although functions vary from regulating the flow, controlling recruitment, and training potential migrants to exploring new markets for labor and actively encouraging nationals to obtain work overseas. Most have also initiated special programs to maximize remittances, such as tax breaks on foreign earnings, special banking facilities at destinations, and the forced remitting of a fixed share of weekly earnings. Many countries have also sought out bilateral agreements with destination countries to supply workers for specific projects, or to protect their nationals working abroad and to provide them services at points of destination. Others have developed special programs to attract back former nationals, especially those with skills or wealth, or to assist labor migrants in readjusting to their home communities. A few countries have set targets for international labor migration and remittances and incorporated them into the national planning process (Hugo 1995*a*). In China, for example, each province has set up a labor export company to encourage and facilitate migration (Qian 1996).

Governments in destination areas usually seek to implement policies that limit and tightly control immigration, and many Asian nations have very restrictionist immigration policies, with Japan being a striking example (Sassen 1993). In some cases, however, Asian governments have played an active role in initiating migration. Examples of such policies include programs to encourage nonpermanent movements (tourists, students, trainees), which later end up spilling over into permanent settlement; business migration programs designed to attract entrepreneurs and investors; the awarding of special preferences to attract skilled immigrants (as in Canada, the United States, Australia, New Zealand); and family reunification provisions that have allowed millions of Asians to settle in traditional countries of immigration.

In short, governments have a substantial independent influence on international labor migration throughout Asia, even though this influence is wielded with little knowledge of the causes or consequences of immigration (Hugo and Singhanetra-Renard 1987). To the degree that policy interventions are based on any theoretical justification at all, it is largely a blind acceptance of the standard model of neoclassical economics.

## *The brain drain*

In the early postwar decades many countries of Asia experienced a significant emigration of immigrants with needed skills and talent, a so-called "brain drain." Although the emigration was limited in its size and demographic impact, it typically involved the exit of highly educated people moving to developed countries such as the United States (Hugo 1996*b*), often persons who had previously studied there. The brain drain to the United States was greatly facilitated by the 1965 amendments to the Immigration and Nationality Act, which eliminated the small Asian quotas (Pernia 1976: 63; Fortney 1972). As the size of Asian immigration increased in the 1980s and 1990s, however, the degree of educational selectivity decreased.

The diversification of outflows to developed countries has had uneven effects across Asia. On the one hand, it appears that refugee movements, moves for family reunion, and labor migration (both legal and illegal) have generally not deprived Asian nations of scarce talent. On the other hand, losses of skilled nationals through "economic" and business migration and the "leakage" of students remaining overseas after completing their studies represents a very clear drain on some nations (Hugo 1996*b*).

In the Philippines, officials are concerned that too many of the nation's best science graduates choose to emigrate (*Manila Chronicle*, March 24, 1994). The U.S. by itself receives three quarters of all Filipino emigrants and the Immigration Act of 1990 almost tripled the number of migrants allowed in under work categories. As a result, the proportion of Filipinos moving to the U.S. in that category doubled. In 1992, around 12 per cent of all Filipino emigrants to the U.S. were professional, managerial, technical, or administrative workers, causing official concern. According to De Peralta (1993), "as Health Secretary Juan Flavier said after discovering the bulk of University of the Philippines 1990 medical school graduates went overseas for employment, ignoring the dearth of doctors in our rural areas, 'It's a shame.' After all, those hundreds of thousands of taxpayers' pesos into their training—only to lose them to other countries."

However, perceptions of the "brain drain" have changed in many Asian countries. Although India expressed dismay at the heavy exodus of highly qualified professionals during the 1960s and 1970s, skilled emigration is no longer seen as a deadweight loss. Whereas Amuzegar in 1968 (1968: 703) estimated that India lost $61 million through the annual emigration of 3,062 natural scientists, engineers, and physicians to the United States, Minocha in 1987 pointed out that "India is not the victim of brain drain, since no evidence has yet been found that a shortage of highly skilled labour exists or that the country's development programs have been harmed by the exodus of professionals. In fact India has a huge surplus of highly skilled labour that cannot be absorbed by its sluggish economy" (pp. 365–6).

Some researchers are referring to there being a "brain overflow" rather than a "brain drain" and point to the positive effects of the massive capital inflows that result when skilled emigrants repatriate their overseas earnings. Hugo (1996*b*) argues that the loss of highly trained personnel has beneficial impacts upon the sending countries because of the mismatch between the origin country's supply of skilled labor and its economy's capacity to absorb it; the sizeable return flow of remittances; the return migration of workers with enhanced skills and capacities; and other economic linkages that migrants forge between origin and destination areas. Nevertheless, there are dissenting views (see Khadria 1991).

## CONCLUSION

Asian labor markets now extend well beyond national boundaries. For highly skilled workers, global labor markets have existed for decades; but increasingly this reality has embraced much unskilled and semi-skilled workers as well. Whereas in the past international migration was part of the calculus of conscious choice only for narrowly defined age, gender, ethnic, and socioeconomic groups, it is now broadly available as an option for Asians to improve their life chances. At the same time, other Asians have little choice but to cross international borders for survival.

Whatever the cause, international migration within Asia can be expected to become more institutionalized, reinforced not only by government policies and organizations but also by the proliferation of private sector agencies facilitating migration for profit. The globalization of information, culture, and business inexorably will increase and impinge on Asia. The region's vast population, dynamic economy, and changing social context will ensure that the already huge reservoir of Asians who are seeking to emigrate will increase at a rate much faster than the total population.

In coming years, it is not difficult to foresee the growth of a large and often disgruntled population of educated young people who cannot be absorbed into their national economies at a level they consider appropriate to their training, skills, and aspirations. Such groups not only have the motivation and assets to migrate, they also have the information to select a destination and the attributes (skills, business experience, education) that qualify them as settlers in one of the major immigration nations, as well as access to social networks to assist them in migration and settlement. In short, the future is probably one of a building pressure for emigration within Asia and a growing pressure on destination countries to absorb it.

International migration in Asia is growing rapidly in its scale and diversity. There are many important research and policy questions in this area which need to be addressed as a matter of urgency, yet our understanding of it is very limited. This is partly a function of the paucity of data on the major movements. Such information is not collected in standard census enumerations and the fact that much of the movement is of a temporary or clandestine nature means that much of it goes undocumented. Detailed study of the movements, their causes, and consequences is also rendered difficult by the fact that the process occurs across nations, cultures, languages, and administrative systems.

## References

Abella, M. I. (1995). "Asian Labour Migration: Past, Present and Future," *ASEAN Economic Bulletin*, 12(2): 125–38.

Amuzegar, J. (1968). *Brain Drain: The Irony of Foreign Aid Policy*. Genoa: Economic Internationale.

Anon. (1984). "Mencari Tuan di Negeri," *Tempo*, 52(xi): 12–17.

Arnold, F. (1989). "Unanswered Questions About the Immigration Multiplier," *International Migration Review*, 23: 889–92.

Asian Regional Programme on International Labour Migration (1990). *Statistical Report 1989: International Labour Migration from Asian Labour-Sending Countries*, Bangkok UNDP-ILO Project.

Athukorala, P.-C., and Wickramasekara, P. (1996). "International Labour Migration Statistics in Asia: An Appraisal," *International Migration*, 34(4): 539–66.

Australian Department of Immigration and Multicultural Affairs (2001). *Immigration: Federation to Century's End*. Canberra: Statistics Branch, Department of Immigration and Multcultural Affairs. (www.immi.gov.au).

Azizah, K. (1997). "International Migration and Its Impact on Malaysia," Paper presented at 11th Asia–Pacific Roundtable Labour Migration in Southeast Asia: The Impact (Political, Economic, Social, Security), Kuala Lumpur, June 5–8.

Bedford, R., and Lidgard, J. (1996). *International Migration in the Asia-Pacific Region in the 1980s and 1990s: Two New Zealand Perspectives*, Population Studies Centre Discussion Paper No. 19, University of Waikato, Hamilton, New Zealand.

Birks, Sinclair, and Associates (1992). *GCC Market Report 1992*. Durham, UK: Mountjoy Research Centre.

Brillantes, J. (1997). "Philippine Labor Export Program and Its Effects on Immigration to Canada," Paper presented at Conference on Asian Immigration and Racism in Canada, University of British Columbia, June 24–27.

Brockett, L. (1996). *Thai Sex Workers in Sydney*. Unpublished MA Thesis, Department of Geography, University of Sydney.

Chin, Ko-Lin (1999). *Smuggled Chinese: Clandestine Immigration to the United States*. Philadelphia: Temple University Press.

Clad, J. (1990). "India Faces Hard Choices As Deficits Widen: The IMF Cometh," *Far Eastern Economic Review*, 84, October 18, 1.

Cross, M. (1990). "A Magnet in Asia," *Far Eastern Economic Review*, December 6: 66.

Dawkins, P., Lewis, P., Noris, K., Baker, M., Robertson, F., Groenewold, N., and Hagger, A. (1991). *Flows of Immigrants to South Australia, Tasmania and Western Australia*. Canberra: AGPS.

De Peralta, G. L. (1993). "Losing our Best and Brightest," *Mainichi Daily News*, May 25, 1993.

—— (1996). *Overseas Student Statistics 1995*. Canberra: DEET, International Division.

Department of Immigration and Ethnic Affairs (DIEA) (1994). *Overseas Students in Australia*, Fact Sheet 18, Canberra: DIEA.

Do Rosario, L. (1995). "Futures and Options." *Far Eastern Economic Review*, 15 June, 21.
Fields, G. S. (1994). "The Migration Transition in Asia," *Asian and Pacific Migration Journal*, 3(1): 7–30.
Fortney, J. (1972). "Immigrant Professionals: A Brief Historical Survey," *International Migration Review*, VI(1): 50–62.
Furuya, K. (1995). "Labor Migration and Skill Development: Japan's Trainee Program," *Asian Migrant*, 8(1): 4–13.
Giddens, A. (1990). "Structuration Theory and Sociological Analysis," in J. Clark, C. and S. Modgil (eds.), *Anthony Giddens: Consensus and Controversy*. New York: Falmer Press.
Goldstein, C. (1994). "Innocents Abroad," *Far Eastern Economic Review*, September: 15, 22–7.
Goss, J., and Lindquist, B. (1995). "Conceptualizing International Labor Migration: A Structuration Perspective," *International Migration Review*, 29(2): 317–51.
Habir, M. (1984). "A Migration Equation," *Far Eastern Economic Review*, April 26, 116–172.
Hicks, G. L. (ed.), (1993). *Overseas Chinese Remittances from Southeast Asia, 1910–1940*, Select Books, Singapore.
Hiebert, M. (1990). "Comrades Go Home," *Far Eastern Economic Review*, 20, May 17, 20.
—— (1996). "Help Wanted—Singapore Scans the Globe for Skilled Professionals," *Far Eastern Economic Review*, June 6, p. 67.
Hugo, G. J. (1975). *Population Mobility in West Java, Indonesia*. Unpublished Ph.D. Thesis, Department of Demography, Australian National University, Canberra.
—— (1980). "Population Movements in Indonesia During the Colonial Period," in J. J. Fox, R. G. Garnaut, T. McCawley, and J. A. C. Mackie (eds.), *Indonesia: Australian Perspectives*. Canberra: Australian National University, Research School of Pacific Studies, pp. 95–135.
—— (1981). "Village-Community Ties, Village Norms and Ethnic and Social Networks: A Review of Evidence from the Third World," in G. F. De Jong and R. W. Gardner (eds.), *Migration Decision Making: Multidisciplinary Approaches to Microlevel Studies in Developed and Developing Countries*. New York: Pergamon Press.
—— (1993). "Indonesian Labour Migration to Malaysia: Trends and Policy Implications," *Southeast Asian Journal of Social Science*, 21(1): 36–70.
—— (1994). *The Economic Implications of Emigration from Australia*, Canberra: AGPS.
—— (1995*a*). "Labour Export from Indonesia: An Overview," *ASEAN Economic Bulletin* 12(2): 275–98.
—— (1995*b*). "International Labour Migration and the Family: Some Observations from Indonesia," *Asian and Pacific Migration Journal*, 4(2–3): 273–301.
—— (1996*a*). "Economic Impacts of International Labour Emigration on Regional and Local Development: Some Evidence from Indonesia." Paper presented at the Annual Meeting of the PAA, New Orleans, May.
—— (1996*b*). "Brain Drain and Student Movements," in P. J. Lloyd and L. S. Williams (eds.), *International Trade and Migration in the APEC Region*. Melbourne: Oxford University Press, pp. 210–28.
—— (1997). "Migration and Female Empowerment," Paper prepared for International Union for the Scientific Study of Population's Committee on Gender and Population's Seminar on Female Empowerment and Demographic Processes: Moving Beyond Cairo, Lund, Sweden, April 21–24.
—— and Gartner, M. (1993). "Evaluation of the Prototype Survey First Wave and Some Recommendations for the Full Survey," Bureau of Immigration Research Prototype Survey for a Longitudinal Survey of Immigrants to Australia (LSIA) Working Paper Series, Working Paper No. 7, April.

—— and Singhanetra-Renard, A. (1987). *International Migration of Contract Labour in Asia—Major Issues and Implications.* Ottawa: IDRC.

Khadria, B. (1991). "Contemporary Indian Immigration to the United States—Is the Brain Drain Over?" *Revue Europeenne des Migrations Internationales,* 7(1): 65–96.

Kritz, M. M., and Caces, C. (1989). "Science and Technology Transfers and Migration Flows," Population and Development Program 1989 Working Paper Series 1.02, Cornell University, Ithaca.

Lewis, P. E. T. (1994). "Singaporean Entrepreneurs—The Australian Connection," *Journal of Enterprising Culture,* 2(2): 709–33.

Lim, L. L., and Oishi, N. (1996). "International Migration of Asian Women: Distinctive Characteristics and Policy Concerns," in G. Battistella and A. Paganoni (eds.), *Asian Women in Migration.* Quezon City: Scalabrini Migration Centre, pp. 23–54.

Low, L., Toh, M. H., and Soon, T. W. (1991). *Economics of Education and Manpower Developments, Issues and Policies in Singapore,* Singapore: McGraw-Hill.

Martin, P. L. (1993). *Trade and Migration: NAFTA and Agriculture.* Institute for International Economics: Washington DC.

—— (1994). "Migration and Trade: Challenges for the 1990s," *Work and Family Life of International Migrant Workers,* 4(3): 1–21.

—— (1996). "Migrants on the Move," *Asia-Pacific Issues* No. 29, East-West Center, Honolulu, Hawaii.

—— Mason A., and Tsay, C. L. (1995). "Overview," *ASEAN Economic Bulletin,* 12(2): 117–24.

Massey, D., Arango, J., Hugo, G., Kouaouci, A., Pellegrino, A., and Taylor, J. E. (1994). "The Evaluation of International Migration Theory: The North American Case," *Population and Development Review,* 20(4): 699–752.

Meng, W. C. (1994). "Taiwan Brain Drain Goes into Reverse," *The Straits Times,* 9 November, p. 19.

Minocha, U. (1987). "South Asian Immigrants: Trends and Impacts on the Sending and Receiving Societies," in J. T. Fawcett and B. V. Carino (eds.), *Pacific Bridges: The New Immigration from Asia and the Pacific Islands.* Staten Island, New York: Center for Migration Studies, pp. 347–74.

New Zealand Immigration Service (2002). *People Approved for Residence in New Zealand by Country of Origin.* Aukland: New Zealand Immigration Service. (www.immigration.govt.nz).

Okunishi, Y. (1995). Japan, *ASEAN Economic Bulletin,* 12(2): 139–62.

Pernia, E. M. (1976). "The Question of the Brain Drain from the Philippines," *International Migration Review,* 10(1): 63–72.

Pieke, F. N. (1997). "Introduction," in G. Beaton and F. N. Pieke (eds.), *The Chinese in Europe,* New York: St. Martin's Press.

Plafker, T. (1995). "China Fights Brain Drain," *International Herald Tribune,* April 24, 3.

Pongsapich, A. (1995). *Recent Trends in International Migration in Asia,* Asian Population Studies Series No. 137, United Nations, New York.

Prasai, S. B. (1993). "Asia's Labour Pains," *Far Eastern Economic Review,* 29 April.

Qian, W. (1996). "The Features of International Migration in China," Paper presented to Conference on European Chinese and Chinese Domestic Migrants, Oxford, July 3–7.

Rallu, J. L. (1996). "Recent Trends in International Migration and Economic Development in the South Pacific," *Asia-Pacific Population Journal,* 11(2): 23–46.

Robinson, K. (1991). "Households: The Effects of Gender and Culture on Internal and International Migration of Indonesian Women," in Gill Bottomley, Marie de Lepervanche and Jeannie Martin (eds.), *Intersexions: Gender, Class, Culture, Ethnicity.* Sydney: Allen and Unwin, pp. 33–51.

Rogge, J. R. (1993). "Refugee Migration: Changing Characteristics and Prospects," Paper presented at Expert Group Meeting on Population Distribution and Migration, Santa Cruz, Bolivia, January 18–22.

Russell, Sharon S. (1992). "International Migration and Political Turmoil in the Middle East," *Population and Development Review*, 18: 719–27.

—— and Teitelbaum, M. S. (1992). "International Migration and International Trade," World Bank Discussion Paper 160, Washington: The World Bank.

—— (1991). *Population and Development in the Philippines: An Update.* The World Bank Asia Country Department II, Population and Human Resources Division, Washington, DC.

—— (1992). "Migrant Remittances and Development," *International Migration*, 30: 267–87.

Salem, E. (1988). "Back to School," *Far Eastern Economic Review*, 59, 25 August, 59.

Sassen, S. (1993). "Economic Internationalization: The New Migration in Japan and the United States," *International Migration Review*, 31(1): 73–102.

Saywell, T. (1997). "Workers' Offensive," *Far Eastern Economic Review*, May 29: 50–2.

Sherry, A., Lee, M., and Vatikiotis, M. (1995). "For Lust or Money," *Far Eastern Economic Review*, December 14: 22–3.

Shozo, F. (1995). *With Sweat and Abacus: Economic Roles of Southeast Asian Chinese on the Eve of World War II*, Singapore: Select Books.

Shu, J., and Hawthorne, L. (1996). "Asian Student Migration to Australia," *International Migration*, 24(1): 65–96.

Skeldon, R. (1994). "Turning Points in Labor Migration: The Case of Hong Kong," *Asian and Pacific Migration Journal*, 3(1): 93–118.

Spaan, E. (1994). "Taikongs and Calos: The Role of Middlemen and Brokers in Javanese International Migration," *International Migration Review*, 28(1): 93–113.

Stahl, C. W., and PECC-HRD Task Force (1996). "International Labour Migration and the East Asian APEC/PECC Economies: Trends, Issues and Policies," Paper presented at PECC Human Resource Development Task Force Meeting, Brunei, June 7–8.

Statistics Canada (2002). *Immigrant Population by Place of Birth and Period of Immigration: 1996 Census, Canada* Ottawa: Statistics Canada. (www.statcan.ca).

Sullivan, G., and Gunaskeran, S. (1993). "The Role of Ethnic Relations and Education Systems in Migration from Southeast Asia to Australia," Sojourn, 8(2): 219–49.

Thuno, M. (1996). "Origins and Causes of Emigration from Qingtian and Wenzhou in Europe," Paper presented to Conference on European Chinese and Chinese Domestic Migrants, Oxford, July 3–7.

Tiglao, R. (1996). "Newborn Tiger," *Far Eastern Economic Review*, 24 October, 66.

Tran, M. (1990). "Brains Behind the US—Brought from Abroad," *Guardian Weekly*, December 30.

UNESCO (1997). *Statistical Yearbook 1997*, Paris: UNESCO.

United Nations Economic Commission for Europe (UNECE) (1994). *International Migration Bulletin*, 4, United Nations, Geneva.

United Nations Population Division (1996). *International Migration Policies* 1995. New York: United Nations.

U.S. Immigration and Naturalization Service (2002). *Statistical Yearbook of the Immigration and Naturalization Service, 1999.* Washington D.C., U.S. Government Printing Office.

Vasuprasat, P. (1994). "Turning Points in International Labour Migration: A Case Study of Thailand," *Asian and Pacific Migration Journal*, 3(1): 93–118.

Wong, D. (1997). "Transcience and Settlement: Singapore's Foreign Labor Policy," *Asian and Pacific Migration Journal*, 6(2): 135–67.

World Bank (1996). *World Development Report 1996*. New York: Oxford University Press for the World Bank.

Zlotnik, H. (1993). "South-to-North Migration Since 1960: The View from the South," in *International Population Conference Montreal 1993*, vol. 2. Belgium: International Union for the Scientific Study of Population, pp. 3–14.

# 6

## Immigration and the Labor Market in Metropolitan Buenos Aires

ALICIA MAGUID

During the first half of the twentieth century, Argentina depended on and actively recruited international migrants from Europe to populate and develop itself. European immigrants affected Argentina's population, labor force, social structure, and culture, but since the 1950s immigration from neighboring countries has become increasingly important. Beginning in the 1960s, these flows have been directed primarily toward greater Buenos Aires, which has become the core of a migration subsystem embracing Chile, Bolivia, Brazil, Uruguay, and Paraguay.

Despite the economy's general instability and deterioration since the mid-1970s, immigration from border countries continues to supply labor force demand generated within Argentina's informal sector. Research in the 1980s revealed a high degree of labor market segmentation and the selective entry of border country immigrants into narrow occupational niches, such as construction and domestic service, jobs normally rejected by native Argentines because of low wages, instability, limited benefits, and hazardous working conditions (Marshall 1979; Maguid 1990).

In this chapter I consider the position of immigrants in the employment structure of greater Buenos Aires circa 1991. National census data reveal that, consistent with earlier patterns, segmented insertion into the workforce continues for immigrants from border countries. Since 1991, however, structural changes in the Argentine economy have affected metropolitan labor markets, yielding a steady increase in unemployment that has reduced opportunities in the industry and construction. By comparing occupational distributions in 1980, 1991, and 1996 I document the effects of these structural changes on immigrants and natives. My analysis reveals that border country immigrants have been relegated to a progressively narrower and more marginalized segment of the labor market.

### INTERNATIONAL MIGRATION TO ARGENTINA

Most European immigrants arrived in Argentina between 1870 and 1929. The Great Depression and World War II truncated the flows, although they revived somewhat during the 1950s and 1960s. All told, between the end of the last century and 1970 some 5.3 million immigrants arrived in Argentina, representing 38 per cent of total net migration into Latin America and the Caribbean (Lattes and Recchini de Lattes 1994). Immigration was responsible for populating Argentina to such a degree that Recchini de Lattes (1989) estimates that the population of 1960 would have been half as large without it.

Since the mid-twentieth century, the volume of immigration has decreased and its composition has shifted to bordering nations. As immigrant origins shifted from Europe to the Southern Cone of South America the flows also feminized (Maguid and Bankirer 1995). At the same time, Argentina shifted from being exclusively a country of immigration to one that also sends out emigrants. During the last few decades, in particular, Argentina has become an important supplier of professional–technical workers to Canada, the United States, and to a lesser extent Europe.

## *Evolution of migration patterns*

Changes in volume of migration since mid-century are reflected in the declining proportion of foreign born persons in Argentina, which rose from 12 per cent in 1869 to peak at 30 per cent in 1914 before declining slowly to reach 5 per cent in the early 1990s (see Table 6.1). The relative number of migrants from bordering countries shows almost no variation over time, indicating the general stability of population movements within the Southern Cone region. As of 1991, foreigners represented 2.6 per cent of the country's 32.6 million inhabitants.

The steady inflow of migrants from the Southern Cone, when combined with the dramatic decline in migration from Europe, greatly increased the proportion of border country nationals in the immigrant flow. Whereas only 9 per cent of Argentina's foreigners were from border countries in 1914, by 1991 the figure had reached 52 per cent. In contrast to the rather gradual increase in the *percentage* of immigrants from neighboring countries, the *absolute number* has fluctuated quite widely during

**Table 6.1.** *Percentage of foreign-born persons and foreigners born in border countries of Argentina, 1869–91*

| Year | Percentage foreign born | Percentage of persons from bordering countries | Percentage of foreigners from bordering countries |
|---|---|---|---|
| 1869 | 12.1 | 2.4 | 19.7 |
| 1893 | 25.4 | 2.9 | 11.5 |
| 1914 | 29.9 | 2.6 | 8.6 |
| 1947 | 15.3 | 2.0 | 12.9 |
| 1960 | 13.0 | 2.3 | 17.9 |
| 1970 | 9.5 | 2.3 | 24.1 |
| 1980 | 6.8 | 2.7 | 39.6 |
| 1991 | 5.0 | 2.6 | 52.1 |

*Source*: Instituto Nacional de Estadística y Censos.

the twentieth century. Periods of rapid immigration are linked to eras of strong labor demand associated with the expansion of Argentina's economy (Marshall 1983).

Political and economic conditions in countries of origin also create push factors from time to time. For example, the Paraguayan Civil War (1946–50) and the 1954 military coup contributed to massive increases in the number of political exiles, who joined the already sizeable flow of Paraguayan workers into Argentina. As Table 6.2 shows, the percentage of Paraguayans increased markedly between 1947 and 1970 and dropped later when many returned home. Authoritarian governments that came to power in Uruguay and Chile during the 1970s also provoked heightened flows into Argentina. Paraguayans and Chileans now represent 30 per cent of Argentina's immigrant population, followed by Bolivians and Uruguayans, each at about 17 per cent, while immigrants from Brazil have dropped to just 4 per cent of the total (see Table 6.2).

### *Settlement patterns*

Argentina's border provinces comprised the main destination for Southern Cone migrants through the 1960s. Thereafter immigrants increasingly went to the Buenos Aires Metropolitan Area, an extensive urban agglomeration formed by the capital city and 19 surrounding districts located in the Province of Buenos Aires. Some writers refer to it as "Greater Buenos Aires" (el Gran Buenos Aires). Between 1960 and 1991 the proportion of border country immigrants going to this zone increased from 25 to 47 per cent, paralleling the movement of internal migrants from Argentina's provinces to the capital.

This metropolitanization of immigration reflects Buenos Aires' prominence in the Argentine political economy. Metropolitan Buenos Aires contains a third of Argentina's population, 35 per cent of its employment, and houses 47 per cent of all workers employed in industry. This remarkable concentration suggests that Buenos Aires functions as a "global city," in the language of world systems theory. Balán (1992) states that by the mid-1980s the Southern Cone had emerged as an independent international migration subsystem with Buenos Aires at its core, created by relatively open migration policies.

**Table 6.2.** *Border country immigrants in Argentina by place of birth, 1869–91*

| Country | 1869 (%) | 1895 (%) | 1914 (%) | 1947 (%) | 1960 (%) | 1970 (%) | 1980 (%) | 1991 (%) |
|---|---|---|---|---|---|---|---|---|
| Bolivia | 15.0 | 6.4 | 8.8 | 15.3 | 19.1 | 17.3 | 15.7 | 17.8 |
| Brazil | 14.3 | 21.3 | 17.7 | 15.0 | 10.4 | 8.4 | 5.7 | 4.2 |
| Chile | 26.3 | 17.8 | 16.7 | 16.5 | 25.3 | 24.9 | 28.6 | 30.2 |
| Paraguay | 7.9 | 12.6 | 13.8 | 29.8 | 33.2 | 39.7 | 34.9 | 31.1 |
| Uruguay | 36.5 | 42.0 | 42.9 | 23.5 | 12.0 | 9.6 | 15.1 | 16.6 |
| Total (*N*) | 41,360 | 115,892 | 206,701 | 313,264 | 467,260 | 533,850 | 753,428 | 841,697 |

*Source*: Instituto Nacional de Estadística y Censos.

Table 6.3. *Location of immigrants born in border countries of Argentina, 1991*

| Region | Border country immigrants | | | Border country immigrants by origin | | | | |
|---|---|---|---|---|---|---|---|---|
| | Total distribution | % of Regional pop. | % of Total foreign pop. | Bolivia | Brazil | Chile | Paraguay | Uruguay |
| Metro Buenos Aires | 47.4 | 3.7 | 42.8 | 38.9 | 27.3 | 18.4 | 65.3 | 80.9 |
| Rest of Buenos Aires | 8.0 | 1.5 | 41.4 | 6.5 | 5.7 | 11.4 | 5.3 | 8.8 |
| Center | 3.8 | 0.5 | 29.7 | 4.6 | 6.4 | 2.9 | 2.4 | 6.5 |
| Cuyo | 5.8 | 2.0 | 63.3 | 10.1 | 2.8 | 12.2 | 0.2 | 0.6 |
| Northeast | 10.6 | 3.2 | 88.1 | 0.5 | 55.3 | 0.2 | 25.6 | 1.2 |
| Northwest | 7.1 | 1.8 | 83.1 | 36.5 | 0.9 | 1.0 | 0.6 | 0.6 |
| Patagonia | 17.3 | 9.9 | 89.7 | 2.9 | 1.6 | 53.9 | 0.6 | 1.5 |
| Total (000) | 841.7 | 21.9 | 43.9 | 143.6 | 33.5 | 244.4 | 250.5 | 133.5 |

*Source*: Instituto Nacional de Estadística y Censos.

As shown in Table 6.3, by 1991 47 per cent of border country immigrants lived in metropolitan Buenos Aires, with exceptionally high concentrations of Uruguayans (81 per cent) and Paraguayans (65 per cent). In contrast, just 39 per cent of Bolivians lived in this region, compared with 18 per cent of Chileans (a majority of whom, 54 per cent, lived in Patagonia). The relative number of border country migrants in the regional population also surpasses the national average in the northeastern provinces of Misiones and Formasa as well as the Patagonian provinces of Santa Cruz and Tierra del Fuego; but metropolitan Buenos Aires region is the only region where all nationalities are represented. Among immigrants in greater Buenos Aires, 43 per cent are Paraguayans, 28 per cent Paraguayan, 15 per cent Bolivian, 12 per cent Chilean, and 2 per cent Brazilian.

## MIGRANTS IN THE BUENOS AIRES LABOR MARKET

According to Beccaria and López (1994, 1996), through the mid-1970s the Argentine labor market differed from those in other Latin American countries in its relatively low rates of unemployment. Despite poor job absorption in the modern sector, the informal sector expanded and offered a reasonable livelihood to workers. From 1975 to 1990, however, production stagnated and monetary instability reduced labor demand and lowered wages, thus, deepening labor market segmentation and stimulating the expansion of precarious jobs in the informal sector. Precarious jobs are unprotected by labor regulations, unstable, and poorly paid.

During the early 1990s, income inequalities widened in spite of a significant increase in productivity and the continued growth of GDP. At the beginning of 1991 the government launched a program to achieve stability and shift the economy away from import substitution industrialization. This restructuring of the Argentine economy along neoliberal lines produced a brief expansion of employment and wages, but by the end of 1992 the situation had once again begun to deteriorate. In 1993 there was a sharp increase in unemployment, particularly among women. The situation worsened thereafter as the gap between labor supply and demand increased. Whereas unemployment fluctuated narrowly between 4 and 6 per cent during 1974–92, afterward it climbed steadily, moving from 11 per cent in 1993 to 18 per cent in 1996. The decline of the economy was also expressed in rates of underemployment, which rose from 8 per cent in 1993 and to 13 per cent in 1996.

Given that unemployment insurance is available to only 5 per cent of the nation's unemployed, and that 90 per cent of those qualifying for unemployment insurance are native Argentines, these trends call the future of labor migration into question. Historically, both internal and international migrants have contributed to the growth of the metropolitan working class and the volume of migration has been linked closely to variations in labor demand. More recently, internal migration has faltered while immigration has increased despite the stagnation of demand, suggesting the intensification of labor market segmentation (see Piore 1979; Marshall 1979, 1983; Maguid 1990).

Data from the 1991 census allow us to investigate how border country migrants have fared in this new labor market compared with native workers. As the census only measures the characteristics of people at the time of the enumeration (rather than at the point of arrival or insertion into the labor market) I also consider intercensal changes in employment patterns during the period 1980–91, when the deepest structural changes occurred. I also combine census data with newer information from the 1996 Permanent Household Survey (*Encuesta Parmanente de Hogares*), which began recording migratory information in 1993. Because the latter corresponds to a sample rather than the population, however, it yields a rather small number of border country immigrants that does not permit detailed analysis.

## *Sociodemographic characteristics*

As Table 6.4 reports, almost three quarters of immigrants from border countries were aged 25–64, a degree of concentration in the labor force ages greatly exceeding that of native (just 46 per cent). Moreover, as the sex ratios show, most migrants are women and females are notably overrepresented compared with the native population. The presence of women among border country immigrants rose substantially between 1980 and 1996, confirming the feminization of migration noted earlier.

Table 6.4 also shows that natives and immigrants have similar educational backgrounds in the intermediate levels. The proportion who have completed primary school is virtually the same across groups (around 55 per cent) as is the percentage who have finished secondary education (about 13 per cent), giving both natives and foreigners the basic qualifications for skilled manual jobs. Migrants are unfavorably positioned at the extremes of the educational ladder, however. Whereas 17 per cent of natives had some higher education, the figure was only 8 per cent for immigrants;

**Table 6.4.** *Composition of total population, native population, and border country immigrants by age, sex, and education in metropolitan Buenos Aires, 1991*

| Categories | Total population (%) | Native population (%) | Border country immigrants (%) |
|---|---|---|---|
| *Age* | | | |
| 0–13 | 24.5 | 26.5 | 6.5 |
| 14–24 | 17.8 | 18.9 | 13.3 |
| 25–64 | 47.3 | 46.1 | 72.7 |
| 65+ | 10.4 | 8.5 | 7.5 |
| *Sex Ratio (M/F)* | | | |
| 1980 | 92.6 | 92.7 | 89.9 |
| 1991 | 91.9 | 92.6 | 82.9 |
| 1996 | 92.1 | 93.2 | 76.2 |
| *Education (Pop. 14+)* | | | |
| Incomplete Primary | 15.8 | 14.6 | 22.1 |
| Complete Primary | 54.5 | 54.7 | 56.2 |
| Complete Secondary | 13.8 | 13.9 | 13.6 |
| Higher Education | 15.9 | 16.8 | 8.1 |

*Source*: Instituto Nacional de Estadística y Censos.

**Table 6.5.** *Education of immigrants from border countries in metropolitan Buenos Aires, 1980–96*

| Education | Immigrants in 1980 | | | Immigrants in 1900 | Immigrants in 1996 | | |
|---|---|---|---|---|---|---|---|
| | Total | Arrived < 1970 | Arrived 1970+ | | Total | Arrived < 1986 | Arrived 1986+ |
| Incomplete primary | 32.5 | 37.7 | 26.3 | 22.1 | 18.4 | 19.3 | 14.4 |
| Complete primary | 53.8 | 51.0 | 57.2 | 56.2 | 62.0 | 61.0 | 65.1 |
| Complete secondary or higher | 13.7 | 11.3 | 16.5 | 21.7 | 19.6 | 19.7 | 20.5 |

*Source*: Instituto Nacional de Estadística y Censos.

and whereas just 15 per cent of natives had not finished primary school, 22 per cent of immigrants had not done so.

Given the historical segregation of border country immigrants in the labor market, it makes sense to consider how stable immigrant schooling has been over time. Table 6.5 indicates a general improvement in educational attainment among immigrants between 1980 and 1996. Over this period the percentage with the lowest educations dropped from 33 to 18 per cent and the share with secondary or higher education climbed from 14 to 20 per cent.

If we focus only on recently arrived immigrants, however, educational levels are even higher. Among those who arrived in the past 10 years, the percentage with low schooling was 26 per cent in 1980 and 14 per cent in 1996, whereas the proportions with some college were 17 and 21 per cent, respectively. This improvement in immigrant education is explained by the expansion of education in sending countries as well as by rising educational requirements for jobs in Argentina's tightening labor market.

## *Insertion into the Metropolitan labor force*

In 1991, the labor force of Metropolitan Buenos Aires was composed mainly of males (62 per cent), whose overall activity rate was quite high (76 per cent—see Table 6.6). Although female participation was rising in the years before 1991, it remained considerably lower at 41 per cent. Bordering country migrants accounted for 6 per cent of the metropolitan area's economically active population, compared with 4 per cent for other foreigners. The participation rate of border country migrants exceeded that of native Argentines, both male and female; but among women the differential was sharpest. As Table 6.6 shows, almost half of immigrant women participated in the labor force in 1991 compared with just 32 per cent of natives. Immigrants also had a lower rate of unemployment than natives, and the differential was once again most pronounced among women. Among females, the rate of unemployment was 7.4 per cent among immigrants but 9.7 per cent among natives, a 24 per cent differential.

Table 6.7 considers the work status of natives and immigrants by gender. As can be seen, 58 per cent of male immigrants were wage earners, but only a small minority of men worked in domestic service. One-third of immigrant males were self-employed, easily exceeding the share for natives. When the data are broken down by time of immigration, those in the self-employed category are mostly long-term, well-established immigrants rather than recent arrivals (see Maguid 1990, 1995). The latter are more likely to be employed as wage-earners, reflecting their need for capital and knowledge as precursors to independent business activities. Among migrant women, the total proportion working for wages is greater than among migrant men once domestic

**Table 6.6.** *Labor force and unemployment rates by sex for population Aged 14+ in metropolitan Buenos Aires, 1991*

| Rate | Total (%) | Natives (%) | Border country immigrants (%) | Percentage difference (%) |
|---|---|---|---|---|
| *Labor force* | | | | |
| Males | 76.5 | 77.3 | 87.8 | 13.6 |
| Females | 40.9 | 32.2 | 49.5 | 53.7 |
| Total | 57.5 | 58.7 | 66.7 | 13.6 |
| *Unemployment* | | | | |
| Males | 6.0 | 6.2 | 5.1 | −17.7 |
| Females | 9.5 | 9.7 | 7.4 | −23.7 |
| Total | 7.3 | 7.5 | 6.1 | −18.7 |

*Source*: Instituto Nacional de Estadística y Censos.

Table 6.7. *Worker status of employed workers in metropolitan Buenos Aires, 1991*

| Workers status | Total (%) | Natives (%) | Border country immigrants (%) | Percentage difference |
|---|---|---|---|---|
| *All workers* | | | | |
| Wage earners | 60.8 | 62.3 | 49.8 | −20.1 |
| Domestic servants | 6.8 | 6.5 | 14.9 | 129.2 |
| Self-employed | 22.2 | 21.4 | 28.0 | 30.8 |
| Employers | 7.6 | 7.2 | 4.5 | −37.5 |
| Family workers | 2.6 | 2.6 | 2.8 | 7.6 |
| *Male workers* | | | | |
| Wage earners | 63.1 | 64.5 | 58.1 | −6.4 |
| Domestic servants | 0.3 | 0.3 | 0.8 | 166.7 |
| Self-employed | 25.4 | 24.5 | 33.9 | 38.4 |
| Employers | 9.3 | 8.8 | 5.5 | −37.5 |
| Family workers | 1.9 | 1.9 | 1.8 | −5.3 |
| *Female workers* | | | | |
| Wage earners | 56.8 | 58.5 | 37.5 | −35.9 |
| Domestic servants | 18.0 | 17.2 | 36.0 | 109.3 |
| Self-employed | 16.7 | 16.2 | 19.2 | 18.5 |
| Employers | 4.6 | 4.5 | 3.1 | −31.1 |
| Family workers | 3.9 | 3.7 | 4.3 | 16.2 |

*Source*: Instituto Nacional de Estadística y Censos.

service is taken into account. Moreover, among women, the proportion of immigrants working as domestic servants is double that of natives: 36 versus 17 per cent.

Table 6.8 considers the skill level of natives and immigrants employed in the metropolitan labor market. In general, only among women are border country immigrants more likely than natives to be employed in unskilled occupations. Whereas 47 per cent of female immigrants held skilled manual jobs, 32 per cent held unskilled manual jobs, and 11 per cent were in the professions, among native females the respective figures were lower at 42, 24, and 24 per cent. Although both immigrant and natives were similarly represented in unskilled jobs among males, among women the percentage of immigrants in unskilled work is 64 per cent higher than that of natives (54 versus 33 per cent), reflecting the high concentration of immigrant women in domestic services.

As can be seen from Table 6.9, which breaks employment down by sector, metropolitan workers are generally concentrated in services (9 per cent domestic, 21 per cent other services), industry (24 per cent), and commerce (23 per cent); and a closer look at the comparative location of immigrants and natives by sector confirms the continued segmentation of the metropolitan labor market. Border country migrants are heavily concentrated in construction, domestic services, and to a lesser extent industry, while being underrepresented elsewhere. Compared with native workers,

**Table 6.8.** *Status of employed workers in metropolitan Buenos Aires, 1991*

| Workers status | Total (%) | Natives (%) | Border country immigrants (%) | Percentage difference (%) |
|---|---|---|---|---|
| *All workers* | | | | |
| Manager–professional–technical | 23.5 | 23.7 | 11.2 | −52.7 |
| Skilled manual | 42.0 | 41.9 | 47.1 | 5.2 |
| Unskilled manual | 24.0 | 23.8 | 32.4 | 36.1 |
| Unknown | 10.5 | 10.6 | 9.3 | −12.3 |
| *Male workers* | | | | |
| Manager–professional–technical | 22.0 | 21.9 | 11.3 | −48.4 |
| Skilled manual | 47.9 | 47.7 | 60.2 | 12.5 |
| Unskilled manual | 18.4 | 18.6 | 18.1 | −2.7 |
| Unknown | 11.7 | 11.8 | 10.4 | −11.9 |
| *Female workers* | | | | |
| Manager–professional–technical | 26.0 | 26.9 | 11.2 | −58.4 |
| Skilled manual | 31.8 | 32.0 | 27.7 | −13.4 |
| Unskilled manual | 33.7 | 32.6 | 53.6 | 64.4 |
| Unknown | 8.5 | 8.5 | 7.5 | −11.8 |

*Source*: Instituto Nacional de Estadística y Censos.

**Table 6.9.** *Sector of employment by sex in metropolitan Buenos Aires, 1991*

| Sector | Total (%) | Natives (%) | Border country immigrants (%) | Percentage difference (%) | Immigrant concentration in sector (%) |
|---|---|---|---|---|---|
| *All workers* | | | | | |
| Industry | 23.9 | 23.7 | 24.2 | 2.1 | 5.5 |
| Construction | 6.6 | 6.2 | 15.4 | 148.4 | 12.7 |
| Commerce–hotel–rest. | 22.5 | 22.1 | 20.8 | −5.8 | 5.0 |
| Transport–communication | 6.6 | 6.7 | 4.3 | −35.8 | 3.6 |
| Finance–ins.–real estate | 8.2 | 8.6 | 4.1 | −52.3 | 2.7 |
| Domestic services | 9.0 | 8.6 | 18.8 | 118.6 | 11.4 |
| Other services | 20.8 | 21.7 | 10.8 | −50.2 | 2.8 |
| Other sectors | 2.4 | 2.4 | 1.6 | −33.3 | 3.7 |
| *Male workers* | | | | | |
| Industry | 28.0 | 27.8 | 29.0 | 4.3 | 6.6 |
| Construction | 10.2 | 9.5 | 25.5 | 168.4 | 12.9 |
| Commerce–hotel–rest. | 24.6 | 24.3 | 25.5 | 4.9 | 5.3 |
| *Female workers* | | | | | |
| Industry | 16.9 | 16.6 | 17.1 | 2.9 | 5.3 |
| Commerce–hotel–rest. | 18.8 | 18.4 | 19.1 | 3.8 | 6.0 |
| Domestic services | 21.7 | 20.7 | 41.9 | 102.4 | 11.5 |

*Source*: Instituto Nacional de Estadística y Censos.

immigrants are 148 per cent more likely to be in construction, 26 per cent more likely to be in domestic services, and 2 per cent more likely to be in industry.

In the latter sector, however, immigrants are relatively unlikely to be employed in the production of durable goods but are overrepresented in the manufacture of nondurable goods, which are relatively labor intensive. Compared with natives, immigrants are 28 per cent more likely to be employed in the production of food, clothing, leather, and furniture and 24 per cent less likely to work elsewhere in industry (data not shown). When the data are disaggregated by gender, moreover, male immigrants are seen to be most strongly overrepresented in construction whereas females are most strongly overrepresented in domestic service. In total, border country immigrants constitute 13 per cent of construction workers and 11 per cent of domestic servants. Neither immigrant men nor women participate much in Argentina's most dynamic sector: finance, insurance, and real estate.

By considering the three labor force dimensions analyzed so far—status, skill, and sector—we can summarize the situation of border country migrants into the Argentine economy as follows. Immigrants generally insert themselves into the labor market as skilled wage earners in industry, skilled wage earners or self-employed workers in construction, or as unskilled wage earners in services. As hypothesized by segmented labor market theory, migrants appear to be recruited into the secondary sector to work at precarious jobs characterized by lower returns to education, skills, and work experience.

The data analyzed so far suggest that immigrant labor market insertion continued to be segmented through 1991. The indicators in Table 6.10 (which are constrained by the availability of information) refer to work underutilization and to other unfavorable insertion conditions in the labor market. The first two indicators measure returns to education: the percentage of workers with secondary or higher education who perform unskilled tasks and the percentage with complete high school or university studies who engage in skilled jobs. These measures not only indicate low returns to education but also a less than optimal utilization of labor resources.

As Table 6.10 shows, compared with the natives, border country immigrants are more seriously underemployed. Whereas 21 per cent of immigrants with a secondary or higher education worked in unskilled jobs, the figure was only 10 per cent among natives. Likewise, 23 per cent of immigrants with college or higher education held skilled manual positions, compared with 15 per cent for natives. In general, the degree of underemployment was greater for men than for women.

Workers engaged in jobs that are unprotected by labor regulations by definition experience tenuous work situations. Whereas almost half (49 per cent) of all border immigrants held an unprotected job, the figure was 32 per cent for natives doing similar work. The disproportion is greatest among migrant women, 65 per cent of whom work in unprotected jobs compared with just 31 per cent of native females.

The proportion of workers living in homes with basic needs unsatisfied is higher likewise much higher among immigrants. Whereas 22 per cent of immigrant males came from households with unmet basic needs, the figure was 14 per cent for native

**Table 6.10.** *Position of workers in the labor market of metropolitan Buenos Aires, 1991*

| Indicator | Total | Natives | Border country immigrants | Percentage difference |
|---|---|---|---|---|
| *Percentage of workers with secondary studies or higher working in unskilled jobs* | | | | |
| Males | 9.7 | 9.7 | 21.2 | 118.6 |
| Females | 11.6 | 10.9 | 14.2 | 30.3 |
| Total | 10.6 | 10.2 | 21.2 | 107.8 |
| *Percentage of workers with university studies or higher working in skilled jobs* | | | | |
| Males | 15.8 | 16.6 | 26.3 | 58.4 |
| Females | 14.6 | 14.5 | 18.6 | 28.3 |
| Total | 15.2 | 15.1 | 22.7 | 50.3 |
| *Percentage of Workers Unprotected by Labor Regulations* | | | | |
| Males | 26.6 | 26.3 | 36.0 | 36.9 |
| Females | 42.7 | 31.4 | 64.9 | 106.7 |
| Total | 33.2 | 32.4 | 49.2 | 51.9 |
| *Percentage of workers in homes with basic needs unsatisfied* | | | | |
| Males | 12.8 | 14.0 | 22.4 | 60.0 |
| Females | 12.0 | 11.6 | 21.7 | 87.1 |
| Total | 12.7 | 11.7 | 22.3 | 90.6 |
| *Indicators of income* | | | | |
| Average Dollars per Hour[a] | 4.20 | 4.30 | 3.20 | −25.6 |
| % in Lowest Income Quintile | 20.0 | 20.3 | 28.2 | 38.9 |
| % in Highest Income Quintile | 20.0 | 20.8 | 8.3 | −60.1 |

[a] Data are for 1996.

*Source*: Instituto Nacional de Estadística y Censos.

males; and among females the differential was even greater: 22 per cent for immigrants compared with just 12 per cent for natives. These differentials carry over into income. The average income per hour was $3.20 for immigrants but $4.30 for natives. As a result 28 per cent of immigrants came from families in the lowest income quintile compared with 20 per cent of natives; and whereas only 8 per cent of immigrants lived in households earning incomes in the highest quintile, 21 per cent of natives did so.

### Labor market segmentation

Thus, available empirical evidence seems to confirm the hypothesis that border country immigrants are relegated to secondary labor market jobs rejected by natives, yielding very unfavorable living conditions, at least through 1991. Since then, however, the Argentine economy and the metropolitan labor market have experienced deep structural changes, with a staggering rise in unemployment accompanied by increasing underemployment and the growth of the service relative to the industrial sector. Tables 6.11 and 6.12 suggest how these circumstances have affected the absorption of migrant workers. Between 1991 and 1996 there was a decrease in the size of the metropolitan labor force, owing mainly to losses in the industrial sector, construction, and community services. The latter sector was affected by cutbacks in government programs and the privatization of state companies, which reduced the number of civil servants. During these 5 years, the finance and insurance sectors grew, along with transportation and communications, but not enough to maintain employment.

The relative number of border immigrants in metropolitan Buenos Aires seemed to stagnate during 1991–6, suggesting an adjustment to decreasing labor demand. Because reliable information on arrivals and departures is not available, however, this observation cannot be confirmed. It is not known whether gross in-migration actually decreased, or whether arrivals and departures simply moved toward a balance. In Table 6.11 a few indicators have been chosen to compare the employment position of border immigrant workers with the situation of all workers in 1980, 1991, and 1996. These data reveal a consistent increase in the proportion of immigrants in domestic service over the period. In contrast, from 1991 to 6 the percentage of self-employed workers among immigrants dropped, although the share still exceeded that in the native population.

**Table 6.11.** *Position of border country immigrants in the employment structure of metropolitan Buenos Aires, 1980–96*

| Indicator | 1980 | | | 1991 | | | 1996 | | |
|---|---|---|---|---|---|---|---|---|---|
| | Total | Migs | %Diff | Total | Migs | %Diff | Total | Migs | %Diff |
| *Status* | | | | | | | | | |
| Wage earner | 69.0 | 63.2 | −8.4 | 60.8 | 49.8 | −18.1 | 66.4 | 56.2 | −15.4 |
| Domestic | 5.5 | 11.4 | 107.3 | 6.8 | 14.9 | 119.1 | 7.5 | 18.4 | 145.3 |
| Self employed | 17.9 | 20.2 | 12.8 | 22.2 | 28.0 | 26.1 | 19.1 | 22.7 | 18.8 |
| *Skill level* | | | | | | | | | |
| Skilled | — | — | — | 42.0 | 47.1 | 12.1 | 44.7 | 49.1 | 9.8 |
| Unskilled | — | — | — | 24.0 | 32.4 | 35.0 | 27.1 | 38.1 | 40.6 |
| *Sector* | | | | | | | | | |
| Industry | 20.9 | 26.8 | 5.9 | 23.9 | 24.2 | 7.2 | 19.9 | 15.9 | −20.1 |
| Construction | 10.0 | 24.6 | 146.0 | 6.6 | 15.4 | 133.3 | 6.2 | 18.7 | 201.6 |
| Commerce | 17.0 | 13.6 | −20.0 | 22.5 | 20.8 | −7.6 | 22.6 | 24.2 | 7.1 |
| Transport | 4.6 | 2.8 | −39.1 | 6.6 | 4.3 | −34.8 | 8.9 | 4.2 | −52.8 |
| Finance | 4.0 | 2.2 | −45.0 | 8.2 | 4.1 | −50.0 | 11.8 | 5.8 | −50.8 |
| Services | 24.0 | 24.0 | 0.0 | 29.8 | 29.6 | −0.7 | 29.8 | 31.3 | 5.0 |

*Source*: Instituto Nacional de Estadística y Censos.

**Table 6.12.** *Employment growth and changes in sectorial distribution of immigrants from bordering countries 1980–91 and 1991–6, Buenos Aires metropolitan area*

| Sector | Total job growth (%) | Percentage change in sectoral distribution (%) | | Concentration of border immigrants within sector (%) | |
|---|---|---|---|---|---|
| | | Total | Immigrants | First year | Last year |
| *Period 1980–91* | | | | | |
| Industry | −5.0 | 14.0 | −10.0 | 4.7 | 5.5 |
| Construction | −10.0 | −34.0 | 32.0 | 13.0 | 12.7 |
| Commerce | 24.0 | 32.0 | 53.0 | 3.5 | 5.0 |
| Services | 43.0 | 24.0 | 23.0 | 5.0 | 5.4 |
| Total | 18.0 | — | — | 5.0 | 5.4 |
| *Period 1991–6* | | | | | |
| Industry | −25.0 | −17.0 | −34.0 | 5.5 | 4.0 |
| Construction | −10.0 | −6.0 | 10.0 | 12.7 | 15.3 |
| Commerce | 9.0 | 0.0 | 16.0 | 5.0 | 5.4 |
| Services | −12.0 | 0.0 | 6.0 | 5.4 | 5.3 |
| Total | −4.0 | — | — | 5.4 | 5.1 |

*Source*: Instituto Nacional de Estadística y Censos.

With respect to occupational skill, in 1996 most border country immigrants could still be found in the skilled category despite an increase in the proportion engaged in unskilled tasks (38 versus 32 per cent in 1991). Although the differential employment of migrants and natives in skilled and unskilled jobs generally remained stable between 1991 and 1996, there were more pronounced differences in sector of employment. Whereas the industrial sector absorbed the largest share of immigrants in 1980, in the ensuing years commerce and services rose to greater prominence. Whereas 27 per cent of immigrants worked in industry in 1980, compared with 14 per cent in commerce and 24 per cent in services, by 1996 the respective figures were 16 per cent in industry, 24 per cent in commerce, and 31 per cent in services. Immigrant participation in construction stood at 25 per cent in 1980, fell to 15 per cent in 1990 and then rose again to 19 per cent by 1996.

Thus, in both 1991 and 1996 the service sector, and within this, domestic service, was the main point of labor market insertion for border country immigrants. The most remarkable change between these years was a drastic reduction in the percentage of migrants working in the industrial sector. These sectoral shifts provoked an increase in immigrant–native differentials in sectoral distribution. The shift is especially striking in the case of construction, where the percentage of migrants grew to be triple that of all workers.

In her analysis of migration and employment in the 1970s Marshall (1983) found that when employment growth was greater in one sector than in others, there tended to be a reassignment of migrant workers into the faster-growing sector, suggesting the greater flexibility of immigrants in adapting to changes in the labor market.

Table 6.12 permits an analysis of how relative change in a sector's growth rate was associated with the sectoral redistribution of migrant workers between 1980 and 1991 and between 1991 and 1996. During the earlier period, industry and construction lost jobs, and border migrants consequently shifted from these sectors towards commerce and services, which were rapidly expanding. These numbers suggest that border immigrants bear the brunt of adjustments to sectoral employment changes. Their share in different sectors shift more dramatically in response to structural change compared with all workers.

Trends for the period 1991–6 generally support segmented labor market theory in accounting for persistent immigration. This theory assumes that a relatively permanent demand for immigrant workers is built into the structure of advanced industrial societies. Although the end of import substitution industrialization in the late 1970s meant that Argentina no longer exhibited the characteristics of an expanding economy, it did manage to maintain a slow growth of employment and a relatively low unemployment rate until 1993.

This pattern demonstrates the capacity of the metropolitan Buenos Aires labor market to absorb workers from neighboring countries even during economic downturns. According to Mármora (1994), migrant workers have always played a complementary and non-competitive role *vis-à-vis* Argentine workers, engaging in jobs rejected by natives due to low pay and unfavorable working conditions while the latter pursued a path of upward occupational mobility. Maguid (1995) and Montoya and Perticará (1995) have shown that border country immigrants are in no way responsible for the rise in unemployment during the 1990s.

In the face of rising unemployment, will Argentines become willing to work in jobs they had previously rejected and abandoned to immigrants? The data in Table 6.12, which correspond to periods of slow (1980–91) and negative (1991–6) employment growth, suggest not. As industrial, construction, and service employment fell sharply from 1991 to 1996, the relative concentration of immigrants generally increased (in construction) or stayed the same (in services). Only the industrial sector registered a decline in the concentration of immigrants (from 5.5 to 4 per cent). Migrant workers, who had already begun to be expelled from this sector during the 1980s, continued to be displaced with greater intensity.

The end result was a reassignment of border migrants to construction, despite the reduction of total employment in that sector. Argentines responded to the drop in construction employment by decreasing their own participation. There has always been an overrepresentation of migrants in construction, but in 1996 the share of border migrants in construction reached its highest historical peak at 15 per cent. Immigrants also moved toward commerce, where they worked as traveling or marginal sellers, cooks, waiters, or as cleaning staff in hotels; but the shift toward services has been more pronounced, led by domestic services.

The data in Table 6.13 reinforce previous findings by showing the differences in sectoral distribution among early and recent immigrants in 1980 and 1996. Whereas recent immigrants in 1980 (those arriving in the last 10 years) were concentrated almost equally in industry, construction, and services, by 1996 recent immigrants were most heavily concentrated in construction (28 per cent), followed by commerce

**Table 6.13.** *Distribution of border country migrants by sector and duration of residence, 1980 and 1996*

| Sector | 1980 Immigrants by arrival time (%) | | 1996 Immigrants by arrival time (%) | |
|---|---|---|---|---|
| | > 10 years ago | Last 10 years | > 10 years ago | Last 10 years |
| Industry | 28.0 | 25.0 | 15.3 | 18.0 |
| Construction | 25.9 | 23.0 | 15.4 | 27.7 |
| Commerce | 12.4 | 15.0 | 24.7 | 21.7 |
| Services | 22.2 | 25.8 | 34.4 | 22.8 |

*Source*: Instituto Nacional de Estadística y Censos.

and services at around 22 per cent each. Industry had slipped to just 18 per cent of recent arrivals.

The data are, thus, consistent in showing that contraction of labor demand increased the sectoral concentration of border country immigrants the detriment of the migrants themselves. During the 1980s immigrants were increasingly employed in construction, commerce, and services where they were increasingly underemployed compared with the skills they possessed. Whether this shift has been accompanied by an absolute reduction in size of the migrant workforce, or whether natives will return to jobs they formerly shunned, are questions that must be left to future research.

## CONCLUSIONS

Until 1991, Argentina, in general, and the Buenos Aires Metropolitan Area, in particular, experienced rising immigration from border countries to fulfill specific demands for labor within certain sectors, in a manner consistent with segmented labor market theory. Structural economic changes in the 1990s had negative consequences for metropolitan employment, as the number of jobs in construction, industry, and services contracted and the unemployment rate climbed to 18 per cent, triple that of the late 1980s. The loss of employment was accompanied by a decrease in the number of sectors employing immigrants and their greater concentration in a few, more marginalized occupations.

Given the narrowing of employment options and the shrinking of metropolitan employment, it is not clear what will happen to immigration from border countries in the future. What role will immigrants play in the coming years if labor demand does not grow? Will their places in the labor market be taken by Argentines? Will immigration decrease as a result, or will it persist owing to the influence of migrant networks, chain hiring, and the worsening of conditions in neighboring countries? And what effect will regional trade treaties such as Mercosur have on the regional population mobility?

The data presented here cannot answer these questions, but they do suggest two critical predictions. As the employment rate falls, border workers will increase their concentration within two sectors—construction and services—and within these sectors they will be unemployed on increasingly unfavorable terms in terms of wages and working conditions. Although Argentina is of particular interest theoretically as the core of a new regional migration subsystem, we currently lack the data to address fundamental theoretical questions, not only with respect to segmented labor market theory, but those pertaining to the other theoretical models reviewed by Massey et al. (1998). To achieve a fuller understanding of the changes that have occurred in the past decade and to anticipate those of the future will require specially designed research that goes beyond the limits of traditional statistics.

## References

Balán, Jorge (1992). "The Role of Migration Policies and Social Networks in the Development of a Migration System in the Southern Cone," in Mary M. Kritz et al. (eds.), *International Migration Systems: A Global Approach*. Oxford: Clarendon Press, pp. 115–32.

Beccaria, Lourdes, and López, Naide (1994). "Reconversión y Empleo en la Argentina," *Revista de Estudios del Trabajo* 7: 110–14.

—— —— (1996). "Notas Sobre el Comportamiento en el Mercado de Trabajo Urbano," *Sin Trabajo: Las Características del Desempleo y sus Efectos en la Sociedad Argentina*. Buenos Aires: UNICEF-LOSADA.

Instituto Nacional de Estadística y Censos (1994). *Clasificador Nacional de las Ocupaciones*. Buenos Aires: Instituto Nacional de Estadística y Censos.

Lattes, Alfredo, and Recchini de Lattes, Zulma (1994). "International Migration in Latin America: Patterns, Determinants and Policies," *International Migration: Regional Processes and Responses, Economic Studies No.7*, Economic Commission for Europe and United Nations Fund for Population Activities, Geneva.

Maguid, Alicia (1990). *Migrantes Limítrofes en la Argentina: Perfil Sociodemográfico y Ocupacional en 1980*. Buenos Aires: Proyecto Gobierno Argentino and United Nations Fund for Population Activities.

—— (1995). "Migrantes Limítrofes en la Argentina: Su Inserción e Impacto en el Mercado de Trabajo," *Revista Estudios del Trabajo*, 10: 22–49.

—— and M. Bankirer (1995). "Argentina: Saldos Migratorios Internacionales 1970–1990," *II Jornadas Argentinas de Estudios de Población*. Buenos Aires: Senado de la Nación.

Mármora, L. (1994). "Sustainable Development and Migration Policies: Their Treatment within the Latin American Economic Integration Blocks," *IOM Latin American Migration Journal*, 12: 112–31.

Marshall, Adriana (1979). "Immigrant Workers in the Buenos Aires Labor Market." *International Migration Review*, 13: 488–501.

—— (1983). "Immigración de Países Limítrofes y Demanda de Mano de Obra en la Argentina, 1940–1980," *Desarrollo Económico*, 23(89): 42–68.

Massey, Douglas S., Joaquin Arango, Graeme Hugo, Ali Kouaouci, Adela Pellegrino, and J. Edward Taylor. (1998). *Words in Motion: International Migration at the End of the Millennium*. Oxford: Oxford University Press.

Montoya, S., and Perticará, M. (1995). "Los Migrantes Limítrofes: Aumentan el Desempleo?" *Novedades Económicas*, 170: 1–2.

Piore, Michael (1979). *Birds of Passage: Migrant Labor in Industrial Societies*. New York: Cambridge University Press.

Recchini de Lattes, Zulma (1989). "Consecuencias Demográficas de los Movimientos Internacionales en la República Argentina, 1870–1960," *Conferencia Mundial de Población*, vol IV. New York: United Nations.

# 7

## Mexican Migration to the United States: The Effect of NAFTA

PHILIP L. MARTIN

Although the United States is the world's major country of immigration and Mexico is the world's major country of emigration, there is a fundamental asymmetry in their situations. Whereas the United States accepts immigrants from many nations, virtually all Mexican emigrants head for the United States (Durand and Massey 1992). In 1996, 164,000 Mexicans entered as legal immigrants and 1.3 million came as non-immigrants for business, pleasure, or temporary work. In addition, Mexican citizens held around 5 million border crossing cards that permitted them to enter the United States and remain in the border zone for up to 72 hours. At the same time, some 1.6 million unauthorized Mexicans were apprehended, mostly just inside the border.

For most of the twentieth century, migration has been a major linkage between the two most populous countries in North America. The slogan "go north for opportunity" is deeply embedded in Mexican culture, especially among rural youth. In 1998, for example, there were about 4 million Mexican-born workers in the U.S. labor market, equaling about one-eighth of Mexico's 32 million paid employees. Between 1980 and 1996, the U.S. received 3.3 million Mexican immigrants, equivalent to 20 per cent of Mexico's net population growth and 30 per cent of U.S. immigration. Most projections assume similar levels of Mexico-to-US immigration for the foreseeable future.

Contemporary Mexico–U.S. migration patterns have their roots in a series of bilateral labor agreements between 1942 and 1964 known collectively as the Bracero Program (Massey et al. 1987: Martin 2003). Under these agreements, some 4.6 million Mexicans entered the United States on a temporary basis to do farm work; some returned year after year, but an estimated 1–2 million Mexicans obtained work experience in the United States as legal guest workers.

The Bracero Program was small during the war years, with Braceros representing under 2 per cent of U.S. hired farm workers in 1944; but the number of Mexicans and the percentage who arrived illegally, as so-called "wetbacks," increased in the late 1940s and early 1950s, as both Mexican workers and U.S. farmers learned they could avoid cumbersome regulations by making private employment arrangements. The usual practice was for a Mexican worker to enter the U.S. illegally, and find a farm job. If the undocumented worker was later apprehended, he was generally returned to the Mexican border, issued work documents, and returned to his U.S. employer, a process termed, even in official government reports, "drying out the wetbacks." The employment of Mexican workers in U.S. agriculture increased even as the number of Braceros decreased, leading one analyst to conclude that "the Bracero program, instead of diverting the flow of wetbacks into legal channels . . . actually stimulated unlawful emigration" (Scruggs 1960: 151).

The perception that Mexico–U.S. migration was out of control in the early 1950s led to "Operation Wetback" in 1954, a massive border control and interior enforcement operation that removed over one million Mexicans and relaxed rules for employing Mexicans as legal Braceros. The ready availability of Braceros permitted California agriculture to expand without raising wages significantly, giving it and the southwest a comparative advantage over eastern states in the production of labor-intensive fruit and vegetable production. California's vegetable production rose 50 per cent and it replaced New Jersey as the "Garden State." According to the U.S. Department of Agriculture, farm worker wages rose 41 per cent from 1950 to 1960 while factory wages rose 63 per cent. Over the course of the decade, therefore, U.S. farmers and Mexican workers grew mutually dependent on each other.

The Bracero Program was strongly criticized by U.S. unions, churches, and Mexican–American organizations. The Mexican government was also critical of the Bracero Program, arguing that its worker protections were rarely enforced. President Kennedy in October 1961 asserted that "the adverse effect of the Mexican farm labor program as it has operated in recent years on the wage and employment conditions of domestic workers is clear and cumulative in its impact" (quoted in Congressional Research Service 1980: 52). When he urged Congress to abolish the program, however, the Mexican government advocated its continuation, as it felt that even an imperfect legal program was preferred to inevitable illegal immigration. In a June 21, 1963 note, the Mexican government asserted that the Bracero Program was "a result of the migration phenomenon . . . [and that] the absence of an agreement . . . would give rise to . . . the illegal introduction of Mexican workers into the United States" (Craig 1971: 195–6).

The Bracero Program was ended unilaterally by the U.S. in 1964, and some ex-Braceros became legal U.S. immigrants. During the 1950s and 1960s, a Mexican could achieve permanent residence on the basis of a letter from a U.S. employer asserting that the Mexican being sponsored was the only person capable of filling the job offered. Most Mexico immigrants in the 1950s and 1960s were former Braceros sponsored in this manner by their U.S. employers. According to one estimate, 80 per cent of the 222,000 immigrants from Mexico between 1957 and 1962 had been Braceros (Taylor 1963: 43). Illegal immigration rose after 1964, but only modestly, as only 110,000 deportable aliens were located in 1965, 212,000 in 1968, 420,000 in 1971, and 788,000 in 1974.

The number of Mexicans apprehended in the United States first reached one million in 1983, after Mexico devalued the peso, and then rose to a peak of 1.8 million in 1986, when the Immigration Reform and Control Act was passed. IRCA included the largest-ever amnesty for illegal foreigners, permitting about 2.3 million Mexicans who had arrived in the 1980s to become legal immigrants. However, the other part of IRCA's "Grand Bargain," sanctions on U.S. employers who knowingly hired illegal workers, did not deter illegal immigration because unauthorized workers could easily purchase and present false documents. One of IRCA's amnesty programs, the Special Agricultural Worker program, legalized about one million Mexican men who claimed doing farm work as illegal aliens in the United States, representing about one in ten of rural Mexico's adult male population.

In the 1990s, the number of legal immigrants and apprehensions from Mexico reached peak levels. The Binational Study on Migration reported (U.S. Commission on Immigration Reform 1997) that there were 7 million to 7.3 million Mexican-born persons in the United States in 1996, up from 4.3 million in 1990. One-third, or 2.3–2.4 million of these people, were unauthorized, despite the legalization of more than two million in 1987–8. Mexican born residents represented about 3 per cent of the U.S. population, and 8 per cent of Mexico's population.

NAFTA was expected to reverse levels of Mexico–U.S. migration that had been ratcheting higher each decade. There were many models that projected NAFTA's economic and labor market effects, and one of the most optimistic projected an additional 60,000 jobs per year in Mexico because of increased trade and investment expected as a result the agreement. However, this is only a small fraction of the number of Mexicans who enter the United States each year to work (estimated at 150,000–200,000) or the number who work illegally for at least part of the year (estimated to be at least 1 million). There was no doubt that NAFTA would, at best, be a long term answer for unwanted Mexico–U.S. migration; but there remained the question of whether it would begin falling from high levels once the agreement was signed, or whether it would first increase and then decrease.

## NAFTA AND DEVALUATION

On January 1, 1994, the North American Free Trade Agreement (NAFTA) went into effect, laying the basis for an eventual free trade area encompassing 380 million people with a combined GDP of $7 trillion. The purpose of NAFTA was to reduce trade barriers and promote investment within the region so that comparative advantage would be maximized. Since Mexico has the lowest wages of the three countries, the expectation was that investment and jobs would flow to Mexico to produce labor-intensive goods, thus creating jobs in Mexico, and decreasing the demand for Mexican workers in the United States.

NAFTA was something of a surprise, mostly because the initiative came from Mexico, which had long sought to maximize its independence from the United States. However, U.S.-trained economist and Mexican President Carlos Salinas de Gortari announced his support for a free trade agreement with the United States in May 1990 and negotiations began in 1991, after opponents in Congress tried but failed to deny President Bush the authority to negotiate it. In November 1993, in a debate carried live on radio and television, the House and Senate narrowly approved NAFTA, allowing it to go into effect on January 1, 1994.

Economic integration generates economic benefits through economies of scale (lower costs and prices per unit at higher volumes) and because of increased specialization, as companies take advantage of different prices and wages (e.g., moving less capital-intensive assembly operations to Mexico). However, the "case for the gains from trade rest heavily on the *restructuring* of national economies... [so that] the dislocations and distributional consequences produced by trade are the flip side of the efficiency gains" (Rodrik 1998: 6).

A number of computable general equilibrium (CGE) models were developed to try to estimate just how this restructuring would affect the economies and labor markets of Canada, Mexico, and the United States (Hinojosa-Ojeda and Robinson 1991). Most of the models examined what would happen in Mexico because (1) the United States and Canada have had a free trade agreement since 1989 and (2) U.S. tariffs on Mexican goods were small before NAFTA (the average U.S. tariff on Mexican imports in 1991 was 4 per cent compared with an average 10 per cent Mexican tariff on U.S. imports—see Lustig 1992).

Virtually all models predicted that Mexico's economy would grow faster, creating more jobs at higher wages than would exist without NAFTA. The U.S. International Trade Commission summarized the various results by noting that Mexico's real GDP was projected to rise by 0.1–11.4 per cent because of NAFTA, Mexican employment was expected to be 7 per cent higher, and that real wages would be 0.7–16.2 per cent greater. The primary mechanism by which these results would be achieved was through greater foreign investment. Capital would flow into Mexico, the argument ran, to bring new technology and new management, thus creating jobs and hope. As a Latin American "tiger," Mexico could run a trade deficit for years as foreign investors built up Mexico's productive capacity and infrastructure, much as South Korea did in the 1960s and 1970s.

Events did not turn out as expected. Although there was an influx of foreign capital in 1993–4, Mexico permitted the peso to become severely overvalued, making imports of both capital and consumer goods cheap. The United States and other foreign investors lent billions of dollars to Mexicans, who used these foreign savings to buy foreign goods, not to build factories and create jobs. Mexican President Salinas wanted to be one of the few Mexican presidents to leave office without devaluing the peso, so he resisted an "orderly" devaluation during the summer of 1994, while his government printed money to buoy the economy in advance of the August 1994 Presidential elections.

The Mexican economy crashed just after newly elected President Zedillo took office on December 1, 1994. Local and foreign investors saw that the $30 billion trade deficit would not be reduced in 1995, and that the Mexican Central Bank was running out of reserves to support the Mexican currency at 3.45 pesos to the dollar. When there were problems renegotiating the new "pacto" that regulated the increase in union wages in Mexico, speculators bet that Mexico would have to devalue its currency, which it did (*Migration News*, 1995–6, various issues).

## DEVALUATION, LEGALIZATION, AND IMMIGRATION

Mexico has had major devaluations at the end of each of the last four presidencies: in 1976, 1982, 1986–7, and 1994–5. After each devaluation, illegal immigration as measured by apprehensions in the United States increased, but there is no consistent relationship between economic troubles in Mexico and illegal immigration to the United States (Escobar 1995). For example, after the 1982–3 peso devaluation, it took about 16 months for the U.S. Border Patrol to notice a significant increase in illegal immigration. In 1987, apprehensions dropped despite a devaluation of the peso, largely because so many Mexicans were becoming legalized US immigrants under the 1986 Immigration Reform and Control Act (IRCA).

The drop in apprehensions in the mid-1980s despite the peso devaluation emphasizes the importance of U.S. policies in determining whether Mexicans respond to economic crises by emigrating. In 1987–8, the United States offered an easy legalization program to illegal farm workers, and almost one million Mexicans took advantage of it to become legal U.S. immigrants. There was less need to risk apprehension when farm worker legalization applications could be filed in Mexico, or Mexicans could come to the border, assert that they qualified for legalization but had no records to prove that they had been employed illegally in U.S. agriculture, and then obtain 90-day entry and work permits (Martin et al. 1995). There was no penalty for filing a false application, or for a person who attempted to enter the United States lawfully at the border by asserting that he was employed as an illegal worker in U.S. agriculture, and needed the 90-day work permit to get proof of that employment and apply for legalization.

One of the major long-term effects of the legalization programs was the support they provided to the fraudulent document industry. It is always difficult to determine whether to make Type I or Type II errors in legalization programs—should the rules be rigorous so that some who should qualify are not legalized, or should the rules be flexible so that all who qualify are legalized but some fraudulently become legal immigrants? The Special Agricultural Worker program was especially vulnerable to fraud. Both farmer and farm worker representatives testified that many illegal aliens had been paid in cash through intermediary farm labor contractors, so individuals were permitted to apply for legalization on the basis of letters from U.S. labor contractors and farmers asserting something to the effect that "Juan Gonzalez picked tomatoes for me for 92 days between May 1985 and May 1986." With only this letter as supporting evidence, about three times more foreigners became legal immigrants on the grounds that they did farm work as illegal aliens than most studies estimated to be the number of illegal alien farm workers; most analyses suggest that over half of those legalized under the SAW program did not do the qualifying farm work (Martin, Taylor, and Hardiman 1988).

Thus, although there were two major devaluations in the 1980s, they had very different migration consequences. The 70 per cent peso devaluation of 1982–3 lowered real wages in urban areas and put Mexican farmers in a cost-price squeeze, but the fact that most Mexican workers kept their jobs and saw their standard of living erode only gradually helps to explain the delayed illegal emigration response (Lustig 1992). The 1986–7 peso devaluation, by contrast, occurred when the United States was offering amnesty to illegal immigrants, the INS was educating employers rather than enforcing sanctions, and the United States enjoyed a period of rapid job growth, all factors that encouraged a massive, seemingly "legal" migration response.

The peso devaluation of 1994–5 occurred in a different climate in Mexico and the United States. One village economic model estimates a migration elasticity with respect to devaluations of 0.7 per cent—a 0.7 per cent increase in emigration for every 1 per cent devaluation of the Mexican peso (Taylor 1995) implying that the 60 per cent devaluation was accompanied by a 42 per cent increase in emigration. It is hard to determine whether this increased migration actually occurred because, beginning in 1993, the United States dramatically changed its border enforcement strategy, making it hard to use apprehensions as a consistent measure of the unauthorized Mexico–U.S. migration flow.

Instead of apprehending illegal aliens inside the United States, processing them, and returning them to Mexico for another attempt, the strategy changed. Operation Gatekeeper in California, Operation Safeguard in Arizona, and Operations Hold-the-Line and Rio Grande in Texas aimed to deter illegal entrants with agents, fences, and lights right on the border and to discourage them from attempting to enter without the help of smugglers. The INS also began to fingerprint and photograph all foreigners apprehended in border areas, but has not yet released any analysis to indicate how many of these people have been caught before.

Since the INS switched from an apprehension to a deterrence strategy in 1993, apprehensions have stabilized at about 1.3 million a year, but what is not yet clear is whether the new strategy will actually deter Mexicans from leaving their homes in the interior of Mexico and traveling to border cities to attempt illegal entry. On the basis of interviews with migrants in Mexico, Massey (1998) concluded that the probability of being apprehended on any attempt had fallen to a new low of about 20 per cent.

The evidence from labor markets that rely on newly arrived Mexican workers tend to support Massey's conclusion that it is still relatively easy for unauthorized Mexican workers to enter the United States and find jobs. The single most labor-intensive activity in North American agriculture requires 40,000–60,000 workers from mid-August to late September to harvest about 200,000 acres of raisin grapes around Fresno, California. Worker surveys find that newly arrived migrants dominate the work force and that enough workers are slipping across the border to keep piece rate wages at about $0.19–0.20 per 25 pounds of green grapes cut and laid on a paper tray to dry in the sun. Workers do complain of both the higher fees charged by smugglers to illegally enter the United States, and the opportunity cost of waiting in Mexican border cities to elude stepped up border controls, and some have responded by remaining longer in the United States because of the cost of re-entry (*Rural Migration News* 1995–9).

## THE MIGRATION HUMP

Immigration was downplayed during the NAFTA debate in order to avoid discussion of an issue that has no easy answer. Instead, the major issue in the United States was whether there would be, in the words of Presidential candidate Ross Perot, a "giant sucking sound" as U.S. jobs went south to Mexico. Most U.S. government statements in support of NAFTA emphasized that an important side benefit of freer trade was likely to be less illegal immigration. For example, U.S. Attorney General Janet Reno said that "we will not reduce the flow of illegal immigration until these immigrants can find decent jobs at decent wages in Mexico" (*San Diego Union-Tribune*, November 14, 1993, p. 1).

Economic theory predicts that, in the long run, Reno will be proved correct: economic growth and job creation accelerated by free trade and investment will promote what has been called "stay-at-home development" (Straubhaar 1988; Appleyard 1989). But emigration pressures do not cease when a migrant-sending country such as Mexico adopts growth-accelerating economic policies. Indeed, the U.S. Commission for the Study of International Migration and Cooperative Economic Development concluded that there could well be a short-term migration hump: "the economic development process itself tends in the short to medium term to stimulate migration."

A migration hump is a temporary increase in migration between two countries that are integrating their economies by increasing trade and investment between them. Economic integration and migration can be short-run complements for many reasons. An analysis of the evolution of factors that initiate and sustain migration in the context of the demand-pull, supply-push, and network factors linking Mexican migrants to U.S. employers concluded that there was likely to be a significant migration hump for several reasons (Martin 1993).

First, economic integration does not suddenly eliminate the demand-pull of jobs in the United States. Instead, economic integration tends to increase exports of U.S. goods produced with migrant workers, as occurred when U.S. fruit and vegetable exports to Mexico increased after 1994. Second, supply-push pressures to emigrate usually increase as a result of closer economic integration, as some industries and sectors prove to be noncompetitive. Mexican agriculture is a case in point. About 30 per cent of Mexico's 95 million people live in rural areas, and depend on agriculture for at least some of their income (U.S. House of Representatives 1993; de Janvry, Sadoulet, and Anda 1994; Cornelius and Myhre 1996). Rural residents have an average per capita income that is only one-third that for Mexico as a whole, and one-fifth of the income earned in Mexico City. As NAFTA liberalizes agricultural trade, crop prices and rural incomes may fall. Mexico has implemented a number of policies that have offsetting effects on farmers.

Third, job growth in Mexico has concentrated in the northern part of the country—over one million of Mexico's 2.5 million manufacturing jobs are in 3000 maquiladoras, most of which are located in border cities. As Mexicans look north for opportunity, some find that their networks lead to jobs in the United States. These networks encompass everything that enables people to move across borders and earn money in another country, from expanded tourism to training programs to easier entry procedures for business visitors (Massey et al. 1987; Massey 1988).

If Mexico–U.S. migration is viewed over several decades rather than several years, then there should eventually be *less* migration with the free trade and the investment policies formalized by NAFTA. A migration hump that adds 10–20 per cent to current Mexican immigration for 10 years, but then reduces economically motivated migration sharply, may be preferable to 200,000–300,000 Mexican immigrants each year ad infinitum (two-thirds of whom are illegal). The migration hump makes explicit the fact that the same policies making immigration controls less necessary in the long run may make them more necessary in the short run. Faster economic and job growth in Mexico should narrow wage differentials as well. If the wage gap between the United States and Mexico can be reduced from the current factor of 8–10 to one to 4–5, and wages grow faster in Mexico than in the United States, much of today's unwanted Mexico–U.S. migration should cease (U.S. Commission for the Study of International Migration and Cooperative Economic Development 1990; Stalker 1994).

## MEXICAN AND U.S. POLICY RESPONSES

Migration between Mexico and the United States forms a substantial part of the North American migration system, one of the largest and best developed migration systems anywhere. Mexico is the source of about one-fourth of the legal immigrants to the United States and over 50 per cent of the unauthorized migrants. The Binational Study on Migration emphasized that demographic and economic factors, which in the mid-1990s produced high levels of emigration, may soon ebb.

First, Mexico in 1997 had 970,000 labor force entrants, but birth rates fell sharply in the 1980s and 1990s, so that the number of new job seekers will fall to 500,000–550,000 per year by 2010. Second, each 1.35 per cent increment to economic growth was associated with 1 per cent job growth in Mexico between 1988 and 1995. If this ratio persists, then 5 per cent economic growth can generate 3.7 per cent job growth, or 1.1 million new jobs each year, enough to employ new job seekers and begin to reduce un- and underemployment. Finally, Mexico is recovering from the devaluation-recession of 1994–5—the number of Mexican workers in formal private sector jobs rose by 400,000 in 1998.

The fastest-growing sector of the Mexican economy in 1998—the maquiladora industry—was launched in the mid-1960s to deter Mexico–U.S. emigration. Foreign direct investment averaged $11 billion a year between 1994 and 1997 and much of it went into maquiladoras, factory assembly operations that are permitted to import components duty free, assemble products with Mexican workers in Mexico, and then re-export the finished product, paying duty only on the value added by Mexican assembly operations. As seen in Table 7.1, there were about 4,045 maquiladoras with one million employees in June 1998, a doubling since 1995, and up sharply from the 1,924 plants and 472,000 workers in 1990.

Maquiladoras currently provide almost 10 per cent of the formal sector jobs in Mexico and about 30 per cent of the manufacturing jobs. Most maquiladoras are located along the U.S.–Mexico border, where unemployment is low and assembly plants recruit workers from the interior of Mexico. About 60 per cent of the employees

Table 7.1. *Maquiladoras and maquiladora employment, 1965–98*

| Year | Number of maquiladoras | Total maquiladora employment |
|---|---|---|
| 1965 | 12 | 3,000 |
| 1970 | 120 | 20,327 |
| 1975 | 454 | 67,213 |
| 1980 | 578 | 119,546 |
| 1985 | 789 | 211,968 |
| 1990 | 1,924 | 472,000 |
| 1995 | 2,206 | 674,692 |
| 1998 | 4,045 | 1,033,527 |

*Source*: U.S.–Mexican Chamber of Commerce, 1998 data are for June, 1998.

in maquiladoras are young women, and most studies of linkages between maquiladoras and migration conclude that the maquiladora workers do not use the assembly plants as stepping stones to the United States. However, young men who accompany women to border cities may migrate northward.

The United States has responded to the Mexican migration hump with a massive expansion of border control efforts, an effort to make more effective what might be called the "island" model of immigration control. An island nation such as Australia has fairly tight entry controls, but no employer sanctions and few interior controls. The alternative "continental" model, reflecting large numbers of smaller countries as in Western Europe permits relatively free movement over borders for tourism and other purposes, and puts primary emphasis on internal controls, usually reinforcing residence and work permit systems.

Until 1986, the United States followed an island strategy, relying primarily on the Border Patrol to deter illegal entry, and exempting most U.S. employers who knowingly hired illegal aliens from sanctions. In 1986, the United States adopted a Grand Bargain—legalization for 3.1 million illegal aliens in the United States in return for employer sanctions to close the door to new immigrants. The legalization program worked; but employer sanctions did not, largely because the unauthorized aliens continued to arrive using false documents to obtain jobs. Enforcement was also insufficient to discourage both foreigners and their U.S. employers from unauthorized hiring.

In 1996, three major immigration laws were enacted, but they continued to emphasize the border control strategy. The new laws effectively created a one-strike system for criminal aliens—one U.S. conviction makes a foreigner subject to removal or deportation. They also made it harder for legal and illegal immigrants to obtain welfare benefits. The new laws were the Anti-Terrorism and Effective Death Penalty Act, signed into law on April 24, 1996; the Personal Responsibility and Work Opportunity Reconciliation Act, signed on August 22, 1996; and the Illegal

Immigration Reform and Immigrant Responsibility Act of 1996, signed on September 30, 1996.

The significance of these responses to continued illegal immigration is that, to the extent that there is a trade-off between numbers and rights, the 1996 legislation maintains high numbers but restricts the rights of foreigners. Legal immigrants who continue to arrive will have restricted access to U.S. social safety net programs, but they as well as unauthorized migrants will have relatively free access to the U.S. labor market.

## CONCLUSION

The catalyst for much of today's Mexican migration lies in past U.S. recruitment of Mexican workers; but solutions to unwanted migration are to be found in both countries. The most important long-run solution for unwanted migration, NAFTA, went into effect in 1994. However, political leaders in both countries have not acknowledged that migration will remain at high levels (or even increase) despite NAFTA, setting the stage for a backlash against Mexican immigration in the United States.

There are three major lessons from the NAFTA experience with using trade to reduce migration. First, the emigration country is generally the major beneficiary of freer trade and investment, suggesting that cooperation on managing migration should be an adjunct to cooperation to promote freer trade. Second, freer trade takes time to increase economic and job growth, and can often seem to be a case of two steps forward and one step back; people in both countries should be warned that the development to reduce migration road is long and winding. Finally, the immigration countries using trade as a substitute for migration should look in their own back yards to reduce the demand for immigrant workers if they want to discourage unwanted migration.

### References

Appleyard, Reginald (1989). "Migration and Development: Myths and Reality," *International Migration Review*, 23: 486–99.

Congressional Research Service (1980). Temporary Worker Programs: Background and Issues. February.

Cornelius, Wayne, and Myhre, David (1996). *The Transformation of Rural Mexico: Reforming the Ejido Sector.* La Jolla: Center for US–Mexican Studies.

Craig, Richard B. (1971). *The Bracero Program: Interest Groups and Foreign Policy.* Austin: University of Texas Press.

de Janvry, Alain, Sadoulet, Elisabeth, and Anda, Gustavo (1994). "NAFTA and Mexico's Corn Producers," Department of Agricultural and Resource Economics Working Paper 275, University of California at Berkeley.

Durand, Jorge, and Massey, Douglas S. (1992). "Mexican Migration to the United States: A Critical Review," *Latin American Research Review*, 27: 3–42.

Escobar Latapi, Augustin (1995). "Restructuring, Social Inequality, and State Action in Mexico: A Labor Systems Approach," Centro de Investigaciones y Estudios Superiores en Antropología Social, Guadalajara.

Hinojosa-Ojeda, Raul, and Robinson, Sherman (1991). "Alternative Scenarios of U.S.–Mexico Integration: A Computable General Equilibrium Approach," Department of Agricultural and Resource Economics Working Paper No. 609, University of California at Berkeley.

Lustig, Nora (1992). *Mexico: The Remaking of an Economy*. Washington: Brookings Institution.

Martin, Philip (1993). *Trade and Migration: NAFTA and Agriculture*. Washington: Institute for International Economics.

—— Taylor, J. Edward, and Hardiman, Philip (1988). "California Farm Workers and the SAW Legalization Program," *California Agriculture*, 4–6.

—— Huffman, Wallace, Emerson, Robert, Taylor, Edward, and Rochin, Refugio (1995). *Immigration Reform and US Agriculture*. Berkeley. Division of Agriculture and Natural Resources Publication 3358.

—— (2003). "Promise Unfulfilled: Unions, Immigration, and Farm Workers," Ithaca: Cornell University Press.

Massey, Douglas S. (1988). "Economic Development and International Migration in Comparative Perspective," *Population and Development Review*, 14: 383–413.

—— (1998). "March of Folly: U.S. Immigration Policy After NAFTA," *The American Prospect*, 37: 22–33.

—— Alarcon, Rafael, Durand, Jorge, and Gonzalez, Humberto (1987). *Return to Aztlan: The Social Process of International Migration from Western Mexico*. Berkeley: University of California Press.

Rodrik, Daniel (1998). "Symposium on Globalization in Perspective: An Introduction," *Journal of Economic Perspectives*, 12: 3–8.

Scruggs, Otey (1960). "Evolution of the Mexican Farm Labor Agreement of 1942," *Agricultural History*, 34: 140–49.

Stalker, Peter (1994). *The Work of Strangers: A Survey of International Labor Migration*. Geneva: International Labor Office.

Straubhaar, Thomas (1988). *On the Economics of International Labor Migration*. Bern/Stuttgart: Paul Haupt.

Taylor, Don (1963). "How Mexico Feels about the Bracero Program," *California Farmer*, April 20.

Taylor, J. E. (1995). *Micro Economywide Models for Migration and Policy Analysis. An Application to Rural Mexico*, Paris: OECD.

U.S. Commission for the Study of International Migration and Cooperative Economic Development (1990). *Unauthorized Migration: An Economic Development Response*. Washington, DC: U.S. Government Printing Office.

U.S. Commission on Immigration Reform (1997). *Binational Study on Migration: Executive Summary*. Washington: US Commission on Immigration Reform.

U.S. House of Representatives, Committee on Government Operations (1993). "Mexican Aagriculture Policies: An Immigration generator?" Washington, DC: Subcommittee on Employment, Housing, and Aviation, October 28.

# 8

## Immigrants in the U.S. Economy

MIN ZHOU

The United States admitted 7.3 million immigrants in the 1980s, almost matching the peak number of 8.8 million admitted during the first decade of the 1900s. Unlike turn-of-the-century immigrants who arrived mainly from Europe, late twentieth century newcomers have been extraordinarily diverse and predominantly non-European. According to the Immigration and Nationalization Service, 87 per cent of those admitted to the United States during the 1980s came from Asia and the Americas. Mexico alone accounted for more than one-fifth of total legal admissions. Along with Mexico, the Philippines, China/Taiwan, South Korea, and Vietnam made up the top five sending countries, followed by the Dominican Republic, India, El Salvador, and Jamaica (Portes and Rumbaut 1996).

These immigrants come from very diverse socioeconomic backgrounds. The 1990 U.S. Census attests to vast differences in education, occupation, and income by national origins. For example, over 60 per cent of immigrants aged 25 or older from India and Taiwan report having college degrees—three times the percentage of Americans; but fewer than 5 per cent of those from Cambodia, Laos, El Salvador, and Mexico report advanced educations. Among employed workers (aged 16+), over 45 per cent of Indian and Taiwanese immigrants hold managerial or professional positions, a percentage more than double that for American workers; but fewer than 7 per cent of those from El Salvador, Guatemala, and Mexico report this employment status. Furthermore, immigrants from India report a median household income of $53,000, compared with $30,000 for the average American household. Those from Cambodia, the Dominican Republic, El Salvador, Honduras, Laos, and Mexico report median household incomes below $22,000.

Such socioeconomic diversity sheds light on the potential pathways to social mobility for recent immigrants. While many new arrivals continue to follow the traditional bottom-up route, a visible proportion have moved directly into mainstream professional occupations and live in middle class suburban communities. The implication for immigrant adaptation to the host society is clear: the current state and future prospects of immigrants and their children are related to the advantages or disadvantages in education, skills, and economic resources that they bring from their homelands (Borjas 1990; Waldinger 1996*a*).

This chapter examines employment patterns of immigrants in the U.S. economy. I first highlight theoretical explanations for the labor market incorporation of immigrants. Second, I describe the general patterns of labor market insertion for major foreign-born nationality groups. Third, I examine intergroup differences in labor force positions, with a focus on levels of underemployment and intergroup differences with respect to gender. In conclusion, I discuss the implications of underemployment for reconceptualizing immigrant labor force dynamics.

## THEORETICAL CONSIDERATIONS

### *Assimilation perspectives*

The sociological literature offers several explanations for different outcomes among immigrants incorporating into the U.S. economy. The long-standing perspective of assimilation envisions incorporation as occurring in multiple stages, usually across one or more generations. Immigrants' economic progress, thus, depends on their length of residence and employment. As members of the first generation acculturate and establish themselves in the U.S. labor market, they increase their contact with, and resemblance to, the native majority. Ethnic groups may remain distinguishable from one another for a long period of time; but according to some sociologists, distinctive ethnic characteristics become increasingly insignificant over time. Eventually, they cease to exist as ethnic groups as they pass through the stages of assimilation, marrying into the majority population and entering mainstream institutions (Gordon 1964; Alba and Nee 1997).

Empirical research has indeed confirmed progressive social mobility across immigrant generations and increasing rates of intermarriage with rising lengths of stay, English proficiency, and exposure to American culture. For example, the descendants of European Catholic immigrants who arrived earlier in the century have now caught up with native-born white Americans in average income and educational attainment, some (e.g. Jewish immigrants) within the span of just one generation, and others (such as the Irish and Italians) within two or three generations. Over time, according to some sociological studies, the distinctive ethnic traits among these European Catholic groups have disappeared (Warner and Srole 1945; Wytrwal 1961; Sandberg 1974; Greeley 1976; Alba 1985).

Other research reveals anomalies that contradict the assimilation perspective. In their study of educational attainment in 25 ethno-religious groups in the United States, Hirschman and Falcon (1985) found that neither generation nor length of U.S. residence significantly influenced educational outcomes. Other studies have found that some immigrant groups, primarily in the first generation, showed remarkable educational and occupational achievements with only limited acculturation and limited U.S. residence (Waldinger and Bozorgmehr 1996). In a contrasting study, second-generation black Caribbean immigrants thoroughly acculturated into American ways suffered worse life chances and faced bleaker mobility prospects than their unacculturated parents (Portes and Stepick 1993; Waters 1994). These findings suggest that the varied pace and differing outcomes of assimilation may not depend entirely on an individual's exposure to the host culture or on a decision to abandon his or her original cultural ways.

### Human capital theory

While the assimilation perspective emphasizes the effects of time and exposure, human capital theory explains differential labor market placement and economic outcomes by level of education, labor market skills, and command of English. Human capital theory predicts that, given sufficient human capital, individuals from diverse racial and national backgrounds have a relatively equal opportunity to succeed. This suggests that the overrepresentation of certain minority group members in the margins of the economic structure is a consequence of their limited human capital. Thus, educational improvement at the individual level is the first step to helping the disadvantaged gain an equal footing in the labor market and eventually rise out of poverty.

Human capital theory has received considerable support from empirical research. Landry (1987) noted that in the past two decades a black middle class emerged from the ghetto as a result of educational and occupational opportunities heretofore unprecedented in the African-American experience, and that many talented and educated blacks were consequently able to obtain jobs comparable to those held by whites with equivalent qualifications. Likewise, Chiswick (1979) showed that male immigrant workers were able to achieve earnings parity with their native born counterparts with comparable human capital credentials. Borjas (1990) concluded that, because of the selectivity of U.S. immigration, those arriving with strong human capital credentials were able to penetrate the primary labor market and compete successfully without starting on the bottom rung of the economic ladder. Hirschman and Wong (1986) found that the remarkable educational attainment of Asian Americans contributed to occupational achievement and earnings parity with whites.

### Structural perspective

Despite evidence supporting human capital theory, other research has shown that the education and experience of successful minority groups are consistently discounted in the labor market and that patterns of educational and economic success are not always duplicated among the minority groups (Bean and Tienda 1987; Tienda and Lii 1987; Model 1991; Zhou and Kamo 1994). Model (1991), for example, found a substantial earnings gap between black men (both foreign- and U.S.-born) and non-Hispanic white men. She noted that this gap was unaccounted for by measurable human capital and marketable skills.

In their investigation of the effects of education and racial/ethnic composition of the labor market on earnings inequality among black, Hispanic, Asian, and white men, Tienda and Lii (1987) found significant intergroup differences in earnings among skilled workers: college-educated non-white men suffered the greatest losses in labor markets with a disproportionate minority concentration; college-educated white men, in contrast, gained the most earnings returns in situations with such concentration. They concluded that both competition based on qualifications and racial discrimination operate to differentiate workers economically along racial and ethnic lines.

Zhou and Kamo (1994) argued that the seeming economic parity of Asian-American men with non-Hispanic white men was due to Asian-Americans' over-achievement in educational attainment, long working hours, and their regional concentration in states with higher incomes. Using paired group comparisons of Asian-American men and non-Hispanic white men, they showed that both native- and foreign-born Asian-American men experienced significant earnings disadvantages relative to white counterparts with identical credentials.

These findings suggest that occupational and earnings inequality may be due not simply to differential human capital and measurable individual traits but to structural factors such as access to formal or informal institutional settings, social capital, and residential locations (Massey and Denton 1987; Portes 1995; Portes and Rumbaut 1996). This structural perspective offers a framework for understanding intergroup differences in immigrant adaptation, focusing on how economic restructuring and globalization influence employment opportunities for immigrant and native workers and taking into account the advantages and disadvantages inherent to the stratified system of social inequality (Wilson 1978, 1987; Kasarda 1983).

Since the 1970s, new technologies have done away with industrial plants dependent on semiskilled workers or facilitated the migration of semi-skilled assembly line operators from high-wage countries to the Third World. Globalization and economic restructuring have consequently transformed America's urban labor markets into a dual structure, with a dominant sector characterized by knowledge-intensive or capital-intensive jobs offering high wages, good working conditions, career stability, and promotion opportunities, and a peripheral sector characterized by low-skilled, labor-intensive work with minimum wages, poor working conditions, and little upward mobility (Edwards 1979; Tolbert et al. 1980).

In this economic structure, only a portion of the American work force benefits economically as information technology and management become more critical to the economy. That segment of the American work force referred to by Peter Drucker as the "knowledge workers" and by former U.S. Secretary of Labor Robert Reich as "symbolic analysts" sees its economic advantages steadily increase (Reich 1992; Drucker 1993). In contrast, blue-collar workers holding those jobs generally available to newly arrived immigrants, not only receive lower pay than in previous years but find that many fewer such jobs exist (Mishel and Bernstein 1992).

As semiskilled manufacturing leaves the central cities, another structural change has occurred: the rapid growth in the corporate and government sectors. This creates opportunities for social and economic mobility for those segments of the minority population protected by union legislation and equal employment legislation (Wilson 1978). For example, it has enabled some educated blacks to move into the middle class. But, as these individuals leave the inner city, a concentration of the most disadvantaged segments of the black population remains. As labor market segmentation reduces demands for unskilled and semiskilled workers in urban centers, it creates a severe condition of skill mismatch that aggravates the problem of unemployment among native minorities, especially minority youth, in the shrinking peripheral sector.

In a study on black–white differences in underemployment during 1970–1982 Lichter (1988), attempt to estimate the effects of industrial restructuring on American workers. He found that young adults, the poorly educated, and blacks suffered most from the eroding employment base in U.S. cities, experiencing an increasing rate of labor force nonparticipation and an incomplete withdrawal from the labor force. He concluded that the shrinking employment base, combined with the economic marginality of urban black youths, was responsible for the deterioration and economic distress of blacks and the urban underclass. These trends suggest that, unlike earlier European immigrants, contemporary immigrants encounter an emerging "hourglass" economy in which opportunities for social mobility shrink even for native-born Americans, creating new obstacles to social mobility despite their strong drive, hard work, and relatively easy access to the labor market.

Other structural theorists disagree about the extent to which economic restructuring causes economic distress among native minorities. These scholars contend that whereas many American workers are negatively affected by economic restructuring, ethnic minority workers disproportionately find their chances for economic mobility lessening. The situation for many dark-skinned and unskilled immigrants is even bleaker (Waldinger 1996*a*). Ethnic minorities, native and immigrant alike, encounter employer discrimination and institutional barriers that block them from equal participation in the labor market.

In a survey exploring what race and ethnicity mean in their hiring and recruitment practices in the Chicago metropolitan area, Kirschenman and Neckerman (1991) found that employers emphasized the color of a person's skin when it came to describing work ethic, attitudes toward work, and causes for tensions in the work place and that they tended to associate some racial minority membership with low productivity, poor work ethics, and interracial tensions. The researchers concluded that racial discrimination in recruitment accounted for economic disadvantages among racial/ethnic minority groups, particularly among members of the inner-city underclass.

Some researchers note the influence of ethnic subsystems in explaining disparities in labor market incorporation of ethnic minority workers. In his book, *Still the Promised City*, Waldinger (1996*b*) concluded that ethnic succession in New York City's labor market allowed immigrants to fill vacant niches that most native-born Americans did not want. Over time these niches were suffused with informal networks, which in turn kept out urban blacks with no connections to these informal employment networks, thus diminishing their employment opportunities.

Similar trends of ethnic niching were also highly visible in Los Angeles's metropolitan labor market, especially in manufacturing (Scott 1996; Waldinger 1996*a*). Some immigrant group members who lacked transferable education, marketable skills, English language ability, formal employment networks, and even legal standing encountered fewer obstacles to entering the labor market than did native-born minorities, even in cities where industrial jobs were believed to be disappearing and economic marginality was said to be worsening (Portes and Zhou 1992; Waldinger and Bozorgmehr 1996).

The above research indicates that native minority group members face severe unemployment and high rates of labor force detachment not simply because jobs that match their skills and human capital credentials are scarce, but because they are excluded from informal social networks attached to job niches in the growing service and manufacturing sectors. This pattern suggests to some that immigrants have diminished the labor market opportunities of low-skilled, native minority workers, and have thereby contributed to the further deterioration of the urban underclass. But other studies using various sources of data to measure the effect of immigration on native workers have found very little evidence to support this view (Borjas 1984; Bean et al. 1988; Reischauer 1989). Immigrant groups may not take jobs away from native workers; they may be simply responding to industrial transformation by creating their own match between available opportunities and ethnic economic and social resources (Light 1972; Waldinger 1989; Portes and Zhou 1992; Zhou 1992).

Overall, the structural perspective is skeptical about eventual assimilation and interethnic accommodation. It focuses on ethnic hierarchies that systematically constrain minorities' equal access to social resources and their opportunities for jobs, housing, and education, resulting in persistent racial–ethnic disparities in income and occupational achievement (Blau and Duncan 1967; Portes and Borocz 1989). On the issue of immigrant adaptation, the benefits of becoming American depend largely on what stratum of American society absorbs the immigrants. The structural perspective takes into account the effects of structural constraints. However, this theoretical framework was constructed to predict macro processes and general patterns of social mobility; it thus lacks the explanatory power to deal with the varied and disparate outcomes of diverse ethnic groups and the members of these groups who themselves display diverse socioeconomic characteristics.

## STUDYING PATTERNS OF LABOR MARKET INSERTION

I use the Public Use Microdata Sample (5 per cent PUMS) of the 1990 U.S. Census (U.S. Bureau of the Census 1993) to examine patterns of labor force participation and underemployment among foreign-born persons aged 25 and 64. I assume that by age 25 a person has completed his or her education and is ready to participate actively in the labor market. I select seven immigrant groups for comparison: Africans, West Indians, Mexicans, non-Mexican-Latinos, Southeast Asians (Cambodian, Laotian, and Vietnamese only), Other Asians (all other Asians), and Europeans. I include a sample of native-born, non-Latino whites as a reference group. Naturally, these broad categories mask differences between specific groups. Previous studies have found significant differences in human capital and cultural capital characteristics and labor market positions between Vietnamese and other Southeast Asian refugee groups, for example (Rumbaut 1989, 1995). The grouping I employ is simply a shorthand way of distinguishing between immigrant and refugee groups.

Using these groupings, I begin my analysis by examining the general pattern of labor market insertion and industry distribution. I then use cross-tabular analyses to examine how immigrant groups differ in the ways they are utilized in the labor force and, based on the Hauser–Sullivan–Clogg Labor Utilization Framework (LUF), how underemployment affects immigrant incorporation into the U.S. labor market (see Hauser 1974, 1977; Sullivan 1978; Clogg 1979; Clogg et al. 1990).

Hauser, Sullivan, Clogg, and others classify labor behavior into seven LUF categories: (1) labor force nonparticipation; (2) sub-unemployment; (3) unemployment; (4) partial employment; (5) underemployment by low wages; (6) underemployment by occupational mismatch; and (7) adequate employment. These categories are mutually exclusive and exhaustive. Because 1990 Census data lack certain information on labor market characteristics, and individual beliefs in job prospects and reasons for working part time or for not working, I modify the seven measures to approximate the original LUF measures, as follows.

*Labor force nonparticipation* includes persons who were nominally in the labor force but who had not worked during the last 2 years. I consider these people to be economically inactive. *Sub-unemployment* includes persons who were not in the labor force but who had worked during the last 2 years. I use this measure as a proxy for the discouraged worker, which assumes that if a person has worked during the last 2 years, he or she may not have voluntarily left the labor force permanently and may reenter the labor force on the belief that jobs are available. In the original LUF scheme, sub-unemployment assumes that a person in the labor force believes that jobs are unavailable (see Clogg 1979: 216). Individuals in this category are often excluded from unemployment statistics, so that joblessness is underestimated by official labor statistics that count only unemployed workers who report that they are actively seeking employment.

*Unemployment* refers to workers who report being unemployed or who had a job but did not work because of layoffs in 1990. The *partial employment* category includes workers who reported that they worked part time year-round, or to those working full time part of the year or part time part of the year in 1990. Part time refers to fewer than 35 work hours a week; part-year to under 48 weeks a year; and full time, full-year to 35 hours or more per week and 48 weeks or more per year. Partially employed workers are assumed to earn lower wages than the adequately employed in proportion to their temporary labor force status. This category is qualitatively distinguished from the next two categories of underemployment because it includes voluntary part-time workers.

*Underemployment by low wages* refers to persons who worked full time year-round, but whose hourly wages were less than or equal to $4.50—about minimum wage in 1990. The original measure for this category is based on poverty thresholds set by the Social Security Administration, which are intended to even up the unequal income effect that these poverty thresholds produce on household heads (or primary wage earners) and on secondary earners (Sullivan 1978; Clogg 1979). Alternatively, using the minimum hourly wage rate is a more direct way to measure low wages at the individual level.

*Underemployment by occupational mismatch* refers to full-time, year-round workers whose level of completed schooling is more than one standard deviation above the overall mean for each of the occupational groups. One drawback of this measure, as Clogg (1979) points out, is that it is not sensitive to the changing demand for skilled labor over time, nor does it respond well to the age effect. I argue, however, that since the examination of underemployment is based on cross-sectional data, cross-time changes in skill demand are minimal. Also, my choice of an older minimum age (25 as opposed to 16), to some extent, reduces the negative effect on younger workers.

Nonetheless, an inherent conceptual problem with this category is that it lumps all persons with similar educational attainment across varied levels of occupations, but it does not reflect the effects of race on occupation and on earnings. A cross-tabulation of income by occupation among the overqualified workers based on the 1990 PUMS showed that blacks and Puerto Ricans who were mismatched in lower-ranking occupations (e.g. operators, transportation workers, and laborers) had higher average earnings than similarly situated workers of other groups (see Zhou 1993). Since it involves a comparison between the group mean and the mean for education of all immigrant groups, the meaning of occupational overqualification may vary for groups with different group means of education and different occupational distributions.

*Adequate employment* refers to workers who reported full-time, year-round work (35 hours per week and 48 weeks per year) in 1990 after all workers in all categories of underemployment by low wages and underemployment by occupational mismatch had been sorted out. In the analyses of underemployment patterns, I exclude this category of workers to focus only on underemployed workers.

## INTERGROUP DIFFERENCES IN UNDEREMPLOYMENT

### *Socioeconomic characteristics*

Table 8.1 profiles able-bodied working aged immigrants by ethnicity and gender. Among males, as shown in the upper panel, Africans and Asians had significantly higher proportions of those in the United States within the past 5 years, while Europeans had only a fraction of new arrivals. With regard to English proficiency, Africans, West Indians, and Europeans had the language advantage, either because they were a highly selective group (e.g. Africans), because they came from English-speaking countries (e.g. West Indians), or because they had been in this country longer (e.g. Europeans). Asians displayed a reasonably good command of English despite their recent arrival. Mexicans showed the lowest level of English proficiency, followed by Southeast Asians and other Latinos.

In terms of human capital characteristics, African and Asian immigrants were by far the best educated: three quarters had attained at least some college education, compared with a little over a half of native whites. Europeans were also better educated on average than native whites. By contrast, Mexican immigrants were the least educated, with a 39 percentage point gap with native whites and a much wider gap with Africans, Asians, and Europeans. Other Latinos, West Indians, and Southeast Asians showed lower levels of education relative to those of native whites

**Table 8.1.** *Selected socioeconomic characteristics of immigrant workers aged 25–64 by ethnicity and gender, 1990*

| Characteristics | African | West Indian | Mexican | Other Latino | Southeast Asian | Other Asian | European | Native White |
|---|---|---|---|---|---|---|---|---|
| *Males* | | | | | | | | |
| <5 Years in U.S. | 27.1 | 17.6 | 17.8 | 17.7 | 19.9 | 26.9 | 11.0 | — |
| Proficiency in English | 96.6 | 92.5 | 52.4 | 69.5 | 66.4 | 82.9 | 95.0 | — |
| College education | 83.6 | 49.9 | 13.5 | 34.0 | 48.9 | 73.2 | 61.3 | 52.8 |
| Aged 25–34 | 49.8 | 36.2 | 49.1 | 36.1 | 43.1 | 66.4 | 28.2 | 31.1 |
| Currently married | 58.5 | 64.1 | 73.4 | 65.5 | 68.4 | 79.0 | 75.7 | 73.1 |
| Poverty | 16.0 | 10.7 | 23.6 | 14.8 | 20.9 | 9.6 | 5.3 | 5.6 |
| Region | | | | | | | | |
| West | 17.7 | 4.2 | 65.9 | 21.1 | 56.7 | 48.7 | 33.7 | 18.3 |
| Northeast | 26.8 | 54.5 | 1.7 | 41.1 | 10.2 | 25.3 | 22.2 | 21.9 |
| South | 43.1 | 38.5 | 24.8 | 32.9 | 23.7 | 15.7 | 28.6 | 32.4 |
| Other | 12.4 | 2.8 | 7.6 | 4.9 | 9.4 | 10.3 | 15.5 | 27.4 |
| Number of cases | 3,484 | 8,341 | 72,485 | 65,070 | 10,411 | 51,897 | 61,833 | 78,704 |
| *Females* | | | | | | | | |
| <5 Years in U.S. | 32.5 | 16.8 | 17.1 | 17.3 | 21.7 | 26.2 | 8.8 | — |
| Proficiency in English | 92.5 | 92.3 | 45.6 | 64.0 | 56.8 | 78.7 | 95.1 | — |
| College education | 67.9 | 42.7 | 13.3 | 31.9 | 31.6 | 60.4 | 51.6 | 49.7 |
| Aged 25–34 | 61.9 | 35.9 | 44.0 | 33.4 | 37.1 | 33.5 | 24.1 | 31.2 |
| Currently married | 62.3 | 51.3 | 71.1 | 59.2 | 72.4 | 79.2 | 75.1 | 72.1 |
| Poverty | 17.6 | 13.7 | 29.3 | 22.0 | 23.7 | 9.0 | 6.7 | 7.9 |
| Region | | | | | | | | |
| West | 18.6 | 4.5 | 65.5 | 21.3 | 55.7 | 51.0 | 33.4 | 18.0 |
| Northeast | 30.4 | 60.4 | 1.3 | 41.8 | 10.4 | 21.9 | 20.4 | 22.0 |
| South | 41.5 | 32.5 | 26.6 | 32.3 | 24.1 | 17.2 | 31.8 | 32.6 |
| Other | 9.5 | 2.6 | 6.6 | 4.6 | 9.8 | 10.9 | 14.4 | 27.4 |
| Number of cases | 1,893 | 9,890 | 60,299 | 72,516 | 10,799 | 62,896 | 78,661 | 82,141 |

*Note*: Native whites sampled at a rate of 1/10 of 5 per cent.

*Source*: 5 per cent Public Use Microdata Sample of 1990 U.S. Census.

and the other best-educated groups. Given the high rate of Mexican and Asian immigration, the trend of both highly skilled and low-skilled labor inflows is quite visible.

All nonwhite immigrants were disproportionately young; in particular, half of the Africans and Mexicans and two-thirds of Asians were ages 25–34, compared with less than a third of native white in this age range. Europeans represented the smallest proportion in this young cohort, an indicator of the ebb of immigration from Europe.

Regardless of race and ethnicity, a clear majority of all working aged men were currently married. Ranked by family poverty status, all nonwhite immigrants were relatively more disadvantaged than their European counterparts and native whites. Mexicans and Southeast Asians had particularly high rates of poverty—almost four times higher than the rate among native whites. Finally, immigrant groups were residentially distributed unevenly across the United States: Africans, West Indians, and other Latinos were highly concentrated in the Northeast and the South; Mexicans, Southeast Asians, and Asians were disproportionately concentrated in the West; Europeans were more evenly distributed but showed greater presence in the West and South.

The profile for female immigrant workers revealed very similar intergroup patterns, as shown in the lower panel. However, relative to their male counterparts, female workers were less proficient in English (among non-English speaking groups), less educated (except for West Indians), and less likely to be in the younger age cohort (except for Africans).

## *Labor force positions*

As shown in the upper panel of Table 8.2, working age immigrant men of all groups displayed fairly low rates of labor force nonparticipation (below 8 per cent), except for Southeast Asians. Southeast Asian workers were more than twice as likely as other workers to be economically inactive. The extremely high rate of labor force nonparticipation among Southeast Asians was due to their status as refugees, many of whom lacked education, English proficiency, job skills, measurable economic resources, and access to employment networks through preexisting ethnic communities (Rumbaut 1995; Zhou and Bankston 1998).

The African immigrant group also included a significant component of refugees from Ethiopia who had a high labor force participation rate. Unlike Southeast Asian

**Table 8.2.** *Labor force participation of immigrant workers aged 25–64 by ethnicity and gender, 1990*

| Characteristics | African | West Indian | Mexican | Other Latino | Southeast Asian | Other Asian | European | Native White |
|---|---|---|---|---|---|---|---|---|
| *Males* | | | | | | | | |
| Not in labor force | 6.7 | 5.1 | 4.3 | 7.9 | 16.2 | 5.6 | 5.0 | 6.2 |
| In labor force | 93.3 | 94.9 | 95.7 | 92.1 | 83.8 | 94.4 | 95.0 | 93.8 |
| Adequate employment | 42.5 | 50.5 | 42.7 | 47.2 | 43.2 | 39.6 | 52.7 | 56.2 |
| Underemployment | 57.5 | 49.5 | 57.3 | 52.8 | 56.8 | 60.4 | 47.3 | 43.8 |
| Number of cases | 3,484 | 8,341 | 72,485 | 65,070 | 10,411 | 51,897 | 61,833 | 78,704 |
| *Females* | | | | | | | | |
| Not in labor force | 17.6 | 10.1 | 35.2 | 28.5 | 34.9 | 23.9 | 25.0 | 20.8 |
| In labor force | 82.4 | 89.9 | 64.8 | 71.5 | 65.1 | 76.1 | 75.0 | 79.2 |
| Adequate employment | 26.1 | 44.1 | 16.3 | 25.6 | 27.7 | 27.9 | 29.2 | 32.4 |
| Underemployment | 73.9 | 55.9 | 83.7 | 74.4 | 72.3 | 72.1 | 70.8 | 67.6 |
| Number of cases | 1,893 | 9,890 | 60,229 | 72,516 | 10,797 | 62,896 | 78,661 | 82,141 |

*Source*: 5 per cent Public Use Microdata Sample of 1990 U.S. Census.

*Note*: Native whites sampled at a rate of 1/10 of 5 per cent.

refugees, however, African refugees (as well as those from Europe) tend to have higher educational attainment, more fluent English, and better access to community-based employment networks.

Mexicans were the most handicapped of all immigrant groups, characterized by a lack of skills and English proficiency. Despite these disadvantages they displayed the lowest labor force nonparticipation rate, probably because most Mexican immigrant workers arrived through extensive employment and migrant networks (Massey 1996). Among those in the labor force, male workers of all immigrant groups, except Europeans, were less likely than native white workers to be adequately employed; over half of them (and over 60 per cent for Asians) were underemployed.

As shown in the lower panel of Table 8.2, intergroup differences are striking. Only 10 per cent of West Indian working aged women stayed out of the labor force, while over a third of Mexican and Southeast Asian women did so. Among those in the labor force, the majority were underemployed, regardless of race or ethnicity. However, West Indian women had a much lower rate than all other groups. Gender differences were also substantial. Relative to their male counterparts, working aged women were generally less likely to participate in the labor force, and when they did, they were more disproportionately underemployed.

### *Industrial distribution, occupation, and self-employment*

Immigrant workers are not evenly distributed in the labor market; rather, they tend to concentrate in certain industries. Significant intergroup differences are revealed in Table 8.3. Patterns among working men showed that Africans, West Indians, and Asians were overrepresented in services; Mexicans in agriculture; and Southeast Asians in manufacturing. Asians were also overrepresented in retail trade. Relative to native whites, Africans and West Indians were underrepresented in manufacturing, and Mexicans were underrepresented in transportation, finance, and services. Yet non-Mexican Latino and European men displayed fairly similar distributions to those of native whites.

Occupationally, African, Asian, and European men were more likely than native white men, and more than twice as likely as other group members, to hold executive or managerial positions; their occupational advantage is apparently linked to their above-average educational attainment. Asians and Europeans were as likely as native whites, but much more likely than other group members, to be self-employed.

Working women displayed rather different distributions by group. Africans and West Indians were overwhelmingly concentrated in services, whereas Mexicans, other Latinos, and Southeast Asians were concentrated in manufacturing. African, West Indian, Asian, and European women were as likely as native white women to hold executive or managerial positions, but women of the other groups fared less than half as well. Self-employment rates for all women were generally lower than for men; but Southeast Asian women, as well as Asian and European women showed higher rates of self-employment than did native white women.

Manufacturing and services employed the largest percentages of immigrant men and women. Within each category, however, were further concentrations by ethnic

**Table 8.3.** *Distribution of employed male and female workers aged 25–64 by industry, occupation, and self-employment, and ethnicity*

| Characteritics | African | West Indian | Mexican | Other Latino | Southeast Asian | Other Asian | European | Native White |
|---|---|---|---|---|---|---|---|---|
| *Males* | | | | | | | | |
| Industry | | | | | | | | |
| Agriculture | 0.5 | 2.7 | 18.0 | 2.8 | 2.7 | 1.3 | 2.4 | 4.2 |
| Mining | 0.5 | 0.1 | 0.8 | 0.2 | 0.3 | 0.3 | 0.8 | 1.4 |
| Construction | 3.0 | 11.3 | 15.2 | 10.8 | 3.5 | 4.4 | 11.6 | 11.9 |
| Manufacturing | 11.0 | 15.4 | 25.5 | 22.8 | 41.8 | 19.4 | 24.4 | 23.1 |
| Transportation | 12.4 | 12.7 | 4.4 | 8.5 | 4.7 | 6.8 | 7.0 | 9.9 |
| Wholesale trade | 3.3 | 3.6 | 5.2 | 5.6 | 4.3 | 5.3 | 5.0 | 5.6 |
| Retail Trade | 15.6 | 12.1 | 13.6 | 15.4 | 16.0 | 20.2 | 12.3 | 11.1 |
| Finance | 6.0 | 6.7 | 1.4 | 5.0 | 2.9 | 6.2 | 5.2 | 5.2 |
| Services | 47.0 | 32.9 | 14.8 | 26.7 | 22.3 | 34.2 | 29.3 | 26.1 |
| Not specified | 0.7 | 2.5 | 1.0 | 2.3 | 1.6 | 2.0 | 2.0 | 1.6 |
| Executive–managerial | 32.1 | 15.6 | 5.1 | 14.8 | 15.5 | 36.8 | 35.1 | 26.4 |
| Self-employed | 7.8 | 7.5 | 7.1 | 10.2 | 9.1 | 14.9 | 17.1 | 14.6 |
| *Females* | | | | | | | | |
| Industry | | | | | | | | |
| Agriculture | 0.4 | 0.6 | 8.9 | 0.7 | 1.1 | 0.8 | 1.3 | 1.6 |
| Mining | 0.1 | 0.0 | 0.1 | 0.1 | 0.1 | 0.1 | 0.2 | 0.2 |
| Construction | 0.8 | 0.7 | 0.8 | 0.9 | 0.7 | 0.7 | 1.6 | 1.7 |
| Manufacturing | 6.5 | 7.3 | 29.6 | 22.7 | 35.6 | 17.9 | 14.3 | 13.2 |
| Transportation | 1.9 | 3.6 | 1.8 | 3.8 | 2.2 | 4.1 | 3.9 | 4.5 |
| Wholesale trade | 1.8 | 1.7 | 4.4 | 3.7 | 3.6 | 3.5 | 2.9 | 3.0 |
| Retail trade | 17.2 | 8.5 | 14.4 | 13.2 | 18.7 | 19.1 | 18.7 | 26.4 |
| Finance | 6.8 | 10.1 | 2.9 | 7.2 | 4.6 | 9.1 | 8.8 | 8.8 |
| Services | 62.7 | 66.1 | 34.6 | 45.7 | 31.3 | 43.6 | 47.6 | 49.3 |
| Not specified | 1.9 | 1.3 | 2.4 | 2.1 | 2.1 | 1.1 | 0.7 | 0.5 |
| Executive–managerial | 23.5 | 19.8 | 5.0 | 12.2 | 9.7 | 23.0 | 24.4 | 25.1 |
| Self-employed | 3.6 | 4.3 | 5.4 | 6.6 | 8.7 | 9.4 | 10.3 | 8.1 |

*Note*: Native whites sampled at a rate of 1/10 of 5 per cent.

*Source*: 5 per cent Public Use Microdata Sample of 1990 U.S. Census.

group and gender. Census data show that over three quarters of Southeast Asian men and two-thirds of Southeast Asian women worked in manufacturing durable goods. In the service sector, over 60 per cent of African and West Indian women were concentrated in business services, health services, and education, with over 40 per cent of African women and half of West Indian women concentrated in health services only.

Case studies and ethnographic observations indicate similar patterns. For example, Southeast Asians in California were mostly employed in the lower segments of electronics, pharmaceutical, and computer industries as assembly-line workers, technicians, machine operators, and office clerks. West Indian men in New York City were mostly engaged in business services, while their female counterparts worked in health and personal services. Mexican, other Latino, and Asian women in Los Angeles who worked in manufacturing were predominantly engaged in labor-intensive industries such as apparels, textiles, and leather products (Baldwin 1984; Foner 1987; Scott 1996; Waldinger 1996*a*).

## *Underemployment*

In general, immigrant workers seem to have relatively few obstacles in gaining labor market entry, although they are disproportionately underemployed. How are these underemployed workers utilized in the labor force? Are there any observable intergroup differences? How do skill and age factors influence underemployment? Tables 8.4 and 8.5 explore these questions (for males and females, respectively). Overall, the various ethnic groups studied were utilized differently in the labor force. Among underemployed men, as shown in the upper panel of Table 8.4, Mexicans and Asians were least represented in the sub-unemployment category "discouraged workers," whereas Asians showed the lowest rate of unemployment. Taking sub-unemployment and unemployment together as an indicator of joblessness for all groups, including native whites, joblessness rates ranged from a high of 29 per cent among West Indians to a low of 14 per cent among Asians, compared with 24 per cent among native whites.

Partial employment seemed to be the modal category among underemployed men of all groups. There was some intergroup convergence, ranging from 38 per cent among Asians to about 48 per cent among West Indians and other Latinos, except for Mexicans, whose partial employment rate was substantially higher at 56 per cent. The next two categories, low-wage employment and overqualified employment, show significant intergroup differences. Among employed male workers, Mexicans were almost twice as likely as other groups to be underemployed by low wages and least likely to be underemployed by occupational overqualification. By contrast, Africans, Asians, and Europeans were more likely to be underemployed by being educationally overqualified for the jobs they held.

It is clear that disadvantages in labor market status do not necessarily pertain to all immigrant groups in the same manner. Of those not able to obtain adequate employment, Mexicans were more likely to be absorbed into partial or low-wage employment, while Africans and Asians were more likely to work in jobs for which they were occupationally overqualified. Do these intergroup differences remain when education and age are controlled for? Previous studies have found that education and age significantly affect underemployment among native black workers, indicating

**Table 8.4.** *Underemployment among male workers aged 25–64 by ethnicity, controlling for education and age*

| Characteristics | African | West Indian | Mexican | Other Latino | Southeast Asian | Other Asian | European | Native white |
|---|---|---|---|---|---|---|---|---|
| *All workers* | | | | | | | | |
| Sub-unemployment | 9.0 | 11.1 | 8.8 | 12.0 | 11.4 | 8.3 | 12.0 | 13.8 |
| Unemployment | 8.5 | 18.0 | 14.9 | 14.4 | 12.4 | 5.9 | 8.3 | 10.2 |
| Joblessness | 17.5 | 29.1 | 23.7 | 26.4 | 23.8 | 14.2 | 20.3 | 24.0 |
| Partial employment | 44.1 | 48.6 | 55.6 | 48.8 | 46.1 | 38.4 | 39.4 | 39.5 |
| Low-wage employment | 5.7 | 8.2 | 17.2 | 11.5 | 8.4 | 8.5 | 6.6 | 9.6 |
| Overqualified employment | 32.6 | 14.2 | 3.5 | 13.4 | 21.7 | 38.9 | 33.7 | 27.0 |
| *Without high school diploma* | | | | | | | | |
| Sub-unemployment | 18.2 | 11.6 | 9.1 | 13.8 | 15.3 | 11.7 | 20.2 | 24.6 |
| Unemployment | 9.9 | 23.0 | 15.9 | 18.2 | 17.2 | 12.1 | 16.3 | 16.8 |
| Joblessness | 28.1 | 34.6 | 25.0 | 32.0 | 32.5 | 23.8 | 36.5 | 41.4 |
| Partial employment | 56.2 | 53.1 | 56.8 | 52.8 | 54.9 | 53.0 | 53.0 | 45.8 |
| Low-wage employment | 15.7 | 12.3 | 18.2 | 15.2 | 12.5 | 23.2 | 10.5 | 12.9 |
| Overqualified employment | 0.0 | 0.0 | 0.0 | 0.0 | 0.0 | 0.0 | 0.0 | 0.0 |
| *Workers aged 25–34* | | | | | | | | |
| Sub-unemployment | 10.9 | 12.2 | 7.5 | 11.4 | 13.3 | 10.8 | 10.8 | 9.8 |
| Unemployment | 8.6 | 18.7 | 13.9 | 14.5 | 12.3 | 5.9 | 8.8 | 12.5 |
| Joblessness | 19.5 | 30.9 | 21.4 | 25.9 | 25.6 | 16.7 | 19.6 | 22.3 |
| Partial employment | 48.3 | 48.2 | 57.0 | 51.6 | 50.4 | 47.6 | 46.2 | 43.4 |
| Low-wage employment | 6.8 | 7.9 | 18.4 | 12.1 | 8.2 | 7.7 | 7.4 | 10.0 |
| Overqualified employment | 25.4 | 13.0 | 3.2 | 10.3 | 15.8 | 28.0 | 26.9 | 24.4 |

*Note*: Native whites sampled at a rate of 1/10 of 5 per cent.

*Source*: 5 per cent Public Use Microdata Sample of 1990 U.S. Census.

that youth and lack of education compound with race to affect adversely the labor market participation of African-Americans (Lichter 1988).

The middle panel of Table 8.4 shows the distribution of underemployment after controlling for education, based on a subsample of male workers who had not finished high school. Intergroup differences followed the same pattern among less-educated workers, but lack of education significantly increased jobless rates for all groups concerned. Changes were more drastic among Africans, West Indians, Europeans, and native whites. Mexicans without high school diplomas continued to show the lowest rate of sub-unemployment, and their unemployment rate did not change much; Asians continued to show the lowest rate of joblessness. Mexicans had relatively high rates of partial and low-wage employment, while all other groups displayed similar proportions in these two categories. The lower panel of Table 8.4 shows the distribution of labor force positions among younger underemployed workers. Based on a subsample of male in the age cohort of 25–34, the intergroup patterns of underemployment remained essentially the same as the overall patterns.

Among underemployed women, the intergroup patterns were quite similar to those of underemployed men (see Table 8.5). However, gender differences were substantial: women appeared to be affected more severely by sub-unemployment,

**Table 8.5.** *Underemployment among female workers aged 25–64 by ethnicity, controlling for education and age*

| Characteristics | African | West Indian | Mexican | Other Latino | Southeast Asian | Other Asian | European | Native white |
|---|---|---|---|---|---|---|---|---|
| *All workers* | | | | | | | | |
| Sub-unemployment | 16.9 | 15.2 | 21.9 | 18.5 | 17.5 | 17.1 | 22.2 | 20.8 |
| Unemployment | 12.6 | 13.4 | 15.9 | 13.6 | 12.1 | 6.9 | 6.2 | 6.0 |
| Joblessness | 29.5 | 28.6 | 37.8 | 32.1 | 29.6 | 24.0 | 28.4 | 26.8 |
| Partial employment | 51.0 | 54.1 | 47.2 | 49.9 | 50.8 | 48.3 | 56.3 | 58.0 |
| Low-wage employment | 5.7 | 10.4 | 13.8 | 12.7 | 11.6 | 9.6 | 7.1 | 8.3 |
| Overqualified employment | 13.9 | 7.0 | 1.2 | 5.2 | 7.9 | 18.0 | 8.2 | 6.9 |
| *Without high school diploma* | | | | | | | | |
| Sub-unemployment | 24.8 | 16.7 | 22.5 | 18.8 | 19.6 | 19.5 | 26.4 | 28.1 |
| Unemployment | 12.8 | 15.4 | 17.5 | 16.3 | 15.0 | 9.6 | 8.6 | 9.7 |
| Joblessness | 37.6 | 32.1 | 40.0 | 35.1 | 34.6 | 29.1 | 35.0 | 37.8 |
| Partial employment | 53.8 | 51.4 | 45.1 | 47.2 | 51.3 | 50.6 | 54.1 | 48.0 |
| Low-wage employment | 8.6 | 16.5 | 14.9 | 17.7 | 14.1 | 20.3 | 10.9 | 14.2 |
| Overqualified employment | 0.0 | 0.0 | 0.0 | 0.0 | 0.0 | 0.0 | 0.0 | 0.0 |
| *Workers aged 25–34* | | | | | | | | |
| Sub-unemployment | 19.1 | 16.7 | 23.1 | 21.1 | 19.1 | 22.0 | 25.6 | 22.4 |
| Unemployment | 12.3 | 14.4 | 15.8 | 14.0 | 13.0 | 7.3 | 6.5 | 7.0 |
| Joblessness | 31.4 | 31.1 | 38.9 | 35.1 | 32.1 | 29.2 | 32.1 | 29.4 |
| Partial employment | 51.0 | 53.7 | 46.2 | 49.0 | 50.9 | 49.7 | 53.5 | 54.7 |
| Low-wage employment | 5.7 | 8.7 | 13.7 | 11.2 | 9.7 | 6.4 | 5.6 | 7.7 |
| Overqualified employment | 12.0 | 7.3 | 1.3 | 4.8 | 7.3 | 14.7 | 8.8 | 8.3 |

*Note*: Native whites sampled at a rate of 1/10 of 5 per cent.

*Source*: 5 per cent Public Use Microdata Sample of 1990 U.S. Census.

unemployment, and partial employment than were their male counterparts, even after education or age was accounted for. While sub-unemployed males may be assumed to be discouraged workers who had detached themselves from the labor market involuntarily, the same assumption may not be applicable to sub-unemployed females. Women may voluntarily withdraw from the labor force because of marriage or childbearing. By the same token, partial employment among men may be viewed as an imposed disadvantage, but partial employment among women may be voluntary or a strategy for supplementing husbands' underpaid family wages.

## *Labor force positions and economic consequences*

Table 8.6 explores the bivariate relationship between labor force positions and economic consequences in terms of average earnings (in 1989 dollars). For men, the intergroup earnings gap was large, with Mexicans at the lowest end, Europeans and Asians at the highest. For women, the intergroup earnings gap was comparatively more narrow, but the earnings of Mexicans were significantly lower than those of other groups. Regardless of race/ethnicity and gender, substantially lower earnings were not only associated with low-wage employment but also with all other forms of underemployment, except for underemployment by overqualification. Underemployed

**Table 8.6.** *Average annual earnings (1989 U.S. dollars) among employed workers aged 25–64 by ethnicity and gender*

| Characteristics | African | West Indian | Mexican | Other Latino | Southeast Asian | Other Asian | European | Native white |
|---|---|---|---|---|---|---|---|---|
| *Males* | | | | | | | | |
| Adequate employment | 26,555 | 26,365 | 21,422 | 27,197 | 26,564 | 37,662 | 40,188 | 35,451 |
| Underemployment | 19,580 | 17,682 | 11,124 | 17,115 | 17,696 | 28,545 | 32,897 | 26,883 |
| Subunemployment | 13,869 | 13,617 | 10,897 | 13,597 | 11,766 | 17,107 | 21,842 | 17,545 |
| Unemployment | 14,793 | 14,278 | 10,378 | 13,635 | 12,689 | 16,585 | 21,662 | 17,658 |
| Partial employment | 13,960 | 14,954 | 10,918 | 14,585 | 13,226 | 18,984 | 23,125 | 20,534 |
| Low-wage employment | 8,657 | 7,916 | 8,383 | 8,309 | 8,157 | 8,948 | 8,469 | 8,516 |
| Overqualified employment | 30,353 | 36,738 | 30,272 | 37,373 | 33,166 | 44,076 | 52,709 | 47,762 |
| *Females* | | | | | | | | |
| Adequate employment | 21,606 | 23,083 | 17,482 | 20,619 | 21,155 | 27,094 | 24,392 | 23,127 |
| Underemployment | 12,865 | 13,149 | 7,260 | 10,403 | 11,295 | 14,927 | 12,894 | 12,043 |
| Sub-unemployment | 8,361 | 10,820 | 5,591 | 8,053 | 8,958 | 9,500 | 8,611 | 7,447 |
| Unemployment | 9,287 | 10,324 | 6,387 | 8,788 | 8,958 | 10,550 | 11,516 | 10,462 |
| Partial employment | 12,177 | 12,837 | 7,613 | 10,200 | 10,174 | 12,763 | 11,776 | 11,526 |
| Low-wage employment | 7,887 | 8,029 | 7,465 | 7,632 | 8,145 | 8,126 | 7,769 | 7,594 |
| Overqualified employment | 23,036 | 30,146 | 22,905 | 26,894 | 25,939 | 27,904 | 32,588 | 32,049 |

*Note*: Native whites sampled at a rate of 1/10 of 5 per cent.

*Source*: 5 per cent Public Use Microdata Sample of 1990 U.S. Census.

workers who were occupationally overqualified did not suffer economically; they actually enjoyed superior earnings advantages.

These findings suggest that for immigrant workers securing a job in the labor market entails not only human capital but also the willingness to take whatever work is available. Current economic disadvantages associated with underemployment may imply a mobility trap, but could also present the first step to social mobility. These averages are calculated based on those who reported positive earnings. Since the majority of the sub-unemployed reported no earnings, their average earnings may be discounted.

## CONCLUSION

Results obtained by applying the LUF to data from the 1990 U.S. Census show that immigrant groups differ according to how they are utilized in the labor force and that differential economic consequences are associated with intergroup differences in labor force utilization. With the exception of Southeast Asians, who are mostly low-skilled refugees, able-bodied immigrants are generally economically active and do not seem to be severely blocked from gaining labor market entry. However, those who have entered the labor force are mostly underemployed: about half of working men of any immigrant groups (over 60 per cent among Asians) and over 70 per cent of working women are underemployed.

Intergroup underemployment patterns vary significantly. Among underemployed men, West Indians, Mexicans, other Latinos, and Southeast Asians seem to be more disadvantaged in their labor force positions than other groups. However, Africans, Asians, and Europeans appear to be able to compensate better for labor force disadvantage by occupational overqualification. Intergroup differences in labor force utilization among women are quite similar, but intragroup gender differences are drastic. Compared with their male coethnics, female workers are more vulnerable to underemployment: 70 per cent or more are underemployed. In particular, joblessness affects all working women, but it hits Mexicans and other Latinos the hardest. African and Asian women seem to bypass the disadvantages of joblessness through overqualified employment, but the proportions in this category are not large enough to offset overall disadvantages. For both men and women, intergroup disparities persist in the labor market, even after taking education and age into consideration.

Do all forms of underemployment accrue to economic disadvantages? The answer is *no* and *yes*, depending on the form of underemployment under consideration. Joblessness is an absolute disadvantage. Partial employment or low-wage employment offers some supplementary earnings, but these earnings are by no means adequate for sustaining a decent living, much less for moving up the socioeconomic ladder. This disadvantage affects Mexican immigrants disproportionately. Although Mexican immigrants have relatively easy access to the U.S. labor market, their labor market positions are largely dictated by the seasonal labor demand of U.S. agriculture, and their employment networks are thus reinforced labor market positions. These structural conditions, in turn, constrain Mexican immigrants' ability to achieve comparable economic success, despite their high rate of labor force participation. Similarly, the current situation of disadvantaged racial/ethnic groups, native and immigrant alike, may not be caused by problems of their own making (the unwillingness to work or to accept low-wage employment for which they are often blamed).

Occupational overqualification turns out to be an effective way to yield a much higher earnings advantage over adequate employment, regardless of race/ethnicity and gender. Even among native whites, this form of underemployment appears to be significant, suggesting that full-time, year-round employment may no longer be adequate for sustaining a decent living. In other words, replenishing job skills and acquiring advanced education are becoming more crucial than ever before to moving ahead socioeconomically because the higher-paying segments of the labor market are pressing higher skill demands on their participants. The underlying message is clear: there is a possible trade-off between joblessness and underemployment by occupational overqualification. In order to succeed in mainstream labor markets, immigrants must not only find ways to educate themselves and replenish job skills but, as an initial first step, to be willing to take jobs for which they are overqualified. For other forms of underemployment, however, the trade-off is less clear-cut, since they are not as closely related to earnings advantages.

While many immigrants start out as low-wage workers and gradually move up in the labor market, others may be stuck in dead-end jobs. Of course, whether one can successfully move out of underemployed positions depends on more than individual human capital or incentive because factors beyond the control of individual group members may intervene. Immigration selectivity is one such factor. Immigrants who have arrived with strong human capital may be able to overcome labor market disadvantages by overqualification. Those who have arrived with little human capital are likely to be employed in low-wage and inferior jobs. These workers usually have few economic resources and cannot afford the time for the retraining that could possibly help them move up in the labor market. However, it would be premature to conclude that those who initially hold entry-level, low-wage jobs are necessarily trapped at the bottom of the labor market. In fact, as immigrants gain labor market experience, many are able to advance within and across industries to better paying positions and even to self-employment (Portes and Zhou 1992, 1996; Zhou 1992).

What are the implications of differential immigrant labor market positions for economic disparities among native-born minority workers? Although this chapter does not address the issue directly, the topic is important. One argument is that immigrant workers, the low-skilled in particular, take jobs away from American workers. When industrial restructuring is eroding employment bases in metropolitan areas where native minorities and immigrant groups are concentrated disproportionately, native minority members are consistently more adversely affected than immigrants. Less educated and young Mexicans face fewer obstacles in gaining labor market entry than similarly situated native minority members, particularly in the low-skilled segment where jobs are said to disappear.

Relocation of industries or businesses places many jobs off limits to most inner-city workers, and historical discrimination in education in the inner city adversely affects minority youth. Inner-city youth, overcrowded in downtrodden neighborhoods where conventional means of achievement are not valued, suffer from extremely high rates of high school dropout, which, in turn, makes these young people less competitive or employable than minority members who either graduate from similar public schools or come from more affluent communities. Moreover, inner-city minority workers are often perceived as undesirable, unreliable, and less productive; they have trouble getting hired, overcoming stereotypes, and maintaining their fragile footholds in the jobs they do acquire (Kirschenman and Neckerman 1991; Wilson 1996).

It is, thus, highly debatable whether low-skilled immigrants out-compete native-born minority workers in metropolitan labor markets. Some immigrant groups, by way of entrepreneurship, are able to regain manufacturing jobs that have out-migrated through industrial restructuring, or to create new jobs and keep those jobs for their coethnics in exclusive ethnic labor markets, giving rise to various ethnic niches (Waldinger 1996*b*). These ethnic enterprises provide opportunities not only for coethnic entrepreneurs but for the coethnic workers disadvantaged by a lack of sufficient human capital, English language ability, and formal employment networks (Light 1972; Portes and Zhou 1992).

Other immigrant groups, by way of informal networking, tap into non-coethnic labor markets (Waldinger 1996*b*). Despite their lack of education and poor command of English, Mexicans do not seem to have high rates of coethnic entrepreneurship, but they have established strong informal networks that enable them to tap into exclusive non-coethnic immigrant labor markets. Given the qualitative differences between native minority and immigrant groups in their mobility strategies and opportunities, race or ethnicity will continue to affect the labor market outcomes in different ways for different groups.

Several implications can be drawn from these varied patterns. One is that human capital alone does not account for the economic success of immigrants. At the individual level, immigrant group members are made to believe that they should be able to market themselves commensurate with their human capital credentials. At the structural level, however, they often encounter barriers based on group membership rather than on individual characteristics that may not keep them from entry but do block their upward mobility within the labor market. Those who are channeled into the labor market by ethnic employment networks, may face mobility traps as well as opportunity.

Accepting low wages or underemployment by means of educational over-achievement can be key to labor market entry. Both, ironically, violate our mainstream cultural value of equity. Consequently, those who have acquired citizenship or who are well acculturated can protect themselves by pushing unions and the government to impose laws excluding cheap labor, strengthening labor regulations, and raising minimum wages. At the same time, they may find themselves out of work and, often, blamed for their unwillingness to work. Immigrants who take odd jobs in their enclaves or take jobs in the larger labor market for which they are overqualified also frequently find themselves unfairly criticized for unfair competition and wage depression posing an economic threat to native workers.

A second implication concerns the difficulty immigrant group members have in fully realizing their human capital and achieving socioeconomic success. While human capital—education and skills—contributes to better labor market placement for minority group members, it alone does not account for intergroup economic disparities. Africans and Asians may provide unfair comparisons because their average levels of education tend to be higher, but compared with less educated groups such as Mexicans, other Latinos, and Southeast Asians, intergroup discrepancies persist in labor force positions and economic status. Strong human capital certainly places Africans and Asians at higher starting points as they move up the socioeconomic ladder, but it does not guarantee equity in occupational and earnings returns.

A third implication pertains to education's importance for the second-generation immigrant. Trends in the inner city that affect native minority youth have started to affect immigrant youth. Herbert Gans (1992) observes that immigrant children from less fortunate socioeconomic backgrounds have a much harder time than middle-class children succeeding in school. A significant number of children of the poor, especially dark-skinned immigrants, can be trapped in permanent poverty in an era of stagnant economic growth and in the process of Americanization because they "will either not be asked, or will be reluctant, to work at immigrant wages and hours as their parents did but will lack job opportunities, skills and connections to do better" (Gans 1992).

Gans predicts that children of the less fortunate may face high rates of unemployment, crime, alcoholism, drug use, and other pathologies associated with poverty and the frustration of rising expectation. Perlmann and Waldinger (1997), however, call this phenomenon "the second generation revolt." They argue that such revolt is not merely caused by exogenous factors like racial discrimination, declining economic opportunities, and exposure to adversarial outlooks of native-born youths, but also by endogenous factors inherent in the immigration process, including pre-immigration class standing and the size and the nature of immigrant inflows.

In conclusion, the results presented in this chapter point to differential labor market positions for immigrant groups and the varied effects of underemployment on economic disparities. These results imply that the forces promoting or impeding economic adaptation into the U.S. economy are well beyond the framework of existing theories and that the economic experiences of immigrant groups vary not only by human capital and structural conditions, but by factors intrinsic to the immigration processes. This chapter highlights the significant situation of economic disparity among immigrant as well as native minority groups. There is a critical need for alternative conceptualizations of, and future research on, labor market dynamics that will examine the significance of race and ethnicity *and* the uniqueness and selectivity of international migration.

**References**

Alba, Richard D. (1985). *Italian Americans: Into the Twilight of Ethnicity.* Englewood Cliffs, NJ: Prentice-Hall.

—— and Nee, Victor (1997). "The Assimilation of Immigrant Groups: Concept, Theory, and Evidence," *International Migration Review*, 31: 826–74.

Baldwin, C. B. (1984). *Patterns of Adjustment: A Second Look at Indochinese Resettlement in Orange County.* Orange: Immigrant and Refugee Planning Center.

Bean, Frank D., Lowell, Lindsay, and Taylor, L. J. (1988). "Undocumented Mexican Immigrants and the Earnings of Other Workers in the United States," *Demography*, 25: 35–52.

—— and Tienda, Marta (1987). *The Hispanic Population of the United States.* New York: Russell Sage Foundation.

Blau, Peter, and Duncan, Otis D. (1967). *The American Occupational Structure.* New York: Wiley.

Borjas, George J. (1984). "The Impact of Immigrants on Earnings of the Native Born," in Vernon M. Briggs, Jr. and Marta, Tienda (eds.), *Immigration: Issues and Policies.* Salt Lake City: Olympus.

—— (1990). *Friends and Strangers: The Impact of Immigrants on the U.S. Economy.* New York: Basic Books.

Chiswick, Barry R. (1979). "The Economic Progress of Immigrants: Some Apparently Universal Patterns," in William Feller (ed.), *Contemporary Economic Problems.* Washington, DC: American Enterprise Institute, pp. 357–99.

Clogg, Clifford C. (1979). *Measuring Underemployment: Demographic Indicators for the United States.* New York: Academic Press.

—— Eliason, Scott R., and Wahl, R. (1990). "Labor Market Experiences and Labor Force Outcomes: A Comprehensive Framework for Analyzing Labor Force Dynamics," *American Journal of Sociology*, 95: 1536–76.

Drucker, Peter F. (1993). *Post-Capitalist Society.* New York: Harper Collins.

Edwards, Richard C. (1979). *Contested Terrain: The Transformation of the Workplace in Twentieth Century.* New York: Harper Torchbooks.

Foner, Nancy (1987). "Jamaicans: Race and Ethnicity Among Migrants in New York City," in Nancy Foner (ed.), *New Immigrants in New York.* New York: Columbia University Press.

Gans, Herbert J. (1992). "Second-Generation Decline: Scenarios for the Economic and Ethnic Futures of the Post-1965 American Immigrants," *Ethnic and Racial Studies*, 15: 173–92.

Gordon, Milton M. (1964). *Assimilation in American Life: The Role of Race, Religion, and National Origins.* New York: Oxford University Press.

Greeley, Andrew M. (1976). "The Ethnic Miracle," *Public Interest*, 45: 20–36.

Hauser, Philip M. (1974). "The Measure of Labor Utilization," *Malayan Economic Review*, 19: 1–17.

—— (1977). "The Measurement of Labor Utilization: More Empirical Results," *Malayan Economic Review*, 22: 10–25.

Hirschman, Charles, and Falcon, Luis (1985). "The Educational Attainment of Religio-ethnic Groups in the United States," *Research in Sociology of Education and Socialization*, 5: 83–120.

Hirtschman, Charles, and Wong, Morrison G. (1986). "The Extraordinary Educational Attainment of Asian Americans: A Search for Historical Evidence and Explanations," *Social Forces*, 65: 1–27.

Kasarda, John D. (1983). "Entry Level Jobs, Mobility, and Minority Unemployment," *Urban Affairs Quarterly*, 19: 21–40.

Kirschenman, Joleen, and Neckerman, Kathryn M. (1991). "'We'd love to Hire Them, but . . . :' The Meaning of Race for Employers," in Christopher Jencks and Paul E. Peterson (eds.), *The Urban Underclass*. Washington, DC: The Brookings Institute, pp. 203–43.

Landry, Bart (1987). *The New Black Middle Class*. Berkeley: University of California Press.

Lichter, Daniel T. (1988). "Racial Difference in Underemployment in American Cities," *American Journal of Sociology*, 93: 771–92.

Light, Ivan (1972). *Ethnic Enterprise in America: Business Welfare among Chinese, Japanese and Blacks*. Berkeley: University of California Press.

Massey, Douglas S. (1996). "The Age of Extremes: Concentrated Affluence and Poverty in the Twenty-First Century," *Demography*, 3: 395–412.

—— and Denton, Nancy A. (1987). "Trends in Residential Segregation of Blacks, Hispanics, and Asians: 1970–1980," *American Sociological Review*, 52: 802–25.

Mishel, Lawrence, and Jared Bernstein (1992). *The State of Working America: 1992–1993*, Washington, DC: Economic Policy Institute.

Model, Suzanne (1991). "Caribbean Immigrants: A Black Success Story?" *International Migration Review*, 25: 248–76.

Perlmann, Joel, and Waldinger, Roger (1997). "Second Generation Decline? Immigrant Children Past and Present—A Reconsideration," *International Migration Review*, 31: 893–922.

Portes, Alejandro (1995). "Economic Sociology and the Sociology of Immigration: A Conceptual Overview," in Alejandro Portes (ed.), *The Economic Sociology of Immigration: Essays on Networks, Ethnicity, and Entrepreneurship*. New York: Russell Sage Foundation, pp. 141–9.

—— and Borocz, Josef (1989). "Contemporary Immigration: Theoretical Perspectives on its Determinants and Modes of Incorporation," *International Migration Review*, 23: 606–30.

—— and Rumbaut, Ruben (1996). *Immigrant America: A Portrait*, 2nd edn. Berkeley: University of California Press.

—— and Stepick, Alex (1993). *City on the Edge: The Transformation of Miami*. University of California Press, Berkeley.

—— and Zhou, Min (1992). "Gaining the Upper Hand: Economic Mobility Among Immigrant and Domestic Minorities," *Ethnic and Racial Studies*, 15: 491–522.

—— (1996). "Self-Employment and the Earnings of Immigrants," *American Sociological Review*, 61: 219–30.

Reich, Robert (1992). *The Work of Nations: Preparing Ourselves for 21st Century Capitalism*. New York: Random House.

Reischauer, Robert D. (1989). "Immigration and the Underclass," *Annals of the American Academy of Political and Social Sciences*, 501: 120–31.

Rumbaut, Rubén G. (1989). "Portraits, Patterns, and Predictors of the Refugee Adaptation Process: Results and Reflections from the IHARP Panel Study," in David W. Haines (ed.), *Refugees as Immigrants: Cambodians, Laotians, and Vietnamese in America*. Totowa: Rowman & Littlefield, pp. 138–82.

—— (1995). "Vietnamese, Laotian, and Cambodian Americans," in Pyung Gap Min (ed.), *Asian Americans: Contemporary Trends and Issues*. Thousand Oaks, CA: Sage Publications, pp. 232–70.

Sandberg, N. C. (1974). *Ethnic Identity and Assimilation: The Polish-American Community*. New York: Praeger Publishers.

Scott, Allen J. (1996). "The Manufacturing Economy: Ethnic and Gender Divisions of Labor," in Roger Waldinger and Menhdi Bozorgmehr (eds.), *Ethnic Los Angeles*. New York: Russell Sage Foundation, pp. 215–46.

Sullivan, Theresa A. (1978). *Marginal Workers, Marginal Jobs: Underutilization in the U.S. Work Force*. Austin: University of Texas Press.
Tienda, Marta, and Lii, D. T. (1987). "Minority Concentration and Earnings Inequality: Blacks, Hispanics and Asians Compared," *American Journal of Sociology*, 92: 141–65.
Tolbert, Charles, Horan, Patrick M., and Beck, E. M. (1980). "The Structure of Economic Segmentation: A Dual Economy Approach," *American Journal of Sociology*, 85: 1095–116.
U.S. Bureau of the Census (1993). *1990 Census of Population and Housing, PUMS (A)*. Washington, DC: U.S. Department of Commerce, Bureau of the Census.
Waldinger, Roger (1989). "Structural Opportunities or Ethnic Advantage: Immigrant Business Development in New York," *International Migrational Review*, 23: 48–72.
—— (1996*a*). "Ethnicity and Opportunity in the Plural City," in Roger Waldinger and Menhdi Bozorgmehr (eds.), *Ethnic Los Angeles*. New York: Russell Sage Foundation, pp. 445–70.
—— (1996*b*). *Still the Promised City: African-Americans and New Immigrants in Postindustrial New York*. Cambridge: Harvard University Press.
—— and Bozorgmehr, Menhdi (eds.) (1996). *Ethnic Los Angeles*. New York: Russell Sage Foundation.
Warner, W. L., and Srole, L. (1945). *The Social Systems of American Ethnic Groups*. New Haven: Yale University Press.
Waters, Mary C. (1994). "Ethnic and Racial Identities of Second-Generation Black Immigrants in New York City," *International Migration Review*, 28: 795–820.
Wilson, William J. (1978). The *Declining Significance of Race: Blacks and Changing American Institutions*. Chicago: University of Chicago Press.
—— (1987). *The Truly Disadvantaged*. Chicago: University of Chicago Press.
—— (1996). *When Work Disappears: The World of the New Urban Poor*. New York: Alfred A. Knopf.
Wytrwal, J. A. (1961). *America's Polish Heritage: A Social History of Poles in America*. Detroit: Endurance Press.
Zhou, Min (1992). *Chinatown: The Socioeconomic Potential of an Urban Enclave*. Philadelphia: Temple University Press.
—— (1993). "Underemployment and Economic Disparities Among Minority Groups," *Population Research and Policy Review*, 12: 139–57.
—— and Bankston, Carl L., III (1998). *Growing up American: The Adaptation of Vietnamese Adolescents in the United States*. New York: Russell Sage Foundation.
—— and Kamo, Yoshinori (1994). "An Analysis of Earnings Patterns for Chinese, Japanese and Non-Hispanic Whites in the United States," *The Sociological Quarterly*, 35: 581–602.

# PART II

# POLICIES IN SENDING NATIONS

# 9

# Remittances, Savings, and Development in Migrant-Sending Areas

J. EDWARD TAYLOR

Migrant remittances and savings represent the most direct and measurable benefits of international migration in migrant-sending areas. Evidence indicates that they contribute both directly and indirectly to income in remittance-receiving households and that this income contribution may be substantial. Economic linkages transmit the effects of remittances and savings to other households in migrant-sending areas, including those that may not participate directly in international migration. These direct and indirect income effects of remittances have potentially profound influences on production, income inequality, and poverty.

The vast majority of research on migrant remittances and savings ignores their indirect effects on migrant-sending economies. As a result, many studies paint a negative picture of the implications of remittances and savings for development. For example, Reichert (1981) calls Mexico–U.S. migration—the world's largest international migration flow—an "illness" or "syndrome" that undermines local development; Wiest (1979) calls it an "addiction"; and Stuart and Kearney (1981) characterize it as a "dangerous dependence." Studies in other parts of the world echo these findings (e.g. see Swanson 1979; Bohning 1981; Rubenstein 1983; Kearney 1986; Diaz-Briquets 1991; for critical reviews see Papademetriou and Martin 1991; Durand and Massey 1992; and Taylor et al. 1996*a*,*b*).

These studies are unduly pessimistic for three reasons. First, the sheer magnitude of migrant remittances is large and often underestimated. Second, in the few studies that have attempted to measure the effects of international remittances on non-remittance income in migrant-sending households, the effect has been found to be positive, indicating that remittances stimulate local production. Third, the few studies that have attempted to measure income linkages among migrant and non-migrant households find that migrant remittances and savings create local income multipliers that are often quite large. Finally, it appears that international migrant remittances in many cases have an equalizing effect on income distributions in migrant-sending areas, particularly at late stages of the development process, providing an avenue for economic mobility for households located at the bottom-to-middle of the income ladder, especially in poor rural areas (Stark, Taylor, and Yitzhaki 1986, 1988).

This chapter examines each of these three sets of potential influences of international migrant remittances and savings on economic growth and development. It then presents a case study to illustrate the diverse array of influences that remittances and savings may have within a major migrant-sending region, in this case the Mexican state of Michoacan.

## QUANTIFYING MIGRANT REMITTANCES AND SAVINGS

Estimation of the size of international migrant remittances is complicated by the fact that an unknown but probably large share of the flows are not channeled through formal banking systems. Microlevel field studies indicate that clandestine or in-kind transfers are substantial (see Lozano Ascencio 1993; Massey and Parrado 1994). In addition, remittances are often in kind, and remittance studies generally do not attempt to put a value on in-kind remittances (or even know how to treat them analytically).

Less-developed country (LDC) governments frequently conceive of emigration as a potential source of savings and foreign exchange. Official estimates from the International Monetary Fund placed total annual remittances from foreign workers at around US$75 billion in 1989. This figure is 50 per cent higher than the total of official development assistance (Russell and Teitelbaum 1992).

In addition to understating the true magnitude of all migrant remittances and savings, this figure masks the importance of remittances to some countries and to specific migrant-sending areas within them. The world distribution of remittances is unequal. Among the world's 21 major recipients of worker remittances, the absolute value of remittances ranged from US$207 million in El Salvador to US$6.2 billion in the former Yugoslavia (see Table 9.1). The ten largest recipients of remittances received 86 per cent of all remittances flowing to these countries. In per capita terms the disparity is even greater. For example, India, far and away the most populous country in Table 9.1, is not among the top ten remittance recipients. In eleven of the countries in the table (Egypt, El Salvador, Bangladesh, Pakistan, Portugal, Turkey, Yugoslavia, Jordan, Yemen, Morocco, and Sudan) remittances constitute more than one quarter of total export revenues (see Taylor et al. 1996). These numbers indicate that migrant remittances constitute a large and important source of capital for many developing countries, contributing to domestic savings, easing foreign exchange constraints, and offering a means to finance trade deficits.

Most micro-level studies that gather data on international migrant remittances do not provide information on total incomes within surveyed households, making it impossible to ascertain the share that remittances comprise of total income within migrant-sending communities. Nevertheless, available evidence suggests that migrant remittances and savings represent an important fraction of total income in many households and regions. For example, income remitted by migrants from rural Mexico accounted for 33–40 per cent of total household income reported on a 1983 survey (Stark, Taylor, and Yitzhaki 1986), based on a survey of two Michoacan villages in 1983. A follow-up survey in 1989 revealed a sharp drop in remittances from

**Table 9.1.** *IMF estimates of total international migrant remittances in 1989 (millions of 1989 U.S. dollars)*

| Country | Total remittances | Per cent of world total |
|---|---|---|
| El Salvador | 207 | 0.63 |
| Jamaica | 214 | 0.65 |
| Sudan | 297 | 0.90 |
| Algeria | 306 | 0.93 |
| Syria | 355 | 1.08 |
| Yemen | 410 | 1.24 |
| Colombia | 467 | 1.42 |
| Tunisia | 488 | 1.48 |
| Jordan | 623 | 1.89 |
| South Korea | 624 | 1.89 |
| Bangladesh | 771 | 2.34 |
| Greece | 1,387 | 4.21 |
| Morocco | 1,454 | 4.41 |
| Spain | 1,861 | 5.65 |
| Pakistan | 1,897 | 5.76 |
| Mexico | 2,277 | 6.91 |
| India | 2,750 | 8.34 |
| Turkey | 3,040 | 9.22 |
| Egypt | 3,532 | 10.72 |
| Portugal | 3,706 | 11.24 |
| Yugoslavia | 6,290 | 19.09 |
| Total | 32,956 | 100.00 |

*Source*: Russell and Teitelbaum (1992).

internal migrants during the economic crisis years of the 1980s, but international remittances continued to account for a persistently large share household income, on the order of 20 per cent. Studies of villages in other regions of Mexico suggest that typical international remittance shares are on the order of 15–25 per cent (see Taylor, Yunez, and Dyer-Leal 1999).

Comparable figures have been obtained elsewhere: 11 per cent of rural household income in a Kenya study by Lewis and Thorbecke (1992), 12 per cent in a Java study (Ralston 1995), 26 per cent in a West India study (Subramanian 1995), 10 per cent in the Sahelian zone of Burkina Faso (Reardon et al. 1992), and 12.5 per cent in a study of rural Egyptian households by Adams (1989). Remittances from migrants in the United States constituted 36 per cent of total income in migrant households in a study of rural households in El Salvador (Taylor and Zabin 1996).

Mexican Migration Project data on 22 migrant-sending communities show that, in the 12 months prior to the survey, household heads who were migrants remitted an average of US$2,383, and other household remitted an average of $2,100.

Returning migrants who were household heads brought back an average of $1,392 in savings; nonheads brought back an average of $858 (Massey and Parrado 1994). Mean family remittances by migrants legalized under provisions of the 1986 U.S. Immigration Reform and Control Act (IRCA) were US$1,1997, or about 7 per cent of total family income, in 1987. They were highest to Mexico ($1,304) and Central America ($1,144) and lower to other Western Hemisphere countries ($930) and countries in the Eastern Hemisphere ($874; U.S. Department of Justice 1992).

## INDIRECT EFFECTS OF HOUSEHOLDS WITH MIGRANTS

The effect of *migrant remittances* on household incomes may not be accurately reflected in the remittances themselves. Migration and remittances may influence the quantity of household income from other sources, as posited by the new economics of labor migration (hereafter NELM), pioneered by Stark (1982) and documented by the few microeconometric studies that have attempted to test it (Lucas 1985; Taylor 1992; Taylor and Wyatt 1996).

In the NELM, migration is hypothesized to be partly an effort by households to overcome market failures that constrain local production. Market failures include missing or imperfect credit and insurance markets, which force household farms to self-finance their production and to self-insure against income risk. Migrants provide their households with liquidity, in the form of remittances, which may be used to finance new production technologies, inputs, and activities. They also offer income insurance, by providing households with access to an income source (migrant remittances) that is uncorrelated—or perhaps negatively correlated—with farm income. If credit and risk constraints are binding and migration enables families with migrants to overcome them, migration should have a positive effect on local production.

The NELM offers a fundamental change in the way that the connection between migration and development is conceptualized and modeled, compared with neoclassical economics and dependency theory. Previous research decoupled the determinants of migration from the effects of migration on sending areas. In NELM, the origins of migration (a household's desire to overcome market failures) imply specific outcomes for development (a positive effect on local production, as remittances and implicit risk contracts with family migrants enable households to overcome market failures).

This view leads to hypotheses about migration and development that are beyond the purview of traditional models, and has provided the inspiration for new surveys to collect data better able to test these hypotheses. NELM-inspired surveys gather data on all aspects of household-farm production and income, not just remittances, because potential correlations between migration and other income sources make it impossible to model migration and other aspects of household-farm economies separately. In other words, they are whole household-farm surveys (Taylor 1992; Adelman and Taylor 1990).

Stark and Katz (1986) formalize the argument that rural-to-urban migration, a labor-market phenomenon, is caused by imperfections in capital markets. Stark and Lucas (1988) and Lucas and Stark (1985) offer theoretical and empirical evidence (from Botswana) that remittances are part of a self-enforcing contractual arrangement between family and migrant, shifting the focus of migration theory away from individual independence (as in the Todaro model) to mutual interdependence.

Stark and Levhari (1982) use a graphical presentation to argue that migration is a means to spread risk, rather than being a manifestation of risk-taking behavior on the part of migrants. Stark's research with Stark and Rosenzweig (1989) and with Lucas (1985) provide some econometric evidence, using household-farm data from India and Botswana, that families insure themselves against risk by placing members in labor markets outside the village, where their incomes are not likely to be positively correlated with local farm incomes.

The importance of the indirect effects of migration on household-farm income turns on the extent to which financial and risk constraints on local production are binding to begin with. If families do not face such constraints, then the indirect income effects of migration in a Stark-type model are minimal, and the family will have little incentive to engage in migration. If credit and risk constraints are binding, then families have a larger incentive to sponsor migrants in an effort to overcome these constraints, and the subsequent indirect effects of migration on family incomes will be large. The net direct plus indirect effects of migration on migrant-household incomes, therefore, are theoretically ambiguous.

Lucas (1985) uses aggregate time-series data on migration from five southern African countries to South African mines to test the Stark hypothesis. His econometric analysis finds that lost-labor effects of emigration are negative and large initially, as production in migrant-sending households falls because less labor is available. In the long run, however, agricultural productivity increases. The productivity increase may be due to the investment of migrant remittances in production activities at home—that is, a loosening of financial constraints on investments that enhance productivity. Alternatively, it may be due to risk spreading, made possible by the diversification of income through migration, which encourages risk-averse households to undertake new agricultural investments. Or it may be some combination of the two.

Adams (1991) finds that households of rural Egyptian migrants have higher marginal propensities to invest than do their non-migrant counterparts. That is, migration has a positive effect on investment that is independent of its contribution to total household income. However, policy biases against agriculture, in the form of depressed prices for farm output, discourage agricultural investments.

Taylor (1992) estimates the marginal effects of migrant remittances on farm incomes and on asset accumulation over time, using matched longitudinal, micro data from farm households in rural Mexico. The initial marginal effect of remittances on household-farm incomes (measured in 1982) is less than unitary; that is, a $1 change in remittances produces a less-than-$1 change in total incomes of remittance-receiving households. This finding implies a negative effect of migrant remittances on non-remittance income. It is consistent with the hypothesis that the marginal product of migrant labor is positive prior to migration. Measured 6 years later, however, the marginal impact of remittances on total income is significantly greater than unitary. That is, over the long run remittances had a *positive* effect on non-remittance income.

These studies, while offering micro, econometric evidence in support of the migration-and-development hypothesis, also suggest that this relationship is not invariant over time or across settings. There appears to be a pattern of first negative and then positive effects of migration on non-remittance income in migrant-sending households. The positive effects clearly depend on the magnitude of migrant remittances and the profitability of investing in new production activities or techniques.

In the Mexican case, poor crop potential on marginal lands often limits families' incentives to invest their remittances in crop production. However, where livestock production is viable, grazing land is available, and transportation and marketing infrastructures are somewhat developed, the development potential of migration may be large. In other settings, profitable investment opportunities may be limited by environmental or market constraints, or else by government policies that turn the terms of trade against agriculture.

A finding that migration negatively affects non-remittance incomes, therefore, could reflect the stage of the migration process at which the study is conducted, or it could be evidence against the migration-and-development hypothesis. In the latter case, policy biases against agriculture may break the migration-and-development link. For example, poor infrastructure or price, credit, and technology policies that discriminate against small farmers may discourage migrant households from investing in new technologies or income activities.

## LOCAL ECONOMY-WIDE EFFECTS OF REMITTANCES AND SAVINGS

A micro household (or household-farm) approach ignores interactions among households. Because of this, even an analysis that treats individual households as whole economies is partial. If economic linkages among households are important, micro household (or household-farm) models may produce misleading findings about the impacts of migration on migrant-sending economies. At the very least, they will tend to underestimate these impacts.

A simple example illustrates the shortcomings of a micro household-farm approach to modeling migration-development interactions. Suppose that a village household (Household A) with a total income of 100 units increases its income to 150 by sending a family member abroad. That is, (a) the remittances the migrant sends home, net of (b) migration costs, minus (c) the income the migrant would have contributed to the household by staying home, plus (d) the migrant's consumption cost at home, equals 50 income units. An econometric estimate of the effect of this income increase on household expenditures finds that all of the 50-unit income increase is allocated to consumption. None is allocated to what most researchers would consider to be productive investment. Such a finding would appear to support the pessimistic view that income from migration is squandered on consumption.

Suppose, however, that the consumption goods whose demand increases are produced by another household within the village (Household B), using 40 units of family labor and 10 units of intermediate inputs "imported" from outside the village. Furthermore, suppose that the investment propensity of Household B is large, say, on the order of 0.20. The second-round effect of the 50-unit increase in Household A's income from migration will be a 50-unit increase in production, a 40-unit increase in Household B's income and an 8-unit (0.20 times 40) increase in village investment. At the end of the second round of the village "remittance multiplier," the total increase in village income will be 90, of which only 50 units are in the migrant household. Estimating the total impact of Household A's gains from migration on income and investment in the village requires carrying this calculation to its limit (this example—and SAM multipliers generally—assume a Keynesian world of underemployed resources).

### *Remittances and household expenditures*

Household expenditures are critical in determining the impact of migration on migrant-sending economies, because they are the means by which income gains in migrant households are transmitted to others in the economy. Understanding the marginal (direct and indirect) effects of migration and remittances on migrant household incomes is a critical first step in estimating the effect of migration on household-farm expenditures. Under NELM, the marginal effect of migration on income also *implies* an influence of migration on household-farm expenditures; that is, on investment in local production activities.

Remittance use surveys focus on expenditures (rather than the marginal income effects of migration) to assess the effect of migration on economic development in sending areas. (For critiques of remittance use surveys see Taylor 1995 and Taylor et al. 1996*b*.) Migration is assumed to have a positive effect on economic development if respondents report spending a large share of their remittance income on "productive investments."

Remittance use studies, however, rest on three shaky assumptions: (1) that observed remittances (net of migration costs) represent the true marginal contribution of migration to household-farm income; (2) that the use of remittances, themselves, accurately reflects the marginal effect of remittances on household-farm expenditure patterns; and (3) that the same families and, in some cases, the same individuals, must be both the source of migration and the agents for transforming migrant earnings into local income growth.

Evidence on non-unitary marginal effects of remittances on incomes in migrant-sending households casts doubt on the first assumption. The second assumption is not reasonable unless remittance checks are earmarked for specific uses and can be treated as separate from other family income sources—that is, unless income is not fungible. If households' marginal propensity to save is positive, income increases from migration should stimulate household-farm savings. In the absence of regional credit markets that tap household-farm savings and channel them outside the village, changes in village savings by definition must equal changes in village investments. This is an accounting identity. Often, the challenge in economic fieldwork is to uncover the specific forms that village investments assume.

If capital markets are missing within the local economy, each household-farm will be bound by a savings-investment constraint. In this case, a positive impact of migration on savings necessarily results in increased investment *by the migrant's household.* Only in this case is the same household necessarily the agent in both migration and investment (assumption 3). If local capital markets exist, migrant households may function as creditors for other villagers who are primarily responsible for carrying out local investments. That is, migrants and investors in local production activities are not necessarily the same. Even if local credit markets are missing or marginal savings rates in migrant households are zero, there are other important channels through which income generated by migration may find its way into local investments. The most important of these channels, paradoxically, is migrant households' use of their income gains for consumption.

The conclusion of many remittance-use studies that remittances are consumed instead of invested often rests on arbitrary definitions of "productive investments." For example, schooling, despite its demonstrated positive effect on household incomes (e.g. Taylor 1986) is often absent from the list of productive investments. This probably is because expenditures on educating family members usually do not create direct, immediate employment and income linkages within migrant-sending economies. Housing expenditures also are off the list of productive investments in many studies, despite their direct stimulus to village construction activities. By contrast, expenditures on farm machinery generally are regarded as productive investments, in spite of the fact that machinery is not produced within the village economy and may even displace labor in village production and produce negative income linkages.

## *Remittance multipliers*

Village remittance multipliers estimated using Social Accounting Matrices (SAM) suggest that economic linkages among households are important in shaping migration's effect on migrant-sending areas. For example, in 1982, remittance multipliers on village income were on the order of 1.87 in a Mexican village studied by Adelman, Taylor and Vogel (1988). Subsequent SAM studies of multiplier effects confirm the importance of inter-household linkages in villages in India (Subramanian and Sadoulet 1990), Java (Ralston 1995), Senegal (Golan 1995) and a Kenyan village-town economy (Lewis and Thorbecke 1992).

SAM multiplier models have been an important advance in village and regional modeling because they highlight the economic linkages among households that transmit exogenous changes in policies or markets through the local economy. SAM remittance multipliers reveal an important finding: *Many of the benefits of remittances accrue to households other than the ones that receive remittances.* Income linkages between migrant and non-migrant households transfer the benefits of migration beyond the remittance-receiving household. They may also be manifested largely outside the traditional farm sectors, as a result of strong linkages between the farm and nonfarm economies (e.g. see Adelman *et al.* 1988; Ravallion and Chandhuri 1994).

The sheer magnitude of remittances and their effect on household incomes and expenditures make it likely that international migration is a major stimulus to LDC economies. Indeed, studies using a new generation of micro economy-wide models (Taylor 1995; Taylor and Adelman 1996) reveal relatively large effects of remittances on local economies, despite the fact that distributional effects of remittances are sensitive to model choice.

## DIRECT AND INDIRECT EFFECTS OF REMITTANCES: A CASE STUDY

A series of studies using data from the author's Michoacan Project offer an in-depth view of the effects of migrant remittances and savings on incomes in a Mexican migrant-sending economy. Taken together, these studies indicate that, far from creating a "dangerous dependence" or a "syndrome," international migration enabled rural households to prosper during a decade of economic malaise in Mexico. It did this by (1) generating large amounts of remittance income; (2) stimulating production in migrant-sending households; and (3) creating expenditure linkages that contributed to income growth in other households within migrant-sending areas.

### *Remittances during the crisis years*

If one looks only at migration and remittance data, it would appear that households' reliance on migration increased during Mexico's economic crisis years. The share of households in the Michoacan sample receiving remittances from migrants in the United States rose from 47 per cent in 1982 to 52 per cent in 1988, and total remittances in the sample jumped by 58 per cent (see Table 9.2—all figures are in 1982 US dollars).

Table 9.2. *Changes in international migrant remittances and incomes in Michoacan Project households, 1982–8*

| | Total income | Remittance income | Non-remittance income |
|---|---|---|---|
| *% Change 1982–8* | 83.0 | 57.9 | 89.9 |
| *share of total income* | | | |
| 1982 | 1.00 | 0.22 | 0.78 |
| 1988 | 1.00 | 0.19 | 0.81 |

*Source*: Tabulations from Michoacan Project data from 1983 and 1989 surveys.

However, increases in non-remittance income exceeded this increase in remittance income; non-remittance income rose by 90 per cent between 1982 and 1988. As a result, total income increased more rapidly than remittance income during the crisis, and the share of remittances in total income declined, from 22 to 19 per cent. These increases in total income are striking in light of the adverse impacts of the crisis in urban areas. For example, real wages in urban Mexico fell by an estimated 32 per cent between 1982 and 1984 (Lustig and Ross 1987).

What explains the combination of rising remittances and a falling share of remittances in total income? Remittances from migrants stimulated non-remittance income in the Michoacan-survey households in three ways. First, they enabled migrant households to purchase inputs (e.g., fertilizer) that increased income in the short run. Second, they provided migrant-sending households with funds to invest in income-producing assets—particularly livestock—which created new sources of local income in the long run. Third, they created expenditure linkages in the local economy that transmitted the positive effects of remittances to other households—including those that did not have migrants in the United States.

## *Short- and long-run remittance effects on migrant-sending households*

Traditionally, microeconomic researchers have treated migrant remittances as simple transfers affecting consumption but not production in migrant-sending households. That is, $1 in remittances translates into $1 of total income. However, the 1989 Michoacan survey data reveal that the marginal impact of remittances on total income was significantly greater than unity: a $1 increase in remittances brought about a $1.85 increase in total household income.

This finding is consistent with the view that remittances loosen constraints on local production, once migrants become established abroad. It contradicts the neoclassical household-farm model (e.g. Singh, Squire, and Strauss 1986), which implies that production is independent of migration and remittances. In the Mexican case, remittances also promoted the accumulation of livestock over time and increased the rate of return to livestock assets (through complimentary investments; see Taylor 1992). The livestock sector's contribution to total income rose from 23 per cent in 1982 to 42 per cent in 1988. When remittances were interacted with household holdings of liquid and illiquid asset, the interaction terms were significant and the direct effect of remittances became insignificant. Just as the new economics of migration theory would predict, the marginal income effect of remittances was greatest in the most liquidity-constrained households (Taylor and Wyatt 1996).

## *Local economy-wide effects*

Village SAM techniques were used to explore the role of income and expenditure linkages in transmitting the impacts of remittances from migrant households to others within migrant-sending economies. Table 9.3 summarizes findings for the

Table 9.3. *Estimated village remittance multipliers, 1988*

| Sector | International migration remittance multiplier | Internal migration remittance multiplier |
|---|---|---|
| *Production* | | |
| Basic grains | 0.15 | 0.20 |
| Livestock | 0.35 | 0.51 |
| Resource extraction | 0.07 | 0.09 |
| Nonagricultural | 0.05 | 0.99 |
| Retail | 1.02 | 0.99 |
| *Value Added* | | |
| Family labor | 0.16 | 0.20 |
| Hired labor | 0.02 | 0.03 |
| Capital | 0.19 | 0.24 |
| Land | 0.22 | 0.31 |
| *Gross Village Product* | 0.60 | 0.78 |
| *Household Incomes* | | |
| Landless | 0.07 (0.04) | 0.17 (0.13) |
| Small landholder | 0.84 (0.56) | 0.36 (0.00) |
| Large landholder | 0.67 (0.39) | 1.22 (0.87) |
| *Investment* | | |
| Physical capital | 0.17 | 0.31 |
| Human capital | 0.03 | 0.05 |

*Note*: Numbers in the table represent the absolute effects of a $1 increase in migrant remittances on the corresponding account total. Numbers in parentheses are shares of the remittance change accruing to each household group.

*Source*: Taylor (1995).

Michoacan survey area. The 1988 remittance multipliers reveal that village income linkages from remittances potentially are large. A US $1 increase in international migrant remittances or savings brought back to the village by migrants results in a $1.60 increase in total village income. That is, it contributes the $1 of remittances and stimulates a $.60 increase in value-added from local production. This "remittance multiplier" does not include the indirect, NELM effects of remittances on migrant households, discussed above.

In the Michoacan case, the direct and indirect benefits of migration are unequally distributed across household groups. On the production side, the largest remittance multipliers are in basic grains, livestock, and especially the retail sectors. A $1 increase in U.S. remittances in 1988 stimulates a $.15 increase in basic grain production, a $.35 increase in livestock output, and a $1.02 increase in the demand for manufactured goods (retail). These numbers illustrate the importance of remittances in generating household demand for village goods. Because the retail sector is essentially a village import sector, the high retail multiplier indicates that remittances also create a significant rural-demand stimulus for industrial production.

Increased production generates value-added within the village that is relatively evenly distributed among family labor, physical capital, and land. Hired labor value-add changes little ($.02). These findings illustrate the family-input intensity of production in this village and a minimal use of hired labor as a substitute for family labor. That is, there is only slight evidence of a functioning local labor market.

Table 9.3 reports total multiplier effects of a $1 increase in U.S. remittances on the income of each household group. These household-income multipliers include the remittances themselves plus the second-round effects of remittances to all household groups on income from village production. The increases in remittances to each household group are presented in parentheses. The differences between the two numbers represent the second-round multiplier effects of the $1 of remittances on household incomes. Even if a household group does not receive remittances, it nevertheless may benefit from second-round effects if remittances stimulate village production activities in which households within the group are engaged.

Remittances from U.S. migrants unquestionably favor small-holder households. These households receive, on average, $.56 per dollar of U.S. remittances, and they benefit handsomely from second-round effects. Their total income increases by 84 cents. In other words, while receiving 56 per cent of U.S. remittances, small-holder households also capture 47 per cent ($.28) of the remittance multiplier on village value-added. Similarly, large-holder households receive $.39 of the average U.S. remittance dollar, and the multiplier effect of one dollar of remittances on their total income is $.67.

In contrast, landless households receive, on average, only 4 cents per dollar of U.S. remittances. They benefit only slightly from second-round multiplier effects of remittances on village production (3 cents, for a total increase of 7 cents in the table). In sum, the first and second-round effects of U.S. remittances favor small-holder households and, to a lesser extent, large-holder households. Landless households do not lose from U.S. migration, but they do not gain much, either.

This finding reflects obstacles to relatively expensive and risky international migration for landless households. International migration risks include those of apprehension during or after illegal border crossings as well as employment risks in migrant labor markets. Family contacts in the United States can substantially reduce migration risks by not only providing job information and placement but also by matching new migrants up with trusted coyotes, or labor smugglers; financing the border crossing; and paying smugglers only after the new migrant is safely in the United States, thus shifting the financial risks of the border crossing from migrant to smuggler.

The finding also reveals weak income linkages to spread the benefits of U.S. migration to the village landless. The multiplier effects of international migrant remittances are different from those of internal migrant remittances. While small-holder households specialize in international migration, internal migrant remittances favor landless (13 per cent) and especially large-holder (87 per cent) households (Column B). As in the case of international migrant remittances, however, the second-round effects do not benefit the landless; only 3 cents of the $.78 multiplier of internal migrant remittances on village value added accrue to this group. By contrast, small-holder households, who do not receive remittances from internal migrants, benefit indirectly by capturing $.36 (46 per cent) of the increased village value-added. The total multiplier effect of internal remittances on large-holder incomes is $1.22, including a direct effect of $.87 and an indirect multiplier effect of $.35.

Production multipliers from internal remittances reflect the relatively favorable impacts of landless households' expenditure patterns and of their investment demand on village production. Basic grains account for a large marginal share of landless-household budgets but not the budgets of the other two household groups. By favoring the landless, internal remittances create a larger stimulus to basic grain production than international remittances. (The internal-remittance multiplier on basic grains production is $.20.) Large-holder households, for which the income multiplier of internal remittances is largest, have by far the highest savings rates of all household groups. In the absence of a well-functioning credit market, these savings are channeled primarily into livestock demand. The livestock-production multiplier is nearly 50 per cent higher from internal remittances ($.51) than from Mexico-to-U.S. migrant remittances ($.35).

Computable General Equilibrium village models (Taylor 1995; Taylor and Adelman 1996) yield similar findings with regard to the total income effects, but not the distributional effects, of international migrant remittances. In these models (and most likely in the real world), migration complements some local production activities but competes with others. The distributional effects of remittances depend critically on the extent to which various household groups are involved in local production activities that are stimulated by the injection of migrant remittances into the local economy. This creates a patchwork of local winners and losers from (some) households' participation in international migration (Taylor 1995).

## REMITTANCES, SAVINGS, AND DEVELOPMENT RECONSIDERED

Migration influences local economies in ways that are usually overlooked by migration research. Direct contributions of migrant remittances and savings to incomes in migrant-sending households typically are large. The new economics of migration posits, and empirical studies document, positive indirect effects of remittances on migrant-household incomes. As a result of these indirect effects, $1 of migrant remittances and savings may contribute more than $1 to total income in migrant-sending households. Expenditure linkages, in turn, transmit the impacts of migration from migrant to non-migrant households. Because of the importance of income linkages in migrant-sending economies, remittance-use surveys of migrant households are likely to offer a limited and distorted picture of the impacts of remittances. Migration and remittances unleash an array of income and price effects which tend to transform village production and influence incomes even in households that do not contain migrants. Many of migration's impacts on local economies are not to be found within the migrant households themselves.

In the short run, the loss of labor to migration and a higher opportunity cost of family time may create trade-offs between migration and local production. However, in the long run, migrant-sending economies benefit from the increased savings made possible by migration. The findings from the Mexico case study presented above support the new economics of labor migration hypothesis that migrants act as financial intermediaries, loosening credit constraints on investment in local production (Stark 1982). They do this by providing their households of origin with access to liquidity, in the form of migrant remittances. They also may promote investments by offering income insurance, promising to assist households in times of economic distress or in the event that new investments fail to produce.

Despite the relatively optimistic picture of migrant remittances, savings, and incomes in migrant-sending areas presented in this chapter, one cannot overemphasize that migration is not a substitute for sound macroeconomic policies and well-designed development strategies in migrant-sending economies. Misguided economic policies both stimulate migration and may seriously limit productive investment opportunities for the savings created by migrants. The migration-and-development literature includes a proliferation of pessimistic case studies in which international migration allegedly did not promote development in migrant-sending areas.

However, none of these pessimistic case studies refer to countries that are models of sound macroeconomic management or growth-oriented development policy. In the Mexican case, in spite of what obviously was a less than ideal policy and economic environment, abundant land for grazing, a new market-oriented development strategy on the part of the Mexican government, and the construction of a new road connecting villages to outside markets probably were critical factors promoting local income growth from remittances.

Where natural resource constraints are more binding, infrastructure is poor, and government policies are not conducive to promoting income growth, the effects of remittances on local incomes obviously will be different: migration may displace local production activities, leading to a "Dutch disease" scenario in which economies specialize in the export of migrants rather than in the production of other "tradables." In economies specializing in "migrant-exports," the possibilities for promoting productive growth linkages from migration are relatively limited.

The policy lesson that stands out from this research is that creating a fertile ground for migration and remittances to contribute to broad-based income growth in migrant-sending areas is the key to promoting migration–development interactions. In most cases, what is needed are not special programs to harness remittances and savings from migrants abroad, but rather sound macroeconomic policies that encourage the productive use of migrant remittances and savings at home.

## References

Adams, Jr., Richard H. (1989). "Worker Remittances and Inequality in Rural Egypt," *Economic Development and Cultural Change*, 38: 45–71.

——(1991). "The Economic uses and Impact of International Remittances in Rural Egypt," *Economic Development and Cultural Change*, 39: 695–722.

Adelman, Irma, and Taylor, J. Edward (1990). "Is Structural Adjustment with a Human Face Possible? The Case of Mexico," *Journal of Development Studies* 26: 387–407.

——Taylor, J. Edward, and Vogel, Stephen (1988). "Life in a Mexican Village: A SAM Perspective," *Journal of Development Studies*, 25: 5–24.

Bohning, Wolf R. (1981). *Black Migration to South Africa: A Selection of Policy-Oriented Research.* Geneva: International Labour Office.

Diaz-Briquets, Sergio (1991). "The Effects of International Migration on Latin America," in Demetrios G. Papademetriou and Philip L. Martin (eds.), *The Unsettled Relationship: Labor Migration and Economic Development.* New York: Greenwood, pp. 183–200.

Durand, Jorge, and Massey, Douglas S. (1992). "Mexican Migration to the United States: A Critical Review," *Latin American Research Review*, 27: 3–42.

——Kandel, William, Parrado, Emilio A., and Massey, Douglas S. (1996). "International Migration and Development in Mexican Sending Communities," *Demography*, 33: 249–64.

Fletcher, Peri L., and Taylor, J. Edward. "Mexico-to-U.S. Migration and the Village Household Economy," Presented at University of Chicago, Conference on New Perspectives on Mexico–U.S. Migration. October 1992.

Golan, Elise H. (1996). "The Village Economy and Tenure Security in West Africa: A Senegalese Village SAM," in J. E. Taylor and I. Adelman (eds.), *Village Economies: The Design, Estimation, and Use of Villagewide Economic Models.* Cambridge: Cambridge University Press, pp. 31–58.

Kearney, Michael (1986). "From the Invisible Hand to Visible Feet: Anthropological Studies of Migration and Development," *Annual Review of Anthropology*, 15: 331–61.

Lewis, B. D., and Thorbecke, E. (1992). "District-Level Economic Linkages in Kenya: Evidence Based on a Small Regional Social Accounting Matrix," *World Development*, 20(6): 881–97.

Lozano Ascencio, Fernando (1993). *Bringing it Back Home: Remittances to Mexico from Migrant Workers in the United States.* Monograph Series 37, Center for U.S.–Mexican Studies, La Jolla, CA: University of California at San Diego.

Lucas, Robert E. B. (1985). "Emigration to South Africa's Mines," *American Economic Review*, 77: 313–330.

——and Stark, Oded (1985). "Motivations to Remit: Evidence from Botswana," *Journal of Political Economy*, 93: 901–18.

Lustig, Nora, and Ross, J. (1987). *Stabilisation and Adjustment Policies and Programmes: Country Study 7, Mexico.* Helsinki: WIDER.

Massey, Douglas S., and Parrado, Emilio (1994). "Migradollars: The Remittances and Savings of Mexican Migrants to the USA," *Population Research and Policy Review*, 13: 3–30.

Papademetriou, Demetrios G., and Martin, Philip L. (1991) (eds.), *The Unsettled Relationship: Labor Migration and Economic Development.* New York: Greenwood.

Ralston, Katherine (1995). "Household Nutrition and Economic Linkages: A Village Social Accounting Matrix for West Java, Indonesia," in J. Edward Taylor and Irma Adelman (eds.), *Village Economies: The Design, Estimation and Application of Village-Wide Economic Models.* Cambridge: Cambridge University Press, pp. 173–213.

Ravallion, Martin, and Chaudhuri, Shubham (1996). "Risk and Insurance in Village India: A Comment," *Econometrica*, 65: 171–84.

Reardon, T., Delgado, C., and Matlon, P. (1992). "Determinants and Effects of Income Diversification Amongst Farm Households in Burkina Faso," *Journal of Development Studies*, 28: 264–96.

Reichert, Joshua S. (1981). "The Migrant Syndrome: Seasonal U.S. Wage Labor and Rural Development in Central Mexico," *Human Organization*, 40: 56–66.

Rubenstein, Hymie (1983). "Remittances and Rural Underdevelopment in the English-Speaking Caribbean," *Human Organization*, 42: 295–306.

Russell, Sharon S. (1992). "Migrant Remittances and Development," *International Migration*, 30: 267–88.

Russell, Sharon S., and Teitelbaum, Michael S. (1992). *International Migration and International Trade*. Washington, DC: The World Bank.

Singh, I., Squire, L., and Strauss, J. (1986). *Agricultural Household Models, Extensions, Applications and Policy*. Baltimore: The World Bank and The Johns Hopkins University Press.

Stark, Oded (1980). "On the Role of Urban-to-Rural Remittances in Rural Development," *Journal of Development Studies*, 16: 369–74.

—— (1982). "Research on Rural-to-Urban Migration in Less Developed Countries: The Confusion Frontier and Why We Should Pause to Rethink Afresh," *World Development*, 10: 70–73.

—— and Katz, E. (1986). "Labor Migration and Risk Aversion in Less Developed Countries," *Journal of Labor Economics*, 4: 134–49.

—— and Levhari, David (1982). "On Migration and Risk in LDCs," *Economic Development and Cultural Change*, 31: 191–6.

—— and Lucas, Robert E. B. (1988). "Migration, Remittances and the Family." *Economic Development and Cultural Change*, 36: 465–81.

—— and Rosenzweig, Mark R. (1989). "Consumption Smoothing, Migration and Marriage: Evidence from Rural India," *Journal of Political Economy*, 97(4): 905–26.

—— Taylor, J. Edward, and Yitzhaki, Shlomo (1986). "Remittances and Inequality," *The Economic Journal*, 96: 722–40.

—— —— (1988). "Migration, Remittances in Inequality: A Sensitivity Analysis Using the Extended Gini Index," *Journal of Development Economics*, 28: 309–22.

Stuart, James, and Kearney, Michael (1981). *Causes and Effects of Agricultural Labor Migration from the Mixteca of Oaxaca to California*. La Jolla: Center for U.S.–Mexican Studies, University of California, San Diego.

Subramanian, Shankar (1995). "Wage Labor, Sharecropping, and Credit Transactions," *Oxford Economic Papers*, 47: 329–56.

—— and Sadoulet, E. (1990). "The Transmission of Production Fluctuations and Technical Change in a Village Economy: A Social Accounting Matrix Approach," *Economic Development and Cultural Change*, 39: 131–73.

Swanson, Jon C. (1979). "The Consequences of Emigration for Economic Development: A Review of the Literature," *Papers in Anthropology*, 20: 39–56.

Taylor, J. Edward (1992). "Remittances and Inequality Reconsidered: Direct, Indirect and Intertemporal Effects," *Journal of Policy Modelling*, 14: 187–208.

—— (1995). *Micro Economywide Models for Migration and Policy Analysis: An Application to Rural Mexico*. Paris: Organisation for Economic Cooperation and Development.

—— (1996). "International Migration and Economic Development: A Micro Economy-Wide Perspective," in J. E. Taylor (ed.), *Development Strategy, Employment, and Migration: Insights from Models*. Paris: OECD.

—— and Adelman, Irma (1996). *Village Economies: The Design, Estimation and Application of Village-Wide Economic Models*. Cambridge: Cambridge University Press.

——————————(1996*a*). "International Migration and National Development," *Population Index*, 62: 181–212.

——Massey, D. S., Arango, J., Hugo, G., Kouaouci, A., and Pellegrino, A. (1996*b*). "International Migration and Community Development," *Population Index*, 62: 397–418.

——and Wyatt, T. J. (1996). "The Shadow Value of Migrant Remittances, Income and Inequality in a Household-farm Economy," *Journal of Development Studies*, 32: 899–912.

——Yunez, Antonion, and Dyer-Leal, George (1999). "Agricultural Price Policy, Employment, and Migration in a Diversified Rural Economy: A Village–Town CGE Analysis from Mexico," *American Journal of Agricultural Economics*, 81: 653–62.

——and Zabin, Carol (1996). "Migration and Development in a Conflict Zone: A Micro Economywide Perspective," Allied Social Science Association Annual Meetings (North American Finance Association), San Francisco, January 5.

United States Department of Justice (1992). *Immigration Reform and Control Act: Report on the Legalized Alien Population*. Washington, DC: U.S. Department of Justice, Immigration and Naturalization Service (March 1992).

Wiest, Raymond E. (1979). "Implications of International Labor Migration for Mexican Rural Development," in Fernando Camara and Robert Van Kemper (eds.), *Migration across Frontiers: Mexico and the United States*. Contributions of the Latin American Anthropology Group, vol. 3. Albany, N.Y.: Institute of Mesoamerican Studies, State University of New York, pp. 85–97.

# 10

## Labor Export Strategies in Asia

GRAEME HUGO AND CHARLES STAHL

Most theoretical work on the initiation and perpetuation of contemporary international migration has given priority to market forces and social networks (see Massey et al. 1993, 1998). Often overlooked is the fact that governments can and do intervene to influence the extent to which migrants with particular characteristics are permitted to enter or leave a country and the nature of their host-country experiences. Nation states are crucial players influencing the scale, direction, and composition of international movement, and policies governing migration and settlement have assumed greater importance politically, economically, socially, and demographically.

Whenever policies have been studied, attention has focused primarily on those countries that experience net gains in overseas contract workers, especially on their efforts to restrict the numbers and characteristics of migrants (see Martin, Mason, and Nagayama 1996). However, in several developing Asian nations, governments have devoted increasing attention to the economic and social implications of labor export, and to the possibility that international migration might be harnessed to improve the prospects for economic development and accomplish specific developmental objectives.

To date, governmental efforts to shape the character, extent, and direction of labor export have preferred international market mechanisms. Most of the major labor-exporting countries—Bangladesh, India, Indonesia, Pakistan, Philippines, Thailand—rely mainly on private recruiters to serve as middlemen between workers and overseas employers. In some countries, rules and regulations have been enacted to curb the excesses of those recruiters who take advantage of the global oversupply of workers to exploit migrants. At times national governments have become actively involved in marketing workers abroad. In the Philippines, for example, the Philippine Overseas Employment Administration has gone beyond simply regulating and registering recruiters and workers; it actively promotes the export of Philippine workers abroad. It and private agencies are together responsible for the fact that in the late 1990s there were some 6.1 million Filipino emigrants spread across 130 different countries (Saywell 1997). In contrast, until recently Vietnam and China have sought to minimize the role of private recruiters, preferring instead to broker deals for labor export on a government-to-government basis. As a consequence, they have played relatively small roles in labor export.

A principal objective of this chapter is to review and assess governmental attempts to shape the extent, character, and direction of labor export. In doing so, we recognize two overlapping systems of international migration: one occurring in the context of officially recognized institutions and the other based on illegal, clandestine, and informal mechanisms. Naturally, there are significant differences in the ability of governments to influence these two migratory systems. A second objective is to consider the future of Asian labor migration by assessing likely changes in the economic and demographic structure of labor-importing societies and their potential influence on the occupational and geographic selectivity of emigration.

## LABOR EXPORT IN ASIA

In the massive expansion of international migration throughout Asia over the last two decades, the movement of contract workers has been greatest. While data relating to workers migrating though official channels are limited, information about the large number who migrate without authorization is almost totally lacking (Arthukorala and Wickramasekara 1996). As of the mid-1990s, Hugo (1997) estimated that there were more than 10 million Asian migrant workers deployed throughout the Middle East and Asia.

Table 10.1 lists the major labor-exporting nations of Asia, along with a rough estimate of the number of workers overseas in the mid-1990s. In absolute terms they range from a low of 60,000 from Vietnam to a high of 6.2 million from the Philippines. Two other countries—India and Indonesia—also exhibited labor exports in the millions (1.4 million workers from the former and 2.4 million from the latter). Pakistan was also a major supplier of international labor with 828,000 expatriate workers.

Official positions with respect to labor export vary considerably from country to country. Although all of the nations in Table 10.1 express general support for overseas workers, some have tried to limit movements to particular types of people at particular times. Others have incorporated labor export as an explicit strategy within a national plan for economic development. Indonesia, for example, listed "Manpower Services Export" as the sixth of seven policy priorities in the labor section of its Sixth National Five Year Development Plan. It explicitly sought to increase the number of Indonesians deployed overseas to augment the inflow of remittances, going so far as to specify the skill profiles migrant workers would need for employment in different labor-importing countries.

### *Benefits of labor export*

Labor-exporting governments have articulated a number of objectives they seek to achieve by encouraging, facilitating, and endorsing international migration. Perhaps the most common is the generation of remittances to pay foreign debts, finance trade

**Table 10.1.** *Asia: Major labor exporting nations and estimates of the number of workers deployed overseas in the mid-1990s*

| Country | Year | Main destination(s) | Number deployed overseas |
|---|---|---|---|
| India | 1992 | Middle East | 1,426,000 |
| Pakistan | 1992 | Middle East | 828,000 |
| Bangladesh | 1992 | Middle East, Malaysia, Singapore, Thailand | 508,000 |
| Sri Lanka | 1992 | Middle East, Malaysia, Singapore, Thailand | 453,000 |
| Myanmar | 1996 | Thailand | 415,000 |
| Philippines | 1997 | Hong Kong, Middle East, Japan, Taiwan, Singapore | 6,100,000 |
| Thailand | 1995 | Middle East, Taiwan, Singapore, Japan, Brunei | 203,000 |
| Indonesia | 1997 | Middle East, Malaysia, Singapore, Hong Kong | 2,404,000 |
| China | 1996 | Japan, Middle East | 380,000 |
| Korea | 1995 | Middle East, Japan | 190,000 |
| Vietnam | 1992 | Europe | 60,000 |
| Malaysia | 1995 | Singapore, Taiwan, Brunei, Japan | 200,000 |

*Source*: Hugo (1997).

deficits, and improve balance of payments. In this sense, sending workers overseas is seen in the same way as the export of any other commodity—as a means of generating foreign earnings.

Although the orthodoxy of the 1970s regarded remittances as minor in scale and modest in effect, larger movements and more accurate measurement in the 1980s changed this thinking substantially. Recent research has established that remittances are substantial in both absolute and relative terms (Russell and Teitelbaum 1992; Massey et al. 1998). Although most remittances go toward consumption, a significant share is inevitably invested in production (Taylor et al. 1996), and even those remittances destined for consumption have significant multiplier effects that strongly promote development (Stahl and Arnold 1986; Stahl and Habib 1989; Taylor et al. 1996).

In addition to the generation of remittances, another objective of labor exportation is relief of under- and unemployment. Although most Asian nations have relatively low rates of open unemployment, underemployment is quite common and many governments view labor export as a partial solution to the lack of jobs. Another justification for labor migration is that it provides workers with training and skills that can be employed later to promote development at home. Yet another rationale is that labor export strengthens bilateral relations to facilitate broader linkages (e.g. trade) that might promote development. Finally, labor migration is seen as a means of alleviating regional imbalances in wealth. In most labor-exporting nations, workers are recruited selectively from certain regions, such as Kerala in India or Java and Nusatenggara in Indonesia. As these provinces are among the poorest, the resulting spatial concentration of remittances will help to promote a more balanced pattern of growth and development (Hugo 1996).

### *Costs of labor export*

Each of the nations listed in Table 10.1 also houses movements that oppose government policies to promote labor export. Their opposition is articulated in the media by academics, parliamentarians, religious leaders, and officials of NGOs. In some cases, opposition takes the form of rebuttals against governmental justifications for labor export; but there have also been other, more principled, objections to labor emigration. Perhaps the oldest and most prominent concerns the "brain drain," the potential loss of people bearing scarce skills, education, and training necessary for domestic development. Another issue concerns the potential abuse of female migrants, who in industries such as domestic service and entertainment are especially vulnerable to exploitation.

A final criticism is that the exportation of labor promotes national dependency. As countries come to depend on remittances to finance trade deficits and generate hard currency for investment, they become vulnerable to external conditions over which they have no control. Critics point to the negative effect of the Gulf War of 1990 on countries such as Pakistan, India, Indonesia, and the Philippines, which not only had to accommodate a sudden influx of returning migrant workers but also suffered a severe loss of foreign exchange (see the articles in the April/June 1992 issue of *Asian Migrant*). An emerging theme in the Philippines is that reliance on labor export and its associated remittances constitutes a source of "national shame."

### *To export or not to export?*

Although labor export may bruise national pride and generate certain difficulties for migrants, families, communities, and governments, it is also true that most labor-exporting Asian nations will not be able fully to absorb additions to their workforce for the foreseeable future, let alone reduce the ranks of the under- and unemployed (Hugo 1998). Job shortages loom large despite the fact that some Asian nations have dramatically reduced fertility levels, undertaken economic restructuring, and are now on the road to rapid, market-led economic growth. Table 10.2 projects nonagricultural wage employment relative to total labor force growth over the next 5–10 years to indicate the scale of the problem these nations will face.

The figures in the last column provide rough estimates, based on recent trends, of the number of nonagricultural wage jobs generated per worker in different Asian labor-exporting nations. A value of 1.0 indicates that projected job growth is expected roughly to equal projected labor force growth, implying that new workers can be absorbed without generating underemployment. A value over 1.0 indicates

**Table 10.2.** *Projected growth of nonagricultural wage employment in selected labor-exporting countries*

| Country | Nonagricultural wage employment as a share of total employment | | Annual growth of nonagricultural wage employment | | Annual growth rate of labor force 1995–2000 | Projected nonagricultural jobs per labor force entrant |
|---|---|---|---|---|---|---|
| | Percent | Year | Rate | Period | | |
| Bangladesh | 29.3 | 1990 | 4.08 | 1985–90 | 2.12 | 0.56 |
| China | 25.8 | 1993 | 6.47 | 1989–93 | 1.08 | 1.54 |
| India | 32.0 | 1996 | 1.36 | 1985–89 | 1.97 | 0.22 |
| Indonesia | 42.8 | 1992 | 1.80 | 1985–92 | 2.53 | 0.30 |
| Pakistan | 38.8 | 1994 | 3.36 | 1985–94 | 3.37 | 0.37 |
| Philippines | 50.6 | 1994 | 3.99 | 1985–94 | 2.70 | 0.75 |
| Thailand | 38.5 | 1991 | 10.28 | 1985–91 | 1.29 | 3.07 |

*Sources*: International Labor Organization (1995); World Bank (1997).

that employment will grow faster than the labor force, and a value less than 1.0 means that job growth will lag behind labor force expansion.

At current rates of growth, for example, Pakistan will only be able to employ 37 per cent of the likely additions to its labor force over the next few years. Prospects for India are even worse: only 22 per cent of additions to the workforce will be absorbed into productive employment. And these figures refer only to new labor force entrants—they do not account for the vast number of workers who are currently underemployed or unemployed workers and still need to be absorbed. Nor do they allow for possible increases in rates of nonagricultural labor force participation.

The latter consideration is particularly relevant in the case of China. Although the table shows that the country is generating nonagricultural wage employment at a rate in excess of the number of new entrants to its labor force, it still has a vast army of surplus labor—in the neighborhood of 100 million workers—within its agricultural sector. At China's current rate of nonagricultural job creation, it would take many years for these surplus workers to be absorbed into productive employment. Hence, emigration pressures are expected to continue in China for the foreseeable future.

In contrast, Thailand has reached a "turning point" in its history of labor migration. The Thai economy is projected to generate nonagricultural jobs at a rate over three times the rate of labor force growth (assuming the growth rates that prevailed before the 1997–8 crisis). This high rate of economic growth has already absorbed thousands of underemployed Thais and hundreds of thousands of workers from surrounding countries (Stahl 1997). As the Thai case indicates, the key to reducing emigration is a reduction in labor force growth rates combined with an effective strategy of economic development. Table 10.2 indicates that the major Asian labor exporters still have a considerable way to go before they reach a similar "turning point" in their histories of labor migration.

While *government involvement* in labor export varies between the countries of Table 10.1, each of them now contains a well-developed *private labor export industry* composed of worker agencies, travel agents, lawyers, and other middlemen who facilitate international movement (Goss and Lindquist 1995). These intermediaries are of crucial importance not only in supporting official flows of documented workers, but even more so in promoting the much larger flows of workers migrating without documents. Indeed, illegal migration could not exist without a private sector dedicated to labor export.

The private labor export industry is highly developed and well organized in most countries and sometimes involves criminal syndicates. In any consideration of Asian labor export, the private entrepreneurs are of fundamental importance in shaping the scale and composition of emigration. Countries differ, however, in the degree to which labor recruitment has been left in the hands of private entrepreneurs. Government policies designed to influence the international export of labor by private actors fall into three categories: those that seek to enhance it, those that seek to control it, and those that seek to maximize the benefits and minimize the costs to promote national development. The various interventions that have been tried to this point are listed in Table 10.3. In each arena, government policies have impinged on both documented and undocumented migration and have varied in the extent and nature of public–private cooperation.

## STRATEGIES FOR LABOR EXPORT

### *Administrative agencies*

Most Asian labor-exporting countries have established one or more governmental agencies to supervise and control labor export. The export agencies created by various Asian governments are summarized in Table 10.4. Although they vary considerably in terms of form and function, they have generally sought to promote labor export in seven basic ways: (1) drawing upon bilateral government-to-government linkages, they have sought to develop new markets for overseas workers; (2) by placing labor attachés in foreign embassies they have sought to identify and develop new possibilities for labor export; (3) by establishing training and pre-departure orientation programs they have sought to provide contract workers with specific and general skills for overseas employment; (4) by establishing regional and local offices throughout the home country, they have sought to provide information about overseas employment opportunities and to facilitate the processing of applications by aspiring workers; (5) by streamlining application and transport, they have sought to minimize the time and money spent by both employers and workers in recruitment; (6) through advertising and propaganda, they have sought to disseminate information about opportunities for overseas work widely throughout the population; and (7) in some countries governments have actually become involved directly in labor export by establishing a recruitment organization to compete with those in the private sector. While most of these export agencies have been set up by national governments, in some large countries local governments have

**Table 10.3.** *Major types of policies relating to labor emigration in Asian countries*

| Policy goal | Government interventions |
|---|---|
| Promote employment | *Foreign market development*<br>1. Establish diplomatic relations<br>2. Strengthen placement services, public and private<br>3. Undertake promotions and marketing missions<br>4. Gather market information and undertake research<br>5. Negotiate bilateral agreements<br>*Manpower supply management*<br>1. Create manpower registry<br>2. Export corporate services<br>3. Implement restrictions against brain drain |
| Protect and promote well-being of migrants | *Standard setting and enforcement*<br>1. Establish minimum standards for employment contracts<br>2. Implement exit control measures<br>3. Make arrangements for social security<br>4. Restrict exit of selected workers (minors and young women)<br>*Supervision of private recruitment*<br>1. License recruitment firms<br>2. Set performance guarantees and penalties<br>3. Limit recruitment fees<br>4. Censure illegal recruitment and clandestine migration<br>*Welfare services*<br>1. Provide information and counseling prior to departure<br>2. Provide labor attaché services on site<br>3. Establish community centers for workers<br>4. Provide support services to families left behind<br>5. Provide returnee training and employment assistance<br>6. Prepare plans for emergency evacuation or repatriation |
| Maximize potential for economic development | *Migrant remittances*<br>1. Implement favorable exchange policies<br>2. Provide remittance policies and services<br>*Migrant savings and investments*<br>1. Create special financial instruments<br>2. Provide information and support services to small investors<br>3. Create special housing programs for migrants<br>*Return of talents and skills*<br>1. Provide special placement services and incentives<br>2. Negotiate bilateral training agreements |

*Sources*: Lim and Oishi (1996); Abella and Abrera-Mangahas (1995).

**Table 10.4.** *Government agencies involved in labor export activities in major Asian nations*

| Country | Institution | Main roles |
|---|---|---|
| Pakistan | Bureau of Emigration and Overseas Employment (BEOE) | 1. Regulate recruiters<br>2. Recruit and place workers |
| Philippines | Philippine Overseas Employment Administration (POEA)<br>Overseas Workers Welfare Administration (OWWA) | 1. Regulate recruiters<br>2. Recruit and place workers<br>3. Promote overseas employment |
| India | Protector General of Emigrants in Ministry of Labor (PGE) | 1. Regulate recruiters<br>2. Set minimum standards for contracts<br>3. Recruit and place workers |
| Bangladesh | Bangladesh Overseas Employment Services Limited (BOESL) | 1. Promotion of overseas employment |
| Sri Lanka | Foreign Employment Division of Department of Labor<br>Sri Lankan Bureau of Foreign Employment (SLBFE) | 1. Recruit and place workers<br>2. Control and monitor recruiters<br>3. Coordinate labor outflows with domestic market conditions<br>4. Administer overseas employment |
| Thailand | Overseas Employment Administration Office (OEAO) | 1. Regulate recruitment<br>2. Promote foreign employment |
| Indonesia | Directorate for Export of Indonesian Workers<br>P. T. Bijak | 1. Survey potential markets for workers<br>2. Provide training to overseas workers<br>3. Regulate recruitment<br>4. Recruit and place workers |

*Sources*: Athukorala (1993); Battistella (1995); Hugo (1995).

established their own agencies to encourage labor emigration from that region. In China, for example, each county has its own labor export company (Qian 1996).

Several labor-exporting nations have specified targets for the numbers and types of workers deployed overseas during particular years. For example, Indonesia's Sixth Five Year Plan outlined an ambitious "National Programme for the Export of Indonesian Workers" (Hugo 1995). It specifically sought to double the number of overseas workers to 1.25 million and raise the inflow of remittances sevenfold to US$8.4 billion between 1994 and 1999. The latter was to be achieved not only by increasing the number of Indonesian workers overseas but also by the gradual replacement of unskilled workers with semi-skilled workers (estimated to earn an average US$275 per month) and skilled workers (US$600 per month). The plan also sought to shift the geographic focus of exports toward Malaysia, where the estimated demand for foreign workers was projected to be 1.2 million over the period, of which Indonesia was expected to provide a total of 800,000 or two-thirds.

On a few occasions governments have attempted to ban particular types of movement to particular countries. In the late 1980s, for example, Bangladesh, Thailand,

and the Philippines banned the sending of women overseas to work in domestic service in countries where they were not protected by labor laws. In 1995 a Filipino maid in Singapore was convicted of murdering another Filipino and a 4-year-old Singaporean child and was executed. Subsequently, the Philippines government announced a ban on sending new domestic workers to Singapore and provided a plan for the voluntary repatriation of those already there.

In each of these cases and others, bans have been ineffective at best and at worst have led to a deterioration in conditions for overseas workers (Battistella 1995). To circumvent the bans, workers simply moved into the illegal migration system or migrate initially to a third country from where they later travel to the banned country. Hence, bans generally have not succeeded in their objective of reducing particular migration flows.

Thus far, we have considered government initiatives that have attempted to shape movements by some form of *direct* intervention, largely restricted to official flows of documented labor. It is also important to consider governmental actions (or in some cases the lack thereof) that influence labor export *indirectly*. Although often quite deliberate, these actions affect the illegal migratory system and the clandestine immigration industry that encourages and facilitates the movement of labor through it. Although governments in few labor-exporting nations have gone so far as to condone undocumented labor migration officially, most only facilitate it to the extent they fail to move against it in any sustained or effective way. Such passive acceptance of undocumented migration is also common in destination countries, although they nonetheless display considerable variation in the vigor of efforts to identify and repatriate illegal workers and to regulate and apply sanctions to businesses found to employ illegal workers.

Again the Indonesian case is illustrative. The migration of Indonesians to East and West Malaysia represents the largest bilateral flow of undocumented migrants anywhere in the region, with up to one million workers moving annually (Hugo 1995; Stahl 1997). Although a former Minister of Labor (Cosmos Batubara) was quoted in the media as fully condoning this illegal flow (see Hugo 1993), it is more the passive acceptance of such high levels of illegal migration that allows the movement to continue virtually unimpeded and relatively openly. The origins of the illegal migrants are well known, the departure points for smuggling boats crossing the Malacca Straits are well established (leaving mainly from East Nusatenggara and Sulawesi), and local officials generally assume that illegal migration is one of the few sources of employment and income available to people in the region. Hence, they are not highly motivated to intervene and there is little official pressure from above to do so.

It may not be clear why aspiring Indonesian overseas workers would opt to travel illegally when there is an officially sanctioned legal system available to them. In general, the government has not been able to devise an official migratory system capable of competing effectively with the unofficial system in a variety of areas. First, the unofficial system is often (but not always) cheaper because legal migrants are frequently forced to make unauthorized payments to officials at various points in the migration process. Nayyar (1996) reports that migrants going through the official system are generally expected to pay a fee equivalent to US$325 (i.e. the average GNP per capita in Indonesia) to go to West Malaysia, whereas the costs of illegal migration range from as little as $25 in Batam (Nayyar 1996) to $200 from West Nusatenggara (Mujiyani, personal communication).

In addition, in the official system migrant workers usually have to make a large up-front payment, which requires them or their families having to raise the funds through a loan from a money lender or by selling property. In contrast, under the illegal system they can work off the cost by having substantial sums taken out of their salaries by the employer at the destination thus requiring up-front outlay. Compared with clandestine migration, the official system is also extremely time consuming and cumbersome, involving the completion of twenty documents and gathering as many as thirty-three signatures (Prijono 1993). As a result, prospective migrants often have to make several costly trips to a designated labor export city and typically experience a delay of 3 months between recruitment and overseas deployment, in contrast to delays of as little as a week in the unofficial system.

Finally, the chain of middlemen involved in conveying illegal migrants to Malaysia often begins with a local *calo* (recruiter) who resides in their home community (Hugo 1993, 1995; Spaan 1994) providing local accountability and security. The fact that the process of legal migration has not been streamlined by government yields a definite advantage to the private sector traffickers. Official acquiescence to the illegal migration industry also extends to the lack of activity in dealing with the burgeoning trade in illegal travel documents and identification papers. Hence, Battistella (1995: 226) points out that "in the Philippines there has been no effective measure to avoid the forging of passports and other documents."

## *Controlling worker characteristics*

Governments of most labor-exporting nations also attempt to exercise some control over the characteristics of workers who are allowed to emigrate by implementing various screening procedures, particularly for women. Table 10.5, for example, lists regulations implemented in different countries to restrict and regulate women seeking to work overseas. These range from bans on women workers in certain occupations to restrictions on the basis of age. These restrictions are mainly meant to protect vulnerable workers, but they often have the effect of forcing some women to resort to illegal channels, which exposes them to greater risks.

A long-standing concern of developing countries has been that labor export involves a "brain drain." This term emerged in the 1960s to describe the selective departure of the most skilled, educated, entrepreneurial, and risk-taking people. The loss of even small numbers of such individuals can have a disproportionately large negative effect on a country and can constitute a significant barrier to economic and social development. In the early postwar decades, there is little doubt that many Asian countries experienced a significant brain drain. Although international emigration from Asia was limited in scale and had little demographic effect, most of the movement involved highly qualified personnel moving to developed countries such

**Table 10.5.** *Restrictions on female worker migration in Asian labor exporting nations*

| Country | Restrictions |
|---|---|
| Bangladesh | Must be aged 25+ for employment as domestic worker<br>Ban on recruitment of entertainers |
| India | Must be aged 30+ for employment as domestic worker in Western Asia or North Africa. Exceptions on case-by-case basis. |
| Indonesia | Must be aged 22+<br>Restrictions on place of employment for household workers<br>Restrictions on ratio of female to male migrant workers<br>Above restrictions may be waived for authorized agents under certain conditions |
| Myanmar | Ban on recruitment except for professionals |
| Nepal | None |
| Malaysia | None |
| Pakistan | Must be aged 35+ for employment as domestic worker<br>Ban on recruitment of nurses |
| Philippines | Domestic workers must be aged 25+; selective bans to certain countries<br>Entertainers must be 23+ and complete academic and skills test, possess artist record book, and undergo pre-departure showcase preview; selective bans to certain countries<br>Nurses must be aged 23+, have B.S. in Nursing, and one year of experience |
| Sri Lanka | Must be 20+ for employment as domestic worker<br>Ban on recruitment of entertainers |
| Thailand | Ban on recruitment of women except for certain countries<br>Entertainers must hold license, diploma from school of art, and must not perform in night clubs |

*Source*: Lim and Oishi (1996).

as Britain or the United States. The brain drain to the latter was greatly facilitated by the 1965 amendments to U.S. immigration law, which created a special preference for skilled workers as it eliminated the ban on Asian immigration (Fortney 1972; Pernia 1976).

According to Adams (1969), the drain from Taiwan and Korea was most serious: in the late 1960s over 90 per cent of students from these countries who arrived for training in the United States never returned home. He estimated that "the United States would have to build and operate 12 new medical schools to produce the manpower provided through immigration... the annual dollar value of this 'foreign aid' to the United States approximately equals the cost of all its medical aid, private and public, to foreign nations" (Adams 1969: 1–2). In fiscal year 1970, of the 13,300 scientists and engineers immigrating to the United States, 56 per cent originated in Asia; and of the 3,200 immigrant physicians and surgeons arriving in the same year, 53 per cent came from this region (National Science Foundation 1972: 3).

During the 1960s, Chang (1992) estimates that only 5 per cent of the 21,248 students who left Taiwan for advanced study abroad returned, while during the period 1971–86 only 15 per cent of the 65,0000 overseas students did so. In the 5 years preceding 1981, one of five college graduates in science and technology went abroad and only 10 per cent ultimately returned.

In the last two decades, however, the situation has become more complex and recent thinking has recognized that in some contexts the emigration of skilled personnel can have beneficial effects on sending countries owing to mismatches between labor supply and demand, inflows of remittances from skilled migrants working abroad, significant return migration with enhanced skills and capacities, and the forging of broader economic linkages between origin and destination countries (Taylor et al. 1996).

Nevertheless, in some Asian countries the brain drain continues to be significant, prompting governments to implement strict exit controls. As Athukorala (1993: 55) points out, "labour legislation in Bangladesh, Sri Lanka, Thailand, and the Philippines provides for the enforcement of restriction/prohibition on the export of workers possessing certain skills or belonging to certain occupational categories except for a few isolated instances." Other countries, however, adopt the opposite stance. India, for example, exempts a growing range of professional workers from the need for emigration clearance. In 1990, exempted categories included medical doctors, engineers, chartered accountants, scientists, lecturers, teachers, advocates, all persons staying abroad for more than 3 years, seamen with accepted qualifications, all income tax payers and persons holding graduate or higher degrees (Athukorala 1993: 54). In other words, the Indian government actively encouraged a "brain drain" as part of a broader effort to secure remittances and alleviate underemployment.

To a considerable degree India is characterized by an "over-production" of highly qualified workers relative to its absorptive capacity, so that remittances and other contributions by emigrants are of greater developmental benefit than underemployment at home (Hugo et al. 1996). In contrast, Indonesia experiences significant labor shortages in many skilled areas. Nonetheless, the government recently announced its intention to increase greatly the number of skilled overseas workers and to phase out unskilled and semi-skilled workers. Since the former are in under-supply and the latter in oversupply, this policy is difficult to understand (Hugo 1995).

## *Regulating labor exports*

A major objective of government agencies involved in Asian labor export is the regulation and control of the movements. In some countries, government sees its role as one of regulating the activities of the private immigration industry rather than trying to play a direct role in the recruitment or deployment of workers overseas. The media in labor-exporting countries is replete with stories of exploitative recruitment practices, including the overcharging of prospective migrants; providing misleading information about working conditions, type of work, and rates of remuneration; offering bogus information about jobs, which turn out to be unavailable when the migrant arrives; colluding with employers to deduct disproportionate amounts from salaries to pay off the "costs" of recruitment and deployment; and providing little or no backup support at the point of destination (see Singhanetra-Renard 1992).

Each labor-exporting country has a set of regulations that specifies the obligations of recruiters toward migrant workers, maximum fees, expected services, qualifications needed by workers recruited in particular categories, etc. However, countries vary considerably in the extent to which they enforce these regulations. Although the Philippines has some of the most comprehensive regulations of all labor-exporting nations, even there:

> Illegal recruitment practices cover a wide range of schemes, from enlisting workers for a job abroad before receiving a job order, promising non-existing jobs, overcharging for placement fees, colluding in contract substitution, to forging documents to facilitate smuggling workers across borders and trafficking workers across borders and trafficking workers for employment in the sex industry. A large number of recruiters compete for limited jobs available abroad and an army of workers willing to be deployed. This situation renders the policing of the sector rather difficult and the industry has admitted to not being capable of disciplining its ranks. (Battistella 1995: 266).

The situation seems worse, if anything, in Thailand where abuses by recruiters are commonplace (Singhanetra-Renard 1992). Although most of the labor-exporting countries set a maximum charge that recruiters can levy to cover commissions, fees for documents, travel costs, tests, etc. these regulations are often ineffective. In reviewing the evidence gathered in several countries, Abella (1989: 120) found that charges for transaction costs are "excessively large and rising" and should be a matter of serious concern for authorities.

Another major area of government regulation relates to the protection and support of nationals working overseas, a vexing issue replete with reports of exploitation and abuse of workers, especially women, at particular destinations. The countries that have satisfied the emigrants' demand for protection are so few that one must question the extent to which the political will exists among labor-exporting governments to take on the issue. The most comprehensive proposals for protecting overseas workers were promulgated in the Philippines through the "Migrant Workers and Overseas Filipinos Act of 1995" (see the July/September 1995 issue of *Asian Migrant*). This legislation attempted to enhance the protection of overseas contract workers at three stages in the migration recruitment process: recruitment, deployment, and during overseas work residence. According to Battistella (1995: 267), the latter is particularly problematic:

> While citizens abroad are covered by a whole range of standards (international law, humanitarian law and bilateral and multilateral agreements) the actual implementation of the law is limited by the standards and practices of the host country. Countries of origin have only their diplomatic offices to ensure that the process is followed, and the threat of international shame and retaliation if such process is disregarded.

There are a number of multilateral conventions which, if actually observed, would guarantee the rights of migrant workers abroad. The United Nations (1990), for example, has developed an "International Convention on the Protection of the Rights of All Migrant Workers and Members of Their Families." In addition, the constitution of the International Labor Organization refers explicitly to the need for migrant workers to receive the same treatment as local workers and this remains the aim of its relevant conventions (Otting 1993). The ratification of these conventions, however, remains very low among the countries that receiving Asian contract workers, as indeed it does also in the sending countries themselves.

Noriel (1993: 159) provides a comprehensive list of measures required of nations to improve the conditions of migrant workers and protect and promote their rights and those of their families:

1. Take all appropriate measures to ensure that the terms and conditions of employment of migrant workers respect the principles of freedom of association and non-discrimination, and the provisions of the relevant ILO instrument.
2. Consider ratification of relevant ILO Conventions concerning the rights of migrant workers and their families.
3. Take appropriate national measures and to cooperate effectively in the field of international assistance, designed to eradicate migration pressures.
4. Take duly into account all pertinent national and international standards when concluding bilateral agreements on migration.
5. Take appropriate action which may include legislation to combat all acts of racism and xenophobia against migrant workers, and to intensify information and educational activities to this end.
6. Ensure that migrant workers have access to information on their rights, including, where necessary, in their own languages.
7. Involve, through appropriate means, workers' and employers' organizations in the formulation and monitoring of the effects of policies which cover recruitment, employment and the working conditions of migrant workers.

It is increasingly realized, however, that Non-Government Organizations (NGOs) are far more effective than the sending states themselves in providing protection to migrant workers overseas (Dias 1993).

## RETHINKING MIGRANT WORKERS' PROTECTION

### *The "Code of Conduct"*

As just noted, there are a number of multilateral conventions which, if observed by host countries, would go a long way toward protecting the rights of migrant workers. The problem is that most of the labor-importing countries are not a party to these conventions and attempts to negotiate supplementary bilateral agreements have, more often than not, been unsuccessful. The failure of host countries to develop national legislation or to ratify international conventions has led some to argue that a more effective approach would be to establish a "code of conduct" for employers: a set of rules pertaining to working conditions and practices that a company, its businesses, subcontractors, and licensees must follow (Porges 1996). Such a code might be aimed at the workforce in general and afford migrants protection under the same provisions; or it might negotiate codes of conduct specifically for companies or industries that employ foreign workers.

The effectiveness of such a code in protecting migrant workers would be circumscribed, however, by the fact that the difficulties confronting migrant workers are wide-ranging and can occur at any point in the migration process, from origin to destination. A typical migrant has to deal with at least one recruiter, a middleman, and an employer. At any point in this process a worker can encounter difficulties. As a result, codes of conduct might be more effective if they were applied at the occupation level, with the nature of the code varying across occupations (see Battistella 1996). Whereas the construction industry in most countries has a relatively high degree of unionization, so that union contracts can provide needed protection for migrant workers, small suppliers and manufacturers (those with fewer than ten employees) are generally not covered by such a contract and would make an appropriate target for a code of conduct established by large corporations to whom the small firms supply inputs (or in some cases final products).

Codes of conduct would be in line with ILO conventions, even if not ratified by the government of the host country. As noted by Battistella (1996), codes pertaining to migrant workers should include, among other things, payment of migration costs by the employer, prohibition of the confiscation of travel documents; equality of treatment with local workers with respect to wages, hours of work, lodging, health care provisions; and the provision of measures allowing for an early termination of contract.

The need to develop codes of conduct to protect the rights of migrant domestic workers and entertainers is particularly acute. Limited protections might derive from codes adopted by recruiting agents and brokers who would assume responsibility for ensuring that employers abide by the adopted codes. Households or nightclubs that violate codes of conduct could be banned by recruiters and security bonds forfeited. Of course, proving employer negligence in a one-to-one employer–employee relationship is necessarily fraught with difficulties, and adopting a code of conduct is far different from ensuring that it is effective. The lack of independent monitoring may lead some firms to cynically adopt codes without any intention of abiding by them (Porges 1996). Labor codes are usually autonomously adopted and monitored by the companies themselves. To be effective, however, they must be independently monitored by persons not unsympathetic to workers.

The enforcement of labor codes may be easier in some industries than others. Consumer boycotts of the products of transnational companies may help to ensure their adherence to the terms of agreed-upon codes. Unfortunately, however, companies that supply inputs for a number of final products may be sufficiently removed from the consumer market that the threat of a boycott will be ineffective. Nonetheless, in a region of the world where very few countries subscribe to ILO and other conventions, the use of codes of conduct may, when combined with other approaches, be of considerable assistance in achieving the objective of migrant worker protection in specific industries.

### *A union of labor-exporting countries*

Sending country officials responsible for protecting overseas nationals are frequently frustrated by their inability to gain the cooperation of host-country officials. To some extent, this lack of cooperation reflects the perception (probably correct) that if one labor-exporting nation bothers a labor-importing nation about worker protection, the latter will just turn to another, more compliant country to obtain its migrant workers. Thus, cooperation on the part of the host country is not necessary to obtain needed access for foreign labor supplies. It is a classic situation in which a few buyers confront many sellers, which typically leads to the exploitation of sellers in the form of lower prices and poorer working conditions.

Of course, the solution to this classic problem is for the sellers to organize to counterbalance the market power of the buyers. In relation to the particular problem at hand, it would, therefore, seem sensible for the labor-exporting countries to form an organization with the specific purpose of negotiating with the labor-importing countries to ensure adequate protection of their overseas workers' rights through the creation of appropriate legislation and institutions. If a labor-importing country refuses to negotiate with the organization then labor exports to that country from organization countries would be banned.

Initially, such an organization might use various international fora to push for the right to negotiate basic conditions for overseas workers and to establish institutional mechanisms to ensure adequate enforcement. Within Asia, the strength of such an organization would lie not only in its potential to control supplies of migrant labor, but in the combined economic clout of 8–10 of the world's larger national economies.

While an organization of labor exporters carries some potential to persuade labor-importing countries to establish standards for migrant workers, it also has certain drawbacks. In the past, attempts to restrict or ban migration to particular destinations have simply resulted in more illegal migration. By turning a blind eye to illegal migration, banned countries could secure access to foreign labor without having to negotiate with any organization representing labor-exporting societies. Indeed, working conditions would probably worsen compared to those that prevailed under the previous legal trade in labor services. Moreover, if a majority of illegal migrants to any banned country came from just one or two organization members, it could threaten the cohesiveness of the organization.

Another threat might be the desire by a member country to increase its share of the labor export market at the expense of other member countries. As noted above, Indonesia is actively planning to increase its deployment of workers abroad, while the Philippines continues actively to promote labor export despite the trauma of the Contemplacion case. Members of any labor-exporting organization would have to accept that they are in competition with each other for a share of the labor export market. However, even given such competition there is considerable scope for cooperation on matters relating to workers' rights. There are many examples of highly competitive firms in the same industry that cooperate through their industry organization to address issues which affect them collectively.

## MAXIMIZING BENEFITS AND MINIMIZING COSTS

A third group of strategies employed by governments in labor-exporting countries seek to maximize the development potential of emigration. These strategies center on migrant remittances and how to make the most of them. Whereas in the past, observers tended to downplay the importance of remittances in promoting economic development, more recently opinion has generally shifted. According to Stahl and Arnold (1986: 918), "although the propensity of remittance recipients to undertake productive investment out of their newfound income is exceedingly low, this does not warrant the conclusion that the developmental value of remittances is negligible. Remittances spent on domestic goods and services are a much needed stimulus to indigenous industries and provide a potentially significant source of development capital."

Stahl and Habib (1989) used an input–output model of the Bangladesh economy to trace through the direct and indirect effects of remittances on domestic output. They found that even when used for apparently "unproductive" ends, remittances, nonetheless, expanded domestic production, not only of consumer goods but also of intermediate products necessary to support that consumption. Because remittances tended to be spent in sectors with strong linkages to the broader economy, they found that "many sectors which do not benefit directly from remittance expenditure will nonetheless experience a growth in demand for their output. It is also anticipated that such a broad expansion of output will enlarge employment opportunities and stimulate demand for investment goods" (pp. 283–4).

Although official data on remittances only reflect the tip of the iceberg of actual flows, Table 10.6 does indicate how important labor export has become to the foreign exchange earnings of many Asian nations. In several nations—Pakistan, India, Sri Lanka, Bangladesh, and the Philippines—remittances are either the most important or among the five biggest sources of foreign exchange, displacing commodities as the most important export. In many countries, remittances are substantially greater than the inflow of development assistance. Remittances, once spurned by commentators as being of little economic significance are now a major element in international financial flows.

In 1991, remittances of $1.55 billion constituted roughly 18 per cent of the Philippines total merchandise exports of $8.75 billion (World Bank 1994). These figures understate the importance of labor export because they do not capture money and goods repatriated through unofficial channels, underscoring the central significance of international migration in the Philippines economy. In 1990, when the Philippine National Bank extended its services to Italy, Amsterdam, Germany, and Madrid, official per capita labor income from Europe more than doubled over the prior year (Russell 1991: 20).

Some significant remittance flows within Asia are necessarily clandestine because of the hostile relationship between nations. For example, until recently the substantial Vietnamese community of the United States was not permitted to remit money or goods to relatives through official channels, but the flows were substantial

**Table 10.6.** *Remittances as a proportion of merchandise exports in selected Asian countries*

| Region and country | Year | Percentage of foreign exchange |
|---|---|---|
| *East Asia* | | |
| China | 1993 | 1.0 |
| Japan | 1994 | 0.1 |
| Korea | 1994 | 0.5 |
| *South Central Asia* | | |
| Bangladesh | 1993 | 25.5 |
| India | 1990 | 9.3 |
| Maldives | 1993 | 0.6 |
| Pakistan | 1993 | 14.7 |
| Sri Lanka | 1993 | 15.2 |
| *Southeast Asia* | | |
| Indonesia | 1993 | 0.8 |
| Laos | 1993 | 2.9 |
| Malaysia | 1994 | 0.2 |
| Myanmar | 1991 | 0.5 |
| Philippines | 1993 | 13.4 |
| Thailand | 1993 | 2.5 |

*Source*: United Nations Population Division (1996).

nevertheless. One interesting flow is that from the 100,000 North Koreans working in Japan back to the Pyongyang regime. Each year it is estimated that the *Chosen Soren*, an association of North Koreans, collects and helps to channel back to North Korea some $600–700 million—about twice the size of the annual North Korean government budget (Smith 1993).

Governments throughout Asia are increasingly aware of the significance of remittances in their national economies. As already noted, several nations have built remittance targets into their development plans. Others have put in place programs to capture as much of the foreign exchange earned by overseas workers as possible. South Korea was a pioneer in this effort, stipulating as a condition for issuing exit permits that at least 30 per cent of earnings had to be remitted through the Korean banking system (Athukorala, n.d.). Although attempts by the Philippines, Pakistan, Thailand, and Bangladesh to do something similar have generally failed (Abella 1992), most Asian countries with substantial labor emigration have established hard currency accounts in domestic banks to attract remittances. These accounts are not subject to foreign exchange regulations and in some cases (India and Pakistan) they offer interest above prevailing world rates (Athukorala, n.d.).

India has been particularly successful in marshaling the financial resources of its large overseas community, especially professionals and business people located in

**Table 10.7.** *Nonresident Indians as a source of foreign investment for India 1983–93*

| Year | Total foreign investment | Percentage made by nonresident Indians |
|---|---|---|
| 1983 | 61.3 | 10.5 |
| 1984 | 99.5 | 13.0 |
| 1985 | 101.9 | 15.1 |
| 1986 | 84.9 | 7.4 |
| 1987 | 83.1 | 19.3 |
| 1988 | 172.2 | 7.4 |
| 1989 | 83.1 | 6.7 |
| 1990 | 73.3 | 4.1 |
| 1991 | 234.9 | 3.7 |
| 1992 | 1,267.2 | 11.6 |
| 1993 (estimate) | 2,152.6 | 5.6 |

*Source*: *Far Eastern Economic Review*, January 26, 1995, p. 51.

developed countries. The so-called NRIs (Non-Resident Indians) have come to be known as the "New Brahmins." They are permitted to open high-interest accounts in the State Bank of India denominated either in British pounds or U.S. dollars that are subject either to no or very low rates of taxation. The upsurge in foreign investment following the government's opening up of the Indian economy in the early 1990s included a significant share from overseas companies owned by NRIs as Table 10.7 shows. During the period 1983–93, overseas Indians have provided 5–20 per cent of total foreign investment.

Detailed studies of the economic effects of remittances are limited in Asia. One study in Bangladesh concluded that the absolute effects of remittances on the income and savings of receiving households was substantial, though it did contribute to an increase in income inequality (Mahmud and Osmani 1980). An econometric analysis based on Philippines data concluded that in that it was a net benefit for that country to train physicians for export (Goldfarb, Havrylyshyn, and Mangum 1984).

Of all policies aimed at increasing the inflow of remittances, the recent liberalization of foreign exchange and trade regimes has undoubtedly had the greatest influence, even if unintended. Prior to this liberalization, exchange rates were often overvalued and tariffs on consumer goods very high, which greatly reduced the incentive to transfer remittances through the formal banking system and encouraged migrants to rely on informal means to transfer money to families back home. It also encouraged returnees to bring back savings in the form of cash for conversion on the black market or consumer goods to which concessionary tariff charges applied and which could be sold for profit.

Even in the newly liberalized financial markets the inflow of remittances and other forms of overseas savings are quite sensitive to market returns. If anticipated real returns on savings are greater in a labor-receiving country than in a labor-sending nation, then it is likely that the flow of remittances will be reduced to that amount essential for family maintenance. Savings will be accumulated in the host country and may remain there after overseas workers return. To the extent that governments can intervene to guarantee that migrant workers receive a rate of return on savings that is at least comparable to those offered in receiving societies, there is still ample scope to increase remittance flows.

## REINTEGRATION OF RETURNING MIGRANTS

A number of labor exporting countries have been concerned with the reintegration of returning overseas workers. Although work in the 1970s and early 1980s criticized migrants for being unwilling to make productive investments in preparation for their return, more recent work has recognized that migrants tend to be workers, not risk-taking entrepreneurs, and that they are cautious in their investments. As Stahl and Arnold (1986: 914) point out, most workers have few resources to fall back on if investments were to fail, so that "everything would be lost, and two, three, or more years of loneliness and drudgery would have been endured for nothing. Under the circumstances it is naive to expect that the overseas work experience will transform a poor working peasant into an industrial entrepreneur."

Nonetheless, numerous schemes have been promoted to encourage returnees to invest their overseas earnings in "productive" enterprises, such as programs to provide small business training and other technical and institutional support. Given the high rate of failure among small businesses, however, Saith (1996: 32) argues that it would be more sensible to devise "reliable and investor-friendly mechanisms and instruments which allow migrants (and other small scale savers) to invest in the capital market without undue exposure to high risk. Such measures could generate strong backward and forward linkages in the domestic economy." This view is similar to that advanced by Stahl and Arnold (1986).

While much attention has been focused on what returning workers do with their earnings upon return, concern also has been directed toward the reintegration of workers. Arif (1995) found that the unemployment rate among returned migrants in Pakistan was significantly higher than that of non-migrants. Although the unemployment differential narrowed over time, even after 18 months the rate among returnees was substantially higher than among non-migrants. Similar results have been found in studies of returned migrants from Bangladesh (Mahmood 1991), India (Nair 1991), the Philippines (Arcinas 1991), and Sri Lanka (Gunatilleke 1991). Arif (1995) also found a statistically significant relationship between the educational attainment of returnees and the probability of being unemployed, and that unemployment was higher among professional and clerical returnees relative to those in other occupational categories. In general, readjustment was relatively easy for low skilled and agricultural workers.

The relatively high rate of unemployment observed among skilled and professional returnees might simply indicate a higher reservation wage, and hence a willingness and financial ability to spend longer looking for a desirable job; but it could also reflect a mismatch between the skills learned and used abroad and those needed in the domestic labor market. Although it may not be entirely clear *why* more skilled workers experience higher rates of unemployment upon return, it is clear that the local economy would benefit by developing a placement service for professional returnees, as long periods of unemployment are likely to erode whatever skills were acquired abroad, thus wasting valuable human capital.

## THE REVERSE BRAIN DRAIN

Another policy being pursued by some Asian nations is the attempt to create a "reverse brain drain" by attracting back home nationals and former nationals who have spent a considerable period of time living and working in a developed country. This movement gathered momentum in the 1990s in association with the burgeoning of economic opportunities in the rapidly growing Asian Tigers, such as Korea, Taiwan, and Hong Kong. Several countries in the region undertook deliberate efforts to attract back former emigrants with particular technical, professional, or business skills.

South Korea offers a good example of such government intervention. According to Yoon (1992: 5), the reverse brain drain in South Korea was not a spontaneous phenomenon, but stemmed from concerted state activity. The involvement of the state went beyond a simple promotional role and was strongly directive in initiating organized repatriation in selected social sectors and setting up procedures to achieve these objectives. State efforts were focused on high-level scientists and engineers for public research and development institutes and beginning in the 1980s were supplemented by vigorous efforts by the private sector. The Ministry of Science and Technology played a crucial role, organizing professional associations of Korean scientists and engineers in the U.S. beginning in 1971 (1990 membership was 6,300), in Europe in 1973 (1,500 members), 1983 in Japan (815 members) and in 1986 in Canada (812 members). In doing so it sought to develop a "reservoir brain pool" for future "reverse brain drain." The government scheme alone repatriated 1,707 Koreans between 1969 and 1989, almost all with doctorates and placed in public research institutes and universities.

Obviously, the extent to which emigrants return to their home country lessens the impact of their loss. Indeed to the extent that they return with enhanced skills, experience, overseas economic connections, and economic assets, they may have a greater positive effect on development than if they had remained home. Naturally, such positive effects are lessened if migrants return at or near the end of their working lives. It is still the case, however, that most contract workers return to their country of origin at the conclusion of their contracts, although there are some exceptions (e.g. Indonesians in Malaysia—see Hugo 1993).

Taiwan also offers strong indications of a reversal of the brain drain. The rate of return among students completing their studies in the US increased from 9 per cent in 1952–61 to 39 per cent in 1988 (Selya 1992: 788). For the last 20 years Taiwan has offered a "no strings attached" travel grant to nationals wishing to return to Taiwan, and between 1990 and 1993 the number taking advantage of this program suddenly doubled. Returnees have included a Nobel Prize winner who established a foundation to support 100 returnees annually and returnees are responsible for eighty-two of the 175 companies located in Asia's Silicon Valley (the Hsinchu Science-Based Industrial Park—see Meng 1994). Most of the *rencai huiliu* (return flow of human talent) accept pay cuts of 30–40 per cent to be closer to aging parents and relatives and what they see as better prospects for upward mobility (see the February 21, 1995, issue of the *New York Times*, p. A1).

There is also evidence of a significant flow back to India from North America (Yatsko 1995). Although much smaller, there is even some evidence of a reverse among the 120,000 students and scholars who left China for the United States between 1987 and 1994. Cities and provinces throughout China have opened returnee centers to lure back business and professional migrants (Rubin 1995: 74). The Shanghai Returned Students Center, for example, has provided assistance for almost 200 foreign-educated Chinese to return and set up businesses. So far, it has been easier to lure back business people than researchers because of the meager salaries paid in universities (Rubin 1995: 75). The Philippines *Balikbayan* program is a long-standing governmental effort to facilitate the return of migrants and assist them in readjusting to life in the Philippines (*Manila Chronicle*, October 23, 1994).

A number of countries have policies and programs to assist the social and economic integration of returning migrants, although there is considerable variation in the number and quality of these programs. Indonesia provides little more than investment advice, whereas the Philippines Overseas Workers Welfare Administration has a number of programs, including one providing loans and support for workers seeking to purchase or build their own homes (*Manila Chronicle*, August 14, 1993). There have been some attempts to mount job creation projects to absorb returning workers, such as those initiated by the ILO in the aftermath of the Gulf War of 1990 (*Manila Bulletin*, February 21, 1991).

Programs that encourage migrant workers to save and accumulate assets while overseas may enhance the value of foreign exchange earnings. Huntoon (1995) found that return migrants with savings were more likely than those without savings to settle in the lagging peripheral regions of their birth rather than in rapidly growing urban centers. Hence, regional development goals are fulfilled by policies to encourage saving.

## RESTRUCTURING LABOR EXPORT

So far we have discussed policies to augment the contribution of labor export to economic development, focusing on the maximization of remittances flows and the reabsorption of returnees. Another policy arena that has been given less attention is human resource development planning that seeks to anticipate changes in the skill-occupational needs of labor-importing countries (Saith 1996: 33–4).

In economic terms, the Asian region was the most rapidly growing during the 1980s and 1990s. In several countries, this growth has led to a demand for labor that has outstripped local labor supplies, offering labor surplus countries in the region the opportunity to identify and fill certain specific occupational and geographic needs. International labor flows within the region are thus increasingly demand-driven and country-specific labor export policies have aimed at filling this demand to ensure that market share is maintained or enhanced. In this sense, labor export policy has been reactive.

The growth process has been associated with fundamental changes in economic and demographic structure and these changes have given rise to corresponding changes in the occupational and skill profiles of labor demand. If labor export is to remain an important adjunct to development policy, as it will for several of the countries of the region, then it is critically important that labor exporters anticipate changes both in skill profile and geographic source of labor demand.

In the past, the demand for production-related workers has derived from acute shortages and wage pressures in manufacturing industries. Immigrant labor has provided relief to these hard-pressed industries, but how long they can continue to operate in this fashion is questionable. The exodus of low-value added manufacturing industries from Japan and the Newly Industrialized Countries to lower wage countries of the region suggest that similar pressures to move abroad will become irresistible in the near future. Saith (1996: 33) argues that labor-exporting countries such as the Philippines should anticipate such moves and provide the human resource infrastructure to become an attractive location for footloose industries. Moreover, such proactive manpower planning policies could tempt both foreign and domestically owned firms in countries of rapidly rising wages (such as Malaysia) to relocate to labor-exporting countries (such as Indonesia), thus obviating the need for the export of production workers.

The exodus of labor-intensive industries from Japan and other aspiring tigers will shift the skill-occupational pattern of labor demand toward services. Rising labor force participation rates among increasingly well-educated women will lead to significant increases in the demand for domestic servants and growth in consumer income will augment the demand for entertainment and, particularly, the demand for meals outside the home. In a tight labor market, these types of jobs are avoided by skilled and educated nationals and become the purview of foreign workers.

These changes in labor demand are driven by changes in economic structure and rising consumer income. Another change that is set to affect the demand for services dramatically is the aging of the population within industrialized countries. Aging will manifest itself in a growth of demand for retirement homes and for para-medical staff, cooks, cleaners, drivers, gardeners, and other service workers.

There are two ways to react to such shifts in the pattern of labor demand. One is to simply follow the market, leaving it up to individuals and their recruiters to identify employment opportunities. The other is to develop such markets actively and to supply them through service sector companies organized specifically for the purpose. The latter strategy implies a need for policies aimed at developing the human resources necessary to sustain such active labor export over the long term. As Saith (1996: 35) recognized, "such a corporate mode of service delivery could remove the stigma attached to some of these personal services by enhancing the dignity of the worker; they could provide a contractual framework where abuses could be curtailed, and where client accountability could be monitored."

Among current labor exporters, the Philippines is probably best placed to take advantage of these developments. It has several internationally recognized medical schools capable of increasing their output of para-medical staff. Moreover, an exceptionally high rate of literacy and a wide understanding of the English language ensures a steady input of personnel into various high-quality training institutions, which could tailor their program to take advantage of this potentially lucrative market niche. Thus, a closer collaboration between market analysts, labor recruiters, and education and training institutions might assist in the development of a corporate service-labor export strategy that could prove highly profitable while ensuring respect and dignity of workers in the host country.

## CONCLUSION

Although a great deal of research attention has focused on government attempts to stop or reduce immigration to developed nations, little has been paid to analyzing policies and programs related to emigration. It is apparent, however, that government activities do strongly influence the scale and composition of emigration, whether legal or undocumented. Across Asia, where wage differentials are on the order of 10 : 1 between NICs and labor surplus economies (Manning 1996: 194), it is apparent that governments in labor-exporting nations have been very active in developing a range of strategies to influence the scale and composition of labor out-migration. Unfortunately, such policies have unfolded in an empirical vacuum and there has been little research available to inform their development and operationalization. There has also been little work to evaluate the effectiveness of existing policies and programs of labor export, despite the fact that they have considerable influence on development in several of Asia's poorest countries and that they impinge upon the well-being of millions of Asians. It is, therefore, of great importance to develop a deeper understanding of the consequences and effectiveness of different labor export policies in years to come.

### References

Abella, Manolo I. (1989). "Pre-migration Costs of Contract Labourers," *Asian Migrant*, 2: 113–21.

—— (1992). "Contemporary Labour Migration from Asia: Policies and Perspectives of Sending Countries," in Mary M. Kritz, Lin Lean Lim, and Hania, Zlotnik (eds.), *International Migration Systems: A Global Approach*. Oxford: Oxford University Press, pp. 263–78.

—— and Abrera-Mangahas A. (1995). *Sending Workers Abroad: A Manual for Low or Middle-Income Countries*. Geneva: Employment Department, International Labor Organization.

Adams, Walter (1969). *The Brain Drain.* New York: Macmillan.

Arif, G. (1995). "International Contract Labour Migration and Reintegration of Return Migrants: The Experience of Pakistan," Ph.D. Thesis, Australian National University.

Athukorala, Premachandra n.d. "Improving the Contribution of Migrant Remittances to Development: The Experience of Asian Labour Exporting Countries," Unpublished paper, Department of Economics, La Trobe University.

—— (1993). "Statistics on Asian Labour Migration: Review of Sources, Methods and Problems in ILO-ARTEP.' *International Labour Migration Statistics and Information Networking in Asia.* Papers and Proceedings of a Regional Seminar held in New Delhi, 17–19 March, UNDP and ILO-ARTEP, Geneva.

—— and Wickramasekara, P. (1996). "International Labour Migration Statistics in Asia: An Appraisal," *International Migration,* 34: 539–66.

Battistella, Graziano (1995). "Philippine Overseas Labour: From Export to Management," *ASEAN Economic Bulletin,* 12: 257–74.

—— (1996). "Employers' Code of Conduct and Migrant Workers," *Asian Migrant,* 9: 119–24.

Chang, S. L. (1992). "Causes of Brain Drain and Solutions: The Taiwan Experience," *Studies in Comparative International Development,* 27: 27–43.

Dias, C. J. (1993). "The Role of NGOs in the Protection and Promotion of Human Rights in Asia," *Asian and Pacific Migration Journal,* 2: 199–222.

Fortney, J. (1972). "Immigrant Professionals: A Brief Historical Survey," *International Migration Review,* 6: 50–62.

Goldfarb, R., Havrylyshyn, O., and Mangum, S. (1984). "Can Remittances Compensate for Manpower Outflows," *Journal of Development Economics,* 15: 1–17.

Goss, Jon D., and Lindquist, Bruce (1995). "Conceptualizing International Labor Migration: A Structuration Perspective," *International Migration Review,* 29: 317–51.

Gunatilleke, G. (1991). "Sri Lanka," in G. Gunatilleke (ed.), *Migration to the Arab World: Experience of Returning Migrants.* Tokyo: United Nations University Press, pp. 290–352.

Hugo, Graeme J. (1993). "Indonesian Labour Migration to Malaysia: Trends and Policy Implications," *Southeast Asian Journal of Social Science,* 21: 36–70.

—— (1995). "Labour Export from Indonesia: An Overview," *ASEAN Economic Bulletin,* 12: 275–98.

—— (1996). "Economic Impacts of International Labour Emigration on Regional and Local Development: Some Evidence from Indonesia," Paper presented at the Annual Meetings of the Population Association of America, New Orleans, May.

—— (1997). "Migration and Mobilisation in Asia: An Overview," Paper prepared at the Conference on Asian Immigration and Racism in Canada, Institute of Asian Research, University of British Columbia, Canada, 24–7 June.

—— (1998). "The Demographic Underpinnings of Current and Future International Migration in Asia," *Asian and Pacific Migration Journal,* 7: 1–25.

—— Massey, J. D. S., Arango, J., Kouaouci, A., Pellegrino, A., and Taylor, J. E. (1996). "Empirical Evaluation of International Migration Theory: The Asian Case," Paper presented for the Meeting of the IUSSP Committee on South-North Migration, San Francisco, 21 June.

Huntoon, Laura (1995). "Return Migration When Savings Differ," *Journal of Urban Affairs,* 17: 219–39.

International Labour Organization (1995). *Year Book of Labour Statistics* 1995. Geneva: International Labour Organization.

Lim, Lin Lean, and Oishi N. (1996). "International Migration of Asian Women: Distinctive Characteristics and Policy Concerns," in G. Battistella and A. Paganoni (eds.), *Asian Women in Migration.* Manila: Scalabrini Migration Center.

Mahmood, R. (1991). "Bangladeshi Returned Migrants from the Middle East: Process, Achievements and Adjustment," in G. Gunatilleke (ed.), *Migration to the Arab World: Experience of Returning Migrants.* Tokyo: United Nations University Press, pp. 238–98.

Mahmud, W., and Osmani, S. R. (1980). "Impact of Emigrant Workers' Remittances on the Bangladesh Economy," *Bangladesh Development Studies*, 8: 1–28.

Manning, Charles (1996). "Labour Markets and Human Resources in Developing East Asia: Different Solutions to Different Problems," *Research in Asian Economic Studies*, 7, Part A: 189–204.

Martin, Phillip M. (1996). "Labor Contractors: A Conceptual Overview," *Asian and Pacific Migration Journal*, 5: 201–18.

——Mason, Andrew, and Nagayama, T. (1996). "The Dynamics of Labor Migration in Asia," *Asian and Pacific Migration Journal*, 5: 2–3.

Massey, Douglas S., Arango, Joquin, Hugo, Graeme, Kouaouci, Ali, Pellegrino, Adela, and Taylor, Edward J. (1993). "Theories of International Migration: A Review and Appraisal," *Population and Development Review*, 19: 431–66.

—— —— —— —— —— —— (1998). Worlds in Motion: Understanding International Migration at the End of the Millennium. Oxford: Clarendon Press.

Meng, W. C. (1994). "Taiwan Brain Drain Goes into Reverse," *The Straits Times*, 9 November.

Nair, P. (1991). "Asian Migration to the Arab World: Kerala (India)," in G. Gunatilleke (ed.), *Migration to the Arab World: Experience of Returning Migrants.* Tokyo: United Nations University Press, pp. 19–55.

National Science Foundation (1972). *Scientists, Engineers and Physicians from Abroad.* Washington, DC: National Science Foundation.

Nayyar, D. (1996). *Indonesia: Emigration Pressures and Structural Change.* Geneva: International Labor Organization.

Noriel, C. C. (1993). "Labor Rights in Selected Asian Countries," *Asian and Pacific Migration Journal*, 2: 147–60.

Otting, A. (1993). "Migrant Workers and the ILO Conventions," *Asian Migrant*, 6: 78–88.

Pernia, E. M. (1976). "The Question of the Brain Drain from the Philippines," *International Migration Review*, 10: 63–72.

Porges, J. (1996). "Developing a Regional Employer's Code of Conduct," *Asian Migrant*, 9: 114–18.

Prijono, O. S. (1993). "People Movement: Social, Cultural and Communication Issues: The Indonesian Case," Paper presented at Conference on Temporary, Long-Term and Permanent Movements of People, Darwin.

Qian, W. (1996). "The Features of International Migration in China," Paper presented to the Conference on European Chinese and Chinese Domestic Migrants, Oxford, 3–7 July.

Rubin, K. (1995). "Homeward Bound," *Far Eastern Economic Review*, 18 May, 74.

Russell, Sharon S. (1991). "Population and Development in the Philippines: An Update," The World Bank Asia Country Department II, Population and Human Resources Division, Washington DC.

—— (1992). "Migrant Remittances and Development," *International Migration Review*, 30: 267–87.

——and Teitelbaum, Michael S. (1992). "International Migration and International Trade," *World Bank Discussion Paper*, 160, The World Bank, Washington.

Saith, A. (1996). "Emigration Pressures and Structural change: Philippines," Unpublished paper, International Labor Organization, Manila.

Saywell, T. (1997). "Workers' Offensive," *Far Eastern Economic Review*, 29 May, 50–2.

Selya, R. M. (1992). "Illegal Migration in Taiwan: A Preliminary Overview," *International Migration Review*, 26: 787–805.

Singhanetra-Renard, A. (1992). "The Mobilization of Labour Migrants in Thailand: Personal Links and Facilitating Networks," in Mary M. Kritz, Lin Lean Lim, and Hania Zlotnik (eds.), *International Migration Systems: A Global Approach*. Oxford: Oxford University Press, pp. 190–204.

Smith, C. (1993). "Cash Lifeline," *Far Eastern Economic Review*, 9 September.

Spaan, E. (1994). "Taikongs and Calos: The Role of Middlemen and Brokers in Javanese International Migration," *International Migration Review*, 28: 93–113.

Stahl, Charles (1997). "International Labour Migration and the APEC/PECC East Asian Economies: Trends and Issues," in *PECC Human Resource Development Outlook 1996–1997*, Asia Pacific Centre for Human Resource and Development Studies, University of Newcastle, pp. 161–186.

—— and Habib, A. (1989). "The Impact of Overseas Workers' Remittances on Indigenous Industries: Evidence from Bangladesh," *The Developing Economies*, 27: 269–85.

—— and Arnold, Fred (1986). "Overseas Workers' Remittances in Asian Development," *International Migration Review*, 20: 899–925.

Taylor, J. Edward, Hugo, Graeme, Arango, Joaquin, Kouaouci, Ali, Massey, Douglas, and Pellegrino, Adela (1996). "International Migration and National Development," *Population Index*, 62: 181–212.

United Nations (1990). *International Convention on the Protection of All Migrant Workers and Members of Their Families*. New York: United Nations.

United Nations Population Division (1996). *International Migration Policies 1995*. New York: United Nations.

World Bank (1994). *World Development Report 1994*. New York: Oxford University Press.

—— (1997). *World Development Indicators 1997*. Washington: World Bank.

Yatsko, P. (1995). "Call Home," *Far Eastern Economic Review*, 26 January, 50–2.

Yoon, B. L. (1992). "Reverse Brain Drain in South Korea: State-led Model," *Studies in Comparative International Development*, 27: 4–26.

# 11

# The Role of Recruiters in Labor Migration

MANOLO I. ABELLA

Although the commercialization of labor migration is a major policy concern in many countries, most notably those in Asia, the issue has received scant attention in the migration literature. Profit-seeking intermediaries increasingly organize the transnational movement of workers and have become significant players in the global labor market. The growing involvement of firms and individuals in labor recruitment is probably more responsible than any other factor for increasing the speed of out-migration and determining the direction of the resulting flows. Private firms presently serve as recruitment intermediaries for around 80–90 per cent of labor migrants from Asia, estimated at around 2 million per year; and middlemen probably underlie a significant share of the outflow from other regions as well, although the data are too weak to determine with confidence the global prevalence of recruitment (International Labor Organization 1994).

Receiving states that are reluctant to organize migration or to involve governmental institutions in the recruitment and placement of foreign workers have—if only indirectly—encouraged commercial recruitment. Before 1973, labor recruitment was often carried out under state auspices, with Germany's *Gastarbeiter* programs being the best-known example (Böhning 1972; Castles and Kosack 1981). Since then, the organization of labor migration has increasingly been left in the hands of private agents whose profitability often comes at the expense of the workers themselves. For this reason, states with active labor exportation programs often pressure receiving country governments to implement measures to protect migrant workers from fraud and excessively high recruitment fees (Hugo and Singhanetra-Renard 1987).

In places where social networks are not sufficiently well-developed to facilitate international movement, those seeking to work abroad must rely either on state employment agencies or on commercial intermediaries. In socialist countries, the recruitment and placement of workers was often a key state function in the central planning apparatus. In some of these nations, recruitment has remained a state monopoly even as the country has moved toward a market economy. In China, for example, special licenses have been issued to hundreds of state-owned engineering and service contractors, as well as to local cooperatives, permitting them to recruit and place workers abroad (Abella 1992).

In most countries, however, the state plays a minor part in recruitment, leaving the task to commercial brokers who make job placements for a fee. Several countries in the former USSR have passed legislation to allow private labor recruitment. Fees are charged either to the employer or the worker, and sometimes to both. Many states, especially those in Europe (Austria, Germany, Ireland, Iceland, the Netherlands, Sweden, United Kingdom), as well as the United Arab Emirates and Uruguay, prohibit recruitment agents from charging any fees to workers. This prohibition is, however, extremely difficult to enforce. In many labor-sending countries with clear policies on the matter, charging fees to workers is not prohibited but fee limitations are set by regulatory bodies and the state imposes financial or criminal sanctions on violators.

The alternatives to profit-seeking intermediaries are not very attractive. Public employment offices are generally less effective in finding foreign jobs than are private firms. Hence, job seekers generally prefer private intermediaries, despite the greater risk of fraud and the possibility of being charged high fees. Several Asian governments have set up specialized organizations to provide free placement for workers wishing to go abroad; but all have failed despite significant state subsidies. In India, for example, five states established "overseas employment corporations." After many years in operation, and at considerable state expense, these corporations have failed to earn a significant share of foreign employment. They mainly manage a few state-to-state recruitment contracts, mostly involving professionals such as medical doctors and nurses, people generally not in need of protection.

## WHAT DETERMINES RECRUITMENT FEES?

People attach value to recruitment services. They represent an economic good because information about jobs and workers is scarce, even in countries where placement services are well-developed. The market for recruitment services has grown rapidly in recent years, especially in technologically advanced economies where the labor requirements are more complex. In the United Kingdom, for example, the number of agencies engaged in placement services rose from 5,000 at the beginning of the 1980s to 13,500 at the beginning of the 1990s (Walwei 1996). Recruitment services are especially useful in acquiring information about jobs or workers located at a geographic or cultural distance. In labor-sending countries where fee-charging agencies are allowed to operate, recruitment services have mushroomed to create, in many instances, an industry of significant size.

Where unemployment is high and jobs are scarce, recruiters have no difficulty finding workers who are willing to pay for placement. Under such circumstances, employers are less inclined to pay than they are during times of labor shortage. It is for this reason that regulations that allow recruiters to charge fees only to employers and not to workers are so difficult to enforce.

The question of how recruitment fees are determined has important policy implications because authorities in labor-sending countries confront the problem of price regulation on a daily basis to minimize the cost of migration for workers. Should national authorities impose legal ceilings on recruitment fees? If regulating fees does not work, what other policy instruments might bring down costs? Would fostering greater competition in the recruitment market lower prices? Unfortunately, not even a proper conceptualization of these issues currently exists to help researchers identify the relevant variables to measure and employ.

## *The recruitment market*

The demand for a recruiter's services is inseparable from the job the worker is being recruited to fill. Job seekers do not purchase a standard service, as when one has one's clothes tailored. In the latter case, the tailor's fee is independent of the cost of the material. In some sense, job placement fees are akin to commissions paid to a sales agent (such as a realtor), except that in recruitment the fee is not determined by the financial value of the good procured, but by the demand itself. As a result, recruiters may get higher fees for unskilled jobs that pay very little than for placements in professional jobs that pay handsome salaries. What the recruiter gets is not a fee for recruitment services per se, but a bribe for the jobs that he or she offers. This value of this "bribe" is a function of several factors, but depends largely on the differential between wages at home and those abroad, and on conditions of demand and supply in the sending country's labor market.

For analogous reasons, the supply of recruitment services is not so much determined by the number and capacities of recruitment firms in the market, but by the conditions of the labor market abroad. This explains some of the perplexing features of this market. On the one hand, one should expect the industry to be very competitive except where legal restrictions bar firms from entering the industry. There are no real economic barriers to new businesses, since recruitment services require low fixed investment and, consequently, there is little by way of economies of scale that would give large firms advantages over smaller ones. On the other hand, some firms reap enormous profits from recruitment, which can only be explained by monopoly or sale of products that nobody else in the market can offer.

## *Sharing the differential*

We start with a simple two-country model in which labor migration is allowed to take place. Figure 11.1 shows the demand for labor in two countries, A and B, with a combined work force of AB, Country A is technologically more advanced than country B, as reflected in the higher productivity of labor ($MPL_a$ compared with $MPL_b$) and higher wages ($W_a$ compared with $W_b$). A has a fully employed work force of $AL_0$, while B has $BL_0$. If A allows some workers from B to enter for employment, say a maximum of $L_0L_1$, its wages will decline to $W'_a$, while wages in B, the country with more abundant labor, will rise to $W'_b$. The migrating workers may be able to earn the wage $W'_a$ in the receiving country, which is higher by the amount DG that they received prior to leaving their own country.

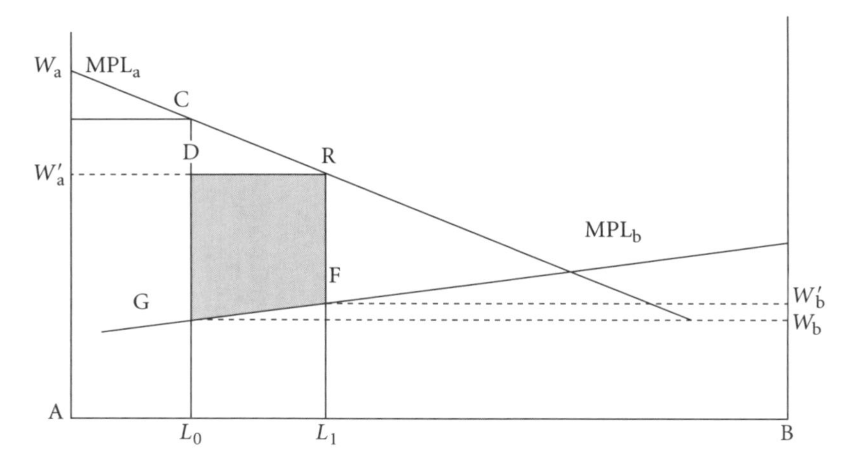


**Figure 11.1.** *Two-country migration model*

Will the migrating workers $L_0L_1$ from country B get the windfall gains, DRFG, by moving to country A? Where there are well-established labor institutions the answer is yes, but in many migration systems workers end up surrendering some or most of their gains to job brokers or recruitment agents. How these gains are shared between worker and recruiter has not been examined systematically in the literature, although this is a practical issue for policymakers. In labor-sending countries where authorities are concerned with how to safeguard the worker's share of windfall gains, laws and regulations have been constructed, but with very little success. Such laws include maximum legal limits to recruitment fees, cancellation of recruitment licenses for violations, requirements barring direct payment of fees to recruiters, etc.

In the model above, the would-be migrant worker, hoping to beat the queue, would consider how much of DG he or she is willing to give up to the recruiter to get a job. Here, we offer a simple paradigm to show how workers' windfall gains are shared. We start with the reasonable assumption that many more workers from B will probably want to go to work in A, except that country A has put a limit of $L_0L_1$ on the number of foreign workers. This "scarcity" of foreign jobs creates a market for job brokers.

How are the workers for $L_0L_1$ selected? We assume that the labor in demand is for unskilled jobs and that all the workers are equally qualified. The market operates by allowing those workers willing to offer money to recruiters to get the job. Evidently, how much workers offer depends on expected wages abroad, or more precisely, the difference between what they can earn abroad and at home. A worker contemplating an offer would presumably compare the expected stream of net income abroad, appropriately discounted, with what the recruiter is asking for.

Information about conditions of employment abroad is also an important variable. If the workers are deceived into thinking that conditions are better than they actually are, they may agree to offer more to the recruiters. Similarly, expectations as to how long they can stay abroad to recover their investment in migrating influence the recruitment fees workers would be willing to pay.

## *Fees and wage differentials*

The critical relationship posited in this chapter is shown in Fig. 11.2: recruitment fees that workers will pay are a function of the wage differential. For simplicity, the wage differential, $W_a - W_b$ is shown as a linear function; it is represented by WF. Everything else being constant, the larger the wage differential, the larger the amount would-be migrants would be willing to pay recruiters for a job offer. In Fig. 11.2a, with a wage differential of $w_1$, workers would be willing to offer a fee of only $f_1$. With a larger wage differential, say of $w_2$, workers will offer a fee of up to $f_2$. At any point above the curve, more job seekers will come forward and offer a higher fee. Below the curve, some job seekers will withdraw from the market because they do not think it worthwhile to go abroad. The intercept of the line shows the minimum wage differential workers would require before considering work abroad. This is a kind of "reservation wage" below which no one will come forward and apply for work abroad.

The WF curve expresses the relationship between wage differential and fees that job seekers are willing to pay in the short run. It is axiomatic that everything else—incomes, skills distribution of the labour force, or stock of migrants abroad—is assumed to be constant. These other factors influence what workers are willing to pay in the *long-run*, but not in the *short-run* model just presented. We later relax this assumption and consider how various factors could influence the relationship between wage differentials and fees.

The curve would have a different elasticity (i.e. slope) in a different labor market. It might, for example, have a steeper slope if there had been previous migration flows and if national communities settled abroad facilitated new migration (a social network effect), thereby substituting for commercial recruiters. In such circumstances, a larger increase in wage differentials would be necessary to support a given increase in fees. Where many job applicants might have relatives abroad to help with job placement, over a period of time one would expect to see the development of social

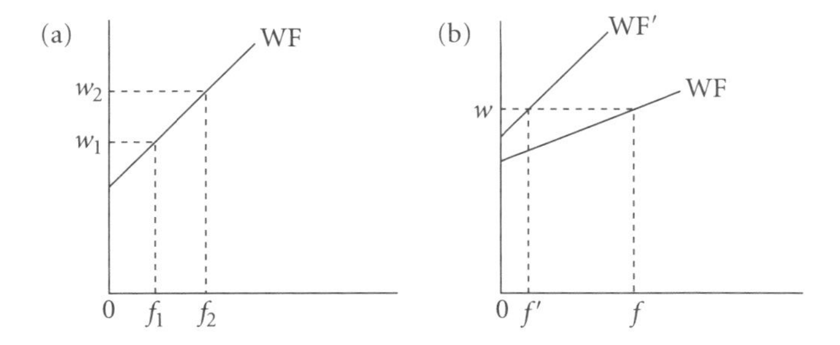


**Figure 11.2.** *Fees determined by wage differentials*

network effects that would drive down recruiter fees, although their impact might be blunted by other countervailing factors.

In a situation where no previous migration has taken place and the only information about migration opportunities comes from private recruiters, without the help of friends or relatives, job seekers have to use private recruiters and will be more likely to pay higher fees. This can be illustrated by a more elastic or flatter WF curve, which indicates that job seekers are willing to pay higher fees to obtain a given increase in wages.

It is very possible for the WF curve to be different for different groups of workers. For example, nurses, for whom there was excess demand in the United States at one time, did not have to pay much in recruitment fees even if their wages were considerably higher than those of other occupations. In Fig. 11.2b, we have two WF curves, one for unskilled workers, WF, and one for professionals, WF′; WF shows that unskilled workers will offer higher fees to recruiters $f$ compared with $f'$ for the same wage differential as professionals, simply because more unskilled workers queue up for fewer jobs.

## *Supply of labor for foreign employment*

In the preceding analysis, an implicit supply of labor corresponds to bids or offers to recruiters. In the following, we attempt to answer the question, How many workers would come forward and offer to go abroad at various levels of recruitment fees?

In the two-country migration model shown earlier, no distinction is drawn between the supply of labor for work at home and for work abroad. Since most people would prefer to stay at home, it is intuitively true that the amount of labor offered at home and abroad will be different at each wage rate. In other words, there is a different supply of labor function for the external labor market. People are likely to require a considerable differential in wages before they will be induced to offer their labor abroad. This is akin to a reservation wage expressed not as an absolute wage but as a differential between the external wage and that prevailing at home. The supply of labor for work abroad can, thus, be represented not as a function of the wage abroad, but of the differential in wages prevailing at home and abroad.

In Fig. 11.3, a supply of labor function is shown with wage differentials on the vertical axis. As with the conventional labor supply function, the number of workers offering their labor rises as wage differentials grow. While a positive slope of the labor supply curve is easy enough to assume, it is not evident how the labor offer curve slope changes as wage differentials widen. This is a matter for empirical verification. In this chapter, we assume that it has the shape of the normal labor supply curve, which rises more and more slowly as wage differentials further widen.

In Fig. 11.3a we assume a supply curve for a homogeneous labor force. This assumption can be relaxed to take into account more realistic conditions in the labor market. For certain analyses it may, for instance, be necessary to consider segmented markets, making distinctions among skills or educational attainments, sex, or age. Generally, it is expected that professionals require larger wage differentials than do

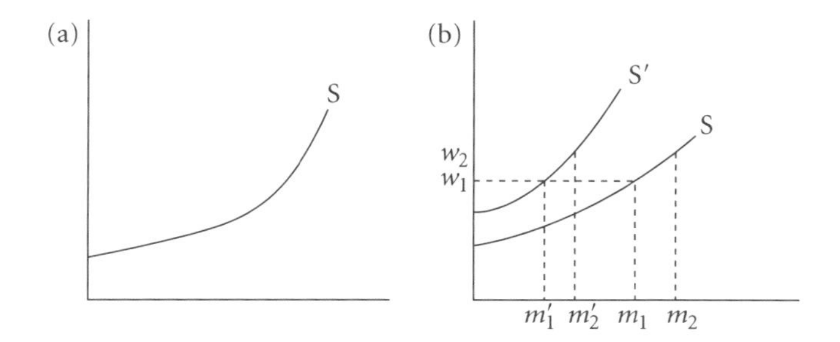


**Figure 11.3.** *Supply of labor for foreign employment*

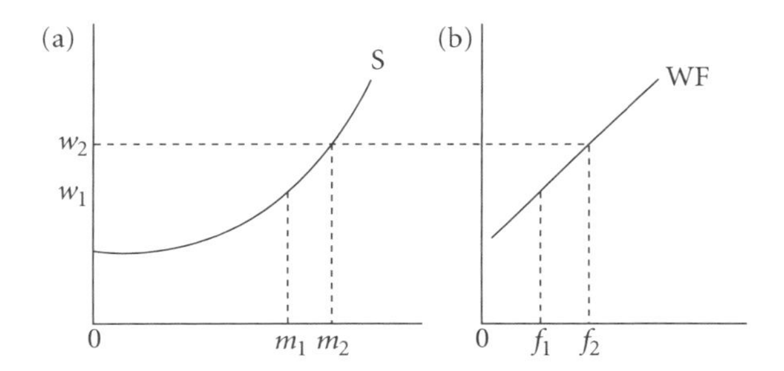


**Figure 11.4.** *Fees and the supply of workers*

unskilled workers to consider employment abroad. In Fig. 11.3b, a given change in the wage differential, from $w_1$, to $w_2$, induces only half as many professionals as unskilled workers to offer their labor abroad.

## *Supply of labor corresponding to level of fees*

Figure 11.4 brings together the supply of labor for work abroad with our wage differential sharing function. With a wage differential of $w_1$, a number $m_1$ of workers seek work abroad (Fig. 11. 4a). These workers are willing to pay a fee of no more than $f_1$ (Fig. 11. 4b). At any fee higher than $f_1$, say $f_2$, workers feel that it is not worthwhile to work abroad unless the wage differential rises to $w_2$.

If government authorities set a legal limit to fees that can be charged, say, equal to $f'$, the regulation will work only if the wage differential happens to be equal to $w_1$. If a higher wage differential exists, for example $w_2$, workers will offer higher bids for the jobs available until the average bids reach $f_2$. This is a typical dilemma faced by authorities when they try to enforce a legal ceiling lower than the fees job seekers are willing to pay.

Legal limits based on a percentage of the contractual wage are used by some countries, for example, Thailand, where recruiters may charge up to a full month's salary.

This is a more practical alternative to fee ceilings because it comes closest to relating the fee to the wage differential and does not need to be periodically adjusted, as is the case with absolute ceilings. There are nevertheless problems with this approach, as when the fee job seekers are willing to pay happens to be many times the size of a monthly contractual salary.

## INSIGHTS FROM EXISTING STUDIES

Despite many violations of government regulations fees charged by recruiters, the cost of recruitment has not been systematically monitored, even in the large labor-sending countries. Documentation of what workers pay to recruiters to obtain jobs abroad comes from a few small sample surveys undertaken by scholars in Asia, and these surveys were not necessarily directed at examining recruitment cost. One such study is by Shah (1996) on the impact of social networks on migration. She interviewed a sample of 800 South Asian male migrant workers in Kuwait to obtain information on how they found employment in Kuwait and what they paid. The sample was divided by country of origin (200 each from Bangladesh, India, Pakistan, and Sri Lanka). For each sub-sample, 100 workers were employed in unskilled and 100 were in skilled occupations.

Table 11.1 provides a summary of some of Shah's findings that are pertinent to this chapter. More than three fourths of the Sri Lankans and slightly more than half of the Bangladeshis in Shah's study were recruited by private agents. Pakistanis and Indians were less dependent on private recruiters, no doubt because of their long history of migration to the Gulf and the existence of established communities to facilitate migration.

**Table 11.1.** *Recruitment fees paid by male South Asian migrant workers in Kuwait: December 1995*

| Variable | Bangladesh (%) | India (%) | Pakistan (%) | Sri Lanka (%) |
|---|---|---|---|---|
| *How work visa obtained* | | | | |
| Through friend or relative | 38.5 | 30.5 | 55.5 | 13.0 |
| From kafeel or employer | 8.5 | 43.5 | 4.0 | 8.5 |
| From recruitment agent | 53.0 | 26.0 | 40.5 | 78.5 |
| No fee paid | 1.0 | 9.0 | 1.5 | 0.5 |
| Fee paid | 52.0 | 17.0 | 39.0 | 78.0 |
| *Amount paid to recruiter* | | | | |
| Less than $700 | 1.0 | 47.0 | 63.0 | 58.0 |
| $700–1,499 | 16.0 | 47.0 | 30.0 | 42.0 |
| $1,499+ | 83.0 | 5.0 | 8.0 | 1.0 |
| Average fee | $1,727 | $900 | $768 | $689 |
| Average monthly wage | $153 | $301 | $373 | $181 |

*Source*: Shah (1996).

Almost all of the Bangladeshis and the Sri Lankans who were recruited by agents paid for their recruitment, in amounts that varied considerably, as shown in the last four rows of Table 11.1. On average, Bangladeshis paid about twice what others paid, a curious find in view of the fact that they were employed in very similar jobs in Kuwait. Only about two out of every five Pakistani migrant workers obtained their jobs through private agents, and they paid, on the average, less than half of what the Bangladeshis did. It is interesting to note the difference that having social networks makes. The Indians (and the Pakistanis) have been in Kuwait much longer than the Bangladeshis or the Sri Lankans. Indians, in particular, constitute an important economic group that has been engaged in trade and commerce in Kuwait and other parts of the region for many centuries. The information in Table 11.1 suggests that these offshore communities have played an important role in the migration of labor from the subcontinent. Many obtained their work visas through friends or directly from employers and sponsors. These were not necessarily cost free, but their jobs, in terms of pay, tended to be better than jobs obtained by the Bangladeshis or the Sri Lankans.

Can wage differentials explain the large differences in fees that these groups of migrant workers paid? Shah's study shows that it will take a Bangladeshi migrant worker 11.2 months to recover money paid to the recruiter for a job in Kuwait, while a Pakistani worker, who makes more than twice the wage but pays less than half the fees, will only need to work 2 months to recover the migration investment. Unfortunately, Shah's survey did not include data on wages earned by workers before they left their countries of origin; therefore, it is impossible to test our hypothesized relationship between wage differentials and fees. Substituting statistics from other sources on earnings of all workers in these countries for individual home wage data will not be satisfactory because one cannot be sure that the data compared are compatible.

An earlier study undertaken by Azad (1989) for the ILO on the cost of migration to the migrant provides us with more detailed information with which to assess the relationship between wage differentials and what workers pay for recruitment. Azad used a sample of 450 returned labor migrants to obtain information on how much they paid for recruitment, passport and medical certificates, preparatory expenses, and passage money. His data on costs for workers migrating to Bangladesh are not for a single point in time but for 17 years, as shown in Table 11.2 along with data on earnings differentials which we derived from Azad's estimates of earnings gaps. Azad calculated earnings gaps as the differential between discounted values of expected earnings abroad (over probable period of stay) and at home, minus the estimated cost of migration.

Over the 17-year period one observes a decline in earnings differentials, due largely to the secular decline in wages of migrant workers in the Middle East. What is intriguing is that migration costs kept on rising during the period, indicating that migrant workers were bidding higher and higher fees for jobs offering lower and lower rewards. This seems to contradict the hypothesis that higher bids will only be made in the expectation of larger wage or earnings differentials.

**Table 11.2.** *Cost of migration and earnings differential for skilled migrants from Bangladesh (in Bangladeshi Takas)*

| Year | Migration cost | Earnings differential |
|---|---|---|
| 1971 | 2,375 | 127,303 |
| 1973 | 42,500 | 234,364 |
| 1974 | 20,000 | 198,581 |
| 1975 | 26,416 | 125,030 |
| 1976 | 35,300 | 125,030 |
| 1977 | 21,100 | 234,194 |
| 1978 | 41,000 | 174,727 |
| 1979 | 44,300 | 132,485 |
| 1980 | 32,770 | 154,848 |
| 1981 | 42,436 | 133,707 |
| 1982 | 58,394 | 127,056 |
| 1983 | 47,620 | 96,630 |
| 1984 | 52,275 | 145,420 |
| 1985 | 59,966 | 111,401 |
| 1986 | 57,083 | 86,208 |
| 1987 | 43,200 | 110,689 |

When the historical migration cost data are plotted against earnings differentials, we do find what looks like a negative correlation. Unfortunately, we have no cross-section data with which to compare these findings. It is, of course, entirely possible that Azad's findings are perfectly compatible with our hypothesis. This would mean that over the long run other determinants swamp the effects of wage differentials that job seekers are willing to pay. These other determinants include changes in the composition of the job seekers over time, expectations about how long one can work abroad, and the probability of finding gainful employment at home. There was indeed a shift in the composition of migrants from Bangladesh towards the less skilled, but this will not have an effect on the findings because the data presented in Table 11.2 are only for skilled workers. One probable difference is that earlier cohorts did not expect to stay long in the Middle East, while their more recent counterparts see greater possibilities of extending their stays. In earlier migration flows, workers were recruited primarily for "time-bound" jobs in construction. In principle, these jobs are indefinite in duration; the only limits are those imposed by the immigration policy of the country of employment.

## CONCLUSIONS

Job brokering for profit has become an important institution in the market for foreign labor, especially where social networks are not yet established to facilitate migration or where states of employment and origin have not agreed on exclusive systems for recruiting labor. Job brokers or recruiters have successfully organized labor migration between many states, especially where few or no political or economic linkages have existed before. However, recruiting activities have been frequently characterized by fraudulent practices and tendencies to "milk" the workers of their expected gains from migration.

Little evidence indicates that public authorities' efforts to protect workers against such practices have been effective. In particular, limits on fees that recruiters can charge workers have been widely disregarded, often with the cooperation of the workers. Private recruiters are generally more effective in finding positions than government agencies, and migrants prefer them despite the greater costs and risks. Governments keen on increasing employment, therefore, often see the need to rely on private agents. The compromise is to closely regulate private recruitment activities. Approaches to regulation, however, are often based on a misunderstanding of how the recruitment market operates. Unlike other services, there is no price for recruitment services per se. What the workers pay is really a share of a wage differential.

Unfortunately, little research on this subject exists to widen the scope for improving policy design and help in choosing policy instruments. From the few studies available, we can draw a less than firm conclusion that many factors, aside from the size of wage differentials, determine how much recruiters get. These studies also show that the existence of social networks is closely associated with lower recruitment costs. Such findings acquire greater significance when set in the context of the analytical paradigm that this chapter has tried to develop.

## References


Azad, Abul Kalam (1989). "The Costs and Financing of Individual Contract Migration: A Case Study of Bangladesh," Working paper, Asian Regional Programme on International Labor Migration, International Labor Organization, Bangkok.

Böhning, Wolf R. (1972). *The Migration of Workers in the United Kingdom and the European Community.* Oxford: Oxford University Press.

Castles, Stephen, and Kosack, Godula (1981). "The Function of Labour Immigration in Western European Capitalism," in P. Braham (eds.), *Discrimination and Disadvantage in Employment: The Experience of Black Workers.* London: Harper and Row, pp. 163–83.

International Labor Organization (1997). "Revision of the Fee-Changing Employment Agencies Convention," Report IV for 85th Session, International Labour Conference, Geneva.

Shah, Nasra (1996). "The Role of Social Networks in Migration to Kuwait Among South Asian Males," Paper presented at the IOM/UNFPA Policy Workshop on Emigration Dynamics in South Asia, Geneva.

Walwei, U. (1996). "Placement as a Public Responsibility and as a Private Service," Labour Market Research Topics 17, Institute für Arbeitsmarkt- und Berufsforschung: Nürnberg.

# 12

# Return Migration in the Philippines: Issues and Policies

GRAZIANO BATTISTELLA

Asia's migration movements include emigrants who resettle permanently in North America and Australia, refugees who seek asylum within the continent in North America and Europe, highly skilled employees working for transnational corporations, and labor migrants. The beginning of labor migration in Asia is usually attributed to labor demand in the Middle East following the oil crisis in 1973. During the first decade (approximately 1973–86), migration flows were mostly absorbed by the Gulf countries, particularly during the construction boom in the Arab states. Then migration began expanding toward East and Southeast Asia (1987–97), with a short increase and then decline toward the Middle East soon after the Gulf War. A third phase was initiated by the Asian financial crisis in 1998, which caused a temporary halt to the decline of flows toward the Middle East and a decrease of intake by Malaysia, Thailand, and Korea. The present phase of Asia's migration will depend in part on the recovery of the Asian economies. However, because the infrastructure of the region's migration system is already in place (migration policies in both countries of origin and receiving countries, the migration recruiting industry and social networks), we can predict that migration will continue even in the presence of economic recession.

Flows originate mainly from South and Southeast Asia and are directed mostly toward West Asia (Middle East) and East Asia. Southeast Asia, however, is a region of both migrant sending and receiving countries. Estimates of annual migration flows indicate that perhaps one million migrants leave South Asia every year, mostly toward the Middle East. Approximately another million leave Southeast Asia for all regions, but increasingly toward East Asia. Considering the flows of migrants that originate in other regions, it is possible to estimate the number of regular migrants in East and Southeast Asia at 4.2 million. However, irregular migration also occurs throughout the region, in the form of migrants overstaying their visas (particularly in East Asia) and of migrants crossing borders in flows that have existed from precolonial times. An estimate of the number of irregular migrants in selected Asian countries is 2.2 million.

This chapter will focus on the return of migrant workers and will ask what policies can be adopted for return migration. To answer this question, we will focus on the case of the Philippines, which is often considered to be ahead of other Asian countries of origin in its migration policies. Specifically, the chapter will describe the extent of return migration experienced by the Philippines and what policies have been implemented. Although return migration is a permanent feature of labor migration, it appears that no adequate return migration policy has been effective anywhere in Asia, including the Philippines.

## RETURN OF LABOR MIGRATION IN ASIA

Initially, labor migration in Asia reflected the same characteristics as labor migration in Europe: single young men with a limited working contract. Whereas migration in Europe became a long-term project and gave migrants the opportunity to settle with their families, however, migration in Asia was conceived to avoid the possibility of integration. Workers cannot be joined by family members, and sometimes they are not allowed to marry local citizens. Female migrants may lose their jobs if they become pregnant. Migrants generally cannot renew their contracts without first returning home; they cannot renew their contracts for extended periods of time; and sometimes they cannot renew beyond a fixed number of years (as in Taiwan). Throughout Asia, migration is strictly temporary and return is mandatory.

Within this labor migration system, return is thus structural, as the system is created to avoid the possibility of remaining abroad. Return migration is considered the final phase of the migration project, or at least a prolonged return to the country of origin. Periodic returns for short vacation followed by overseas employment within the same migration project is not considered return migration, at least for this discussion. Given this understanding, a simple matrix can be constructed, with four types of return identified with respect to timing and decision-making.

The first type—voluntary return at the end of the migration project—implies that migrants' objectives were achieved. In the second type, other factors—unsatisfactory or intolerable working conditions, changes in motivation or aspirations, family issues—prompt a return before the end of the contract, constituting a setback for the original project. In a third type, the end of the contract coincides with the completion of the economic activity for which the migrant was hired, as in the case of project-tied workers. The final type is generated by crises (retrenchment, repatriation for health or legal reasons, or situations of *force majeure*, like war).

Although also useful for policy analysis, the matrix has a simple descriptive purpose; it is not intended to describe in depth the determinants of return migration (for studies on that specific subject see Rogers 1984). While economic factors are the most relevant motivation for the decision to migrate, personal and family aspects seem to play a more important role than economics in the decision to return (Dumon 1986). Although migration theory has accumulated some knowledge regarding the factors that originate migration (see Massey et al. 1993), much less effort has been dedicated to explaining return.

## RETURN MIGRATION IN SELECTED ASIAN COUNTRIES

Return migration remains an elusive subject because official data are generally unavailable. Countries that regulate and record exits do not record returns from abroad except via disembarkation cards, which are voluntarily and often hastily filled out by returning passengers. Because matching embarkation and disembarkation cards has proven difficult, surveys are the main source of information on this subject. Although the different structures and purposes of surveys discourage quick comparisons, they do ask similar questions of returning migrants, providing a basis for generalization about the reasons for return, employment reintegration, social adjustments, use of remittances, and effects of return migration policies.

## *Reasons for return*

Termination of contract is the overwhelming reason for return. Two-thirds of Pakistanis, 56 per cent of Indians, 55 per cent of Bangladeshis, and 41 per cent of Thais surveyed gave this reason as their motivation for return (Khan 1991; Mahmood 1991; Nair 1991; Pongsapich 1991). Early termination of contract by the migrant worker involved 15 and 20 per cent of respondents (mostly skilled workers, who could afford to walk off the job). Other reasons, such as family issues, played minor roles. Differences between early returnees and normal returnees were studied by Eelens (1992), who focused on Sri Lankans returning from the Middle East. He found that the rate of early return was much higher for housemaids (12 per cent within the first year versus 8 per cent for other workers), and that their average duration of stay was shorter (24 months) compared with other workers (37 months).

Two major areas of determinants for return are presented by Eelens: reasons related to work (motivating 68 per cent of housemaids and 86 per cent of others) and reasons related to family (19 and 3 per cent, respectively). Of reasons related to work, housemaids were particularly affected by heavy workload and bad health. Other workers were affected by premature expiration of contract (24 per cent), lack of work (15 per cent), and illness (13 per cent). The greater importance of family reasons among housemaids derives primarily from the maids being mostly women, who are more involved in the care of children.

The probability of early return among housemaids was higher for migrants coming from a slum residential area of origin, who were married, above 25 years of age, working in Saudi Arabia or the United Arab Emirates, earning less than Rs. 2,500 per month, and abroad for a second or third term. Obviously, early returnees face more problems than migrants who complete their contracts. The major problem is insufficient savings to pay the cost of migration (19 per cent of housemaids who returned within one year had not met their placement fees). Other problems relate to low pay for high effort and a perception of lower status than in the place of origin.

## *Economic reintegration*

Studies generally agree that return migration brings problems, particularly in the area of economic reintegration. The proportion of migrants unemployed upon return is significant and usually higher than before migration. In the case of Pakistan, for instance, only half of returnees were able to find employment immediately after return and almost 30 per cent remained unemployed after 2 years (Gilani 1986). The same result was found in Kerala (Nair 1991) and unemployment among returnees was double the figure before migration in Sri Lanka (Gunatilleke 1991) and 41 per cent in Bangladesh (Mahmood 1991).

Sometimes migrants remain unemployed because they are not actively seeking jobs or are seeking self-employment, but the preponderant factor is unavailability of jobs. When return is to more developed countries (such as Korea or Thailand), the possibility of finding work is much greater. Some Korean migrants working for Korean companies abroad were reassigned to jobs within seven to 11 weeks of their return. Thus, the rate of unemployment among these returnees was much lower (Seok 1991).

Employment upon return entails a change of occupation for some migrants, particularly those previously employed in agriculture. In the case of Thailand, for instance, the percentage of workers employed in agriculture decreased from 77 per cent before migration to 42 per cent after return (Roongshivin et al. 1986). Unskilled workers generally face more difficulties in finding jobs and experience a higher rate of occupational change.

To help conceptualize return migration, several typologies have been proposed. That of Cerase (1974) is based on the propensity of migrants to serve as potential innovators in their places of origin. Although many migrants indicate a desire to establish businesses, however, few do so. Most do not have sufficient finances for self-employment or lack managerial expertise, and often the area of return does not present attractive opportunities for investment (Abella 1986). Local opportunities for self-employment are important in shortening the length of unemployment among returning migrants, and naturally countries with better economic prospects provide better entrepreneurial opportunities. In Korea, for example, the number of self-employed workers increased from 26 to 37 per cent after return (Seok 1991) and in Thailand one in ten returnees had started his or her own business (Pongsapich 1991).

Some researchers emphasize migrants' lack of skill acquisition while working at unskilled jobs or domestic services. Others indicate the gap or mismatch between skills demanded in migration and skills required in the returnee's national labor market. Some retraining is usually necessary even for returning migrants trying to find employment in the occupational sector in which they were employed while abroad (Saith 1989).

## *Social adjustments*

Social adjustment upon return has generally been considered a minor problem. In most cases, the extended family system prevalent in Asian countries provides for a migrant's children (Battistella and Gastardo-Conaco 1998) and offers mechanisms to cope with the absence of the migrant. In addition, the new role assumed by wives of absent husbands in managing the household sometimes confers on them a new status (see Go and Postrado 1986) and new opportunities for deepening their marital relationship. Researchers have not detected major issues in adjustment to the community or changes in cultural values. Time spent abroad is relatively short so changes in the home community are usually not significant or visible. Most difficulties are psychological and associated with drops in income and changes in consumption habits related to unemployment or low-wage employment upon return.

### *Remittances*

Four conclusions emerge from the various studies concerning the remittances of temporary migrants. First, they are substantial and significant for the origin country's balance of payments. Second, they are mostly spent in three areas: improvement of housing and purchase of land, education of children, and consumption. The proportion of savings invested in housing and land was the following: Sri Lanka 41 per cent, Thailand 57 per cent, Bangladesh 45 per cent, and Pakistan 50 per cent (Amjad 1989). Third, remittances are responsible for increasing income disparities within the origin population and for fueling inflation. Finally, researchers emphasize the non-productive use of remittances by focusing on the fact that in most cases remittances are not used to establish businesses or for investment projects.

Countering the latter point are those who credit migrants with the rational utilization of remittances given the constraints of their personal, local, and national situations. Consumption habits, for instance, are considered relevant for their indirect effect on the economy (Mahmud 1989), and the propensity to save is higher among migrant workers than commonly believed (Amjad 1989). Criticisms of migrant spending patterns typically do not consider that risky investments are not among a migrant's priorities or that the amount available to migrants is usually insufficient for entrepreneurial activities (Farooq 1987).

Remittances also positively affect, in an indirect way, communities of origin by providing "improvements in public services, commercial trade, education and health facilities, communication and transport wherever there are substantial numbers of migrants' families" (Abella 1986). As to whether remittances increase disparity in income distribution, Gilani (1986) found that "no other net inflow of resources to the public at large has historically been as equally distributed over the national population as remittances."

In general, then, research on return migration indicates both widespread satisfaction among migrants for their achievements and problems present in the system, such as the cost of migration, which places many migrants in a position of dependence, vulnerability, and debt. Moreover, migration is not necessarily successful for everyone (especially those moving across occupational categories). Two things appear to be essential for a successful experience: clear goal setting before the migration process, and wise management of resources and planning for return (Gunatilleke 1991).

### *Policies*

Asian countries in general have not had policies or official programs for reintegrating migrants. Although India devoted much attention to attracting remittances and savings from migrants with policies formulated for highly skilled immigrants living permanently abroad, it did little for the reintegration of low-skilled workers (Nayyar 1989). Examples of local initiatives in support of returnees are found in Kerala. While the Kerala State Industrial Development Corporation promoted the idea of industrial investment among migrants, the Kerala Financial Corporation sought to intensify investment by migrants in small industries (Nair 1989).

Thailand, at one time, considered establishing a registry of those who have worked abroad, developing computerized employment information, and establishing advisory services to help migrants set up their own business enterprises (Tingsabadh 1989). In Pakistan, the Overseas Pakistani Foundation limits its services to supplying information on existing investment opportunities to returning migrants. In the Philippines, the Overseas Workers Welfare Administration offers loans of $2,000–20,000 to support the business ventures of returning migrants. In Sri Lanka the Bureau of Foreign Employment has cooperated with the Merchant Bank to provide training courses for entrepreneurship. In general, where government initiatives exist, they are intended to facilitate entrepreneurship; but they usually benefit only a small number of people—namely those with sufficient savings and education to enter into a business venture (Farooq 1987).

## RETURN MIGRATION TO THE PHILIPPINES

The Philippines is the largest labor-exporting country in Asia. Its annual outflow of workers has remained above or close to 500,000 throughout the 1990s, not counting seafarers. From its early concentration on the Middle East (83 per cent of migrants in 1984), the Philippines has increasingly diversified destinations for its migrant workers. In 1997 deployments to East and Southeast Asian countries surpassed those to the Middle East, although the trend reversed in 1998, mainly because of the economic crisis. The Philippines also has the most developed migration system in Asia, with three government agencies in charge of its administration and hundreds of employment agencies dedicated to expanding opportunities for overseas workers. Some programs do exist for reintegration, but returnees seem to be of little concern to the government, at least until the appoinment of an undersecretary for reintegration of migrants within the Department of Labor and Employment.

Like most other countries, the Philippines does not have a system to collect data on returning migrants. The arrival card to be filled out before entering the Philippines through airports does request information from returning migrant workers. However, not much is known from processing the cards, and no actual matching between arrival and departure cards takes place. The department in the Philippine Overseas Employment Administration only counts the so-called *balik-manggagawa* ("rehires") who have returned at the end of their contracts but whose contracts have been renewed for another term. The number of these "balik-manggagawa," therefore, does not reflect the number of true returnees, but only the number of those who are departing again under renewed contracts. The distinction between new hires and rehires only indicates some trend of the migration flow. A high percentage of new hires could predict expanded deployment of migrant workers, while a high percentage of rehires could indicate a declining trend. Nevertheless, this indicator is not very accurate.

Lack of firm data on returnees makes it almost impossible to determine the current number of migrants or the approximate number of those who have been migrants. Government estimates place the number of Filipinos abroad in 1998 at 6.97 million, of whom 2.94 are migrant workers, 2.15 are immigrants, and 1.88 are undocumented migrants. If only new hires are considered, 4.58 million Filipinos have been processed for deployment since 1975. This figure can be considered a maximum, since not all processed workers are actually deployed. In addition, one is considered a newly hired worker even when going abroad for a second or third time, given a lapse of more than six months between contracts or a change in country of destination. Subtracting from the number of all migrants the estimate of those currently abroad—using a more conservative estimate than that the government provides and not counting irregular migrants—yields a figure of approximately 2.5 million migrants who have permanently returned to the Philippines.

Analysis of the 1988 National Demographic Survey (including all migrants) and the 1991 Survey of Overseas Workers did not produce an estimate of the number of returnees but provided other insights. For instance, return usually occurs between 3 and 6 years after migration and is significantly affected by the unemployment situation in the region of return. In fact, a 1 per cent increase in unemployment diminishes the probability of return by 12–20 per cent; and obviously immigrants with permanent visas have lower rates of return (Rodriguez and Horton 1996).

Increasingly important are two specific groups of labor migrants: trainees and irregulars. Trainee programmes were adopted by Japan in 1991 and by Korea in 1993. In the former nation, trainees from the Philippines have exceeded 3,000 every year since 1990 (Oishi 1995), while a little over 5,000 trainees had been deployed to Korea since 1996 (Casco 1996). Trainees are bound to return after completion of the training program and be absorbed by the local industry or into joint ventures. Unfortunately, trainee migration has been used less for technology transfer than to allow businesses to employ migrant workers while circumventing migration policies. As for irregular migrants, there is no way to confirm government estimates and irregular migrants are unlikely to avail themselves of reintegration programs. When caught in difficult situations, however, they pose a serious problem and often require official intervention, both in regard to protection as well as to repatriation.

Here, it is useful to return to the matrix presented earlier and distinguish between the four types of returnees to the Philippines: those who achieved their migration goal, those for whom the migration process has been completed, those who had to return early, and those who were victims of external crises. Groups one and two, the majority of returnees, can be estimated to equal that of new hires—approximately 200,000 every year. As for returnees who suffer a setback due to personal and family reasons, or because of abuse and victimization, the available numbers come from cases brought to the attention of the Philippines Overseas Workers Administration—7,747 in 1997. It is generally assumed that this number understates the actual instances of abuse, but it is not possible to determine how many of the complainants are returnees. Finally, people who return because of a major crisis constitute a special group and are normally the object of contingency plans and ad hoc policies.

## POLICIES OF RETURN MIGRATION IN THE PHILIPPINES

Intervention in favor of returning migrants was traditionally delegated to the Overseas Workers Welfare Administration (OWWA), a private fund originally established with contributions from employers, but now largely sustained by contributions given by migrants before going abroad. However, the Migrant Workers and Overseas Filipinos Act of 1995, which was intended as an overall approach to migration, includes a provision concerning return migration. Articles 17 and 18 provide for the establishment and the function of the Replacement and Monitoring Center. The Center aims at reintegration, employment promotion, and the utilization of migrant skills for development. Specifically, it is to develop livelihood programs, coordinate with private and government agencies for the utilization of migrant potential, establish a database system on skilled migrant workers, periodically assess job opportunities for returnees, and develop and implement other appropriate programs.

The text of the law reflects the basic compromises inherent in the evolution of the legislation. The House of Representatives was preoccupied with wooing Filipinos back to the country, while the Senate was leaning more toward providing protection to migrants overseas (Battistella 1998). The initiative's major shortcoming was its lack of implementation. Although the law was adopted in 1995 and became effective in 1996, the Center was not established until early 1999. Even before the establishment of the Replacement and Monitoring Center, Philippine policy on returning migrants was enacted in three ways.

### *Economic reintegration*

Economic reintegration has been high on the list of government concerns regarding returning migrants. Micro studies in the early 1980s determined that only 44 per cent of returnees to the Philippines sought wage employment, and only half of these found jobs, usually within 5 months. Another, 17 per cent sought self employment, while 39 per cent did not seek local employment because wages were too low or because they were still looking for another job overseas (Go 1986). More than half of those who had returned from the Middle East were without jobs when a study by the United Nations University was conducted in the late 1980s. For the 42 per cent who had found employment, the mean waiting time was 30 months due to job shortages or unacceptably low wages. Of those who found employment, construction workers were the largest group and service workers were the smallest. Return also implied change of occupation for most. Only 3 per cent returned to agriculture, and almost 50 per cent of technical, administrative, and clerical workers had to change occupation. In contrast, only 23 per cent working in construction left that occupation (Arcinas 1991).

The government's primary concern has been to capture and use remittances. The Philippines experimented with a policy mandating that a fixed percentage of the migrant's salary be sent home; but that policy was discontinued (except for seafarers, who still remit 80 per cent of their salaries). Incentives were then considered as a more effective way to capture the flow of remittances, through the Overseas Investment Act of 1991. The law intended to maximize the inflow of remittances by offering returnees ways to use remittances through nonofficial channels for debt conversion, through official institutions for loan and investment funds and other incentives. However, the act's provisions were never enacted since the implementing rules were never prepared.

What government policies and incentives did not achieve, the general improvement of the economy in the mid-1990s finally did. Remittances to the Philippines have quadrupled since 1991. The first notable increase occurred between 1991 and 1992 (31 per cent) and the second between 1994 and 1997. Remittances represented 9 per cent of GDP in 2001. This rapid increase cannot be explained by increased numbers of migrants for the years 1991–4. In fact, while the number of migrants increased by 27 per cent in 1991 and by 10 per cent in 1992 before leveling off and then declining by 10 per cent in 1995, remittances increased by 32 per cent in 1992, 24 per cent in 1994 and 1995, and 25 per cent in 1997.

The latest increases warrant additional explanation. In fact, they coincide with the elimination of restrictions in foreign exchange transactions and with renewed growth in the Philippine economy. In addition to the improved capacity of Filipino banks to service migrant workers through branches established abroad, the Filipino economy became an attractive area for investment. The increase in 1997, when the currency was devalued by 34 per cent, can be explained by the attraction of the country's higher exchange rate.

In response to criticisms of the "nonproductive" use of remittances, the International Labor Office launched a pilot project in the Philippines in 1989–91 with financial support from the European Union and the Philippine government. It sought to establish the institutional basis for assisting migrants who select self-employment upon return. By the end of the project, 300 migrants or their families were supposed to have established sustainable businesses and a network of non-governmental organizations (NGOs) was to deliver support services to the nascent entrepreneurs and to self-employed overseas workers. In the end, just 210 enterprises benefited from the project. Fewer than half were start-ups, while the remaining involved improvements of existing businesses.

In terms of size, 44 per cent were micro, 53 per cent were cottage, and 4 per cent were small enterprises. Most of them involved services (33 per cent) and manufacturing (31 per cent); the rest, trade and agriculture and fisheries. The project was most successful in Cebu, which was at the time oriented toward rapid development. The least successful were in Metro Manila and Tacloban because of the high costs and few market opportunities there. Sustainability was not sufficiently addressed, particularly in establishing a network of NGOs to provide services in this area.

Among the conclusions of the project were the following (International Labor Organization 1991): migrants are not necessarily more entrepreneurial than other people; the decision to establish some form of business should be made early, while the migrant is still abroad, implying that information regarding options and opportunities is rendered as soon as possible and that relatives of migrants play an important role in the planned venture; training courses must target potential entrepreneurs and must emphasize the risks involved in investing hard-earned earnings; access to financing is of great importance, and, to avoid conflicts of interest, those who help package loan requests should not be involved in approving the loans; NGOs should not count too much on fees from clients but must rely on external subsidies; the most relevant factor for successful entrepreneurship by migrants is the overall condition of the economy.

Economic reintegration was also pursued by OWWA and took various forms eventually becoming the Expanded Livelihood Development Program, which had the objective of providing credit to returning migrants. A 1996 evaluation of the program concluded that 5,466 projects were funded for a total amount of P152 million, benefiting 6,609 individuals and generating jobs for more than 12,000 workers. Projects were mostly in service (42 per cent), trading (38 per cent), agribusiness (12 per cent), and manufacturing (8 per cent). The evaluation also concluded that repayment of loans was unsatisfactory even though the ceiling for nonperforming loans was established at 30 per cent. In addition, the program generally did not benefit the most needy migrants, as land was required for loan collateral, processing time was long (9 months or more), and the loan ceiling of P50,000 was inadequate. The final conclusion was that the credit program for reintegration was "a financially losing proposition" and should be left to a bank or other financial institution (Overseas Worker Welfare Administration 1998).

The understanding that services to returnees involve the cooperation of more than one government agency originated in Kabuhayan. Available to both migrants and their dependents, the program offered referrals for assistance in entrepreneurial services, investments, and training; but it was minimally implemented. Perhaps its most significant result was to establish cooperatives under the coordination of the Cooperative Development Authority. Some forty-five cooperatives were formed throughout the nation, mostly in Luzon (twenty-six) and mostly of a non-agricultural mixed type.

### *Social reintegration*

Social reintegration was envisioned as the twin component of economic reintegration in the Integrated Return Program for returning migrants designed by OWWA. The program was to function as community organizing to create an environment in which migrants could reintegrate as active participants. However, the programme never really took off and has been reassessed within the overall approach of the Replacement and Monitoring Center.

Welfare activities have been carried out by both OWWA and the Philippines Overseas Employment Administration (the latter handles approximately 6,000 cases every year). While not all these cases concern returning migrants, the numbers indicate an established need for services to migrants or their families in the Philippines. Where the government cannot reach, NGOs and migrant organizations have stepped in to provide services. Although most NGOs concentrate on advocacy, training, and community organizing, they also offer counseling, legal and paralegal services, and livelihood programs. There have been some successful examples of cooperative ventures initiated by NGOs, and some micro-credit initiatives have been carried out in cooperation with other NGOs in the region (International Catholic Migration Commission 1998).

### *Contingency plans*

In addition to the steady, invisible flow of people returning at the end of their contracts, migrants sometimes become entangled in events that require them to be repatriated as a group. Repatriation of a large number of returnees obviously involves an extraordinary effort. A typical policy in these situations is to establish a contingency plan. During the past 10 years such a plan has had to be prepared or enacted on several occasions.

The Gulf War caused 1.5 million migrants to be evacuated, 500,000 of them to Asian countries. The Philippines, whose major contingent in the Middle East was in Saudi Arabia, was not among the most affected countries. Nevertheless, a contingency plan had to be implemented to repatriate 29,728 Filipino migrants from Kuwait and Iraq. The plan was effective, in part because 15,398 were repatriated by the International Organization for Migration. Expenses for repatriation of the others and for emergency family assistance loans benefiting 7,326 families were shouldered by OWWA. However, major gaps became apparent during the crisis: a lack of reliable data on the number of Filipinos in the affected region, a lack of coordination among agencies, inadequate personnel at the foreign posts, and strained relations between Filipino officials and the migrants themselves (Santo Tomas and Tigno 1992). Moreover, the contingency plan was not severely tested, as the crisis ended quickly and migrants were soon redeployed abroad.

The need for a contingency plan was recognized in 1997, when Sabah instituted a regularization program for irregular migrants in its territory out of concern that many Filipinos might be repatriated. It was estimated that perhaps 400,000 Filipinos were in Sabah as a result of strife in Mindanao dating back to the early 1970s. Between March 1 and August 31, 1997, 413,832 unauthorized migrants were regularized, including 119,128 Filipinos. However, authorities estimated that about 80,000 irregular migrants failed to register (Kurus 1998). As it turned out, the threat of massive repatriation was exaggerated, as only a few thousand Filipinos returned.

Contingency plans were also discussed in view of the return of Hong Kong to China on 1 July 1997. Approximately 130,000 Filipino migrants were present in Hong Kong, 93 per cent as domestic workers. In spite of assurances from the Chinese authorities, Filipino domestic workers feared being displaced by domestic workers from Mainland China. Research concluded that no immediate change occurred, yet it was unlikely that this situation could remain unchanged forever (Asis et al. 1997).

Possibilities for reabsorbing workers back into the Philippine economy were examined by assessing the skill potential of the migrant population in Hong Kong (Samonte 1997). Answers to a multiple-response questionnaire indicated that among the jobs this population had held before migrating were: domestic helper (71 per cent), salesperson (27 per cent), secretary/clerk (13 per cent), factory worker (9 per cent), teacher (6 per cent), overseas worker (6 per cent), sewing machine operator (6 per cent), and self-employment (6 per cent). This exercise confirmed that the percentage of graduate women employed as domestic workers was no longer so high, and it revealed a disparity between migrants' goals and their actual opportunities and preparation.

The survey also confirmed the relevance of information and training programs for self-employment. Once again, however, there was no need to implement a contingency plan. A pilot project was implemented jointly by ILO and IOM with the assistance of UNDP to facilitate the reintegration of Filipinos from Hong Kong. The project targeted migrants intending to return within 18 months and who had accumulated at least P50,000 or owned 300 $m^2$ of land. A total of 129 participants were selected to participate in the project.

A successful repatriation of Filipinos in distress was carried out when civil war broke out in Cambodia. However, the small number of persons involved (about 160, mostly not migrant workers), does not make that case a good example of how contingency plans can be successfully implemented. When Malaysia and Thailand announced massive repatriation campaigns in the wake of the financial crisis, however, countries of origin began to worry. Repatriation proved more complex than expected because both countries met opposition from employers who could not find easy replacements for the work that migrants did. In addition, Malaysia's plan to redirect migrants from urban jobs to plantations was more difficult than authorities had expected. Large repatriations did occur (news reports estimated about 300,000 from Thailand to Myanmar and 300,000 from Malaysia to Indonesia and Bangladesh); but these were ultimately fewer than announced (Battistella and Asis 1999).

Most Filipino migrants were not in countries directly affected by the Asian financial crisis. Only a few thousands were in Thailand and Korea, for example. The reduction of workers in Korea might have involved about 7,000 Filipinos. As for Malaysia, most Filipinos were in Sabah, where there was no massive reduction of the foreign labor force. Thus, the real effect of the crisis on Philippine migration was a reduction in employment opportunities. A simulation conducted by Böhning (1998) concluded that between 1997 and 1999 the Philippines lost approximately 94,000 overseas job opportunities. Actual data for 1998 indicate a loss of deployment to Malaysia and Korea, but not an overall decline in labor migration.

Thus, the Asian financial crisis did not create massive return migration to the Philippines. If anything, the Philippines has increasingly become a receiving country, at least for Indonesian immigrants in the south of the country. However, those Filipinos who did return found fewer and worse opportunities for employment, as the economy barely escaped recession in 1998, and no specific policies were adopted for returning Filipinos because of the crisis. In fact, government policy was to encourage migrants to remain abroad and to renegotiate their contracts at lower standards to maintain their jobs. This policy was sometimes imposed. In Hong Kong, for example, Filipino domestic workers were forced to accept a 5 per cent salary reduction, which ultimately was not enough to prevent their replacement by Chinese amahs.

## DISCUSSION AND RECOMMENDATIONS

Return migration has been insufficiently considered by researchers, administrators, and policymakers. Researchers have limited themselves to local surveys because of the difficulty of locating a dispersed and sometimes invisible population. Administrators have not set up registration mechanisms for returnees that might be useful in evaluating migration's consequences. Policy makers have been wary of providing benefits to migrants already perceived as economically fortunate. As a result, existing programs have not been implemented in earnest, contingency plans for crisis-related mass returns have not been really tested, and assistance for social integration has relied only on the intervention of civil society.

This review of research on return migration in the Philippines and elsewhere yields five basic conclusions:

1. Finding employment is the biggest difficulty returnees face. Unemployment is normally higher among migrants after return than before departure. Employment abroad is responsible for this situation to some extent, as migrants find it hard to adapt to the lower salaries of employment at home and to adjust consumption habits that have been changed by remittances. Return migration often also requires a change of occupation.
2. Skills acquired abroad are not necessarily helpful for reintegration. First, many migrant jobs require skills that workers already have. Second, workers with degrees or diplomas often find jobs as migrants that do not allow them to develop skills in their respective professions. Finally, on their return to a country of lower economic development, jobs at a level appropriate to their education may not exist. At the same time, however, initiatives carried out by NGOs during migration offer some training to domestic workers that can be helpful for reintegration.
3. Although a significant proportion of migrants plan to use savings for self-employment upon return, this goal is realized by only small group. The typical enterprises undertaken by migrants are in services and transportation. The major obstacles to self-employment are insufficient investment money, lack of expertise, and adverse local economic conditions. Assistance by way of providing adequate information and management skills to entrepreneurial migrants has yielded meager results because the single most relevant factor is the country's overall economic situation. Entrepreneurship is successful only in regions that provide economic environments hospitable to development.

4. Migrants have been maligned for irrational use of remittances and savings, which have mostly gone to improving housing, purchasing land, educating children, and consumption. However, many studies now support these choices as perhaps the most rational given migrants' circumstances (Taylor et al. 1996). A real increase in remittance flows and their use for sustainable enterprises depend mostly on the economic health of the country. Thus, recent increases in remittances to the Philippines coincided with a period of notable economic growth.
5. The social effect of return migration depends on the overall time a migrant spends abroad. However, the relatively frequent returns that are mandated for most labor migration from Asia usually keep migrants from becoming estranged from their families and places of origin. Strict return requirements also minimize problems associated with second-generation migrants, since family reunification in receiving countries is not allowed. Problems in the education of children left behind are often experienced despite support from the extended family, particularly when the mother is absent (Battistella and Gastardo-Conaco 1998).

Policy recommendations must begin with the understanding that some programs should be geared toward all returnees while others are tailored to specific situations. Information appears to be a needed service that governments can offer. Some government policies already mandate the periodic provision of information on the skills of returnees and opportunities in local areas, but early planning of migration objectives makes a big difference. Therefore, information on economic trends, jobs, and training possibilities should be part of predeparture seminars offered to migrants so that they and their home communities can apply this knowledge to prepare for and pursue realistic goals.

Programs for economic reintegration have general validity, whether migrants return at the end of the migration project, before its conclusion, or unexpectedly because of external crises. Unfortunately, attention in entrepreneurship programs has focused too much on spectacular results, possible only in a few cases, whereas a more helpful goal would be to reach a wider population with more modest results. Experience in some regions indicates that programs designed by local entities, rather than by national agencies, are more likely to succeed and that cooperative ventures can provide more sustainability than individual projects (International Catholic Migration Commission 1998).

In view of the increasing feminization of labor migration in Asia, reintegration programs should include gender-sensitive provisions. Migrant women (61 per cent of those workers newly hired from the Philippines) are primarily confined to stereotypical female occupations such as services (54 per cent) and entertainment (18 per cent), occupations for which they find no employment upon return. Their experience abroad in those sectors is usually not helpful for reintegration into the Philippine labor market, where they face competition because of age and other factors.

Provision of credit at favorable rates is another important economic reintegration issue. The less than positive results reached by government loan programs suggest that credit should be left to competent credit institutions rather than to administrative agencies. Where government action is needed is in the macroeconomic direction of the economy, to ensure that the cost of money is not prohibitive for small investors.

Social reintegration assistance is most needed by migrants who return because of abuse or conflict at the job site. Such help has been offered primarily by NGOs and migrant organizations, which seem to be more effective than government agencies in providing quality services. However, organizing the welfare services offered by NGOs, perhaps even their accreditation with the appropriate government agency, would ensure some commitment beyond the voluntary efforts of civil society (International Catholic Migration Commission 1998).

Unforeseen and dramatic circumstances will continue to create instances of massive displacement. Such events present management problems, which might strain the resources of any government, particularly that of a developing country. Nevertheless, countries with significant migration programs must prepare contingency plans to face such situations. Based on shortcomings revealed in previous crises, it is clear that an adequate information database and effective coordination among government agencies is especially needed (Santo Tomas and Tigno 1992).

After examining the specific issue of return labor migration in Asia, and particularly in the Philippines, one cannot avoid asking whether there is really a need for return migration policies at all. The question emerges because of Asia's poor record in this area, partly due to the political implications of such programs, being perceived as discriminatory by a local labor force that views migrant households as more privileged. The answer to the question is yes, however. The very real needs of migrants who have been away for some time and whose work brings economic dividends to the home country justifies return migration programs. In the successful return of migrants lie two possibilities: breaking the vicious cycle of a labor migration (which forces workers to go abroad again and again) and eliciting the cooperation of migrants for social transformation and economic development.

The best policies are not those specifically designed for migrants, but those designed for the entire home population from which migrants can benefit. Moreover, successful reintegration programs originate from cooperation between countries of origin and receiving countries. Such cooperation, which should be extended to all aspects of the migration process, has not received much attention in Asia. It is particularly necessary in the case of migrants going abroad as trainees. Cooperation should begin with the design of the trainee programs and involve assistance from receiving countries to ensure that trainees do not become disguised migrants and that their return is facilitated by joint international ventures. Return migration cannot continue to be neglected in practical and effective terms. Successful reintegration spells the difference between migration that benefits the development of migrants and their home countries, and migration that becomes a revolving door of labor exportation.

## References

Abella, Manolo (1986). "Epilogue: Impacts and Adjustments," in Manolo Abella and Yogesh Atal (eds.), *Middle East Interlude: Asian Workers Abroad*. Bangkok: United Nations Economic Social and Cultural Organization, pp. 336–48.

Amjad, Rashid (1989). "Economic Impact of Migration to the Middle East on the Major Asian Labour Sending Countries: An Overview," in Rashid Amjad (ed.), *To the Gulf and Back*. New Delhi: International Labor Organization, pp. 1–27.

Arcinas, F. R. (1991). "Asian Migration to the Gulf Region: The Philippine Case," in Godfrey Gunatilleke (ed.), *Migration to the Arab World: Experience of Returning Migrants*. Tokyo: United Nations University Press, pp. 103–49.

Asis, Maruja, Tigno, Jorge, and Baviera, Eileen (1997). "Hong Kong after 1997: Prospects for Migrant Workers and Philippines–Hong Kong Relations," *Asian Migrant*, 10: 13–22.

Battistella, Graziano (1998). "The Migrant Workers and Overseas Filipinos Act of 1995 and Migration Management," in Benjamin V. Cariño (ed.), *Filipino Workers on the Move: Trends, Dilemmas and Policy Options*. Diliman: Philippine Migration Research Network, pp. 81–112.

—— and Gastardo-Conaco, Cecilia (1998). "The Impact of Labour Migration on the Children Left Behind: A Study of Elementary School Children in the Philippines," *Sojourn: Journal of Social Issues in Southeast Asia*, 13: 220–41.

—— and Asis, Maruja M. B. (1999). *The Crisis and Migration in Asia*. Quezon City: Scalabrini Migration Center.

Böhning, W. Roger (1998). "Conceptualizing and Simulating the Impact of the Asian Crisis on Filipinos' Employment Opportunities Abroad," *Asian and Pacific Migration Journal*, 7: 339–67.

Casco, Liberty T. (1996). "Developing an Approach for Technological Cooperation from the South Korea Trainee Program," Unpublished Thesis for Master in Public Management, Development Academy of the Philippines.

Cerase, Francesco P. (1974). "Expectations and Reality: A Case Study of Return Migration from the United States to Southern Italy," *International Migration Review*, 8: 245–62.

Dumon, W. (1986). "Problems Faced by Migrants and their Family Members, Particularly Second Generation Migrants, in Returning to and Reintegrating into their Countries of Origin," *International Migration*, 24: 113–28.

Eelens, Frank (1992). "Early return of Sri Lankan Migrants in the Middle East," in Frank Eelens, T. Schampers, and J. D. Speckmann (eds.), *Labour Migration to the Middle East: From Sri Lanka to the Gulf*. London: Kegan Paul International, pp. 183–97.

Farooq-I-Azam, M. (1987). *Re-integration of Return Migrants in Asia: A Review and Proposals*. New Delhi: International Labor Organization.

Gilani, Ijaz S. (1986). "Pakistan," in Manolo Abella and Yogesh Atal (eds.), *Middle East Interlude: Asian Workers Abroad*. Bangkok: United Nations Economic, Social, and Cultural Organization, pp. 109–74.

Go, Stella (1986). "Returning Filipino Overseas Contract Workers: The case of Barangay Vergara, Metro Manila," in *Returning Migrant Workers: Exploratory Studies*. Bangkok: ESCAP, pp. 55–69.

—— and Leticia T. Posirado (1986). "Filipino Overseas Contract Workers: Their Families and Communities," in Fred Arnold and Nasra Shah (eds.), *Asian Labor Migration: Pipeline to the Middle East*. Boulder and London: Westview, pp. 125–44.

Gunatilleke, Godfrey (1991). "Sri Lanka," in Godfrey Gunatilleke (ed.), *Migration to the Arab World: Experience of Returning Migrants*. Tokyo: United Nations University Press, pp. 290–352.

International Catholic Migration Commission (1998). "A Situational Analysis of Reintegration Needs and Response Programmes for Returned Overseas Filipino Workers," Unpublished Manuscript, Regional Liaison Office, Manila.

International Labor Organization (1991). "Entrepreneurship on Migrant Earnings in the Philippines: Results and Experiences from an ILO Project," Geneva: International Labor Organization.

Khan, Fahim M. (1991). "Migrant Workers to the Arab World: The Experience of Pakistan," in Godfrey Gunatilleke (ed.), *Migration to the Arab World: Experience of Returning Migrants.* Tokyo: United Nations University Press, pp. 195–237.

Kurus, Bilson (1998). "Migrant Labor: The Sabah Experience," *Asian and Pacific Migration Journal*, 7: 281–95.

Mahmood, Raisul A. (1991). "Bangladeshi Returned Migrants from the Middle East: Process, Achievement, and Adjustment," in Godfrey Gunatilleke (ed.), *Migration to the Arab World: Experience of Returning Migrants.* Tokyo: United Nations University Press, pp. 283–9.

Mahmud, Wahiduddin (1989). "The Impact of Overseas Labour Migration on the Bangladesh Economy," in Rashid Amjad (ed.), *To the Gulf and Back.* New Delhi: International Labor Organization, pp. 55–94.

Massey, Douglas S., Arango, J., Hugo, G., Kouaouci, A., Pellegrino, A., and Taylor, J. E. (1993). "Theories of International Migration: A Review and Appraisal," *Population and Development Review*, 19: 431–66.

Nair, Gopinathan P. R. (1989). "Incidence, Impact and Implications of Migration to the Middle East from Kerala (India)," in Rashid Amjad (ed.), *To the Gulf and Back.* New Delhi: International Labor Organization, pp. 344–64.

—— (1991). "Asian Migration to the Arab world: Kerala (India)," in Godfrey Gunatilleke (ed.), *Migration to the Arab World: Experience of Returning Migrants.* Tokyo: United Nations University Press, pp. 19–55.

Nayyar, Deepak (1989). "International Labour Migration from India: A Macro-Economic Analysis," in Rashid Amjad (ed.), *To the Gulf and Back.* New Delhi: International Labor Organization, pp. 95–142.

Oishi, Nana (1995). "Training or Employment? Japanese Immigration Policy in Dilemma," *Asian and Pacific Migration Journal*, 4: 367–85.

Overseas Workers Welfare Administration (1998). "The Evaluation Report on the Expanded Livelihood Program," Unpublished manuscript, Overseas Workers Welfare Administration, Manila.

Pongsapich, Amara (1991). "Migrant Workers to the Arab world: Thailand," in Godfrey Gunatilleke (ed.), *Migration to the Arab World: Experience of Returning Migrants.* Tokyo: United Nations University Press, pp. 150–94.

Rodriguez, Edgard R., and Horton, Susan (1996). "International Return Migration and Remittances in the Philippines." in David O'Connor and Leila Farsakh (eds.), *Development Strategy, Employment and Migration: Country Experiences.* Paris: Organization for Economic Cooperation and Development, pp. 171–200.

Rogers, Rosemarie (1984). "Return Migration in Comparative Perspectives," in Daniel Kubat (ed.), *The Politics of Return.* Staten Island, NY: Center for Migration Studies, pp. 277–99.

Roongshivin, Peerathep, Piyaphan, Suchai, and Suraphanich, Piya (1986). "Survey of the Situation of Thai Returned Migrant Workers for Development of a Reintegration Policy for the Sixth Five-Year Plan, 1987–1991: A Case Study in Khon Kaen," in *Returning Migrant Workers: Exploratory Studies.* Bangkok: ESCAP, pp. 81–107.

Saith, Ashwani (1989). "Macro-Economic Issues in International Labour Migration: A Review," in Rashid Amjad (ed.), *To the Gulf and Back*. New Delhi: International Labor Organization, pp. 28–54.

Samonte, Elena L. (1997). *Filipino Migrant Workers in Hong Kong: Inventory of Skills and Long-Term Plans*. Manila: University of the Philippines Center for Integrative and Development Studies and Philippines Overseas Employment Administration.

Santo Tomas, Patricia, and Tigno, Jorge (1992). "Philippine Lessons from the Gulf Crisis: Anatomy of a Contingency Plan," *Asian Migrant*, 5: 49–54.

Seok, Hyunho (1991). "Korean Migrant Workers to the Middle East," in Godfrey Gunatilleke (ed.), *Migration to the Arab World: Experience of Returning Migrants*. Tokyo: United Nations University Press, pp. 56–102.

Szanton Blanco, Cristina (1996). "Balikbayan: A Filipino Extension of the National Imagery and of State Boundaries," *Philippine Sociological Review*, 44: 178–93.

Taylor, J. Edward, Arango, Joaquin, Hugo, Graeme, Kouaouci, Ali, Massey, Douglas S., and Pellegrino, Adela (1996). "International Migration and Community Development," *Population Index*, 62: 397–418.

Tingsabadh, Charit (1989). "Maximizing Development Benefits from Labour Migration: Thailand," in Rashid Amjad (ed.), *To the Gulf and Back*. New Delhi: International Labor Organization, pp. 304–42.

# 13

# International Migration, Identity, and Development in Oceania: A Synthesis of Ideas

RICHARD BEDFORD

Everywhere they go—to Australia, New Zealand, Hawaii, mainland USA, Canada, and even Europe—they strike roots in new resource areas, securing employment and overseas family property, expanding kinship networks through which they circulate themselves, their relatives, their material goods, and their stories all across their ocean. The resources of Samoans, Cook Islanders, Niueans, Tokelauans, Tuvaluans, I-Kiribatis, Fijians, Indo-Fijians, and Tongans, are no longer confined to their national boundaries; they are located wherever these people are living permanently or otherwise. This is as it was before the age of Western imperialism (Hau'ofa 1994*a*: 155–6).

This chapter is about people of the sea; an appropriate theme for a conference which was held in Barcelona, the major coastal city of a country whose famous seafaring explorers "discovered" (for Europe at least) the peoples and places of Oceania over 500 years ago. For the people who inhabit the thousands of islands in Oceania—many so small that the cartographer finds it difficult to represent them on a map of the Pacific Basin—the sea is the essence of history and geography. Whether as a route way or as a barrier, or as a source of sustenance or a destructive force, the sea has been and remains critical to geopolitics, social organization, and economic development. If one works in the island countries of Oceania (and I include here my own country, Aotearoa, or New Zealand as it was renamed by the Dutch explorer, Abel Tasman), the answers to many critical questions require reference to this ever-present, all pervasive, constantly moving, sea.

At the turn of the millennium, new geographies and histories are being rewritten for many parts of what was once termed Spain's "new world." Inhabitants of islands scattered across the ocean that Magellan referred to as "Pacific" have participated actively in this rewriting. Especially important in this regard are the novels and poems of Samoan Professor of English Literature at the University of Auckland, Albert Wendt (1973, 1974, 1977, 1979, 1982, 1991) and Tongan Professor of Sociology and novelist at the University of the South Pacific in Fiji, Epeli Hau'ofa (1981, 1987, 1994*a*,*b*, 1998). Ideas gleaned from the writings of Wendt and Hau'ofa surface in several places in this discussion; they capture the essence of a new geography of islands which departs from a Eurocentric fascination with the smallness, fragmentation and isolation of the thousands of atolls, reef islands, volcanic cones, and continental islands which comprise the region termed Oceania.

At the heart of my assessment of mobility, identity, and development in Oceania is a perspective on an island world, and its inhabitants, which is predicated on a particular geography. It is a geography that invokes Hau'ofa's (1994*a*) metaphor of a "sea of islands," rather than the more conventional approach that identifies and differentiates between numerous, fragmented, isolated microstates scattered across a vast ocean. In this alternative geography, the sea is incorporated at the outset into the definition of place; it is not considered to be simply a barrier separating one cluster of small, fragmented landmasses from another.

As Hau'ofa (1994*a*) has argued, Oceania is a large world, full of places in which to make homes, where generations of seafaring peoples, who habitually roamed the seas, continue to travel vast distances in order to enlarge the range of options they have for economic and social development. It is a world which, early in the twenty-first century, includes the largest cities of New Zealand and Australia as well as Los Angeles and Vancouver on the west coast of the United States and Canada, respectively.

Just as the ancestors of today's Pacific Islanders made the longest sea crossings for successful settlement ever made before the seventeenth century (Ward 1997: 179), a second diaspora of Pacific peoples over the past 40 years has proved to be one of the most interesting in modern times in terms of motivations, complexity, and economic and social consequences. Ward (1997: 179–80) observes that international migration in Oceania since the 1950s has resulted in an unusual, if not unique, creation of transnational social and economic relationships at family levels which in some respects transcend the state as the primary socioeconomic grouping for whole peoples:

> [T]hese transnational linkages ... are some of the most interesting features of the current diaspora in Oceania, and may give us clues to future socio-cultural developments and networks in other parts of the world as people everywhere become more mobile and migration does not carry the old implication of almost complete social and economic separation at the household level.

## STRUCTURE OF AN ARGUMENT

Having introduced a geographical context for my discussion, I will situate my concern with international migration in Oceania into the wider literature about what Miller and Denemark (1993: 1) have called the "new salience of international migration issues." I will address the theme of migration and development in the Pacific by exploring four approaches to the subject that dominate much of the contemporary literature on population movement in this part of the world. These are, respectively, the literatures on (1) demographic and resource imperatives for migration, (2) remittance flows and dependency/interdependency structures in the region, (3) Pacific identities and the socio-cultural dimensions of contemporary mobility, and (4) the effects of structural adjustment programs and globalization on transformations of Pacific societies.

The concluding section agrees with Connell (1997), Macpherson (1997), and Ward (1997) that there is scope for articulating some theoretical synthesis about contemporary mobility in Oceania around concepts of culture and society that are no longer linked to particular locations or territories. As Macpherson (1997) observes, with particular reference to migration in Oceania, there has been a tendency to regard the sea as something which separates communities of migrant origin and destination, and to view these as two distinctive worlds. In the second half of the twentieth century, however, modern telecommunications and transport systems have overcome the "tyranny of distance" that reinforced this separation. Macpherson (1997) now conceives of multi-local "meta" societies encompassing migrant sources and destinations.

These "meta" societies and cultures, which are by no means restricted to Oceania, use complex social and technological networks to promote movement of ideas, commodities, and people between places. In Connell's (1997: 199) view, such a cultural perspective is useful when theorizing transnational migration because it brings together "an understanding of the economic position of countries within the global and regional economic system, and the relationship between economic dislocations, unemployment and restructuring; the current political, economic, racial and gender structuring of the core countries, which provide employment for migrants, but neither the economic security nor equal incorporation into the body politic (or other historical institutions); and the construction by migrants of multiple networks, meanings and identities as means of simultaneously participating in and resisting their subordination."

## A MOBILITY SYSTEM

In an earlier conference paper, I outlined the evolution of the contemporary patterns of mobility which dominate international flows of people in Oceania (Bedford 1992). Papers by Chapman (1991), Hayes (1991), Bedford (1991, 1992, 1994), Connell (1991*a*, 1997), Crocombe (1994), Macpherson (1992, 1997), Overton (1993*a*, 1996), and Ward (1993, 1997), among others, contain a wealth of information on recent population movements in this world of islands. It is not intended to detail the structure of contemporary mobility in Oceania again. Rather, the following very brief summary of salient characteristics of the region's mobility system provides a backdrop to a more detailed consideration of four perspectives on migration and development in Oceania.

Linkages between island groups and the metropolitan countries on the southern and north-eastern rims of the Pacific Basin intensified rapidly after World War II. In the Pacific, as in other parts of the world, there was a massive increase in the volume of international mobility both to the region as well as between the various island countries (see Crocombe 1992, 1995 for comprehensive analyses of the manifold links between the Pacific Islands on the one hand, and New Zealand and the United States on the other).

One component of this population movement is temporary labor circulation, sometimes structured by intergovernmental agreements, but more commonly encompassing spontaneous and often clandestine migration in search of work, which has been almost impervious to effective policy intervention by receiving countries (Macpherson 1981). This form of movement is particularly important in the context of linkages between island states in Polynesia (the eastern Pacific) and Micronesia (the northern Pacific) on the one hand, and four of the metropolitan countries on the rim: Australia, New Zealand, Canada, and the United States.

The largest component of contemporary population movement between metropolitan countries in the region and island states, as well as to Oceania from countries in other parts of the world, is flows of tourists and short-term visitors (Bedford 1992; Crocombe 1992, 1995). Pacific Islanders traveling to Australia, New Zealand, Canada, and the United States tend to be called "visitors"; many have kinsfolk in Auckland, Sydney, Vancouver, and Los Angeles. This short-term migration between countries in the region is one of the products of globalization—the greatly increased international flows of capital, technology, goods, services, and resources which reflect deepening interdependence in both the regional and the global economies (Bedford 1999*a*).

Net migratory losses from the island states to countries of the Pacific rim had produced a situation by the mid-1990s whereby more than 400,000 people of Pacific Island ethnicity (those who could claim Pacific Islander identity by birth) were living in rim countries of the Pacific (Ward 1997: 185). There could be as many as 50,000 more living in other countries (such as the traditional European colonial powers of France, Germany, and the United Kingdom). Around half of these Pacific Islanders would have been born in countries on the rim, especially New Zealand and the United States. The total number of Pacific Islanders in countries on the rim is the equivalent to around 75 per cent of the total resident population of countries in Polynesia. For example, more Cook Islanders, Niueans, and Tokelauans live overseas than in the "home islands"; and of all Samoans and Tongans approximately 40 and 30 per cent, respectively, live overseas (Bedford 1999*b*).

As Ward (1997: 195) notes, "this extremely high proportion of expatriates in the total population of the Polynesian and Micronesian ethnic groups is a unique feature of this diaspora." Migration from the islands to selected Pacific rim countries, while appearing to be a process of dispersal from the homelands is, in respect of the modern world economy, a process of concentration into major regional or international economic cores (Ward 1997: 186). Accidents of colonial history have a lot to do with the initial flows from particular island groups to New Zealand and the United States in particular (see Crocombe 1992, 1995). Over the past 40 years, economic transformations in these two countries have attracted increasing numbers of Pacific Islanders as migrants and visitors. Over time, tens of thousands of visitors ended up staying on and becoming residents in their new metropolitan homes. However, this did not mean that they had lost contact with or an interest in events in their former island homes.

An enduring, and very important feature of migration in Oceania is the high level of circulation between the islands and countries on the Pacific rim. This circulation is, in turn, an integral component of an ongoing process of expanding the worlds of action and interaction among islanders—a process that has been going on for centuries in this sea of islands, but which has accelerated very rapidly in the past 20 years.

## PERSPECTIVES ON MOBILITY IN OCEANIA

Almost 15 years ago, in a review of migration in the Pacific Islands prepared for the 1983 Pacific Science Inter-Congress in Dunedin, I identified four major research perspectives in the literature (Bedford 1984, 1986). The oldest, and most pervasive of these was one that emphasized demographic imperatives for emigration from small, crowded islands. This perspective was embedded in quantitative analyses of people–environment relations common to geography and demography in the 1950s and 1960s (Bedford and Heenan 1987).

The second perspective had its roots in the writings of anthropologists and sociologists concerned with the adaptation of migrants to new situations in alien metropolitan destinations—a literature which drew much of its inspiration from debates about "assimilation" and "integration" in societies which had yet to be identified as "multi-cultural."

The third perspective drew inspiration from the dependency paradigm which gained popularity in the evolving neo-Marxist post-colonial literature of the 1960s and 1970s—one that emphasized the increasing marginalization of "satellite" states in a world capitalist economy dominated by the Euro-American core. A final, and related perspective, favored mainstream Marxist ideas about the articulation of different modes of production in social formations dominated by capitalism, by placing more emphasis on the structural conditions within which immigrant unskilled workers were exploited in the labor markets of countries with advanced capitalist economies.

At the dawn of a new century, it is again possible to identify four major research perspectives in the migration literature on Oceania. There is some continuity with the perspectives favored by writers in the 1970s and early 1980s, especially with reference to issues having to do with resource use and environmental constraints in small island countries, and the deepening dependence of island economies on aid and remittances from metropolitan countries on the Pacific rim. The population–environment perspective has been extended to encompass debates about the implications of global climate change and possible sea-level rise, especially for the inhabitants of coral atolls and the coastal zones of small volcanic islands.

The dependency perspective has taken on new dimensions in a lively debate about the relevance of a model for economic development that relies on international migration, remittance flows, foreign aid, and the growth of jobs in the bureaucracy—the so-called MIRAB economics. There is a very extensive literature on migration and remittances in Oceania that is not possible to review in detail in this chapter. An extended discussion of this perspective can be found in Bedford (1999*b*).

There have also been some shifts in thinking. Earlier concerns with migrant adaptation have been broadened to encompass a more holistic perspective on the meaning of mobility for peoples whose societies and cultures are better conceptualized as being multi-local in character, rather than being defined in terms of distinctive and quite separate places of migrant origin and destination. This literature places considerable emphasis on the nature of linkages between families in the islands and overseas, and the articulation of these linkages to further the economic development of individuals and groups in both the source and destination areas. Again only a summary of the main issues developed in this literature on Pacific "meta" societies can be presented here; a more extensive discussion can be found elsewhere (Bedford 2000).

Debates about the articulation of modes of production have been superseded by a more focused assessment of the latest phase of capitalist development, one equated with the rather slippery phenomenon of "globalization." There are two other key dimensions to this approach to the study of migration and development in Oceania. One concerns the effects of economic restructuring in major overseas destinations on Pacific migrants, especially in New Zealand. The second deals more specifically with the implications of globalization for island countries, especially the internationalization of industrial production, finance markets, labor circulation, structural adjustment programs, and information transfers, and the effects these have on population movement.

The development of Oceanic "meta" societies as well as the macro-scale economic transformations associated with globalization and restructuring have, in turn, been influenced by the recent "Asian financial crisis." In the conclusion to an earlier paper, I suggested that "in the last decade of the twentieth century and in the next century, the South Pacific migration system is likely to be much more heavily influenced by proximity to Asia than by its links to a distant Europe, which have dominated the transformations in society and economy since the late eighteenth century" (Bedford 1992: 59).

The 1990s certainly witnessed the extensive expansion of Asian interests into both the island states as well into as the "traditional" countries of immigration on the Pacific rim (Australia, Canada, New Zealand, the United States of America). However, at century's end, the island peoples of Oceania still remained more closely linked into and affected by societies and economies in Australasia and North America than by the "tigers" of Northeast and Southeast Asia (Connell 1998).

The seas and forests of Oceania are another matter: Asian exploitation of the marine and timber resources of the Pacific is extensive, and while the migrant destinations remain focused on countries on the southern and eastern rim, the destinations for many of the region's resources are countries to the west. Proximity to Asia is, again, becoming a much more important reality to the people of Oceania, as it did in the 1940s when the Japanese bombing of Pearl Harbor and the invasion of other countries on the Asian Pacific rim seriously challenged the hegemony of the United States and its western allies in the "sea of islands."

## THE POPULATION–ENVIRONMENT PERSPECTIVE

It is impossible to generalize about the links between international migration in Oceania and the relationships between people and the island environments. There is no simple relationship between population pressure and emigration to overseas destinations anywhere in the region, even though the restricted carrying capacity of small islands for people was a major concern for demographers and geographers writing about international migration in the 1960s and 1970s (Bedford 1986).

The main reason for the complicated situation with regard to population–environment relations is that the majority of small island states in the northern and eastern Pacific have relationships with countries on the Pacific rim which allow access to jobs or residence overseas (Crocombe 1994). This fact does not negate entirely a concern with rates of population growth in different parts of the region and, as Haberkorn (1995) and Campbell (1995) show, these remain quite high in a number of island states which have limited land areas. Population growth per se rarely features as an argument in its own right for access to international migration opportunities in the 1990s, except in the occasional "doomsday" projections of futures for Pacific states (e.g. Gallick 1993).

Crocombe (1994: 311–12) provides a useful summary of countries in the region in terms of the access their inhabitants have to a metropolitan country. He groups island countries into three categories: highest (those with free access to a metropolitan country), medium (those with significant access to one or more metropolitan countries), and very limited external access. The significance of different levels of metropolitan access for demographic dimensions of population–environment relations is obvious. Most of the small coral atolls, reef islands, and mixed coral–volcanic islands have a form of "safety valve" in terms of at least one overseas destination for potential emigrants. In some countries, such as the northern Pacific island groups in Micronesia, or the Polynesian countries whose inhabitants automatically qualify for New Zealand citizenship, all of the population could theoretically move to a Pacific rim country. This potential for emigration has led at least one authority to postulate that in the next century a number of small island states could be completely depopulated in terms of permanent inhabitants, and become holiday resorts for the descendants of the former residents (Ward 1989, 1993).

The complete depopulation of island countries seems unlikely given current growth rates, migration patterns, and the identification of island-born Oceanic peoples to their homelands, unless significant environmental or economic changes render existing settlement and agricultural systems unsustainable. There has been a lively debate in the literature about the possible implications of climate change for Pacific populations and islands. A very useful review of the relevant literature can be found in Campbell (1995), who emphasizes the difficulty of generalizing about these implications in such a large and diverse region, notwithstanding the significance of coastal settlement in nearly all countries.

The countries that are most prone to adverse effects of sea level rise, or changes in precipitation, are the atoll territories of the central Pacific, especially Kiribati, Tuvalu, and Tokelaus (Connell and Lea 1992). These countries are seen most frequently as potential sources of climate change-induced "environmental refugees" seeking new homes overseas. The Tokelauans already have an outlet through their New Zealand citizenship; Tuvaluans and I-Kiribati do not yet have such easy access to overseas destinations for emigrants. Consideration has been given to the possible plight of these atoll inhabitants by policy makers in New Zealand and Australia, but until the problem becomes a real one it is unlikely that changes will be made to existing immigration policies (Brookfield 1989; Bedford 1991, 1992).

A more serious problem, both in terms of the likelihood of people–environment pressure and the actual numbers of people affected in the longer term, is the effect of sustained and rapid population growth for some densely settled agricultural regions in countries that do not have ready access to an overseas outlet for permanent emigration. The most important forms of population movement in Papua New Guinea, the Solomon Islands, Vanuatu (Melanesia), Kiribati (Micronesia), and Tuvalu (Polynesia) are internal, either from rural to urban areas, or within rural areas.

There has been considerable population redistribution in all countries over the past two centuries, much of it determined in large part by the policies of former colonial governments (Bedford 1980, 1981; Chapman and Prothero 1985; Connell and Lea 1993). In countries like Papua New Guinea and Kiribati attempts to resettle people from densely settled areas in places where there seemed to be opportunities for making more intensive use of land continued following independence (Connell 1987*a*,*b*). However, options for resettlement tend to be more promising in theory than in practice.

In recent years, internal redistribution of people has been inhibited by a reluctance on the part of indigenous land owners to make available blocks of land for "strangers" (Chapman 1992). In addition, there have been attempts to discourage migration to towns, especially where prospects for employment are limited (Chapman 1991, 1992; Connell and Lea 1993). In the longer term it is likely that there will be increasing population pressure on local land resources which may prove difficult to resolve without some international outlets for emigrants.

Another issue creating a sense of pressure on available land resources in some parts of the region, is the retention of property rights by absentee landowners. This problem has been discussed at some length in a review of land tenure customs and practices in the Pacific (Ward and Kingdon 1995). The rights of absentee landowners vary quite markedly depending on the extent to which indigenous land tenure systems were codified by European colonial administrations. Where there has been detailed codification, and the imposition of strict inheritance principles guaranteed by law, as there was in the Cook Islands, Fiji, and New Zealand, the rights of absentees tend to be more persistent than in those places where the flexibility of precolonial arrangements still prevails (see, for example, Overton 1993*b*; Hooper and Ward 1995).

In addition to its direct implications for population growth and, by extension, for population densities, especially in rural areas, and for rural labor supply and land use, international migration has a number of economic and social impacts on Pacific communities. These are related, in part, to the age-selectivity of migration, and the adjustments made by those who remain behind to cope with a redistribution of work in the home as well as in the subsistence gardens and cash-earning activities (Connell 1987*a*; Bedford 1987; Bayliss-Smith et al. 1988).

In addition there are the profound effects that transfers of money, goods, and "human remittances" between resident communities in the islands and expatriate kin overseas have on economy and society at "home" and abroad. These transactions tend to be discussed in the context of the dependency relationships associated with the MIRAB economies which have evolved in many parts of Oceania. Such relationships form the substance of the next section.

## MIRAB ECONOMIES AND THE DEPENDENCY PERSPECTIVE

One of the most pervasive themes in Oceania's literature on migration and development over the past decade has been the role of remittances in the transformation of island societies and economies. The literature on migrant remittances is enormous, and it is not possible here to do justice to the very substantial academic debates on this subject in Oceania. Useful reviews include Hayes (1991), Connell (1991*b*), Brown and Connell (1993), Brown (1994, 1998), Brown and Foster (1995), Brown, Foster, and Connell (1995), Connell and Brown (1995), Bedford (1999*b*). In this section attention is focused on a model of the economies of small island countries which has generated considerable debate about the nature, magnitude, use, and sustainability of migrant remittances between Pacific Island communities in the metropolitan countries on the rim and their island "homes."

In the mid-1980s an economist, Geoff Bertram and a geographer, Ray Watters, both based at the Victoria University of Wellington in New Zealand, articulated a model of the economies of those small Pacific countries which had extensive expatriate communities overseas (American Samoa, Cook Islands, Niue, Samoa, Tokelaus, Tonga), or which relied heavily on transfers of income from contract labour employed overseas (Kiribati, Tuvalu). The model, known by the acronym MIRAB (Migration, Remittances, Aid, Bureaucracy), applies in situations where external resource transfers, rather than productive activity within the country, actually drive the economy (Bertram and Watters 1985, 1986).

Thus, in MIRAB economies international migration generates remittance flows which fuel internal consumption of imported goods in the islands and raise expectations for higher material living standards. Aid transfers from former colonial powers and multilateral agencies, which have either a vested interest in or a sense of obligation towards the development of countries which are perceived to have limited potential for endogenous economic growth, contribute to the improvement of infrastructure and expansion of the state bureaucracy which becomes the largest single employer of salaried staff in the country (Bertram and Watters 1985; Watters 1987).

The perpetuation of MIRAB economies was seen to be contingent upon regular flows of remittances and continued dependence on international aid (Bertram and Watters 1986; Bertram 1986, 1993). Both were seen to be sustainable in the case of several small island countries of Polynesia, partly because of the access which their inhabitants had to metropolitan countries on the Pacific rim (thus ensuring access to employment opportunities for migrants), and partly because of the commitments which successive governments in New Zealand and Australia had made to furthering the development of Pacific microstates.

Bertram and Watters (1985, 1986) recognized the potential fragility of economies which relied for their survival on external resource transfers which reflected "good will" rather than economic necessity. However, in the particular circumstances which surrounded the dynamics of these transfers in parts of Oceania, they considered this dependency to be both sustainable and positive in terms of its contribution towards the development of the island peoples concerned. The MIRAB concept has generated considerable debate, especially amongst sociologists, anthropologists, and geographers in Australia, New Zealand, and the Pacific Islands.

For example, Bertram (1997) has reviewed both the evidence for the persistence of MIRAB economies as well as some of the critiques of the model. Recapitulating on the nature of the MIRAB economy, he observed:

> In a MIRAB economy the indigenous population maximize their material well-being by management of the globalization process. Subsistence production from land, most of which remains under unalienated customary tenure, puts an insurance floor under living standards by providing for basic needs, and possibly some modest sales of cash produce to urban or export markets. However, it is the release of family members and family savings from village agriculture and fishing, and their outward movement to other sectors, other islands, and other countries, that opens the way to securing higher incomes. Released factors and cash are allocated across whatever geographical and economic space the local population has access to, with the resulting income shared between migrants and their home communities by means of remittances. This process includes employment in the large aid-supported government sectors, which puts cash in the hands of all households with members engaged in such employment. (Bertram 1997: 5)

He goes on to add that remittances, interest and dividend payments, aid, and other official transfer payments, which are sources of disposable income that do not arise directly from the sale of commodities, can therefore be classed as rent incomes. Economies whose populations rely heavily on these income sources are rentier economies and incomes in such economies can be sustained as long as the flows of remittances and aid continue (Bertram 1997: 5). It is here that much of the debate begins: just how sustainable are unrequited transfers, such as remittances and aid for material welfare?

The Pacific literature on remittance flows demonstrates that they have been much more durable over time and in terms of consistency of volume, than conventional remittance decay models suggest. Brown (1998) has reviewed the Pacific situation well, while Stark (1991*a*,*b*) contain useful general discussions. Relying largely on anecdotal evidence, Bertram and Watters (1986) argued that a persistent stream of new immigrants from the islands into countries like New Zealand and Australia, coupled with strong social networks linking overseas migrants with their kin back in the island "homes," and a long-term intention on the part of migrants to return to the islands, would ensure that remittances did not decline over time.

There are few longitudinal studies of remittance behavior among Pacific Islanders living overseas, but studies by Tongan graduate students in Auckland

(Fuka 1985; Vete 1995) and Sydney (Tongamoa 1990) showed that the pattern of flows over time is complicated because remittances tended to fluctuate somewhat, with those individuals still remitting after 15 years sending the greatest per capita amounts home. Connell and Brown (1995: 18) concluded after reviewing a range of survey data and anecdotal evidence that "while the propensity to remit was negatively related to the age of the migrant, it was positively related to the migrant's length of absence from home."

Detailed statistical and econometric analyses which Foster (1995), Walker and Brown (1995), and Brown (1998) have carried out on remittance determinants of Tongan and Samoan migrants, and on the nature of remittance decay functions for Pacific migrant communities, provide support for the view that remittance levels do not appear to decline with length of absence away from the migrant's home country in Oceania (Brown, Foster, and Connell 1995: 171). However, not all researchers are convinced by the recent data on remittance "stability" from cross-sectional surveys among migrants New Zealand and Australian cities as well as in the islands.

Cluny Macpherson, a prominent writer about Samoan migration, has commented as follows on the sorts of conclusions Brown (1998) and others have been reaching from cross-sectional data on remittance behavior:

> There are real epistemological issues with this approach and attempts to generate some "notional" Pacific Islander who behaves in some "typical" way with respect to remittances. This "isolate the modal response"... has now largely been discredited because it was shown to be a poor reflection of empirical reality... People's views of the significance of their place of birth change over time and with circumstances. The death of parents for instance produces in many Samoans a significant shift in their feelings about Samoa. Changing attitudes to customary titles occurs with increasing age for some Samoan men and produces a shift in their orientation to Samoa and in their willingness to remit. It was this problem that led me to look longitudinally at what a panel of people did and to show that there was not one "notional" response but in fact a number and that these were all shaped by migrants' understanding of what they were trying to achieve and how they could most effectively do it. It certainly gave lie to the notion that Samoans, let alone Pacific Islanders as a whole, do either one thing or another when they remit. (Macpherson, pers comm. August 1997)

The issue of remittance decay has assumed greater significance in Oceania in recent years, following the extensive restructuring of economies in New Zealand and, to a lesser extent in Australia, since the mid-1980s, and the decline in employment opportunities in both countries for unskilled and semi-skilled migrant labor (Larner 1991*a*,*b*; Bedford 1993*a*,*b*). There has also been a significant reassessment of foreign aid commitments in the Pacific both by the governments of New Zealand and Australia in the 1990s, and this has made their counterparts in a number of Pacific countries nervous about the sustainability of external unrequited resource transfers (Appleyard and Stahl 1995; Cuthbertson and Cole 1995).

Finally, the "bureaucracy" (B) component of MIRAB has been substantially reduced in some countries (especially the Cook Islands) as a result of external pressure to reduce government deficits (Mellor 1997). This, in turn, has stimulated emigration of the more highly qualified Pacific Islanders made redundant at home, thus reinvigorating the remittance flows.

The use of remittances has also attracted considerable attention in the literature on international migration in Oceania (see Walker and Brown 1995 for a useful review). It is generally argued that remittances raise levels of consumption without creating a firm basis within the domestic economy to sustain higher consumption in the future. Indeed, as Walker and Brown (1995: 90) note, remittance dependence feeds on itself in the sense that it increases the need for further migration. As the private transfers associated with remittances (both in cash and in kind) become more pronounced in the domestic economy, lack of investment in productive activities becomes more pronounced, thus reinforcing stereotypes of the "migrant syndrome" and the "frozen" domestic economy (Walker and Brown 1995).

Brown and Connell (1993) and Walker and Brown (1995) challenge this conventional wisdom about remittance use. Using the evidence from their econometric analyses of both secondary data on remittances and savings for Tonga and Samoa, as well the survey data on Tongan migrants in Brisbane and the recipients of remittances in Tonga, they argue that "migrants do not remit only for purposes of family support but also for reasons of investment in both financial and productive assets in their home countries" (Walker and Brown 1995: 110–11). The authors go on to suggest that: "Remittances in kind can, in some instances, therefore be best understood in the context of the economic activities of a migrant family-based 'transnational corporation,' where the sending of remittances in the form of goods is an integral part of the family's international trade and investment activities" (Walker and Brown 1995: 111).

The notion of family-based "transnational corporations" lies at the heart of Bertram and Watters' (1985, 1986) model of MIRAB economies. Following the anthropologist Marcus (1981), they used the felicitous expression "transnational corporation of kin" to refer to the social context of their economic system. The concept of Pacific Island kin groups as transnational economic entities has attracted considerable attention from social scientists working in Oceania during the 1980s and 1990s (see, for example, Brown and Connell 1993; Cowling 1990; Hayes 1991; Hooper 1993; James 1991, 1993; Munro 1990; Underhill 1989; Watters 1990).

The original conception of the transnational corporation of kin as an extended family working in harmony to maximize resources and opportunities amongst its members in several places (including overseas locations) was attacked on the grounds of what Hayes (1991: 43) termed the "fallacy of misplaced familism." There is abundant ethnographic evidence of conflict and tension within Pacific Island kin groups, and Bertram (1997: 16), in his review of the MIRAB concept 12 years on, agrees that "the continual dialectic between centrifugal forces of individualism and the centripetal pull of family solidarity (backed by a variety of sanctions and rewards) makes it clear that a much richer story of the behavioral, microeconomic foundations of migration and remittance flows is required."

Notwithstanding criticisms of the notion of "transnational corporation of kin," Bertram (1997: 16) argues that there is still mileage to be obtained from an analogy between extended family decision-making and the operation of transnational corporations, especially in the context of multi-local, multinational communities of kin such as those which characterize contemporary Polynesian societies. He cites recent work by a French economist, Bernard Poirine (1994, 1997, 1998) as being supportive of the notion of a transnational family enterprise. Poirine's vision of the family, according to Bertram (1997: 16–17) is

> a coalition of individuals grouped into overlapping generations, engaged in a repeated game over time. Individuals are bound into the coalition by self-interest because Pareto gains are available to all family members from joint decision-making on the education and allocation of family members for each of whom a life strategy is planned and pursued. Migration and remittances are thus the implementation of a complex set of contractual relationships within the family, and the ethnographic evidence of tension, conflict and use of social control mechanisms against errant individuals are interpreted as the usual institutional arrangements for enforcing contracts and overcoming problems of moral hazard.

To some economists, at least, there is still great mileage to be made in exploring the MIRAB model. Bertram (1997), Poirine (1998), and Brown (1998) consider that one of its advantages "is that it provides optimising micro foundations for its macroeconomic propositions, in contrast to the usual World Bank approach to Pacific development, which is restricted to manipulating disembodied economic aggregates" (Bertram 1997: 17). Portes (1996: 3), renowned theorist of the economics of labor migration has also taken up the task of giving "theoretical form to the concept of transnational communities, a less noticed but more potentially potent counter to the more visible forms of globalization."

The debate about processes of resource allocation and decision making within Pacific Island extended families continues and is being enriched by a parallel debate about the multi-local and multinational identities which increasing numbers of Pacific peoples have. These identities have, in the words of Kerry James (1993: 147) made possible "a great deal of ingenious indigenous entrepreneurial endeavor as people create durable income-producing arrangements from the opportunities which the expansion of external relations offers them." Multiple identities, and the opportunities they afford for both economic and social activity are addressed in the next section in the context of what some sociologists are suggesting are the "meta" societies of Oceanic peoples.

## "META" SOCIETIES AND NEW CULTURAL PERSPECTIVES

In the conclusion to his assessment of the implications of migration for the "expanding worlds of Oceania," Ward (1997: 194) questions "whether it is realistic to consider the 'Western Samoan economy,' or the Tongan or other island economies, as something bounded by the territorial extent of the state." He notes that transnational households clearly do not regard the economy in this way and suggests that "perhaps the most far reaching implication of the diaspora of Oceania would be to question the basic premises of nationalism and statehood in this part of the world" (Ward 1997: 194). Ward's questions echo concerns which Hau'ofa (1994*a*,*b*, 1998), Macpherson (1997), and Connell (1997), amongst others, have about contemporary

Oceanic social realities—these are not well captured in many parts of the region by the current spatial division into territories and states whose existence occupies less than 200 years of the more than 30,000 years of human habitation of some islands.

A critically important component of mobility systems anywhere is the creation of new identities and, with these, new social realities. Hau'ofa (1994*a*,*b*, 1998) is convinced that much of what is meaningful for the daily lives of "ordinary people" in Oceania lies outside the prevailing development discourses which are premised on very narrow economistic and geographically deterministic views of an oceanic world. Such views tend to "overlook culture history, and the contemporary process of 'world enlargement' carried out by tens of thousands of ordinary Pacific islanders right across the ocean from east to west and north to south, under the very noses of academic and consultancy experts, regional and international development agencies, bureaucratic planners and their advisers, and customs and immigration officials, making nonsense of all national and economic boundaries, borders that have been defined only recently, crisscrossing an ocean that had been boundless for ages before Captain Cook's apotheosis" (Hau'ofa 1994*a*: 151).

Hau'ofa's perspective on Oceania has generated considerable debate (see the comments by academics, poets, planners, amongst others, contained in the collection edited by Waddell, Naidu, and Hau'ofa (1993) as well as Sissons' (1998) critical assessment of Hau'ofa's ideas). Notwithstanding the criticisms, there is no question that his search for a more meaningful frame of reference for contemporary social realities in Oceania, especially as these relate to peoples from the eastern and northern islands, has had a profound impact on recent writing about migration in the region. At the heart of a "new" cultural perspective into interpretations of the social context for contemporary international mobility is the notion of what Macpherson (1997) has termed the "meta" societies of contemporary Polynesia and Micronesia.

The core to Hau'ofa's argument is that Oceanic peoples have always been mobile, often traversing considerable distances in their social and economic exchanges before the division of their "sea of islands" into colonial territories, and some consequential restrictions on ocean-going canoe travel, confined them to specific islands and island groups. While not disputing that some of the peoples of the eastern and northern Pacific did make very long journeys, Ward (1997), amongst others, cautions against too ready an acceptance of an argument that "ordinary people" in all parts of Oceania were highly mobile between island groups until relatively recently. Drawing on evidence from both oral tradition and the interpretations of "indigenous society" which linguists, anthropologists, and other "cultural constructionists" (Hau'ofa 1994*b*: 2) have written, Ward (1997: 180–1) goes on to argue as follows:

> Two centuries ago the known world of most Pacific Islanders was restricted to a relatively small area. On the larger islands and island groups of Melanesia many communities had very restricted worlds, limited by the environmental barriers of mountains, swamps or forest and with severely limited contacts with other communities. They had little sense of any wider worlds, of other languages, customs, economies and identity. The extremely large number of separate languages, some 1,200 (nearly one-quarter of the world's total) in Melanesia alone, most with a very small number of speakers in world terms, reflected the isolation and micro-scale of the interacting

groups. Identity lay with the immediate neighborhood and community and wider concepts of people, nation, or state were lacking.

The situation in the 1990s is very different, especially for the peoples of the eastern and northern Pacific, and Ward (1997) is in full agreement with Hau'ofa's claim that migration has become the norm for an unusually high proportion of people. The reasons for this seem to lie as much in the ability of Pacific Islanders to adapt to and to adopt new cultural models, as to their time-honored tradition of mobility within a "sea of islands." Following Crocombe (1994), Ward (1997: 182) suggests that

> [p]erhaps the great success of Pacific Islanders as long distance migrants has bases not only in deep cultural history but also in recent educational policies which have tended to fit people for occupations most readily practised outside their natal areas, and frequently overseas, and in factors such as the remarkably thorough incorporation of Pacific Islanders into the broad world of Christian ideas which gives some intellectual or social link to the mores of their new homelands.

A distinguishing feature of the recent diaspora of Pacific Island peoples is the strength of linkages between the island and rim-based communities. These linkages, which are sustained by complex networks of communication, trade, and circulation of people and ideas, are constantly changing Pacific cultures and, in the process, generating a number of subcultures which have distinctive characteristics associated with their locations. Thus, the Samoan culture of villages in Samoa is different in many ways from Samoan culture in Auckland or in Los Angeles. With the emergence of multiple levels of identity amongst Samoans, the differences between these subcultures become acceptable; they enable people to have real personal identification with different places and different cultures as they move between the multiple centers of Samoan residence in the contemporary world (Macpherson 1997).

Some critical questions about this multinational social reality do emerge, and these can create tensions for those who wish to move for some length of time from the islands to one of the rim homelands (or vice versa). While there is little disagreement amongst members of the island and rim-based communities that the cores of Tongan and Samoan culture are located in the islands, a question can be raised with reference to Niuean or even Cook Island Maori culture (Macpherson 1997). In both of these cases there are far more Niueans and Cook Island Maori living in Auckland than in the islands. Does the weight of population distribution affect the relative cultural weight of island communities in the rim? The issue is not trivial, especially for the second and third generation descendants of Pacific migrants in New Zealand and, increasingly, the United States and Australia.

Over the past three decades, the diversity of lifestyles experienced by Pacific Island migrants in the rim cities as well as in the island homelands has required inevitable acceptance of culture clashes, discrimination, and disappointment, notwithstanding the fact that there will always be some individuals who "move easily between islands, oblivious to difference, sheltered in the confines of transnational aiga [Samoan extended families]" (Connell 1994: 276). Much more cosmopolitan populations of

Samoans, Tongans, Cook Islanders, Niueans, and Tokelauans now inhabit both the villages in the islands and the cities on the rim than was the case in the 1960s and early 1970s when the most recent Oceanic diaspora commenced. These people are much more at ease with the multiple identities that are required to cope effectively with living in many locations.

There are costs associated with the increasingly ambiguity in identity which accompanies the successful cosmopolitan. As Wendt himself said, "when you don't belong completely to any culture... you will always be an outsider and suffer from a sense of unreality... I know I can't live away from Samoa for too long. I need a sense of roots, of home—a place where you live and die. I would die as a writer without roots; but when I go home I'm always reminded that I'm an outsider, palagified [Europeanised]" (cited in Connell 1994: 276–7). Ambivalence remains the norm for most Pacific Island migrants and their children living in cities on the rim.

As Connell (1994: 277) suggests, capturing some of the essence of Chapman's (1991) powerful paper:

> In an uncertain global political economy, even the most cosmopolitan Samoan must ensure that Samoa is not merely a nostalgic fantasy, but a potentially real destination... Migration is rarely absolute, unambivalent or final; it is not a cause and consequence of a definite break with a cultural life that is part of history, but a partial and conditional state, characterised by ambiguity and indeterminacy. A fixed status presupposes that the future can be foretold. Uncertainty defines the experience of migration, even in second generations.

The recent experience of economic restructuring in New Zealand, and an associated reduction in welfare support by the state, has certainly challenged the senses of security many Pacific Island migrant families have had in the largest urban concentration of Polynesians in the world. The final section of the chapter deals with the impacts of structural adjustment programs and globalization on the transformations of Pacific societies. Pacific Island peoples, both living in the islands and in the rim cities have had to cope with a pervading economism in the discourses about "development." Such discourses have produced bleak outlooks for all Pacific Island states, as well as for increasing numbers of individuals and families living in Australia, New Zealand, and the North American Pacific rim cities. It was these bleak views that stimulated Hau'ofa (1994*a*) to challenge the conventional wisdom about the prospects for people living in "small islands in a far sea."

## RESTRUCTURING AND THE GLOBALIZATION PERSPECTIVE

For more than a decade most economic commentaries on the Pacific Islands have been gloomy (see, for example, the regular reports contained in journals such as *Island Business Pacific* and *Pacific Island Economies*). The legacies of a century or more of colonialism in the region are quite diverse, but one which has proved to be particularly problematic in all island countries is expensive state-paid infrastructures, comprising large bureaucracies and costly public-good services such as health and transport systems, and a totally inadequate tax base from which to fund the costs of this infrastructure. Indeed, a central premise of the MIRAB economy model is that government expenditure is greatly in excess of revenue and that this imbalance will persist in small island states.

Aid in the form of development assistance to improve transport networks, health and education infrastructures, and promote greater productivity in the export sectors of the economies, as well as budgetary assistance to cover some of the costs of the civil service in a number of countries, has been, and remains a central part of the economies of Oceania. Through the 1980s and 1990s, a priority for international agencies such as the World Bank, the International Monetary Fund, and the Asian Development Bank, as well as governments in Australia and New Zealand (major aid donors in Oceania), has been reducing the need for this aid and improving the balance of payments situations of countries in the region. External intervention in the direction of economic policy has remained heavy, notwithstanding the shift in status from colonies to independent states for most of Oceania's countries between 1960 and 1990.

Attempts to make Pacific economies more productive and more self-sufficient (especially in terms of reduced dependence on foreign aid) have been occurring at the same time as the economies in New Zealand, Australia, and the United States have been variously "restructured." Transformations in the global capitalist economy since the early 1970s, commonly labeled "globalization," have impacted strongly on all of the countries in Oceania, albeit in different ways and times. These transformations have had important implications for international migration throughout the region and, in turn, have generated new perspectives on this movement.

At the heart of globalization is a communications revolution: a revolution in modes of transport (especially the development of rapid transit systems which can move large quantities of freight and large numbers of passengers within and between countries), a revolution in modes of telecommunication (especially the shrinking costs of telecommunication that have accompanied use of satellites and more effective types of cables), and a revolution accompanying the use of computers for a wide range of electronic communication tasks.

These various revolutions have profoundly altered the nature of linkages between peoples and places in Oceania, not always in directions which can be considered "improvements" everywhere, but generally in ways which have fostered the development of international communication between the islands and the countries on the Pacific rim. Kissling (1984) and Ward (1993, 1995) contain useful reviews of the revolutions in sea and air transport and telecommunications linkages which have ensured that people living in different parts of the region have remained strongly influenced by colonial heritage.

Over the past 30 years telecommunication has become critically important for maintaining links between the island-based and rim-based communities of Pacific peoples. In societies with limited traditions of written communication, telephone calls are extremely important for sustaining interpersonal contact. Telegraphic transfers of money are also a vitally important component of remittance flows, especially when funds are needed urgently for a major family event or to cover the cost of an airfare. International communication, including visiting friends and relatives, is often easier than internal communication and travel, reflecting a colonial and post-colonial history of concentration of comparative advantage in a few places, and the increasing spatial (and socioeconomic) disadvantage of many others.

The comparative advantages of places continue to be transformed, often very rapidly, by the increasing internationalization of production, financial markets, and commodity culture. This was reflected graphically in the impact of economic restructuring on the advantages of residence in Auckland for Pacific Island peoples in the late 1980s and early 1990s. While all of the major Pacific rim destinations for migrants from island countries in Oceania have experienced forms of economic restructuring during the 1980s and 1990s, the most comprehensive and rapid transformations have taken place in New Zealand. The details of New Zealand's "experiment" can be found elsewhere; there are a number of excellent studies available dealing with aspects of the political, economic, and social transformations (Le Heron and Pawson 1996; Kelsey 1997).

The implications of the changes induced by economic restructuring for the Pacific Island communities resident in New Zealand have been less well studied, although Bedford (1989, 1993*a*, *b*, 1994, 1996), Larner (1991*a*, *b*), Macpherson (1991*a*, *b*, 1992, 1994, 1997), Ongley (1991), Bedford and Larner (1992), and Krishnan, Schoeffel, and Warren (1994), have examined selected aspects. A major concern has been the implications of a dramatic decline in the manufacturing industry labor force between 1986 and 1991 for employment of Pacific Island men and women in New Zealand.

During this 5-year intercensal period, for example, 100,000 jobs were lost, mainly in manufacturing industries such as food processing firms (especially freezing works) and an extensive import-substitution car assembly industry. A fluctuation in the fortunes of the main global share markets in October 1987 manifested itself in a major "crash" in New Zealand. This event, combined with the significant changes in government policy concerning subsidies for producers, import tariffs to protect domestic manufacturing, and the withdrawal of the state from provision of commercial services and ownership of productive enterprises, all contributed to a massive transformation in the occupational composition of the labor force.

Macpherson (1992) has examined the implications for Samoan families in New Zealand of rising unemployment and a reduction in benefit entitlements after 1991 when the New Zealand government commenced a comprehensive restructuring of the welfare state. He was particularly concerned with the effects of restructuring on remittance behavior and on the capacity of the New Zealand-based Samoan families to continue to support long-stay "visitors" from the islands. His conclusions were similar to those of Stanwix and Connell's (1995) for Fijians in Sydney: increasing tensions were emerging between the demands for cash to support a very modest life style in the cities on the rim and the demands for cash and goods by kin in the islands. Maintaining a viable livelihood in New Zealand was seen to be the top priority amongst families who chose to stay.

An interesting consequence of a major shift from employment in manufacturing to service industries, especially from the mid-1980s, has been a shift from male-generated incomes to female-generated incomes in Samoan households (Larner 1991*a*,*b*; Bedford and Larner 1992). This has created a number of tensions and social problems which have contributed to a flow of "human" remittances back to the islands. James (1991) has described this phenomenon well in her Tongan village studies. Some of the children had been sent home because life for children in the village was perceived to be better and safer than in the stressed households and alienating street environments of Auckland and Los Angeles.

A comprehensive assessment of the effects of "globalization" on the Pacific Island communities living in cities on the rim has yet to be completed. Clearly there have been major changes in the structures of the advanced capitalist economies and their labor markets over the past two decades, and Pacific Island migrants, who are disproportionately concentrated in the lower segments of the labor market, have been disadvantaged by many of these changes (Gibson 1983; Bedford and Gibson 1987; Ongley 1991). There have also been significant changes in the structures of welfare support for all residents, especially in New Zealand, and also in the United States and Australia specifically for people who are not citizens of the country. A renewed emphasis on citizenship as a basis for entitlement to particular privileges is emerging in many parts of the "developed" world, often stimulated by concerns about immigration (Castles and Miller 1993; Castles 1997; Spoonley 1997; Spoonley and Bedford 1997).

For some Pacific Islanders who cannot be citizens of their own country as well as a country on the rim, this is posing some major dilemmas. Choices about "belonging" to a country have rarely been an issue for legal migrants on the rim; permanent residence used to guarantee virtually all of the same privileges as citizenship, and still does in New Zealand (Bedford et al. 1998). For the illegal migrants, usually referred to as "overstayers" in the New Zealand and Australian literature, the situation is more problematic.

Another characteristic of "globalization" in New Zealand and Australia has been a concern to "tighten up" on illegal immigration, coupled with attempts to make the process of selecting desired immigrants more transparent and less discriminatory in terms of sources of migrants (Bedford 1992, 1994, 1996; Bedford and Lidgard 1997). However, as Smith (1994 cited in Connell 1997: 214) argues: "Efforts to marginalise, silence and exclude undocumented 'others' are a sign of failures of the nation-state and the economy to incorporate new immigrants, by means that proved effective in the past—factory work, unions, public education and urban politics—as all these historic institutions wither away: globally restructured, weakened and fragmented."

The story of globalization is not just a story of transformation towards a more homogeneous global capitalist economy where cultural differences have been obliterated by the "coco-colonization of the world" (Gibson-Graham 1998). As Gibson-Graham (1996: 146) argues in her provocative essay "Querying Globalization," it is important to "explore the ways in which we might resist and rethink the representation of globalization as the social disciplinarian that polices all economic transformations—forcing them into line, into direct competition and equilibration—and thereby establishes a Kingdom on earth in which the local is humbled." It is important to give space to local reactions and counterattack.

Responses by Pacific Island peoples to the manifestations of globalization in the rim cities have been diverse. There has been some return migration to the islands (see, e.g., Bedford 1994; Connell 1994; Rallu 1996). There have also been attempts to exploit new opportunities in the more flexible, "open" market economies. Particularly important here has been the creation of much semi-skilled work, and this has favored multiple-job holding as well as job-sharing, especially for women (Larner 1991*b*, 1996). Exploitation of labor is rife in these more "flexible" employment conditions, but, equally, opportunities for more diverse approaches to access to paid work are possible. As Soja (1996: 5), amongst others, emphasizes, it is advisable to "set aside the demands to make an either/or choice and to contemplate instead the possibility of a both/and also logic, one that not only permits but encourages a creative combination of postmodernist and modernist perspectives, even when a specific form of postmodernism [such as casualisation of the labor market] is being highlighted."

Niche markets have been created for specialist types of food and clothing in the increasingly multicultural societies of Pacific rim cities. The Pacific Island "flea" markets of Sydney, Auckland, and Los Angeles have become much larger and more dynamic in recent years, as demand for fresh island produce has increased, and distinctive styles of clothing worn by Pacific Island peoples have become more fashionable. Growth in these "flea" markets, and a number of specialty shops marketing produce from the islands, has accompanied a reciprocal growth in "flea" markets in the islands (Brown and Connell 1993).

There have also been social reactions; Pacific Island cultures are distinctive, despite an attempt by majority populations to conflate all under the one label of "Pacific Islanders" (or PIs as they have become known, in New Zealand). Maintaining cultural distinctiveness is a complex process, as Wendt (1973), Connell (1994), Macpherson (1997), and Ward (1997) show in their representations of the Polynesian diaspora. Wendt (1973: 97–8), for example, pointed out that Samoans in New Zealand tended to consider themselves superior to the indigenous Polynesian Maori population and, in the 1970s at least, believed the same racist myths about Maoris as the white New Zealanders (pakeha) did. Samoans also did not get on particularly well with Tongans, Niueans, Tokelauans, or Cook Islanders. There were conscious efforts made to sustain fa'a Samoa (the Samoan way of life) in New Zealand, and to ensure that children were raised to accept their "true" identity as Samoans. Over time, Samoan children, especially those born in New Zealand, have become increasingly aware of the commonalities with the children of other Pacific island migrants with whom they have been raised and educated (Macpherson 1997). As Macpherson (1997: 95) goes on to observe:

> In this process a new Pan-Pacific identity has started to emerge in the social space between their parents' Pacific Island societies and the predominantly European or Pakeha society. It seems also to occur at certain periods of life in which children start to consider Samoan identity consciously as they are increasingly exposed to others outside the home, and as they encounter challenges to their self-nominated identity from other Samoans (Anae 1995), particularly in adolescence. Known to themselves as variously as the "PIs" or "Polys" or "NZ

Borns" this group is creating a new social space in which elements of their parents' culture and society are combined with elements of others found in the city to produce a new patois, new music, new fashion, new customs, and practices which mark their distinctness.

Reaction to and counterattack against the pervasive influences of globalization are little documented in the migration literature on Pacific Island communities in New Zealand and Australia. Yet, evidence from the street, in the form of the competing graffiti of the "Tongan crips" and their Samoan equivalents, suggest that distinctive identities (and territories) remain critically important in the "tossed salads" (Connell 1997: 215) that now characterize the social, cultural, political, and spatial domains of the modern Pacific rim metropolis.

## TOWARD A SYNTHESIS

The contemporary literature on international migration in Oceania indicates that the "scholarly impasse," which Chapman (1991: 264) argued was stifling effective examination of population movement in the island Pacific, may have passed. His concern that the images and metaphors being used to capture the essence of the region's mobility were "rooted in the realities of a previous and now eclipsed generation" no longer seems to apply to an increasing volume of research on international migration. As this paper has demonstrated, the imagery associated with terms such as "emigration" and "depopulation" is rarely conveyed in the most recent writings of people like Brown, Connell, Hau'ofa, Hooper, James, Macpherson, Ward, and Wendt—all contributors of ideas on contemporary international migration in the region. Their writings certainly capture the "contemporary ebb and flow of Pacific island movement, [and] its inherently volatile and ambiguous character" (Chapman 1991: 264).

Chapman's concerns with "metaphors of misunderstanding" are more relevant when it comes to the language used to speculate about prospects for development in the region. As noted earlier in this paper, a prevailing view is that significant "structural adjustment" is needed if national economies are to become more self-reliant and sustainable. It is this literature about dependent development that depresses people like Hau'ofa (1994*a*, 1998) so much, just as the prevailing hegemony of discourses about inevitable "domination" of global capitalism everywhere concerns feminist scholars such as Gibson-Graham (1996). Both have sought ways to challenge the prevailing orthodoxy about development; both have searched for images and metaphors which better capture the "both/and also" logic which Chapman (1991: 288), Soja (1996: 5), and many feminist scholars favor, rather than the demands of an either/or choice which continues to dominate mainstream academic discourse.

Discourses about development in the eastern and northern Pacific have to be couched in terms of transnational networks of kin because the transactions within these networks now dominate the economies of many countries. These ideas, which have been around in the literature about international migration in Polynesia for at least two decades, have gained added potency in the 1990s as discourses about multiple identities, multiple locations, and the diminishing relevance of the nation state have come to dominate writing about the meaning of "self-reliance" and "sustainable development" in particular national and international contexts.

It is also important to appreciate that the emphasis on multiple identities and multi-local populations in recent studies of international migration in Oceania, traverses ideas and concepts which have been around for a long time in research on internal migration in the region, especially in the western Pacific, or Melanesia. For almost 30 years there has been an ongoing debate about the significance of population circulation, rather than a process of permanent relocation of people from rural communities to towns.

Chapman's numerous contributions to the literature on internal mobility have been particularly influential in the development of ideas about the meanings of mobility in cross-cultural context (Bedford 1999*b*). Connell (1997: 215–17), in his recent plea for more attention to be focused on flexibility, paradoxes, and the essential ambiguity of international population movement, quotes several of Chapman's (1991) observations about mobility. In this regard, there are some significant continuities in discourses about mobility, identity, and development in Oceania. Multi-local Melanesian communities, encompassing urban nodes and one or more rural nodes within different parts of a country, between which there are complex exchanges of people, goods, money and ideas through kinship networks which span several regions and types of location, have been discussed at length by migration specialists in Oceania.

Chapman's (1991: 288) plea for conceptualizations of mobility which capture "the essence and meaning of a people's mobility as an active dialogue between different places, some urban, some rural, some both and some neither, as incorporating a range of times simultaneously ancient and modern, and as the most visible manifestation of a dialectic between people, communities, and institutions," resonates well with Hau'ofa's (1994*a*: 153–4) plea for a conceptualization of Oceania as a "large sea full of places to explore, to make homes in . . . a large world in which peoples and cultures moved and mingled unhindered by boundaries of the kind erected much later by imperial powers." Neither writer has any time for the efforts by western writers to impose a kind of rationality or logical structure onto the texts of indigenous traditions and behavior; both ask why epistemologies set within the western intellectual tradition of the European Enlightenment should represent the exclusive philosophical basis for the study of socioeconomic transformation in different societies (Hau'ofa 1994*b*: 3; Chapman 1995: 258).

Notwithstanding the parallels between aspects of long-established discourses on internal mobility, identity, and development in the western Pacific, and the more recent debates about "blood, behaviour, boundaries and belief" (Crocombe 1994) in the context of international migration and the creation of identities in contemporary Polynesia and Micronesia, there are some new developments in the recent literature which are linked to the intellectual turmoil surrounding discourses about modernity and postmodernity. Connell (1997: 214) makes the most explicit reference to these debates when he questions the significance of a global–local duality which "was at the core of modernization theory and some early anthropology and implicit in the presumed confusion and awkward juxtapositions of post-modernism." Citing several scholars who have contributed to the geographical literature on the meaning of place in the changing global, regional, and local networks of social relations, he invokes the imagery and metaphors of the postmodern "turn" when he writes

> The reprocessing of identity, of places and people, by those who once saw—or experienced—their lives as more or less predictably constrained by the given established order, may produce new emancipatory social movements. But, even in the most propitious circumstances—and migrants, particularly labour migrants, are rarely in these—the emergence of new transnational subjects, operating outside officially/traditionally constructed categories of identity, often results in new efforts by established power structures (from California to Singapore) to impose discipline and surveillance over them ... [Yet] Attempts to control the geography of migrants have also achieved little; migrants have created their own geographies, established new ideologies and boundaries and redefined historic notions of race and gender. (Connell 1997: 214–15)

It is in this genre of writing, which invokes a dialectic where "there is no local or international ... [where] journeys have many meanings, many endings and much inbetweenness" (Connell 1997: 217) that there appears to be scope for producing some new wine in some new barrels of contemporary international migration scholarship. It is a dialectic which challenges us to keep our critical geographical imagination creatively open to redefinition and expansion in new directions (Soja 1996: 2). It is a dialectic which is sympathetic to Hau'ofa's (1994*a*: 160) plea to the peoples of Oceania that they "overturn all hegemonic views that aim ultimately to confine us again, physically and psychologically, in the tiny spaces which we have resisted accepting as our sole appointed place, and from which we have recently liberated ourselves."

## References

Appleyard, Reginald T., and Stahl, Charles W. (1995). "South Pacific Migration: New Zealand Experience and Implications for Australia," *International Development Issues* No. 24, Australian Agency for International Development, Canberra.

Anae, M. (1995). "Papalagi redefined: towards a New Zealand-born Samoan identity," Paper presented at the New Zealand Association of Social Anthropologists, August 1995, Wellington.

Bayliss-Smith, T. P., Bedford, Richard D., Brookfield, H. C., and Latham, M. (1988). *Islands, Islanders and the World: the Colonial and Post-Colonial Experience in Eastern Fiji.* Cambridge: Cambridge University Press.

Bedford, Richard D. (1980). "Demographic Processes in Small Islands: The case of Internal Migration," in H. C. Brookfield (ed.), *Population-Environmental Relations in Tropical Islands: The Case of Eastern Fiji.* Paris: UNESCO Press, pp. 29–59.

—— (1981). "Overview of Recent Research on the Variety and Forms of Population Mobility in Southeast Asia and Melanesia: The Case of Circulation," in G. W. Jones and H.V. Richter (eds.), *Population Mobility and Development: Southeast Asia and the Pacific*. Canberra: Australian National University, pp. 17–49.

Bedford, Richard D. (1984). "The Polynesian Connection: Migration and Social Change in New Zealand and the South Pacific," in Richard D. Bedford (ed.), *Essays on Urbanisation in Southeast Asia and the Pacific*. Christchurch, NZ: University of Canterbury.

—— (1986). "La Filiere Polynesienne: Migrations et Changements Sociaux en Nouvelle-Zelande et dans le Pacifique Sud," *L'Espace Geographique*, 25: 172–86.

—— (1987). "Pacific Populations in the 1980s: An Overview," in H. Buchholz (ed.), *New Approaches to Development Co-operation with South Pacific Countries*. Saarbruchen: Verlag Publishers, pp. 85–114.

—— (1989). "Out of Fiji... A perspective on Migration after the Coups," *Pacific Viewpoint*, 30:142–53.

—— (1991). "Migration and Development in the Pacific Islands: Reflections on Recent Trends and Issues," in R. Thaker (ed.), *The South Pacific*. London: Macmillan, pp. 145–68.

—— (1992). "International migration in the South Pacific region," in Mary M. Kritz, Lin Lean Lim, and Hania Zlotnik (eds.), *International Migration Systems: A Global Approach*. Oxford: Clarendon Press, pp. 41–62.

—— (1993*a*). "Migration and Restructuring: Reflections on New Zealand in the 1980s," *New Zealand Population Review*, 19: 1–14.

—— (1993*b*). "Holding the Fort? Pacific Island Polynesian Women in the Workforce, 1991," in D. Brown et al. (eds.), *Ethnicity and Gender: Population Trends and Policy Challenges in the 1990s*. Wellington: Population Association of New Zealand, pp. 251–65.

—— (1994). "Pacific Islanders in New Zealand," *Espaces Populations Societes*, 94: 187–200.

—— (1996). "International Migration and National Identity," in R. Le Heron and E. P. Pawson (eds.), *Changing Places: New Zealand in the Nineties*. Auckland: Longmans, pp. 340–50.

—— (1999*a*). "Culturing Territory," in R. Le Heron and L. Murphy (eds.), *Encountering Place: Explorations in Human Geography*. Auckland: Oxford University Press, 121–150.

—— (1999*b*). "Mobility in Melanesia: Bigman Bilong Circulation," *Asia-Pacific Viewpoint*, 40: 3–17.

—— (2000). "Meta-Societies, Remittance Economies and Internet Addresses: Dimensions of Contemporary Human Security in Polynesia," in N. Poku and D. Graham (eds.), *Migration and Human Security*. London: Routledge, 110–137.

—— and Gibson, K. (1987). *Migration, Employment and Development in the South Pacific*. New Zealand: Noumea. International Labor Organization and South Pacific Commission.

—— and Heenan, L. D. B. (1987). "The People of New Zealand: Reflections on a Revolution," in P. Holland and W. B. Johnston (eds.), *Southern Approaches: Geography in New Zealand*. Christchurch: New Zealand Geographical Society, pp. 133–78.

—— and Larner, W. (1992). "Pacific Islanders in New Zealand in the 1980s," in P. Spoonley and A. Trlin (eds.), *International Migration in New Zealand: Digest and Bibliography No. 2*. Auckland: Department of Sociology, Massey University of Palmerston North, pp. 65–81.

—— and Lidgard, J. M. (1997). "Visa-Waiver and the Transformation of Migration Flows Between New Zealand and Countries in the Asia-Pacific Region, 1981–1996," in Lee Boon-Thong and Tengku Shamsul Bahrin (eds.), *Vanishing Borders: The New International Order of the 21st Century*. Aldershot: Ashgate, pp. 111–30.

—— Goodwin, J. E., Ho, E. S., Lidgard, J. M., Macpherson, C., and Spoonley, P. (1998). "Regulating International Migration: A New Zealand Perspective," *Aotearoa/New Zealand Migration Research Network Research Papers*. School of Sociology and Social Work, Massey University, Auckland.

Bertram, I. G. (1986). "Sustainable Development in South Pacific Micro-Economies," *World Development*, 14: 809–22.

—— (1993). "Sustainability, Aid and Material Welfare in Small South Pacific Island Economies," *World Development*, 21: 247–58.

—— (1997). "The MIRAB Model Twelve Years On," Paper presented at the Pacific Science Inter-Congress, Suva, Fiji, July.

—— and Watters, R. F. (1985). "The MIRAB Economy in South Pacific Microstates," *Pacific Viewpoint*, 26: 497–519.

—— —— (1986). "The MIRAB Process: Earlier Analyses in Context," *Pacific Viewpoint*, 27: 47–59.

Brookfield, H. C. (1989). "Global Change and the Pacific: Problems for the Coming Half-Century," *The Contemporary Pacific*, 1: 1–17.

Brown, R. P. C. (1994). "Migrants' Remittances, Savings and Investment in the South Pacific," *International Labour Review*, 133: 1–19.

—— (1995). "Hidden Foreign Exchange Flows: Estimating Unofficial Remittances to Tonga and Western Samoa," *Asian and Pacific Migration Journal*, 4: 35–54.

—— (1998). "Do Migrants' Remittances Decline Over Time? Evidence from Tongans and Western Samoans in Australia," *The Contemporary Pacific*, 10: 107–51.

—— and Connell, J. (1993). "The Global Flea-Market: Migration, Remittances and the Informal Economy in Tonga," *Development and Change*, 24: 611–47.

—— and Foster, J. (1995). "Some Common Fallacies about Migrants' Remittances in the South Pacific: Lessons from Tongan and Western Samoan Research," *Pacific Viewpoint*, 36: 29–45.

—— ——, and Connell, J. (1995). "Remittances, Savings and Policy Formulation in the South Pacific," *Asian and Pacific Migration Journal*, 4: 169–85.

Campbell, J. R. (1995). "Contextualizing the Effects of Climate Change in Pacific Island Countries," in T. W. Giambelluce and A. Henderson-Sellers (eds.), *Climate Change: Developing Southern Hemisphere Perspectives*. Chichester: John Wiley, pp. 349–74.

Castles, Stephen (1997). "Globalization and the Ambiguities of National Citizenship," *Aotearoa/New Zealand Migration Research Network Research Papers*. School of Sociology and Social Work, Massey University (Albany Campus), Auckland, pp. 3–20.

Castles, Stephen, and Miller, Mark J. (1993). *The Age of Migration: International Population Movements in the Modern World*. New York: Guilford Press.

Chapman, M. (1991). "Pacific Island Movement and Socio-economic Change: Metaphors of Misunderstanding," *Population and Development Review*, 17: 263–92.

—— (1992). "Population Movement: Free or Constrained?" in R. Crocombe and E. Tuza (eds.), *Independence, Dependence, Interdependence: The first 10 years of Solomon Islands Independence*. Suva: Solomon Islands College of Higher Education and Institute of Pacific Studies, University of the South Pacific, pp. 75–97.

—— (1995). "Island Autobiographies of Movement: Alternative Ways of Knowing?" in P. Claval and Singaravelou (eds.), *Ethnogeographies*. Paris: L'Harmattan, pp. 247–59.

—— and Prothero, R. M. (1985). *Circulation in Population Movement: Substance and Concepts from the Melanesian Case*, London: Routledge & Kegan Paul.

Connell, J. (1987*a*). *Migration, Employment and Development in the South Pacific: General Report*. Noumea: International Labour Organisation and South Pacific Commission.

—— (1987*b*). "Migration, Rural Development and Policy Formulation in the South Pacific," *Journal of Rural Studies*, 3: 105–21.

—— (1991*a*). "Island Microstates: The Mirage of Development," *The Contemporary Pacific*, 3: 251–87.

——(1991*b*). *Migration and Remittances in the South Pacific Forum Island Countries*. Sydney: Department of Geography Monograph, University of Sydney.
——(1994). "In Samoan Worlds: Culture, Migration, Identity and Albert Wendt," in R. King, J. Connell, and P. White (eds.), *Writing Across Worlds: Literature and Migration*. London: Routledge, pp. 263–79.
——(1997). "A False Global-Local Duality? Migration, Markets and Meanings," in P. J. Rimmer (ed.), *Pacific Rim Development. Integration and Globalisation in the Asia-Pacific Economy*. Sydney: Allen and Unwin, pp. 197–221.
——(1998). "The Regional Crisis and the Pacific," Paper presented at the Australian Migration Research Network Workshop, Canberra, October.
——and Brown, R. P. C. (1995). "Migration and remittances in the South Pacific: Towards New Perspectives," *Asian and Pacific Migration Journal*, 4: 1–34.
——and Lea, J. P. (1992). "My Country Will Not Be There: Global Warming, Development and the Planning Response in Small Island States," *Cities*, 9: 295–309.
————(1993). *Pacific 2010: Planning the Future—Melanesian Cities in 2010*. Canberra: National Centre for Development Studies, The Australian National University.
————(1995). *Pacific 2010: Urbanisation in Polynesia*. Canberra: National Centre for Development Studies, The Australian National University.
————(1998). "Island Towns: Managing Urbanization in Micronesia," Occasional Paper No. 40, Centre for Pacific Island Studies (University of Hawai'i at Manoa) and Research Institute for Asia and the Pacific (University of Sydney), Sydney.
Cowling, W. (1990). "Motivations for Contemporary Tongan Migration," in P. Herda, J. Terrell and N. Gunson (eds.), *Tongan Culture and History*. Canberra: Department of Pacific and Southeast Asian History, The Australian National University.
Crocombe, R. (1992). *Pacific Neighbours: New Zealand's Relations with Other Pacific Islands*. Christchurch: Macmillan Brown Centre for Pacific Studies, University of Canterbury.
——(1994). "The Continuing Creation of Identities in the Pacific Islands: Blood, Behaviour, Boundaries and Belief," in D. Hooson (ed.), *Geography and National Identity*. Oxford: Blackwell, pp. 311–30.
——(1995). *The Pacific Islands and the USA*. Suva: Institute of Pacific Studies, University of the South Pacific.
Cuthbertson, S., and Cole, R. V. (1995). *Population Growth in South Pacific Island States: Implications for Australia*. Canberra: Australian Government Publishing Service.
Foster, J. (1995). "The Relationship Between Remittances and Savings in Small Pacific Island States: Some Econometric evidence," *Asian and Pacific Migration Journal*, 4: 117–38.
Fuka, M. L. A. (1985). "The Auckland Tongan Community and Overseas Remittances," Unpublished MA Thesis in Geography, University of Auckland, Auckland.
Gallick, R. (1993). "A Doomsday Scenario?" in R.V. Cole (ed.), *Pacific 2010: Challenging the Future*. Canberra: National Centre for Development Studies, The Australian National University, pp. 1–11.
Gibson, K. (1983). "Political Economy and International Labour Migration: The Case of Polynesians in New Zealand," *New Zealand Geographer*, 39: 29–42.
Gibson-Graham, J. K. (1996). *The End of Capitalism (As We Knew It): A Feminist Critique of Political Economy*. Oxford: Blackwell Publishers.
——(1998). "Islands: Culture, Economy and Environment," in E. Bliss (ed.), *Islands: Economy, Society and Environment*. Hamilton: New Zealand Geographical Society, pp. 1–5.
Haberkorn, G. (1995). "Pacific Populations in the 1990s," *New Zealand Population Review*, 21: 1–26.

Hau'ofa, E. (1981). *Tales of the Tikongs.* London: Penguin Books.
—— (1987). "The New South Pacific Society: Integration and Independence," in A. Hooper et al. (eds.), *Class and Culture in the South Pacific.* Suva: Centre for Pacific Studies, University of Auckland and Institute of Pacific Studies, University of the South Pacific, pp. 1–2.
—— (1994*a*). "Our sea of islands," *The Contemporary Pacific*, 6: 147–62.
—— (1994*b*). "Pasts to Remember," Paper presented at the Pacific Writers Forum, East-West Center, August 1994, Honolulu, Hawaii.
—— (1998). "The Ocean in Us," *The Contemporary Pacific*, 10: 391–410.
Hayes, G. (1991). "Migration, Metascience, and Development Policy in Island Polynesia," *The Contemporary Pacific*, 3: 1–58.
Hooper, A. (1993). "The MIRAB Transition in Fakaofo, Tokelau," *Pacific Viewpoint*, 34: 241–64.
—— and Ward, R. G. (1995). "Beyond the Breathing Space," in R. G. Ward and E. Kingdon (eds.), *Land, Custom and Practice in the South Pacific.* Cambridge: Cambridge University Press, pp. 250–64.
James, K. (1991). "Migration and Remittances: A Tongan Village Perspective," *Pacific Viewpoint*, 32: 1–23.
—— (1993). "The Rhetoric and Reality of Change and Development in Small Pacific Communities," *Pacific Viewpoint*, 34: 135–52.
Kelsey, J. (1997). *The New Zealand Experiment: A World Model for Structural Adjustment?* Wellington: Auckland University Press and Bridget Williams Books.
Kissling, C. (1984). *Transport and Communications for Pacific Microstates: Issues in Organisation and Management.* Suva: Institute of Pacific Studies, University of the South Pacific.
Krishnan, V., Schoeffel, P., and Warren, J. (1994). *The Challenge of Change: Pacific Island Communities in New Zealand 1986–1993.* Wellington: New Zealand Institute for Social Research and Development Ltd.
Larner, W. (1991*a*). "Labour Migration and Female Labour: Samoan Women in New Zealand," *Australian and New Zealand Journal of Sociology*, 27: 19–33.
—— (1991*b*). "Women and Migration," in P. Spoonley, D. Pearson, and C. Macpherson (eds.), *Nga Take: Ethnic Relations and Racism in Aotearoa/New Zealand.* Palmerston North: Dunmore Press, pp. 51–66.
—— (1996). "Feminisation of the Labour Force," in R. Le Heron and E. Pawson (eds.), *Changing Places: New Zealand in the Nineties.* Auckland: Longman Paul, pp. 97–101.
Le Heron, R. and Pawson, E. P. (1996). *Changing Places: New Zealand in the Nineties.* Auckland: Longman Paul.
Macpherson, C. (1981). "Guest-Worker Movements and their Consequences for Donor and Recipient Countries: A Case Study," in G. W. Jones and H. V. Richter (eds.), *Population Mobility and Development: Southeast Asia and the Pacific.* Canberra: Development Studies Centre, The Australian National University, pp. 257–77.
—— (1991*a*). "Pacific Islanders," *Pacific Viewpoint*, 32(2): 139–46.
—— (1991*b*). "The Changing Contours of Samoan ethnicity," in P. Spoonley, D. Pearson, and C. Macpherson (eds.), *Nga Take: Ethnic Relations and Racism in Aotearoa/New Zealand.* Palmerston North: Dunmore Press, pp. 67–86.
—— (1992). "Economic and Political Restructuring and the Sustainability of Remittances: The Case of Western Samoa," *The Contemporary Pacific*, 4: 109–35.
—— (1994). "Changing Patterns of Commitment to Island Homelands," *Pacific Studies*, 17: 83–116.
—— (1997). "The Polynesian Diaspora: New Communities and New Questions," in Ken'ichi Sudo and Shuji Yoshida (eds.), *Contemporary Migration in Oceania: Diaspora and Network.* Osaka: Japan Center for Area Studies, pp. 77–100.

Marcus, G. E. (1981). "Power on the Extreme Periphery: The Perspective of Tongan Elites on the Modern World System," *Pacific Viewpoint*, 22: 48–64.

Massey, D. S., Arango, J., Hugo, G., Kouaouci, A., Pellegrino, A., and Taylor, J. E. (1994). "An Evaluation of International Migration Theory: The North American Case," *Population and Development Review*, 20: 699–751.

Mellor, C. S. (1997). "Economic Restructuring in Cook Islands: A Review," *Pacific Economic Bulletin*, 12: 17–24.

Miller, Mark J., and Denemark, R. A. (1993). "Migration and World Politics: A Critical Case for Theory and Policy," Occasional Paper No. 8, Center for Migration Studies, Staten Island, New York.

Munro, D. (1990). "Transnational Corporations of Kin and the MIRAB System," *Pacific Viewpoint*, 31: 63–66.

Ongley, P. (1991). "Pacific Islands' Migration and the New Zealand Labour market," in P. Spoonley, D. Pearson, and C. Macpherson (eds.), *Nga Take: Ethnic Relations and Racism in Aotearoa/New Zealand*. Palmerston North: Dunmore Press, pp. 17–36.

Overton, J. (1993*a*). "Pacific Futures? Geography and Change in the Pacific Islands," *New Zealand Geographer*, 49: 48–55.

—— (1993*b*). "Farms, Suburbs, or Retirement Homes: The Transformation of Village Fiji," *The Contemporary Pacific*, 5: 45–74.

—— (1996). "Restructuring Oceania: Regional Reconfigurations of Economic and Political Relations in the Pacific," in Yue-Man Yeung (ed.), *Global Change and the Commonwealth*. Hong Kong: Hong Kong Institute of Pacific Studies, Chinese University of Hong Kong, pp. 131–56.

Poirine, B. (1994). "Rent, Emigration and Unemployment in Small Islands: The MIRAB Model and the French Overseas Departments and Territories," *World Development*, 22: 1997–2009.

—— (1997). "A Theory of Remittances as an Implicit Family Loan Arrangement," *World Development*, 25: 22–81.

—— (1998). "Should we Love or Hate MIRAB?" *The Contemporary Pacific*, 10: 65–106.

Portes, Alejandro (1996). "Globalization from Below: The Rise of Transnational Communities," in W. P. Smith and R. P. Korczenwicz (eds.), *Latin America in the World Economy*. Westport, CT: Greenwood Press, pp. 151–68.

Rallu, J.-L. (1996). "Return Migration to the Cook Islands," *New Zealand Population Review*, 22: 45–68.

Sissons, J. (1998). "Conspiracy, Class and Culture in Oceania: A View from the Cook Islands," *The Contemporary Pacific*, 10: 164–78.

Smith, M. P. (1994). "Can You Imagine? Transnational Migration and the Globalization of Grassroots Politics," *Social Text*, 39: 15–33.

Soja, E. W. (1996). *Thirdspace: Journeys to Los Angeles and Other Real-and-Imagined Places*. Oxford: Blackwell Publishers.

Spoonley, P. (1997). "Migration and the Reconstruction of Citizenship in Late Twentieth Century Aotearoa," *Aotearoa/New Zealand Migration Research Network Research Papers*. School of Sociology and Social Work, Massey University (Albany Campus), Auckland, pp. 21–40.

—— and Bedford, R. D. (1997). "Migration Issues in Aotearoa/New Zealand," in P. Brownlee and C. Mitchell (eds.), *Migration Issues in the Asia Pacific*. Wollongong: Centre for Multicultural Studies-Institute for Social Change and Critical Inquiry, University of Wollongong, pp. 1–22.

Stanwix, C., and Connell, J. (1995). "To the Islands: The Remittances of Fijians in Sydney," *Asian and Pacific Migration Journal*, 4: 69–88.

Stark, O. (1991*a*). *The Migration of Labor*. Oxford: Basil Blackwell.

Stark, O. (1991*b*). "Migration in LDCs: Risks, Remittances and the Family," *Finance and Development*, 28: 39–41.
Tongamoa, T. (1990). "Migration, Remittances and Development: A Tongan Perspective," Unpublished MA Thesis in Geography, University of Sydney, Sydney.
Underhill, Y. (1989). "Population Mobility as a Household Strategy: The Case of Manihiki Atoll, Cook Islands," Unpublished MA Thesis in Geography, University of Hawai'i.
Vete, M. F. (1995). "The Determinants of Remittances among Tongans in Auckland," *Asian and Pacific Migration Journal*, 4: 55–68.
Waddell, E., Naidu, V. J., and Hau'ofa, E. (1993). *A New Oceania: Rediscovering our Sea of Islands*. Suva: School of Social and Economic Development, University of the South Pacific.
Walker, A., and Brown, R. P. C. (1995). "From Consumption to Savings? Interpreting Tongan and Western Samoan Sample Survey Data on Remittances," *Asian and Pacific Migration Journal*, 4: 89–116.
Ward, R. G. (1989). "Earth's Empty Quarter? The Pacific Islands in a Pacific Century," *Geographical Journal*, 155: 235–46.
——(1993). "South Pacific Futures: Paradise, Prosperity or Pauperism?" *The Contemporary Pacific*, 5: 1–21.
——(1995). "The Shape of Tele-cost Worlds: The Pacific Islands Case," in A.D. Cliff, P.R. Gould, A.G. Hoare, and N.J. Thrift (eds.), *Diffusing Geography: Essays for Peter Haggett*. Oxford: Blackwell, pp. 221–40.
——(1997). "Expanding Worlds of Oceania: Implications for Migration," in Ken'ichi Sudo and Shuji Yoshida (eds.), *Contemporary Migration in Oceania: Diaspora and Network*. Osaka: Japan Center for Area Studies, pp. 176–96.
——and Kingdon, E. (1995). *Land, Custom and Practice in the South Pacific*. Cambridge: Cambridge University Press.
Watters, R. F. (1987). "The Political Economy of Decolonisation and Nationhood in Small Pacific Societies," in A. Hooper et al. (eds.), *Class and Culture in the South Pacific*. Suva: Centre for Pacific Studies, University of Auckland and Institute of Pacific Studies, University of the South Pacific, pp. 32–55.
——(1990). "Comment on 'Transnational Corporations of Kin and the MIRAB System: The case of Tuvalu,'" *Pacific Viewpoint*, 31: 67–68.
Wendt, A. (1973). *Sons for the Return Home*. Auckland: Longman Paul.
——(1974). *Flying Fox in a Freedom Tree*. Auckland: Longman Paul.
——(1977). *Pouliuli*. Auckland: Longman Paul.
——(1979). *Leaves of the Banyan Tree*. Auckland: Longman Paul.
——(1982). "Towards a New Oceania," in G. Amirthanayagam (ed.), *Writers in East-West Encounter: New Cultural Bearings*. London: Macmillan Press, pp. 202–15.
——(1991). *Ola*. Auckland: Penguin.

# PART III

# POLICIES IN RECEIVING NATIONS

# 14

# Have the Occupational Skills of New Immigrants to the United States Declined Over Time? Evidence from the Immigrant Cohorts of 1977, 1982, and 1994

GUILLERMINA JASSO

Immigration to the United States is a topic that excites the interest of scholars, policymakers, and the general public—the general public because they seek simultaneously to honor their heritage and safeguard their future, policymakers because they cannot ignore the competing claims of aroused constituencies, and scholars because immigration combines and exemplifies a rich array of behavioral, historical, constitutional, and legal questions. The behavioral questions have long attracted social scientists from diverse disciplines: Who comes, and why? How long do they stay? What happens to their identity, and to their pocketbook? What happens to their children? How long does it take to become an American? An early example is the monumental work by Thomas and Znaniecki (1918–20), *The Polish Peasant in Europe and America.*

Often, however, the questions asked are not well posed, and the data used to address them are not a good fit to the questions. The results are thus far from satisfying—neither scholars nor policymakers nor the general public obtain conclusive answers.

In this chapter I consider one important question—whether the occupational skills of entering cohorts of immigrants to the United States have declined over time. Specifically, I analyze the question, assess the data required to address it, and present new evidence.

A large body of recent research indicates that immigrant occupational skills have declined over time (see, for example, Borjas 1994; LaLonde and Topel 1992). However, the data used to reach that conclusion are not exactly appropriate to the

This is a revised version of a paper presented at the Conference on "International Migration at Century's End: Trends and Issues," Barcelona, Spain, May 1997. Early versions of portions of this paper were also presented at the annual meeting of the American Economic Association, New Orleans, Louisiana, January 1997, and at the Conference of the International Sociological Association, Research Group on Migration, New York, New York, June 1997. I am grateful to participants at all those meetings for many helpful comments, but especially to Joaquín Arango, Harriet Duleep, Douglas T. Gurak, Ali Kouaouci, Lin Lean Lim, Adela Pellegrino, Mark Regets, T. Paul Schultz, Georges Tapinos, J. Edward Taylor, Min Zhou, and Hania Zlotnik.

question. For example, data that do not distinguish between immigrants and non-immigrants are used to assess the skills of entering cohorts of immigrants. Thus, the finding that more recently arrived foreign-born have lower work attachment and earnings could be due to different legal composition across groups with different duration, given that the more recently arrived are less likely to be permanent resident aliens—with permission to work—than those with longer tenure in the United States. Moreover, differences across time among recent arrivals could reflect changes in the mix of immigrants and nonimmigrants.

Relatedly, labor force participation among foreign-born women is particularly difficult to assess in such data, given that the spouses of many nonimmigrants are not permitted to work, so that what appears to be lack of a work ethic may instead be compliance with the law (or, alternatively, concealment of unauthorized employment). The lack of fit between questions and data has prompted efforts to obtain better assessments using more appropriate data and, more fundamentally, to obtain better data. In this chapter, I report preliminary new evidence on cohort effects based on a different body of data, data which do identify legal immigrants.

## THE QUESTION AND THE DATA

### *Change in cohort quality*[1]

New immigrants to the United States bring with them a given level of human capital, observable, *inter alia*, in their schooling, occupation, and wages. Because the decision to migrate involves a comparison of prospects in the origin and destination countries, the distribution of human capital among a cohort of immigrants reflects conditions in their origin countries and conditions in the United States—not only economic conditions but also social, political, and, importantly, legal conditions. For example, through its immigration laws, the United States plays a part in shaping the immigrant human capital distribution; and, so, too, through their educational and occupational policies, do origin countries. Because conditions both in the United States and around the world change over time—laws change, there is economic development, periodically there are natural disasters and political upheavals, etc.—the human capital distribution among new immigrants also changes.

Cohort change in the human capital distribution among immigrants may appear as a trend; and the trend may be positive or negative. Alternatively, there may be trendless changes, depending on the underlying changes in country conditions. *A priori* we can imagine several components of cohort change, not all of them producing a trend. Here are three examples.

First, consider the popular story of declining immigrant quality due to the family reunification provisions of U.S. immigration law. In essence, this story says that the greater the obstacles to migration, the higher the quality of the immigrant; pioneer immigrants are, thus, of higher quality than the relatives who follow. As family

1. Following conventional usage, the term "quality" is used as a convenient shorthand for the level of occupational skills; of course, there are other forms of quality not correlated with occupational skills.

reunification becomes entrenched, new immigrants represent the third, fourth, and higher-order links in the chain started by the pioneer immigrant; hence, there should be a diminution in immigrant quality over time. This story is eminently plausible, and recent research appears to support it.

Now consider a second scenario. Periodically, there are natural disasters and political upheavals around the world, and periodically there are streams of refugees. Sometimes the refugees are poor and uneducated—perhaps the earthquake or famine struck in poor areas—and sometimes the refugees are wealthy and cultivated—perhaps the coup struck directly at them. To the extent that the United States provides a haven for refugees, and there is no trend in the targets of natural or political upheavals, the refugee component of U.S. immigration will exhibit cohort change in quality but no trend in such change.[2]

Finally, consider a generalization of both the family reunification and refugee stories, one based on migration networks. This story highlights the links between prospective immigrants and individuals or organizations in the destination country. The links—and hence the networks—may be based on a variety of characteristics or activities, for example, on kin relationships or on professional relationships. Thus, several kinds of migration networks can be identified, including employment networks, family networks, marriage-market networks, friendship networks, and philanthropic-organization networks. Building on work by Burt (1995), Massey (1990), Portes and Sensenbrenner (1993), and others, we can conjecture that there are (at least) two mechanisms by which migration networks operate and that these two mechanisms have opposite effects: By reducing the costs of migration, they reduce the intensity of self-selection and hence immigrant productivity, but by increasing access to information, networks enhance productivity.[3]

Meanwhile, the human capital distribution of the native-born U.S. population also changes over time. Studies of immigrant cohort quality typically investigate not only cohort changes among the immigrants but also cohort changes relative to the U.S. population. It is possible, for example, for a positive absolute trend in immigrant skills to coexist with a negative relative trend.

The study of cohort effects raises several additional questions, among them two basic questions: First, what do we mean by "immigrant"? Second, what do we mean by "year of entry"?

*Immigrants*

When policymakers think about "immigrants," they think about immigration policy; they think about changing this or that provision of immigration law. The term

2. Sometimes a given refugee stream may exhibit declining quality over time. This occurs if the danger—and the urgency to flee—is correlated with skills. See Jasso and Rosenzweig (1990: 358–81) for discussion and evidence concerning this "wave" effect.

3. An important question concerns the relative strength of both the positive and negative effects of each type of network. Further hypotheses involve the effects of contact with several networks, conditioned by the networks' interrelationships—for example, following Burt's (1995) notion of "structural holes," the lesser the overlap across networks, the greater the benefit.

"immigrant" has a precise meaning in U.S. law: An immigrant is a person admitted for permanent residence in the United States. An immigrant has a substantial set of rights, including the right to engage in most occupations and, later, the right to become a citizen.[4]

When social scientists study the behavior of a set of individuals, it is assumed that those individuals constitute a meaningful class of some kind, that they share certain behaviorally relevant features. Thus, in studying the employment decisions of immigrants (and comparing them to those of natives or across origin countries), it is assumed that the "immigrants" share the feature that they have the right to engage in most occupations, that they can engage in job search, and so on. The interests of scientists and the interests of policymakers thus coalesce—the human object of study is a holder of a permanent resident alien visa.[5]

*Year of admission*

"Cohort" is given the proper name of the year of admission to lawful permanent residence. For example, an immigrant is said to belong to the 1975 immigrant cohort or the 1948 immigrant cohort, etc. All members of the cohort share certain formative experiences. They have complied with the law in effect at that time; and the cohort date marks the inception of their "permanent residence." Because the rights of immigrants differ sharply from the rights of nonimmigrants (i.e. holders of a temporary visa)—for example, in the work sphere—life as an immigrant may differ sharply from life as a nonimmigrant. Thus, the cohort of interest when we study immigrants refers to the date of admission to permanent residence. Although time in the United States as a nonimmigrant may play important parts in language acquisition or in job or marital search, the defining date for an immigrant cohort is the date of admission to permanent residence.[6]

4. Legislation enacted in 1997 reduces the rights of nonnaturalized immigrants, including the rights of certain immigrants to obtain certain forms of public assistance. However, employment rights remain unimpaired.
5. According to U.S. law, an immigrant is an alien (i.e. not a citizen or national of the United States) who is granted the right to reside permanently in the United States. Some equivalent phrases are: Becoming an immigrant, gaining admission to permanent residence, getting a "green card." (Note, however, that confusion sometimes arises because the "green card" is physically produced after admission to permanent residence, and thus there is an interval of several weeks between admission to permanent residence and the new permanent resident's receipt of the actual physical card; during this interval the immigrant's proof of permanent resident status is a special stamp on his or her passport.)
6. A third, deeper, question involves the fit between "year of entry," however defined, and the "cohort" underlying the "cohort effects." Ideally, the date of immigration signals the origin-country events propelling the move. In an earlier time, before the United States established numerical controls on immigration, date of immigration told a story; the story might be of the Irish potato famine or of the Russian Czar's conscription initiatives. But immigration restriction has produced lengthy waiting lists for admission to permanent residence (3.6 million in January 1997) and, though some types of visas are available immediately, others may take as long as twenty years (e.g. in May of 1997 family-fourth-preference visas—for siblings of U.S. citizens—for Philippine applicants were available only to applicants who had been approved since before 22 December 1977). Thus, the date of immigration is no longer a direct indicator of the origin-country events propelling the move.

The study of cohort effects in immigration thus asks about changes in the quality of immigrant cohorts over time, where immigrant cohorts are defined as the set of persons who became permanent resident aliens during a specified period of time, usually a year. Because immigration is an official matter, and the United States government follows fiscal years, immigrant cohorts are defined by the fiscal year; since 1976, the U.S. fiscal year starts on the first of October and carries the name of the following calendar year.[7]

*Mechanisms for cohort changes*

As noted above, the family reunification provisions of U.S. immigration law governing visa allocation would appear to promote a decline in cohort quality. The system currently in place has its roots in the 1965 amendments to the Immigration and Nationality Act of 1952. The 1965 Act placed great emphasis on family reunification, so that relatively few slots were available for prospective immigrants from Eastern Hemisphere countries who did not have kin in the United States; concomitantly, it placed, for the first time, a numerical ceiling on immigration from the Western Hemisphere. However, the Western Hemisphere retained first-come/first-served visa allocation until 1977, when it, too, came under the family-reunification preference system. The 1990 Immigration Act changed the law, allowing more immigrant visas to non-kin, for example, 55,000 diversity visas and a minimum of 140,000 employment-based visas per year to non-kin workers (the 140,000 including their spouses and children, however). Nonetheless, the majority of immigrant visas are still awarded on the basis of kinship.

There are three broad types of family members whose immigration is facilitated by current law. First, U.S. law permits the unlimited immigration of the spouses, minor children, and parents of (adult) U.S. citizens. Second, U.S. law permits the numerically limited immigration of the siblings and adult children of U.S. citizens and the spouses and children of permanent resident aliens (immigrants who have not yet naturalized). Third, U.S. law permits the immigration of the spouses and minor children of most numerically limited immigrants; these are sometimes called "derivative" immigrants or simply dependents of the principal immigrant. For example, the spouse of a U.S. citizen is an immigrant principal, but the spouse of an employment-based visa holder is a derivative immigrant and not an immigrant principal.

Cross-cutting these three types of family immigrants recognized in U.S. immigration law is a behavioral dimension—the distinction between family formation and family reunification. Family reunification implies that previously divided families are being reunited; and that is indeed the case when parents, siblings, and biological children immigrate—the sponsor is reunited with his or her parent or his or her sibling or his or her offspring. Family reunification also occurs when a married person or a parent who becomes a permanent resident in a visa category which does not allow accompanying family members (i.e. derivative spouses and children) subsequently sponsors the spouse's or children's immigration. Sponsorship of a spouse,

7. In the previous system, which ended on 30 June 1976, the U.S. fiscal year started on the first of July and carried the name of the following calendar year.

however, need not be for family reunification; it may be for family formation, as when a U.S. citizen decides to marry a foreign-born person. Similarly, sponsorship of the new spouse's children or of adopted children also reflects family formation rather than family reunification. Given the five years' residency requirement for the naturalization of immigrants, it is probably the case that most immigrants sponsored as the spouses of U.S. citizens are family-formation immigrants and most immigrants sponsored as the spouses of permanent resident aliens are family-reunification immigrants.

As for non-kin immigrants, current law provides for the immigration of three main types: (1) employment-based immigrants, and their spouses and children; (2) refugees and asylees, and their non-refugee/non-asylee spouses and children; and (3) diversity immigrants (immigrants from countries which have been under-represented in recent immigration), who win a visa by lottery, and their spouses and children (who need not be from the under-represented countries).

The visa class is useful in distinguishing between "pioneer" and subsequent immigrants. Spouses of U.S. citizens, refugees and asylees, and diversity immigrants are likely to be pioneer immigrants; employment-based principals and spouses may both be pioneer immigrants. Siblings of U.S. citizens are definitely not pioneer immigrants. Note that the law can lead to immigration "chaining," so that with the passage of time an increasingly larger fraction of the family immigrants are not only non-pioneer immigrants but are farther removed from the pioneer generation.

Visa class is also useful for distinguishing, albeit crudely, among the several types of migration networks. Specifically, the following links can be made: Immigrants admitted as spouses of U.S. citizens can be classified as having access to a marriage-market network, employment-based immigrants can be linked with employment networks, immigrants admitted as siblings or parents of U.S. citizens with family networks, and refugees with philanthropic-organization networks. Moreover, it is possible that diversity immigrants are involved in friendship networks. Unfortunately, visa class information alone does not permit assessment of multiple networks (e.g. siblings involved in employment networks, etc.).

Of course, there may be other mechanisms that would bring about a trend in cohort quality. Consider the immigration of spouses of U.S. citizens. If there is positive assortative mating, then the immigrant spouses will resemble their American sponsors; and if the quality of Americans going abroad or socializing with foreigners changes, then the immigrants' quality will also change. Similarly, shifts in the U.S. economy or in the tastes of employers may lead to shifts in the occupational distribution of new immigrant cohorts.

Finally, U.S. law and policy alter immigrant cohort quality by other mechanisms besides that of family reunification. These include amnesty programs, refugee programs, diversity-immigrant programs, and shifts in eligibility requirements for employment-based visas. Refugees, as discussed, may differ in quality over time. Persons granted amnesty may exhibit especially reduced quality; they had no family networks (who might have sponsored them) and seemingly neither the skills nor attractiveness to acquire an employment sponsor or a spouse sponsor. With respect to shifts in requirements for employment visas, a case in point concerns medical doctors, who, under the provisions of the Act of October 12, 1976, effective January 10,

1977, are now required to have passed Parts I and II of the National Board of Medical Examiners Examination as a condition of eligibility for an employment-based visa.[8] Finally, the diversity-visa program requires that the immigrant have completed high school or its equivalent (or have at least two years of work experience in an occupation requiring at least two years' training or experience).

Note that the sponsors of immigrants are crucial to understanding U.S. immigration and cohort change. If cohort quality declines, then we might ask whether the sponsors have also declined in quality.

## *Data—required and available*

The most basic data requirement for studying cohort quality is that the data pertain to immigrants, that is, to persons admitted to lawful permanent residence. From either the scientific perspective—seeking to understand the behavior of persons who have chosen (and been chosen) to make a permanent life in the United States—or the policy perspective—seeking to increase the effectiveness of U.S. immigration policy by allocating scarce immigrant visas to the worthiest applicants (however worthiness might be defined)—the proper object of study is immigrants. It makes little sense to study changing cohort quality in samples which include not only immigrants, but also a broad assortment of nonimmigrants—temporary workers, World Bank personnel, students and their spouses, etc.[9]

The data currently available in the United States, however, are far from perfect. The most frequently used data are from the Decennial Censuses and the Current Population Surveys (CPS). These may be characterized as providing abundant information on the wrong sample, as respondents are described by nativity and not by visa status. The data with the best information on visa status, the annual immigrant cohort data made available by the U.S. Immigration and Naturalization Service (INS), unfortunately provide only one piece of information for assessing skills—occupational title. We discuss briefly key data elements.

### *Immigration status*

Table 14.1 provides a diagrammatic view of the coverage of foreign-born persons in several available data sets. It highlights the principal visa statuses—naturalized immigrant, permanent resident, nonimmigrant with permission to work, nonimmigrant without permission to work, and illegal aliens. As shown, INS new-immigrant data cover permanent resident aliens and include, for those immigrants who are

8. See Jasso and Rosenzweig (1995) for description of pertinent provisions of the 1976 legislation as well as follow-up legislation in 1981, which exempts from examination physicians who were already practicing in the United States in a nonimmigrant status as of January 1978. For extended discussion of physician immigrants, see Stevens, Goodman, and Mick (1978) and Mejia, Pizurki, and Royston (1980).
9. For assessing assimilation, moreover, another basic requirement is that the data be longitudinal. Only longitudinal data enable disentangling cohort and experience effects, and only longitudinal data prevent biases associated with emigration selectivity.

**Table 14.1.** *Measurement of migrant's legal status in the United States: Selected U.S. data sets*

| Data set | Naturalized citizens | Legal immigrants | Legal nonimmigrants | | Deportable migrants |
|---|---|---|---|---|---|
| | | | Permitted to work | Cannot work | |
| Census/CPS | | | | | |
| INS | | | formerly | formerly | formerly |
| LPS | | | | formerly | formerly |
| LA | | | | | |
| UC-EDD | | | | | |
| NAWS | | | | | |
| NIS-P(1) | | | formerly | formerly | formerly |
| NIS-P(2) | | | | | |

*Notes*: INS: INS immigrant and naturalization files; LPS: Legalized Population Surveys; LA: Los Angeles Migration Study; UC-EDD: University of California, Davis, Farmworker Survey; NAWS: National Agricultural Worker Survey; NIS-P(1): New Immigrant Survey, Pilot Study, primary sampled individual; NIS-P(2): New Immigrant Survey, Pilot Study, family/household members.

Subsets identified in the data are denoted by closed rectangles. Missing rectangle denotes the absence of persons in the data set currently in that legal status. The set of deportable migrants includes legal nonimmigrants who violate the terms of their visa as well as entrants without inspection. INS immigrant files contain limited information on previous nonimmigrant and undocumented status, for immigrants adjusting from a nonimmigrant or undocumented status. Primary sampled individuals in the NIS-P became legal immigrants in FY 1996 and were not yet eligible for naturalization.

adjusting from a nonimmigrant status, the type of nonimmigrant status; annual data on naturalization cohorts are also available.

Census/CPS data distinguish naturalized citizens, but the remaining types cannot be identified. Moreover, measurement of naturalization in the census is problematic, producing possibly serious overestimates of the size of the naturalized population. It is widely believed, for example, that naturalization has been over-reported in the censuses of 1950, 1970, 1980, and 1990 (Shryock and Siegel 1975: 274; Warren and Passel 1987; Passel and Clark 1997), a point to which we return below.

*Year of admission*

Immigration and Naturalization Service data provide the month and year of admission to permanent residence. They also provide, for the subset who are adjusting from a nonimmigrant status, date of admission to that nonimmigrant status; however, long residence with a succession of nonimmigrant visas is ignored except for the final nonimmigrant status. Immediately prior residence in illegal status is recorded for a small subset, notably for persons acquiring the immigrant visa under the registry provisions or suspension of deportation.[10]

Census and CPS data provide information on year of "entry" that is difficult to interpret. Both the 1980 and the 1990 Censuses asked the question, "When did this person come to the United States to stay?" Little is currently known about how immigrants and other foreign-born (nonimmigrants and illegals) respond, behaviorally, to this question. An immigrant who arrives for the first time in the United States in possession of an immigrant visa and who never leaves will have no difficulty; such a person "came to stay" on the date of admission to permanent residence. However, for others, the question is problematic. It is not known whether immigrants who adjusted from a nonimmigrant status reply with the date of admission to permanent residence or the date of admission to the nonimmigrant status or, when there is a string of nonimmigrant statuses, which date they choose as the date when they "came to stay." As for nonimmigrants and illegals, officially they cannot have "come to stay," so it is not clear how they answer the question.[11]

Additionally, the instruction for the year-of-entry question differs across the two census years, in 1980 tapping the "first" year the person came to stay and in 1990 the "latest" year the person came to stay.[12] Immigrants who naturalize and who have had several spells of U.S. residence after becoming legal immigrants may appear at first

10. The registry provisions of U.S. law grant permanent residence to individuals who have resided illegally in the United States for many years. Currently, as fixed by the Immigration Reform and Control Act of 1986, the requisite period of residence must have begun on or before January 1, 1972. Prior to this legislation, the registry cutoff date was 30 June 1948.
11. The new data collection initiative to obtain longitudinal information from successive cohorts of new immigrants—the New Immigrant Survey—includes questions designed to learn how foreign-born residents answer census-type questions.
12. In the 1980 Census, according to the Data Users' Guide (p. K-21), "Persons who had entered this country more than once were asked to respond in terms of the first year they came to stay permanently, disregarding any departures for vacation or temporary business." In the 1990 Census, the instruction for the question on year of entry states, "If the person has entered the United States (that is, the fifty states and the District of Columbia) more than once, fill the circle for the latest year he/she came to stay." The shift in the instructions for the 1980 and 1990 year-of-entry questions—from "first year" to "latest year" that persons came to stay—illustrates the notorious difficulty of using census data for studying immigration processes.

blush to misreport that they are naturalized, given the residency requirements for naturalization.[13]

*Sponsor characteristics*
If sponsors choose immigrants, then in order to understand the characteristics at entry and the progress of immigrants it is necessary to understand the characteristics of sponsors. Excepting the new data collection initiative in the New Immigrant Survey, information about the sponsors of immigrants is limited to a single data set, compiled by the General Accounting Office (GAO) and containing the nativity of the sponsors of immediate-relative immigrants in FY 1985. From that data set comes the information available in the past decade about the nativity of sponsors—for example, that 80 per cent of the sponsors of immigrant spouses are native-born U.S. citizens.

## EMPIRICAL FRAMEWORK

### *Data and measures*

As noted, all data currently available for studying U.S. immigration have serious shortcomings. Census and CPS data provide excellent information on the wrong sample, and INS data provide limited information on the right sample. Much recent work has relied on census samples of the foreign-born, neglecting INS data on immigrants. In this paper we address the question of cohort effects using INS immigrant data.

We use three data sets available from INS; these provide information on the entire cohorts who became permanent residents in Fiscal Years 1977, 1982, and 1994. These cohorts were chosen for three reasons: (1) The years represent years in which three distinct law regimes were in effect; (2) the FY 1977 and 1982 data sets are the only two data sets currently available which match entire immigrant cohorts to the naturalization records of subsequent years (a feature exploited in other ongoing research); and (3) the FY 1994 data set describes recent immigrants. All three data sets contain all publicly available, electronically stored information obtained at admission to permanent residence; the two matched samples also provide information obtained at naturalization.

The FY 1977 cohort includes both immigrants who qualified for their visa before passage of the 1976 amendments to the Immigration and Nationality Act as well as immigrants who qualified afterwards. The principal changes were (1) to apply to the Western Hemisphere the preference category system of allocating numerically limited visas; and (2) to apply the 20,000 per-country limit to the Western Hemisphere. Approximately one-third of the Western Hemisphere immigrants

13. For example, over 100,000 Mexico-born persons in the 1990 Census report that they entered in 1985–90 and that they are naturalized—an unlikely number, given residency requirements, if entry coincides with admission to permanent residence. While undoubtedly some are misreporting naturalization (perhaps confusing it with admission to permanent residence), others may be correctly reporting both that they are naturalized and that the latest year they came to stay occurred in the 1985–90 period.

holding numerically limited visas qualified for them under the old first-come/first-served system.[14]

The FY 1994 cohort reflects the substantial changes made by the Immigration Act of 1990 and its legislative successors. Three provisions in particular deserve comment. First, the number of visas to be awarded on the basis of skills (to employment-based principals plus their spouses and minor children) was increased more than twofold—from 54,000 numerically limited plus a few thousand numerically unlimited "special immigrants" (e.g. ministers of religion and former employees of the U.S. government abroad) to 140,000 numerically limited (incorporating the formerly unlimited "special immigrants"). Concomitantly, the requisite skill level was upgraded; for example, the annual number of visas available to "unskilled" workers and their immediate family members declined from a maximum of 27,000 (in the old sixth preference category designated for needed skilled or unskilled workers) to 10,000 per year in the "other workers" subcategory of the new employment third preference category.

Second, provision was allowed for "new seed" immigrants from countries which in the wake of the family reunification provisions of the 1965 Act had been underrepresented in recent immigration; the FY 1994 visa allotment to diversity immigrants was 41,056, of which 40 per cent were to go to persons from Ireland.

Third, additional visas were made available for the spouses and children of aliens legalized under the Immigration Reform and Control Act of 1986 (IRCA), up to 55,000 (depending on the previous year's usage of immediate-relative visas) in each of three years, FYs 1992–4. The figure for FY 1994 was set at 32,776 (INS Statistical Yearbook 1994: A. 2-2); because immigrant visas are valid for four months, the actual number of immigrants admitted in FY 1994 under the legalization provisions was 34,074 (INS Statistical Yearbook 1994: 35).

Finally, we note that although the FY 1994 cohort includes 6,022 IRCA-legalized adjustments to permanent residence (INS Statistical Yearbook 1994: 32), the public use data file does not contain their records.[15]

INS data provide the month and year of admission to permanent residence, age at admission, the country of birth, whether the person is adjusting from a nonimmigrant status and, if so, the year admitted to that status, and occupation. We used the INS information to construct several new variables, as follows.

Occupation is the only indicator of skill in the INS data sets. Three different coding schemes were used across the almost twenty years covered by the data.

14. A small fraction of the immigrants admitted as natives of the Western Hemisphere obtained their visas under the Silva Program, which, starting in July of 1977 and under court order, provided to queued applicants 144,946 visas to compensate for that number of visas which had been used for the adjustment of Cuban refugees and charged to the Western Hemisphere ceiling (INS Statistical Yearbook 1982: 213). The INS Statistical Yearbooks from 1978 to 1983 record a total of 145,468 Silva immigrants.
15. Note also that the 1990 Act provides for adjustment of numerical limits based on the previous year's usage. Thus, for example, the number of visas available on the basis of employment in FY 1994 was 143,213, rather than 140,000 (INS Statistical Yearbook 1994: 15).

For comparability, I recoded occupation onto a single scheme, using the twenty-five occupation groups in the 29-category variable devised by INS based on the 1980 Census and used by INS since 1983. Next, I constructed an earnings measure by coding the twenty-five occupation groups in the 29-category variable (the other four categories are for students, housewives, etc.) by the mean earnings for all men aged 18 and over who were employed full-time year-round in 1979, based on published tabulations from the 1980 U.S. Census (U.S. Bureau of the Census 1984). The resulting occupational earnings measure may be thought of as a broad measure of skills. It captures shifts in earnings due to shifts in occupation, but not earnings differences within the broad occupation category. An advantage of this measure is that it is not sensitive to changes in skill prices.

Caution is required in interpreting occupation. For immigrants who acquire employment-based visas, occupation refers to the occupation which enabled visa acquisition. For all others, occupation refers to the self-reported occupational title. Among immigrants who adjust status, occupation probably refers to actual or intended occupation in the United States. However, for newly arriving, non-employment-based immigrants, it is not known whether the occupation they report refers to occupation in the home country or in the United States.[16]

We used information on class of admission to construct indicator variables for twelve major visa classes. These are spouse of U.S. citizen, parent of (adult) U.S. citizen, employment visa principal, spouse of employment visa principal, sibling of U.S. citizen, spouse of sibling of U.S. citizen, refugee/asylee, spouse of refugee/asylee, diversity principal, spouse of diversity principal, legalization principal, and dependent of legalization principal.

Four remarks about the visa-class binary variables: First, for comparability with the 1977 and 1982 cohorts, we exclude from the employment-visa indicator variables the FY 1994 employment fourth and fifth preference categories, which cover religious workers, former employees of U.S. government units abroad, investors, and others formerly outside the employment visa categories. Second, we include in the refugee-asylee classification rather than in the employment classification a set of visa categories which highlight the origin country as a reason for visa entitlement; these include, for example, visa categories for Soviet scientists and Chinese students (from the employment second and third preference categories, respectively). Third, the legalization principals class includes persons granted permanent residence under a variety of registry and suspension-of-deportation provisions.[17] Fourth, as already

16. Consider, for example, a person who is a lawyer in the origin country but, the law being a less transferable skill than, say, symphony conducting, the person either reports no occupation or reports something like "library card checker," a post already offered to him or her by a U.S. university.

17. We excluded from the legalization category individuals whose legalization reflects admission via the regular immigration categories. For example, we include in this category persons with a "Z33" visa—"Person in whose case record of admission for permanent residence was created. Must have entered prior to July 1, 1924."—but exclude persons with a "Z13" visa—"Alien granted suspension of deportation (other than crewman) and adjusted as immediate relative of U.S. citizen or special immigrant."

noted, the 1994 cohort data do not include aliens legalized under IRCA, of which there were 6,022 admitted to permanent residence in FY 1994; however, the data do include 34,074 legalization dependents as well as other legalizations, as described above.

The cohort year is represented by binary variables. Origin country is represented by country of birth; the immigrants come from 223 countries.

## *Specification and estimation*

*Cohort effects*

To assess the operation of cohort effects we compare the occupation distribution and the average occupational earnings across the three years—1977, 1982, and 1994. To quantify cohort effects, we regress the natural log of occupational earnings on two binary variables representing the 1982 and 1994 cohorts; the coefficients of the two-year variables represent the log difference in earnings relative to the (omitted) 1977 cohort. Because, as discussed above, the dynamics of cohort change may differ across country and visa class, it is useful to assess the operation of cohort effects separately by region and selected countries of birth as well as by visa class. Moreover, cohort change dynamics may differ by sex. Accordingly, analyses are carried out separately by visa class and origin region/country as well as separately for men and women.

To assess average cohort decline in the full sex-specific populations, we also estimate an equation that allows each of the major visa classes to have its own intercept, but that constrains the cohort decline to be the same for all visa classes and a second equation that additionally controls for a full set of country fixed effects. The full version that controls for both visa class and country of birth is written:

$$\ln(\text{earn}) = \beta_0 + \beta_1\text{FY82} + \beta_2\text{FY94} + \Sigma\delta_k\,\text{Visa}_k + \Sigma\gamma_k\,\text{COB}_k + \varepsilon. \qquad \text{Eqn. 1}$$

# RESULTS

## *Preliminary findings*

Table 14.2 reports the occupational distributions among the three immigrant cohorts, separately for men and women aged 21–65 at admission to permanent residence. As shown, the proportion of men reporting an occupational title decreased from 87 per cent in 1977 to 71 per cent in 1982, with only a smaller subsequent decrease to 70 per cent in 1994; among women, the proportion reporting an occupational title decreased moderately from 41 per cent in 1977 to 38 per cent in 1982, with a subsequent negligible increase to 1994. Among men, the proportion in the two top summary occupation groups—managerial/professional and technical—declined slightly between 1977 and 1982—from 45 per cent to 43 per cent—recovering to 44 per cent by 1994, while among women there was a negligible decline between 1977 and 1982—from 53 per cent to 52 per cent—followed by a slight increase to almost the 1977 level.

**Table 14.2.** *Occupational distributions, immigrants age 21–65 at admission to permanent residence: FY 1977, 1982, and 1994 cohorts*

| Occupation group | 1977 Cohort | | 1982 Cohort | | 1994 Cohort | |
|---|---|---|---|---|---|---|
| | Men | Women | Men | Women | Men | Women |
| *All immigrants* | | | | | | |
| % Reporting occupation | 86.6 | 40.7 | 71.2 | 37.9 | 70.0 | 39.0 |
| % Students | 4.6 | 2.5 | 8.2 | 5.1 | 5.7 | 4.6 |
| *N* (000) | 130.9 | 153.7 | 173.2 | 173.2 | 217.0 | 275.6 |
| *Immigrants reporting occupational title* | | | | | | |
| Managerial-professional | 32.4 | 29.4 | 30.4 | 27.9 | 32.1 | 31.6 |
| Tech-sales-administrative | 12.7 | 23.7 | 12.4 | 24.4 | 12.0 | 21.2 |
| Service | 9.1 | 19.7 | 10.3 | 21.8 | 14.5 | 21.7 |
| Farming–Forestry–Fishing | 4.9 | 0.9 | 6.2 | 4.1 | 4.4 | 3.7 |
| Precision–Crafts–Repair | 18.1 | 7.7 | 17.2 | 9.7 | 11.2 | 4.9 |
| Operators–Laborers | 22.8 | 18.7 | 23.7 | 12.1 | 25.9 | 17.0 |
| Average earnings (000) | $21.2 | $18.8 | $20.0 | $18.6 | $19.6 | $18.6 |
| *N* (000) | 113.2 | 62.6 | 123.1 | 65.6 | 151.9 | 107.6 |

*Notes*: Figures for fiscal year 1982 exclude 14,062 cases for which information was missing. Figures for fiscal year 1994 exclude 6,002 legalized under IRCA provisions. Lower panel excludes cases reporting a military occupation.

Interpreting the decline in the proportion reporting an occupational title is no easy matter. Neither eliminating the proportion in school (shown in Table 14.2) nor restricting further the age group (not shown) eliminates the decline. One may speculate in a number of ways. First, perhaps persons in transition from one occupation to another (e.g. a refugee who was a hunter in the origin country) are less likely to report an occupational title. Second, perhaps individuals who immigrate via non-employment visas and who are in occupations which disqualify or make difficult an employment visa (e.g. physicians) are less likely to report an occupational title. Third, perhaps the proportion of immigrants who are independently wealthy has increased over time. Fourth, immigrants with non-employment-based visas who are adjusting from a nonimmigrant status prohibiting employment may be unemployed or, alternatively, reluctant to disclose their occupation. Fifth, individuals arriving with an immigrant visa from countries with exit restrictions may have been reluctant to state their occupation at the U.S. consular office abroad.

To explore the question of reporting an occupational title, I looked more closely by country of origin and class of admission. Reporting an occupational title varies both by country and over time; for example, among women born in Mexico, the proportion reporting an occupational title grew steadily across the three cohorts, from 22.5 per cent in 1977 to 44.9 per cent in 1994, a figure almost six percentage points larger than the corresponding cohort total of 39 per cent.

Inspection of visa class indicates that adjusting status is strongly associated with failure to report an occupational title—among women, the proportions reporting an occupational title are 44 per cent of non-adjusters and 32 per cent of adjusters, and among men, the corresponding figures are 87 per cent and 59 per cent. Thus, reluctance to disclose occupation is more likely to be associated with U.S. conditions than with origin-country conditions. Moreover, immigrants who do not report an occupational title (and are not students) are concentrated in two classes—refugees and spouses of U.S. citizens. Refugees, of course, are adjusting status; and the proportion adjusting status among spouses of U.S. citizens exceeds that for the non-refugee immigrant population as a whole. Over half of the spouse adjustments are adjusting from a tourist visa. Future research might investigate the determinants of reporting an occupational title; here, we note only that different mechanisms may be at work for refugees and spouse adjustments.[18]

Table 14.2 also reports average occupational earnings in 1979 dollars. As shown, occupational earnings declined across the three cohorts, from $18,765 to $18,591 for women and from $21,184 to $19,625 for men. The magnitude of the decline is trivial among women ($174), but not insubstantial among men ($1,559).

Overall, the figures of Table 14.2 suggest a decline in cohort quality among men between 1977 and 1994—unless the propensity to report an occupational title is inversely correlated with earnings. Among women, however, the decline in occupational earnings is trivial, and the proportion reporting an occupational title increased between 1982 and 1994.

Of course, there were also marked compositional shifts during the period, so that these results may mask differential trends across subsets of new immigrants. We turn now to examine occupational earnings separately by major visa classes and by region and selected countries of birth. In both the visa and the country analysis, I first describe the patterns of occupational earnings and then turn to examine cohort change.

## Occupational earnings by visa class

### *Earnings differences across visa class*

Table 14.3 reports occupational earnings, separately by the major visa classes; we look at earnings levels before turning to cohort effects. Among men, the top earners are employment principals (as expected), and the bottom earners are refugees and spouses of refugees and, in 1994, legalization principals and dependents. Among women, the top earners are the wives of employment principals, and the bottom earners include refugee and legalization immigrants and, in FY 1977, mothers of U.S. citizens.[19]

18. The New Immigrant Survey will also enable probing the behaviors associated with reporting an occupational title and choosing a title to report.
19. Table 14.3 omits earnings figures for the FY 1977 immigrants who obtained visas under the old first-come/first-served system for natives of the Western Hemisphere, a group making up approximately one-third of the Western Hemisphere immigrants holding numerically limited visas in the FY 1977 cohort. Average occupational earnings among male Western Hemisphere principals were lower than for any visa class except spouses of refugees; male spouses of Western Hemisphere principals, however, had higher earnings than all other visa classes except the employment and sibling-based. Among women, both principals and spouses in the Western Hemisphere category had the lowest average occupational earnings.

**Table 14.3.** *Average occupational earnings (1979 U.S. dollars) among immigrants age 21–65 at admission, by visa class: FY 1977, 1982, and 1994 cohorts*

| Visa class | 1977 Cohort | | 1982 Cohort | | 1994 Cohort | |
|---|---|---|---|---|---|---|
| | Men | Women | Men | Women | Men | Women |
| *Kin of U.S. citizen* | | | | | | |
| Spouse | $19,322 | $18,768 | $18,834 | $18,904 | $18,667 | $19,158 |
| Parent | 19,798 | 17,155 | 20,066 | 17,131 | 19,049 | 17,465 |
| Sibling | 20,758 | 18,912 | 21,000 | 18,838 | 20,055 | 18,924 |
| Spouse of Sibling | 20,662 | 19,604 | 22,048 | 19,405 | 20,548 | 19,199 |
| *Employment* | | | | | | |
| Principal | 31,640 | 23,255 | 28,850 | 17,965 | 24,316 | 20,405 |
| Spouse | 24,253 | 25,667 | 22,652 | 20,804 | 22,013 | 21,734 |
| *Refugee/asylee* | | | | | | |
| Principal | 18,574 | 17,248 | 17,554 | 17,493 | 17,437 | 17,654 |
| Spouse | 17,910 | 16,966 | 17,712 | 17,725 | 18,404 | 17,031 |
| *Diversity* | | | | | | |
| Principal | — | — | — | — | 19,784 | 18,908 |
| Spouse | — | — | — | — | 19,849 | 19,211 |
| *Legalization* | | | | | | |
| Principal | 18,838 | 18,933 | 19,991 | 16,810 | 17,172 | 17,345 |
| Spouse | — | — | — | — | 15,890 | 15,295 |
| *All immigrants 21–65* | $21,184 | $18,765 | $20,001 | $18,602 | $19,625 | $18,591 |

*Note*: Figures are for all immigrants age 21–65 at admission who report an occupational title.

Thus, the wives of men who qualify for an employment visa are, on average, the most highly skilled women, more skilled than women who qualify for such visas on their own, suggesting the joint interplay of assortative mating, labor-market, and marriage-market factors. For example, there may exist a lower-earnings occupation track for women employment principals (including, say, child care occupations).

A visa class frequently targeted for elimination is that of siblings of U.S. citizens. Table 14.3 shows that siblings, as well as their spouses, do well. Among men, siblings ranked third in earnings in 1977 and fourth in 1982 and 1994; among women, spouses of sibling principals ranked third in 1977 and second in 1982 (and would have been third in 1994 except for the new presence of diversity immigrants). Sisters of U.S. citizens do slightly less well—their highest rank in occupational earnings was fourth in 1982.

Spouses of U.S. citizens constitute a visa class not likely to be eliminated. Table 14.3 shows that wives of U.S. citizens outrank husbands of U.S. citizens in occupational earnings. While wives ranked third in 1982 and fifth and sixth in 1994 and 1977, respectively, husbands of U.S. citizens ranked sixth, seventh, and eighth across the three cohort years. These results, too, suggest the operation of assortative mating, given that, among U.S. citizens, men outearn women.

Spouses of legalization immigrants have the lowest earnings in the set of visa classes, among both men and women. Diversity immigrants and their spouses ranked sixth and fifth, respectively, among men and seventh and third among women.

To explore further the operation of assortative mating, I examine the relevant pairs of figures in the employment, sibling, refugee, and diversity categories, constructing an array in which the average earnings of the male principals in a given visa category are paired with the average earnings of the female spouses of principals in that visa category, the earnings of female principals are paired with the earnings of male spouses of principals, etc. The highest earners in all three cohorts are male employment principals and their wives; and the second highest earners in two of the three cohorts are female employment principals and their husbands. Brothers of U.S. citizens have the same rank as their wives in 1977 (third) and in 1994 (fourth).

The correlation between the average occupational earnings of the men and women in the array is high. It also increases over the period, from 0.72 in FY 1977 to 0.74 in FY 1982 to 0.98 in FY 1994, suggesting the operation of two possible mechanisms: (1) Positive assortative mating in occupational skills is increasing worldwide; and (2) egalitarian couples are more drawn to the United States now than fifteen years ago (reflecting perhaps the increase in restrictions on women in some countries).[20]

If visa class signals operation of migration networks, then these results suggest that employment networks produce the most skilled immigrants, followed by marriage-market and kin networks. At the bottom are the philanthropic-organization networks, which appear to produce less skilled immigrants, notably refugees and, to a lesser extent, legalization dependents. Note, however, that immigration law and world conditions strongly influence the skill mix in some of the visa classes. A fair test of the effects of networks would compare the skill mix across various kinds of networks, holding constant visa eligibility requirements. Moreover, it is possible that the effects of networks are more clearly discernible over time, as the new immigrant adjusts to the United States.

*Cohort change in occupational earnings across visa class*

As shown in Table 14.3, there is a mix of increases and decreases across cohort. The most dramatic change is in the occupational earnings of employment principals. Among both women and men, occupational earnings declined sharply between 1977 and 1982, followed by increases (modest for men) between 1982 and 1994. This pattern suggests a change in the occupational mix, which, as noted, reflects U.S. law (via restrictions on physicians, for example), the U.S. economy, and the tastes of employers. Immigrants admitted as the spouses of employment principals exhibit somewhat similar patterns (except that among men there is no upturn between 1982 and 1994).

20. Of course, these figures provide only crude assessments of assortative mating. A better approximation using INS public-use data would restrict the comparison to married individuals in the visa categories. Still better, the New Immigrant Survey will enable precise assessment of assortative mating, given that information on earnings is collected from actual husband–wife pairs.

To look more closely at cohort effects by visa class, I report in Table 14.4 the difference in average log earnings, relative to 1977, obtained, as discussed above, via regressions of the log of occupational earnings on the two cohort binary variables. As shown, cohort changes differ both by visa class and by gender. Cohort changes are not uniform by gender for any visa class except for employment principals and their spouses—all registering declines (as known from Table 14.3). If we restrict attention to changes between 1977 and 1994, however, changes are the same for both sexes in the spouse of sibling category (negative), the refugee/asylee principal category (negative), and the spouse of refugee/asylee category (positive), besides the two employment categories.

Mothers of U.S. citizens increased in occupational skill, but fathers' occupational skill increased only in 1994. Between 1977 and 1994, mothers' skill increased by almost three percentage points, while fathers' skill decreased by almost 3.5 percentage points.

Husbands of U.S. citizens declined in occupational skill, but wives of U.S. citizens increased. This result can be variously interpreted. If there is positive assortative mating, then the quality of the U.S. citizens marrying foreign-born persons changed differentially by gender—U.S. citizen women declining in quality and U.S. citizen men increasing in quality. Alternatively, U.S. citizens with a taste for foreign spouses saw a changing marriage market, such that high-quality foreign men were less likely to marry American women, while high-quality foreign women grew more likely to find marriage to an American attractive. This could be due to changing opportunities in origin countries as well as in the United States (via employment-based visas).

**Table 14.4.** *Cohort change in natural log of occupational earnings among immigrants age 21–65 at admission, relative to 1977 cohort, by visa class*

| Visa class | Men | | Women | |
|---|---|---|---|---|
| | 1982 | 1994 | 1982 | 1994 |
| *Kin of U.S. citizen* | | | | |
| Spouse | −0.0225 | −0.0319 | 0.0024 | 0.0069 |
| Parent | 0.0120 | −0.0366 | −0.0002 | 0.0211 |
| Sibling | 0.0064 | −0.0417 | −0.0086 | −0.0102 |
| Spouse of Sibling | 0.0459 | −0.0183 | −0.0136 | −0.0253 |
| *Employment* | | | | |
| Principal | −0.1981 | −0.1749 | −0.2127 | −0.0847 |
| Spouse | −0.0548 | −0.0779 | −0.1403 | −0.1006 |
| *Refugee/asylee* | | | | |
| Principal | −0.0433 | −0.0575 | 0.0130 | 0.0123 |
| Spouse | −0.0275 | 0.0154 | 0.0281 | 0.0144 |
| *Legalization* | | | | |
| Principal | 0.0408 | −0.0743 | −0.1008 | −0.0744 |
| *All immigrants 21–65* | −0.0365 | −0.0511 | −0.0044 | −0.0034 |

*Note*: Figures shown are change in natural log of occupational earnings.

The figures of Table 14.4 are dominated by the sharp decline in occupational earnings among employment-based principals. Why did skill decline so much among employment visa principals? This decline is especially interesting given that the Immigration Act of 1990 explicitly sought to upgrade the employment categories. Examination of the data reveals that the decline is largely due to the decline in the number of physicians, consistent with the 1976 legislation discussed above. Focusing on employment principals, 24.1 per cent of immigrant men in FY 1977 (1,755 persons) were physicians; that figure dropped to 2.8 per cent in FY 1982 and 2.5 per cent in FY 1994. Among women, the corresponding proportions dropped from 8.7 per cent in FY 1977 (337 persons) to 1.02 and 1.3 per cent, respectively, in FYs 1982 and 1994. Thus, much of the observed cohort decline among employment principals is due to the restrictions placed by U.S. immigration law on the immigration of physicians.

Overall, the data show a trivial decline in occupational earnings among women (less than half of one percentage point) between 1977 and 1994 and a small decline among men of five per cent. It is striking that among men occupational earnings declined between 1977 and 1994 in every one of the nine identified visa classes except that of spouses of refugees. Among women, on the other hand, occupational earnings declined between 1977 and 1994 in only five of the nine visa classes, registering increases among wives and mothers of U.S. citizens and women with refugee-based visas.

## *Occupational earnings by region/country of birth*

*Earnings differences across region/country of birth*

Table 14.5 reports average occupational earnings by continent and selected countries, again for each cohort and separately for men and women. As shown, the two American continents rank lowest in occupational earnings; Africa ranks highest in 1977 and 1982, dropping to third and second place among men and women, respectively. Europe ranks third among women and fourth among men. Asia is never lower than third, and among women in 1994, those from Asia rank highest.

Of course, there is substantial variation within continent. Among the countries shown, such variability is especially noticeable in North and Central America and Asia. For example, in 1977, among men, the difference between the highest and lowest average occupational earnings among a continent's countries is about $10,000 in both Asia and North and Central America. Among the countries shown, Mexico ranks consistently at or near the bottom, and India at or near the top.

*Cohort change in occupational earnings across region/country of birth*

Table 14.6 reports, for all six continents and for selected countries, the cohort change in 1982 and 1994, relative to 1977. Country and gender-specific components of immigration behaved differently. Among men, cohort effects were negative for all continents except Europe and, in 1994, Oceania. Among women, cohort effects were negative for all continents except Europe, South America, and, in 1982, North and Central America. Among men, the largest declines were seen among immigrants from Africa, with immigrants from Asia a far second. Among women, the largest declines were small relative to those seen among men and about the same for immigrants from Asia and Africa.

**Table 14.5.** *Average occupational earnings (1979 U.S. dollars) among immigrants age 21–65 at admission, by region and selected countries of birth*

| Region and country of birth | 1977 Cohort | | 1982 Cohort | | 1994 Cohort | |
|---|---|---|---|---|---|---|
| | Men | Women | Men | Women | Men | Women |
| *North & Central America* | | | | | | |
| Total | 18,640 | 16,845 | 17,965 | 17,087 | 17,393 | 16,810 |
| Canada | 26,417 | 19,655 | 24,073 | 19,634 | 24,253 | 20,803 |
| Cuba | 18,524 | 16,863 | 18,975 | 17,918 | 16,935 | 17,584 |
| Dominican Republic | 17,821 | 16,172 | 17,965 | 16,851 | 17,292 | 19,209 |
| Haiti | 18,778 | 16,766 | 18,935 | 17,256 | 18,356 | 17,977 |
| Mexico | 16,733 | 16,415 | 16,560 | 16,423 | 16,251 | 15,614 |
| *Asia* | | | | | | |
| Total | 24,506 | 21,295 | 21,217 | 19,582 | 21,064 | 19,911 |
| P.R. of China | 22,148 | 20,280 | 20,088 | 17,833 | 20,733 | 20,160 |
| Hong Kong | 22,308 | 19,044 | 22,864 | 19,868 | 23,016 | 21,465 |
| India | 31,649 | 31,216 | 26,282 | 25,720 | 24,129 | 24,487 |
| Japan | 20,667 | 19,183 | 20,294 | 19,317 | 22,839 | 19,387 |
| Korea | 21,297 | 19,308 | 21,072 | 18,773 | 21,019 | 19,092 |
| Philippines | 22,781 | 20,122 | 22,973 | 20,584 | 20,182 | 19,509 |
| Taiwan | 24,924 | 21,108 | 26,180 | 22,297 | 24,945 | 22,207 |
| Vietnam | 25,115 | 19,692 | 17,349 | 17,393 | 16,043 | 16,178 |
| *Europe* | | | | | | |
| Total | 20,207 | 19,247 | 20,790 | 19,148 | 20,308 | 19,195 |
| Ireland | 22,958 | 18,294 | 21,664 | 20,208 | 20,021 | 19,027 |
| Italy | 18,463 | 17,395 | 19,480 | 19,521 | 20,722 | 21,557 |
| Poland | 19,149 | 18,206 | 18,896 | 18,476 | 18,798 | 18,773 |
| *South America* | 20,037 | 17,309 | 19,419 | 17,791 | 19,065 | 18,421 |
| *Africa* | 27,936 | 21,636 | 21,801 | 20,462 | 20,670 | 19,829 |
| *Oceania* | 22,037 | 19,108 | 21,339 | 18,481 | 21,638 | 18,950 |
| *All immigrants* | 21,184 | 18,765 | 20,001 | 18,602 | 19,625 | 18,591 |

Table 14.6 contains many interesting country-specific patterns and results. These include: (1) The strong performance of women immigrants from Italy (+16.8 per cent), the Dominican Republic (+14.3 per cent), and Hong Kong (+11.5 per cent); and (2) the discrepant declines between women and men from Vietnam.

## *Average cohort declines, net of visa class and region/country of birth*

The results presented above provide strong evidence of cohort effect dynamics that differ by gender, visa class, and country of origin. Although worldwide there is evidence of a small cohort decline among men and a trivial one among women, the average decline masks a mix of both large increases in occupational earnings (e.g. among Italian women) and large decreases in occupational earnings (e.g. among employment-based immigrants and among African and Asian men).

**Table 14.6.** *Cohort change in natural log of occupational earnings among immigrants age 21–65 at admission, relative to fiscal year 1977 cohort, by region and selected countries of birth*

| Region and country of birth | Men | | Women | |
|---|---|---|---|---|
| | 1982 | 1994 | 1982 | 1994 |
| *North & Central America* | | | | |
| Total | −0.0267 | −0.0557 | 0.0093 | −0.0090 |
| Canada | −0.0688 | −0.0535 | 0.0031 | 0.0581 |
| Cuba | 0.0283 | −0.0744 | 0.0515 | 0.0234 |
| Dominican Republic | 0.0190 | −0.0125 | 0.0398 | 0.1426 |
| Haiti | 0.0129 | −0.0117 | 0.0225 | 0.0691 |
| Mexico | −0.0073 | −0.0198 | −0.0027 | −0.0442 |
| *Asia* | | | | |
| Total | −0.1152 | −0.1156 | −0.0670 | −0.0440 |
| P.R. of China | −0.0908 | −0.0562 | −0.1354 | −0.0199 |
| Hong Kong | 0.0263 | 0.0493 | 0.0340 | 0.1146 |
| India | −0.1463 | −0.2104 | −0.1539 | −0.1701 |
| Japan | −0.0052 | 0.1151 | 0.0105 | 0.0121 |
| Korea | −0.0087 | −0.0109 | −0.0294 | −0.0152 |
| Philippines | −0.0091 | −0.0898 | 0.0102 | −0.0104 |
| Taiwan | 0.0758 | 0.0401 | 0.0579 | 0.0612 |
| Vietnam | −0.2600 | −0.3281 | −0.0879 | −0.1546 |
| *Europe* | | | | |
| Total | 0.0440 | 0.0197 | 0.0007 | 0.0012 |
| Ireland | −0.0090 | 0.0791 | 0.0699 | 0.0297 |
| Italy | 0.0423 | 0.0985 | 0.0907 | 0.1676 |
| Poland | −0.0034 | −0.0014 | 0.0170 | 0.0429 |
| *South America* | −0.0130 | −0.0338 | 0.0269 | 0.0506 |
| *Africa* | −0.1956 | −0.2456 | −0.0430 | −0.0695 |
| *Oceania* | −0.0034 | 0.0057 | −0.0298 | −0.0061 |
| *All immigrants* | −0.0365 | −0.0511 | −0.00444 | −0.0034 |

Notwithstanding the evidence in support of specifications with visa-specific and country-specific cohort effects we now estimate pooled models (separately by sex, of course) in which the twelve visa classes studied above are allowed to have a unique intercept in a ln earnings equation but the cohort effects are constrained to be the same across all visa classes.

Table 14.7 reports estimates of two initial basic versions of eqn (1). The estimates labeled "Ordinary least squares" (OLS) include as regressors only the two cohort binary variables and the twelve visa class binary variables; the estimates marked "Fixed effects" (FE) include as well a full set of binary variables for all the countries of birth represented in the data. The omitted cohort is FY 1977.

**Table 14.7.** *Cohort effects on natural log of occupational earnings among immigrants age 21–65 at admission, net of visa class (ordinary least squares) and net of both visa class and country of birth (fixed effects)*

| Variable | Men | | Women | |
|---|---|---|---|---|
| | Ordinary least squares | Fixed effects | Ordinary least squares | Fixed effects |
| 1982 | −0.0452 | −0.0385 | −0.0150 | −0.0091 |
| 1994 | −0.0749 | −0.0765 | −0.0151 | −0.0025 |
| *Constant* | 9.8845 | — | 9.7789 | — |
| $R^2$ | 0.0952 | 0.2068 | 0.0374 | 0.1380 |
| *No of countries* | 230 | | 222 | |
| *No of observations* | 388,190 | | 235,831 | |

*Note*: Both ordinary least squares and fixed effects specifications include binary variables for the twelve visa classes shown in Tables 14.3 and 14.4. Their coefficients are not reported. Fixed effects specifications include binary variables for the full set of countries in the data. Omitted cohort is FY 1977.

The first vivid result is that, consistent with all the figures seen earlier, cohort decline appears to be largely a male phenomenon. Average earnings in the female immigrant stream register a slight decline between 1977 and 1982, but thereafter hold steady in the OLS estimate, and in the FE estimate increase between 1982 and 1994. The magnitude of the decline is 1.5 percentage points in the OLS estimate, and in the FE estimate is less than one percentage point in the first five years and a quarter of a percentage point for the entire study period.

Among men, occupational earnings declined by three to four percentage points from 1977 to 1982 and by another three to four percentage points from 1982 to 1994. Given that the second interval is more than twice as long as the first, these results indicate that the decline was considerably steeper between 1977 and 1982 than at the later period. Recall that it was in that first interval that the employment-based immigrants registered major declines and that it coincides with the change in the law affecting the immigration of physicians.

Comparison of the OLS and FE results suggests that, among men, the cohort decline may not be due to shifts in origin country composition or solely to such shifts, as the coefficients change only slightly. Put differently, and consistent with the results in Table 14.6, there appear to have been cohort declines within country, on average. Among women, however, the 1.5 percentage decline in the OLS estimate is substantially diminished in the FE estimates, suggesting that compositional shifts in origin country account for most of that 1.5 percentage decline.

These results suggest three main conclusions: (1) Cohort decline is largely a male phenomenon; (2) on average, there was cohort decline within country; and (3) on average, there was cohort decline within class of admission. These results also provide evidence for the operation of several mechanisms. Cohort decline within visa class suggests operation of a demand mechanism such that both U.S. law (via occupational restrictions and amnesty and refugee programs), sponsors of workers, and sponsors of spouses and other family members sought out less-skilled immigrants in 1982 and 1994, relative to 1977, and/or a supply mechanism such that within the class of foreign-born eligible for U.S. immigrant visas, those attracted to the United States in 1994 were less skilled than those similarly attracted in 1982 and 1994.

Cohort decline within refugee-and-country groupings is consistent with the wave effect discussed earlier. Cohort decline within blood-kin categories is consistent with the diminution of skills thought to be a by-product of family-reunification policies under the assumption that the immigrants in each successive cohort are farther removed from the pioneer immigrant.[21]

## CONCLUDING NOTE

In this chapter I examined the question whether immigrant occupational skills have declined over time, using data collected by the U.S. INS on the cohorts of new immigrants admitted in Fiscal Years 1977, 1982, and 1994. The data contain one measure of skill, occupation; to construct a quantitative measure of skill I used a measure of occupational earnings, defined as the average earnings of full-time, year-round workers in the occupation group.

Results indicate that average cohort quality declined slightly among men, but only trivially among women. Cohort change dynamics differ by gender, visa class, and origin country, producing a mix of increases and decreases in occupational earnings. On average, however, there is evidence of cohort declines both within origin country and within visa class. The pattern of results suggests that a portion of the decline is due to changes in U.S. immigration law and policy other than family reunification: Restricting the entry of physicians, granting amnesty to large numbers of undocumented aliens who did not qualify under other provisions of the law, providing refuge to individuals with few skills marketable in a modern economy. As well, results suggest the operation of both sponsor-demand and immigrant-supply mechanisms leading to a slight diminution in occupational skills of male immigrants.

Our results pertain to immigrants' occupational skills at admission to permanent residence. Full assessment of cohort changes requires examination of assimilation

21. For example, the estimated decline between 1977 and 1994 among fathers of U.S. citizens (Table 14.4) provides evidence for the family-reunification quality-decline hypothesis only if one assumes that U.S. citizen sponsors of fathers in 1994 were farther removed from the original immigrant in the chain than U.S. citizen sponsors of fathers in 1977. To illustrate, the 1977 sponsors may have been predominantly drawn from among employment-based immigrants, and thus their fathers would constitute the second link in the immigration chain; in contrast, the 1994 sponsors may have been predominantly drawn from among spouse-of-sibling immigrants (sponsored by a previous immigrant), and thus their fathers would constitute at least the third link in the immigration chain. Note that this example forces us to think harder about exactly what is meant by the family-reunification quality-decline hypothesis.

patterns of immigrants from different cohorts and of the children of immigrants. It may be that the children of the least skilled will make the longest strides, as they and their parents find themselves in an environment that richly rewards investment in human resources.

Meanwhile, directions for further research include investigation of the determinants of reporting an occupational title, refined assessment of the operation of assortative mating and of network mechanisms, and exploration of the quality-decline hypothesis in chains of family-reunification immigrants.

## EPILOGUE

The work just reported was followed by a larger-scale study incorporating all the U.S. immigrant cohorts for which Public Use Data were available—immigrant cohorts from FY 1972 through FY 1995 (Jasso, Rosenzweig, and Smith 2000). The new work indicates that immigrant skill declined until the late 1980s and subsequently began to increase. Consistent with the work reported in this chapter, immigrant skill was lower in 1994 than in 1982 and lower in 1982 than in 1977. However, the decline was reversed in the late 1980s, with 1994 representing only a local low point in an otherwise upward trend. The lowest average occupational earnings was recorded in FY 1987, and by FY 1990, immigrant skill was higher than it had been in any year since 1982. The results also showed considerable volatility in the occupational earnings of new immigrant cohorts, such that obtaining a clear picture of trends requires inspection of the entire annual series; relying on selected years, just like relying on decennial censuses, may obscure the true picture. Other recent work (Barrett 1996; Funkhauser and Trejo 1995) provides additional evidence that the decline in immigrant skill ended in the late 1980s, followed by an upswing in the 1990s.

The analysis also suggests the operation of U.S. immigration law in shaping the occupational skills of new immigrant cohorts. As discussed in this chapter, the early downturn in immigrant occupational earnings coincides with the decrease in the number of physician immigrants due to changes in pertinent U.S. law, and the high point in post-reversal occupational earnings occurs in 1992, the first year of the new law which increased the number of employment-based visas available for high-skilled immigrants. Moreover, if refugees are excluded, the upturn in immigrant skill is even more dramatic.

## REFERENCES

Barrett, Alan. (1996). "Did the Decline Continue? Comparing the Labor-Market Quality of United States Immigrants from the Late 1970's and Late 1980's," *Journal of Population Economics*, 9: 57–63.

Borjas, George J. (1994). "The Economics of Immigration," *Journal of Economic Literature*, 32: 1667–717.

Burt, Ronald S. (1995). *Structural Holes: The Social Structure of Competition*. Cambridge, MA: Harvard Belknap.

Chiswick, Barry R. (1978). "The Effect of Assimilation on the Earnings of Foreign-Born Men," *Journal of Political Economy*, 86: 897–921.

Duleep, Harriet Orcutt, and Regets, Mark C. (1996). "Admission Criteria and Immigrant Earnings Profiles," *International Migration Review*, 30: 571–90.

Funkhauser, Edward, and Trejo, Stephen J. (1995). "The Labor Market Skills of Recent Male Immigrants: Evidence from the Current Population Survey," *Industrial and Labor Relations Review*, 48: 792–811.

Jasso, Guillermina, and Rosenzweig, Mark R. (1990). *The New Chosen People: Immigrants in the United States.* A volume in "The Population of the United States in the 1980s: A Census Monograph Series." New York: Russell Sage.

—— and ——. (1995). "Do Immigrants Screened for Skills Do Better Than Family-Reunification Immigrants?" *International Migration Review*, 29: 85–111.

—— —— and Smith, James P. (2000). "The Changing Skill of New Immigrants to the United States: Recent Trends and Their Determinants," in George J. Borjas (ed.), *Issues in the Economics of Immigration.* Cambridge, MA: NBER Press, pp. 185–226.

LaLonde, Robert J., and Robert H. Topel. (1992). "The Assimilation of Immigrants in the U.S. Labor Market," in George J. Borjas and Richard B. Freeman (eds.), *Immigration and the Work Force.* Chicago: University of Chicago Press.

Massey, Douglas S. (1990). "The Social and Economic origins of Immigration," *Annals of the American Academy of Political and Social Science*, 510: 60–72.

Mejia, Alfonso, Pizurki, Helena, and Royston, Erica. (1980). *Foreign Medical Graduates: The Case of the United States.* Lexington, Massachusetts: Lexington Books.

Passel, Jeffrey S., and Clark, Rebecca L. (1997). "How Many Naturalized Citizens Are There? An Assessment of Data Quality in the decennial Census and CPS," Paper presented at the annual meeting of the Population Association of America, Washington, DC, March 1997.

Portes, Alejandro, and Sensenbrenner, Julia (1993). "Embeddedness and Immigration: Notes on the Social Determinants of Economic Action," *American Journal of Sociology*, 98: 1320–50.

Shryock, Henry S., and Siegel, Jacob, and Associates. (1975). *The Methods and Materials of Demography*, third printing (revised). Washington, DC: U.S. Government Printing Office.

Stevens, Rosemary, Goodman, Louis Wolf, and Mick, Stephen S. (1978). *The Alien Doctors: Foreign Medical Graduates in American Hospitals.* New York: Wiley.

U.S. Bureau of the Census. (1984). *1980 Census of Population. Volume 2. Subject Reports, PC80-2-8B: Earnings by Occupation and Education.* Washington, DC: U.S. Government Printing Office.

U.S. Immigration and Naturalization Service. (1943–1978). *Annual Report of the Immigration and Naturalization Service.* Washington, DC: U.S. Government Printing Office.

______. (1979–1992). Statistical Yearbook of the Immigration and Naturalization Service. Washington, D.C.: U.S. Government Printing Office.

Warren, Robert, and Passel, Jeffrey S. (1987). "A Count of the Uncountable: Estimates of Undocumented Aliens Counted in the 1980 United States Census," *Demography*, 24: 375–93.

# 15

## Admissions Policies in Europe

CATHERINE WITHOL DE WENDEN

Everywhere in Europe the right to migrate is threatened, with pressures of public opinion, racist violence in Germany, debates on identity in France, and fears in southern European countries towards their extra-European neighbors. Tougher policies have been designed and implemented: reform of asylum rights in Germany (1993), Pasqua and Debre laws in France (1993 and 1997) followed by the so-called consensual Chevènement Law (1998), visa systems and expulsions of illegals in all European countries, problems for the undocumented in France, Spain, Italy, and Portugal.

### BORDER CONTROL

Despite a general consensus that each state or country has a right to control its own borders, the kind of control to be imposed remains unclearly defined, creating contradictions between states. Based on the historical and geographical specifics of each country, differing interpretations of the United Nations Convention on Asylum of 1951, and variations in nationality rights, admissions policies differ strongly from country to country.

Most European countries decided to stop labor migration in 1973–4, as did the United Kingdom in 1962. Most countries that have experienced more recent immigration, such as Italy, Spain, Portugal, and Greece, adopted new immigration policies during the 1980s. These policies all differ from those of the United States, Canada, and Australia, which combine an emphasis on selective or family immigration with repression at entry.

In Europe, entrance is generally determined before migrants arrive at the border, via visa systems in effect since 1989. Paradoxically, at the same time that countries are trying to reinforce Fortress Europe by restricting immigration, they are encouraging tourism and travel, with the result that most illegal migrants in Europe enter legally and simply overstay.

Economic crisis has changed the types of immigrants European countries want: highly skilled "brain drain" versus less skilled and nonworker categories of immigrants. While one can observe a diversification in the kinds of immigrants coming to the European Union (those seeking family reunification, asylum seekers, students, ethnic migrants, highly skilled workers, Europeans, seasonal workers), access to legal residence and citizenship is tightening, as evidenced by recent debates on nationality codes, access to welfare, and the opening or closing of local political rights to non-Europeans. In general, the more that access to welfare is opened, the stricter entrance controls become.

In spite of the convergence of European positions on immigration policy, in the context of free trade, globalization, and transnational networking, border control is not so strong as it may seem in the public eye. Control has costs, both economic and political. Alternative policies that have been proposed or implemented (quotas, bilateral agreements, legalization programs), hardly reflect public opinion. The philosophy of control is not debated, because it may bring unexpected effects, such as long-term settlement, if immigrants lose the freedom to enter, leave, and return. It also implies an uneasy selection of immigrants on the basis of money, networks, or color of the skin.

Most European countries are abandoning the goal of zero immigration because they realize that it is impossible to achieve, given the influences of human rights conventions, asylum rights, family reunification principles, and labor market needs. But these policies do not frankly reflect public opinion. In spite of border enforcement, migrant flows continue while popular European responses are dissuasive, reactive, and repressive.

Everywhere in Europe, mass migration has been considered a historical exception involving a provisional stay and quick expulsion if necessary. However, return policies have largely failed since the mid-1970s. The abandonment of nation-state sovereignty over European borders is not always easily accepted by the populace, but the logic of economics dominates over that of politics.

Commonly shared and enacted procedures for migrant entrance, residence, and departure are necessary for Europe. The absence of a consistent policy creates a strong pull factor leading migrants from one country to another. Examples of the inconsistent European policies include the legalizations in southern Europe, discrepancies between asylum procedures and nationality codes, and diverse positions on holding the line in the Mediterranean and Eastern Europe. Most countries in Europe have an extra-European neighbor attracted to their labor markets, higher salaries, and welfare benefits. Some countries, such as Germany, are victims of the prosperous images they project outside Europe; other images related to human rights or culture can also be attractive. A sharing of the burdens of recent migrant flows has been proposed by Germany and Austria; but the main obstacles to greater diplomatic cooperation between European nation-states is the growing dependence of policymakers on public opinion, discrepancies between nationality codes, and the continuing strength of national sovereignty in a field so rich in symbols. Intergovernmental policy at the European level is still up-to-date, in spite of the Treaty of Amsterdam.

## EUROPEAN TOOLS

Immigration policies are now covered by intergovernmental agreements within the European Union, adopted first with the Schengen Agreements and then by all

European countries in the Trevi and Dublin Accords, before a transition from the third pillar of the Maastricht Agreement (intergovernmental) to the latest (monetary union). But this harmonization policy is challenged by the interests of each European state, by the existence for some of colonial pasts, and by public perceptions that immigration is a threat.

## *Agreements and treaties*

According to the Schengen Agreements (signed on June 14, 1985), France, Germany, and the Benelux nations defined the notion of common external borders and decided to suppress internal border controls while implementing policy and judicial cooperation in their response to people entering Europe illegally and overstaying their visas. On June 19, 1990, a convention on implementation was settled, creating a European experiment for common border controls, circulation, computerization of information on illegal migrants, and international judiciary cooperation. Italy (in November of 1990) and Spain and Portugal (June 1991), followed by Greece, Austria, and Finland (1995) all eventually joined the Schengen area. Readmission agreements have been added at the discretion of European countries and extra-European ones; these oblige the states of origin from which illegal migrants entered the Schengen area to take them back.

Since March of 1996, European citizens have not been submitted to internal border control within the Schengen space. But the Schengen Agreements created another internal border: one between non-European residents, who are obliged to hold visas, and Europeans, who are beneficiaries of the new freedoms for circulation, settlement, and work.

The Dublin Convention, signed in June of 1990, held each state was responsible for examining and adjudicating asylum seekers. It tried to address two issues—that of multiple asylum seekers who apply to several countries at once, and that of asylum seekers sent from one country to another when no single country considers itself responsible for the asylum application. The Dublin Convention reasserted the principles of the Geneva Convention of 1951, its enlargement in 1967, and its implementation by each country's national law.

Other concepts have been added to these regulations: that of "safe countries of origin" (those from which no one can ask for asylum) and that of "manifestly unfounded demand" (where there is no compelling evidence of persecution). Sanctions can be imposed on air companies carrying illegal migrants into the Schengen zone, and the treatment of asylum applications has been coordinated to avoid the long-term settlement of applicants who are likely to be refused. The Dublin Agreements were implemented in 1997.

## *Other resolutions*

Other resolutions have been adopted for admission policies, harmonizing policies for family reunification (June 1993), employment (1994), and long-term residency

(1995). Some discrepancies still exist, however, in humanitarian situations, where each country determines its own response. The effectiveness of resolutions and criteria is problematic for some states, and most policies are inspired by restrictive positions. The European frame exists, but each state has final control over its implementation.

### *Fighting illegal migration*

In accordance with the CIREA (the Center for Information, Discussion and Exchange on Asylum approved by the Council of Europe in 1997) and the CIREFI (Center for Information, Discussion and Exchange on the Crossing of Frontiers and Immigration, adopted in 1994 to cover trafficking and expulsion practices), the home ministries of European countries have established computerized information systems for illegal migration control. In October of 1994, readmission agreements were signed; but here, too, some areas have been neglected, such as illegal work, expulsion decisions, and choice of country of destination. The absence of any common framework for establishing such policies and various practical obstacles has left a large degree of autonomy to EU member states.

A paradox arises in most European countries. Inside each nation-state, those most opposed to the Europeanization of police and immigration control are also the strongest supporters of national security policies, reflecting the challenges to sovereignty within Europe. Between the nation-states, in contrast, cooperation in policing escapes democratic control. This creates tensions within and between countries.

## NATIONAL POLICIES

Recent general trends appearing in national policy include (1) the strengthening of restrictive policies inspired by public opinion hostile to alternative immigration policies (border controls, immigrant quotas, cooperation with migrant-source countries) and to more Europeanization; and (2) the effect of restrictive policies in western European countries, which has led first to a decrease in regular entrants and asylum applications since 1993 before the rise of the last five years.

### *France*

In France, since 1974 immigration control has focused on (1) economic migration only involving Europeans, seasonal workers, and qualified workers; (2) family reunification; and (3) asylum seekers, students, and trainees. Immigration flows have been stable since the mid-1980s (an average of 100,000 per year; 95,000 in 1995). They are unavoidable because they are protected by law and by international agreements.

For 20 years the French government has produced a host of immigration legislation: the 1981 laws on entrance and duration of stay; the law of 1984 establishing the

10-year residence card; the law of 1986 ("Pasqua law") on entrance and stay; the law of 1989 ("Joxe Law"); the law of 1993 ("new Pasqua Law"); the law of 1997 ("Debré Law"); and the law of 1998 ("Chevènement Law"). New bills are presently being discussed in 2003. All of these pieces of legislation focus on entrance and duration of stay, coupled with measures against illegal migration and work (1989), the legalization of undocumented migrants (1982 and 1998), and asylum reform (the reform of 1989 and the constitutional reform of 1993 to incorporate the Schengen principles). In spite of recurring debates about uncontrolled migration, the foreign population in France has stabilized at about 3.6 million (6.3 per cent of the total population). Half of all entrances involve family reunification, but we have observed a decline in immigration flows and asylum seeker entrances (from 28,000 to barely 20,000 from the beginning to the end of the 1980s), and then a return to growth after 2000 (reaching 47,000 in the year 2002).

### *Germany*

Like most European countries, Germany stopped its recruitment of workers in 1973; but recently it formally recognized itself as a country of immigration and has sought to promote return migration as a tool for controlling immigration. After a peak number of entrances in 1993, due to surge in asylum seekers the arrival of ethnic Germans from the east, Germany's foreign population has grown from 5 to 7 million, not counting the 2.5 million ethnic Germans settled since 1989. Since the 1993 reform of asylum rights (Article 18 of the Fundamental Law), asylum admissions have fallen to 125,000 per year, out of a total of 800,000 annual admissions. The most highly represented nationalities within Germany are Turks (2 million), former Yugoslavs (1 million), Italians (500,000), Greeks (350,000), and Poles (250,000).

### *United Kingdom*

The United Kingdom formally closed its borders to settlement applicants in 1962. The majority of its resident foreigners come from countries of the British Commonwealth, and the Law of 1948 facilitated their access to entrance and settlement. Among the 3 million so-called nonwhites living in the United Kingdom, almost 500,000 are Pakistanis; 850,000 are Indians; and 163,000 are Bangladeshis. Since the 1993 reform of asylum rights (Article 18 of the Fundamental Law), asylum admissions have fallen to less than 100,000 per year, out of a total of 800,000 annual admissions. Asylum entrances are higher in the U.K. than in France (81,000 in 1995).

### *Benelux nations*

In Belgium, foreigners represent 9 per cent of the total population and are approaching one million persons, the largest number of whom are Italians (25 per cent) and Moroccans (16 per cent). In the Netherlands, flows have reached 80,000 per year into a stock of 850,000, with a decrease in asylum applications (to 21,000 in 1996). In Luxembourg, a country strongly dependent on foreign labor, foreigners represent

33 per cent of the total population (150,000 settled), with a majority of Portuguese followed by Italians.

## *Southern Europe*

All of the former European emigration countries have become countries of immigration. By the end of the 1980s, Italy, which has a very attractive labor market, counted one million foreigners in its population, including Europeans (at 15 per cent) and "extra-community" immigrants, of which Moroccans make up the largest group. Two laws (one in 1986 and the "Martelli Law" of 1990), followed by legalization of undocumented migrants and delayed implementation of the Schengen Agreements (in September 1997), characterize the Italian approach. Asylum has decreased since 1991 (dropping from 25,000 to 17,000 per year).

Spain, with half a million settled foreigners (mostly Europeans, Latin Americans, and Moroccans), has a very attractive labor market, in spite of the progressive tightening of its immigration policy and the implementation of the Schengen Agreement (1996). Massive legalizations, bilateral agreements on readmission with Morocco, and the enactment of a new status for foreigners (in 1996) have greatly increased the public's consciousness of immigration issues.

Portugal, like Spain, has witnessed a large decrease in emigration since 1974. The freedom of circulation for Portuguese, established with its entrance with Spain into the European Union followed by free labor mobility in 1992, changed the image of Portuguese immigrants in Europe, who were formerly viewed as illegal migrants. Instead, Portugal has become an immigration country, with 170,000 foreigners in 1995, a majority of whom are from its former colonies compared with 30 per cent from Europe and 25 per cent from Latin America. There have been several legalization initiatives in recent years, modeled on those in Spain and Italy in the 1990s, and the passage of a law in 1993 to establish rules for entrance and length of stay.

Greece, with 300,000 foreigners and a tradition of emigration, is confronted with great immigration pressure, taking in 80,000 entrants per year to a population that already constitutes 10 per cent of the total, adding to the large number of persons of Greek origin being "repatriated" from Russia and Albania. Since 1991, the Greek government has adopted a restrictive policy that authorizes the repatriation of illegal migrants, expulsions, repression of illegal work, and police cooperation with other European partners, all justified by Greek's isolation from European borders and its geographic position as a buffer zone.

## *Switzerland and Austria*

Like Luxembourg, Switzerland's share of foreigners is very high (around 18 per cent of its total population) with a significant volume of annual and seasonal entrants attracted by its labor market, which depends heavily on immigrant workers. This country traditionally welcomes asylum seekers (e.g. it had 17,000 applications in 1995). In spite of Switzerland's refusal to enter the European Union in 1993, its admissions policies have several points of convergence with those of other European countries: liberalization of entries for qualified and highly skilled workers and the loosening of employment limits for them; the simplification of entry procedures for border commuters; and an increase in annual authorizations for family reunifications.

For a long time Austria has been considered a 'second choice' immigration country. But since the fall of the Berlin Wall in 1989, it has become a door of entry from East to West. The number of entering foreigners doubled between 1989 and 1993 and now represents 9 per cent of the total population. This formerly welcoming country for Eastern refugees has also received overseas refugees due to a visa system established in 1972. In spite of a decrease in refugee status recognition since 1990, transitory refugees and migrants to Austria have increased since 1989. The foreign population is composed approximately of one-third Western European and American citizens, one-third Eastern Europeans, and one-third foreigners from the Balkans. Unlike Germany, Austria has no equivalent return of "Ethnic Austrians" and has a very dissuasive policy regarding citizens from countries on its eastern borders. It is also the first European country to have adopted an explicit quota for immigration (20,000–25,000 entries per year, from which refugees are deducted). After its entrance into the European Union, Austria joined the Schengen Agreements in 1997.

## *Finland, Sweden, and Denmark*

Finland, with the lowest proportion of foreigners in all of Europe (its 68,000 foreigners constituted just 1.3 per cent of the population in 1995), is mostly a welcoming country for former USSR citizens (16,000), Baltic citizens and Swedes (who are often Finns who emigrated earlier and wish to return). Since the 1990s, this former country of emigration has faced strong immigration pressures from refugees and to returnees. A new training policy for skilled former USSR citizens has been implemented, as have visas for former Yugoslav asylum seekers. The Schengen Agreements were signed by the six countries of the Nordic Free Market in December of 1996.

With more than 1.6 million foreigners (1995), Sweden is an important immigration country for Nordic citizens and refugees. Since 1989, its foreign population has been strongly diversified, mainly owing to asylum seekers and family reunifications. Like Finland, Sweden has to reconcile its entrance into the European Union with its place in the Nordic free labor market, which also includes Norway and Iceland. Finns are the most important immigrant group and Swedish immigration policy now includes bilateral agreements with the Baltic States.

Denmark, an emigration country during the nineteenth century, has become an important immigration destination for seasonal workers, border commuters, and refugees, with 222,000 foreigners in 1995. In 1970 Denmark closed its labor market to foreigners except for Europeans and members of the Nordic free labor market. Denmark has also been confronted with the repatriation of Danes from Greenland and the Faeroe Islands. Asylum seekers (5,900 in 1995, out of 50,000 statutory refugees) are now decreasing.

## CONCLUSION

In spite of the persistence of certain idiosyncratic characteristics owing to the distinctive histories and geographies of European states, the trend in Europe's immigration policies is one of convergence in two basic areas: border control and residence rights. Everywhere in Europe, border control is a priority, and the principle of closure to foreign workers is maintained, except for Europeans. The right to entrance for family reunification, students, highly skilled workers, asylum seekers, tourists with visas, and people dependent on health care has become increasingly restricted. At the same time, residence rights are linked more to length of a former stay than to work, even if such a residence criterion is challenged by the new distinction between Europeans and non-Europeans.

In spite of the growing similarity of basic principles among European states, discrepancies remain in the rights each country grants to foreigners, including right to remain, residence status, social rights, and access to work and to citizenship. The most salient differences between European countries in their approaches to immigration policy include: differences in the right to enter, involving various implementations of asylum rights and interpretations of the Geneva Convention of 1951; the lack of a common policy regarding length of residence card validity or access to citizenship, welfare, or work for families in reunification; the existence of different tools for managing illegal migrants (sanctions against employers, career sanctions, legalization programs, selected categories for entrance, visa practices); and, finally, divergences in the degree of Europeanization and a growing adherence within states to nationalist policies in response to pressure from national public opinion.

On the whole, however, convergence of policy seems to dominate, in strong trends (dissuasion strategies) as well as weak ones (employer sanctions, police networking to manage illegals and asylum seekers, visa systems, expulsions and repatriations, and a rapid increase in the Europeanization of decision-making processes). The Amsterdam Treaty of 1997 raised new issues about the decline of nation-state sovereignty with the transition from the "third pillar" (intergovernmental decision-making processes for immigration and asylum) to a "first pillar" (a communalization of decisions) after a 5-year transition period.

Perhaps the Amsterdam Treaty will lead to the end of European national immigration policies, and thus to the end of citizen control over such decisions. For several years, immigration flows have challenged the traditional categories of public policy and nation-state order by creating transnational networks, minorities, diasporas, illegal migrants—all part of globalization and to a lesser extent Europeanization.

As transnational organizations such as the Council of Europe and the U.N. High Commissioner for Refugees come to limit national autonomy, immigration and asylum issues (involving minority rights, family reunification, asylum, and non-European status) have increased tensions between human rights advocates and those insisting on national sovereignty. How long will sovereignty resist? Underground policies may bring unexpected effects but a de-politicization of immigration issues may bring some hope.

# 16

## A New Paradigm for the European Asylum Regime

DANIÈLE JOLY AND ASTRI SUHRKE

This chapter discusses trends in the concept and practice of asylum over the last two decades of the twentieth century. Most of these changes took place in the industrialized world, particularly Europe—hence, the chapter will emphasize the European context. The most striking development has been a series of attempts to restrict the rights to asylum under the 1951 Geneva Convention. These attempts took many forms: restricting rights to file applications, stricter interpretation of the Convention's articles, the development of non-Convention forms of temporary protection, and new measures for reception in regions of origin. In effect, these changes amount to a new asylum regime.

As the path toward asylum has narrowed, however, policies to deal with the refugee problem as a whole have widened. This tendency is expressed in what has come to be called "a comprehensive refugee policy," which basically consists of interventionist policies that provide protection and humanitarian assistance within countries of origin so as to preempt mass outflows. Since these two trends—restricted access to asylum and interventionist policies to prevent large-scale exits—developed in tandem as closely linked responses to the same underlying problem, both will be considered here.

This chapter assesses policy developments rather than social scientific thinking about policies or immigration. The reason is simple: the social scientific literature about changes in the contemporary asylum regime is quite limited. The literature mostly consists of documentary material produced by actors seeking to codify or justify policies and reports and information compiled by activist critics to evaluate existing policies and advocate alternatives. Both will be reviewed here. Although the literature on the emergence of a comprehensive refugee policy overlaps with a much larger literature on the causes and resolution of social conflict, that portion focusing on the refugee dimension is discussed here. The relevant legal literature is also rapidly growing, and only that dealing with one critical aspect of the new asylum regime—the concept of temporary protection—will be considered here.

### ASYLUM BEFORE THE END OF THE COLD WAR

The international asylum regime that developed after World War II was, in reality, two different regimes. In Europe and North America, asylum was founded on the

1951 Geneva Convention in legal terms, and supported by important political and social forces. First, there was a sense of guilt over the atrocities perpetrated by Nazi Germany against the Jews and other minorities, many of whom had been refused asylum in Europe and the United States. Second, once the backlog of refugees from World War II was cleared, the next refugees seeking to reach the West were from communist countries, and therefore politically desirable. In this respect, the Cold War had a decisive and liberal impact on the asylum regime in the West.

Economically, refugees were also welcome because the West needed a large supply of labor for postwar reconstruction, and this fact also led governments to adopt liberal immigration policies. Finally, neither governments nor citizens harbored a fear of being overwhelmed: exit from the communist bloc was severely restricted and refugees came either in a trickle or in rare flows occasioned by intermittent upheavals (as in Hungary during 1956 and Czechoslovakia in 1968). As a result, asylum in the industrialized West developed into a strong and very liberal institution that lasted for several decades.

This liberal asylum regime had several notable characteristics. Access to claims was not restricted. Convention status or equivalent rights were readily granted (in the case of the Scandinavian countries, a humanitarian status introduced at the time conferred virtually the same rights as Convention status). The Convention was used to determine the status of both individuals and groups. Group determination occurred in response to the arrival of massive flows from Eastern Europe or, in the case of the United States, was granted to specific nationalities such as Cubans and Soviet Jews). There was no expectation that refugees would ever return home—after all most had "voted with their feet" to leave Communist countries. As a result, host governments typically granted Convention rights that permitted long-term residence and eventual civic integration into society.

In the developing world, especially in Asia and Africa, the asylum institution evolved quite differently. Few countries were initially signatories to the 1951 Geneva Convention, and the particular circumstances of Africa led to the promulgation of a separate regional convention (1969 Convention of the Organization of African Unity), which provided a much broader foundation for asylum than the 1951 Convention and implicitly recognized the actual pattern of mass inflows and group determination. Unlike in Europe, refugees in Africa at this time were not an exceptional occurrence but a frequent fact of life, and states and local communities adjusted accordingly. Although there were cases of mass deportations and some formal permanent settlement, mostly migrants were placed in long-term settlements or camps to await changes at home that would permit return. As a result, mass influxes and temporary protection were defining characteristics of asylum in independent Africa and Asia some two to three decades before being introduced in Europe.

Restrictions on asylum in the West had begun to appear before the end of the Cold War, but were powerfully reinforced by the latter event. In North America, large inflows from Cuba and Haiti in 1979–80 marked a watershed. In Europe, the large increase in spontaneous asylum seekers from the developing world in the second half of the 1980s constituted an equivalent marker. On both continents, for the first time it became manifestly clear that industrialized countries would increasingly be called upon to host asylum seekers from the "third world," where the potential pool of applications was very large indeed. The collapse of state socialism in the Soviet Union and East and Central Europe also raised the specter of conflict and upheaval on the doorsteps of Western Europe. With the barriers to exit down, both officials and the public feared that asylum inflows from these areas would swell rapidly.

The result was increasingly divergent paths of asylum between developed and developing countries. In the industrialized states—now reconceptualized as "the North" rather than "the West"—governments took strong steps to restrict asylum, at first individually but increasingly in cooperation with each other. Over time states in Eastern and Central Europe were pulled into cooperation. The European Union took the lead in building what has come to be known as "Fortress Europe." Indeed, the timing and dynamic of the new policies were heavily influenced by the pace of European integration as the progressive dismantling of internal frontiers led to greater harmonization of policies for the purpose of controlling the common external border (Santel 1995; Brochman 1996).

In the developing world, meanwhile, asylum was jeopardized by declining economies, population pressures, and a growing awareness of the environmental costs of hosting large refugee populations. But a policy of *de facto* mass asylum continued amid intermittent attempts to restrict entry. Overall, it was a pattern in which strong states exercised their power to exclude asylum seekers, while the weak granted mass asylum by default (Suhrke and Newland 1996).

## THE NEW ASYLUM REGIME

### *Temporary protection*

Temporary protection à l'Européenne arose in the context of profound changes in the asylum regime during the 1980s and constituted a cornerstone of the new regime. The eruption of war in the Balkans in the early 1990s gave it further shape. Even though an array of new restrictive measures demonstrated the deep reluctance of Europeans to accept more refugees into the European Union, a major crisis exploded on its doorstep. After procrastinating, E.U. officials yielded to the pleas of the United Nations High Commissioner for Refugees (UNHCR) to accept refugees from the former Yugoslavia on a temporary basis. They could not simply ignore the civil war and the masses of displaced people resulting from the worst massacres in Europe since the Nazi period. *Realpolitik* led the UNHCR to suggest a scheme that E.U. states were willing to consider. The result was the formulation of the concept of temporary protection status.

In a first formal step, the UNHCR called an international meeting on humanitarian aid for victims of the conflict in the former Yugoslavia on July 29, 1992 and proposed a comprehensive response to deal with the several hundred thousand persons who had by then been displaced. Temporary protection, one of seven components in the plan, was defined to include "at a minimum, admission to the country where such protection is being sought, respect for the principle of non-refoulement and basic human rights, and repatriation when conditions so allow in the country of origin" (U.N. High Commissioner of Refugees 1992: 4).

The European Union and UNHCR were the twin architects of the evolving concept and practice of temporary protection, although the European Union emerged as the dominant partner. The UNHCR advised the European Union in asylum issues, but critics argued the agency yielded too readily to E.U. demands and failed to establish adequate standards of treatment for temporary protection. In the end, many countries awarded more than the minimum requested by the UNHCR and its officials could have insisted on a minimum of parity and harmonization between receiving countries. Criticism came from activist institutional and social actors—including scholars—who attempted to influence the course of events.

The question of temporary protection also involved other institutions and bodies concerned with asylum in Europe: the Council of Europe, the European Council on Refugees and Exiles (ECRE—an umbrella organization of NGOs), other national and international NGOs, the Organization for Security and Co-operation in Europe (OSCE), the Intergovernmental Consultations on Asylum (a structured network of European and North American governments), individual European governments, and UNHCR itself. All issued declarations and resolutions to mark their positions.

## *Status and instruments*

Temporary protection of various kinds had been granted earlier within Europe. For instance, in 1936 *temporary refuge* was granted in France and Britain to persons fleeing the Spanish Civil War (Perluss and Hartman 1986). Successive historical examples of *temporary asylum* have been documented by Thorburn (1995), including the case of Hungarians in Austria and Yugoslavia in 1956 and the Czechs in Austria in 1968. According to Luca (1994), the current form of temporary protection can be traced back to the early 1980s, when the notion of temporary refuge was developed in the context of the refugee crisis in South East Asia. She defines it as a flexible measure pending resettlement or repatriation without any direct reference to protection.

There is no international convention or declaration on temporary protection—just UNHCR documents originally drafted for countries outside of Europe (such as ExCom Conclusion 15 on Refugees without an asylum country, ExCom Conclusion 19 on Temporary Refuge 1980 and ExCom Conclusion 22 1981 on the Protection of Asylum-seekers in situations of large-scale influx). These documents remain terse and succinct, but they have been supplemented by subsequent UNHCR texts drafted in response to the situation in the former Yugoslavia.

A form of temporary protection did exist in the 1930s (Hathaway 1984; Joly 1996) but it was the only status available and not in addition to the universal and "generous standards of protection provided by the 1951 Convention" (Rudge 1996*a*: 3). The temporary protection created for persons from the former Yugoslavia can, therefore, be considered as a qualitatively new status, although the UNHCR argues against this interpretation. According to the UNHCR, the temporary element is implicit in 1951 Convention provisions for asylum, as evidenced by the existence of a cessation clause. Nevertheless, it is clear that European states in the past consistently implemented the Geneva Convention in a way that granted permanent residence and integration. When the question of return arose, it generally fell upon the refugees themselves to petition European governments and E.U. institutions to set up return programs (Joly 1996).

The present European version of temporary protection relies on a positive group determination based mostly on nationality and an assessment of vulnerability. A similar group determination was commonly used in the 1930s and early 1940s, but the 1951 Geneva Convention introduced universal criteria for status determination and is commonly interpreted to imply individual determination. Thus, the differences between the old and the new asylum regime are clearly evident.

## *Instruments and practice*

Two E.U. documents on refugees from the former Yugoslavia were issued in 1992 and 1993. They constitute the first regional instruments on temporary protection and are also the first pan-European texts to establish a status for a refugees (EU Council of Ministers 1992, 1993). As nonbinding recommendations, however, they permit each state to control the numbers and mode of implementation. As a result, there are large discrepancies in application of these instruments throughout the European Union and in the rest of Europe.

Only a few states have actually passed specific legislation governing temporary protection. Most preferred to adapt existing statuses or use *ad hoc* measures (Joly, Kelly, and Nettleton 1997). For instance, Denmark, The Netherlands, and Spain developed a specific legal basis for temporary protection. Belgium prepared one but later abandoned it, while Germany could not implement what it had formulated. Only recently Sweden prepared specific legislation to cover former Yugoslavs.

By avoiding legislation, European host states did not have to specify the duration of "temporary" or provide specifics about renewals for permission to stay. In other words, the process of granting temporary protection was neither definitive nor static. Each new step established a potential model for the future, yet variations in its implementation gave ample room for discussion. Contributing to this debate were various resolutions and declarations on temporary protection by other institutions, including the Council of Europe, the European Commission, the European Parliament, the OSCE, the Intergovernmental Consultations on Asylum, ECRE, and other NGOs.

Non-refoulement is the first requirement set by the UNHCR for temporarily protected refugees (U.N. High Commissioner of Refugees 1981, 1992). This principle, which prohibits extradition to a state where a deportee is subject to torture, was generally reserved for designated groups among former Yugoslavs, at least once a border had been reached. Given the well-known atrocities taking place in the war area, it was nearly impossible to return asylum-seekers in large numbers (Secretariat of the Intergovernmental Consultations 1995). This was in line with the general practice in Western Europe to apply the non-refoulement clause much more widely than the granting of refugee status itself.

Access to protection was not made easier for persons from the former Yugoslavia than for other asylum-seekers, except for vulnerable groups such as detainees or people in need of medical treatment. As soon as the number of asylum seekers from the war zone grew, most countries imposed visas (European Parliament 1996). This measure, combined with carrier sanctions, made access to application for non-refoulement difficult, as noted by the UNHCR (1994*c*). However, those who managed to reach a border spontaneously generally benefited from the principle non-refoulement.

Most countries observed a distinction between "invited persons" and spontaneous arrivals. The former (various groups of "vulnerable persons") were treated in a manner similar to "quota refugees" in that they had easy access to procedures that granted temporary protection status and concomitant rights. In such cases, processing usually took place in the country or the region of origin. Yet, many had problems escaping from the zone of danger and reaching safety and for spontaneous arrivals the first-country rule applied (applications had to be made in the country of first arrival). This led to the dispersal of families and their near impossibility of being regrouped. Nor could such refugees apply for protection in more than one country since the 1992 E.U. document stipulated that people had to come "direct from combat zones" (E.U. Council of Ministers 1992: 2).

Since non-refoulement was practiced throughout the European Union for designated groups from the former Yugoslavia, a visa permitted physical presence and gave *de facto* temporary protection. Some countries even felt the necessity to soften the visa requirement. Denmark, for example, established a foreign service mission in Zagreb which issued visas to applicants and thus facilitated access. Compared to the earlier visa-free period, however, the new measures slowed down the intake and enhanced recipient government control over the process (Brochman 1995). The "Zagreb office" solution devised by Denmark offered one version of the concept of "processing in the region" that, as shown below, was developed by the Intergovernmental Consultations on Asylum (Secretariat of the Intergovernmental Consultations 1994).

To define eligibility for temporary protection, the UNHCR proposed several broad criteria: persons fleeing areas affected by conflict and violence; persons who have been or would be exposed to human rights abuses (including ethnic or religious persecution); and persons who, owing to their specific situations, felt compelled to flee as a result of a conflict (U.N. High Commissioner of Refugees 1993: 2). The latter provision was subsequently changed and broadened to include "persons who for other reasons specific to their personal situation are presumed to be in need of protection," thus incorporating those whose need for protection was based on other circumstances than the place of origin (U.N. High Commissioner of Refugees 1994*a*–*c*: 2).

A 1992 E.U. resolution first established a criterion based on the area of origin, limiting temporary protection to those from the former Yugoslavia, and then added two further considerations: the state of the conflict in the actual place of origin if they came "direct from combat zones" (European Council on Refugees and Exiles

1994: 2); and the degree of vulnerability of those who "have been in a prisoner-of-war or internment camp and cannot otherwise be saved from a threat to life or limb; are injured or seriously ill and for whom medical treatment cannot be obtained locally; are under a direct threat to life or limb and whose protection cannot otherwise be secured; have been subjected to sexual assault, provided that there is no suitable means for assisting them in safe areas situated as close as possible to their homes" (Council of Europe 1993).

In its 1995 Resolution on burden-sharing, the European Union reiterated the above criteria in relation to other "situations of armed conflict or civil war" (European Council on Refugees and Exiles 1995: 1). However, for the first time in a regional instrument, women were specifically identified as a group worthy of protection if they had been subjected to sexual assaults. A European Commission (1997: 5) proposal for joint action concerning temporary protection broadly follows similar guidelines on beneficiaries but stresses that it "relates solely to mass influx situations."

Most E.U. member states gave temporary protection to vulnerable groups, but in other respects they adapted and modified the guidelines considerably. Some limited it to Bosnians or a few other groups from the former Yugoslavia; others extended it to all nationals from the former Yugoslavia. In addition, the status awarded differed not only between countries but sometimes also within the same country, depending upon the modality of arrival. Analyzing the pattern, the E.U. Commission noted that states had generally adopted one of two approaches: (1) those which had introduced special, often nationality-related temporary protection mechanisms, clearly defining the beneficiaries, and (2) others which chose a more vague approach "based on the general principle that the beneficiaries would be those who do not fulfill the requirement of Article I of the Geneva Convention, but whose return to the country of origin would otherwise cause special hardship" (E.U. Commission 1996: 3). The Commission considered the first approach to be the more straightforward, but failed to declare which one it supported.

Both the European Parliament and the Council of Europe have advocated wider, all-embracing criteria for granting temporary protection. The Parliament would include all persons fleeing generalized violence who may not fall within the specific definition of refugees (Arnold 1996). The Council of Europe would embrace humanitarian refugees fleeing regions beset by war, civil strife or natural disasters such as from Rwanda, Afghanistan, Liberia, Somalia, Sudan, as well as those defined by UNHCR to fall under its mandate, and also adds a new category of people fleeing from "natural or ecological" disasters (Arnold 1996: 3).

In most E.U. countries, temporary protection could not run concurrently with standard asylum procedures, and persons given temporary protection had their asylum applications frozen, postponed, or not considered at all. The relationship between the two procedures has in most countries changed over time, however. As temporary protection became prolonged, a kind of norm developed in several European countries to set a limit to temporariness, and persons with long-term temporary status were given access to the Convention asylum procedure or to a humanitarian status.

The question of the relationship between access to asylum procedures and temporary protection is important, especially when "temporariness" becomes prolonged and the issue of return arises. The UNHCR initially did not insist on access to the asylum procedure, a position that E.U. states welcomed in their 1992 Conclusion on former Yugoslavia (European Council on Refugees and Exiles 1992). But asylum advocates, especially ECRE, requested that from the beginning persons benefiting from temporary protection be given access to the asylum procedure if they so wished. In the few instances where temporarily protected persons had access to the procedure, they were often advised to delay their applications, as filing a claim would change their status from that of the relative security of temporary protection to the vulnerabilities of an asylum-seeker whose application might be denied, leading to deportation.

The Council of Europe has stressed the importance of examining applications for asylum in parallel with temporary protection "in the shortest possible time and at the latest within a given lapse of time" without giving a time limit, although it quotes the two-year deadline in Denmark and the three years used in Norway (Arnold 1996: 8). The European Parliament has been more forthcoming, declaring that "four years is too long and it ideally should last only two years. After this time alternative solutions should be considered; the provision of permanent status being clearly the most appropriate solution" (European Parliament 1996: 11). This is also the view expressed by ECRE (Rudge 1996*b*).

Before question of returning to the former Yugoslavia arose, the UNHCR (1994*a*) asked governments to consider three possibilities for regularizing persons with temporary protection: (1) recognition as Convention refugees; (2) granting to all or certain groups a humanitarian status; or (3) a set of *ad hoc* measures as close as possible to Convention status. Looking to the time when return might be possible, the European Parliament called for giving all persons under temporary status at least access to the normal asylum procedures prior to repatriation (European Parliament 1996).

## *Policies of return*

With the conclusion of a peace agreement for the former Yugoslavia in 1995, the modalities of return for persons under temporary protection became an urgent issue. The UNHCR lifted temporary protection in December, 1996, and took the general position that the optimal solution is voluntary return of refugees to their place of origin under safe conditions. In practice, return clearly raises three questions of when, how, and where? Since conflict has continued in some areas and expanded to others, the requirement of safe return is not met for all prospective returnees and their temporary protection should, therefore, be extended. The Dayton Agreement recognized that no support or legitimization for ethnic cleansing must be given—hence, in theory refugees should be able to return to their place of origin.

In practice, as ECRE (1996) has pointed out, this provision has created a dilemma of what to do when the place of origin is dominated by an ethnic group that is hostile to prospective returnees. Will host countries force refugees to return nonetheless? On the one hand, return to areas other than the place of origin would confirm ethnic cleansing and contravene the spirit of the Dayton agreement, although it is not legally binding on third parties. On the other hand, it would harmonize with the E.U. interpretation of Article 1A of the Geneva Convention on internal flight alternatives/relocation. Another option is to convert temporary protection into permanent status in the country of exile (a Convention or humanitarian status).

The Yugoslav case illustrates the point noted above: temporary protection is not simply a replacement of humanitarian status. Rather, it presupposes its existence since not all temporarily protected persons will be able to return or qualify for Convention rights. Unlike Convention refugees, temporarily protected persons could fall under forcible repatriation orders and at least one country (Germany) has done so. Even some liberal sources of opinion, such as the Council of Europe, while stating that voluntary return is the basic principle, accept that returns other than on a voluntary basis cannot be ruled out. The Council allows exceptions only for Convention refugees, and certain groups such as victims of torture and those who have suffered the traumas of war and rape (Arnold 1996: 9).

The UNHCR, as already noted, upholds as a general principle that return must be voluntary and occur under conditions of safety and dignity. It has proposed that host states permit refugees from the former Yugoslavia to prepare their return, that repatriation be implemented in an orderly manner, and that it take place in a phased sequence according to geographic, ethnic, and familial criteria. In terms of geography, internally displaced persons should return first, then refugees from neighboring states, then those from other countries. In terms of ethnic criteria, the first returnees should be those who constitute the ethnic majority in their home area, followed by those who wish to relocate to new areas where their ethnic group is the majority, and lastly by those going to areas where returnees constitute the minority. Finally, in terms of family status, the first to return should be childless adults or adults where spouses or children are still living in the former Yugoslavia, followed only later by return families (European Council on Refugees and Exiles 1996).

In the Dayton Peace Agreement on Refugees and Displaced Persons of 1995, safe return has been defined as return "without risk of harassment, intimidation, persecution, or discrimination, particularly on account of... ethnic origin, religious belief, or political opinion." The importance of a good return program is generally accepted by host states. The Commission on Security and Cooperation in Europe in 1993 advocated the creation of programs to assist the dignified return not only of refugees, but also of foreigners who did not qualify for permanent immigration (Commission on Security and Cooperation in Europe 1993).

Some E.U. countries have organized special return programs for refugees and asylum seekers. For unsuccessful asylum seekers, some countries have agreed to take back their own nationals in return for financial compensation (Italy/Albania, Germany/Romania) (Muus et al. 1993). In 1990, Germany prepared a reintegration and reemigration plan for asylum-seekers from Sri Lanka (German Federal Ministry of the Interior 1990). Repatriation programs for accepted refugees constitute another category. Scandinavian countries, for instance, set up a return program for Chilean refugees in the early 1990s. The Norwegian government introduced its own program for former Yugoslavs, building on the established scheme for Chilean refugees. It included benefit payments, a travel grant, health insurance for one year, development aid to the nation of origin targeted to the local area of return, and a 2-year period for returnees with permanent residence permits to change their minds (Brochman 1995). Similar programs have been set up for the former Yugoslavs in other Scandinavian countries.

Obviously, safeguards need to be an integral part of any return program. The European umbrella organization for refugees and asylum rights, ECRE, emphasizes that states should grant returning refugees a legal right to come back into the host country within 6 months (Conseil Européen pour les Réfugiés et les Exiles 1996). This safeguard could be an incentive for the refugees to attempt repatriation. ECRE also stresses the need to support "le retour volontaire des réfugiés en toute sécurité, dans la dignité et... accompagné de moyens suffisants pour le retour à une vie normale" (Conseil Européen pour les Réfugiés et les Exilés 1996: 1).

Dignity as well as security is also a precondition for return in the discourse of agencies and individuals concerned with the interests of refugees. The determination of when a return may be accomplished with dignity involves a complex combination of factors in the legal, material, and emotional domain. According to the E.U. Commission (1997: 7) a safe return under humane conditions involves five elements: the right to return freely to homes of origin; physical and legal safety; non-discrimination and respect for fundamental human rights such as freedom of movement, respect for family life, freedom of opinion and religion, and property rights; access to assistance and shelter; and an effective system for monitoring the reintegration process.

Repatriation issues naturally affect not only refugees and their countries of asylum but also their countries of origin. As de Jong (1996) points out, mass return may be destabilizing for origin countries whose social and economic fabric has been torn by civil war and internecine violence. Ferris (1997) argues that post-conflict governments may thus find it in their "best interest... for the refugees to remain in exile." Returning refugees, she points out, may jeopardize the fragile stability of the home country because of their ethnicity, past involvement in the conflict, or because of their anticipated political and welfare demands, such as claims to land, which may raise complex issues of land tenure and property restoration.

In addition, the return of refugees probably means decreased remittances to the home country, and thus delayed reconstruction. In the case of El Salvador, for instance, remittances from a large and mixed community of refugees and migrants in the United States in the early 1990s (shortly after the peace accords were signed) were estimated to be three times the value of the country's major export crop and a principal factor in "saving the economy from a considerably worse fate" (Spence et al. 1995: 21).

The return of refugees from the former Yugoslavia is seen by some as the acid test of temporary protection—determining whether it will indeed be temporary

(Secretariat of the Intergovernmental Consultations, quoted in Rudge 1995). It is increasingly becoming clear, however, that return is complicated, as the map of the homeland has *de facto* changed and many refugees cannot return to their former residence. About 200,000 Bosnian refugees returned mostly to majority areas during 1996 and 1997, 95,000 from Germany alone in 1997. Forced returns included 929 from Germany, 90 from Austria and 49 from Switzerland (U.S. Committee for Refugees 1998). Minority returns have progressed slowly and remained problematic, despite the "enormous efforts" of the UNHCR (Ogata 1997: 5), whose "open cities" initiative has not yielded expected results. In a joint statement, both the European Council on Refugees and Exiles and the International Council of Voluntary Agencies (1998) have underscored the effective barriers to return: basic human rights that are not safeguarded, continued harassment of minorities, the presence of war criminals, the issue of missing persons, and the need to reconstruct civil society.

### *Standards of treatment*

The defining characteristic of temporary protection is that it did not offer the possibility of integration. On the contrary, in several countries it included features designed to prevent integration in the host society, such as requiring education in one's own mother tongue rather than the host country language. Other features of temporary protection varied considerably from country to country, but there were several commonalities. First, the social rights granted were not as good as those granted to persons with Convention or humanitarian status, although they were slightly better than those of asylum-seekers. Second, the implementation of these reduced rights further varied across countries, and also within a single country depending upon the modality of admittance. In France, for example, the prohibition on refoulement created a paradoxical situation that enabled people to stay but without any status that conferred social rights.

The initial standards set by UNHCR remained very limited, in accordance with those formulated by its Executive Committee for the benefit of poor non-Europeans (ExCom 22, U.N. High Commissioner of Refugees 1981). After 1992, when a plea was made for temporary protection, over a year went by before UNHCR recognized the need to review standards (U.N. High Commissioner of Refugees 1993). Subsequently the agency put forward a request for an improvement stating that "when the period of temporary protection has to be prolonged, improved standards of treatment might be called for" on the grounds that "unlike asylum-seekers, whose claims were not yet examined, the need of the person concerned for international protection was already established" (U.N. High Commission for Refugees 1994*a*: 2). Only in 1995 did the UNHCR advocate standards "close to that which recognised refugees are entitled" (U.N. High Commissioner of Refugees 1995*b*: 3) including family reunification, employment, education, and a certain degree of integration over a protracted period of time.

In reaction, ECRE voiced concern with the effect of temporary protection on the treatment of refugees in general: "what we are witnessing is the downgrading of the entire European asylum system to the lesser protection level afforded by temporary protection" (see Rudge 1996*a*: 8). To prevent this, the European Council on Refugees and Exiles proposed that temporary protection only be implemented if accompanied by training and educational program, a right to family reunification, a guarantee of decent living conditions, social benefits, opportunities for gainful employment, identity papers, and travel documents as afforded to other refugees (European Council on Refugees and Exiles 1994). The E.U. Commission (1997) sets out a number of minimum rights which include nuclear family reunification, employment, social security and education on a par with Convention refugees (p. 16).

## *Scholarly engagement*

Scholarly writings on temporary protection are few and recent. Almost all share a concern for the ethics of protection, which committed scholars perceive as being jeopardized by current developments in asylum policies and practices. Goodwin-Gill (1996: 3–5) elaborates on "threats" to refugee protection from the state and from the UNHCR, while Hathaway (1996: 4) argues that we are facing "an impending fundamental breakdown of the protection regime." One legal scholar argues that temporary protection is not part of public international law, but represents a pragmatic approach that combines "administrative and political efficiency" (Kälin 1996: 25).

Other scholars see temporary protection as "a functional step towards an eventual solution" (Marx 1994: 16; Thorburn 1995: 465), and Kjaerum (1993) identifies its purposes as saving administrative and economic resources, facilitating the return of the refugees politically, and sending a signal to the public that it is a matter of protection and not of immigration. It is generally assumed that temporary protection in and of itself cannot function effectively; it must be viewed as an integral part of a broader, more comprehensive approach to the refugee crisis that addresses sources of conflict and possibilities for return (Thorburn 1995; Hathaway 1996; Kälin 1996).

More positively, some legal scholars view temporary protection as a "link between non-refoulement and a durable solution" (Kjaerum 1993: 3) or at least as a means to bridge two protection gaps (Kälin 1996). The first gap is between the binding principle of non-refoulement and the discretionary character of admission and asylum (see Goodwin-Gill 1996). The second gap is between the protection of Convention refugees and non-Convention refugees forced to flee the dangers of armed conflict or systematic and widespread human rights violations (Kälin 1996: 26). Kälin finds other benefits deriving from temporary protection. Protection can be offered to non-Convention refugees without undermining the permanent institution of asylum. It also allows suspending provisions regarding the "safe third country" clause, thus permitting more burden-sharing of asylum among states.

On balance, however, scholarly analyses of the concept or practice of temporary protection are mostly critical. Goodwin-Gill, who in 1994 had looked favorably on a comprehensive approach to protection, in 1996 leveled sharp criticism at the UNHCR for "substituting 'humanitarian action' for the duty to provide protection" (1996: 5). Hathaway (1996: 32) strongly disapproves of the standard of treatment given to those awarded temporary protection, accusing the UNHCR of giving "tacit approval to the use of temporary protection as an opportunity or excuse to restrict refugee rights."

Some scholars have sought to systematize the conditions under which temporary protection is justifiable. Kälin (1996) defines two main parameters: (1) the existence of a mass influx and (2) the presence of persons who are not Convention refugees but who largely come under the definition of the OAU Convention and Cartagena declaration. He further adds another two conditions: an international process to restore a situation permitting return in safety and dignity, and an appropriate intergovernmental forum and a mechanism for burden-sharing.

As for the duration of temporary protection, scholars differ. Kälin (1996) deems a maximum of 5 years as reasonable, while Kjaerum advocates a shorter period, arguing that if repatriation does not "take place after a period of two years the situation of the refugee should be normalized" (Kjaerum 1993: 15).

Standards of treatment and appropriate levels of social rights for persons in temporary protection have attracted considerable interest. Two arguments have been put forward to support an improvement of standards which may overlap in practice, although not in legal terms. The first is to limit the time period for humanitarian reasons, a suggestion that has generally been accepted. The second is to improve the quality of life the longer the term of residence in the host country. The Geneva Convention carefully constructed a regime that bestowed rights as a function of a refugee's attachment to the asylum state (Hathaway 1996), yielding a gradual improvement of treatment by duration of lawful residence, domicile, or habitual residence (Kälin 1996).

Grounds for an improvement of standards are also found in the International Covenant on Civic and Political Rights (ICCPR) and the International Covenant on Economic, Social and Cultural Rights. Hathaway (1996: 35) argues that the simple presence of a refugee does not constitute a "public emergency which threatens the life of the nation" as required for emergency suspension of rights under the ICCPR. He proposes a set of guidelines for temporary protection that include non-refoulement, security, dignity, and self-sufficiency. Kjaerum (1993) concentrates instead on rights to employment and family reunion. He finds arguments in favor of the latter in the European Convention of Human Rights, citing Article 8 as the basis for "an obligation for any European state to admit family reunion on their territory if the reunion cannot take place elsewhere" (Kjaerum 1993: 11).

As for the question of return, Goodwin-Gill (1996: 9) argues that it has currently lost its connection with humanitarian ideals and has become "a political end, to be achieved by whatever means are available and regardless of principle." Kälin posits that a durable solution in the form of return or integration has to be found since resettlement is unlikely. He further recommends modalities to ensure return in safety and dignity. Hathaway (1996: 15) identifies the conditions for a successful repatriation, emphasizing that it must be safe and feasible to return, and that refugees should be "encouraged to explore, without penalization the feasibility of return. Finally, repatriation is meaningless without reintegration, and reintegration requires careful bridge-building between returnee and stayee communities."

## *Burden-shifting and sharing*

The restrictive asylum regime that developed in Europe included three dynamics of burden-shifting. First is simple burden-shifting, which occurs when exclusionary measures in one state increase the demand for asylum in other states. To what extent such burden-shifting actually occurred is difficult to document empirically, and evidently there have been no systematic efforts to do so. Second is complex burden-shifting, which occurs when exclusionary measures in one state are linked to compensatory measures (usually financial aid) to another state to induce it to take in refugees or rejected seekers. This approach was developed by the European Union members with respect to several Eastern and Central European states. Third is the mixed model, where in asylum seekers are held and processed in regions of origin. Based on a Dutch proposal in 1993, the idea was to shift protection to the country or region of origin, which—depending on which form it took—could be a simple or complex burden shifting (Secretariat of the Intergovernmental Consultations 1994, 1995).

The Dutch initiative had ambiguous implications that were hard to sort out in advance. As the proposal moved through the Inter-Governmental Consultation (IGC) process in 1994 and 1995, all participating states affirmed in principle that temporary protection within designated areas of "the region of origin" (defined as those outside the IGC states) would not completely substitute for asylum in the IGC states. Yet, the potential for policy to develop in this direction was clearly inherent in the plan given that the main thrust of the proposal was to manage conditions for receiving, and keeping, refugees in regions outside the industrialized North.

All three mechanisms implied a form of burden shifting that was criticized by activists and concerned scholars. The consequences, it was feared, would further weaken the international refugee regime based on the 1951 Convention and the Statutes of the U.N. High Commissioner of Refugees, first by undermining the individual's right to asylum as delineated in international refugee law and human rights law, and second by breaching political–ethical principles of equity among states in caring for the world's refugees. Establishing separate mechanisms for processing in regions of origin, moreover, could also weaken the political authority and financial basis of the UNHCR by giving rise to a parallel and competitive refugee regime (European Council on Refugees and Exiles 1995). More fundamentally, Richmond (1994) criticized the evolving asylum system as representing a "global apartheid" that was morally corrupt and politically counterproductive.

The current distributive function of the contemporary international asylum system combine arbitrary elements with a systematic bias against poor and violent regions of the world. This system was assessed by an international team of scholars organized by York University (Canada) in the early 1990s with a view to propose legal reforms for "responsibility sharing" (York University 1995). Mobilizing legal scholars and social scientists, the York project explored ways to combine temporary protection with a globalized redistribution scheme reflecting the ability of host states to provide protection as well as the preferences of refugees. The aim was not only to secure protection for individuals, but to produce a redistribution that would undercut the current systemic biases which lead to refugee accumulations in the poorer parts of the world, or in states that happen to be situated next to conflicts.

Similar ideas had been put forward two decades earlier by Grahl-Madsen (1977), who proposed that states take in refugees according to national wealth and population. These proposals came to naught, and the York reformulation project similarly ended up without clear, consensual recommendations. While the principle of burden sharing (relabeled as "responsibility sharing") to ensure greater protection for refugees and equity among states was endorsed, there were doubts on other grounds. Some participants feared that temporary protection would undermine the present safeguards, however imperfectly realized, in the 1951 Convention. Others questioned the practical and moral basis for shifting refugees across regions, and noted that earlier redistribution schemes had occurred only under exceptional circumstances (after World War II and after the Vietnam war). Nor was it clear which criteria for redistribution were most compelling, or what could be most meaningfully shared: financial transfers or refugees?

The less radical idea of burden-sharing within regions seemed a priori more feasible and has been explored by scholars and policymakers. As noted in one paper prepared for the York project, states within a region are less able to avoid the consequences of political disorder in their own neighborhood, more likely to be concerned, and—given existing patterns of cooperation—more likely to have some stake in cooperation for mutually beneficial trade-offs (Suhrke and Hans 1995).

Not surprisingly, in the early 1990s those governments most affected by refugees from the former Yugoslavia were the first to propose cost-sharing schemes within the European Union, and during the mid-1990s several smaller E.U. states (notably Sweden, Denmark, and the Netherlands) continued to promote the idea as a general insurance scheme. The obstacles were formidable, however, as demonstrated when a new crisis erupted in Albania in early 1997 and no E.U. member came forward to share the costs with Italy, which bore the brunt of the refugee outflow. The reasons for this state of affairs have been analyzed in an insightful paper by Noll (1997). Using the logic of game theory, he argues that states are caught in a "prisoner's dilemma" whereby the uncoordinated pursuit of individual self-interest results in mutual damage.

## TOWARD A COMPREHENSIVE REFUGEE POLICY

The accumulated pressures and fears that generated a more restrictive asylum regime in the North also led to a renewed emphasis on prevention in refugee sending regions. Partly to justify the new restrictions, governments called in the 1990s for new measures to prevent conflict and so control the causes of outflow. The UNHCR likewise moved more openly into the political realm by drawing attention to the political causes of humanitarian disasters, demanding that these be recognized and dealt with, and claimed for itself a modest if definite preventive role.

The latter view represents a marked departure from the position of UNHCR during most of the post-World War II period, when a studied apolitical stance was cultivated.

It recalled the position of an earlier era, for in 1938 the High Commission of German Refugees had declared that "*in the present economic conditions of the world, the European States, and even those overseas, have only a limited power of absorption of refugees. The problem must be tackled at its source if disaster is to be avoided*" (see Coles 1988: 409).

## *Development of the new UNHCR doctrine*

Within the UNHCR, the preventive idea was wrapped in the cloak of a "comprehensive refugee policy." Recognizing the very limited willingness of other European states to provide asylum to refugees from the former Yugoslavia, the High Commissioner convened a ministerial-level meeting in July 1992 where she first proposed a "comprehensive response" to the crisis. The plan had two key elements. The first was the novel concept of "preventive protection," clearly inspired by the UN Secretary General's emphasis on "preventive diplomacy" in his 1992 *Agenda for Peace*. Conceived as protection in place that would make flight unnecessary, "preventive protection" in the Yugoslav case was defined as humanitarian measures taken to reduce violence within a theater of war, including the monitoring of human rights and international humanitarian law. The second element, as already discussed, was temporary protection for victims of war in states away from the conflict.

To explore the preventive concept more generally, the UNHCR and International Labor Organization jointly sponsored a major conference in May 1992. Composed of scholars and practitioners, the conference focused on foreign aid as an instrument to reduce South–North migration, but also discussed a "comprehensive response" to refugee flows that could be preemptive and preventive. Writing in the preface to the publication of the conference papers, the UNHCR co-author of the volume, Schloeter-Paredes, noted that the emergence of complex and large population flows of migrants and refugees had made it more difficult for the UNHCR to determine who needed protection. As a result, the UNHCR had to reappraise its traditional approaches.

In particular, "coherent strategies for the prevention of refugee flows" had to be developed in a multilateral context and with broad international cooperation. Two principal strategies were emerging:

> [H]umanitarian aid alone cannot be effective without concomitant political initiatives aimed at resolving conflicts. Peace, conflict mediation and conflict resolution are crucial to make possible the return of refugees and to prevent further or new outflows... The promotion of democratic forms of government, the strengthening of human rights monitoring mechanisms, institution-building and support for legal reforms are all important components of preventive strategies. (Böhning and Schloeter-Paredes 1994: 8)

Similarly, since extreme poverty was seen as a likely cause of violent internal conflict, "better targeted development assistance" was viewed as a means to reduce or prevent refugee outflows. Seen in this perspective, strategies to resolve conflict or modify its causes differ from the more limited strategy of providing "preventive" protection and assistance within the theater of conflict. The former were in the tradition of an earlier generation of efforts to address the "root causes" of refugee flows, which developed in the highly politicized climate of the U.N. General Assembly of the early 1980s. Root causes were identified as structural conditions of inequality, oppression, racism, authoritarianism, and totalitarianism that were located within states as well as in the international system at large.

The more limited strategy of "preventive protection" represented a new departure in the 1990s, and it took many forms. The most ambitious were the creation of "safe havens" and other types of "safe humanitarian zones" that were designed to protect civilians and prevent refugee outflows within conflict areas. The achievements have been mixed, at best. Attempts by the U.N. to establish protective space in Bosnia met with little success, as did efforts by the U.S. led coalition in Northern Iraq in the aftermath of the Gulf War in 1991 and French efforts to delineate southwest Rwanda as a humanitarian zone in the aftermath of the 1994 genocide (Loescher 1993; Tiso 1994; Adelman and Suhrke 1996; Dowty and Loescher 1996). Less ambitious or less structured ways of providing protective presence were also tried in the form of open relief centers (pioneered in Sri Lanka) and the creation of "humanitarian space" by relief assistance and human rights monitoring (Nicolaus 1994; Donini 1996).

By the time the ILO-UNHCR conference volume was published (1994), the notion of a "comprehensive refugee policy" had been elevated to the status of policy doctrine in UNHCR. It is indicative that whereas the subtitle of the 1993 issue of *The State of the World's Refugees* (*SOWR*) (the biannual publication of the High Commissioner's office) was "The Challenge of Protection," the 1995 issue was more appropriately subtitled "In Search of Solutions." Written in-house by UNHCR staff but in cooperation with external experts, and drawing on a range of legal and social science literature, the second volume noted the changing role of asylum. The traditional approach to protection had been "reactive, exile-oriented and refugee-specific" (p. 30) and had associated asylum with resettlement in the host state or third countries. In the wake of the end of the Cold War, however, increasing restrictions on both asylum and third country resettlement had demonstrated the inadequacy of the traditional approach and forced a reorientation.

The new orientation was "proactive, homeland-oriented, and holistic" (p. 43), reflecting a shift of attention to the "country of origin" and associated preventive-preemptive approaches. The SOWR 1995 affirms as an emerging "fundamental principle" that refugee flows can be "averted" if action is taken to reduce or remove the threats that force people to flee. A list of such activities includes monitoring and early warning, diplomatic intervention, economic and social development, conflict resolution, institution building, the protection of human and minority rights, and the dissemination of information to prospective asylum-seekers. The role and experiences of the UNHCR in these activities are then reviewed.

Echoing the argument made by Schloeter-Paredes, the 1995 SOWR report claims that conventional categories such as "refugees," "returnees," "internally displaced persons," and "resident population" had broken down. In conflict areas or in repatriation situations, persons often moved from one category to another, making it difficult for the UNHCR to aid one without helping the other. As a result, a pronounced "mission creep" developed, complete with a new vocabulary. Terms such as "displaced people," "uprooted populations" or "involuntary migrants" increasingly replaced conventional concepts of refugee as defined in the 1951 Convention (see p. 38). The UNHCR no longer protected only "refugees," but also "peoples of concern" to the UNHCR more broadly.

## *Intrusive control to preempt refugee flows*

The doctrine of a comprehensive policy drew support from a parallel reorientation towards prevention and intrusive control that appeared in the U.N. system after the end of the Cold War. Traditional barriers in a world based on nation-states had to be scaled, Secretary General Boutros Boutros-Ghali declared in 1992. States that did not observe "the needs of good internal governance" could not expect to hide from international censorship behind the protective shield of national sovereignty. "The time of absolute and exclusive sovereignty... has passed," the Secretary General said, thus opening the way for international intervention against repressive regimes of the kind that historically have been major causes of refugee flows (Boutros-Ghali 1992: 8–9).

The U.N. General Assembly also nibbled cautiously at the principle of national sovereignty. Prompted by a wish to provide more effective humanitarian aid to victims of internal warfare or natural disasters, the General Assembly adopted two French-sponsored resolutions (in 1988 and 1990) promoted by then-Minister of Humanitarian Affairs, Bernard Kouchner, that widened the scope for humanitarian relief efforts within states. More decisively, (for the U.N. at least) the resolution established a new U.N. Department of Humanitarian Affairs and in 1992 affirmed the legitimacy of intrusive international aid in emergencies. The seminal resolution (46/182) stated that humanitarian assistance should be provided "in principle" after an appeal from the affected country, thereby implying there might be exceptions. While not going as far as humanitarian activists who have affirmed a duty to intervene, these were bold words for a body representing the interests of states.

About the same time, and at the request of the U.N. Commission on Human Rights, the Secretary General established a special representative to consider the issue of international protection for internally displaced persons. The initiative was a central element in the emerging country-of-origin doctrine in the U.N. system. A mechanism that provided effective protection to vulnerable people within their own country would have the side-effect of reducing the number and legitimacy of international refugees. In his first report in 1993, the special representative, the former Sudanese diplomat Francis Deng, echoed the principle of limited sovereignty invoked in the *Agenda for Peace*, arguing that the principle of subsidiarity permits the international community to move in if states fail to protect their subjects (United Nations 1994).

In the European Community, a similar ideological reorientation towards root causes and country of origin was taking place. In its first "communication" on immigration and asylum policies, the E.C. Commission identified what it saw as three basic policy tasks: (1) dealing with causes; (2) controlling borders; and (3) integrating foreigners already legally resident in member states. With respect to causes, the 1994 report emphasized the need to improve human rights conditions and limit collective violence. E.U. member states were encouraged to emphasize greater "respect for human rights and the rule of law in their external relations." Refugee policy was broadly defined to encompass a range of traditional foreign and security policies intended to prevent armed conflict, as well as provide humanitarian assistance.

The new focus on countries of origin was controversial both inside and outside the UNHCR. Critics noted that the new doctrine was inspired less by an appreciation of its feasibility than by the growing number of asylum seekers. Declarations of the need to modify causes of refugee movements, critics argued, were a smokescreen for restricting protection abroad. "Preventive protection" could be seen simply as a device to prevent refugee outflows. No matter how it was viewed, however, it was of questionable effectiveness.

In this perspective, "a comprehensive refugee policy" both detracted from and undermined the primary mission of the UNHCR to secure asylum. Among the most vocal external critics was international law expert James Hathaway. Basing himself in international refugee law, which is only designed to address the symptoms of conflict by providing "interim and palliative" protection, Hathaway argued that asylum must be the principal focus of the international refugee regime. The causes of flight are properly a subject of the international human rights and security regime of the U.N., and dealing with them involves different legal norms and policy tools (Hathaway 1995: 8–9). Given the manifest difficulties of addressing the underlying causes of refugee movements, and the inadequacy of "preventive protection" in conflicts such as ex-Yugoslavia, these objections have some merit. UNHCR, for instance, tacitly admitted as much by quietly dropping the term "preventive protection."

By the middle of the 1990s, a related concern had developed, prompted by growing awareness of the political, and often unintended consequences of humanitarian assistance designed to assist and protect civilians in situations of armed conflict. Did humanitarian assistance actually help to fuel the conflict and was it thus counterproductive in the long run? The question was discussed by the aid agencies, and appeared in a growing literature by concerned scholars and practitioners (Christian Michelsens Institutt 1997). By the late 1990s, the new conventional wisdom in the U.N.-system was that humanitarian assistance and preventive protection at best could buy limited time to find a political solution (Jesse-Pedersen 1997).

## References

Adelman, Howard, and Suhrke, Astri (1996). *Early Warning and Conflict Management.* Study II of the Joint Evaluation of Emergency Assistance to Rwanda. Copenhagen: Danida.

Arnold, May (1996). "Preliminary Draft report on Temporary Protection of Persons Forced to flee their Country," Committee on Migration, Refugees and Demography, Parliamentary Assembly Council of Europe, Strasbourg: 18 September.

Böhning Wolf R., and Schloeter-Paredes, M. (1994). "Introduction," in W. R. Böhning and M. Schloeter-Paredes (eds.), *Aid in Place of Migration.* Geneva: International Labor Office, pp. xx–xx.

Boutros-Ghali, Boutros (1992). *Agenda for Peace.* New York: United Nations.

Brochman, Grete (1995). *Bosnian Refugees in the Nordic countries: Three Routes to Protection.* Oslo: March.

——(1996). *European Integration and Migration from Third Countries.* Oslo: Scandinavian University Press.

Conseil Européen pour les Réfugiés et les Exilés (1996). "Position Prise par le Conseil Européen pour les Réfugiés et les Exiles sur la Question des Réfugiés de l'ex-Yugoslavie," Paris, Conseil Européen pour les Réfugiés et les Exilés, Avril.

Christian Michelsens Institutt (1997). *Humanitarian Assistance and Conflict. A State of the Art Report.* Bergen: Christian Michelsens Institutt.

Coles, Gervase (1988). "Approaches to the Refugee Problem Today," in Gil Loescher and Laila Monahan (eds.), *Refugees and International Relations.* Oxford: Clarendon Press, pp. 212–24.

Commission on Security and Cooperation in Europe (1993). "CSCE Human Dimension Seminar on Migration, Including Refugees and Displaced Persons, Consolidated Summary," Office for Democratic Institutions and Human Rights, Commission on Security and Cooperation in Europe, Warsaw, 20–23 April.

Council of Europe (1993). "Human Rights at the Dawn of the 21st Century: Proceedings of an Interregional Meeting Organised by the Council of Europe in Advance of the World Conference on Human Rights," Strasbourg: Council of Europe Press.

de Jong, Cornelius (1996). "Elements for a More Effective European Union Response to Situations of Mass Influx," *International Journal of Refugee Law*, 8: 156–69.

Donini, Antonio (1996). "The Politics of Mercy: UN Coordination in Afghanistan, Mozambique and Rwanda," Providence, R.I.: Thomas J. Watson Institute for International Studies, Brown University, Occasional Paper #2.

Dowty, Alan, and Loescher, Gil (1996). "Refugee Flows as Grounds for International Action," *International Security* 21: 43–71.

E.U. Commission (1994). "Communication from the Commission to the Council and the European Parliament on Immigration and Asylum Policies," European Union Commission, Brussels.

——(1996). "Temporary Protection: A Subject for 'Common Action'?" European Union Commission, Brussels.

——(1997). "Proposal to the Council for a Joint Action based on Article K.3 (2)(b) of the treaty on European Union Concerning Temporary Protection of Displaced Persons." European Union Commission, Brussels, COM(97)98.

E.U. Council of Ministers (1992). "Conclusion on People Displaced by the Conflict in the Former Yugoslavia," E.U. Council of Ministers, London 10518/92.

——(1993). "Resolution on Certain Common Guidelines as Regards the Admission of Particularly Vulnerable Persons from the Former Yugoslavia," E.U. Council of Ministers, Copenhagen: 1 June.

——(1994*a*). "Note from the Presidency to Migration Working Party (Admission) of Steering Group (Asylum and Immigration) Draft Council Resolution on Burden-Sharing with Regard to the Admission and Residence of Refugees," E.U. Council of Ministers, Brussels, 1 July.

——(1994*b*). "Report from the Presidency to Permanent Representatives Committee/Council (JAI): Burden sharing with Regard to the Admission and Residence on a Temporary Basis of Displaced Persons," E.U. Council of Ministers, Brussels, 17 November.

——(1995). "Council Resolution of 25 September 1995 on Burden-Sharing with Regard to the Admission and Residence of Displaced Persons on a Temporary Basis," *Official Journal*, No. 262, 07/10/95.

European Council on Refugees and Exiles. (1992). "Position on Refugees from the Former Yugoslavia." London: European Council on Refugees and Exiles.

—— (1994). "A European Refugee Policy in Light of Established Principles," European Council on Refugees and Exiles, London, April.

—— (1995). "Summary of Views on Processing in the Region of Origin: Informal Report," European Council on Refugees and Exiles, London.

—— (1996). "Position on Refugees from the Former Yugoslavia by ECRE: Update December," European Council on Refugees and Exiles, London.

—— and International Council of Voluntary Agencies (1998). "Statement to the U.N. High Commissioner of Refugees and the Humanitarian Issues Working Group," European Council on Refugees and Exiles and International Council of Voluntary Agencies, Geneva, 26 June 1998.

—— (1995). "Resolution on the Communication from the Commission to the Council and the European Parliament on Immigration and Asylum Policy," *Official Journal*, C103, 24.7.1977, p. 1.

—— (1996). "Temporary Protection: The Protection of Refugees from the former Yugoslavia by the Member States," Draft, European Parliament, Strasbourg.

Ferris, Elisabeth (1997). "After the Wars are Over: Reconstruction and Repatriation," Paper presented at the Conference on Forced Migration, New School for Social Research, Center for Ethnicity, Migration and Citizenship, New York, April 4.

German Federal Ministry of the Interior (1990). "Report by the Inter-ministerial Working Group on a 'Refugee Concept'," Federal Ministry of the Internal, Bonn, September 25.

Goodwin-Gill, Guy (1996). "Refugee Identity and the Fading Prospect of International Protection," Paper presented at the Conference on Refugee Rights and Realities, Nottingham, England, November 30.

Grahl-Madsen, Atle (1977). *Territorial Asylum*. Stockolm: Almqvist & Wiksell International.

Guicherd, Catherine (1995). "Securing Stability in Central Europe: Will the Stability Pact Do?" Unpublished paper, Institute for Public Policy Research, London, March.

Hathaway, James (1984). "The Evolution of Refugee Status in International Law: 1920–1950," *International and Comparative Law Quarterly*, 33: 348–80.

—— (1995). "Reformulation of Refugee Law," Preliminary paper presented at York University, Toronto.

——(1996). "Towards the Reformulation of International Refugee Law: A Model for Collectivized and Solution-Oriented Protection," Paper presented at Consultative Workshops in London and Washington, October 4 and 11.

Intergovernmental Consultations (1994). "Reception in the Region of Origin," Intergovernmental Consultations, Geneva, November.

—— (1995). "Reception in the Region of Origin," Intergovernmental Consultations, Geneva, September.

Jesse-Pedersen, Soeren (1997). Address to the Conference on Forced Migration, New School for Social Research, Center for Ethnicity, Migration and Citizenship, New York, April 4.

—— (1996). *Haven or Hell? Asylum Policies and Refugees in Europe*. Basingstoke: Macmillan.

—— Nettleton, Clive, and Poulton, Hugh (1992). *Refugees: Asylum in Europe?* London: Minority Rights Group.

—— Kelly, Lynette, and Nettleton, Clive (1997). *Refugees in Europe: the Hostile New Agenda*. London: Minority Rights Group.

Kälin, Walter (1996). "Towards a Concept of Temporary Protection. A Study Commissioned by UNHCR," University of Bern, November 12.

Kjaerum, Morten (1993). "Temporary Protection in Europe in the '90s," Paper presented at the Council for Security and Cooperation in Europe Expert Seminar on Migration Including Refugees and Displaced Persons, Council for Security and Cooperation in Europe, Warsaw, 20–24 April.

Loescher, Gil (1993). *Beyond Charity: International Cooperation and the Global Refugee Crisis.* New York: Oxford University Press.

Luca, Donatella (1994). "Questioning Temporary Protection, Together with a Selected Bibliography on Temporary Refuge/Temporary Protection," *International Journal of Refugee Law*, 6: 535–62.

Marx, Reinhart (1994). "Temporary Protection: Refugees from the former Yugoslavia, International Protection or Solution Oriented Approach?" European Council on Refugees and Exiles, London, June.

Muus, Philip J. (1993). "Reception Policies for Persons in Need of International Protection in Western European States," United Nations High Commission of Refugees, Geneva, September.

Nicolaus, P. (1994). "UNHCR's Protection Role in Sri Lanka," *AWR Bulletin*, 32: 1–2.

Noll, Gregor (1997). "Prisoner's Dilemma in Fortress Europe," Paper prepared for the Second Informal Expert Meeting on Legal Aspects of Temporary Protection. Stockholm University, March 14–15.

Ogata, Sadako (1997). Statement by Mrs Sadako Ogata of the U.N. High Commission of Refugees at the Inter-governmental Consultations on Asylum, Refugee and Migration Policies in Europe, North America and Australia (IGC). Washington, May 6.

Richmond, Anthony (1993). "Reactive Migration: Sociological Perspectives on Refugee Movements," *Journal of Refugee Studies*, 6: 7–24.

—— (1994). *Global Apartheid.* Toronto: Oxford University Press.

Rudge, Philip (1995). Interview, 21 November.

—— (1996*a*). "Foreign Policy for Refugees and Migration: Efforts within Europe Concerning Migration," Paper presented at the University of Bern, November 6.

—— (1996*b*). "Rights of Persons Under Temporary Protection," Presented at the Parliamentary Hearing on Temporary Protection for People Forced to Flee their Country, Committee on Migration, Refugees, and Demography, Parliamentary Assembly, Council of Europe, Paris, April 12.

Santel, Bernhard (1995). "Loss of Control: The Build-up of a European Migration and Asylum Regime," in Robert Miles and Dietrich Thranhardt (eds.), *Migration and European Integration.* London: Pinter.

Secretariat of the Intergovernmental Consultations (1994). Working Paper on Reception in the Region of Origin, Secretariat of the Intergovernmental Consultations on Asylum, Refugee and Migration Policies in Europe, North America, and Australia, Geneva, September.

—— (1995). "Report on Temporary Protection in States in Europe, North America, and Australia." Secretariat of the Intergovernmental Consultations on Asylum, Refugee and Migration Policies in Europe, North America and Australia, Geneva: August.

Spence, J., Vickers, G., and Dye, D. (1995). *The Salvadorean Peace Accords and Democratization.* Cambridge, MA: Hemispheric Initiatives.

Suhrke, Astri, and Newland, Kathleen (1996). *States and Refugees.* Paper prepared for the World Development Report 1997, Carnegie Endowment for International Peace, Washington, DC.

—— and Hans, Asha (1995). "Responsibility Sharing," *Study III of the Reformulation of Refugee Law Project*, York University, Toronto.

Thorburn, Joanne (1995). "Transcending Boundaries: Temporary Protection and Burden-Sharing in Europe," *International Journal of Refugee Law*, 7: 459–82.

Tiso, Christopher (1994). "Safe Haven Refugee Programs: A Method of Combating International Refugee Crisis," *Georgetown Immigration Law Journal*, 8: 112–20.

—— (1980). "Temporary Refuge," Executive Committee—31st Session, Ex Com Conclusion 19, No.19 (XXX1).

—— (1981). "Protection of Asylum Seekers in Situations of Large-scale Influx," Executive Committee—32nd Session, ExCom Conclusion, No.22 (XXXII).

—— (1983). "The Problem of Manifestly Unfounded or Abusive Applications for Refugee Status or Asylum," Executive Committee—34th Session, ExCom Conclusion 30, No.30 (XXXIV).

—— (1992). "A Comprehensive Response to the Humanitarian Crisis in the Former Yugoslavia," Paper presented at the International Meeting on Humanitarian Aid for Victims, Geneva.

—— (1993). "Background Note," Prepared for the Informal Meeting of Government Experts on Temporary Protection, U.N. High Commissioner for Refugees, Geneva, January 21.

—— (1994*a*). "Background Note," Prepared for the Informal Round Table on Temporary Protection in the Broader Context, U.N. High Commissioner for Refugees, Diyonne, June 30.

—— (1994*b*). "Note on International Protection," Submitted by the U.N. High Commissioner for Refugees, Geneva, September 7.

—— (1995*a*). *The State of the World's Refugees: In Search of Solutions*. Geneva and London: Oxford University Press.

—— (1995*b*). "Information Note," Prepared for the Informal meeting of Government experts on the Implementation of Temporary Protection, Geneva, April 20.

—— (1995*c*). "The Scope of International Protection in Mass Influx, I: Introduction," Presented to the Subcommittee of the whole on International Protection 26th meeting, U.N. High Commissioner for Refugees, Geneva, June.

—— (1996). "Working Paper for the Development of a Policy Package in Europe," U.N. High Commissioner for Refugees, Geneva, June.

United Nations (1994). "Addendum: Profiles in Displacement: Sri Lanka," *Human Rights, Mass Exoduses and Displaced Persons*. New York: United Nations.

U.S. Committee for Refugees (1998). "World Refugee Survey 1998," Washington D.C.: U.S. Committee for Refugees.

York University (1995). *Reformulation of Refugee Law Project*. Toronto: Centre for Refugee Studies, York University.

# 17

## Immigrants and the Welfare State in Europe

MARTIN BALDWIN-EDWARDS

The relationship of noncitizens to European welfare systems is perhaps one of the most complex yet under-researched areas of contemporary policy. What little comparative literature exists spans the gamut of possible analyses, from Freeman (1986), who suggests that European welfare states are almost uniformly exclusive owing to their citizen-based provisions; through Baldwin-Edwards (1991), who argues that different states interact very differently with their immigrant populations; and more recently, Soysal (1994) and Jacobson (1996), who both claim that European countries are almost uniformly inclusive of their resident aliens owing to the massive impact of international human rights law.

At the beginning of the twenty-first century, not only is there no consensus about the effect of immigration, but the issues are becoming politically dangerous. Increasingly, immigration is blamed for financial crises, particularly when assistance given to asylum seekers and refugees is highly visible (Bauboeck 1994). Almost all available evidence suggests that immigrants contribute far more than they receive from welfare arrangements (see Barabas et al. 1991; Ruland 1994). Immigration is often blamed for causing unemployment, yet both legal and undocumented migrants work in highly segmented labor markets with little or no competition from the indigenous labor force.

As immigrants reach high concentrations in vulnerable industries such as textiles, however, unemployment among the immigrant populations has risen (Bauboeck 1994; Organization for Economic Cooperation and Development 1994). Rising rates of unemployment are sometimes taken as clear evidence that immigration itself causes unemployment. By the late 1990s, immigrant unemployment rates had in most European countries reached levels between two and three times those for native populations, with some nationalities experiencing levels as high as 50 per cent (Africans in France), 36 per cent (Turks in the Netherlands), and 31 per cent (non-Nordic foreigners in Sweden), while in Australia, Canada, and the United States the rates remain comparable to those for the indigenous populations (Leslie et al. 1997; Organization for Economic Cooperation and Development 1998).

As almost all European countries approach the predicted demographic crisis of having few of working age to support many pensioners, immigration may seem an ideal solution. There are major problems with this view, however. First, the level of immigration would have to be phenomenally high—and this would be unacceptable politically. Second, these "guestworkers" too would inevitably remain, changing the country's ethnic composition substantially after some time. It should be noted, however, that the German pension scheme has been sustained for some time by migrant workers, whose contributions exceed payments by a factor of 3–4 (Ruland 1994: 85).

Thirty years ago, expanding European economies were able to absorb immigrants and also develop extensive welfare systems, whereas today unskilled immigrant labor is mostly unwelcome and welfare systems are undergoing major reform. These reforms are being undertaken with little or no regard for immigrant participation: the only policy being developed to fill labor shortages is a "skilled guestworker" policy or temporary employment of foreigners (Organization for Economic Cooperation and Development 1998). Two important questions arise from these diverse national policies: Is there adequate social protection for the workers? And is their presence really temporary?

One should not ignore the significant extent of illegal or illegally working immigrants across the European continent. The informal economy has been identified as a "postmodern" aspect of advanced capitalism, with its informalization of the labor market (Sassen 1991, 1994). Southern European countries in particular have large informal sectors with high immigrant participation (Baldwin-Edwards 1999); but all of Europe has seen increased numbers of illegal immigrants working in the economy. The financing of European welfare states through high taxation and social insurance costs has made illegality an attractive option for both employers and some employees: the social consequences have yet to be realized.

In this chapter, I first sketch the evolution of European welfare states, their various phases, and their broad relations with immigrants. Then I address the question of migrants' welfare needs by migrant category based on a life-cycle hypothesis. I go on to examine the relative successes of different welfare systems in satisfying these needs, insofar as available evidence permits. Finally, I identify some conclusions and underlying problems, with a tentative comment on future possibilities.

## THE EUROPEAN WELFARE STATES

Welfare states emerged across Europe at different times, with different programs and with different institutional forms (Esping Andersen 1990). Strong and ethnically homogenous labor movements were one possible common factor in the evolution of European welfare states (Stephens 1979). In contrast, Faist (1995) has argued that ethnic heterogeneity, like that found in the United States, has led to a small welfare state and to race-class cleavages.

Welfare systems are explicitly tied to the evolution of most nation states and their coceptualization of national citizenship (Marshall 1950), yet it is unclear how immigrant populations should relate to welfare systems. Given that immigrant populations were not formative in their development, their participation was not considered. Formal participation could always be enabled by the acquisition of legal nationality: other intermediate statuses were *perhaps* to be negotiated.

Following Esping Andersen, I identify four welfare regimes in Europe: the social democratic (in Scandinavia); conservative (on continental Europe); liberal/ social democratic (in the United Kingdom); and the southern European (Esping Andersen 1990; Baldwin-Edwards and Gough 1991; Ferrera 1996). The particular arrangements of these regimes have implications for immigrant participation, discussed below.

The social democratic model of welfare has as its linchpin the concept of social citizenship—universalist, tax-financed, residence-based, and delivering high levels of benefits with top-up schemes maintaining some differentiation. The system is expensive and requires high levels of employment and taxation.

The system prevailing in the United Kingdom is a mix of liberal and social democratic philosophies, with the former predominating in the last two decades. Rights to social benefits in law are weak, financing is a mix of contribution and taxation, and only medical services via a distinct National Health Service are universal (otherwise benefits tend to be means-tested and occupational and status differentiation are low). The private sector is extensive and runs alongside a centralized state sector.

The conservative regime exhibits law-based rights to a wide range of benefits, with social insurance as the principal mode of organization and services delivery. Occupationally differentiated benefits are delivered by para-state institutions. In addition a set of means-tested benefits exist for those who fall outside of the insurance system.

The southern European model resembles an underdeveloped version of the conservative regime. However, there are distinct differences that encourage viewing it as a separate categorization. First, the coverage of the population is low, with very few or no benefits means-tested for those who fall outside the system. Second, the differentiation of benefits is far greater than would reflect occupational earnings differentials, with privileged groups obviously benefitting. Third, a massive asymmetry of pensions expenditure exists alongside undeveloped unemployment benefits and inadequate universal national health systems. Finally, the management of the para-state funds is not transparent, and in certain cases management is heavily subsidized by taxation in clientalist fashion (Ferrera 1996).

## INCORPORATION OF IMMIGRANTS INTO WELFARE SYSTEMS

There are, I suggest, four basic mechanisms by which immigrants can be incorporated into a national welfare system: (1) as "privileged aliens" by means of a treaty affecting specific nationalities; (2) through international human rights norms enforced by the courts (case law); (3) by "structural acceptance," or toleration by the system; and (4) as a denizen, or through some explicit, active immigrant policy. In the ensuing paragraphs I discuss each of these mechanisms in turn.

### *Privileged aliens*

Privileged aliens are beneficiaries usually of bilateral treaties concluded between countries with historically close ties, such as Portugal and Brazil, which grant reciprocal or sometimes nonreciprocal rights (e.g. those based on post-colonial relations) to nationals. Of specific note are the well-known rights of migrants within the European Union (E.U.). There are two mechanisms through which a third country national might benefit. The first is simply as a family member of an E.U. national; the second is through the direct applicability of agreements entered into by the E.U. and a third party (such as the E.U./Turkey Association Agreement, the E.U./Maghreb Cooperation Agreements; and the so-called Europe Agreements with Eastern Europe). The latter give substantial rights to legally resident nationals in the European Union, sometimes approximating the rights of nationals and E.U. citizens themselves.

The role of the European Union in developing social protections for migrants' rights is crucial. Already the jurisprudence of the European Court of Justice has benefited considerably those nationalities covered by third-country agreements. Suggestions for extending E.U. coordinating rules on social security to third-country nationals are now being made (see Pieters 1995). In fact, the Court has more or less taken these provisions as a baseline for interpreting the Association and Cooperation Agreements.

### *International Human Rights Law*

Throughout the postwar period, an encyclopedic collection of multilateral and bilateral treaties has emerged to cope with the increasing migration of workers and to protect human rights in general (Baldwin-Edwards 1991; Hollifield 1992). Multilateral conventions governing migrants' social rights include the European Convention on Human Rights (ECHR) and its additional protocols; the European Convention on Establishment of 1955; the European Social Charter of 1961; and the European Convention on Social Security of 1972. Of these, the most significant for case law is the ECHR, although many E.U. countries have signed the other conventions and incorporated them into domestic law.

The trend of governments has been to diminish the rights of legal migrants, whereas courts have been enforcing established rights and even extending them. Judicial activism is now one of the principal innovating forces in this area. Several recent cases demonstrate this: in Germany's Molenaar case, the Court found that the nonexportability of pensions was unconstitutional. Also in Germany, the Administrative Court of Gottingen found that a refugee and his family expelled for claiming social assistance must be allowed to stay in order to keep the family united. Likewise, the European Court of Human Rights, in a case brought against Austria, found for the plaintiff, a Turk who had applied for social assistance when his unemployment benefits ran out. The court found unlawful discrimination in property rights under Article 1 of Protocol 1 of the ECHR.

Similarly, the ruling in February 1997 of the Court of Appeal in the United Kingdom (where local authorities appealed against applying the National Assistance Act of 1948 to allow asylum seekers to claim housing assistance and social security benefits) must be seen as a landmark decision. Essentially, U.K.'s Asylum and Immigration Act of 1996 removed the right of an estimated 13,000 asylum seekers to claim benefits and the courts restored them, in what amounts to constitutional fashion.

### *Structural acceptance by welfare systems*

The extensive labor migration of the 1960s coincided with the expansion and consolidation of most European welfare systems. Yet patterns of public policy, although showing some degree of convergence, still retain clear differences (Esping Andersen 1990). What seems unequivocal is that migration has had few structural effects on welfare systems. Any modifications have been fragmented attempts to rationalize what are increasingly irrational, nationally focused welfare systems in an interdependent global economy.

Using the earlier typology of welfare regimes, one might expect the social democratic to be the most inclusive, the conservative to benefit migrants after substantial periods of employment and residence, the United Kingdom to be ambiguous, and the southern European to be exclusive. In broad terms this analysis holds, although there are specific problems associated with each regime type (discussed further below).

### *Denizenship*

Only two European countries (Sweden and the Netherlands) have developed active immigrant policies (Hammar 1985). Others have granted equality with nationals for their recruited guestworkers in certain areas of social policy and most have been obliged to concede substantial social rights for their long-term residents, often referred to as "denizens." In the case of France, assimilation into French society and the acquisition of French nationality is taken for granted. The granting of permanent residence rights varies greatly across Europe, as shown in Table 17.1. Only recently has permanent status become even a theoretical possibility in southern Europe, and elsewhere, the qualifying periods of residence remain highly diverse.

These different residency requirements of alien laws (immigration regimes) coincide almost precisely with the Esping Andersen typology of welfare regimes (Baldwin-Edwards 1991; Faist 1995). France is anomalous, although recently it has shifted to a position more typically continental. The southern European countries' underdeveloped immigration systems correspond with the level of development of their welfare systems, with Greece and Portugal lagging well behind in both areas.

## IMMIGRANTS AND WELFARE

The greatest problem in analyzing the relationship between immigrants and welfare systems is its complexity. In each country, two things are critical for this relationship: the legal status of the migrant and the migrant's nationality. The first is important

Table 17.1. *Residence period required to receive the status of legal permanent resident*

| Country | Years |
|---|---|
| Switzerland | 10 |
| Austria | 10 |
| Germany | 8 |
| Belgium | 5 |
| Netherlands | 5 |
| UK | 4 |
| France | 3 |
| Denmark | 2 |
| Sweden | 2 |

*Source*: Niessen (1989) cited in Soysal (1994).

because of the interaction between aliens law and social law; the second because of the existence of bilateral or multilateral treaties benefiting specific nationals. It is not possible to identify migrants' social rights without analyzing their relationship to aliens law. Theoretical entitlements can be misleading, since claims can lead to a refusal of residence permit renewal. The strongest claims are by denizens and by those with Convention refugee status. Others may risk their residence status by claiming social rights, most particularly social assistance.

An alternative approach to this analysis is made by Wenzel and Bös (1997), who identify two structural variables as critical: the complex categories of legal immigration status and the administrative rationale of each welfare provision. Clearly—as they emphasize—the rules of each welfare program are crucial. They suggest that underlying rationales have structured different sorts of welfare states, to the extent that we can identify some patterns of immigrant/welfare relations.

Various legal categories of immigrants exist. For present purposes I identify the following: undocumented aliens and undocumented (but legally resident) workers; guestworkers; permanent residents; Convention refugees; and "tolerated" refugees. A sixth and major category is asylum seekers. The situation of the latter is constantly changing and impossible to assess. Generally, they are prevented from working and allotted assistance benefits at a lower rate than the indigenous population, particularly in southern Europe, where few facilities are provided. The worst provision appears to exist in Greece.

Table 17.2 offers a very rough guide, based on my assessment, to the situation of migrants by category. This table ignores the provisions benefiting "privileged aliens" by treaty or E.U. law. As can be seen, there are variations in the treatment of each group across Europe. The classification indicates the general position only, with variation within categories indicated by a question mark. The welfare service most readily given is school education for migrants' children, although access to higher education is restricted. Health care also is generally available, sometimes even to illegal migrants.

**Table 17.2.** *Characterization of immigrants' welfare rights*

| Legal status | Education | Healthcare | Pensions | Unemployment insurance | Social assistance | Public housing |
|---|---|---|---|---|---|---|
| Undocumented | Y | ? | N | N | N | N |
| Guestworkers | Y | ? | Y | ? | N | N |
| Permanent residents | Y | Y | Y | Y | Y | ? |
| Convention refugees | Y | Y | ? | ? | ? | Y |
| Tolerated refugees | Y | ? | N | N | ? | ? |

*Notes*: Y: generally available; ?: wide variation and/or doubt; N: generally not available.

Pensions, however, tend to be linked with employment status and records, and therefore exclude those without formal status. Unemployment benefits are available if the migrant meets the basic requirements. Social assistance (which is generally means-tested) is rarely available and, even when it is, it can threaten the residence status of the applicant. Public housing is sometimes available in principle, but in practice, immigrants are given low priority.

Looking at benefits by category of migrant, we see that the best protected are Convention status refugees and those with permanent residence rights (denizens). The least protected are illegal immigrants and workers, followed by "tolerated" refugees. These categories vary significantly from one European country to another, with sometimes quite large differences in the statuses of "temporary worker" and "guestworker," for example. Thus, as the table shows, any attempt at comparison is necessarily approximate and little more than impressionistic.

## SOCIAL NEEDS OF MIGRANTS OVER THE LIFE CYCLE

Little attention has been paid in the literature to the life cycle of immigrant populations. The principal effect of most social policy regimes is to redistribute across the life cycle rather than across the general population. This fact might explain the general lack of interest in the area. Unlike the life cycle of indigenous populations, where the greatest burden is found in youth and old age, the immigrant life cycle needs most support in intermediate stages, which should have implications for social policy. A final life-cycle distinction is that immigrant pensioners may choose to return to their country of origin. If they do not have the legal right to receive their pensions there (i.e. to "export" their pension rights), they are unlikely to exercise that option.

Figure 17.1 gives a diagrammatic representation of the "migration cycle," adapted from older literature (Garnsey 1987). It views the migration cycle as consisting of four basic phases, the first of which is *young guestworker recruitment*. Here, the existing

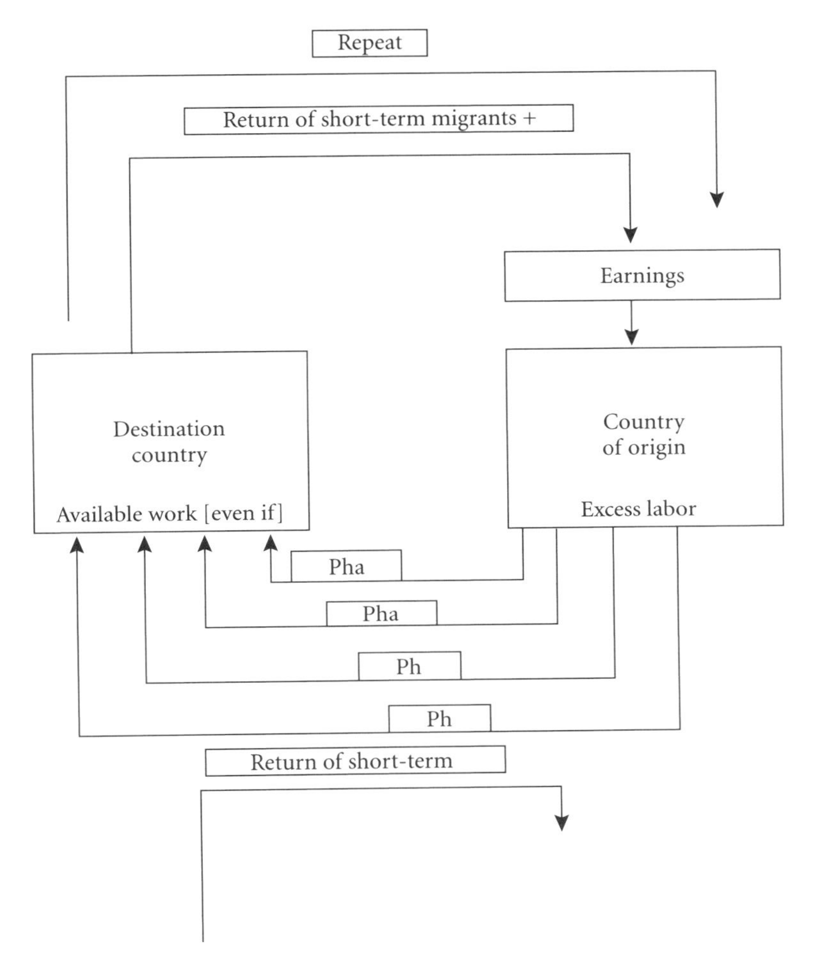


**Figure 17.1.** *The migration cycle*

*Source*: Adapted from Garnsey (1987).

legal provisions of most bilateral recruitment agreements are adequate. The worker is likely to make few demands on welfare services, owing to his or her age, and, if legally working, he or she is likely to be a net contributor to the welfare system. Phase 2 is that of *older migrants*. Although not traditional "target migrant," older migrants, possibly with families, may be longer-term guestworker or recurrent migrants. More recently, many have simply been unable to find work in their country of origin and leave out of desperation. Others are refugees or displaced persons who have emigrated involuntarily. The potential claims of these migrants on the welfare system are greater than in Phase 1, primarily because of age and higher probability of health problems.

Phase 3 corresponds to *family reunification.* When joined by family members, the needs of the migrant are far greater. Obviously, families with children are likely to need the most: education, health care, housing. Once established in a new country, the problems of relocation, particularly those relating to children and their education, may be so great as to lead to geographical immobility and periods of unemployment or partial employment.

Finally, Phase 4 is that of *ethnic community formation.* The process of social integration begins here. Depending on the particular location of an immigrant group in any country, welfare state participation may be more or less similar to that of comparable socioeconomic groups of natives. Many migrants will retire and remain in the host country, while some will return to their country of origin. It is imperative that they should have the financial resources to permit this, which basically means the right to "export" the pension to which they have entitlement. This requires either the general possibility of exportable benefits in the welfare system, or specific provision by treaty for certain nationalities.

This life-cycle hypothesis characterizes the traditional guest worker migrant. The principal forms of immigration over the last 10 years, however, have been family reunion, illegal migration, and asylum-seeking. The last two present serious difficulties, for both the state and for the migrant.

## PATTERNS OF POLICY ACROSS THE LIFE CYCLE

### *Phase 1*

Given that few guestworkers are presently being recruited (except for highly skilled professional workers), the first phase of the life cycle seems to apply principally to illegal migrants and undocumented workers, for whom little information is available. Clearly, the level of protection is very low across the European Union, although we might expect one country, the United Kingdom, to come out looking more generous. This is because the U.K. welfare system is to a large extent residential and tax-based, with the assumption of legal residence of all in the territory. This assumption exists because of the emphasis on external border control in immigration policy. What little evidence exists tends to support this hypothesis.

The social democratic regimes seem to be less tolerant of illegal migrants, owing to the high degree of regulation in the system. There are probably few problems, as illegal migration is better detected. Generally, there is more of a problem with illegal residents in continental Europe. Under conservative regimes, illegal migrants are likely to exist completely outside of the system, whereas in southern Europe limited evidence suggests that insurance contributions are exacted from employees who will never be able to claim the associated benefits. In both southern Europe and many other continental countries, periodic legalization programs attempt to attract illegal migrants into the formal sector, with limited success.

## *Phases 2 and 3*

The research of Von Maydell (1995) across seventeen countries concludes that there is little discrimination against legally resident third-country nationals in social law, although there is a lack of transparency in many countries. The report is confined to the social provisions of EEC (Reg. 1408/71, the coordinating rules for E.U. nationals) thereby omitting the two problem areas of social assistance and housing. Furthermore, the study omits any consideration of interaction with aliens law. There is no consideration given to empirical research, and great emphasis is placed on theoretical legal provision.

Social democratic regimes are generally perceived to present few problems, with substantial support for long-term residents and their families. In other countries, the interaction with aliens law is crucial: if the head of household has permanent residence status, there may be few problems other than poor housing and potential unemployment. Without this status, it may be impossible even to achieve family reunion. One perverse "negative welfare" effect is the general requirement of a minimum income and suitable housing before a migrant can exercise the right to family reunion. This requirement minimizes potential of welfare claims by migrants, despite the fact that they may have contributed fully in insurance and tax contributions. (Across the European Union, only two states do not have this requirement, Denmark and Sweden.) Thus, family reunion may be effected illegally owing to the difficulty of achieving it legally (Bauboeck 1994). Subsequently, children are not schooled in order to avoid detection of the family.

In southern Europe, phases 2 and 3 are completely neglected. Not only are the welfare systems highly skewed, but aliens regulations award permanent residence to few. This, in combination with the very large number of illegal aliens, represents the most socially unprotected geographical area for migrants.

## *Phase 4: Ethnic communities and welfare*

Research from the United Kingdom shows that even native-born ethnic communities tend to have higher unemployment rates than native whites (Leslie et al. 1997). By this measure, there is a low degree of assimilation in the United Kingdom. Immigrant communities across Europe exhibit high unemployment rates along with low participation rates (Organization for Economic Cooperation and Development 1998). This implies that there is considerable participation in the informal economy, with all its associated social and legal disadvantages. Limited research data are available, with apparently no cross-country comparisons, for specific welfare sectors. Here, we examine two areas of the welfare state important for families with children—health care and education (data are drawn from limited national research).

### *Availability and utilization of health services*

Studies of Belgium (Leman 1997; Buekens et al. 1998) and Spain (Prad Martínez et al. 1998) identify phenomena and problems that may prevail across

Europe, and at the very least serve as hypotheses for future cross-national research. High perinatal mortality of North Africans in Belgium, contrary to studies in the United Kingdom, is not linked with low birth weight and poor socioeconomic conditions. Diet and smoking patterns are suggested as possible causes, but no hard data is available.

Looking at the adult population, Leman (1997) uses a threefold typology of medical afflictions of immigrants: imported pathologies, acquired diseases, and adaptive pathologies. The latter two are the most important because they relate respectively to life conditions in the host country (nutrition, housing, climate, employment) and socio-cultural adaptation (mainly psychological and social). In the category of acquired diseases, Leman notes that the recorded rate of industrial accidents is twice as high for immigrants as for the native population. This is un-researched, but is probably linked to the overrepresentation of immigrants in high-risk occupations. Also exhibited are more frequent illnesses among immigrants and earlier retirement. Poor-quality housing leads to higher rates of lead and other toxic poisonings and to respiratory diseases. Poor diet and smoking are identified as causes of higher incidences of diabetes and gastrointestinal disorders.

In the category of adaptive diseases, Leman notes the physical consequences of social and mental problems, along with post-industrial accident psychological disorders. De Muynck (1998), in studying Turks and Moroccans in Belgium's Flemish region, notes serious problems, despite universal health provision for all legal immigrants. Immigrants are shown in the literature to have lower health status than natives and to use preventive and curative services less than natives. Health-care providers also pay less attention to immigrants. The health system does not require or facilitate "special provisions," and although 29 per cent of providers with immigrant patients do provide services, special provisions are necessary for adequate communication between doctor and patient.

Following this problem, Verrept and Louckx (1998) examine the use of "health advocates" in Belgium. Moroccan and Turkish women there were recruited to minimize the language and cultural barriers for patients of those ethnic groups when using health services. Their conclusion is that although the program had positive effects, on both utilization and even patient health, these were limited by the poor understanding of issues by the doctors and the low status of the health advocates. Thus, their research identifies ethnocentricity as a problematic, one that cannot be remedied by interpreters alone.

Ugalde (1998), in a study of immigrants and the Spanish health system, confirms the observations of Leman in Belgium. In particular, a small sample of Moroccan (73) and Spanish (95) construction workers showed, from their last symptoms prompting a medical consultation that the Moroccans were more prone to headaches, chest pains, general malaise, and stomach aches than their Spanish co-workers. These mental and psychosomatic disorders totaled 67 per cent as compared with 15 per cent reported by the Spaniards. When the same workers were asked why they had *not* used health services when they had felt ill, 33 per cent gave illegal status as the reason, followed by 27 per cent expressing fear of losing their employment.

Ugalde (1998) notes the role of NGOs in health care for immigrants, commenting that due to limited resources, some have pressured the public sector to provide such services. In Barcelona and Madrid this pressure was successful in garnering improved care for all immigrants and all registered immigrants; in the Madrid metropolitan area it was not.

With the paucity of cross-national data, it is difficult to identify patterns with respect to health care provision. It seems that even where there is universal health treatment, as in Belgium, the United Kingdom and Sweden, immigrants encounter serious difficulties in using it. For those countries with insurance-based systems, there clearly are greater problems, even including access to services.

*Education and language acquisition*

In all E.U. countries, immigrant children's access to the school system has never before been an issue. It has only recently started to become more problematic in two respects: (1) recognition of minority rights and the right to difference (e.g. the wearing of head scarves by Muslim girls) and (2) difficulty with illegal immigrant children. There appears to be no comparative research on the latter, and little in the way of national data.

A traditional problem for migrant children is language acquisition, preferably while maintaining links with the mother tongue. In fact, a 1977 European Community Directive set up guidelines for policy, but applied it only to children of E.U. nationalities. It has never been extended to non-E.U. nationals. Immigrant minority language instruction (IMLI) has begun to be recognized across Europe as bridging the gap between school and home, and thus an important tool in combating disadvantage. Nevertheless, Broeder and Extra (1997), in their outstanding comparative analysis, conclude that France and the U.K. are so focused on their national languages that IMLI is "tolerated at the margins," while arguments for IMLI have been stronger in Belgium, the Netherlands, and Germany. In Sweden, cultural–political motives have been dominant. In none of these countries have immigrant minority languages been revalued in the educational system.

## RETIREMENT TO COUNTRY OF ORIGIN

Recent research has started to shed some light on this area. Bolderson and Gains (1994), in their study of the exportability of benefits among OECD countries, link outcomes with the original structures of the welfare systems. The insurance-based systems might be expected to grant exportability of pensions and some other benefits: in fact, the conservative regimes—in this study, France and Germany—are the ones that, in principle, prohibit such claims. Two southern European countries—Italy and Portugal—allow exportability in principle. One other country, the Netherlands, is noted as deliberately constructing its pension system to allow exportability, in contrast with its other benefits. The Swedish system has serious difficulties with restrictions, and, as in France and Germany, displays discrimination against non-nationals in its arrangements. The United Kingdom is seen as discouraging portability of pensions in principle, and it makes no distinction on nationality grounds. Generally, Bolderson and Gains conclude, the most difficult regimes for exportability are noncontributory and means-tested.

The generalized "structural" study cited above does not account for the existence of bi- and multilateral treaties deviating from the general principles. Ruland (1994) examines such provisions in the case of Germany and concludes that recent changes will improve the situation by requiring the exportability of all insurance benefits, although without treaty provision the estimated value of the federal subsidy will be deducted. Only 56 per cent of insured foreigners are covered by explicit treaty. The data supplied shows the payments made to be surprisingly low, especially for Turks who are covered by both bilateral treaty and E.U. law. This suggests that a possible impediment exists, such as bureaucratic difficulty or simply ignorance of legal entitlement.

Bonniol (1994) examines the fifteen African treaty arrangements in the case of France. She offers few concrete conclusions, except to note that pension provisions are highly developed and that there is great complexity and difficulty in implementation give such a variety of schemes. In 1990, 86,000 families received family allowances, and 200,000 pensions and annuity payments were made.

Tamagno (1994) notes, however, that few agreements exist with developing countries. Most have been made between developed countries. He attributes this to lack of political pressure from immigrant communities in developed countries, along with the low priority accorded by the governments of developing countries. We can see for pension arrangements, welfare systems that have adapted *ad hoc* through multiple treaty arrangements. Furthermore, the coverage is not good. It may be that the bureaucratic cost of implementing these complex arrangements is at least as great as simply conceding the general principle of exportable contributory benefits.

## CONCLUSIONS AND A PROGNOSIS

We have seen that the social protection of migrants across the European Union is fragmented and sometimes tenuous: not only is the variation between countries very great (as one would expect) but so is the protection afforded in different phases of the immigrant life cycle for immigrants of different legal statuses and different nationalities. Thus, the claims of Soysal and Jacobson are exaggerated and unhelpful in assessing policy outcomes and options. On the other hand, Freeman is quite incorrect in asserting that European welfare states exclude immigrant participation.

My contention is that European welfare regimes reflect not only citizenship conceptions and other ideologies, but also their principles of inclusion and exclusion. These welfare state structures have evolved over the twentieth century, always reflecting majority interests. The relationship of immigrants to such welfare systems is either accidental (structural toleration), juridical (international treaties and human rights case law), or ideological (active immigrant policies).

These piecemeal adaptations of welfare systems to immigrants are complex and costly to implement. It is possible that excluding immigrants from welfare services has cost as much as including them. Since welfare regimes are now undergoing (or are about to undergo) radical restructuring, there is the possibility of incorporating noncitizens in a rational, ordered manner. The OECD suggests in one report that current labor market trends should be the basis of social policy (Organization for Economic Cooperation and Development 1996) and that income transfers should be used less and other measures found to help the social and labor market position of those in need. It is doubtful, though, that European countries will be able to escape their histories of racial exclusion and construct inclusive, market-based welfare systems.

Several serious problems have received little academic or political attention. The first obvious problem is the lack of comparative research across Europe, as noted by some authors such as Abel-Smith et al. (1995) and Broeder and Extra (1997). Little political interest in remedying the deficit is evident. Following from this fact and from the complexity of the matter, no understanding exists for the practical purpose of making welfare provisions for immigrants across the European continent.

The second problem is that even where theoretical provision exists, it may not be adequately utilized. The most common explanation is the ethnocentric nature of welfare provisions. Small inroads have been made, for example, the introduction of "health advocates," or the use of IMLI, yet these have not challenged the prevailing structures. Even Sweden, the most multicultural and inclusive of European states, has a problem assimilating its immigrant populace. Thus, migrants' pensions in Sweden are not exportable to their home country, regardless of their contribution levels.

The third problem is that the real needs of the large immigrant populations across Europe are not only disregarded, but unknown. I have suggested here an alternative life-cycle hypothesis, but it lacks rigorous empirical substance. Again, proper comparative research is required. If the hypothesis is broadly correct, then alternative welfare provisions—special measures—could be implemented. There is no reason why such measures should cost more, especially if they redistribute in the individual or family life cycle.

A fourth problem extends way beyond social policy. This is the increasing phenomenon of illegal immigration and employment. The only obvious remedy, in northern Europe at least, is tighter enforcement of employer sanctions, putting the emphasis on the exploiters rather then the exploited. However, there must also be a recognition that labour markets are using unskilled cheap labor and that this labor is cheap in part because the workers are foreign, and in part from illegality. The implication may be that legal immigration of the unskilled is again desirable, along with affordable social protection for these workers.

What has been the role of the European Union and the Commission in all of this? The answer appears to be, precisely none. One official (Rasmussen 1997) explains this in the area of migrants' health needs:

> There is little or no action or attempt to put together a coherent strategy, for three reasons. First, there are no funds or staff available for such action. Second, migrants have no strong pressure groups or lobbyists to plead their cause. Third, it would imply interference in national affairs.

He concedes that the Commission has the power to encourage exchange of information between member states about policies for migrants and setting up infrastructures such as hospitals and medical services for multicultural users through the Structural

Funds. But this would require the tacit consent of member states, and no government has shown any interest. Furthermore, we should again note a lack of interest in funding comparative research in these areas: policy-oriented academic research should be the current basis of future action.

The Commission does spend money enthusiastically for funding non-governmental organizations (NGOs). These have been identified by the OECD as important in the delivery of welfare services. This view is supported by the research of Room and Perri (1994), who mount a critique of Esping Andersen's class-coalition-based approach for ignoring mobilization in the nongovernmental sector. Although NGO provisions predominate in the less-developed welfare systems of southern Europe (with the exception of Greece) and play a significant role in "conservative" regimes, this sectoral location is likely to be a poor predictor of behavior. Furthermore, as Room and Perri show, whereas the third sector traditionally has been subsidized by the state, increasingly NGOs draw on E.U. resources and even engage in lobbying at the community level (Room and Perri 1994).

What of the future? The mobilization of migrants, particularly through migrant associations at both the national and European levels, must become a major mechanism for reform. NGOs can be a socio-political force and have the unique capacity to incorporate and represent illegal migrants. Furthermore, migrant groups may well constitute an unattached electoral force in a future "federalized" Europe: such political power—along with NGO self-help, albeit with state and EU financial support—constitutes the most likely route for the emancipation of Europe's migrant communities.

## References

Abel-Smith, B., Figueras, J., Holland, W., McKee, M., and Mossialos, E. (1995). *Choices in Health Policy: An Agenda for the European Union.* Aldershot: Dartmouth.

Baldwin-Edwards, Martin (1991). "The Socio-Political Rights of Migrants in the EC," in G. Room (ed.), *Towards a European Welfare State?* Bristol: School for Advanced Urban Studies, University of Bristol, pp. 189–234.

——(1999). "Where Free Markets: Alien in the Twilight Zone," *South European Society and Politics* 3(3): 1–25.

——and Gough, Ian (1991). "European Community Social Policy and the UK," in N. Manning, *Social Policy Review 1990–91.* Harlow: Longman, pp. 147–68.

Barabas, G., Gieseck, A., Heilemann, H. D. von Loeffelholz (1991). "Gesamwirtschafteliche Effekte der Zuwanderung 1988–91," *RWI-Mettelungen*, 4: 133–54. Rhine-Westphalian Economics Research Institute, Germany.

Bauboeck, Rainer. (1994). "The Integration of Immigrants," Unpublished Report prepared for the Council of Europe, Brussels.

Bolderson, H., and Gains, F. (1994). "Comparison of Arrangements for Exporting Benefits Relating to Age, Disability and Widowhood in Twelve OECD countries," in *Migration: a Worldwide Challenge for Social Security.* Geneva: International Social Security Association, pp. 53–74.

Bonniol, F. (1994). "Coordination of Social Security Legislation Between Developed and Developing Countries: The Relations Between France and Fifteen African Countries," in

*Migration: a Worldwide Challenge for Social Security.* Geneva: International Social Security Association, pp. 211–26.

Broeder, P., and Extra, G. (1997). "Language," in H. Vermeulen (ed.), *Immigration Policy for a Multicultural Society.* Brussels: Migration Policy Group, pp. 57–100.

Buekens, Pierre, Dewaux, Térèse, Godin, Isabelle, Basuy-Stoobant, Godelieve, and Alexander, Sophie (1998). "Prenatal Outcomes of North African Immigrants in Belgium," in Antonio Ugalde and Gilbert Cardenas (eds.), Health and Social Services among International Labor Migrants: A Comparative Perspective. Austin: University of Texas Press, pp. 39–50.

Churches' Council for Migrants in Europe (Various Dates) *Migration News Sheets.* Brussels: Churches Council for Migrants in Europe.

De Muynck, Aimée (1998). "How do Flemish Health Providers Take care of their Turkish and Moroccan Patients?" in Antonio Ugalde and Gilbert Cardenas (eds.), *Health and Social Services among International Labor Migrants: A Comparative Perspective.* Austin: University of Texas Press, pp. 51–66.

Departamento de Relaçiones Internacionais e Convençiones de Segurança Social (1995). "Social Security in Europe: Equality between Nationals and Non-nationals," *Proceedings of a Conference Held in November 1994.* Oporto: Departamento de Relaçiones Internacionais e Convençiones de Segurança Social.

Esping Andersen, Gosta (1990). *The Three Worlds of Welfare Capitalism.* Cambridge: Polity Press.

Faist, Thomas (1995). "Ethnicisation and Racialisation of Welfare State Policies in Germany and the USA," *Ethnic and Racial Studies,* 18: 219–50.

Ferrera, M. (1996). "The Southern Model of Welfare in Social Europe," *Journal of European Social Policy,* 6: 17–37.

Freeman, Gary (1986). "Migration and the Political Economy of the Welfare State," *Annals of the American Academy of Political and Social Sciences,* 485: 51–63.

Garnsey, E. (1987). "The Immigration Cycle in Post-war Britain," In R. Knudsen, I. Henriksen and H. Holt (eds.), *Migrant Women in the European Community.* Strasbourg: E.U. Commission.

Hammar, T. (1985). *European Immigration Policy.* Cambridge: Cambridge University Press.

Hollifield, James (1992). *Immigrants, Markets and States.* Cambridge: Harvard University Press.

International Social Security Association (1994). *Migration: A Worldwide Challenge for Social Security.* Geneva: International Social Security Association.

Jacobson, David (1996). "Rights Across Borders: Immigration and the Decline of Citizenship," Baltimore: Johns Hopkins Press.

Leman, J. (1997). "Health Care and Immigrants in Belgium," *Studi Emigrazione,* 34: 41–9.

Leslie, Derek, Blackaby, David, Drinkwater, Stephen, and Murphy, Philip (1997). "Unemployment, Ethnic Minorities and Discrimination," Paper presented in the Seminar Series on Unemployment, Schuman Centre, European University Institute, Florence, February 28.

Marshall, T. H. (1950). "Citizenship and Social Class," in T. H. Marshall and T. Bottomore (eds.), *Citizenship and Social Class.* London: Pluto Press, pp. 3–51.

Organization for Economic Cooperation and Development (1994). *Trends in International Migration: SOPEMI Report.* Paris: Organization for Economic Cooperation and Development.

—— (1996). "Beyond 2000: The New Social Policy Agenda," Unpublished paper, Paris: Organization for Economic Cooperation and Development.

Organization for Economic Cooperation and Development (1998). *Trends in International Migration: SOPEMI Report.* Paris: Organization for Economic Cooperation and Development.

Pieters, D. (1995). "Enquiry into the Legal Foundation of a Possible Extension of Community Provisions on Social Security to Third Country Nationals Legally Residing and/or Working in the European Union," in Departamento de Relaçiones Internacionais e Convençiones de Segurança Social, *Proceedings of a Conference Held in November 1994.* Oporto: Departamento de Relaçiones Internacionais e Convençiones de Segurança Social, pp. 189–244.

Prado Martínez, Dolores M., Marradón Seuvano, Mavía D., Sánchez-Andrés, Ángeles, Gutiérrez Ramero, Esperanza, Avevedo Cantero, Paula and Sebastian Herranz, Julia (1998). "Cycle and Reproductive Paterns among women in Spain," in Antonio Ulgade and Gilbert Cardenas (eds.), Health and Social Services among International Labor Migrants: A Comparative Perspective. Austin: University of Texas Press, pp. 109–20.

Rasmussen, L. (1997). "International Migration and Health in the European Union," in Antonio Ugalde and Gilbert Cardenas (eds.), *Health and Social Services among International Labor Migrants: A Comparative Perspective.* Austin: University of Texas Press, pp. 1–8.

Room, G., and Perri, T. (1994). "Welfare States in Europe and the Third Sector," in T. Perri and I. Vidal (eds.), *Delivering Welfare: Repositioning Non-profit and Co-operative Action in Western European Welfare States.* Barcelona: Centro de Iniciativas en Economía Social.

Ruland, F. (1994). "Impact of International Migration on Social Security: The Example of Old Age Insurance in Germany," in International Social Security Association, *Migration: A Worldwide Challenge for Social Security.* Geneva: International Social Security Association, pp. 77–96.

Sassen, Saskia (1991). *The Global City: New York, London, Tokyo.* Princeton: Princeton University Press.

—— (1994). *Cities in a World Economy.* Thousand Oaks, CA: Sage.

Soysal, Yasemin (1994). *Limits of Citizenship: Migrants and Postnational Membership in Europe.* Chicago: University of Chicago Press.

Stephens, John D. (1979). *The Transition from Capitalism to Socialism.* London: Macmillan.

Tamagno, E. (1994). "Coordination of Social Security Programmes of Developed and Developing Countries," in International Social Security Association, *Migration: A Worldwide Challenge for Social Security.* Geneva: International Social Security Association, pp. 227–42.

Ugalde, Antonio (1998). "Health and Health Services Utilization in Spain among Labor Immigrants from Developing Countries," in Antonio Ugalde and Gilbert Cardenas (eds.), *Health and Social Services among International Labor Migrants: A Comparative Perspective.* Austin: University of Texas Press, pp. 87–96.

Verrept, Hans, and Louckx, Fred (1998). "Health Advocates in Belgian Health Care," in Antonio Ugalde and Gilbert Cardenas (eds.), *Health and Social Services among International Labor Migrants: A Comparative Perspective.* Austin: University of Texas Press, pp. 67–86.

Von Maydell, B. (1995). "Treatment of Third Country Nationals in the Member States of the European Union in terms of Social Law," in Departamento de Relaçiones Internacionais e Convençiones de Segurança Social, *Proceedings a Conference Held in November 1994.* Oporto: Departamento de Relaçiones Internacionais e Convençiones de Segurança Social, pp. 137–54.

Wenzel, U., and Bös, M. (1997). "Immigration and the Modern Welfare State: The Case of USA and Germany," *New Community*, 23: 537–48.

# 18

# The Legacy of Welfare Reform for U.S. Immigrants

MICHAEL FIX AND WENDY ZIMMERMANN

In 1996, the U.S. Congress undertook a major reform of America's welfare system in order to discourage dependency and unwed childbearing while encouraging work and marriage. It sought to do this by ending the unrestricted entitlement of families to state financial support and setting time limits on the receipt of transfer payments. The legislation also marked a sharp exclusionary turn in U.S. immigrant policy by imposing new and unprecedented bans on the receipt of public benefits by legal immigrants. Although in the 2 years following the law's passage, some benefits were restored to certain classes of immigrants, it nonetheless represents a watershed in U.S. immigration history.

Welfare reform also ushered in a number of normative and institutional changes that, when taken together, also served to limit immigrants' use of public benefits, even when they remained eligible. Administrative data from Los Angeles County (home to the largest number of immigrants in the United States) indicate that between January 1996 and January 1998 monthly approvals for welfare payments and public medical assistance fell by 71 per cent among legal immigrants, while the number of monthly approvals for citizens did not change. The shift occurred despite the fact that the eligibility of legal immigrants for these benefits did not change in the state of California. The results, then, suggest that U.S. welfare reform, along with related policy changes, has had a profound "chilling effect" on the use of public services by immigrants.

## EARLY REVERSALS AND LONG-TERM LEGACIES

Like many Western industrialized nations, the United States has sought to reduce its welfare expenditures by restricting benefits to citizens. Few Western countries though, have reversed their immigrant eligibility policies so sharply in so short a time. The 1996 Personal Responsibility and Work Opportunity Reconciliation Act (more commonly known as the 1996 Welfare Reform Act) signaled a striking shift from a rather inclusive social welfare policy that made legal immigrants eligible for public benefits largely on the same terms as citizens to a new policy that systematically discriminated against noncitizens.

Realizing, perhaps, that it had gone too far, in August of 1997 Congress restored the eligibility of most immigrants who were already present in 1996 to receive certain disability payments. At the same time, individual states, which had been granted new authority to deny public benefits to legal immigrants, generally chose not to, and continued to extend medical assistance and welfare benefits to immigrants. In June of 1998, moreover, Congress voted to restore eligibility for food subsidies to those immigrants who were elderly, disabled, or under 18 and were in the U.S. when the law passed.

Despite these reversals of the 1996 bill, the legislation had a number of far-reaching and largely overlooked legacies for immigrants. First and foremost, it restricted noncitizens' and especially *new* noncitizens' eligibility for public benefits. Second, it signaled a change in societal norms regarding immigrants' use of public benefits, norms that influenced the law's later implementation and seemed to affect the willingness of immigrants to apply for benefits, even when eligible. Finally, the law revolutionized the governance of immigrant policy by devolving immigrant eligibility decisions to state and local authorities. In doing so, it imposed new verification and reporting requirements on state and for the first time fused immigrant and social welfare policies. Indeed, the issue of immigrant eligibility was explicitly layered onto virtually *all* decisions to create or expand social programs. Together, these legacies introduced deep structural changes in civic membership, social policy, and federalism that will be hard to undo.

## *Immigrant-specific provisions*

Immigrant policies are public actions that affect immigrants' integration into society after their arrival. As enacted, the 1996 welfare reform transformed immigrant policy in several important ways. First, it barred most immigrants from receiving Supplemental Security Income (SSI—a cash assistance program to help the aged, blind, and disabled) and federal food stamps (a food subsidy program for poor families). Second, the law excluded not only "current" immigrants who were already in the United States at the time the law was enacted , but also prohibited receipt of benefits by new or "future" immigrants who had yet to enter the country. Third, the law barred new immigrants for 5 years from receiving any "federal means-tested benefits," which were defined to include Temporary Assistance for Needy Families (TANF—transfer payments to poor families) and Medicaid (which covers essential health care costs care for people otherwise unable to pay). Fourth, the 1996 law gave states the option of barring immigrant who were in the U.S. on or before August 22 from receiving TANF, Medicaid, and Social Services Block Grants, and it allowed them to prohibit those arriving after August 22 from getting TANF or Medicaid payments following the expiration of the mandatory 5-year ban.

The 1996 law did exempt certain categories of legal immigrants from the foregoing restrictions, including refugees during their first years in the United States, legal immigrants who had worked for 10 years or whose spouse or parents had done so, and noncitizens who had served in the U.S. military. At the same time, however, it prohibited "unqualified immigrants" from all "federal public benefits" and required public agencies to verify the legal status of all applicants for services. "Federal public benefits" were defined to include any retirement, welfare, health, disability, assisted housing, public housing, post-secondary education, food assistance, unemployment benefit, or any similar benefits to which payment or assistance is provided to an individual, household or family eligibility unit by an agency of the United States using appropriated funds (Public Law 104–193, Section 401(c)). "Unqualified immigrants" not only included undocumented immigrants but other persons who had legal authority to remain in the United States without permanent residence.

## *Early implementation: Mitigating the impacts*

In the wake of the legislation, many public officials quickly sought to soften the law's potentially devastating impact on immigrants. Indeed, upon signing welfare reform into law, President Bill Clinton announced that he wanted the immigrant provisions scaled back, and their subsequent history has largely—but not entirely—followed his advice. This systematic softening can be traced to several converging developments. First was the forging of new and strong interest-group coalition between immigrant advocacy organizations such as the National Immigration Law Center and broad-based policy groups such as the Center on Budget and Policy Priorities. Softening was also prompted by extensive and unfavorable media coverage of the negative effects of SSI and food stamp cuts on immigrants (see, for example, Magagnini 1997; Wong 1997). The policy reversals also reflected a delayed Congressional recognition of the nation's changed demographics, and a bipartisan concern within high immigration states that the costs of federal restrictions would be passed on to state tax payers. Finally, of course, the restoration of federal benefits was carried out against the economic backdrop of an unexpectedly large federal budget surplus.

How were the originally draconian immigrant measures actually softened in practice? At the *federal level*, Congress and the Administration restored SSI eligibility to qualified immigrants who were receiving benefits when the bill passed, as well as to anyone in the country on that date who might later qualify. They also restored food stamp eligibility to elderly and disabled immigrants and to legal immigrants under 18 who were in the U.S. when the law passed. They narrowed the definition of "federal means-tested public benefits." Instead of the 60–100 programs initially envisioned, the ban was limited to TANF, food stamps Medicaid, SSI, and the state Child Health Insurance Program.

In addition to these measures, the period that refugees were eligible for SSI, Medicaid, and food stamps was extended from 5 to 7 years after arrival and the definition of a "qualified alien" was expanded to include immigrants and children who were victims of domestic violence. Certain Cuban and Haitian immigrants and Amerasians were also made eligible for benefits on the same terms as refugees. Private, nonprofit organizations were exempted from having to verify the immigration status of applicants for services or benefits, several child-oriented public benefit programs were also exempted from verification requirements (notably the Head Start and Maternal and Child Health Care programs).

At the *state level*, meanwhile, in what marks a striking development in fiscal federalism, officials made unexpectedly generous implementation decisions. Eighteen states, including all of the major immigrant receiving states, developed their own food stamp replacement programs, usually targeted to elderly or disabled immigrants and immigrant children. All states chose *not to* bar unqualified immigrants, including undocumented aliens, from a food supplement program for women, infants, and children (the WIC program), despite their new-found power to do so; and almost all states retained the eligibility of current immigrants for TANF and Medicaid, as well as services provided under the Social Service Block Grant. (The only exceptions are Alabama and Utah which did not provide TANF; Wyoming, which did not provide Medicaid; and South Dakota which did not provide either.) A few states (most notably California) also provided state-funded TANF and Medicaid to new or "future" immigrants, who were explicitly barred from federally funded programs for 5 years. They did so despite the fact that the full costs of these programs were borne by state treasuries (Zimmerman and Tumlin 1999).

## IMMIGRANT ELIGIBILITY IN THE WAKE OF REFORM

### *Food stamps*

Despite these efforts to blunt welfare reform's effects, many immigrants still lost eligibility for public benefits. Only one quarter of the approximately 935,000 non-citizen immigrants whose eligibility for food stamps was taken away had them restored, and future immigrants were left out altogether, yielding a projected $3.7 billion in savings over 6 years (U.S. Congressional Budget Office 1996). Since SSI is a program for the elderly and disabled, nearly all current immigrants regained their eligibility for SSI. But by following the SSI population "model," Congress left out the largest group of needy immigrant food stamp recipients: working age adults. It also left out a significant subset of the elderly non-disabled population: those aged 60–65 years and those who turned 65 after August 22, 1996.

State food replacement programs offer a window onto the post-devolution world of immigrant policy set in motion by welfare reform. The key fact here is the limited reach of state replacement programs: only about 21 per cent of the immigrants who lost eligibility for federal food stamps by August 1997 had their eligibility restored by the states (see O'Neal 1998). Two explanations stand out for the fact that so few immigrants were covered by state-funded food benefits. First, like the federal restorations, many state programs left out working age adults (California was an exception). Second, thirty-two states offered no replacement program at all, and although they were generally not the major immigrant receiving states, immigration to such non-traditional destinations was rising rapidly. According to tabulation of the March 1997 Current Population Survey done by the Urban Institute, the number of immigrants settling in the forty states with the smallest immigrant populations rose by 50 per cent between 1990 and 1996.

There are other, less global, reasons for the limited reach of the state programs. In two large immigrant receiving states (Texas and Florida), for example, access to state food stamps was conditioned on past receipt. In Texas, only those immigrants who received food stamps during the year before August 1997 were deemed eligible in the future. In Florida, benefits were extended only to those immigrants who happened to be receiving federal food stamps in the month of August of 1996. As a result, the number of immigrants losing eligibility in these states was far from negligible.

### *Mixed families with citizen children*

One little-noticed population edged out of the safety net by welfare reform's immigrant provisions was U.S.-born citizen children of legal and undocumented immigrants, whose households witnessed an inevitable decline in resources. Contrary to popular belief, families do not fall neatly into two categories: those composed of citizens and those made up of noncitizens. According to the 1997 Current Population Survey, one in ten American children lives in a mixed status family (with at least one noncitizen parent and one citizen child). In places where immigrants are concentrated, the numbers are even more striking. In the Los Angeles metropolitan area, for example, 45 per cent of all families are of mixed status, and in New York the figure is 29 per cent. The percentages are even higher among poor families—those with incomes below 200 per cent of the poverty level. In Los Angeles, two-thirds of such families were mixed and in New York the share was one-third. Although citizen children retained eligibility for benefits themselves, their families, nonetheless, had less total money to spend on food once their noncitizen parents lost their benefits. Neither the federal restorations nor any of the state food stamp replacement programs solved this problem since they did not cover working age adults. As a result, immigrant-targeted food stamp cuts were probably felt by more children—and by more citizen children—than the framers of federal policy probably intended.

Given that *noncitizen children* of immigrants remain eligible for food benefits under state programs, why provide aid to working age adults who, in the words of Texas Senator Phil Gramm, should be coming to America "with their sleeves rolled up and ready to work, not to get food stamps"? (*Wall Street Journal* 1998). The fact is, many recipients already *are* working. According to Urban Institute tabulations from the March 1997 Current Population survey, about half of all noncitizen parents in food stamp eligible households had worked during the prior year.

Furthermore, while the welfare reform law also severely limited food stamps that native able-bodied childless adults could receive, those living in areas with high unemployment who were unable to find jobs, nonetheless, retained eligibility. In one of the clearest examples of discrimination against immigrants embedded in new policy, however, this exception is not made for legal immigrants who lost their food stamps. They lost their benefits whether or not there was work to be found in their locality.

### *New or "future" immigrants*

Perhaps, the clearest line drawn by welfare reform is not the one separating legal immigrants from citizens, but that dividing noncitizens in the United States as of

August 22, 1996 from those arriving afterward. As already noted, the latter are barred from receiving TANF and Medicaid payments for 5 years and from SSI and federal food stamps until they naturalize. The access of new immigrants to public benefits was further constrained by new sponsor "deeming" requirements. "Deeming" refers to the allocation of income earned by an immigrant's sponsor to the immigrant himself or herself. Each family- and employment-based immigrant must have a sponsor, who is required to sign an "affidavit of support" that promises to support the immigrant materially. Before 1996, support only had to be guaranteed for 3 years, but afterward the coverage of the affidavit was extended to the point of citizenship (a minimum of 5 years). Moreover, the new law required that all of the income reported in the affidavit of support be allocated to the immigrant (in addition to his or her own income) for purposes of determining benefit eligibility. In practice, this procedure (deeming) effectively worked to deny assistance to most immigrants. If that were not enough, the new law also expanded deeming to Medicaid, whereas before it had applied only to TANF, food stamps, and SSI (although the 1996 Illegal Immigration Reform and Individual Responsibility Act did allow a one year exemption for immigrants whose sponsors could not provide support, thus, leaving them without food and shelter).

In contrast to their relatively generous treatment of current immigrants, most states followed the federal government's lead and did not provide substitute benefits to new immigrants. Moreover, even the comparatively small number of states that continued to provide TANF and Medicaid to new immigrants imposed stricter sponsor-deeming requirements that limited the number of immigrants eligible for assistance. This systematic discrimination against new immigrants occurred at a time when the new immigrant population is growing rapidly—by roughly 800,000 to 1 million persons per year. As a result, the effects of the exclusion are steadily becoming less and less abstract over time, especially in the major immigrant-receiving states.

### *Time limits on refugee eligibility*

Welfare reform retained the preferential treatment historically extended to refugees by exempting them for a limited time from federal bars to benefits. Refugees' eligibility for food stamps, SSI, and Medicaid terminated 7 years after arrival, and access to TANF ended 5 years after arrival, assuming they did not meet another exemption and do not naturalize. The exemptions for TANF and Medicaid were only relevant in states that opted to bar current noncitizens from benefits or to extend the 5-year ban on new immigrants.

These time limits may, nonetheless, leave many poor refugees without access to a social safety net. According to 1997 data, approximately 59 per cent of the 1.6 million noncitizen refugees have been in the United States for more than 5 years and 40 per cent have been present over 7 years. About two-fifths of each group had incomes below 125 per cent of the federal poverty level (the cutoff for food stamp eligibility is generally 130 per cent). A recent Urban Institute study of New York's immigrant population revealed that even after 5 years in the United States, refugee incomes trailed those of all other classes of immigrants, including the undocumented (Passel and Clark 1998). The study also found that the principal source of refugee income was welfare payments and that refugees who came to the U.S. fleeing political persecution tended not to have financial sponsors to whom they could turn for support if they lost public benefits.

### *Immigrants who do not naturalize*

One often overlooked population excluded from public benefits includes immigrants who have sought to naturalize but were unable to do so. By limiting the access of noncitizens to benefits, welfare reform introduced a strong new incentive to naturalize. The power of this incentive was especially strongly felt among working age immigrants ineligible for food stamps and new immigrants arriving after August 22, 1996, whose eligibility for all major benefit programs was suddenly conditioned on naturalization.

Making citizenship a criterion for access to the welfare state has unquestionably contributed to an increased demand for naturalization. Annual applications for naturalization rose from just 200,000 in 1991 to 1.3 million in 1996. The inducement to naturalize was particularly acute in segments of the immigrant population that earned less, had lower educational credentials, and spoke less English.

Many such noncitizens confronted significant barriers to naturalization, including waiting periods that average upwards of 18 months across the country and reach 24 months in large immigrant-receiving communities such as Miami. While waiting most immigrants remain ineligible for benefits. In addition, the fee for naturalization is $95 per person, a nontrivial amount for those already eligible for public benefits (which the INS proposed doubling). Immigrants must also pass an English test and a U.S. civics test in order to naturalize. These tests can prove quite difficult for those who have not had opportunities to learn English or who have low literacy levels in their own language.

### *Unqualified immigrants*

By barring unqualified immigrants from all "federal public benefits," welfare reform not only excluded undocumented immigrants from virtually all public benefits, it also disenfranchised various classes of immigrants who were arguably present with the nation's consent, including applicants for asylum and recipients of temporary protected status. While illegal immigrants historically have been eligible for few public benefits, a number of child-oriented services have generally been made available to immigrants regardless of legal status. Although the reach of new restrictions on "federal public benefits" is less broad than some observers anticipated (the Head Start and Maternal and Child Health programs were excluded), unqualified immigrants would no longer be able to use services provided under the Social Service Block Grants, which funded two key services: child protective and child care services.

To the extent these functions can be provided by nonprofit agencies that are not required to verify immigration status, however, the effects will be muted.

Despite the fact that providing benefits to illegal immigrants is beyond the bounds of current political discourse, the undocumented represent a large and growing share of the immigrant population and a powerful demographic reality. Over one-third of the recent immigration flow and 20 per cent of all foreign-born residents are presently estimated to be undocumented (Passel and Kahn 1998). Indeed, there are over one million undocumented immigrant children under age 18 in the United States (see Passel and Kahn 1998; Clark et al. 1994). Although lower birth rates and increased job production in Mexico, along with stepped-up enforcement of immigration controls, might eventually slow the flow of illegal immigrants, these demographic and economic changes are not likely to be felt in the short run. Moreover, the new requirement that immigrant sponsors earn at least 125 per cent of the poverty level might foreclose legal entry for many low-income immigrants. The new sponsorship requirements will likely shift a share of the immigration flow from legal to illegal channels. According to our earlier estimates, over one-third of all families headed by a foreign-born person, and half headed by an immigrant from Mexico or Central America, do meet the new sponsor income requirements (Fix and Zimmerman 1997).

The size of the undocumented population is not only increasing because of new entrants, but because the path to gaining legal residence has become longer and more difficult. Immigration reform legislation passed in 1996 makes it considerably more difficult for immigrants to acquire legal status if they have spent more than 6 months in the United States illegally. At the same time, new fingerprinting requirements introduced to screen immigrants for criminal histories have created a backlog not only in naturalization applications, but also those for green cards. Together, these developments mean that being undocumented may become less of a transitional status than it has been historically, making the class of immigrants barred from public benefits larger *and* more permanent. These issues affect a significant share of the new immigrant population, as at least 20 per cent of new immigrants have entered the U.S. illegally at either their first or last trip to the U.S. (Jasso et al. 2000).

## BEYOND ELIGIBILITY: NORMATIVE AND INSTITUTIONAL EFFECTS

The immigrant provisions of welfare reform ushered in a host of other changes that went beyond simple shifts in eligibility for public benefits. New norms, new complexity, new and inexperienced decision makers, along with fewer due process protections and expanded verification and reporting requirements, could counteract the efforts to blunt welfare reform's impacts described above. These shifts and the chilling effects on benefits use that they introduce, may have more far-reaching impacts than eligibility changes and stand as welfare reform's real legacy for immigrant policy.

### *New verification and reporting requirements*

In addition to shifting decision-making and fiscal responsibilities to states, the 1996 welfare reform law mandated that a host of federal, state, and local institutions had to verify clients' immigration status for the first time. Since verification is required for all benefits classified as "federal public benefits," the reach of the new responsibilities was directly tied to the way in which federal officials defined this simple but consequential phrase. Some benefits were expressly exempted from the immigrant restrictions, such as emergency medical services funded under Medicaid. In addition, non-profit, charitable organizations were also relieved of verification requirements. Finally, federal regulations make clear that agencies had only to verify the immigration status of the individual to receive (versus apply for) the benefit. Agencies, then, did not have to verify the status of undocumented parents applying for benefits on behalf of their citizen children.

Institutions not mandated to verify citizenship and immigration status may, nonetheless, be compelled—or believe they are compelled—to do so. Although charitable nonprofit organizations were exempted from verification requirements, the law set up an inherent conflict: unqualified immigrants were barred from federal public benefits but organizations that provide such assistance did not have to enforce the bar. Further, the law required verification only for federal public benefits, even though it banned unqualified immigrants from receiving state and local, as well as federal, public benefits. To comply with the law, then, states had to screen for immigration status when providing their own public benefits.

California, in particular, took an expansive approach to implementing the bar on state public benefits, extending welfare reform's reach beyond welfare offices to a wide array of agencies and service providers. The state not only screened for immigration status in public assistance programs, but required all holders of California professional and commercial licenses to prove citizenship or legal residence before renewing their licenses (*Los Angeles Times*, February 28, 1998). This new requirement affects over three million people who are licensed by the state each year, including the 573,000 commercial driving licenses issued by the California Department of Motor Vehicles, mandating that applicants prove they are citizens or legal residents before their licenses can be renewed. As a result, state bureaucrats with no expertise in immigration matters, who license professions ranging from acupuncturists to jockeys to pest control inspectors, were forced to distinguish immigrants legally present from those who were not.

The new verification rules were accompanied by new requirements that certain state agencies report undocumented immigrants to the INS. State agencies administering federal housing assistance, SSI, and TANF were required to report any person they "know" to be unlawfully resident in the United States at least four times a year. This new verification and reporting requirement was introduced at the same time that welfare reform announced new bars on state and local "sanctuary laws," which had prohibited city employees from asking about immigration status or reporting immigrants to the INS. New York City fought the bar on local sanctuary laws but lost (see *City of New York and Rudolph W. Giuliani* v. *The United States of America and Janet Reno*, Civ. No. 96-7758 (JGK) (S.D.N.Y., July 18, 1997)).

New York, Chicago, and Los Angeles—cities that collectively contain roughly a third of all foreign born persons in the United States—have all enacted sanctuary laws of some type. Taken together, these new verification and reporting mandates have had far-reaching effects on immigrants' willingness to trust public and private community institutions. Indeed, the requirements might even keep eligible U.S. citizens and legal residents from applying for and receiving benefits if they feared that contact with a state or local agency could lead to the deportation of an undocumented relative. This fact again underscores the complicated issue of mixed status families.

## *New complexity*

The implementation of the law's new verification and reporting requirements leads to another of welfare reform's legacies: increased complexity. In fact, few immigration-related laws required such an immense dedication of energy and resources to interpret their meaning. It is axiomatic that complexity leads to decision errors, especially when thrust upon inexperienced new actors. In the first place, benefit-providing agencies had to wade through the 70+ pages of INS verification guidelines and proposed rules to determine whether it had to verify the immigration status of a prospective client. If the answer appeared to be "yes," the staff had to understand and implement many new legal status distinctions the law drew among different groups of immigrants, for in addition to the distinction between "qualified" and "not qualified" immigrants, eligibility also depended, among other things, on whether the immigrant entered before or after August 22, 1996, whether the immigrant or members of his or her family had worked 40 quarters, and whether the immigrant's sponsor signed an old or a new affidavit of support. Constantly changing eligibility rules also complicated matters.

The intricate nature of the new eligibility rules and exemptions also promoted misunderstanding of the law by immigrants themselves. Particularly following the partial restoration of eligibility for food stamps and SSI, many immigrants must have been left confused over whether they did or did not qualify for benefits. The full complexity of the law will only become apparent with time, as litigation over its many controversial provisions and differing state and federal interpretations proceeds.

## *Changing social norms*

Welfare reform sends a number of implicit and explicit messages to immigrants that indicate the attitude of the American public toward their use of public benefits. Just a few of the simple, and often very misleading, messages that have been communicated to immigrants by this very complex law include the following: that immigrants—including legal residents—are not entitled to public benefits; that legal immigrants will not be able to naturalize if they get benefits; that legal immigrants will not be able to reenter the United States if they receive benefits; that legal immigrants will have to repay benefits to reenter the country; and that legal immigrants will not be able to sponsor relatives if they receive benefits.

Shifting social norms led to an overly broad interpretation of the law's restrictions on benefit use. Specifically, the U.S. State Department, the Immigration and Naturalization Service, the state of California, and other state governments misapplied public charge laws to require repayment of benefits by immigrants trying to reenter the country, obtain a green card or naturalize. In fact, immigrants are not required to repay benefits in most instances (see Limón 1997; Richardson 1997). While the chilling effects of changing norms and this controversial use of public charge will only emerge in the long run, data on declines in approved applications for public benefits in Los Angeles County provide a window onto the early impacts.

### *Compounding effects of other changes*

Welfare reform's immigrant restrictions did not occur in a vacuum. Many changes occurring in other policy domains also limited immigrants' access to public benefits and served to compound the challenges faced by public service-providing organizations. The shift toward Medicaid managed care, for example, generally limited immigrants' choice of health care providers and assigned them to health maintenance organizations that were often not conveniently located or culturally competent. Medicaid managed care also appears to have placed additional financial burdens on public hospitals, making it harder for them to provide services to uninsured legal immigrants who no longer qualify for Medicaid.

Immigrants were not only affected by welfare reform provisions that specifically applied to noncitizens. Everyone who remained eligible for TANF payments was subject to new time limits and work requirements, citizen and noncitizen alike. Increased emphasis on job placement rather than education and training seems to have had a particularly profound effect on immigrants and refugees who lack English and other job skills. It remains to be seen whether states will take into account the specific language and cultural needs of immigrants as they design their welfare-to-work programs.

In addition, welfare reform's goal of restricting immigrant access to public benefits was interwoven with an expanded use of the public charge doctrine, yielding considerable confusion over its correct application. Public charge is a term the INS and the State Department use to describe immigrants who have or will become dependent on public benefits. In practice the public charge test is used to determine whether a noncitizen should be barred from entering the United States or should be deported because of their past and expected dependence on state and federal benefits. While public charge considerations historically were routinely taken into account in decisions to issue green cards, they were rarely invoked in decisions regarding reentry or as grounds for deportation (National Immigration Law Center 1997).

Under the new law, immigrants seeking to obtain a green card must prove they are not likely to become a public charge. Use of public benefits may, but does not necessarily, affect their chances of getting a green card. No public charge test, however, is applied to an applicant for naturalization and a legitimate use of public benefits should not, therefore, affect an immigrant's chances of becoming a U.S. citizen.

As already mentioned, federal and state officials have invoked the public charge doctrine to condition immigrants' adjustment to legal status (including getting a green card) and legal immigrants' reentry into the United States on the repayment of public benefits they previously received. Although these uses of public charge were challenged in court (see National Immigration Law Center 1997), confusion over the consequences of benefits receipt and the misapplication of rules served to magnify the chilling effect that welfare reform had on immigrants' use of public services.

At the same time that welfare reform was telling immigrants that they were less welcome than before, 1996 immigration reform legislation also reduced the due process protections offered to them, such as judicial review extended to noncitizens facing deportation or removal. The reduced protections only exacerbated the concerns of immigrants and further chilled their willingness to seek public benefits for which they remained eligible.

## *Chilling effects: Data from Los Angeles County*

We suggest that changing norms, new verification and reporting requirements, decision errors that flowed from the increased complexity, the overly broad use of public charge doctrine, and reduced due process protections combined to create a "chilling effect" on eligible immigrants contemplating access to public benefits. Data from the Department of Public Social Services (DPSS) of Los Angeles County strongly support this contention. As Table 18.1 indicates, between January 1996 and January 1998 there was no change in the number of newly approved citizen-headed cases or families for welfare benefits (called AFDC before 1996 and TAF or CalWORKs afterward) and the California version of Medicaid, known as Medi-Cal. During that same time period, though, the number of noncitizen-headed cases approved fell to 52 per cent, going from about 3,000 approved cases per month in early 1996 down to about 1,500 cases per month for most of 1997. This shift reflected a decrease in applications not a rise in denials: overall denial rates held steady over the period.

The fall-off in applications was equally steep for the citizen children of immigrants: monthly approved applications for welfare benefits fell by half while there was a slight increase among the children of citizens (Table 18.2). This sharp decline in approved cases occurred despite the fact that there was no change during this period in immigrants' eligibility for these two programs under California law. California opted to keep all qualified immigrants eligible for its welfare benefits program, using state funds to pay for new immigrants during the federal 5-year bar. As the table clearly indicates, however, the drop among noncitizens reflects a fairly steady decline over the course of the two years and is not a one-time phenomenon (Zimmerman and Fix 1998).

The decline in approved cases is greater for households headed by legal immigrants (−71 per cent) than for households headed by illegal immigrants (−34 per cent) who are applying for assistance on behalf of their eligible citizen children. In both instances, though, the principal beneficiaries are typically citizen children.

**Table 18.1.** *Cases newly approved for welfare benefits (AFDC or TANF with Medi-Cal) in Los Angeles County by immigration status of household head*

| Month and year | U.S. citizens | Noncitizens | Legal immigrants | Illegal immigrants |
|---|---|---|---|---|
| *Calendar Year 1996* | | | | |
| January | 4,085 | 3,177 | 1,545 | 1,632 |
| February | 4,468 | 3,168 | 1,650 | 1,518 |
| March | 4,623 | 3,283 | 1,588 | 1,695 |
| April | 4,626 | 3,068 | 1,542 | 1,526 |
| May | 4,520 | 2,873 | 1,403 | 1,470 |
| June | 4,119 | 2,490 | 1,218 | 1,272 |
| July | 4,726 | 3,089 | 1,548 | 1,541 |
| August | 3,570 | 2,066 | 1,036 | 1,030 |
| September | 5,078 | 2,808 | 1,420 | 1,388 |
| October | 5,072 | 2,621 | 1,307 | 1,314 |
| November | 3,833 | 1,951 | 963 | 988 |
| December | 4,037 | 1,702 | 529 | 1,173 |
| Change 1/96–1/97 (%) | −17 | −38 | −59 | −19 |
| *Calendar Year 1997* | | | | |
| January | 4,042 | 1,967 | 641 | 1,326 |
| February | 3,923 | 1,731 | 564 | 1,167 |
| March | 4,173 | 1,705 | 532 | 1,173 |
| April | 4,272 | 1,491 | 457 | 1,034 |
| May | 3,765 | 1,255 | 444 | 811 |
| June | 3,819 | 1,387 | 441 | 946 |
| July | 4,148 | 1,433 | 476 | 957 |
| August | 4,170 | 1,457 | 472 | 985 |
| September | 4,413 | 1,619 | 505 | 1,114 |
| October | 4,774 | 1,696 | 489 | 1,207 |
| November | 3,554 | 1,270 | 368 | 902 |
| December | 4,466 | 1,702 | 454 | 1,248 |
| Change 1/97–1/98 (%) | −6 | −23 | −30 | −19 |
| *Summary* | | | | |
| January 1998 | 4,072 | 1,519 | 450 | 1,069 |
| Change 1/96–1/98 (%) | −23 | −52 | −71 | −34 |

*Note*: Households are classified by "first adult" in the household, typically the parent.

*Source*: Los Angeles County Department of Public Social Services.

One explanation for the sharp decline in approved immigrant cases during a time when there was no change in newly approved citizen cases could be higher levels of naturalization. That is, it may be that some immigrants are still applying for benefits but as citizens rather than noncitizens, though it is unlikely that naturalization accounts for such steep declines. Moreover, similar patterns appear in the monthly approvals for county-funded general relief. General relief provides cash assistance to poor persons who are ineligible for AFDC/TANF or SSI benefits.

**Table 18.2.** *Children newly approved for welfare benefits (AFDC or TANF with Medi-Cal) in Los Angeles County by immigration status of household head*

| Month and year | Citizen children of citizen adults | Citizen children of non-citizen adults | Citizen children of legal immigrant adults | Citizen children of illegal immigrant adults |
|---|---|---|---|---|
| *Calendar Year 1996* | | | | |
| January | 6,148 | 5,144 | 2,741 | 2,403 |
| February | 6,586 | 4,984 | 2,803 | 2,181 |
| March | 6,917 | 5,178 | 2,689 | 2,489 |
| April | 6,926 | 5,075 | 2,761 | 2,314 |
| May | 6,644 | 4,418 | 2,288 | 2,130 |
| June | 6,100 | 3,882 | 2,086 | 1,796 |
| July | 7,161 | 4,815 | 2,531 | 2,284 |
| August | 5,496 | 3,147 | 1,630 | 1,517 |
| September | 7,761 | 4,415 | 2,348 | 2,067 |
| October | 7,846 | 4,359 | 2,294 | 2,065 |
| November | 5,834 | 3,111 | 1,613 | 1,498 |
| December | 6,161 | 2,868 | 1,025 | 1,843 |
| Change 1/96–1/97 (%) | −17 | −39 | −56 | −19 |
| *Calendar Year 1997* | | | | |
| January | 6,245 | 3,160 | 1,203 | 1,957 |
| February | 5,799 | 2,831 | 1,068 | 1,763 |
| March | 6,208 | 2,819 | 1,000 | 1,819 |
| April | 6,356 | 2,446 | 860 | 1,586 |
| May | 5,643 | 2,193 | 914 | 1,279 |
| June | 5,880 | 2,325 | 871 | 1,454 |
| July | 6,360 | 2,442 | 886 | 1,556 |
| August | 6,454 | 2,395 | 900 | 1,495 |
| September | 6,858 | 2,788 | 998 | 1,790 |
| October | 7,454 | 2,924 | 932 | 1,992 |
| November | 5,615 | 2,136 | 684 | 1,452 |
| December | 7,176 | 2,982 | 916 | 2,066 |
| Change 1/97–1/98 (%) | +4 | −15 | −23 | −9 |
| *Summary* | | | | |
| January 1998 | 6,501 | 2,693 | 921 | 1,772 |
| Change 1/96–1/98 (%) | +6 | −48 | −66 | −26 |

*Note*: Households are classified by "first adult" in the household, typically the parent.

*Source*: Los Angeles County Department of Public Social Services.

## *The fusion of immigrant and social welfare policy*

In the wake of welfare reform, virtually all federal benefit and support programs were classified as either a "federal public benefit" or a "federal means-tested benefit" for the purposes of determining immigrant eligibility. By forcing policymakers to classify all benefit programs in these terms, virtually all social policy actions suddenly had to confront questions of immigrant policy and membership, an imperative that took on new meaning in an era of budget surpluses. States, which must bar unqualified immigrants from state and local public benefits, had to take immigration issues more explicitly into account when they addressed benefits policy.

This new classification system inevitably led to controversial results. The new state Children's Health Insurance Program (CHIP) offers a good example. Like Medicaid, this block grant provides funds to states to expand poor children's health coverage and were duly defined as a "federal means-tested benefit," meaning that a state that funds a health program for poor residents with a combination of federal CHIP funds and its own revenues will be subject to the same immigrant restrictions as the Medicaid program. As a result, some state health care programs that were once available to legal noncitizens were barred to new immigrants.

Moreover, the 5-year bar on means-tested benefits restricts immigrants' access to the programs they need most at the time their need is greatest. In the case of the children's health insurance program, new qualified immigrants are ineligible even though poor immigrants are nearly twice as likely to be uninsured (52 versus 26 per cent) as poor natives (see Richardson 1997). Furthermore, immigrants' incomes are lower during their first years after arrival than they are after being in the U.S. for 5 or 10 years (Passel and Clark 1998). Although new immigrants' sponsors have pledged to support them, paying for health care for an uninsured immigrant who falls ill can be prohibitively expensive.

## *The devolution of immigrant policy*

Welfare reform marks a sharp departure from the federal government's exclusive role in determining immigrants' eligibility for public benefits. Before welfare reform, states were prohibited from setting their own eligibility standards for immigrants, as Supreme Court rulings from the 1970s onward held that the power to discriminate on the basis of citizenship status was reserved to the federal government (see *Graham* v. *Richardson*, 403 US 67 (1971); *Mathews* v. *Diaz*, 426 US 67 (1976)). The 1996 law essentially overruled this judicial doctrine and gave states broad new authority to determine immigrants' eligibility for benefits.

But welfare reform represents more than a simple transfer of authority to the states. It also can be viewed as a cost shift, as states choosing for political or other reasons to extend benefits to new or future immigrants must now pay the full costs. As the state food stamp experience indicates, where costs are shared between the states and the federal government, the states were generous in retaining noncitizens' eligibility for benefits. But where there is no cost sharing they were significantly less generous, and there was greater variation. Because it has been mainly the large immigrant-receiving states, such as California and New York, that have extended state-funded food stamp programs, the inequitable and disproportionate share of immigration-related costs they now absorb is much wider than it was before.

Welfare reform does not represent an expansion of state power in all instances, however. While welfare reform increased state power with respect to determining legal immigrants' eligibility for public benefits, it reduced state discretion in the framing of policies to deal with illegal immigrants. The 1996 law limited state power in several ways. First, it required states wishing to provide services to undocumented and other "unqualified" immigrants to enact a new law that explicitly announced the state's intent to do so. Second, states were barred from retaining "sanctuary laws" that prohibited state or local officials from reporting illegal immigrants to the INS. Third, the law imposed on state agencies a host of new verification and reporting mandates (Fix and Zimmermann 1997).

## CONCLUSION

Even though the federal government has scaled back some of the welfare law's more draconian restrictions, welfare reform's immigrant provisions leave a number of far-reaching legacies for the nation's immigrants and for immigrant policy. In the first place, almost three quarters of noncitizens who lost federal food stamps, most of them working age adults, have little prospect of having their eligibility restored. The effect of this continuing ban will be forcefully felt by citizens as well as noncitizens because of the large numbers of mixed families containing noncitizen parents and citizen children. Moreover, the rapidly expanding population of immigrants arriving after August 22, 1996 did not benefit from Congress's second thoughts about immigrant bars to public benefit programs. They remain excluded from most such programs at both federal and state levels.

Second, welfare reform's legacies go beyond eligibility restrictions to encompass the law's profound chilling effects. In Los Angeles County, the number of monthly approved applications from legal immigrant-headed families for welfare payments fell dramatically between January 1996 and January 1998 despite the fact that there was no change in legal immigrants' eligibility for the program. During the same time period, there was no change in monthly approved applications for citizen-headed families. These declines translate into a commensurately sharp reduction in the number of citizen children of legal immigrants who no longer receive welfare payments to which they remain entitled.

Third, welfare reform has transformed the governance of immigrant policy by devolving authority to state and local governments. As the demographic significance of immigration continues to rise, responsibility for incorporating newcomers will increasingly fall to state and local governments whose capacity and inclination to respond generously will vary widely. Immigrants in states with strong economies, developed advocacy networks, and enough sympathetic voters may end up with substantially greater access to health and nutritional benefits than their counterparts in other states.

### References

Clark, Rebecca L., Passel, Jeffrey S., Zimmermann, Wendy N., and Fix, Michael (1994). *Fiscal Impacts of Undocumented Aliens: Selected Estimates for Seven States.* Washington, DC: The Urban Institute, September.

Fix, Michael, and Zimmermann, Wendy N. (1997). *Welfare Reform: A New Immigrant Policy for the United States.* Washington, DC: Immigrant Policy Program, The Urban Institute, April.

Jasso, Guillermina, Massey, Douglas S., Rosenzweig, Mark, and Smith, James (2000). "The New Immigrant Survey Pilot Study: Overview and New Findings About U.S. Legal Immigrants at Admission," *Demography*, 37: 127–38.

Limón, Lavinia (1997). Letter to State TANF Directors from Lavinia Limón, Director, Office of Family Assistance, Administration for Children and Families, Department of Health and Human Services, December 17, Washington, DC.

*Los Angeles Times* (1998). "Licensing to Require Legal Residency," *Los Angeles Times*, February 28.

Magagnini, Stephen (1997). "Suicide Illustrates Welfare Reform's Toll Among Hmong," *Sacramento Bee*, November 9.

National Immigration Law Center (1997). "Public Charge," Unpublished Paper, National Immigration Law Center, Washington, DC, July.

O'Neal, Bonnie (1998). Comments of Bonnie O'Neal, Food and Consumer Service, U.S. Department of Agriculture, at the National Conference on Immigrants and Welfare, convened by the National Immigration Law Center, January 27, Washington, DC.

Passel, Jeffrey S., and Kahn, Joan R. (1998). *Immigration, Fertility, and the Future American Work Force.* Washington, DC: The Urban Institute.

—— and Clark, Rebecca (1998). *Immigrants in New York: Their Legal Status, Incomes and Taxes.* Washington, DC: The Urban Institute.

Richardson, Sally K. (1997). Letter to State Medicaid Directors from Sally K. Richardson, Health Care Financing Administration, Department of Health and Human Services, December 17, Washington, DC.

U.S. Congressional Budget Office (1996). *Federal Budgetary Implication of the Personal Responsibility and Work Opportunity Reconciliation Act of 1996.* Washington, DC: Congressional Budget Office.

*Wall Street Journal* (1998). "Cost of Highway Bill Endangers Plan to Restore Food Stamps to Immigrants," *Wall Street Journal*, April 3.

Wong, Doris Sue (1997). "Food Pantries See Sharp Increase in Demand," *The Boston Globe*, November 29.

Zimmermann, Wendy, and Fix, Michael (1998). *Declining Immigrant Applications for Medi-Cal and Welfare Benefits in Los Angeles County.* Washington, DC: The Urban Institute.

—— and Tumlin, Karen (1999). *Patchwork Policies: State Assistance for Immigrants under Welfare Reform.* Washington, DC: The Urban Institute.

# 19

# Controlling International Migration through Enforcement: The Case of the United States

FRANK D. BEAN AND DAVID A. SPENER

Recent referenda and legislation in the United States (Proposition 187 in California, the Omnibus Crime and Control Act, the anti-terrorist legislation of 1995, and the 1996 welfare and immigration bills) indicate that the motivation to try to control immigration to the United States has in recent years once again reached high levels of intensity. This tendency is not unique to the United States, of course, but is shared to some degree or other with other industrialized democracies (Miller 1994). Nations increasingly seek to control the various kinds of flows (legal immigrants, refugees, unauthorized migrants, and non-immigrants) across their borders, but often find that the policy instruments employed to achieve such control seem inadequate to the task (Cornelius, Martin, and Holliefield 1994). It often seems that the more countries resort to various enforcement measures, the less successful their attempts at control.

One of the most conspicuous and in many ways interesting cases in this regard is the United States, not only because of the long border it shares with Mexico and its dominant international economic and political position, but also because the United States has to a considerable extent defined itself as a nation of immigrants, certain aspects of which it ironically now finds itself repudiating. To the extent that this is an accurate description of the recent situation with respect to migration enforcement mechanisms, it raises interesting questions about the effectiveness of states as control agents in an era that increasingly emphasizes the importance of relatively unrestricted global markets, especially financial and commercial ones. The apparent failure or inability of states to control migration flows invites the conclusion that at least certain kinds of flows are either uncontrollable or so strongly sustained by existing social and economic forces that effective control would be prohibitively expensive in either financial or political terms.

Deciding whether this conclusion bears scrutiny requires that we first ascertain if efforts to control migration and enforce regulations have been of sufficient scope and seriousness to warrant the charge that they are ineffective. The conclusion that migration flows to industrial democracies in general and the United States in particular are uncontrollable through enforcement mechanisms requires that the answer to this question be "yes." If the answer is "no," then while it might still be the case that flows are uncontrollable (or governed by forces that are so strong that control is exceedingly difficult), observers will not be able to discern this from the evidence available.

These considerations raise the issue of the recent nature and effectiveness of immigration enforcement in the United States, focusing on the 1986 Immigration and Reform and Control Act (because of its novel and primary goal of trying to control unauthorized migration through the adoption of employer sanctions) and the 1993 U.S. Border Patrol Operation known as "Hold-the-Line" (because of its attempt to tighten restrictions at the U.S./Mexico border). Examining these enforcement efforts means devoting attention to the U.S./Mexico border, because it is migration from Mexico that constitutes the greatest concern of policymakers in the United States, even though this concern is frequently masked either by rhetoric about immigration in general or illegal migration in particular.

In this chapter we ask to what extent recent employer sanctions and border interdiction efforts have been effective in controlling Mexican migration to the United States. What conclusions can be drawn about the possibility of controlling migration from the evidence that has emerged so far about the effectiveness of these tactics? In seeking to answer these questions, this chapter is organized into four sections. The first focuses on IRCA and the research that has been conducted on the effectiveness of its enforcement efforts. The second focuses on recent efforts to tighten enforcement directly at the U.S./Mexico border, particularly Operation Hold the Line, which represents a more intensive effort that has heretofore been attempted to limit unauthorized migration flows. The third section examines as an alternative one particular mode of entry that crossers presently use and might increasingly resort to if border controls prove effective. It thus provides an illustration of how effectiveness in enforcing one control mechanism can be thwarted by entry through other means. The fourth presents conclusions and policy implications.

## EMPLOYER SANCTIONS AS AN ENFORCEMENT MECHANISM

The major post-World War II initiative to curtail illegal migration was the 1986 Immigration Reform and Control Act (IRCA—see Bean, Vernez, and Keely 1989). IRCA attempted to reduce the flow and stock of Mexican undocumented immigrants through several means: (1) the legalization of many undocumented immigrants already residing in the United States; (2) a prohibition against hiring undocumented workers; and (3) the allocation of increased resources for border enforcement activities. An important criterion by which IRCA's effectiveness can be judged is, thus, the extent to which unauthorized flows were actually reduced and the size of the resident unauthorized population diminished, beyond the decrease brought about solely by legalization programs. Apart from changing the status of resident undocumented migrants, did IRCA reduce illegal entries?

The main source of evidence that has been relied upon to answer this question is INS apprehensions statistics, which come from monthly tallies of the number of times persons crossing into the United States illegally are apprehended by the U.S. Border Patrol or other INS enforcement personnel. The data suffer well-known limitations: they do not distinguish among different types of migrants, they include statistics for persons apprehended multiple times, and they do not reflect that persons may return to Mexico before the end of the year in which they are apprehended.

Thus, the peak number of 1,767,400 apprehensions in fiscal year 1986 enormously overstates the size of the undocumented population entering and settling in the United States. Conversely, the statistics can also lead to underestimates if many entrants go undetected. Even with these problems, apprehensions statistics are of considerable use in making assessments of unauthorized migration flows to the United States, and are useful for gauging changes in the flows over time because they are the only large scale data that can be used to measure, however roughly, such flows. Because almost all apprehensions (92 per cent in fiscal year 1987, for example) involve Mexicans, they are particularly useful in gauging Mexican flows.

What do they indicate about IRCA's effectiveness? Border Patrol apprehensions declined in the years immediately after IRCA's passage, from 1,767,400 in 1986 to roughly 1.2 million in 1987, to 1 million in 1988, to 954,253 in 1989 (here and elsewhere INS data refer to the U.S. government's fiscal year, which extends from October 1 through September 30, not to the calendar year). However, this trend reflects, in part, the level and vigor of INS enforcement. The number of hours the Border Patrol devotes to interdiction has fluctuated over the years. Thus, it is most useful to examine apprehensions per hour of effort expended by the Border Patrol and per so-called "linewatch" hour (the hours spent in *direct* patrolling of the border) (Bean, Vernez, and Keely 1989; Bean et al. 1990; Espenshade 1990, 1995).

Data on line-watch apprehensions, line-watch hours, and line-watch apprehensions per hour are presented for fiscal years 1977–95 in Table 19.1. Five distinct periods emerge. From 1977 to 1982, a relative boom period in the Mexican economy, line-watch apprehensions were relatively stable or declined slightly. From 1983 to 1986, after the slowdown in the Mexican economy and before the passage of IRCA, line-watch apprehensions jumped sharply (by almost 46 per cent from 1982 to 1983). After a lag, line-watch hours also increased. Most importantly, line-watch apprehensions per hour climbed substantially (by more than 47 per cent compared to the 1977–82 period).

The next period covers 1987–9, the fiscal years immediately after IRCA's passage. During this period, apprehensions declined, as did line-watch apprehensions per hour. However, line-watch apprehensions did not fall to their 1977–82 levels. To what extent might IRCA have been responsible for the post-1986 decline? While the legislation stemmed some of the increase in illegal flows that resulted from the 1982 recession in the Mexican economy, it did not reduce illegal crossings to earlier levels.

The fourth period covers 1990–3, the "late" IRCA/pre-NAFTA period. During this time, apprehensions again moved upward, closer to pre-IRCA levels, indicating that deterrent effects were dissipating. The final period covers 1994–5, the post-NAFTA and (in 1995) post-peso devaluation period. Apprehensions data are hard to interpret during this period unless enforcement changes are explicitly taken into account.

**Table 19.1.** *Line-watch apprehensions, line-watch hours, and line-watch apprehensions per line-watch hour, 1977–95*

| Fiscal year | Line-watch apprehensions | Line-watch hours | Line-watch apprehensions per hour |
|---|---|---|---|
| 1977 | 441,265 | 1,740,446 | 0.254 |
| 1978 | 481,612 | 1,762,616 | 0.273 |
| 1979 | 488,941 | 1,935,926 | 0.253 |
| 1980 | 428,966 | 1,815,797 | 0.236 |
| 1981 | 452,821 | 1,929,448 | 0.235 |
| 1982 | 443,437 | 1,871,173 | 0.237 |
| 1983 | 646,311 | 1,976,126 | 0.327 |
| 1984 | 623,944 | 1,843,179 | 0.339 |
| 1985 | 666,402 | 1,912,895 | 0.348 |
| 1986 | 946,341 | 2,401,575 | 0.394 |
| 1987 | 750,954 | 2,546,397 | 0.295 |
| 1988 | 614,653 | 2,069,498 | 0.297 |
| 1989 | 521,899 | 2,436,788 | 0.214 |
| 1990 | 668,282 | 2,549,137 | 0.262 |
| 1991 | 711,808 | 2,390,500 | 0.298 |
| 1992 | 814,290 | 2,386,888 | 0.341 |
| 1993 | 840,326 | 2,713,024 | 0.310 |
| 1994 | 687,163 | 3,074,060 | 0.224 |
| 1995 | 480,580 | 1,891,413 | 0.254 |
| *Mean values* | | | |
| 1977–82 | 456,174 | 1,842,568 | 0.248 |
| 1983–6 | 720,750 | 2,033,444 | 0.354 |
| 1987–9 | 629,169 | 2,350,894 | 0.268 |
| 1990–3 | 758,677 | 2,509,887 | 0.302 |
| 1994–5 | 699,247 | 2,973,337 | 0.235 |

*Source*: INS Statistical Yearbooks and special INS tabulations.

When these factors are considered, there is reason to believe that 1995 increases in Mexican flows are at least as much the result of U.S. conditions as they are the consequence of Mexican conditions, meaning that they cannot be attributed solely to the peso devaluation (Bean and Cushing 1995).

In general, the evidence from analysis of apprehensions data indicates that IRCA brought about a reduction in undocumented Mexican immigration during the three years immediately following its passage. Subsequently, the results of research suggest that undocumented immigration was again on the rise. While IRCA's legalization programs accounted for a substantial share of the post-IRCA reduction simply by removing "at-risk" migrants from the apprehension pool, the threat of sanctions against U.S. employers and the likely perception of a closing labor market seems to provide a plausible explanation of the residual (Bean, Edmonston, and Passel 1990). However, the gradual implementation of sanctions over a 3-year period argues against sanctions as a prime source of the decline, since the greatest reductions in apprehensions took place in the first and second years of implementation when enforcement was weakest.

Decreased flows, thus, seem not to be attributable to the deterrent effects of sanctions. A more likely possibility is that they reflect the influence of generalized patterns of rumor and anxiety about the effects of the law. Once it became clear to potential migrants that IRCA was not going to lead to draconian enforcement against migrants, the undocumented labor migration process resumed unabated. While this result might appear to support the conclusion that employer sanctions have been ineffective, it is difficult to embrace this conclusion with certainty because the employer sanctions provisions passed in the 1986 legislation have never been enforced very strongly, nor has INS allocated sufficient resources to sanctions enforcement to provide a test of their effectiveness (Fix and Hill 1990). And even if this were not the case, sanctions might prove ineffective because undocumented workers can use fraudulent documents to obtain employment. Thus, the only conclusion supported by the evidence that has emerged to date is that an adequate test of the effectiveness of employer sanctions as an enforcement mechanism has yet to occur in the United States.

## BORDER INTERDICTION AS AN ENFORCEMENT MECHANISM

If firm conclusions about the effectiveness of employer sanctions are difficult to reach, what about conclusions concerning border interdiction efforts? How effective have interdiction attempts been as mechanisms of control? The most notable effort to date on which research has been conducted is Operation Hold-the-Line, which was launched on Sunday, September 19, 1993, in El Paso, Texas. The Operation represented a major change in strategy for controlling the border in the El Paso sector.

Whereas previous emphases had been on apprehending suspected illegal migrants once they had crossed the border, the new tactic was to enhance linewatch operations by maintaining a high profile along a stretch of approximately 20 miles of border in the metropolitan El Paso area. The idea was to discourage the unregulated flow of illegal migration of individuals from Mexico into El Paso and the United States by stopping people before they crossed the border. Prior to the initiation of the Operation, the Border Patrol had concentrated less on illegal migrants crossing the border and more on tracking them down and arresting them after they crossed and as they moved on to other destinations.

The major reason for conceiving and implementing Operation Hold-the-Line was to curtail illegal entry into El Paso (and through El Paso into the United States). To what degree was that objective achieved? Understanding the effects of the Operation on border crossings requires a recognition that there are many different reasons for crossing, and that either legal or illegal means may often be used to achieve various crossing objectives. This means that it is useful to consider a taxonomy of different kinds of border-crossers. Just as it has been useful to consider different kinds and national origins of illegal entrants to the United States in estimating the magnitude of stocks and flows of illegal migrants (Bean, Edmonston, and Passel 1990), so too is it useful to consider different kinds of border-crossers in seeking to assess the effects of Operation Hold-the-Line on flows in El Paso-Juárez.

Two major distinctions among kinds of crossers are important at the outset. The first is between legal and illegal crossers. The second is between long-distance and local migrants (or local crossers). When combined with certain other characteristics of crossers, these distinctions yield eight possible kinds of crossers we think it is useful to consider (Bean et al. 1994). One consists of persons who cross illegally with the intention of moving on to other destinations in the United States to find work. These might be termed "illegal long-distance labor migrants." A second consists of persons who cross illegally in order to seek work or to set up street vending operations in El Paso. These might be termed "illegal crossers, illegal workers." A third consists of persons (mostly teenage males) who cross illegally in order to "hang-out," to have a good time, or just for the experience of crossing. Much of the petty vandalism often attributed to migrants may be committed by this type of crosser, who might be termed "local juvenile crossers." A fourth type consists of persons who cross legally using "mica" cards (the local resident commuting card) but who work illegally as maids, gardeners, or other kinds of workers in El Paso. These might be termed "legal crossers, illegal workers." A fifth type consists of persons who cross illegally to engage in some nonwork related activity, including shopping, visiting friends and relatives, and seeking medical services. These might be termed "illegal non-labor crossers." A sixth type consists of persons who cross legally (using the mica card) to pursue a similar variety of legal activities. These might be termed "legal temporary crossers." A seventh type consists of "legal crossers, legal workers" (U.S. citizens living in Juárez, or legal long-distance labor migrants, for example). An eight type of crosser lives illegally in El Paso and crosses into the United States illegally upon returning from visits with friends and family in Mexico.

Operation Hold-the-Line may have affected each type of crossers differently. Long distance labor migrants, for example, may have been strongly motivated to find a way to enter despite increased efforts at deterrence. If so, their crossings may have been inconvenienced but not substantially deterred by Operation Hold-the-Line. In particular, it is reasonable to ask if these border crossers sought simply to go around the end of the line outside of El Paso, or cross into the United States at other points along the border where surveillance was less intense. In order to shed light on such questions, we examined monthly, sector-specific data on apprehensions before and after the Operation. These data are counts of the number of times persons entering the country illegally were apprehended by the Border Patrol or other INS enforcement personnel within a given period of time.

We focused on INS Border Patrol apprehensions at the U.S./Mexico border. Border Patrol arrests are of two types—line-watch and non-line-watch apprehensions. The former result from time spent guarding the border against smuggling and illegal entry of aliens. They include apprehensions by Border Patrol agents engaged in surveillance; tower watch; patrolling along the border on foot, horseback or in some kind of vehicle; as well as other operations designed to prevent illegal entry. As implied by the nature of the activity, nearly every line-watch apprehension (roughly 97 per cent) is of a person apprehended trying to enter the United States without appropriate entry documents. Non-line-watch operations involve several kinds of activities—non-line-watch patrols, farm and ranch checks, traffic checks, transportation checks, city patrols, and other activities.

Information on changes in the number of Border Patrol linewatch and non-line-watch apprehensions, thus, provides a partial basis for assessing whether the monthly number of illegal southern border crossings into the United States (or the magnitude of the undocumented "flow") changed after Operation Hold-the-Line began. We assess this change by examining line-watch and non-line-watch apprehensions data from 1989 through April of 1994. Moving from West to East, the U.S./Mexico border is divided into nine Border Patrol sectors: San Diego, El Centro, Tucson, Yuma, El Paso, Marfa, Del Rio, Laredo, and McAllen. Table 19.2 shows the average monthly values for both line-watch and non-line-watch apprehensions and enforcement hours for the first 7 months of fiscal years 1993 (October 1992 to April 1993) and 1994 (October 1993 to April 1994).

The average gross number of apprehensions along the entire U.S./Mexico border declined by nearly 12,000 per month from 1993 to 1994 (from about 66,300 to about 54,500 per month). Most of this decline occurred because of the sharp decline occurring in the El Paso sector (see the second line in Table 19.2), where apprehensions dropped by over 10,000 per month. Thus, as measured in these terms, Operation Hold-the-Line clearly substantially reduced the number of linewatch apprehensions in the El Paso sector and, by implication, the flow of illegal crossers into the United States.

The patterns for enforcement hours and non-line-watch apprehensions also indicate, however, that this decline may have occurred to some extent at the price of non-line-watch apprehensions. Prior research has shown that both line-watch and non-line-watch apprehensions vary directly with enforcement hours (Bean, Edmonston, and Passel 1990; North 1988), a relationship that derives from the enforcement strategy followed by the Border Patrol of trying to intercept aliens after entry. Thus, the results in Table 19.2 show that, except in the El Paso sector, apprehensions generally go up when enforcement hours rise and decline when hours drop.

The change in strategy involved in Operation Hold-the-Line, however, turned this relationship upside-down. By stationing agents right at the border in order to prevent illegal entry before it occurs, fewer apprehensions were made because fewer illegal crossings occurred. Thus, while line-watch enforcement hours more than doubled during the Operation in comparison to the same months of the previous year (from 32,000 per month to almost 67,000 per month), apprehensions in the El Paso sector dropped to less than one-fourth of their previous level.

The effects of Operation Hold-the-Line are further revealed by examining changes in the number of apprehensions per hour (Table 19.3). From the same months in

**Table 19.2.** *Average monthly line-watch and non-line-watch apprehensions and enforcement hours by sector grouping, fiscal years 1993–4 (first 7 months)*

| Sector | Line-watch hours (000) | | Apprehensions (000) | |
|---|---|---|---|---|
| | 1993 | 1994 | 1993 | 1994 |
| *Linewatch* | | | | |
| Entire border | 214.9 | 261.1 | 66.3 | 54.5 |
| El Paso | 32.0 | 66.9 | 14.3 | 3.9 |
| All but El Paso | 182.9 | 194.2 | 52.0 | 50.6 |
| Arizona | 34.4 | 37.1 | 4.9 | 6.8 |
| California | 76.9 | 80.9 | 37.3 | 32.3 |
| Texas (not El Paso) | 71.6 | 76.3 | 9.8 | 11.5 |
| *Non-Line watch* | | | | |
| Entire border | 170.0 | 145.8 | 27.6 | 23.9 |
| El Paso only | 40.9 | 23.4 | 6.8 | 2.0 |
| All but El Paso | 129.1 | 122.4 | 20.8 | 21.9 |
| Arizona | 16.8 | 18.3 | 3.4 | 4.8 |
| California | 38.1 | 35.0 | 8.3 | 7.7 |
| Texas (not El Paso) | 74.2 | 69.1 | 9.1 | 9.4 |

*Source*: Immigration and Naturalization Service, Statistics Division.

**Table 19.3.** *Line-watch and non-line-watch apprehensions per hour by sector grouping, fiscal years 1993–4 (first 7 months)*

| Sector | Line-watch | | Non-line watch | |
|---|---|---|---|---|
| | 1993 | 1994 | 1993 | 1994 |
| Entire border | 0.309 | 0.209 | 0.162 | 0.164 |
| El Paso only | 0.447 | 0.058 | 0.166 | 0.085 |
| All but El Paso | 0.284 | 0.261 | 0.161 | 0.179 |
| Arizona | 0.142 | 0.183 | 0.202 | 0.262 |
| California | 0.485 | 0.399 | 0.218 | 0.220 |
| Texas (Not El Paso) | 0.137 | 0.151 | 0.123 | 0.136 |

*Source*: Immigration and Naturalization Service, Statistics Division.

fiscal year 1993 to the Operation months in fiscal year 1994, the number of apprehensions per hour in the El Paso sector declined by 87 per cent (from 0.45 to 0.06 per hour). A smaller decline (about 50 per cent) occurred in the case of non-line-watch apprehensions. In all other groupings of sectors except California, and in the case of both line-watch and non-line-watch apprehensions, the average number per hour increased, suggesting that illegal flows increased in sectors outside just to the west and east of the El Paso corridor. Thus, based on an examination of a wide variety of evidence, there is little doubt that Operation Hold-the-Line curtailed illegal crossings into El Paso.

The Operation resulted in other intended and unintended effects as well. One intended effect was to reduce street vending by Mexican nationals in El Paso's downtown commercial district and in certain residential neighborhoods close to the border. The Operation was indeed successful in reducing the participation of illegal crossers in this activity. One study conducted by the University of Texas at El Paso interviewed forty-six of the several hundred downtown street vendors operating downtown before the blockade, and found that 41 per cent of these referred to themselves as "illegals" who lacked papers to work in the United States (Staudt 1994). An unintended effect of the Operation, as suggested by interviews with residents of Juárez (Bean et al. 1994), was to encourage some Juárez commuter workers, particularly women domestic workers, to find places to live in El Paso in order to keep their jobs.

Overall the Operation was more successful in curtailing illegal migration among local crossers than among long-distant migrants. The latter could go around the "line" drawn through El Paso, either with the help of "pasamojados" (people smugglers) or by choosing another entry point along the 1900-mile border. Moreover, Operation Hold-the-Line made the apprehension of long-distance migrants passing through El Paso even less likely, insofar as Border Patrol agents formerly deployed "inland" were moved right to the border itself.

Among local crossers, differences in the extent to which the Operation was successful differed by type of crosser, working best among "illegal crossers/illegal workers" (particularly street vendors and others, like older female domestic workers for whom crossing became especially difficult), and (especially) "juvenile crossers." These types of crossers tended to be the poorest of the Juárez crossers (see Bean et al. 1994 for information about socioeconomic heterogeneity within these categories).

"Long distance labor migrants" and "legal crossers/illegal workers" typically have greater financial resources at their disposal; otherwise they could not finance their long distance migration or qualify for a Border Crossing Card. "Legal crossers/illegal workers," as long as they have valid crossing documents and believable reasons for entering the United States, were perhaps even more free to work illegally, given the decreased presence of the Border Patrol throughout the city of El Paso. And these illegal crossers, including non-labor crossers, who are well-integrated into the social fabric on both sides of the border, were still able to find ways to cross, including obtaining false documents and staying for longer periods with friends and relatives (who may also be illegal) in El Paso.

In short, what decreased the most in response to Operation Hold-the-Line, apparently, was the participation of illegal crossers in petty crime and street vending in south El Paso, activities most associated with juvenile crossers and other youths and adults from Juárez who sought to extend their informal economic subsistence activities to the U.S. side.

## THE BORDER CROSSING CARD AS AN ALTERNATIVE MODE OF ENTRY

The effects of Operation Hold-the Line documented so far tend to support two conclusions: (1) that saturation efforts aimed at interdicting unauthorized Mexican flows are effective in curtailing certain kinds of border-crossers, and (2) that when confronted with such efforts, many types of crossers will seek other points or modes of entry.

What is an example of another mode of entry? Federal immigration law, as given in Title 8 of the *Code of Federal Regulations* (CFR), has established many different categories of non-immigrant visas for foreign citizens who wish to visit the United States on a nonpermanent basis. A special type of non-immigrant visa available at the Mexican border is the border crossing card (BCC), which is held by hundreds of thousands of Mexican citizens residing in frontier cities. The border crossing card is known by several names to Mexican border residents: "pasaporte local," "mica," and "permiso de cruce." The BCC is not to be confused with the "tarjeta verde" (green card) held by legal permanent residents of the United States (which is no longer green, but is still called by its original name), or with the "pasaporte provisional" (Mexican Form 13), which is one of the documents that applicants must present in order to be issued a BCC.

Bearers of border crossing cards, which have no expiration date, are entitled to admission to the United States "as a border crosser or non-immigrant visitor for a period not to exceed 72 hours to visit within 25 miles of the border" (CFR, Title 8, § 235.1). The BCC may be issued to Mexican residents by officers of the INS at official ports of entry to the United States located on the southern border. The BCC is a small, laminated wallet-sized card that, unlike a passport, is easily carried by its bearer and inspected by INS officers at ports of entry to the United States.

The BCC may be issued to Mexican residents by officers of the INS at official ports of entry to the United States located on the southern border. A recipient of the BCC need not bear a valid Mexican passport, but may instead present proof of Mexican residency by presenting a valid Mexican Form 13 (the pasaporte provisional) (CFR, Title 8, §212.6). As is the case with any non-immigrant visa, BCC applicants must demonstrate that they do not intend to abandon their Mexican residence in favor of one in the United States, and that they do not intend to seek employment in the United States (CFR, Title 8, §1184 (b) ). As with any visa, whether immigrant or non-immigrant, BCC applicants must also demonstrate that they are "not otherwise inadmissible" to the United States (CFR, Title 8, §212.6)—that they are not members of a class of "excludable aliens" and they have not broken any other U.S. immigration laws. There is no limit on the number of BCCs that may be issued at any official port of entry to the United States in a given year.

For most practical purposes the answers to the separate questions of whether the BCC applicant should be regarded as an immigrant or non-immigrant entrant and whether he or she belongs to a class of excludable aliens hinge on the answer to another question: Is the applicant, in the estimation of the INS, financially solvent?

Applicants who are financially solvent, based on their employment or their assets, are presumed to be less likely to be immigrants posing as temporary visitors to the United States. Their solvency helps to establish a claim of eligibility for a non-immigrant visa such as the BCC.

It also helps applicants to demonstrate that they do not belong to the three classes of excludable aliens who are most likely to apply for a BCC: (1) paupers, professional beggars, or vagrants (less common exclusions are the mentally retarded, the insane, drug addicts, convicted criminals, polygamists, and prostitutes); (2) persons seeking to enter the United States to perform skilled or unskilled labor; and (3) persons who are likely to become "public charges." INS officers, according to the relevant statutes, may require entrants to answer questions regarding or present written documentation of their solvency. Failure on the part of applicants to provide such answers or evidence at the time of application constitutes sufficient grounds for denying issuance of the BCC. Failure to provide such requested information to an INS officer at the moment of entry with the BCC can result in its confiscation and revocation.

In order to avoid issuing the BCC to likely illegal immigrants or cross-border commuter–workers, the INS requires applicants to present substantial written documentation of their permanent Mexican residence and stable employment. Every BCC applicant must present either a valid Mexican passport or a Form 13, which is issued by Mexican federal government offices in the northern border cities. In addition, applicants are required to present utility receipts in their name to demonstrate further their Mexican border residency. To indicate financial solvency, the INS asks applicants who are employees to present original pay stubs demonstrating employment over the last 12 months, a letter from employers verifying employment, as well as proof of Mexican Social Security registration and bank account statement.

From a U.S. perspective, it would seem that almost any employed person in the workforce thus would quickly be able to meet the "common sense" requirements of the BCC application process. The Mexican reality in general, and the border reality in particular, however, do not correspond very well to a U.S. perspective on routine documentation of an individual's socioeconomic status. First of all, thousands of employed residents of Mexican border cities, including many employed by U.S.-owned maquiladora plants, live in self-constructed housing in vast squatter settlements called colonias. Residents of such areas often own no official title to their lots, pay no rent, and receive no public utilities. Many colonia residents have a difficult time in documenting their Juárez residence in the ways requested of BCC applicants by the INS.

Second, a large proportion of the population all over Mexico, but especially in Northern border cities, is employed in the so-called informal economy. The term informal economy refers not only to the petty commerce of street vendors and market stall operators, but also to a wide range of economic activities undertaken by small-scale establishments and the self-employed that take place largely beyond the reach of government regulation (Castells and Portes 1989). Informal sector workers typically are not registered with Mexican Social Security, do not appear on any official payroll, have no taxes deducted from their wages, and are not protected by state health and safety regulations (Zenteno 1993).

One of the largest groups of poor people living in the Mexican border cities are the employees of maquiladoras, the U.S.-owned export assembly plants set up as part of the binational Border Industrialization Program (Tamayo and Fernández 1983; Tiano 1987; Young and Christopherson 1986). Unskilled personnel working full-time in the maquiladoras made an average of $146 per month in 1988, including fringe benefits (Insituto de Estadística, Geografía, e Informática 1989), and populate many of the poorer colonias in the border cities, where they live side by side with participants in the informal economy—street vendors, construction workers, owners of small stores, and repair shops, etc. (Alarcón and Lozano 1991).

It is the relatively low wages of maquiladora workers—who are also the largest single group of formal economy workers in cities like Juárez—that pull mean and median wages of formal sector workers below those of informal workers. The fact that maquiladora wages have been high enough to attract thousands of migrants to the border from poorer regions in Mexico while at the same time remaining a small fraction of prevailing wages on the U.S. side of the border has prompted concern among some analysts that maquiladora employment could be used by many as a springboard to migration to the United States. Although most researchers believe that the net effect of maquiladora employment is to actually reduce illegal migration flows (Carrillo Huerta 1990; Cornelius and Martin 1993; Dávila 1990).

The existence of the BCC both reflects and facilitates the historical economic and social integration of border "twin" cities like Ciudad Juárez-El Paso, the two Laredos, and Tijuana-San Diego. Mexican residents who possess the BCC use it to pass freely back and forth between the U.S. border city and their homes in Mexico to conduct all sorts of personal affairs—to shop, pay social visits, change currency, deposit money in U.S. banks, attend cultural and sporting events, receive medical services, go out to eat, etc. Many also use the BCC to conduct economic business—to meet with business or trading partners, purchase supplies, deliver orders of goods produced or assembled in Mexico, use communications, financial, or repair services, and, in some cases, to go to work (illegally).

Most border cities are extraordinarily dependent economically upon Mexican nationals for the dollars they spend on personal consumption items as well as the kinds of business transactions they conduct there, both of which serve to integrate the U.S. and Mexican economies. Without the free, legal, and routine cross-border movement of thousands of Mexican nationals facilitated on a daily basis by the BCC, the economies of border cities like El Paso would suffer substantially. An indication of just how dependent border businesses are upon Mexican consumers is that in the Texas border cities retail sales fell over 40 per cent in 1982 as a result of the Mexican government's radical devaluation of the peso (Institute for Manufacturing and Materials Management 1991). Similar downturns in Christmas season retail sales were reported in these cities this year following the peso's latest, and least-expected devaluation (*Wall Street Journal* 1995).

While there is no way of knowing how many BCCs are in circulation, the Encuesta Socioeconómica Anual de la Frontera (ESAF) of 1987, as reported by Alegría (1990) showed that 48 per cent of workers in Juárez, 58 per cent of workers in Tijuana, and

**Table 19.4.** *Estimated percentage of resident workers who enjoy legal border-crossing privileges in three Mexican border cities, 1993*

| | Nuevo Laredo–Laredo | Juarez–El Paso | Tijuana–San Diego |
|---|---|---|---|
| Economically active population | 78,408 | 336,007 | 286,045 |
| % with legal border-crossing privileges | 66 | 48 | 58 |
| Number with legal border-crossing privileges | 51,749 | 161,283 | 165,906 |

*Sources*: U.S. and Mexican Censuses of Population 1970, 1980, and 1990; Encuesta Nacional de Empleo Urbano, fourth quarter 1989.

66 per cent of workers in Nuevo Laredo possessed some kind of nonresident visa that allowed them to visit the United States. The visa possessed by the majority of these workers undoubtedly was the BCC. Applying these percentages to the economically active populations of each city in 1993 produces estimates of the numbers of workers residing in these cities who have border crossing privileges, shown in Table 19.4. While no comprehensive data are available on the nationality or legal status of persons entering and leaving the United States through official ports of entry along the Mexican border, qualitative observation and interviews with border residents and INS officials indicate that the majority of Mexican nationals crossing the border routinely do so with a Border Crossing Card (Bean et al. 1994).

Historically, many residents of Mexican border cities have sought and gained employment in the U.S. cities immediately across the border from them. These Mexicans commute back and forth between their homes in Mexico and their jobs on the U.S. side on a routine basis (Alegría 1992; Martínez 1978, 1994). For many years, this practice was tolerated by immigration authorities in places like El Paso (Bean et al. 1994), where well-to-do residents relied upon Mexican commuters to provide them with low-cost domestic housekeeping, gardening, and child-care services (Nathan 1991; Ruíz and Tiano 1987). As recently as 1993, for example, it was possible to stand on any of the international bridges connecting the downtowns of El Paso and Juárez and watch rowboats ferry passengers illegally from Mexican to U.S. territory without interference, in broad daylight. Indeed, a rationale for launching Operation Hold-the-Line was to put a stop to this kind of blatant disregard of legal entry procedures, which had become a source of acute embarrassment for the Border Patrol in the early 1990s.

In El Paso, the Border Patrol surveyed around 600 undocumented migrants it apprehended in the weeks immediately preceding the Operation, and ascertained that at least 60 per cent of them resided in Juárez and had no destination in the United States other than the El Paso metropolitan area (Bean et al. 1994). To date, the El Paso District is the only one that has systematically attempted to collect data on the origins and intended destinations of Mexican nationals it has apprehended.

**Table 19.5.** *Estimates of cross-border commuting by residents of three Mexican border cities, 1993*

| | Nuevo Laredo–Laredo | Juarez–El Paso | Tijuana–San Diego |
|---|---|---|---|
| Number of commuters | 2,980 | 16,128 | 22,312 |
| Economically active: Mexico | 78,408 | 336,007 | 286,045 |
| Economically active: U.S. | 58,732 | 286,528 | 1,503,229 |
| % of Mexican econ active | 3.8 | 4.8 | 7.8 |
| % of US econ active | 5.1 | 5.6 | 1.5 |

*Sources*: Mexican and U.S. Censuses of Population and Housing, 1970, 1980 and 1990; Encuesta Nacional de Empleo Urbano, fourth quarter 1989.

**Table 19.6.** *Estimated legal status of cross-border commuters in three Mexican border cities, 1993*

| Sector | U.S. citizen | Resident | Card | Entrant | Total |
|---|---|---|---|---|---|
| *Nuevo Laredo* | | | | | |
| Number | 924 | 596 | 1,281 | 179 | 2,980 |
| Per cent | 31 | 20 | 43 | 6 | 100 |
| *Juarez* | | | | | |
| Number | 6,290 | 3,871 | 5,322 | 806 | 16,128 |
| Per cent | 39 | 24 | 33 | 5 | 100 |
| *Tijuana* | | | | | |
| Number | 2,454 | 9,148 | 9,594 | 1,116 | 22,312 |
| Per cent | 11 | 41 | 43 | 5 | 100 |

*Sources*: Encuesta Socioeconómica Anual de la Frontera, 1987; Mexican Census of Population and Housing, 1970 and 1990.

Table 19.5 presents rough, synthetic estimates of the number of cross-border commuters residing in three Mexican border cities in 1993, both in absolute terms and relative to the economically active population of the metropolitan area on either side of the border. Of those who worked illegally in the United States, the vast majority possessed a BCC or other valid visa to enter the United States; those who crossed into the United States illegally ("entered without inspection" in INS parlance) constituted a small minority even of those persons who worked illegally (Table 19.6).

Hundreds of thousands of current Mexican border-city workers and their dependents possess valid border crossing cards, and thousands of these use them to work illegally in U.S. border cities. To date, no data have been collected by any agency of the U.S. or Mexican governments that permit even rough estimates of the per cent of Mexican residents residing illegally in the United States who entered by using a valid border crossing card. In 1994, the INS estimated that of the 823,000 Mexicans believed to be residing illegally in the United States, 743,000, or 90 per cent had "entered without inspection," that is, had sneaked across the border illegally. Only 10 per cent, according to the INS had "overstayed" their time-limited visa (Warren 1994).

The existence and widespread use of the BCC confounds these estimates, however, for there is no reliable way of identifying persons who have used it to establish U.S. residence. In making its estimates, the INS lumped BCC-abusers with Mexicans who "entered without inspection." The BCC has no expiration date and allows for multiple entries into the 25-mile border strip in the United States. At the border, no data is collected on how many BCC-holders (or Mexican bearers of other types of multiple-entry, non-immigrant visas) enter the U.S. versus leave it over time.

Many Mexican migrants, both legal and undocumented, that settle in California and the Midwest traditionally have come from "interior" Mexican states such as Jalisco, Michoacán, and Guanajuato which are far from the border (Massey et al. 1987; Durand and Massey 1992), without first sojourning in the Mexican border cities before migrating to the United States. Such persons are not potential abusers of the BCC, which is issued only to border residents. There is also evidence that a great deal of "stage" migration—that is, the migration of residents of Mexico's northern border states and cities to cities immediately across the border in the United States—has also traditionally occurred (Martínez 1978, 1994; Portes and Bach 1985; Weeks and Ham-Chande 1992). Since the 1970s, the populations of cities like Tijuana and Juárez have burgeoned with the arrival of migrants from all over Mexico; as these cities continue to grow in size, the potential for the growth of filter migration grows as well, and can be facilitated by the widespread misuse of the BCC.

It is ironic, then, that the BCC has come to be seen by Mexican workers as one of the major fringe benefits of a maquiladora job, as interviews with residents of Juárez colonias have showed in our research. Maquiladora jobs are relatively easy to get, and provide workers with the documentation that the INS requires for obtaining the BCC, including letters of employment, pay stubs, and social security "pink sheets." Young adults working in the maquiladoras are able to get BCCs for other family members living with them, including their parents, based on their maquiladora employment.

People interviewed for the study who did not work in the maquiladoras generally regarded maquiladora employment as low paying and otherwise unattractive, except for the fact that such employment facilitated obtaining the BCC. The stability of employment in maquiladoras is also questionable. Turnover rates among assembly-line workers have been fabulously high, averaging 12 per cent per month in recent years (Carrillo 1990). Cerrutti and Roberts (1994) found that working class women's employment in the border cities is extremely volatile, with frequent job changes and entries and exits into and out of the work force in the same year. This was also true of women maquiladora workers.

It would seem, then, that the 12 months of pay stubs from the same employer that the INS insists that BCC applicants present may not, in the case of many maquiladora workers, reflect the stability of their employment, but rather their knowledge of the requirements of the BCC. A number of working men in one colonia reported that they could earn 2.5–3 times more as informal laborers in construction than they could in the maquiladoras as machine operators, but that as construction workers they would never be able to produce the documentation of their employment the INS requires for the BCC.

It is impossible to know how many maquiladora workers and their dependents have obtained the BCC and subsequently used it to establish a U.S. residence, although some of the people interviewed in our research had either done so themselves or had friends or family members who had. Carrillo Huerta (1990) reports that a survey of 1,200 maquiladora workers in Tijuana, Ciudad Juárez, and Matamoros conducted in 1988–9 showed that nearly 30 per cent of those workers who had migrated to the border from elsewhere in Mexico believed that working in a maquiladora would help them get a job in the United States, although few (under 10 per cent) actually planned to migrate across the border. The survey did not, however, explore whether the 30 per cent based their belief on their ability to use maquiladora employment to obtain border-crossing privileges.

## SUMMARY AND CONCLUSIONS

Estimates of illegal Mexican residents of the United States who "entered without inspection" may be significantly inflated by Mexicans who have used the BCC as a means of entering to establish a U.S. residence. While no one knows how many valid BCCs are currently held by Mexican nationals living on either side of the U.S.–Mexico border, synthetic estimates indicate that the number of adult workers possessing a BCC who reside in just three of Mexico's northern border cities is in the hundreds of thousands. And the estimates presented above exclude dependent relatives of these workers who also have valid BCCs.

These findings have several implications for U.S. immigration policy. Foremost among them is that focusing exclusively on the prevention of illegal border crossing by Mexican nationals will not prevent many other Mexicans from entering the country legally in order to work and/or live illegally. Increased surveillance and fortification of the international boundary itself, as exemplified by Operation Hold-the-Line in El Paso, Texas and Operation Gatekeeper in San Diego, California, are highly visible and politically popular measures, but they ignore the fact that for thousands of Mexican residents of cities like Tijuana and Ciudad Juárez, the effective (and unfortified) border is located 25 miles into the U.S. interior. In the case of Operation Hold-the-Line, which was most effective at reducing the number of illegal crossings made by Juárez residents whose only U.S. destination was El Paso (Bean, et al. 1994), the INS took the inconsistent approach of launching a massive police action against one group of violators of U.S. immigration laws—illegal border-crossers—while mostly ignoring a larger group of violators—BCC abusers. Adding to the irony is that the social characteristics of illegal crossers and BCC abusers may not be particularly different, since INS procedures for issuing the BCC are unable to truly distinguish between "admissible" and "inadmissible" applicants as reflected in their stable employment and residence in Mexico. This situation is not without precedent in the history of U.S. immigration policy. During Operation Wetback in the 1950s, thousands of Mexicans working on U.S. farms in the Southwest were deported while simultaneously thousands more were imported as part of the Bracero Program (Calavita 1992).

In conclusion, evidence about the effectiveness of enforcement mechanisms employed by the United States to control unauthorized migration is mixed. Employer sanctions do not appear to have been effective, but this conclusion must be tempered by the fact that the will and resources to enforce them have largely been lacking. Operation Hold-the-Line was sufficiently effective in that it implied that border interdiction efforts more generally could possibly work. As our discussion of the use of Border Crossing Cards as a mode-of-entry indicated, however, the apparent success of a measure like Hold-the-Line can be offset by increased recourse to other ways of entering the country. This "balloon" effect (push it in one place and it pops up in another) does not mean, however, that interdiction is necessarily foredoomed to failure, although it does imply that enforcement efforts will have to attain a degree of scale and comprehensiveness not heretofore attempted if they are to have any chance of working, and even this may not guarantee success as long as other channels of interchange between countries (commerce, tourism, etc.) remain open, thus ensuring alternative routes of entry. Thus, it seems difficult to think that the gap between enforcement efforts to control migration and the degree of success those efforts achieve will close anytime soon.

## References

Alarcón, Eduardo, and Lozano, José Carlos (1991). *Necesidades de Vivienda en los Trabajadores de la Industria Maquiladora de Nuevo Laredo*. Nuevo Laredo, Tamaulipas: Universidad Autónoma de Tamaulipas.

Alegría, Tito (1992). *Desarrollo Urbano en la Frontera México-Estados Unidos*. Mexico City: Consejo Nacional para la Cultura y las Artes.

——(1990). "Ciudad y Transmigración en la Frontera Norte con Estados Unidos," *Frontera Norte*, 2: 7–38.

Bean, Frank D., and Cushing, Robert G. (1995). "The Relationship Between the Mexican Economic Crisis and Illegal Migration to the United States," *Trade Insights*, 5: 1–4.

——Edmonston, Barry, and Passel, Jeffrey S. (1990). *Undocumented Migration to the United States: IRCA and the Experience of the 1980s*. Washington, DC: The Urban Institute Press.

——Thomas J. Espenshade, Michael J. White, and Robert F. Dymowski (1990). "Post-IRCA Changes in the Volume and Composition of Undocumented Migration to the United Sates: An Assessment Based on Apprehensions Data," in J. S. Passel, F. D. Bean, and B. Edmonston (eds.), *Undocumented Migration to the United States: IRCA and the Experience of the 1980s*. Washington, DC: The Urban Institute Press, pp. 111–58.

——Vernez, George, and Keely, Charles B. (1989). *Opening and Closing the Doors: Changing U.S. Immigration Patterns and Policies*. Santa Monica, Washington, DC: RAND and Urban Institute.

——Chanove, Roland, Cushing, Robert G., de la Garza, Rodolfo, Freeman, Gary, Haynes, Charles W., and Spener, David (1994). *Illegal Mexican Migration and the United*

*States/Mexico Border: The Effects of Operation Hold-The-Line on El Paso and Juárez.* Washington, DC: U.S. Commission on Immigration Reform.

Calavita, Kitty (1992). *Inside the State: The Bracero Program, Immigration, and the INS.* New York: Routledge.

Carrillo Huerta, Mario M. (1990). "The Impact of Maquiladoras on Migration in Mexico," Working paper. Washington, DC: Commission for the Study of International Migration and Cooperative Economic Development.

Castells, Manuel, and Portes, Alejandro (1989). "World Underneath: Origins, Dynamics, and Effects of the Informal Economy," in Alejandro Portes, Manuel Castells, and Lauren Benton (eds.), *The Informal Economy: Studies in Advanced and Less Developed Countries.* Baltimore: The Johns Hopkins University Press, pp. 11–37.

Cerrutti, Marcela, and Roberts, Bryan (1994). "Entradas y Salidas de la Fuerza de Trabajo: La Intermitencia del Empleo Femenino en Mexico," Unpublished Paper, Population Research Center, University of Texas at Austin.

Cornelius, Wayne A., and Martin, Philip L. (1993). *The Uncertain Connection. Free Trade and Mexico-U.S. Migration.* La Jolla: Center for U.S. – Mexican Studies, University of California, San Diego.

—— Martin, Philip L., and Hollifield, James F. (1994). *Controlling Immigration: A Global Perspective.* Stanford: Stanford University Press.

Dávila, Alberto (1990). "Effect of Maquiladora Employment on the Monthly flow of Mexican Undocumented Immigration to the U.S., 1978–1992," *International Migration Review*, 27: 484–512.

Durand, Jorge, and Massey, Douglas S. (1992). "Mexican Migration to the United States: A Critical Review," *Latin American Research Review*, 27: 3–42.

Espenshade, Thomas J. (1995). "Using INS Border Apprehension Data to Measure the Flow of Undocumented Migrants Crossing the U.S.–Mexico Frontier," *International Migration Review*, 29: 545–65.

—— (1990). "Undocumented Migration to the United States: Evidence from a Repeated Trials Model," in Frank D. Bean, Barry Edmonston, and Jeffrey S. Passel (eds.), *Undocumented Migration to the United States: IRCA and the Experience of the 1980s.* Washington, DC: The Urban Institute Institute Press, pp.159–81.

Fix, Michael, and Hill, Paul T. (1990). *Enforcing Employer Sanctions, Challenges and Strategies.* Santa Monica and Washington: The RAND Corporation and The Urban Institute Press.

Institute for Manufacturing and Materials Management (1991). *Paso del Norte Regional Economy: Socioeconomic Profile.* El Paso.

Instituto Nacional de Estadística, Geografia, e Informática (1989). *Estadística de la Industria Maquiladora de Exportacíon.* Aguascalientes: Instituto Nacional de Estadística, Geografia, e Informática.

Martínez, Oscar J. (1978). *Border Boom Town: Ciudad Juarez Since 1848.* Austin: University of Texas Press.

—— (1994). *Border People: Life and Society in the US–Mexico Borderlands.* Tucson: University of Arizona Press.

Massey, Douglas, Alarcón, Rafael, Durand, Jorge, and González, Humberto (1987). *Return to Aztlán: The Social Process of International Migration from Western Mexico.* Berkeley: University of California Press.

Miller, Mark J. (1994). "Strategies for Immigration Control: An International Comparison," *The Annals* 534: 1–219.

Nathan, Debbie (1991). *Women and Other Aliens: Essays from the US–Mexico Border*. El Paso: Cinco Puntos Press.

North, David (1988). *IRCA's Batting Averages (Memo #2)*. Umpublished Paper, Transcentury Development Associates, Washington, DC.

Portes, Alejandro, and Bach, Robert (1985). *Latin Journey*. Berkeley: University of California Press.

Ruíz, Vicki, and Tiano, Susan (1987). *Women on the U.S.–Mexico Border: Responses to Change*. Boston: Allen and Unwin.

Staudt, Kathleen (1994). "Struggles Over City Space in El Paso/Juárez: Comparative Policies, Enforcement, and Collective Action," Paper presented at the XVIII International Congress of The Latin American Studies Association, V, Atlanta (March 11).

Tamayo, Jesus, and Fernández, Jorge Luís (1983). *Zonas Fronterizas*. Mexico City: Centro de Investigatión y Docencia Económicas.

Tiano, Susan (1987). "Maquiladoras in Mexicali: Integration or Exploitation?" in Vicki Ruíz and Susan Tiano (eds.), *Women on the U.S.–Mexico Border: Responses to Change*. Boston, MA: Allen and Unwin, pp. 17–39.

*Wall Street Journal* (1995). "After the Fall: Predicting Effects of the Peso's Drop." *The Wall Street Journal*, January 4, 1995, P. T1.

Warren, Robert (1994). "Estimates of the Undocumented Immigrant Population Residing in the United States, by Country of Origin and State of Residence: October 1992," Unpublished Paper, Immigration and Naturalization Service, Statistics Division, Washington, DC.

Weeks, John R., and Ham-Chande, Roberto (1992). *Demographic Dynamics of the US-Mexico Border*. El Paso: Texas Western Press.

Young, Gay, and Christopherson, Susan (1986). "Household Structure and Economic Activity in Ciudad Juárez," in Gay Young (ed.), *The Social Ecology and Economic Development of Ciudad Juárez*. Boulder: Westview Press, pp. 65–95.

Zenteno, René (1993). "El Uso del Concepto de Informalidad en el Estudio del Empleo Urbano," *Frontera Norte*, 5: 67–93.

# PART IV

# PROSPECTS AND POLICIES RECONSIDERED

# 20

## Back to the Future: Immigration Research, Immigration Policy, and Globalization in the Twenty-first Century

DOUGLAS S. MASSEY AND J. EDWARD TAYLOR

When considering international migration in the twenty-first century, it is important to bear in mind the oft-quoted aphorism of the philosopher George Santayana: "Those who cannot remember the past are condemned to repeat it." Today's international migrant flows did not emerge in a vacuum, of course; rather, they are intimately connected to broader processes of economic integration that for the past half century have been shrinking the globe. Places that are linked to one another by flows of goods, capital, commodities, and information also tend to be linked by flows of people, in a process that many people today refer to as "globalization." What many observers fail to realize is that the current wave of globalization is not the first in human history. Indeed, to a remarkable extent the current era replicates an earlier period of globalization that crested during the first decade of the twentieth century, when, for example, the share of foreign born in the U.S. population was far higher than it is today. This first period of globalization has far more in common with our own era than with the period from 1914 to 1990.

### GLOBALIZATION PAST AND PRESENT

The decades preceding the outbreak of World War I were characterized by an expanding international economy based on free trade and mobile capital. Then as now the integrity of the trade system was safeguarded by a hegemonic nation capable of projecting its power throughout the world to safeguard global lines of transportation and communication. Under the protection of the British navy, international commerce thrived, yielding a rising volume of international exchange in goods, commodities, and natural resources and growing international investment (Kenwood and Lougheed 1999). To facilitate the transnational movement of capital, materials, and goods, a rudimentary but functional set of international institutions had evolved, and trading nations moved steadily toward liberal democracy even as the societies themselves became more unequal with respect to wealth and income.

The emergence of this first transnational economy was closely associated with the migration of labor (Hatton and Williamson 1998). Within nations, migration led to rapid urbanization; between nations it produced massive immigration. From 1800 to 1929 more than 50 million people left Europe for destinations in the Americas, Oceania, and elsewhere (Ferenczi 1929). These large-scale population movements were rooted in structural transformations that overcame nations as they were incorporated into the emerging transnational economy and began to industrialize (Massey 1988). Once begun, international population flows were supported by an expanding infrastructure of interpersonal networks and social organizations that linked people and communities in distant places.

Given the falling costs of transportation and communication and technological innovations that permitted rapid movement, international migration by 1900 had become substantially circular (Wyman 1993). Large outflows of emigrants from eastern and southern Europe were counterbalanced by large return flows of both migrants and remittances from the Americas and Oceania (Nugent 1992). Returning migrants and their remittances played an important, but often largely unappreciated, role in the social transformation and economic growth of European sending nations (Massey 1988).

The growing prosperity, optimism, and cosmopolitanism that accompanied the first wave of globalization came to a sudden end with the outbreak of world war in August 1914. Over the next 4 years the leading industrial powers of Europe engaged in an unprecedented and massive destruction of land, labor, and capital, and most of the participants assumed crushing, unpayable debts. When the war finally ended, political stability was gone. The regimes of most belligerent nations had been overthrown, the hegemonic power of Britain was fatally wounded, and the nascent system of international institutions crafted in the late nineteenth century was in tatters (James 2002). World War I opened a Pandora's box of contradictory forces, and it would take most of the next century to reconcile them: the intensification of the struggle between labor and capital, the polarization of political ideology between communism and fascism, and the widespread retreat from liberal democracy among former trading nations.

The period 1918–45 brought the collapse of international trade, the rise of autarkic economic nationalism, and the implementation of chauvinistic restrictions on trade, investment, and immigration (James 2001). Although the world economy hobbled along for a while on the strength of wealth accumulated in the New World during World War I, by 1929 it all came crashing down. Following a decade of worldwide economic depression, the ideological contradictions unleashed in 1914 were partially resolved on the battlefield between 1939 and 1945, as a coalition of communist and liberal democratic states arose to defeat fascism in World War II, which in many ways was simply the final battle of the first war.

The end of World War II did not bring about a full resumption of the global regime of free trade because of the armed standoff between the liberal capitalist democracies and communist dictatorships, with a new superpower at the core of each block: the Soviet Union and the United States. In the west, the United States took the lead in rebuilding the transnational market economy in a way that sought to correct the mistakes of the earlier era and avoid another catastrophic war. It joined with other liberal states to charter a new and more effective set of international institutions that together could guarantee international security, liquidity, convertability of currencies, investment, and trade: NATO, the United Nations, the World Bank, the International Monetary Fund, the General Agreement on Tariffs and Trade, and eventually the World Trade Organization. At the same time, the United States supported the economic reconstruction of Europe and worked to facilitate its integration as a union of liberal capitalist democracies, leading ultimately to the formation of the European Union.

These innovations led to a revival of trade, first among the nations of the OECD, and then, as decolonization proceeded, between the first and the third worlds. As the reconstruction of Europe and Japan drew to a close, agencies such as the U.N., the IMF, and the World Bank shifted to promote economic growth in developing nations and to facilitate their entry into the global trading system (Stiglitz 2002). The increasing flows of capital, goods, raw materials, and information were accompanied by a renewed large-scale movement of labor, first within the OCED and later between the Third and the First Worlds. Emigration from poorer nations usually did not spring forth spontaneously, however. It had to be instigated deliberately by developed nations in the 1950s and 1960s, via a series of negotiated international agreements to arrange the recruitment, transportation, and employment of temporary "guestworkers" from developing countries (Martin and Miller 1980; Reichert and Massey 1982).

Until 1990, however, international migration was never in a position to reach its full potential because of the Cold War, which isolated nearly a third of the human population from the global market economy (the citizens of China, the Soviet Union, and nations in their spheres of influence) while miring many Third World nations in proxy confrontations and political machinations. Although western democracies maintained liberal asylum and refugee policies, these were predicated on the assumption that communist nations would work assiduously to prevent emigration from occurring in the first place. The west agreed to take in refugees who managed to escape, but only on the tacit assumption that communist-block countries would do their utmost to stop them from leaving.

When this implicit agreement on the regulation of emigration collapsed with the end of the Cold War, the expansive refugee and asylum policies of Western countries quickly disappeared. It is only with the end of the Cold War that the world returned to the stage of political and economic development that it had reached in 1914. The contradictory forces set in motion by World War I were not fully reconciled until the fall of the Berlin Wall in 1989. Only then were conditions ripe for the full flowering of an international trade and the emergence of the new global economy.

The link between global trade and immigration is illustrated using U.S. data in the bar graph shown in Fig. 20.1. The clear, left-hand bars show the number of immigrants to the United States (in millions) by decade during the century. The shaded, right-hand bars show international trade as a percentage of the U.S. gross national product. The statistical correlation between these two variables is high: 0.84. As can be seen, early in the century trade and immigration ran at very high levels. During 1901–10, for example, a record 8.8 million immigrants entered the United States, and

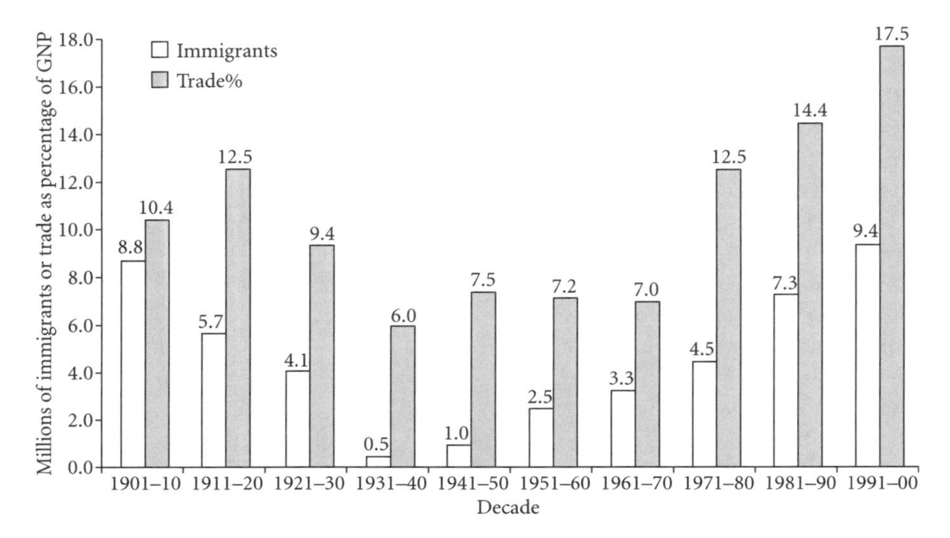


**Figure 20.1.** *U.S. immigration and foreign trade by decade*

trade comprised roughly 10 per cent of total GNP. World War I truncated immigration in the ensuing decade, even as it boosted trade, which rose to nearly 13 per cent of GDP; but the effect of isolationist policies in the 1920s is clearly evident as immigration declined to 4.1 million and trade fell to 9 per cent of GNP.

During the 1930s, international trade and immigration both reached a nadir. From 1931 to 1940, only 500,000 persons entered the United States and international trade accounted for a mere 6 per cent of U.S. economic activity. The 1930s and the subsequent three decades constitute a kind of interregnum between global trading regimes. From 1950 to 1970, trade fluctuated around 7 per cent of GNP while immigration slowly increased, going from 1.0 million during the 1940s to 3.3 million in the 1960s, still only a fraction of the level achieved during the first decade of the century and lower than any decade from 1870 through 1930.

The revival of trade and immigration really began in the 1970s. In that decade, trade increased sharply, finally coming to equal the share of GNP achieved during 1911–20 (12.5 per cent). At the same time, immigration surpassed the level it had last achieved during the 1920s. Over the remaining decades of the twentieth century, both international migration and trade expanded to reach new and unprecedented heights. By the last decade of the century, immigration had surged to 9.4 million persons while trade rose to comprise almost 18 per cent of GNP.

At the dawn of the new century, in other words, the United States found itself at the center of a new global economy characterized by massive cross-border movements of people, goods, commodities, services, and information. As in the earlier period of globalization, there is a hegemonic nation capable of projecting its power worldwide to safeguard transportation and communication, an evolution toward liberal democracy among trading partners, rising inequality within and between nations, and the existence of functional institutions to solve the many problems inherent to international transactions. As a result, markets for land, commodities, capital, goods, raw materials, and information are increasingly global in scope, yielding a rising volume of international movements of all kinds.

As before, the flows of goods, capital, commodities, and information are accompanied by a rising volume of immigration, and once again emigration is rooted in structural transformations that follow countries' incorporation into the global market economy. Once begun, the migration flows are sustained by a complex web of interpersonal networks and informal institutions that support and facilitate international movement. The principal difference between the current period of globalization and its predecessor is that today's core economic powers all seek to impose controls and limitations on the movement of people. Before 1914, in contrast, no controls effectively existed. Even as the United States, Canada, the European Union, Australia, and Japan presently work to ensure that borders are porous for movements of goods, capital, land, raw materials, services, commodities, and information, they are unwilling to accept free flows of people across international boundaries (except within the European Union). On the contrary, developed nations have increasingly sought to apply restrictive measures to limit international migration.

The contradiction is again well-illustrated using data from the United States. As a result of restrictions on immigration, increases in the *rate* of immigration (proportionate to population) have not paralleled increases in the *rate* of trade (proportionate to the size of the economy). Indeed, as Fig. 20.2 shows, the rate of immigration to the United States during the 1990s is quite low by historical standards. Although the absolute number of immigrants may be at record levels, the United States population

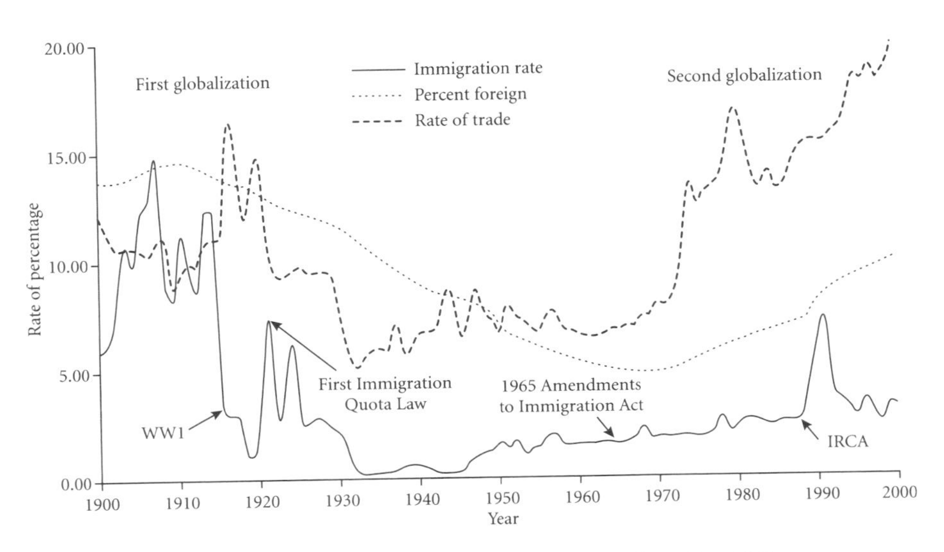


**Figure 20.2.** *Annual rates of trade and immigration 1900–2000*

is now much larger than earlier in the century. Whereas the rate of immigration was 12 per thousand in the years immediately preceding World War I, at no time since 1970 has it exceeded 8 per thousand. The rate of immigration surged briefly to 7.2 in 1991 as result of legalization programs authorized by the 1986 Immigration Reform and Control Act (IRCA). Apart from this unusual episode, however, the rate of immigration has grown very modestly, increasing from just 1.8 per thousand in 1970 to reach 3.2 per thousand in the year 2000, a far cry from the 15 per thousand recorded in 1907. In contrast, foreign trade as a proportion of GNP rose from 8 to 20 per cent between 1970 and 2000. Thus, immigrants, despite their growing visibility, are far less common demographically than they were during the first period of globalization prior to 1914.

In essence, today's global economy is characterized by the deregulation and globalization of all markets save that for labor. Whether this contradiction can be sustained is one of the fundamental questions of the twenty-first century, and how it is resolved—through the termination of global trade or the opening of countries to freer immigration—will determine much about the population size, composition, and structure of the world's developed nations.

## LESSONS FROM THIS VOLUME

The chapters included in this volume are consistent with our view of international migration as an integral part of the spread of markets and global trade. As markets for financial capital, goods, commodities, and services have globalized, so have markets for human capital and labor, yielding rising international flows of migrants. Emigration does not stem from a lack of development, but from development itself, as nations are structurally transformed through their incorporation into global regimes of trade and politics. Contrary to much popular opinion, emigration from the Third World does not arise from demographic pressures. In her chapter, Zlotnik conclusively shows that the degree of emigration from a country is *in no way* related to the underlying rate of population growth. Rapidly growing nations do not necessarily produce the most emigrants, nor do slowly growing populations produce the fewest.

The role of structural economic transformation in generating international migration is highlighted by Okólski's chapter on Central and Eastern Europe. During the Soviet Era, most countries experienced little international movement and what little migration occurred generally followed the structure of exchange within the socialist COMECON block. The collapse of the Soviet Union, however, brought about a shift from command to market mechanisms which radically transformed the structure and organization of former Soviet societies and displaced millions of workers from state-run industries and planning bureaucracies, ended subsidies on housing, food, and medical services, and created new needs for income, capital, credit, and insurance. The result was a surge in international migration, much of it directed toward market economies in the west, with which economic contact had been restored.

While nations of Central and Eastern Europe experienced a rising tide of emigration following their integration within the global economy and the shift from command to market mechanisms, emigration from Sub-Saharan Africa languished as the region became increasingly marginalized from the world economy (Centeno, Louch, and Hargittai 1999). As Adepoju's chapter reports, in two-thirds of African nations population growth exceeded economic growth during the 1990s, bringing about an absolute decline in per capita income. Despite the fact that Africans stood to gain more than Asians or Latin Americans from international migration, relatively few left the continent. Among immigrants to the United States during the 1990s, for example, just 4 per cent originated in Africa.

Although millions of Africans find themselves outside their countries of birth, most were displaced persons fleeing ethnic violence, civil war, or ecological degradation, and most were located in neighboring countries. One exception to this pattern of calamity-based migration is the system of labor migration that emerged in South African following the demise of apartheid. In many ways, this system of regional attraction parallels that centered on Argentina in South America. Both countries historically had attracted significant numbers of immigrants from Europe; but by the end of the century each had scaled back to attract principally intra-continental migrants. According to Zlotnik (1998), two-thirds of immigrants to South Africa came from the neighboring countries of Botswana, Lesotho, Mozambique, Namibia, Swaziland, and Zimbabwe. Maguid, in her chapter in this volume, shows that more than half of all immigrants to Argentina in the 1990s came from the bordering nations of Bolivia, Chile, Paraguay, Uruguay, and Brazil, up from just 9 per cent during the first decade of the century. She argues that immigrants to Argentina arrived to satisfy a strong demand for low-wage labor that originated in a highly segmented labor market characteristic of metropolitan Buenos Aires, a structure that seemed to intensify during periods of economic recession.

Such a pattern of labor market segmentation is typical of developed nations. As Zhou's analysis of data from the United States reveals, immigrants readily find jobs and encounter few barriers to entering the U.S. labor market; but once employed their prospects for mobility are less certain. A majority of immigrants are underemployed in the sense that they are overqualified for the jobs they hold. Among female immigrants, 70 per cent are underemployed. Migrants from the West Indies, Southeast Asia, Mexico, and other Latin American nations appear to be most disadvantaged in the U.S. labor market, and show clear signs of being stuck in dead-end jobs that offer few prospects for economic mobility, consistent with segmented labor market theory (see Piore 1979).

In addition to North America, another migratory system of long duration is that prevailing in Oceania. According to Bedford, migratory exchanges between islands of the Polynesian archipelago are hundreds, if not thousands of years old. During the 1990s, however, well-structured migratory circuits based on social networks and trade emerged, with island states increasingly integrating to form a coherent transnational economy, society, and culture held together by flows of migrants, remittances, and foreign aid that helped to sustain local bureaucracies—the so-called MIRAB model of development.

Hugo's chapter points out that, in addition to small island nations, the Pacific region also contains some of the world's largest and most dynamic economies, with nations such as Australia, Japan, Taiwan, South Korea, Singapore, and Malaysia emerging as key nodes within the global marketplace during the 1990s. Not coincidentally, all of these nations also became countries of immigration, importing workers from other Asian nations that themselves were in the process of transformation, including Thailand, Indonesia, the Philippines, Pakistan, India, and Bangladesh.

The latter countries also contributed significant numbers of migrants to Europe, North America, and the Persian Gulf. Indeed, as Hugo and Stahl report in their chapter, migrant-sending countries in Asia and the Pacific have been at the forefront of using labor migration as a tool to promote national economic development, creating programs and sometimes entire ministries to promote the export of labor and establishing mechanisms to capture remittances and channel them toward productive investment.

By the mid-1990s, migrant earnings accounted for around 37 per cent of total exports from the Philippines, making labor the country's most important single export. Remittances also represented an important source of foreign exchange for many Asian countries. According to Hugo and Stahl, during the early 1990s, migrant remittances constituted 26 per cent of foreign exchange earnings in Bangladesh, 15 per cent in Pakistan and Sri Lanka, and 13 per cent in the Philippines.

Not only do migrant remittances and savings have direct effects on incomes of migrant-sending households, they also have important indirect effects by increasing household liquidity and enabling productive investments that otherwise would be impossible. In his chapter, Taylor documents the importance of remittances in promoting economic growth within migrant-sending regions. His survey suggests that each $1 of migrant remittances actually generates more than $2 in household income once indirect effects are taken into account. At the aggregate level, spending enabled by migrant remittances also has strong multiplier effects, thus generating additional employment, production, and income throughout the national economy.

By the mid 1990s, some 120 million persons lived outside of their country of birth (Zlotnik 1998), and as of the year 2000, these international migrants together remitted home some $60 billion per year (International Monetary Fund 2001). Given these numbers, it is hardly surprising that the recruitment and transport of international migrants, both authorized and unauthorized, has become a large and lucrative business. According to the data marshaled in Abella's chapter, job-brokering for profit has become an important institution supporting international migration throughout the world, especially during the early stages of migration when social networks have not yet been established. Even when official labor recruitment is available, migrants often prefer to pay higher fees to private agents so as to gain quicker access to foreign employment, and given the self-interested collusion of migrants and agents, state attempts to regulate and control international labor recruitment have been largely unsuccessful.

Battistella observes in his chapter that reintegration is another problem faced by policymakers in migrant-sending countries. Returning overseas migrants often face difficulty in finding suitable employment at home, having grown accustomed to higher salaries and acquired elevated consumption habits while working abroad. Although many migrants seek to use their savings to launch themselves in self-employment, few are successful in realizing this goal. Moreover, the longer a migrant has been abroad the more difficult and less successful reintegration tends to be. Inevitably, however, the success or failure of reintegration efforts lie outside the control of the migrants themselves. As Battistella notes, it depends substantially on the macroeconomic health of the country.

As economies have integrated on a global scale, developed nations have moved uniformly toward greater restrictions. Withol de Wenden's chapter reveals that nations of the European Union have moved toward tighter border controls and more restricted residence rights for immigrants, even as they have moved to promote the free movement of E.U. citizens within the union itself. The shift toward restriction, in turn, has placed greater pressure on the asylum regime as the only door to Europe left ajar. Nevertheless, according to the chapter of Joly and Suhrke, the consequent surge in asylum applications during the 1990s led to state actions to curtail this avenue of entry as well. Countries of the European Union moved in concert toward a comprehensive and more limited refugee policy that places a greater emphasis on the prevention of departures from sending regions, essentially reducing the number of asylum claims by blocking refugees from reaching the European Union in the first place.

While countries of the European Union have moved toward harmonizing policies of border enforcement, asylum, and residence, Baldwin-Edwards points out that they remain fragmented with respect to the social rights of immigrants. Given the strain that social welfare programs are under from Europe's aging population and rising dependency burden, the question of which immigrants are eligible to receive what benefits and in which quantity is one of fundamental importance. In the absence of immigration, current levels of social spending simply cannot be sustained. Yet most governments in the European Union are reluctant to accept the necessity or even the reality of immigration. They likewise have strong incentives to restrict granting access to social welfare to those immigrants who are admitted for work and residence. As a result, Baldwin-Edwards suggests that reforms, if they do come, will occur as a result of the political mobilization of immigrants rather than the unilateral actions of states.

The contradictions involved in stopping immigration within a globalizing economy are nowhere better illustrated than in the United States. The United States is the hegemonic power and the core market for producers around the world. Since the early 1990s it has pursued a strategy of regional market consolidation and integration parallel to that of the European Union, but without a broader framework to promote the free movement of labor. The North American Free Trade Agreement unites Mexico, Canada, and the United States to create a free trade zone characterized by the cross-border movement of capital, goods, commodities, services, and information, but it makes no provision for the movement of labor within this integrated North American market. As Martin notes in his chapter, "cooperation on managing migration should be an adjunct to cooperation to promote freer trade... [because]... freer trade takes time to increase economic and job growth."

Rather than approaching Mexican immigration as a bilateral issue to be managed jointly with Mexico, the United States has moved in the opposite direction. Since 1986, in an effort to halt undocumented migration unilaterally, U.S. authorities have criminalized the hiring of undocumented workers and dramatically increased the size and budget of the U.S. border patrol. At the same time, to discourage the migration of legal as well as illegal immigrants, the U.S. Congress in 1996 curtailed the access of non-citizen foreigners to various social services.

According to evidence summarized in the chapter by Bean and Spener, these actions were unsuccessful in reducing unauthorized Mexican migration. If anything, the militarization of some parts of the border simply reallocated unauthorized migrants to new points along the border or pushed them from a pattern of surreptitious entry to one of legal entry followed by a subsequent violation of visa regulations (working or staying too long). Massey, Durand, and Malone (2002) also show that the odds of apprehension have actually dropped as migrants were pushed into more remote and lightly patrolled sectors of the border.

Restricting the access of immigrants to U.S. social welfare services also did not deter Mexicans from coming to the United States, but Fix and Zimmerman indicate that it had a profound "chilling" effect on immigrants, discouraging even those who qualify for benefits from exercising their rights to them, thus creating a marginalized immigrant population. If anything, stripping non-citizens of their rights to social welfare simply encouraged additional immigration by inciting a massive shift toward naturalization. Obtaining U.S. citizenship confers a series of entitlements to support the legal immigration not only of spouses and dependent children, but also mothers, fathers, brothers, sisters, and grown children.

## FUTURE RESEARCH

The worldwide advent of international migration in the late twentieth century offers many formidable challenges. The globalization of capital and labor markets and the internationalization of production pose strong challenges to the very concept of the nation state and the idea of national sovereignty itself, requiring people to move beyond current conceptions of territory and citizenship, and to expand them to consider the transnational spaces that are currently being formed around the world through massive immigration. These changes are especially daunting because they will occur at a time when the forces of globalization are also producing downward pressure on wages and incomes in developed nations. Because immigrants and immigration policies will necessarily be discussed in a very heated and politicized environment, social scientists have special responsibilities to policymakers and the public.

First, they must establish the basic facts about immigrants and immigration. Among the three fundamental fields of demography—fertility, mortality, and migration—the latter remains the least well-developed methodologically. Unlike birth or death, mobility is more of a social than a biological event. The definition of a move requires fixing a line and agreeing that it has been crossed; but *where* that line is drawn geographically and administratively is very much a social and political construction. Although international migration, by definition, involves crossing a national boundary, the simple act of boundary-crossing does not necessarily mean that immigration has occurred, for this depends on who is doing the crossing and what their intentions are.

Consider, for example, two men of the same age from the same town in Poland who cross the border into Germany. Both speak Polish exclusively and neither has ever before been abroad; yet if one person has a grandparent born in Germany, he will be classified by state authorities as a returning German while the other will be considered a foreigner and possibly an immigrant. He is only "possibly" an immigrant, because it also depends on the purpose of the border-crossing. If it is to visit relatives for a short time and return, the state classifies him as a tourist. If his purpose is to reunite with a German bride and settle in Germany, he will be a legal immigrant. If he tells authorities he is just visiting but then violates his tourist visa by taking a construction job in Berlin, he will be considered by the state to be an undocumented, illegal, or unauthorized migrant. The conceptual problems multiply when one considers that intentions may change over time: the "returning" German may discover that he dislikes Germany and goes home; the sincere tourist may encounter an unexpected job opportunity and decide to stay; or the undocumented migrant may marry a German woman and legalize to appear suddenly as an "immigrant."

Obviously, where and how a state's politicians and bureaucrats choose to draw geographic, political, and administrative boundaries determines the number of immigrants and their characteristics. Although demographers have developed objective criteria to define international migrants (see Zlotnik 1987), no country has adopted them, and wide variations exist between countries in the way that migration statistics are tallied and reported. Under these circumstances, the responsibility of researchers is threefold: first, to pressure national statistical offices and census bureaus to adopt scientific standards for collecting and tabulating data on international migration; second, to disentangle the government statistics that *are* reported to reveal the objective numbers and characteristics of international migrants as well as their patterns and processes of assimilation; and third, to go beyond official statistics to develop independent and more detailed sources of data on international population movements.

In addition to establishing the basic facts about immigration, researchers should test various theoretical explanations comparatively across nations and migratory systems to determine which ones prevail under what circumstances and why. Although Massey et al. (1998) concluded that alternative theoretical explanations were mostly complementary rather than competing, they were not able to state with any precision which theories were most important empirically in accounting for variations in the number, rate, and characteristics of immigrants over time and whether and why different theories may prove more or less efficacious in accounting for immigration patterns in different times and places. Relatively little research has been done to compare the strength of effects hypothesized under various theories, and what little has been done is confined to the North American system, and within that system, mainly to the case of Mexico–U.S. migration. More research needs to be done on immigration in different countries and systems, and more of it needs to compare alternative hypotheses directly within the same statistical analysis.

Finally, researchers not only have an obligation to establish the fundamental facts of international migration and to explain them theoretically, they must also communicate their findings to state officials and the public in ways that are simple and nontechnical yet accurate and intuitively sensible. International migration and the interethnic relations it produces will be among the most important and potentially divisive topics of public debate in the next century, but all too often social scientists confine their writing to professional journals and their speaking to scholarly conferences. As a result, public discussions of immigrants and immigration policy have been dominated by myths, misinformation, and, at times, outright lies that are grounded in ideology rather than scientific understanding. It is the responsibility of social scientists not only to generate knowledge about immigration, but also to make sure that this knowledge finds its way into the public arena where it can accurately inform debate, and hopefully, yield more enlightened and efficacious policies to regulate the entry and integration of immigrants.

## FUTURE POLICY

Most policymakers and citizens in developed capitalist nations *think* they know why foreigners seek to enter their nations. Standards of living are low in the Third World and high in the developed, capitalist world, and by moving between the two migrants can expect to realize a gain in their material well-being. In practical terms, migrants are assumed to make a cost-benefit calculation that weighs the projected costs of moving against the expected returns, monetary and otherwise, from living and working in a developed country. Since this balance is large and positive for most people outside the nations of the OECD, they rationally choose to emigrate.

However, the chapters included in this volume, along with the earlier review of migration theory and research published by Massey et al. (1998), suggest that reality is more complicated than this simple scenario suggests. Policies, if they are to be successful, must be grounded in scientific truth, yet most policymakers in the world today base their actions on the limited framework of neoclassical economics, which sees migration as a cost-benefit decision made by individuals. The two decades of theoretical and empirical research summarized by the chapters in this volume reveal several basic truths about international migration, and policymakers should be aware of them.

First, contrary to common belief, *international migration does not stem from a lack of economic growth and development, but from development itself.* As industrialization spread across Europe after 1800, its onset triggered waves of emigration in country after country; and in the current day, the poorest and least developed nations do not send the most international migrants today. The fact of the matter is that no nation has undergone transition to a developed market economy without experiencing a massive displacement of people from traditional livelihoods, which are mainly located in the countryside; and in numerous cases a large fraction of these people have ended up migrating abroad.

A second basic truth is that *immigration is a natural consequence of broader processes of social, political, and economic integration across international borders.* When the upheavals of market creation occur, those who adapt to changing circumstances through emigration do not scatter randomly, nor do they necessarily head for the *nearest* wealthy society. Rather, they go to places to which they are *already linked* economically, socially, and politically. Economic links reflect broader relations of trade and investment. Political links stem from formal treaties, colonial administration, and military deployments. Social ties stem from any institutional arrangement that brings people into contact with one another on a regular, sustained basis, such as overseas military deployments, student exchange programs, diplomatic missions, tourism, trade, and multinational corporate activities.

Third, when they enter developed capitalist nations, *immigrants are generally responding to a strong and persistent demand that is built into the structure of post-industrial economies.* Owing to shifts in the technology of production, the emergence of the welfare state, and the embedding of market relations in broader social structures, labor markets in developed nations have become increasingly segmented into a primary sector containing "good" jobs attractive to natives and a secondary sector of poorly paid "bad" jobs that natives shun. To fill the latter, employers turn to immigrants, often initiating flows through direct recruitment. If there were no demand for their services, immigrants, particularly those without documents, would not come, as they would have no means of supporting themselves at the destination.

A fourth basic fact about immigration that surprises many people is that *migrants who enter a developed country for the first time generally do not intend to settle permanently.* Settlement intentions reflect underlying motivations for migration. The motivation that most people imagine when they think about immigrants is their desire to maximize earnings, which indeed would involve permanent relocation. In reality, however, many if not most moves are motivated by a desire to overcome limited economic opportunities related to incomplete or missing markets for capital, credit, and insurance in the source area. That is, people become migrants to solve economic problems *at home.* They seek to work abroad *temporarily* to generate earnings that can be repatriated to diversify risks, accumulate cash, and finance local production and consumption.

Recognizing the diversity of immigrant motivations yields another basic observation: that *international migration is often less influenced by conditions in labor markets than by those in other kinds of markets.* Immigration policies to date have implicitly assumed that immigrants come to maximize earnings and policies have consequently sought to influence conditions in labor markets. If migrants are moving to self-insure, acquire capital, or substitute for credit, however, then lowering expected wages may not eliminate or even reduce the impetus for international migration.

More leverage on migration decisions might well be had influencing other markets in sending countries, through programs designed to improve the performance and coverage of those markets.

Whatever a migrant's original intentions, a sixth basic truth is that *as international migrants accumulate experience abroad, their motivations change, usually in ways that promote additional trips of longer duration, yielding a rising likelihood of settlement over time.* Although most migrants begin as target earners, they are changed by the migrant experience itself. Living and working in an advanced, post-industrial economy exposes them to a consumer culture that inculcates new tastes and motivations that cannot be satisfied through economic activities at home. Rather, the easiest path to their satisfaction becomes additional foreign labor. As migrants spend more time abroad, they acquire social and economic ties to the host country and begin to petition for the entry of family members. Over time, temporary migrants thus have a way of turning into permanent settlers.

A seventh basic fact about international migration is that *it tends to build its own infrastructure of support over time.* As a result, migratory flows acquire a strong internal momentum that makes them resistant to easy manipulation by public policies. As politicians in country after country have discovered to their chagrin, immigration is much easier to start than to stop. The most important mechanism sustaining international migration is the expansion of migrant networks, which occurs automatically whenever a member of a some social structure emigrates to a high-wage country. Emigration transforms ordinary ties such as kinship or friendship into a potential source of social capital that aspiring migrants can use to gain access to a high-paying foreign jobs.

Finally, despite strong tendencies toward self-perpetuation and settlement, *immigrant flows do not last forever—they have a natural life that may be longer or shorter but are necessarily of limited duration.* Data indicate that most European nations underwent an "emigration transition" from low to high to low emigration rates with economic development. Historically, this process took eight or nine decades, which is admittedly a long time to accept immigrants while waiting for economic conditions to improve in sending regions; but recent experience suggests that the "migration hump" is considerably shorter now than in the past. Not only is mass emigration temporally limited; evidence suggests that the time required for the emigration transition has shortened dramatically.

Immigration policy is often cast as a Hobson's choice between open and closed borders, between the free and unhindered movement of immigrants and the imposition of strict limitations on their numbers and characteristics. Whether they realize it or not, public officials generally rely on the conceptual apparatus of neoclassical economics when thinking about immigration. They see a world filled with millions of desperately poor people who, unless they are forcibly blocked or at least strongly discouraged, will surely seek to improve their lot by moving to developed nations. When framed in these stark terms, the necessity of a strict immigration policy seems self-evident, and given the conceptual tools offered by neoclassical economics, the only realistic policy is to attempt to raise the costs and lower the benefits of immigration.

Such has been the logic employed by policymakers throughout the developed world in recent decades. As we have seen, however, the causes of international migration are by no means limited to those specified under neoclassical economics. International migration stems as much from mechanisms specified by the new economics of labor migration, social capital theory, segmented labor market theory, and world systems theory as those described by neoclassical economics. If a comprehensive understanding of international migration requires a synthesis of different theoretical viewpoints, so too does the formulation of an enlightened and efficacious immigration policy.

This realization suggests a *third way* between the extremes of an open border and draconian restrictions on international movement. Rather than attempting to discourage immigration through unilateral repression—seeking to stamp out flows that global trade policies otherwise encourage—policymakers should recognize immigration as a natural part of global economic integration and work multilaterally *to manage it more effectively*. Much as flows of capital, commodities, and goods are managed for the mutual benefit of trading partners by multilateral agreements and institutions such as GATT and the WTO, labor migration can also be cooperatively managed to maximize the benefits and minimize the costs for both sending and receiving societies. In short, international migration must be recognized as an inextricable part of economic globalization and be brought under the aegis of broader multilateral agreements regulating trade and investment.

## References


Centeno, Miguel, Louch, Hugh, and Hargittai, Eszter (1999). "Phonecalls and Fax Machines: The Limits of Globalization," *Washington Quarterly*, 22: 83–100.

Ferenczi, Imre (1929). *International Migrations, Volume I: Statistics.* New York: National Bureau of Economic Research.

Hatton, Timothy J., and Williamson, Jeffrey G. (1998). *The Age of Mass Migration: Causes and Impact.* New York: Oxford University Press.

International Monetary Fund (2001). *Balance of Payment Statistics Yearbook.* Washington, DC: International Monetary Fund.

James, Harold (2002). *The End of Globalization: Lessons from the Great Depression.* Cambridge: Harvard University Press.

Kenwood, A. George, and Lougheed, Alan L. (1999). *The Growth of the International Economy 1820–2000: An Introductory Text.* London: Routledge.

Martin, Philip L., and Miller, Mark J. (1980). "Guestworkers: Lessons from Western Europe," *Industrial and Labor Relations Review*, 33: 315–30.

Massey, Douglas S. (1988). "International Migration and Economic Development in Comparative Perspective," *Population and Development Review*, 14: 383–414.

——Arango, Joaqín, Hugo, Graeme, Kouaouci, Ali, Pellegrino, Adela, and Taylor, J. Edward (1998). *Worlds in Motion: Understanding International Migration at the End of the Millennium.* Oxford: Oxford University Press.

——Durand, Jorge, and Nolan Malone (2002). *Beyond Smoke and Mirrors: Mexican Immigration in an Age of Economic Integration.* New York: Russell Sage Foundation.

Nugent, Walter (1992). *Crossings: The Great Transatlantic Migrations 1870–1914*. Bloomington: Indiana University Press.

Piore, Michael J. (1979). *Birds of Passage: Migrant Labor and Industrial Society*. New York: Cambridge University Press.

Reichert, Joshua S., and Massey, Douglas S. (1982). "Guestworker Programs: Evidence from Europe and the United States and Some Implications for U.S. Policy," *Population Research and Policy Review*, 1: 1–17.

Stiglitz, Joseph E. (2002). *Globalization and its Discontents*. New York: W.W. Norton.

Wyman, Mark (1993). *Round-Trip to America: The Immigrants Return to Europe, 1880–1930*. Ithaca: Cornell University Press.

Zlotnik, Hania (1987). "The Concept of International Migration as Reflected in Data Collection Systems," *International Migration Review*, 21: 925–46.

—— (1998). "International Migration 1965–96: An Overview," *Population and Development Review*, 24: 429–68.

# Index